That Most Precious Merchandise

THE MIDDLE AGES SERIES

Ruth Mazo Karras, Series Editor

Edward Peters, Founding Editor

A complete list of books in the series is available from the publisher.

THAT MOST PRECIOUS MERCHANDISE

The Mediterranean Trade in Black Sea Slaves, 1260–1500

Hannah Barker

PENN

UNIVERSITY OF PENNSYLVANIA PRESS

PHILADELPHIA

Published by
University of Pennsylvania Press
Philadelphia, Pennsylvania 19104-4112
www.upenn.edu/pennpress

Printed in the United States of America on acid-free paper
1 3 5 7 9 10 8 6 4 2

Library of Congress Cataloging-in-Publication Data

Names: Barker, Hannah, author.
Title: That most precious merchandise: the Mediterranean trade in Black Sea slaves, 1260–1500 / Hannah Barker.
Other titles: Middle Ages series.
Description: 1st edition. | Philadelphia: University of Pennsylvania Press, [2019] | Series: The Middle Ages series | Includes bibliographical references and index.
Identifiers: LCCN 2019006688 | ISBN 9780812251548 (hardcover)
Subjects: LCSH: Slave trade—Mediterranean Region—History—To 1500. | Slavery—Mediterranean Region—History—To 1500.
Classification: LCC HT983.B37 2019 | DDC 306.3/6209822—dc23
LC record available at https://lccn.loc.gov/2019006688

Contents

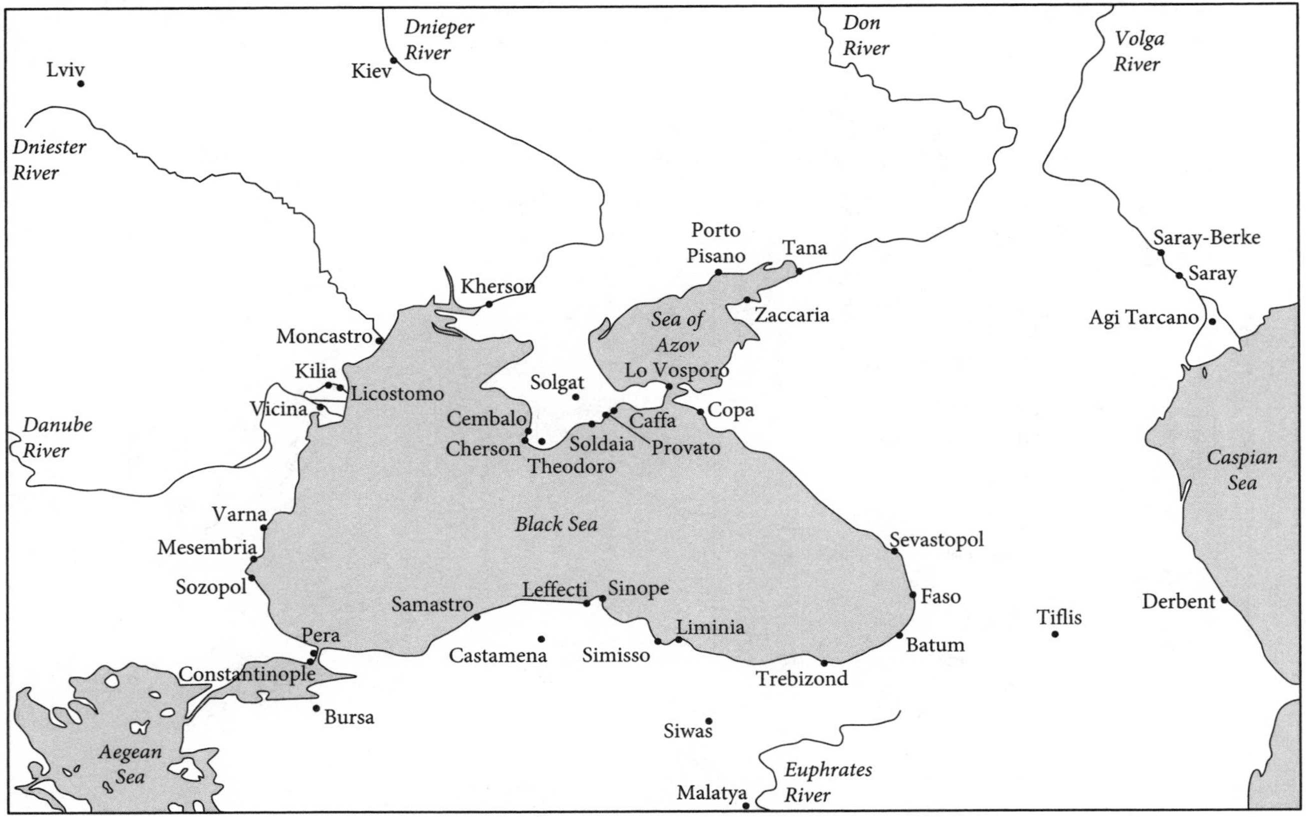

Map 1. The Black Sea. Map created by Hannah Barker using data from naturalearthdata.com.

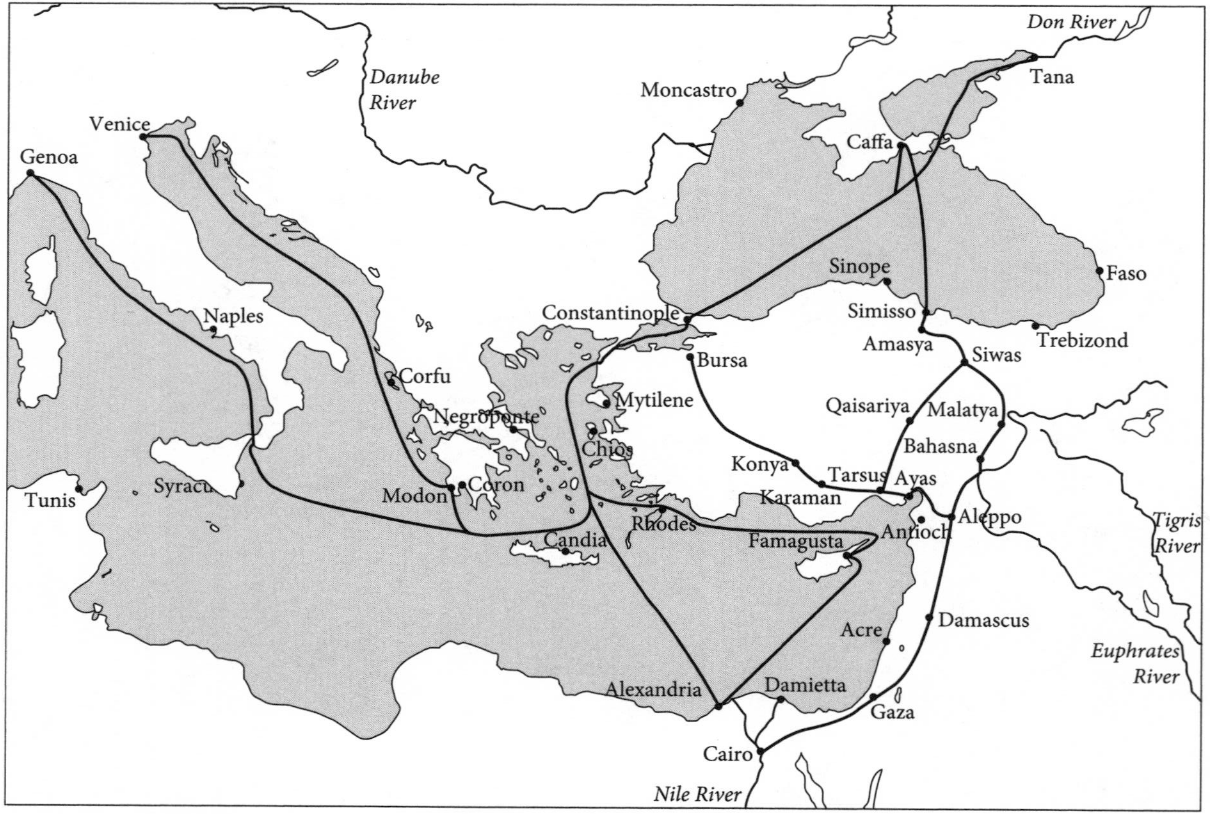

Map 2. Slave Trade Routes. Map created by Hannah Barker using a template from Daniel Dalet (d-maps.com).

Introduction

On September 19, 1363, a ten-year-old Tatar boy named Jaqmaq was sold as a slave in the Black Sea port of Tana. His first owner had probably been a Christian, as he had already been baptized with the name Antonio. His second owner was a local Muslim named Aqbughā, the son of Shams al-Dīn. Aqbughā sold Jaqmaq/Antonio to his third owner, Niccolò Baxeio of the parish of St. Patermanus in Venice, for 400 aspers. Niccolò also bought a fifteen-year-old Tatar girl from Aqbughā and a twelve-year-old Tatar boy from another local man. All three children were to be delivered to different people in Venice. Jaqmaq/Antonio was destined for Gabriel Teuri of the parish of St. Severus, who would be his fourth owner.

About twenty years later, another boy named Jaqmaq, this time a Circassian, was also sold as a slave in the Black Sea. He was purchased by a merchant named Kazlak, who brought him to Egypt. There Kazlak sold him to a military commander, the amir ʿAlī ibn Ināl, who trained him as a mamluk, a military slave. Once his education was complete, Jaqmaq accompanied ʿAlī's mother on a pilgrimage to Mecca. Upon his return, he discovered that his older brother was also serving as a mamluk in another household, that of the sultan of Egypt. When the sultan found out, he took Jaqmaq away from ʿAlī ibn Ināl and added him to the royal household, reuniting the brothers. After some additional training, the sultan freed Jaqmaq and made him a page at court. Over the course of several decades, Jaqmaq rose through the ranks in the court and army. In 1438, he himself became sultan and enjoyed a long reign until 1453. During that period, he purchased thousands of slaves to staff his household and serve as mamluks in his army. His successor, al-Manṣūr ʿUthmān, was his son by a Turkish slave woman named Zahrāʾ.

The life of the first Jaqmaq, the Tatar boy sold to Venetians, is documented only through a single entry in the register of the notary who drew up the contract for his sale.[1] As a result, we know a great deal about the circumstances under which he was sold but nothing about what happened to him before or afterward. The life of the second Jaqmaq, the Circassian boy sold to Egyptians, is documented in numerous chronicles, biographical dictionaries, and other narrative sources.[2] There are coins minted in his name, and the school (*madrasa*) that he endowed still stands in Cairo today. Yet these sources reveal more about his political career than his early life as a slave. What binds the two Jaqmaqs together, despite their radically different fates in both life and the historical record, is their involuntary participation in the Mediterranean trade in Black Sea slaves.

The history of the Black Sea as a source of Mediterranean slaves stretches from ancient Greek colonies to human trafficking networks in the present day. During the medieval period, the trade in Black Sea slaves peaked between the mid-thirteenth and mid-fifteenth centuries. More precisely, it was in the 1260s that the Byzantine emperor Michael VIII Paleologus granted commercial privileges in the Black Sea to the rulers of Genoa, Venice, and the Mamluk kingdom of Egypt and Greater Syria (*bilād al-Shām*). On the basis of those privileges, Mediterranean merchants settled in the Black Sea and exported various goods, including slaves. Slave exports continued until 1475, when Ottoman forces conquered Caffa, Genoa's chief colony on the Crimean Peninsula. Although the Black Sea slave trade did not end in 1475, it was reorganized to serve Ottoman rather than Italian or Mamluk needs.

Even at its height during the fourteenth and early fifteenth centuries, the Black Sea slave trade was never the sole source of Mediterranean slaves.[3] Genoese and Venetian merchants bought the captives taken in conflicts throughout the Mediterranean region. The Genoese bought slaves from ongoing wars between Christian and Muslim kingdoms in Iberia, and they also enslaved Sardinians caught up Genoa's war with Pisa. The Venetians bought slaves from pirates and raiders in the Balkans and the Aegean Sea. Both Genoa and Venice enslaved captives taken from North Africa and the Ottomans. When allowed to do so, they also purchased African slaves in Alexandria, Tunis, and other North African ports. However, the greatest demand for slaves in the medieval Mediterranean was concentrated not in Italy but in Cairo, home of the Mamluk sultan and his amirs, the commanders of his army. The Mamluks preferred Black Sea slaves for military service, but they also imported large numbers of African slaves for domestic service as well as slaves from the Balkans, the Aegean, Central Asia, and the Indian Ocean when they were available. Yet within this diverse population of slaves, those from the Black Sea were the single largest group. The trade in Black Sea slaves provided merchants with profit and prestige; states with military recruits, tax revenue, and diplomatic influence; and households with the service of enslaved women and men.

The trade system that carried slaves from the Black Sea into the Mediterranean is the subject of this book. Genoa, Venice, and the Mamluk sultanate, the three most significant importers of Black Sea slaves, have never been studied together. The main obstacle has been language: an integrated study of the Mediterranean trade in Black Sea slaves must draw on sources in both Latin and

Arabic.[4] Yet once the Latin and Arabic sources are examined together, it becomes clear that Christian and Muslim inhabitants of the Mediterranean shared a set of assumptions and practices that amounted to a common culture of slavery.[5] These included the ideas that slavery was legal and socially acceptable, that slave status was based on religious difference, that religious difference could be at least partially articulated through linguistic and racial categories, and that slavery was a universal threat affecting all free people. It also included practices related to slave conversion, the inspection process and contractual language for buying and selling slaves, the use of slaves as social and financial assets, a strong preference for slave women over men, the widespread use of slave women for domestic and sexual service in urban households, and the status of children born to slave women and free men.

In addition, examining the Arabic and Latin sources together shows that the Genoese, Venetian, and Mamluk slave trades were thoroughly entangled and that this had wide-ranging effects.[6] Genoese–Venetian rivalry for control of the Black Sea slave trade was an important element in their broader rivalry for commercial dominance of the Mediterranean. Mamluk sultans required a steady supply of slaves to maintain military and political stability, so they offered generous incentives to slave traders from the entire Mediterranean region. Because several of the ports used by these traders were Genoese colonies, Genoese diplomats used their control over the flow of slaves to negotiate with the Mamluks for privileges in lucrative markets like Alexandria. That strategy was risky though: choosing to disrupt the Mamluk slave trade led to reprisals against Italian merchants living in Mamluk cities, while choosing not to disrupt the Mamluk slave trade led to scathing public criticism by supporters of the crusade movement. The rulers of Genoa and Venice therefore managed the slave trade with care, seeking to reap its profits and defuse its conflicts. Their regulations played a greater role than the actions of individual merchants in shaping the Mediterranean trade in Black Sea slaves.

Medieval Sources on the Slave Trade

Scholars of the Mediterranean trade in Black Sea slaves have a rich source base. The difficulty lies not in finding appropriate sources but in bringing together disparate sources from different genres in a coherent way. The most useful Latin sources are notarial registers. Notaries were required to keep a register of all the documents they drew up and to deposit those registers with the state. As a result, the state archives of Genoa and Venice contain hundreds of notarial registers with information about the sale, rental, donation, inheritance, and manumission of slaves as well as disputes concerning them. Although many notarial registers have been lost or destroyed over the centuries, those that have survived hold thousands of legal acts involving slaves, enough to create a database and conduct simple statistical analyses.

Yet the data provided by notarial registers can address only certain aspects of the slave trade. Sources from other genres are needed to round out the picture. Tax records give economic context for the individual acts of import, export, sale, possession, and manumission of slaves recorded by notaries.[7] Legal context comes from medieval collections of Roman, canon, and civil law, with their learned commentaries and notarial formularies.[8] Treaties governing the slave trade and crusade propaganda help to fill in the political context.[9] Finally, there are anecdotes culled from letters, merchants' accounts, travelers' tales, sermons, and literary works that flesh out the intellectual, cultural, and social contexts of the slave trade.[10]

The most valuable Arabic sources are slave-buying advice manuals.[11] This genre evolved from ancient Greek texts that addressed slavery in the contexts of household management (Bryson's *Management of the Estate*), social order (Aristotle's *Politics*), geography (Hippocrates' *Airs, Waters, Places*), and physiognomy (Polemon's *Physiognomy*). Muslim scholars gathered the Greek material; translated it into Arabic, Persian, and Turkish; and made revisions and updates to suit their own times. The most famous slave-buying advice manual, Ibn Buṭlān's *General Treatise on the Skills Useful in the Purchase and Examination of Slaves* (*Risāla jāmiʿa li-funūn nāfiʿa fī shirā al-raqīq wa-taqlīb al-ʿabīd*), was composed in Baghdad in the eleventh century.[12] Three lesser-known manuals have survived from the late Ayyubid and Mamluk periods: the anonymous *Inspection in Slave-Buying* (*Al-Taḥqiq fī shirā' al-raqīq*) from the thirteenth century, Ibn al-Akfānī's *Observation and Inspection in the Examination of Slaves* (*Al-Naẓir wa-al-taḥqīq fī taqlīb al-raqīq*) from the fourteenth century, and al-ʿAyntābī's *The Apt Statement on Choosing Female and Male Slaves* (*Al-Qawl al-sadīd fī ikhtiyār al-imā' wa-al-ʿabīd*) from the fifteenth century.[13] Both Ibn al-Akfānī and al-ʿAyntābī were physicians associated with the Manṣūrī hospital in Cairo. Their slave-buying advice manuals offered medical as well as ethnographic advice for choosing slaves.

Because some Mamluk slaves entered the ruling elite, many other sources deal directly or indirectly with the slave trade. Normative legal sources are especially abundant. They include compilations of religious law and legal opinions according to the four Sunni schools (all of which had a presence in Mamluk Cairo),[14] *shurūṭ* manuals that provided model documents for scribes,[15] *ḥisba* manuals for market inspectors,[16] and treaties governing the slave trade.[17] These genres all show how the slave trade was supposed to operate.

Unfortunately, there are relatively few descriptive sources against which to check the normative sources. No tax registers and few documents of sale or manumission survive from the Mamluk period.[18] Instead, a great deal of anecdotal information comes from narrative sources about the lives of elite slaves. These include chronicles,[19] geographical treatises,[20] biographical dictionaries,[21] and travel accounts.[22] Although narrative sources are mainly concerned with the political and religious activities of the elite, they sometimes repeat stories about the origins and early lives of prominent mamluks. Such tidbits are most useful when read together with evidence drawn from other genres and from the Latin sources.

The most intractable obstacle to the study of this slave trade is the lack of material from the Golden Horde, the Mongol state north of the Black Sea, where many of the slaves originated. The Golden Horde's administrative archive was destroyed by Timur (Tamerlane) in the early fifteenth century.[23] Archeologists have excavated medieval sites in the Black Sea region, but most of their findings have been published in Russian.[24] Surviving texts from Georgia, Bulgaria, and other medieval states in the region seem to say little about either slavery or trade. In fact, the most substantial surviving archive produced within the Black Sea comes from Genoa's colony at Caffa. The colonial administration there made clean copies of its most important records, such as treasury (*massaria*) registers, and sent them back to Genoa for official review.[25] Genoese and Venetian notaries who worked in the Black Sea colonies kept registers and deposited them with the state when they returned home.[26] Both Italian and Mamluk travelers in the region wrote about their adventures.[27] There is undoubtedly room for further research on the basis of Greek, Russian, Ottoman, and possibly Georgian sources, but given the limitations of time and language that constrain a historian working alone, my analysis is restricted to Latin and Arabic sources. My hope is that the present book will provide others with a helpful framework for studying Black Sea slavery using a wider variety of sources and languages.

Modern Mentalities: Erasing the Medieval Slave Trade

Two historical narratives have shaped modern scholarship on slavery: the antislavery narrative of Christian amelioration and the Marxist narrative of modes of production. The Christian amelioration narrative, spread by the late eighteenth-century antislavery movement in Britain, held that Christian principles of spiritual equality and brotherly love were incompatible with slavery. It therefore asserted that the Christianization of the Roman Empire had caused the gradual disappearance of slavery from Europe. This was imagined to be a slow process, as Christian principles acted indirectly to mitigate masters' behavior and state policies over the course of centuries. Proponents of Christian amelioration dated the end of slavery in western Europe between the sixth and twelfth centuries, depending on whether they considered serfdom to be an extension of slavery or a new and different status.[28] Others acknowledged the persistence of slavery into the later Middle Ages but insisted that the treatment of slaves continued to improve gradually.[29] Either way, the sixteenth-century resurgence of slavery in European colonies was portrayed as a reversal of civilizational progress.[30] The good news was that this lost progress could be restored through abolition. Although the proslavery movement in the late eighteenth century also used Christian texts to support its position, the antislavery movement's eventual success meant that its historical narrative of Christianity as a force for the amelioration and abolition of slavery became the dominant one.[31]

The second narrative ascribed the disappearance of slavery in Europe to economic rather than religious forces. Karl Marx presented human history as a series of developmental stages in the mode of production. Over time, the ancient class structure of citizens and slaves was replaced by the medieval class structure of nobles and serfs, followed by the modern class structure of capitalists and workers.[32] Although slavery, feudalism, and capitalism all involved a class of property owners dominating a class of producers, each mode of production was characterized by a distinct form of domination and of class struggle. Among twentieth-century historians of slavery, the Marxist narrative has generated debates over the role of capitalism in the rise and abolition of Atlantic slavery[33] and over the timing and significance of the medieval transition from slavery to feudalism.[34] Thus the Marxist narrative erased medieval slavery in two ways.[35] First, because it presented feudalism as the quintessential medieval mode of production, it simply did not occur to most historians that slavery could play a significant role in the Middle Ages. Second, most historians have assumed, like Marx, that slavery was primarily a mode of agricultural production. Because medieval slaves tended to be women engaged in domestic and sexual service in urban households, their presence was easily ignored or dismissed.

Medieval historians who noticed the presence of slaves in their sources have struggled to respond to these two narratives. One approach has been to test the boundaries of the Marxist narrative by debating exactly when and how Roman agricultural slavery in Europe died out. The answer seems to be that the process unfolded over many centuries, varied significantly from region to region, and involved more than two forms of unfreedom (i.e., slavery and serfdom are not sufficient to express the multiplicity of early medieval practices).[36] Another approach has been to document the existence of urban slavery in exhaustive detail. Relying heavily on notarial registers, this literature has focused on the slave trade, the demography of the slave population, and the labor performed by slaves.[37] There have been efforts to combine these approaches by linking the end of agricultural slavery with the emergence of urban slavery.[38] A third approach has been to draw attention to the gendered nature of medieval slavery and the significance of women's labor.[39] Finally, scholars have addressed slavery in medieval law[40] and in parts of northern Europe beyond the reach of direct Roman influence.[41]

Nevertheless, although the Christian amelioration narrative and the Marxist narrative are both more than a century old, they continue to shape the study of slavery. The influence of the Marxist narrative is openly acknowledged, and an economic emphasis has been the norm for scholarship on medieval slavery. In contrast, the influence of the Christian amelioration narrative, especially the static and monolithic role it ascribes to Christianity, has rarely been questioned.[42] Since the appearance of Charles Verlinden's seminal work *L'Esclavage dans l'Europe médiévale* in 1955 and 1977, it has been clear that Christians owned slaves throughout the Middle Ages and that the Church as an institution not only tolerated slavery but owned slaves itself. Nevertheless, there remains a sense that this *should not* have been the case. Historians who study medieval slavery still feel compelled to condemn it on moral grounds.[43] This is not simply a matter of anachronism, of holding medieval society to modern standards. Rather, it is the Christian amelioration narrative that suggests that medieval slave owners were behind their own times, not fully imbued with Christianity, sinful and corrupt.

Nineteenth-century proponents of Christian amelioration certainly interpreted late medieval slavery (when they acknowledged its existence at all) as a sign of moral corruption, namely, the corruption of Christian principles by sinful greed or the nefarious influence of the Orient.[44] Either way, Italians and Spaniards were seen as especially guilty. Their persistence in keeping slaves could be attributed to regional backsliding, associated in the nineteenth century with backward southern European Catholicism as opposed to forward looking northern European Protestantism. Their failings, therefore, did not reflect on Christianity as a whole. The association between slavery, moral corruption, and greedy Italian merchants has been repeated by generations of medieval historians, as discussed in Chapters 4 and 6. Its effects on Anglophone scholarship have been especially pervasive, since Christian amelioration was closely associated with the British Protestant antislavery movement and the civilizing mission of the British Empire.[45] But it has influenced medieval historians of other backgrounds too.

Unquestioning adherence to the Christian amelioration narrative has sometimes led to the misinterpretation of medieval sources. For example, the fifteenth-century Genoese lawyer Bartolomeo de Bosco drew up an advisory brief (*consilium*) in which he defended the inheritance of the son of a former slave woman and her master. Other members of the master's family had challenged the son's status as an heir (but not his status as a freeman) because his mother had been a slave at the time of his conception; the son contended that his mother had been manumitted and that his father had declared him legitimate. Bosco's advisory brief began with a warning that "a judge ought not to decide simply following conscience, but ought to form [his opinion] according to the things which were mentioned and proved pertaining to the truth of the actions."[46] Since Bosco supported the son's claim to inherit, he was advising the judge not to follow his conscience, which would lead him to rule against the son of a slave, but rather to examine the facts, which would show the son to be a legitimate heir. Bosco's own conscience could not have been too deeply troubled by the institution of slavery, because he himself owned a female slave.[47]

Yet a recent article discussing this brief has interpreted it as a statement in opposition to slavery: "Bosco accepted that slavery was a normal, legal, human condition for some, but he knew that in a perfect world it would not exist. His long consilium on this case reveals his pleasure in defending this colonial family."[48] This is the reverse of Bosco's own statement, which assumed that conscience would favor slavery, and it illustrates how misleading the Christian amelioration narrative can be when studying medieval attitudes toward slavery.[49]

The study of slavery in the medieval Islamicate world is part of a different historiographical tradition. The Eurocentric nature of the Marxist narrative combined with the relative lack of surviving economic sources from the Islamicate world means that an economic approach has not gained much traction.[50] Instead, scholars have focused on legal history, for which there are excellent sources; and social history, with special attention to questions of race, gender, and sexuality.[51] The object of this scholarship has sometimes been framed in ahistorical terms as "Islamic slavery," but recently, there has been more attention to variations in the practice of slavery by Muslims living in specific times and places.[52] Conversations with historians and anthropologists of slavery in Africa have also enriched the study of slavery in Islamicate societies.[53]

The study of mamluks, or military slaves, under the Mamluk sultanate in Egypt and Syria has been shaped by an additional set of questions. One question is the extent to which military slavery was distinctive to Islamicate societies; comparative research has shown that it was not.[54] Another question concerns the legal status and political legitimacy of Mamluk sultans. The Mamluks were unusual among societies with military slaves because Mamluk sultans were former slaves ruling in their own names, de jure as well as de facto. This system of government was possible only because mamluks were manumitted at the end of their training. Their status as freedmen was essential to their legal and political ability to govern: they were not and could not be slave rulers.[55] Their previous enslavement mattered politically, however, because the education imposed on them as slaves shaped their careers after manumission. It is this formative aspect of slavery that has occupied the attention of most scholars of the Mamluk system.[56]

Although the Christian amelioration narrative would seem to have little to do with the history of slavery in the Islamicate world, it has influenced the field in subtle ways. British antislavery societies and representatives of the British state pressured nineteenth-century Muslim rulers to abolish slavery to demonstrate their civilizational progress.[57] Their defensive reaction to British pressure coalesced into an Islamic amelioration narrative. According to the Islamic amelioration narrative, Islam held slave owners to a high moral standard and caused Muslims to treat their slaves far better than Christian slave owners ever had. Thus Christians had no moral high ground with regard to slavery. This discourse has developed, on one hand, into an Islamic case for abolition and, on the other hand, into a debate about whether the slaves of Muslim masters were truly well treated.[58] A new chapter has recently been added by the Islamic State's decision to legalize slavery within its territory and to enslave Yazidi captives, a decision that has been condemned by Muslims in other parts of the world.[59]

Like the Christian amelioration narrative, the Islamic amelioration narrative encourages generational chauvinism: the idea that modern people are inherently better or wiser than medieval people and therefore qualified to judge them.[60] Thus, like the Christian amelioration narrative, the Islamic amelioration narrative should be challenged and discarded as anachronistic. Stronger arguments are available to activists who wish to oppose slavery in the present day. As for slavery in the past, arguments about good and bad treatment have not been productive for several reasons. First, an individual slave's experience of slavery depended on the behavior of his or her individual master and on the overarching legal and social structures that governed slavery. Second, because of the common culture of slavery in the late medieval Mediterranean, the overarching legal and social structures were remarkably similar across Christian and Muslim societies. Finally, because Christians and Muslims in the late medieval Mediterranean acquired their slaves from the same sources in the Black Sea, those slaves were subject to the same violence of capture, the same humiliation of sale, and the same vulnerability of status regardless of where they were eventually taken or who eventually bought them.

Outline of Chapters

This book is not a comparative history of slavery in medieval Italy and Egypt. Mamluks, Genoese, and Venetians shared a common culture of slavery, and they participated together as partners and competitors in the Black Sea slave trade. To present an integrated picture, this book is divided into two parts. The first part, Chapters 1 through 4, defines slavery as it was instituted in the late medieval Mediterranean and highlights some aspects of the common culture of slavery, especially those related to trade and the market. The second part, Chapters 5 through 7, examines the various forces that shaped the slave trade from the Black Sea into the Mediterranean.

The book begins by defining slavery within a specific context: the Mediterranean in the thirteenth through fifteenth centuries. Chapter 1, "Slavery in the Late Medieval Mediterranean," presents fundamental assumptions about slavery in that context. Slavery was legal and socially acceptable among Christians, Muslims, and Jews living in the late medieval Mediterranean. Although enslavement was a universal threat that affected everyone living in the region, slave status was based on religious difference: people were not supposed to enslave adherents of the same religion as themselves. However, once enslaved, slaves were expected to convert to the religion of their masters, and their conversion did not require manumission. Because religious belief was a difficult quality to prove in court, the second chapter, "Difference and the Perception of Slave Status," discusses how language and race were used as shorthand for categorizing individuals as enslaveable or not enslaveable in a particular society.

Chapter 3, "Societies with Slaves: Genoa, Venice, and the Mamluk Sultanate," sketches the demography of the late medieval Mediterranean slave population. It then explores the experiences of slaves and the kinds of labor and service they performed. Gender, race, and the master's identity all played a role in the services demanded of individual slaves. Chapter 4, "The Slave Market and the Act of Sale," describes the locations and operations of the major slave markets in Genoa, Venice, Cairo, and Alexandria. It walks through the process of inspecting a slave, explaining how a slave sale differed from the sale of any other commodity. It presents the surviving data for the changing prices of slaves as well as various factors that might affect the price of a particular slave. Finally, it highlights certain unusual contractual clauses specific to the sale of slaves, such as the health warranty and the consent clause.

Chapter 5, "Making Slaves in the Black Sea," surveys the evidence for violent capture and sale by relatives as the chief mechanisms for enslaving free people around the Black Sea. It then examines regional and local conditions that governed the slave trade across the Black Sea. The long-standing rivalry between Genoa and Venice for control over major ports and shipping in the Black Sea and in the Mediterranean was one important factor. Another was the Mamluk–Golden Horde alliance, established in the mid-thirteenth century, and the Mamluks' desire to ensure safe passage for their merchants and a steady supply of slaves. Political changes in the states surrounding the Black Sea, especially during the mid- and late fourteenth century, also affected which groups of people were most vulnerable to enslavement.

The heart of the book is Chapter 6, "Constraining Disorder: Merchants, States, and the Structure of the Slave Trade." It profiles individual merchants who bought and sold slaves in small numbers and in bulk, for themselves and as agents for others. It also traces the routes those merchants used; the ways in which they cooperated and competed with one another; the risks and logistical challenges they faced; the rewards they received; and the role of states in constraining, directing, and taxing their activities. It shows that the Black Sea slave trade was not conducted by professional slave traders—there were no specialists who made their living chiefly by trading or shipping slaves. Instead, the slave trade was conducted by opportunists, buying and selling slaves alongside other commodities and transporting them in mixed-cargo ships.

The final chapter, "Crusade, Embargo, and the Trade in Mamluk Slaves," situates the Black Sea slave trade within the religious and diplomatic contexts of the late medieval crusade movement and the broader struggle between Christian and Muslim powers for control of the Mediterranean. Christian proponents of the crusades asserted that Christian merchants, especially the Genoese, were strengthening the enemy by supplying the Mamluks with military slaves from the Black Sea. They advocated that slaves be included in the papal embargo policy against the Mamluks. Although Genoa did play an important role in facilitating the Mamluk slave trade, it was the state rather than individual merchants that negotiated the terms of engagement with the Mamluks, and it was the state that struggled to reconcile its slaving and crusading activities. Thus the Mediterranean trade in Black Sea slaves should be understood not only as an economic activity carried out by merchants but also as an area of state regulation with significant diplomatic and religious consequences.

Chapter 1

Slavery in the Late Medieval Mediterranean

When medieval Christians imagined an ideal society, order was among its guiding principles. The ideal society envisioned by Thomas Aquinas, for example, was set in the Garden of Eden, where he believed that humanity had existed in a sinless natural state.[1] Because he also believed that humanity was naturally sociable, the inhabitants of Eden must have lived together in a society. Within that society, there would be naturally occurring differences of gender, age, and physical stature, as well as the differences of goodness and knowledge that would emerge as individuals exercised their free will. Those who cultivated goodness and knowledge would have dominion over the others, but without coercion. Dominion was necessary in Eden, according to Aquinas, for two reasons. First, society needed a ruler to look after the common good. Second, the wisest and best members of society were obligated to use their virtues for the benefit of all. Thus differences among people, both those naturally occurring and those developed through free will, led to social hierarchy. Accepting one's place in the hierarchy was necessary for peace and order; refusing it constituted pride, the greatest sin.[2]

The ideal society imagined by medieval Muslims was different. Its setting was paradise, the Garden of the afterlife, where believers experienced never-ending joy surrounded by every kind of beauty and abundance. One aspect of this joy was reuniting with family members across generations. In early descriptions of the Garden, all the branches of an extended family were depicted living together in an infinitely spacious tent or pavilion, thus combining the pleasures of sociability and privacy. They would enjoy banquets together without the work of preparing and serving food. Instead, a retinue of beautiful male *ghilmān* and female *ḥūr* would serve the food, fill the cups, and provide the entertainment.[3] The *ghilmān* and *ḥūr* were not human and had never experienced worldly life. Their sole function was to serve. Like splashing fountains and fragrant trees, they can be understood as living elements of the Garden's adornment. Over time, depictions of the Garden evolved such that female *ḥūr* came to be portrayed as singers and sexual partners for the enjoyment of male believers, while female believers and male *ghilmān* faded into the background.[4]

Real societies in the late medieval Mediterranean were, of course, not anyone's ideal. Real rulers used force to exercise dominion over their subjects, and real households depended on the labor of real people for their meals. The lowest position in the human hierarchy was in reality filled by slaves. It can be difficult today to understand how masters could recognize the humanity of their slaves while still denying them freedom, but it was precisely their humanity that made slaves valuable. Simply by existing at the bottom of the hierarchy, slaves enabled free people to feel superior. Their presence in a household enabled its head to display his skills as a ruler. Slaves' reason and capacity for decision-making made them capable administrators and soldiers; their capacity for love and companionship made them suitable nurses for children and the elderly as well as sexual partners for their masters.

Christians and Muslims shared three fundamental assumptions about slavery in addition to its place at the bottom of the human hierarchy: that it was legal, that it was based on religious difference, and that it was a universal threat. These assumptions formed the core of a common culture of slavery in the late medieval Mediterranean. All free adults knew that they could legally purchase a slave. They expected the slaves available for sale to come from religious backgrounds different than their own. At the same time, they were aware that they themselves could become enslaved if captured by pirates or raiders in the wrong place at the wrong time.

The line between slavery and captivity in the late medieval Mediterranean was hazy. Captivity ended with a return home after the payment of a ransom or some other mechanism of exchange, and it was not necessarily associated with religious difference.[5] Slavery was ideologically based on religious difference, and it was usually permanent. It is only clear in retrospect which individuals would be ransomed from captivity and which would remain in slavery. Ransoms, however, were easier to arrange for captives held in geographical or social proximity to their homes than for captives taken far away. In the western Mediterranean, ransoms and exchanges between Iberia and North Africa were mediated by friars, merchants, confraternities, and monarchs.[6] In the eastern Mediterranean and the Black Sea, merchants and diplomats usually arranged ransoms.[7] But for slaves transported over long distances, from the Aegean to Catalonia or from the Black Sea to Italy, no ransom could be expected.

This distinction between captivity and slavery shaped expectations regarding conversion. Captives taken across religious boundaries might or might not be pressured to convert, depending on how their masters believed conversion would affect their ransom.[8] Slaves, for whom a ransom was not expected, were converted to the religion of their masters, and such conversions did not confer freedom. Christians who purchased Muslims, Jews, and pagans expected them to convert to Christianity while remaining enslaved. Muslims who purchased Christians, Jews, and pagans as slaves expected them to convert to Islam while remaining enslaved. Jewish law allowed partial conversion to Judaism for slaves, with the possibility of full conversion after manumission.[9]

One consequence of assuming slave conversion without manumission was a rhetoric of competition for slave souls. Conversion was one of the justifications given for slave ownership, because it increased the number of souls belonging to the "right" religion. In the late Middle Ages, some Christians also argued that it was better for Christians to purchase Christian slaves than to allow them to be purchased and converted by Muslims. In other words, they used the rhetoric of competition for slave souls to justify the enslavement of Christians by Christians. As a result, thousands of Christians from the eastern Mediterranean and the Black Sea were kept as slaves in the central and western Mediterranean. Some challenged their status in court, arguing that legal slavery had to be based on religious difference. A few won their freedom. Muslim scholars in the late medieval Mediterranean never presented an intellectual argument for the enslavement of fellow Muslims; whether they enslaved fellow Muslims through negligence is a different question. Given such complications, this chapter explores how slave status was defined in the late medieval Mediterranean and how the boundary between free and slave status was enforced.

Terminology

The English language has only two words, *slave* and *serf*, to indicate a person of unfree status. The vocabulary of Latin and Arabic is richer. In classical Arabic, all of the following terms may be translated as slave: *ʿabd*, *raqīq*, *ghulām*, *fatan*, *khādim* and *khādima*, *mamlūk* and *mamlūka*, *waṣīf* and *waṣīfa*, *jāriya*, and *ama*.[10] In Mamluk-era texts, a male slave was usually called *ʿabd*, *raqīq*, or *mamlūk*; a female slave *jāriya*; and a eunuch *khādim* or *fatan*. Both freeborn and manumitted people were *ḥurr*, but *ʿatīq* was specific to manumitted people. Certain terms, like *ghulām* and *khādim*, were used for both slaves and free servants. Others, like *mamlūk* and *ʿabd*, were adopted by free people to convey respect in formal contexts, as English speakers once used the phrase "your humble servant." The term *mamlūk* has also entered English in two forms. With a lowercase *m*, *mamluk* refers to both slaves and former slaves in military service. With an uppercase *M*, *Mamluk* refers to the state that governed Egypt and Greater Syria from 1250 to 1517, a state headed by mamluks.

In medieval Latin, the range of terms for unfree people was similarly broad, including *servus* and *serva*, *sclavus* and *sclava*, *mancipium*, *colonus*, *villanus*, *emtitus*, *famulus*, *verna*, *ancilla*, and others. *Servus* was by far the most commonly used term. In classical Latin, it meant "slave," but over time, its meaning evolved to include serfs and others of unfree status. According to the thirteenth-century jurist Rolandinus Passeggieri, the division between *servi* and free people was one of six fundamental divisions that characterized humanity.[11] An invented etymology connected *servus* with the verb *servare*, "to save," on the basis that slaves were those saved and not killed in war. Iacopo da Varagine, archbishop of Genoa in the late thirteenth century, listed four types of *servi*: those born into slavery, those captured in battle, those purchased with money, and those hired to serve.[12] Even those who voluntarily served a great man might count as *servi*.[13] The term *sclavus* (and its vernacular equivalent *schiavo*) was coined in the eleventh century to distinguish slaves from serfs and other *servi*, but it was not widely adopted until the fourteenth century.[14] Because most of the authoritative legal texts of the late Middle Ages were compiled in the twelfth and thirteenth centuries, they used *servus* for all unfree people. The multiple meanings of *servus* thus complicated the work of both medieval and modern interpreters.

Other Latin terms for unfree people appeared less frequently. *Ancilla*, exclusively for female slaves, and *verna*, the Roman term for a slave born into the master's household, remained in use.[15] *Mancipium* and *emtitus* carried associations of purchased property or chattel, as did the vernacular *testa*. *Famulus* changed its meaning: a Roman *famulus* was a slave member of the household, but a late medieval *famulus* was a free servant, usually an apprentice serving to learn.[16] Terms such as *colonus*, *ascriptus*, and *villanus* for people bound to the land or to agricultural service indicate an unfree status more like serfdom than slavery.[17] Every free person was *liber*. *Ingenui* were born free; *liberti* or *libertini* were manumitted.

Finally, a quirk of grammatical gender has affected scholarly analysis of late medieval slavery. In both Arabic and Latin, the masculine plural form is used for groups of mixed gender. As a consequence, the presence of female slaves is often hidden behind grammatically masculine forms.[18] Authors of legal texts resorted to gendered pairs of plural nouns (*sclavi et sclavae*, *mamālik wa-jawārī*) to refer unambiguously to male and female slaves as a group. In genres other than law, it is common to find only the masculine plural noun in cases where slaves of both genders were probably intended.

Slavery in Christian and Islamic Thought

Slavery was legal throughout the late medieval Mediterranean, and there was a broad consensus about what slavery as a legal status entailed. In Christian Europe, slave status was defined by the *ius commune*, the amalgam of Roman and canon law taught by the law faculties of medieval universities.[19] The Roman law curriculum was based on the Justinianic Code, while the canon law curriculum was based on Gratian's *Decretum*, compiled around 1140, and the *Liber Extra*, compiled by Raymond of Peñafort and issued in 1234.[20] All three works circulated with standard glosses that elaborated on and challenged the original text. The glosses also referenced biblical and Aristotelian texts, many of which were taught in medieval universities as part of the liberal arts curriculum that was a prerequisite for the study of law. For practical use, jurists created reference manuals with collections of model documents and discussions of the underlying legal principles, including slave status. These were called notarial formularies. The most widely copied and the first to appear in print was that of Rolandinus Passeggieri.

In contrast, Sunni Islamic law was divided into four schools (*madhhab*, pl. *madhāhib*): Mālikī, Ḥanafī, Shāfiʿī, and Ḥanbalī. Each school had its own legal texts and commentaries based on the Quran and *ḥadīth* (sayings and acts of Muḥammad), refined over the course of centuries. Most Islamic rulers favored one legal school over the others, but the Mamluk sultan was advised by judges from all four. The Mamluks also had a civil judicial system (*maẓālim*) through which subjects could petition the sultan and his administration, but *maẓālim* courts tended to hear cases concerning land rather than moveable goods like slaves.[21] Delving into the full ramifications of slavery in Islamic law is beyond the scope of a single book.[22] Instead, the following discussion will highlight the aspects of slavery on which all four schools agreed.

Both Christians and Muslims agreed that freedom was the original state of humanity and that free status should be assumed in ambiguous cases.[23] In its Christian formulation, freedom implied both a natural capacity (reason) and a legal capacity (property in oneself).[24] Slaves retained the natural capacity but lost the legal capacity: they had reason, but they were the property of others. Manumission meant "restoring them to their former origins and to the right of free birth, and declaring them Roman citizens, and restoring them to the primeval right according to which all men are born free."[25] Because the Roman empire no longer existed in the thirteenth century, gaining Roman citizenship meant gaining equal status to those born free. The Islamic formula for manumission made the former slave "free among the free Muslims, what is for them is for him and what is upon them is upon him."[26]

Because the original state of humanity was freedom, slaves' legal status did not affect their spiritual status. According to Iacopo da Varagine, a late thirteenth-century archbishop of Genoa, "all, whether slave or free, are created from earth and born nude and wailing . . . all, whether slave or free, have the same place, namely the same world, the same earth, the same air . . . all, whether slave or free, will die, dissolve into ash, and rot . . . all, whether slave or free, have one Lord . . . all, whether slave or free, will come to the judgment of God."[27] Ibn Manẓūr, the author of the fourteenth-century Arabic dictionary *Lisān al-ʿarab*, made a play to similar effect on *ʿabd*, a word that has two plural forms, *ʿabīd* and *ʿibād*. All people were *ʿibād* (worshippers) of God, but some were also *ʿabīd* (slaves) of God's creatures.[28] Thus slaves were not spiritually inferior and could take part in religious rites alongside free people.

Having accepted the principle of original freedom for slaves, medieval jurists were most interested in situations where obedience to God might conflict with obedience to a master. In general, they held that "if the master commands that which is not contrary to holy scriptures, let the slave be subject to the master. But if in fact he orders the contrary, let him obey the master of the spirit more than [that] of the body."[29] Christian slaves were not to be ordained as priests or admitted to monasteries, while Muslim slaves were not allowed to lead communal prayer.[30] Jurists were also interested in slave marriages, because they could produce conflicts between the rights of a spouse and those of a master.[31]

However, there were some who disputed the idea of spiritual equality for slaves on the basis that slavery was a consequence of sin. The rhetoric of spiritual enslavement to the passions was common in both Christian and Islamic texts, but it was Christian authors who spelled out a direct connection between spiritual and juridical slavery.[32] They linked slavery with original sin,[33] with Hagar and Ishmael (implying Christian superiority over Islam),[34] and with the Israelites' captivity in Egypt (implying Christian superiority over Judaism).[35] Although they also cited the curse of Ham as a divinely instituted basis for slavery, that story played a more important role in early modern ideologies of slavery than in medieval ones.[36]

The Quranic stories of Adam and Eve, Noah and Ham, Hagar and Ishmael, and Moses were not connected with slavery. When the Quran mentioned slavery, it was as an aspect of pre-Islamic society rather than as a consequence of sin, so Muslims were less likely than Christians to posit a connection between sin and juridical slavery. Nevertheless, Quranic references to slavery were interpreted by all four schools of Islamic law as divine authorization for the continued existence of slavery in the Islamic era.[37]

In addition to scripture, those arguing for the inherent inferiority of slaves adopted the concept of natural slavery from Aristotle's *Politics* and *Ethics*. Those texts were less popular among Muslim scholars than Plato's *Republic*, so Aristotelian natural slavery had relatively little influence on Islamic thought.[38] But because Aristotelian texts formed the bedrock of the Christian university curriculum, Christian scholars were more willing to embrace natural slavery.

The *Politics* was translated into Latin in the thirteenth century, and scholastic commentaries appeared almost immediately.[39] The commentators tended to harden Aristotle's statements on slavery, seeking consistency in a flexible text. One flexible element was the relationship between natural and juridical slavery. In some passages, Aristotle declared that juridical slaves were also slaves by nature, while in other passages, he conceded that natural masters might find themselves juridically enslaved. To address this inconsistency, the commentators tried to identify natural slaves in their own era, but what they found depended on which aspects of Aristotle's definition they chose to emphasize.[40] Those who emphasized rulership concluded that citizens, the ruled, were Aristotle's natural slaves. Those who emphasized physiognomy concluded that artisans or peasants were natural slaves because they were large and strong. Those who emphasized lack of reason concluded that barbarians were natural slaves. Because Aristotle associated barbarism with Scythians, the inhabitants of the Black Sea, this final answer came closest to the reality of late medieval slavery.

In his *Summa theologica*, the thirteenth-century theologian Thomas Aquinas famously endeavored to reconcile the truths of scripture and of Aristotle. The result was a powerful argument for the natural inferiority of slaves. Part of Aquinas' argument was outlined at the beginning of this chapter: he saw the dominion of some people over others as a natural aspect of human society from the moment of creation. However, drawing on Aristotle, he identified two forms of dominion.[41] In the civil form, the ruler exercised power over the ruled for the benefit of the ruled. This was the dominion exercised by the free over the free, rulers over citizens, and husbands over wives, and this was the dominion that existed in Eden. In the second, servile form of dominion, the ruler exercised power over the ruled for the ruler's own benefit. This form of dominion emerged from sin and was thus appropriate to the fallen world. It was exercised by tyrants over subjects and masters over slaves.

Setting aside philosophical debates about freedom and the nature of humanity, both Christians and Muslims recognized slavery in practice as a legitimate institution arising from and defined by human law.[42] They agreed that some slaves were born into slave status and that free people could be legally enslaved if they were unbelievers captured in war.[43] Penal enslavement and the sale of free people into slavery were forbidden by Islamic law.[44] The Justinianic Code permitted parents to sell their children into slavery; canon law also permitted it "in greatest necessity."[45] Selling oneself into slavery was forbidden, but the punishment for doing so was permanent enslavement.[46] Both the Justinianic Code and canon law also prescribed enslavement as a punishment for certain crimes.[47] In theory, for example, the concubines of priests could be sold into slavery, but in practice, the harshest punishment they suffered was exile.

Slave status involved both legal objectification and legal weakness. In the context of property law, slaves were objects and not persons. They could be bought, sold, gifted, rented, pledged, and otherwise disposed of like any other type of property.[48] The injury or death of a slave was considered property damage. Slaves were often grouped with animals in legal texts because both were living property.[49] In the context of family and criminal law, slaves were recognized as persons but were legally weak. They could not own property, inherit or bequeath property, conduct business, hold positions of legal authority, testify in court, execute a will, or serve as a legal guardian.[50] If slaves were found guilty of a crime, their masters might be held responsible for the associated fines or punishments. Some aspects of slaves' legal weakness could be mitigated by their masters. For example, Islamic law allowed a master to authorize a slave to conduct business.[51] Slaves of both Muslims and Christians could own a small amount of personal property, a *peculium*, which nominally belonged to their masters but in practice could be used to buy freedom. In certain respects, the legal weakness of slaves was comparable to that of women, minors, and the mentally ill.

Slavery and Religious Difference

Although slavery was legal in the late medieval Mediterranean, there were norms regarding who could enslave whom. Late medieval Mediterranean slavery was intrusive, meaning that slaves were supposed to be outsiders brought into the slaveholding society rather than insiders excluded or degraded from the slaveholding society.[52] The main criterion used to distinguish outsiders from insiders with respect to slavery was religion. Adherents of the same religion should not enslave one another, but adherents of different religions could enslave one another.[53] The special status granted to certain religious groups included both protection from enslavement and restrictions on slave ownership. Muslim authorities did not allow local Christians and Jews to own Muslim slaves, but they also forbade their enslavement by local Muslims.[54] Christian authorities did not allow local Muslims and Jews to own Christian slaves, but they also forbade their enslavement by local Christians, except in cases where enslavement was the judicial punishment for a crime.[55] When state protection was withdrawn, as when the Jewish population of Spain was expelled by Ferdinand and Isabella in 1492, these groups became vulnerable to enslavement.[56] Apart from protected groups, Christians were allowed to enslave Muslims, Muslims were allowed to enslave Christians, Jews were allowed to enslave Muslims in Christian states and Christians in Muslim states, and everyone was allowed to enslave pagans.

In addition to the expectation that slaves must come from different religious backgrounds than their masters, there was also an expectation that slaves would convert to the religion of their masters and that such conversions did not require manumission.[57] On the Islamic side, jurists permitted the forcible conversion of certain types of people, including women, children, and prisoners of war.[58] Converting slaves without manumission was thus legally straightforward. On the Christian side, canon law considered forcible conversions invalid because the sacrament of baptism required an intention to convert on the part of the person baptized. Late medieval missionaries, however, argued that masters with pious intentions could baptize enslaved children because they did not yet have the ability to form intentions or make binding vows themselves.[59] Still, manumission was not required, because the conversion of a slave was not an act of free will and because slavery was closely associated with sin. As explained by Franco Sacchetti, the son of a free Florentine man and a slave woman, "he who does not believe in the reward of Christ ought not to be free . . . for the most part they are like oxen to baptize. He does not even agree to become Christian through baptism. One is not held to free him, although he may be Christian, if he does not desire it. I do not say, that if he seems good and has the will to be a good Christian, that you do not do [an act of] mercy by freeing him, just as it would be bad and a sin, having a slave man or woman of guilty condition, as the greater part are, although he might be Christian, to free him."[60] In other words, converted slaves should remain under the paternalistic control of their masters for their own moral good.

The apparent simplicity of slavery based on religious difference was complicated by sectarianism. The Sunni–Shiʿite split within Islam was used to justify enslavement during the Ottoman era but not under the Mamluks.[61] More important to late medieval slavery was the Catholic–Orthodox split within Christianity. Although the schism had begun in the eleventh century over such issues as papal primacy, the addition of *filioque* to the Nicene Creed, and the use of leavening in eucharistic bread, bitter hostility between ordinary Catholics and Orthodox did not arise until the thirteenth century.[62] In the wake of the Fourth Crusade, Catholic powers including the papacy, the newly created Latin Empire of Constantinople, and Frankish states in the Aegean all adopted crusading as their framework for interacting with the Orthodox. Crusade preaching spread the image of the schismatic Greek, and repeated campaigns in the Aegean hardened attitudes on both sides. At the same time as Catholic crusades began to target Orthodox people, the Aegean was being colonized by Genoa and Venice and raided by Catalan and Turkish pirates. Both processes generated large numbers of captives.

In theory, Catholic and Orthodox Christians should not have enslaved one another no matter how much they hated each other. In practice, they did enslave one another, although Catholics had the upper hand and therefore enslaved more Orthodox than the reverse.[63] In the early fourteenth century, after the restoration of the Byzantine Empire in Constantinople, Byzantine authorities complained vigorously about this. Patriarch Athanasius I wrote to the Byzantine emperor in 1303–1305 about the misery of Greeks captured by Turks and Italians, "those who escape half-dead from the Ishmaelites and the very Italians . . . who were able to take them into captivity on account of the magnitude of general lawlessness, their disregard for God, and their scorn and neglect of the divine commandments."[64] Emperor Andronicus II Paleologus protested to Genoa in 1308 that "certain Genoese induced certain Greek boys and girls from Constantinople and from other countries in Romania [i.e., Greek territory], promising to do many good things for them, if they would come to Genoa with them. Many boys and girls came, and when they were in the city of Genoa they sold them as slaves, which is unjust."[65] In response, Genoa's colonial governor in Pera agreed to declare the enslaved Greeks free and permit them to leave. Andronicus II also wrote to Venice in 1319 to complain that Venetian pirates were selling Greeks as slaves in Rhodes and Cyprus.[66] In 1339, Andronicus III Paleologus sent envoys to Pope Benedict XII to discuss ecclesiastical union and an alliance against the Turks. Among various proposals for improving Catholic–Orthodox relations, he asked the pope to order that "all Greeks who were sold by Latins, wherever they are, should be freed, and in addition that Greeks should not be sold, and if certain people buy or sell them, or go against them, they should be excommunicated."[67] Benedict XII ignored this suggestion.

Most fourteenth-century Catholics seem to have felt that Orthodox people deserved enslavement. An anonymous English pilgrim in the 1340s observed that because the Orthodox priests of Cyprus did not accept papal primacy, "their punishment, when captured, is life servitude (*perpetua servitus*), nor does the Church of Rome, although it is a work of charity to ransom slaves (*servos*), lift a hand for their liberation."[68] Another pilgrim in the 1340s, Niccolò of Poggibonsi, also used Orthodox rejection of papal primacy to justify their enslavement:

> The Greeks hate us Latins more than they hate the Saracens, and through this great hatred they are separated from the Roman Church. As we make the pope, the vicar of God, to be the head of the Roman Church for Christians, likewise the Greeks make a vicar for themselves. In the place of the pope, they make the patriarch of Constantinople, and he makes the bishops. . . . Every Sunday the pope communicates with all those who obey him; but the pope treats them [the Greeks] in this way, that he allows others to take them and then sell them as slaves. And many times I saw merchants who had a great line, and they led them thus to sell at the market, as they do beasts; and when a merchant wants to sell this sad

> merchandise, he has them cried by the auctioneer; and whoever offers the most money, to him they are sold. O Greeks, who were masters of the world, and now are made slaves, resold throughout the world, priced like beasts![69]

The early fourteenth-century crusade propagandist William of Adam offered a more moderate expression of this position: the pope did not have a pastoral duty toward Orthodox Christians but nevertheless deplored their enslavement by Muslims.[70]

Controversy over Catholic ownership of Orthodox slaves continued into the fifteenth century. In 1388, the bishop of Barcelona persuaded King John I of Aragon to restrict ownership of Greek slaves, but in 1401, the city council of Barcelona obtained a privilege from Pope Martin I that not only permitted ownership of Greek slaves but also prevented slaves "of the nation of the Greeks or who are Armenians, Albanians, Russians, Bulgars, Walachs, or from the parts or regions subject to the emperor of Constantinople" from challenging their status in court.[71] An envoy from John VIII Paleologus to Venice in 1418 protested that a Venetian man in Modon was selling Byzantine subjects to the Catalans and holding others for ransom.[72] The Venetian Senate denied the claims on the basis that its castellan in Modon would never allow such behavior. Bans by later popes on the sale of Greek slaves were quickly revoked.[73] In the 1430s, a Burgundian visiting Constantinople reported that the Greeks "had reached the point of damning the Pope who had held a general council in which they were declared schismatics and damned and that they were a race of slaves (*tous fussent serfs à ceux qui estoient serfs*)."[74]

Although the status of Greek slaves attracted the most attention and debate, the majority of Orthodox slaves owned by Catholics were not Greek. In fifteenth-century Genoa, for example, Russians and Circassians were the two most common categories of slaves.[75] Russians had adopted Orthodox Christianity in the tenth century, around the same time that Scandinavians had adopted Catholicism. Orthodox Christianity was also well established in the Caucasus.[76] The kingdom of Georgia was a regional bastion of Orthodoxy, although it also had suzerainty over small Muslim principalities, such as Samtzkhe. Coastal Circassian and Abkhaz communities maintained close ties with Constantinople. Inland, however, the situation was murkier. Circassian and Abkhaz nobles treated religious allegiance as a political decision and could therefore be flexible about their professions of faith. During the fourteenth century, as Genoa established hegemony in the Black Sea, a few professed Catholicism.[77] Circassian and Abkhaz villagers practiced a syncretic religion that blended Orthodoxy with animism. They decorated sacred trees with crosses and attached the attributes of older deities like Merise, the goddess of bees, to Christian figures, such as Mary.[78] As a result, Catholic authors claimed fellowship with Georgians, Circassians, and Abkhaz when they wanted to emphasize the extent of the world's Christian population but disavowed them in the context of slavery.

Other Christian groups were enslaved in smaller numbers. They included Armenians, Alans, Crimean Goths, Kipchak Turks,[79] and the Ruthenians of Galicia and Volhyna.[80] In the 1430s, rumors circulated that Black Sea Christians were descendants of mythical Catholic crusaders who had detoured around the perfidious Greeks of Constantinople.[81] Other rumors suggested that the Crimean Goths were related to the Visigoths, the Germans, or the Scots.[82] Nevertheless, slaves from all of these groups could be found in Genoa, Venice, and their colonies.[83] In consequence, scholars have dismissed centuries of Christian life in the Black Sea, claiming that the region was mostly pagan or that its religious diversity enabled merchants to pick and choose non-Christian slaves rather than acknowledge that Catholic Christians systematically enslaved Orthodox Christians.[84]

The possibility of Muslims enslaving Muslims has also been dismissed by modern scholars. Despite the fact that Islam was the dominant religion of the Golden Horde and its Tatar subjects, modern scholars have assumed that mamluks of Tatar origin were pagan or that the Islamization of the Golden Horde was superficial and therefore legally and ethically irrelevant.[85] Upon investigation, however, it is clear that many mamluks from the Black Sea must have been Muslim.[86] Scholars at the time were aware that Islam was widespread among Tatars and Alans and that many mamluks were of Tatar or Alan origin.[87] In recounting his life story, the amir Taghrī Barmish al-Jalālī revealed that he had been born in Anatolia and that his father was Muslim.[88] Another amir, Yalbughā al-Sālimī, was born in Samarqand to a Muslim family and given the name Yūsuf.[89] A popular epic glorifying Baybars, the first Mamluk sultan, said that his original name was Maḥmūd and that he was the son of the Muslim king of Khurasan.[90] Although this story is untrue, it suggests an awareness among ordinary Mamluk people that some of their slaves had Muslim origins. One reason why mamluks were given the patronymic Ibn ʿAbd Allah, "son of a servant of God," may have been to veil the names of their Muslim fathers.[91]

Mamluk-era scholars showed equally scant concern for the enslavement of Muslim women from peripheral areas like the Black Sea. When al-Subkī, a fifteenth-century Mamluk jurist, was asked about how to avoid buying slave concubines of Muslim origin, his response departed from the legal principle of assuming freedom in ambiguous cases.[92] Instead, he ruled that men could keep concubines of probable Muslim origin as long as there was any possibility at all that they might be descended from slaves. Al-Subkī's response stands in sharp contrast to that of Aḥmad Bābā, a seventeenth-century jurist from Timbuktu, who advised traders in the Saharan oasis of Suwāt about how to avoid buying Muslim slaves.[93] Aḥmad Bābā listed African peoples known to be Muslim and urged the traders not to buy slaves from those groups.

Therefore, despite the fact that religious difference was the legal basis of slavery in the late medieval Mediterranean, both Christians and Muslims enslaved their coreligionists from the Black Sea and were aware of what they were doing. How did they justify this conflict between the ideology and practice of slavery? One part of the answer lies in the significance of conversion. By forcing their slaves to convert, masters claimed to increase the number of souls belonging to the "right" religion. This claim fostered a competitive attitude toward slaves' souls and, in some cases, a desire to accumulate slaves to prevent their conversion to the "wrong" religion as well as to enforce their conversion to the "right" one.

Chapter 7 explains how in the context of the crusades, the Mamluk system of military slavery came to be perceived by both Muslims and Christians as a means to win slaves' souls for Islam and defend the Islamic world against attacks by pagans and Christians. Similarly, canon law required Christian communities to buy Christian slaves and potential converts from Jews to protect them from conversion to Judaism, while Jewish communities in Egypt regarded the integration of slave converts as a victory for their faith.[94] The fourteenth-century Dominican William of Adam dramatized the plight of Christian slaves in Muslim hands with two tales. The first was that of a Greek slave woman on the road to Persia who gave birth to a son. She debated whether to kill the child to prevent him from apostatizing or whether to keep him alive and rely on God's mercy. William characterized this as a struggle between faith (*fides*) and love (*pietas*), with the faithful decision being to kill her son.[95] The second tale was that of a slave convert in India who felt abandoned by God: "The Lord has turned His back to us, not His face; He has stricken us with His heel, utterly destroyed, and uprooted, and deserted us as useless logs cut for burning and has apparently deleted us from His memory. What shall we do? . . . Although I believe and know that it is better to put down the burden of the flesh than to lose eternal life, I have not been granted by heaven the gift of dying for the faith which I hold in my heart."[96] Putting words in the mouths of both real and fictional characters was a common medieval rhetorical device, and William may have invented these two tales to make a point. That point was the spiritual violence of slavery. Conversion was the greatest fear and most painful injury suffered by William's imagined slaves.[97]

By the fifteenth century, the Castilian traveler Pero Tafur was able to claim that "the Christians have a Bull from the Pope, authorizing them to buy and keep as slaves the Christians of other nations, to prevent their falling into the hands of the Moors and renouncing the Faith. They are Russians, Mingrelians, Abkhaz, Circassians, Bulgars, Armenians, and other diverse Christian nations."[98] Tafur explained his own purchase of three Christian slaves by juxtaposing it with the Mamluk slave trade taking place around him. If he had not purchased them, they would have been purchased by Mamluk merchants and converted to Islam.

The fifteenth-century humanist Giovanni Gioviano Pontano also offered an explanation for the phenomenon of Christians enslaving Christians. He believed that Muslims (Turks and Africans) observed the prohibition against enslaving fellow Muslims, but

> among us, Christians also serve. For as I heard from the ancients, the custom was that Thracians and also Greeks who inhabit the Black Sea be sold: who, lest they be in the service of the barbarians, merchants sailing the Black Sea, having redeemed them from the Scythians, were offering them for sale. For it seemed more honorable to serve them for a short time, while they repaid the money paid per head, than to be the plunder of barbarians and submissive to perpetual servitude, also with the greatest disgrace of the Christian name. . . . Therefore this great injury to humankind is made the law of humanity.[99]

In other words, Pontano thought it better for Orthodox Christians from the Black Sea to be purchased by Catholics and serve them in repayment than to be purchased by non-Christians.

In merchant circles, respect for property rights was sometimes given priority over the threat of slave conversion. This caused an outcry in 1445 when a fourteen- or fifteen-year-old slave described as a Christian from the land of Prester John (probably Ethiopia) fled from the house of his Muslim master in Alexandria to a ship belonging to the famous French merchant Jacques Coeur.[100] The ship captain took the boy to Montpellier, where he was placed as a servant in the archbishop's household. But Coeur feared that French galleys might no longer be allowed to trade in Egypt because his captain had violated an agreement with the Mamluks about the return of fugitive slaves. He ordered the boy shipped back; upon his return to Alexandria, the boy converted to Islam. This shocked the French Church, especially the religious orders dedicated to ransoming Christian captives from Muslims. French merchants who did business with Muslims maintained that Coeur had acted correctly. The resulting controversy played a role in Coeur's fall from royal favor.

I have found only one medieval expression of remorse for the enslavement of coreligionists. Leontios Makhairas, a Greek Cypriot chronicler of the early fifteenth century, felt that the 1373 Genoese conquest of the island was divine punishment for Cypriot enslavement of their fellow Orthodox Christians:

> And if you wish me to tell you how it was that Famagusta was taken, I say that this was allowed by God because of our sins. And not Famagusta only: it would have been just that they should have taken all Cyprus as well, because of our many sins. And to tell you about it openly: first of all was the sin of the slaves. The land of the Greeks was being ravaged, and the men were being brought over to the islands as slaves and captives, and our people treated them so hard-heartedly, that they used to throw themselves down from the roofs and kill themselves, and some of them cast themselves into pits, and others hanged themselves, for the heavy torments which they made them endure, and because they were famished. . . . And they went against the face of God, who says: "Six years your servant shall serve you, and in the seventh you shall set him free." . . . For this reason God punished them, and the Bulgarians took horse against them; the slaves also and the Genoese; and they robbed them and carried them off captive, and took away their women and their goods, and humbled them to the ground.[101]

Makhairas' remorse was limited, however. Elsewhere in his chronicle, he criticized Greek, Bulgar, and Tatar slaves for supporting the Genoese invasion. His contemporaries in Cyprus did not cease to buy Orthodox slaves.[102]

Slavery in Court

Because slavery was a matter of human law (*ius gentium*) in the Christian context, cases of slave status were adjudicated in civil rather than ecclesiastical courts. Each Italian city-state had its own law code (*ius proprium*), a set of local customs, and a system of courts to enforce them. However, because most Italian jurists studied law at the university in Bologna, the principles of Roman law and the *ius commune* underpinned most local legislation on slavery.[103] Since the Justinianic Code provided an authoritative and comprehensive legal framework for slave status, legislators in Venice and Genoa largely confined themselves to regulating the use and behavior of slaves.[104] Only the Genoese legal code attempted to define slave status: "let male and female slaves be understood . . . as those who were possessed or detained by any person as male or female slaves."[105] In another passage, slaves were defined as submissive persons.[106] In a third passage, a slave was defined as "she who is held and owned as a slave by her master or mistress, and she who is considered and held to be a slave by the neighborhood of the said master or mistress."[107] These definitions are more or less circular, although they do highlight the role of reputation and witness testimony alongside written documents in determining slave status.

In Venice, cases of disputed status were handled by the Senate. For example, a Venetian patrician returning from Beirut in 1399 brought with him a manumitted Tatar who wished to convert to Christianity and live in Venice.[108] Upon their arrival, the patrician entrusted him to another Tatar freedman, Antonius, a *vacinarius* who prepared cow- and oxhides. Instead of helping him, Antonius sold him as a slave for twenty ducats to Zanino Calcaterra, who sold him again to a Catalan man. When the case came to light, the Venetian Senate condemned Antonius to a beating, three months in prison, and compensation for Calcaterra, but it did not mention the fate of the wrongfully enslaved Tatar.

The most famous and long-running case of disputed status was that of the *anime*. In 1386, the Senate first ruled against importing Albanian children from Durazzo who "can easily be sold and treated as slaves, which is done wrongly and against God and the honor of our dominions," explaining that "because they are Christian, they ought not to sell them nor cause them to be sold in any way."[109] Such children were called "souls" (*anime*). The punishment for selling *anime* was a fine of one hundred lire and six months in prison for each child. All previous sales of *anime* were annulled, and sellers were required to compensate buyers for their losses. The *anime* already present in Venice were not to be exported to other cities, such as Florence, Siena, or Bologna, where their slavery might become permanent.[110] However, the *anime* had to repay the freight charges for their shipment to Venice. The debt was set at six ducats for those older than ten and three ducats for those younger; those with no money could work for four years in lieu of payment.

This ruling proved difficult to enforce, and in 1387, the *capisestieri* complained to the Senate. The Senate responded that masters who could show documents (*cartas, instrumenta, vel probationes*) to prove that their child slaves came from beyond Corfu (outside the Adriatic) could keep them.[111] In 1388, the Senate received another complaint that the *anime* were "rustic and of rude intellect" so that "no utility or benefit can follow from them" after liberation.[112] In fact, said the complaint, their masters had done them a service by rescuing them from the Turks and supporting them. The Senate's response was to raise the price of freedom to eight ducats or ten years of service, but *anime* still had to be registered with the *capisestieri* and could not be exported. Their status remained a problem as late as 1453, when the penalty for evading registration was extended from the owners of *anime* to the ship captains who imported them.[113]

In Genoa, cases of disputed status were decided by the *sindicatori*. They usually took the form of petitions by slaves claiming freedom on the basis of Christian origin or prior manumission. For example, a slave who had been manumitted in the will of Augustinus Iahele of Savona was nevertheless handed over to Oliverius de Maris in Genoa.[114] With Oliverius' consent, she petitioned the *sindicatori* to recognize her manumission by Augustinus and officially declare her free.

The process began when the slave designated a procurator, a Genoese citizen with full legal rights, to petition the *sindicatori* on her behalf. Her master was then called upon to respond: he might do so in person or designate a procurator to represent him. Each side presented legal arguments and evidence, including written documents and oral testimony. For example, three Genoese merchants and a ship captain were called upon as witnesses to the free status of Maurus, a Greek sailor whom a Genoese merchant attempted to sell as a slave in Palermo in 1328.[115] An extract from Genoa's tax cartularies was offered as evidence in the case of Caterina, a Greek woman from Cephalonia, and a sale document in the case of Cali, also known as Theodora.[116]

Having heard the arguments of each side, the *sindicatori* would arrive at a decision and order its execution. Thus, in 1479, the *sindicatori* decided that "Maria has been established as a Hungarian in law and in the presence of the honorable lords *sindicatori* of the commune of Genoa."[117] Through her ethnicity, Maria's religion and legal status were made clear: "the said Maria was and is a Hungarian and a Christian, and by consequence free, and cannot be retained as a slave, but rather must and ought to be held as free."[118] Therefore the *sindicatori* manumitted her by decree and required her to pay 150 lire, an enormous sum, to compensate her former masters for all expenses associated with her purchase in Chios, including the purchase price, taxes, and freight charges. She was given ten days to arrange payment and three months after that to make payment in full. If she failed to pay on time, the decree of manumission would lapse. No punishment was imposed on Maria's former masters despite the ruling that she had been enslaved illegally.[119] This was normal; the *sindicatori* rarely penalized either the sellers or the owners of wrongfully enslaved Christians, and in many cases, the slave herself was ordered to compensate her former owner for the loss of her value.

We do not know whether Maria was able to pay her owner in time. The consequences of failure are represented by the case of an Albanian woman named Theodora.[120] The *sindicatori* declared her Christian and therefore free in August 1479. One year later, they added a fine of twenty-five lire to cover her initial price, associated expenses, and taxes in response to a petition from the heirs of her former master. Theodora failed to pay the fine within ten days. On July 18, the *sindicatori* had her detained by the commune until she paid the twenty-five lire plus three soldi in additional expenses.

Although it might seem impossible for a newly manumitted slave to find enough money to compensate her owner within ten days, a woman named Maria managed to do so in 1481. Once Maria was declared free of Melchionis de Monleone, she immediately designated Petrus de Camulo as her new procurator. His first task was to pay eighteen ducats to Melchionis as required by the *sindicatori*. He also took responsibility for defending Maria in court, in general and specifically against Melchionis. Finally, he committed "to renting and pensioning the same Maria in the city of Genoa to that person or those persons of good condition and reputation, and for that price and salary which can best be had."[121] Once Petrus found work for Maria as a free domestic servant, she would repay him for his assistance.

In the courts of Genoa, some slaves were more successful at challenging their status than others. A clear case of wrongful enslavement was that of Maria, a young woman from Naples who petitioned the *sindicatori* in 1492. Three years earlier, she had been living with her parents in Naples. A ship's scribe had enticed her to leave, promising that she would be his servant and mistress, but then he sold her as a slave in Genoa. Fortunately, Maria's parents were able to locate her. Ladislaus Doguorno, a canon of Salerno, and Antonio Soprano of Naples both traveled to Genoa and testified on her behalf. Ladislaus' testimony has survived: he told the *sindicatori* that he knew both Maria and her parents and that Maria was recognized as a Christian in Naples and elsewhere by those who knew her. He protested that her enslavement was illegal "because Christians cannot be sold or obligated."[122] Maria was duly declared free.

Other slaves of Catholic origin also petitioned for freedom on the basis of shared religion. In 1487, a slave appealed to the *sindicatori* because she had been sold as an Iberian Muslim (*mora*) but was actually an Iberian Christian (*hispana*).[123] In 1455, a Hungarian woman named Anna designated a procurator to petition for freedom on the grounds that "she is Christian and free, conducting herself as a free person, and of Hungarian origin who cannot be sold as a slave either by law or by the form of the ordinances of the city of Genoa."[124] However, Hungarian Catholics who succeeded in petitioning for freedom were still required to pay compensation.[125] Georgius was freed in 1405 but ordered to serve an additional nine years without a salary. Elena was freed in 1418 but ordered to pay ninety lire, which she did by contracting to serve Cattaneo Doria for fourteen years. Maria, mentioned previously, was freed in 1479 but ordered to pay 150 lire in 1479. Caterina was also freed in 1479 but ordered to pay 180 lire.

Italians, Iberians, and Hungarians were widely known to be Catholic. In 1394, a Catholic Tatar slave "presented himself in [the Genoese colony of] Chios before the lord podestà of Chios in his court, asserting himself to be a Christian of the Catholic nation and never a slave but rather free and a man of his own right. The lord podestà of Chios, having seen the witnesses produced by the said slave, liberated him."[126] Antonio Coca, a broker in Pera who had sold this slave about one month previously, was ordered to reimburse the buyer. The fact that a Tatar slave won his freedom in a Genoese colonial court on the basis of shared Catholicism should stand as a warning to modern historians not to rely too much on apparent correlations between ethnicity and religious affiliation.

Among Orthodox Christians, some had more success in petitioning for freedom than others. An Armenian woman named Marta was freed in 1417 but required to pay fifty lire, which she did by arranging to serve Isotta Bracelli for seven years (reduced to five years if she worked as a wet nurse).[127] Two Albanian women also had success with the *sindicatori* in 1479 and 1480.[128] We do not know the outcome of three more petitions by Albanians, one of whom identified herself as the daughter of the late Amzrendari Aragi and asserted that she was "free and born from free parents and of Christian race and therefore cannot nor ought to be detained in servitude."[129] A woman from Sclavonia designated procurators to present her petition in 1487, but the outcome of her case is not recorded either.[130] Finally, the podestà of Lucca heard a case in 1413 in which a procurator argued for the freedom of a slave woman "because she was of Bosnian origin and Christian, and in that region Christ the Lord is worshipped, through whose blood all believers are redeemed, and entirely exempt from any yoke of servitude."[131] His argument is one of the more explicit statements linking redemption or manumission from juridical servitude with Christ's redemption of humanity from sin.

There were a number of successful petitions from Greek Orthodox slaves.[132] In 1398, a Greek woman who had served Babilanus Alpanus as a free servant (*famula*) appointed a procurator when she heard that Babilanus intended to make her a slave (*sclava*). She protested that this was illegal because "she was begotten of Greek parents."[133] In 1479, a Greek woman named Anna was freed because Greeks should not "be sold nor bought nor kept as a slave as accustomed by law and by justice," while her owners were urged to accept the decision "lest the soul of the said late Ilarius [Anna's deceased former owner] suffer on account of such retention."[134] Similar cases are documented in Genoa in 1424 and 1489 as well as in Caffa in 1380 and 1398.[135]

Orthodox Christians from Bulgaria were treated inconsistently by the *sindicatori*. Many Greek slaves based their petitions for freedom precisely on the fact that they were not Bulgar. Thus, in 1380, a slave woman who demonstrated herself to be a Greek from Constantinople and not a Bulgar was freed on the grounds "that all Greeks should be free and held and treated as free in the city and district of Genoa."[136] The Christianity of Bulgars apparently did not warrant the same protection. Yet when Michael, a male slave, was determined to be Bulgar and not Tatar in 1391, the *sindicatori* chose to manumit him on the condition that he serve for another eight years without salary.[137] A controversy over the baptism of a fugitive slave in 1488 turned on whether she was Hungarian and therefore already Christian, or Bulgar and therefore apparently not Christian enough.[138] The case of a slave named Cali or Theodora depended on whether she was a Greek from Constantinople, as she herself testified, or a Tatar purchased in Cyprus, as her owners claimed.[139]

Finally, there is no record of a Christian from Russia or the Caucasus being freed on the basis of shared religion. There are records of Mingrelian, Circassian, and Abkhaz women petitioning the *sindicatori* because their previous manumissions were not being honored, but none cited Christian origin as a factor in her defense.[140] This is odd, because Russians and Caucasians made up the majority of the Genoese slave population during the fifteenth century and because most of the inhabitants of both Russia and the Caucasus were Orthodox Christians at that time. Some possible reasons for the discrepancy will be offered in Chapter 2.

In the Mamluk sultanate, disputes over slave status were heard by a *qāḍī*, a judge belonging to one of the four schools of Islamic law.[141] If the religion of the alleged slave was at issue, the slave herself was allowed to testify. If the dispute arose from a mistake in the act of manumission, witness testimony played an important role. The cases that received the most attention were those of mamluks whose manumission had not been correctly performed and whose status therefore had to be rectified before they could hold government posts.[142] For example, an amir named Aytamush was about to be made a general (*atabak*) when Sultan Barqūq was informed of a problem with his manumission. Aytamush had belonged to another mamluk named Asandamur, who in turn had belonged to Jurjī, the governor of Aleppo. When Jurjī died in 1370, an amir named Bajjās took possession of both Asandamur and Aytamush and manumitted them, but this manumission was invalid because Bajjās had acquired them illegally. Technically, Aytamush still belonged to the estate of Jurjī. So before Aytamush could become a general, Sultan Barqūq had to contact the heirs of Jurjī, buy Aytamush, and remanumit him.

The Universal Threat of Slavery

"God has given you the right of ownership over them; He could have given them the right of ownership over you."[143] This was not a platitude. Slavery in the late medieval Mediterranean threatened everyone, and no group was exempt from its dangers. After encountering prisoners begging for money and children displayed for sale in Cairo, the Franciscan Paul Walther de Guglingen and his fellow pilgrims "lamented the misery of such people, praising God, our creator, who had hitherto kept us safe from such things, and asking him strenuously that he keep us safe from these miseries and bring us back in health to the land of the faithful."[144] They did not seek to rescue anyone but simply hoped to reach home safely themselves.

Free people from all parts of the Mediterranean were vulnerable to capture in war. Holy war offered the best opportunity for taking slaves (as opposed to captives), because by definition, it involved opponents of different religions.[145] As a result, the late medieval crusades generated many slaves. Frankish residents of Tripoli were enslaved after the fall of that city in 1268, as were Frankish residents of Acre in 1291.[146] Five thousand Muslim residents of Alexandria were captured by Peter of Cyprus in 1365, some of whom were ransomed and the rest of whom were enslaved.[147] The Mamluk conquest of Cyprus in 1426 generated large numbers of slaves.[148] This is not to mention the slaves, both Franks and Turks, taken in crusades against the Ottomans.[149] *Corso* (holy war conducted through piracy) threatened everyone who traveled by sea.[150] The arrival of a ship that had captured thirteen Christian sailors en route from Libya to Alexandria was marked by public celebration.[151] In Valencia, Muslims captured by Christian pirates were displayed publicly for the satisfaction of local Christians who feared the same fate at the hands of Muslim pirates.[152] Pero Tafur, a fifteenth-century Castilian traveler, told a story about Castilian and Catalan pirates who preyed on Muslim shipping until they themselves were captured and forced into piracy against Christians on behalf of the sultan.[153]

Travelers and free people living along the coast were also vulnerable to enslavement by ordinary pirates and raiders. The Greek population of the Aegean was prey to Venetians, Genoese, and Catalans as well as Turks from the emirates of Menteshe, Aydin, and the Ottoman sultanate. Caterina, a Greek woman from Negroponte, petitioned the *sindicatori* of Genoa for freedom after having been captured by the trireme of Domenicus de Nigrono and sold as a slave.[154] Pilgrims bound for Jerusalem were advised not to wander along the seashore in the eastern Mediterranean, "lest [they] be suddenly seized by pirates and reduced to perpetual and miserable servitude, which often happens."[155] Shipwreck, a danger in itself, might also cast travelers ashore among enemies who "would have carried us into a strange land and sold us all."[156]

In the late medieval Mediterranean, ship captains could not even be trusted to protect the freedom of their own passengers and crew. For example, in 1316, a Venetian captain decided to enslave and sell several Greeks whom he had taken on board as sailors in Monemvasia.[157] A different Venetian captain enslaved and sold some Greek merchants whom he had accepted as passengers in Salonika.[158] The same thing happened to a group of Tunisian merchants who arranged passage from Cairo to the Barbary coast on a Catalan ship in 1408; the captain sailed to Barcelona instead and sold the merchants as slaves.[159] In 1440, a Venetian man named Petrus Marcello decided to kidnap Hajji Ibrahim, a Muslim merchant from Acre who owed him money. He then sailed to Beirut to negotiate with Ibrahim's son Hassan. Marcello invited Hassan and ten other men to come aboard his ship but then sailed away to Rhodes and sold all twelve as slaves. After the Mamluk sultan complained to Venice, Marcello was ordered to find and release them. Seven of the men had apparently been shipped to Nice, so Marcello asked his family to contact the duke and duchess of Burgundy and find out who had purchased them.[160] We do not know whether he ever succeeded in locating the people he had sold.

The threat of capture and enslavement affected the powerful and noble as well as ordinary sailors, merchants, and fishermen. Al-Ḥasan ibn Aḥmad al-Razī, a learned judge and physician who spent most of his life in Damascus, was enslaved in 1299 during the Mamluk–Ilkhan war and sold to a Frankish master in Cyprus.[161] In 1311–1312, a ship carrying Mamluk and Mongol ambassadors was captured by Genoese pirates based in Chios.[162] The pirates tried to sell the ambassadors and their retinue, about sixty people in total. No one would buy them because Sultan al-Nāṣir Muḥammad had ordered the retaliatory arrest of all Frankish merchants, both Genoese and non-Genoese, who lived in Alexandria, Damascus, and other Mamluk cities. Eventually, Segurano Salvaygo, a Genoese noble in Mamluk service, was able to negotiate the release of both the ambassadors and the merchants. A similar incident occurred in 1388, when Frankish pirates captured the sister of Sultan Barqūq and the daughter of his nephew en route from Syria to Egypt.[163] In 1319, a Byzantine ambassador was captured and sold by Venetian pirates while traveling to Venice on official business.[164] In 1387, the master of the Hospitaller order in the Peleponnese was captured in battle, sold as a slave, and vanished from the historical record.[165]

The risk of enslavement applied even to the inhabitants of the Black Sea slaving ports. In 1341, Nicoletto Gata, a Venetian merchant resident in Tana, arranged to send a slave back to his wife in Venice. Yet seven years later, Nicoletto himself was sold as a slave in Saray, the capital of the Golden Horde, because he was unable to pay his debts. He was fortunate to have business associates to whom he could appeal for help.[166] Filippo Lomellini, the Genoese castellan of Cembalo in the Black Sea, was not so lucky. He was captured in battle and sold in the 1450s, and he never resurfaced.[167]

Although slavery and captivity were ever-present dangers in the eastern Mediterranean and the Black Sea, the distinction between them could be hazy. Slavery was usually based on religious difference, whereas captivity did not have to be. Slavery was permanent, at least in theory, whereas captivity was expected to end in ransom or exchange. As a rule of thumb, sale marked the transition from captive to slave because it generated a written legal document and witnesses that could serve as evidence of slave status later on. For example, after triumphing over Byzantine forces in 1352, the victorious Genoese general Paganino Doria agreed to release all of his Greek captives, except those who had already been sold. This clause in the peace treaty led to a lawsuit thirteen years later in Genoa. A Greek woman named Lucia petitioned the *sindicatori* for freedom in 1365 because she had been captured by Doria but never sold as a slave.[168] Lucia's mistress, Violante, argued that Doria had sold Lucia and other captives to Bartolomeo Lercario and Antonio Pellavicino. Lercario and Pellavicino took Lucia to the market of Theologum in Turkish territory and sold her to Iacobus de Guaterio, Violante's brother, who in turn gave her to Violante as a gift. Lucia, however, testified that she remembered being captured but did not remember being sold to Lercario, Pellavicino, or Guaterio. The outcome of this case is not known, but the result clearly depended on whether Lucia had been sold.

In most cases, the distinction between slavery and captivity was not so clear. Captives sold into slavery might still be ransomed, especially if they remained close to home. In Tana, a Russian woman named Maria was ransomed by her brother after three years in slavery, but on the condition that she stay with her master for two additional years to nurse their baby daughter before returning home.[169] Greek slaves were occasionally sold within the Aegean Sea with a clause requiring their new masters to accept future offers of ransom. Leo, a Greek slave from Samos, was sold to a physician in Crete "in perpetuity, except however that if his father or any of his relatives want to ransom him, you [the buyer] are bound to return him."[170] Notaries sometimes facilitated the process. Nicola de Boateriis, a Venetian notary in Famagusta, seems to have used his connections in Negroponte to organize the ransom of several slaves.[171]

On the other hand, ransom did not necessarily mean an immediate return to freedom. Captives ransomed by a charitable stranger instead of a family member were expected to compensate their redeemers with money or service. This expectation may have been rooted in the Roman concept of *postliminium*.[172] It may also have been influenced by canon law, which required pagan slaves redeemed from Jewish or Muslim masters to compensate their Christian redeemers.[173] When service was offered as compensation, the term was usually five years, but some jurists allowed the redeemer to keep the ransomed captive indefinitely.[174] In other words, ransom might simply mean slavery under a different master.

In the eastern Mediterranean, ransoms by charitable strangers were often formalized with a document of sale in which the stranger purchased the slave followed by a document of manumission in which the stranger promised to free the slave after a certain period of service. For example, in 1427–1428, Giorgio of

Milan purchased three Greek slaves in Alexandria who had been taken in the recent Mamluk conquest of Cyprus.[175] He immediately freed two but retained the third, a widow, to serve him until she was able to pay back the forty ducats of her ransom. Likewise, Elena, a Greek slave in the house of Andrea de Moneglia in Chios, petitioned the bishop of Chios for freedom.[176] The bishop arranged for her to be redeemed by another Genoese man, Nicolaus Pichaluga of Sampierdarena, who paid twenty-five ducats for her. In return, Elena agreed to serve Nicolaus for five years. During that time, she would receive food, drink, and clothing; she would be treated well; and Nicolaus would not dismiss her against her will. These clauses were standard in the employment contracts of free servants. At the end of five years, her debt would be repaid, and she would be entirely free.

In the interval between the ransom payment and the fulfillment of the terms of manumission, the ransomed captive was technically a slave of his or her redeemer. This precarious position sometimes led to permanent enslavement. An extreme case was that of Stefano di Posaga. In 1439, Nicolo Morosini, the captain of an official Venetian galley returning from Tana, stopped at Ponterachia, a Turkish port, to take on water. There he rescued a fugitive slave, Stefano di Posaga. However, when the galley arrived in Venice, Morosini sent Posaga to work on his land in Padua, "holding him as a slave (*servum*)."[177] After four years, he sold Posaga to another ship captain, who was supposed to take him to Syracuse. Posaga finally contested his status in Syracuse, where the judges freed him. Judges in Venice then fined Morosini 200 lire. This is one of the rare cases in which a medieval judge penalized someone for wrongful enslavement. The fact that Posaga was an Italian man and not a Russian woman is undoubtedly relevant to the punishment of his enslaver.

How a person's status might slip from ransomed captive to permanent slave is illuminated by an unusual passage in a document from Kilia, a Black Sea port at the mouth of the Danube River. In the document, a Genoese woman named Iohanna sold a Greek slave woman named Maria. However, the document deviated from the usual legal formulas to include a statement about the circumstances behind the sale:

> This is the slave whom the said Bartolomeo, Iohanna's husband, redeemed from Saracens in Asprocastro [i.e., Moncastro], in which place she was a slave, as the aforesaid Iohanna and the slave Maria both assert. Maria asserts the aforesaid things to be true, and that it is also true that she, Maria, was and is a slave of the said Iohanna and Bartolomeo on account of the aforesaid redemption, allowing it to be true that there is not any instrument or document concerning the aforesaid matters.

> And Iohanna made the aforesaid sale, as she asserts, on account of the need which she has for money for the subsistence of life for herself and her two daughters, because she said that the said Bartolomeo her husband does not do and has not done any good for Iohanna or for her daughters, several months having now elapsed, but he stays in Maurocastro [i.e., Moncastro] with a certain woman whom he keeps, and also in order to pay one *sommum* of silver to a certain priest to whom the said Iohanna is obligated, as she asserts.[178]

In other words, Maria was trapped in the gray area between captivity and slavery. She had been enslaved by Muslims in the Black Sea port of Moncastro and ransomed by a Christian stranger, Bartolomeo de Azano. Bartolomeo brought her to his home in Kilia, where she served his wife, Iohanna, and their two daughters. When Bartolomeo abandoned his family and moved to Moncastro to live with another woman, Iohanna was no longer able to support her daughters. She decided to sell Maria to raise money and pay the debt she had already contracted with a priest. Slaves were expensive, and Maria may well have been Iohanna's single most valuable possession.

When Bartolomeo acquired Maria, was he redeeming a captive or purchasing a slave? Maria and Iohanna said that Maria had been redeemed (*redemit*), but in the next line, Maria testified that she was a slave (*sclava*). This is surprising, because slaves were not legal persons and did not have the capacity to give legal testimony. Nevertheless, Maria also testified that there was no formal document or instrument concerning her redemption and thus no written evidence of her status, the price that Bartolomeo had paid for her, any promise of freedom he might have made, or any obligation she might have undertaken to serve or repay him. There was also no indication of how long she had served Bartolomeo's family or whether she was close to fulfilling the standard five-year term of service.

The testimony in the document was elicited from Maria by her buyer, Precival Marchexano of Genoa. Among the witnesses to the contract was Thomas de Via, a Genoese citizen who acted as an interpreter between Greek (for Maria) and Latin (for Precival). Precival probably intended to take Maria into the Mediterranean and resell her.[179] Recording this story would increase her resale value by legitimizing her status as a slave. At the time of her sale in Kilia, Maria's status was dubious. She was Greek, possibly of free birth, had no documented history as a slave, and had been redeemed from Muslims under conditions that normally entailed manumission after completion of a fixed period of service or payment of a fixed sum of money. However, the testimony in the document emphasized Iohanna's possession of Maria and right to sell her despite all the factors in her favor. Moreover, Maria testified that she "was and is a slave." This statement, once carried into the Mediterranean in the register of the notary Antonio di Ponzò, would make it difficult for her to challenge her status later.[180] A boilerplate clause in many slave sales was a promise on the part of the seller to uphold the buyer's right of ownership in court. With written affirmation of Maria's slave status, Precival could confidently defend his ownership of her and right to sell her onward.

We can only speculate about why Maria testified that she was a slave rather than a ransomed captive. One factor may have been the difficulty of challenging Iohanna's claim to ownership. Maria did not have any proof of ransom, origin, or free status at birth. She may not have been aware of Genoese laws and norms governing the treatment of Greek captives. She was also facing a language barrier and may not have been able to find a translator willing to help her defend her status. Violence, threats, or other forms of coercion may also have affected her testimony.[181] In any case, the fact that her testimony was recorded provides us with an unusual glimpse into the precarious zone between slavery and captivity.

Conclusion

Today we consider slavery an insult to human dignity, and we study slaves' agency as a way of affirming their humanity.[182] We imagine that anyone who owned slaves must have denied their humanity or failed to recognize it. The inhabitants of the late medieval Mediterranean, however, had a different understanding of both slavery and the human condition. They believed that hierarchy and menial labor would exist even in ideal societies like the Garden of Eden or the Garden of paradise. In those ideal societies, the lowest level of the hierarchy would be occupied by free people, and menial labor would be done by specially created nonhuman beings. In the real world, slaves occupied the lowest level of the hierarchy and did the menial work. Their humanity was never in question, but the restrictions and humiliations imposed on them were considered legal and socially acceptable.

Acceptance of both slavery and the humanity of slaves was supported by the perception of slavery as a universal threat. A slave owner one day, whether an Italian merchant or a noble Mamluk lady, might realistically find himself or herself enslaved the next. Slaves were considered the most miserable and unfortunate of people, a status that one wished to avoid for oneself but might choose to alleviate or exploit in others. For example, the fifteenth-century German pilgrim Felix Fabri pitied the slaves he observed in Alexandria, sympathizing with their desire to flee and deploring the horrible punishments they faced if recaptured.[183]

Yet he and his fellow pilgrims thought it funny to be mistaken for slaves in the Cairo slave market, where they might well have been sold in reality if their ship had been captured by pirates. After the misunderstanding was cleared up, one of his companions tried to purchase an Ethiopian slave in the same market where he himself had just been haggled over.

The universal threat of enslavement was just one aspect of the common culture of slavery in the late medieval Mediterranean. Christian and Muslim authorities agreed that the natural status of humanity was freedom but that slavery was a legitimate aspect of human law. They agreed that individuals could be enslaved through birth and capture in war, but Christian authorities also allowed the sale of free people into slavery and recognized enslavement as a judicial penalty. They agreed that religious difference was the principle underlying slave status, but in practice, they were more concerned with protecting souls from apostasy than bodies from slavery. Catholic authorities were willing to authorize the purchase of Orthodox slaves to protect their souls. Yet they were more likely to grant petitions for freedom by Greeks than by Russians. What made the enslavement of Russian Orthodox Christians in Genoa more acceptable than the enslavement of Greek Orthodox Christians? The next chapter delves more deeply into how the inhabitants of the late medieval Mediterranean understood difference in the context of slavery.

Chapter 2

Difference and the Perception of Slave Status

Religious difference was the legal and ideological basis of slavery in the late medieval Mediterranean. In theory, anyone might be captured and enslaved by adherents of another religion. In practice, some people were more likely to be enslaved than others, and some were enslaved by coreligionists. Russian Christians, for example, were more likely to be enslaved and less likely to be judicially manumitted than Greek Christians in Christian Italy. Such patterns show that despite the legal and ideological importance of religious difference, it was not the only factor at work in determining slave status.

For medieval jurists, the problem with a system of slavery based on religious difference was the difficulty of proving the religion affiliation of specific slaves. Religious belief was an immaterial quality of the spirit, fully accessible only to God and the individual believer himself or herself.[1] Religious practices like circumcision might leave visible marks on the body, but because most late medieval slaves were women and circumcision applied only to men, their affiliation could not be proven in this way.[2] Some Mediterranean societies used badges or special clothing to signal religious affiliation, but clothes were easy to change.[3] In theory, Christians, Muslims, and Jews followed distinctive dietary laws; in practice, slaves were not asked to eat pork or drink wine as a religious test. Slaves were sometimes able to prove their affiliation by reciting a prayer or creed (the *shahāda* for Muslims; the Pater Noster, Ave Maria, or Credo for Christians), but they were not able to give binding legal testimony about themselves.[4] Moreover, newly enslaved people who had not yet learned the language of their masters would struggle to communicate anything about their religious background.

The difficulty of categorizing slaves by religion caused legal and economic problems. People enslaved illegally did have opportunities to challenge their status, as discussed in Chapter 1, and occasionally, they were successful. No master wanted to take on the potential expense and inconvenience of a slave whose status was doubtful. A seller might need to show a contract for his or her initial purchase of a particular slave to verify that slave's status.[5] Slave sale contracts often included a clause in which the seller promised to uphold the legality of the sale in court. But there were other ways to categorize slaves and thereby assess the validity of their status. Previous scholarship has shown that medieval people used language, law, customs, descent, and geographical origin along with religion to identify themselves and categorize others.[6] Of these options, language and race were the most relevant in the context of slavery.

The difficulty of categorizing an individual slave in a reliable way can be illustrated by two descriptions of the same young woman, a slave purchased by Biagio Dolfin in Alexandria in 1419 and sent to Niccolò Dolfin in Venice. Her sale contract, composed in Arabic, described her as "a female slave of Nubian race, called Mubāraka, a Christian woman." In a letter to Niccolò composed in Venetian, Biagio described her as "a little slave girl, black, Saracen, about fourteen years old."[7] These two descriptions are fundamentally inconsistent. Was Mubāraka a Nubian Christian or a Saracen (an Arab Muslim)? The answer is that, in the context of slavery, both racial and religious categories were dictated by the master. Mubāraka was a Nubian Christian in Alexandria because that categorization made her legally enslaveable in Alexandria, and she was an Arab Muslim in Venice because that categorization made her legally enslaveable in Venice.

Before embarking on a detailed discussion of language and race as they operated in the late medieval Mediterranean culture of slavery, however, several caveats are in order. First, although sources in Arabic and Latin used many of the same terms to categorize their slaves, we cannot assume that those terms meant precisely the same thing in both languages. Both Latin and Arabic, for example, used the word Turk to categorize slaves. In Latin sources, it referred to people from Anatolia, but Arabic sources were more likely to call people from Anatolia *rūmī*.[8] The term Turk in Arabic sources could be used in multiple ways, but it was associated with nomads, people living in the north, and speakers of Turkic languages.

Second, the use of these terms varied according to genre. In Italy, legal documents and travel narratives used contemporary terms (Tatar, Circassian) for Black Sea people, while literary and scholarly works used classical Greco-Roman terms (Scythian, Sarmatian).[9] Though it is frustrating for the historian to find multiple terms used to signify one group of people, it serves as an excellent reminder of the cultural construction of race. In the late medieval Mediterranean, racial categories were used inconsistently because different genres constructed them differently.

Finally, it should be noted that few of the slaves originating from the Black Sea were black by either medieval or modern standards. The subject of race in the Middle Ages is a complex one, contested among specialists and frequently misunderstood by nonspecialists.[10] Studies of racism in medieval slavery have generally limited their analysis to black and white rather than engage with this complexity. I argue that the complexity of the medieval framework of race was essential to the medieval framework of slavery. When categorizing a slave by religion did not serve the needs of the master, either because religious affiliation was too difficult to prove in court or because it would lead to the slave's manumission, masters turned to the much more complex and flexible category of race to justify their ownership. I also find that reexamining the powerful and deeply engrained association between black skin color, race, and slavery in a historical context where slavery was correlated with race but not with skin color helps show the ways in which modern racial thinking is historically contingent.

Language

Language was associated with outsider status in the late medieval Mediterranean culture of slavery. Slaves' poor command of their masters' languages, whether or not it was true, was often cited by medieval sources as evidence of their foreign, heathen origin.[11] Slaves were also renamed by their masters in ways that marked their status as social outsiders. However, Christians and Muslims perceived the connection between language, outsider status, and slavery in different ways. Christians saw linguistic diversity as a reflection of the diversity of the Christian community and of humanity in general, whereas Muslims saw the Arabic language as a unifying force for the Muslim community.

Muslims placed great weight on Arabic as the language of Islam because it was the language in which God had revealed the Quran. Non-Muslims in disguise could be unmasked through their poor command of Arabic, but Muslims unable to speak Arabic might go unrecognized as believers.[12] Under the wrong conditions, this could lead to their enslavement. For example, two Christian ships arrived in Tunis in 1462 with a group of captives for ransom. A passing traveler, ʿAbd al-Bāsiṭ ibn Khalīl, visited the ships and found one captive left unransomed by the locals, "an excellent Muslim of Turkish race, knowing only Turkish and the language of the Franks."[13] Since ʿAbd al-Bāsiṭ spoke Turkish as well as Arabic, he was able to speak with the captive and explain to the locals that he was a Muslim. They hastily ransomed him too and tried to excuse their mistake: "'By God,' he said to me, 'we didn't know his language at all, we believed that he was an infidel'" because he didn't speak Arabic.[14] Later in his journey, ʿAbd al-Bāsiṭ was shocked to encounter a group of Berbers who did not recognize him as a Muslim even though he was "addressing them in Arabic speech and confessing the two *shahāda*."[15] In fact, the Berbers "didn't know Arabic at all: their language is Berber, and they don't distinguish between the language of the Arabs and that of the Franks. They astonished me greatly."

The assumption that all Muslims could speak Arabic was also the basis of a slave market scam practiced in al-Andalus during the thirteenth century.[16] A female slave was offered for sale at a very high price with the claim that she was a fresh captive from Christian territory. After the sale had been concluded and the seller had gone away, the woman addressed the unwary buyer in perfect Arabic. She threatened to complain to the local judge that she was a free Muslim who had been unjustly enslaved, tarnishing the buyer's reputation as well as costing him the purchase price. Then she would suggest that he resell her to another dupe and split the proceeds with her, perpetuating the scam but reducing his own losses.

In contrast, Christians interpreted linguistic diversity as a sign of religious diversity within the Christian community.[17] Latin and Greek were used as shorthand to represent Catholic and Orthodox Christians. A crusade proposal of 1332 asserted the correctness of Catholicism against the "many Christian peoples of diverse languages who do not walk with us in faith or in doctrine."[18] Pilgrims and travelers used linguistic diversity to express their amazement at the variety of people they encountered. At Christmas celebrations in Bethlehem, the fourteenth-century pilgrim Niccolò of Poggibonsi explained that "each generation (*generazione*) celebrates in its own rite, in its own tongue, so that it is a marvel to see so many people thus disguised in tongue and attire (*in lingua e in vestimenta*)."[19] He mentioned both spoken and written language in his description of the diversity of Cairo, where "one generation is distinguished from another in language and letters and dress."[20] According to Alberto Alfieri, fifteenth-century Caffa was "ornamented by the tongues of its diverse peoples."[21] Arnold von Harff used linguistic diversity to indicate the sheer length of his physical journey: "I will, with God's help and according to my small understanding, now describe [my journey] from country to country, from town to town, from village to village, from mile to mile, from one day's journey to another, from language to language, from faith to faith, together with all that I have seen and experienced."[22]

What may appear to be a loose association between language and religion was nevertheless used to distinguish groups of people in law and in the courts. In 1224, a plaintiff speaking through an interpreter appeared before the archbishop of Genoa to challenge the status of a slave woman named Maimona. The archbishop ruled that Maimona's enslavement was legitimate because "she did not seem to him to be from the land of Egypt, rather she seemed to be from the Maghrib on account of her language."[23] Venice offered to confer citizenship on fifty people in the Black Sea region to boost its presence there, but the offer was open only to those who were "Latin by origin and language."[24] In 1368, Venice forbade its merchants from importing slaves "of the Tatar language."[25] As for Circassians, the Venetian humanist Giorgio Interiano claimed that they were so uncivilized that they did not even have a written form for their language.[26] A man named Johan won freedom in Valencia by proving that he was a Hungarian Christian and not a Muslim Turk. His case rested upon the testimony of four Germans who conversed with him in the German and Hungarian languages as well as a doctor who verified that he was not circumcised.[27]

In Italian documents, the connection between language and religion appeared most often in relation to names. Masters frequently renamed their slaves. Roughly 80 percent of slave women in Genoa were given one of six names (Caterina, Lucia, Maddalena, Margherita, Maria, or Marta).[28] These names were also given to freewomen, but the pool of names for freewomen was much larger. Giorgio was a common name among male slaves, far more common than among freemen. Certain names were given only to slaves: Cita (quick), Bona (good), Picenina (little), Benvenuta (welcome), Pucella (handmaiden), Divizia (riches), Melica (musical), and Aspertus or Expertus (experienced).[29]

Legal documents included both old and new names, often presenting the distinction between them in terms of language and religion. Sometimes language was emphasized: "Caron in Tatar, Paul in our language" or "Chotlu by name, and thereafter called Christina in Latin."[30] Other times religion was emphasized: "called Stoilana in her language, by the grace of baptism Marta" or "not baptized, and is called Achzoach in her language, and in baptism ought to be named Bona."[31] Sometimes language and religion were explicitly connected, such as the woman "called Margarita at baptism and in Latin."[32] A Venetian correspondent writing to the Pratese merchant Francesco Datini notified him of the purchase of a new slave and advised him to "have her baptized and give her a name in your own way."[33]

Because the imposition of a Latin name was sometimes linked with baptism, scholars have tended to assume that all slaves with recognizably Latin names had been baptized.[34] That is not necessarily true. Some masters gave their slaves Latin names without the sacrament of baptism.[35] Also, there were numerous slaves whose old and new names were both associated with Christianity. An Abkhaz girl named Maria was renamed Barbara; a Russian Maria was renamed Marta.[36] In such cases, did the conferral of a new name imply a second baptism, or were these slaves renamed without baptism? A woman "called Caterina in her language and Antonia in baptism" was certainly baptized once and may have been baptized twice.[37] A Circassian girl "called Serafina in her language but in our idiom Magdalena" seems to have been renamed without a sacrament.[38] Baptizing the same individual twice was theologically unsound, even if the two baptisms were performed in different rites. Nevertheless, some Catholic priests seem to have performed rebaptisms, since Pope Martin V threatened to excommunicate anyone who rebaptized Greek slaves.[39]

Adding race to the set of connections between names, languages, and religions can be misleading too. The name Caracossa might derive from Saragossa in Spain, from Circassia in the Black Sea, from the Greek name Karakouttis, or from a Tatar name.[40] Each onomastic possibility carries a different set of linguistic, religious, and racial associations. Some slaves had names that reinforced their linguistic or racial categorization, such as Jarcaxa or Jarcaxius for a Circassian.[41] Others had ethnonyms that did not match their linguistic or racial categorization, such as a Tatar woman named Cataio (Chinese), a Circassian woman named Gota (Goth), and a Laz woman named Comana (Cuman).[42] Nasta, usually considered a Greek name, belonged to a girl categorized as Tatar.[43] The name Chotlu or Cotlu was attributed to Alan, Mongol, Russian, and Tatar women.[44] The result is that names cannot be relied upon to categorize a slave by language, religion, or race.

In contrast, Mamluk slaves were usually given non-Islamic names. Domestic slaves and eunuchs were given the names of desirable objects or qualities like Amber or Nightingale.[45] Young mamluks, as well as some of their slave concubines, were given distinctive names composed of Turkic and Persian elements like Aqbirdī or Qarābughā.[46] Names constructed in that way signaled a slave's membership in the elite military class, not his or her original language. Of the distinctive mamluk names, some were invented in Egypt, but others had roots in the Black Sea.[47] Comparing mamluk names with the original names of male slaves in Italian documents can reveal which names were used in the Black Sea. The name Jaqmaq, common among mamluks, also appeared as Zachmach or Iacomacius in seventeen Italian documents from Tana, Venice, Genoa, and Pera.[48] Thirteen were categorized as Tatar and one as Circassian. Only two mamluks named Jaqmaq were assigned a racial category in the Mamluk sources: one was a Circassian and the other a Circassian or Turkman.[49] Other male slave names that appeared in both Italian and Mamluk sources were Quṭlūbughā/Cotluboga, Qarābughā/Charaboga, Jarkis/Charcaxius, Kitbughā/Katboga, and Tangrībirdī/Tangriberdi. Female slave names that appeared in both sets of sources were Mughāl/Mogal, Ṭughay/Tochay, and Tulū/Tholu.

Mamluk slave names were marked by another distinctive feature. The names of free people included a chain of patronymics, but slaves and former slaves had only one patronymic, Ibn ʿAbd Allah (son of a servant of God). This naming convention erased the slave's biological family and signaled his or her foreignness from Mamluk society.[50] Many Mamluk names also included a *nisba* or *laqab*, an adjectival nickname. A single mamluk could have multiple nicknames referring to different facets of his identity, such as his patron (al-Nāṣirī for a client of the sultan al-Nāṣir Muḥammad), his affiliation with a legal or theological school (al-Mālikī for a jurist of the Mālikī school), his physical appearance (al-A'war for a man with one eye), or his place of origin (al-Asqalānī for a man from Ascalon). Nicknames that appear to indicate a place of origin can be misleading, though. Al-Jarkasī, for example, might refer to a mamluk of Circassian origin or to a mamluk with a previous owner named Jarkas.[51]

Race in the Late Medieval Mediterranean

We have become used to thinking about slavery as a hierarchy of power built on a racial binary, white over black. This framework does not fit late medieval Mediterranean slavery. First, late medieval Mediterranean slavery was a hierarchy of power built on religious, not racial, difference. Second, neither religious nor racial differences were perceived as binary in the late Middle Ages. Third, racial differences were not articulated in terms of skin color in the late Middle Ages, although skin color was one of many physical characteristics that could carry racial associations. The significance of religion for late medieval Mediterranean slavery was addressed in Chapter 1. The remainder of this chapter addresses the roles played by race, skin color, and other aspects of physical appearance.

To approach race from a new perspective, historians may benefit from conversation with psychologists, anthropologists, and sociologists about how human categories arise and function. The private human self is a consciousness located within a body; it develops by interacting with the world around it. The result is the creation of a social self, "a bundle of perceptions held about an individual by a social world," in addition to a private self.[52] Although individuals may try to maintain their social selves in harmony with their private selves, their social worlds may not allow them to do so. This is certainly the case with slaves. While the private selves of slaves are a fascinating and elusive topic of research, the following discussion seeks only to understand certain aspects of their social selves, namely, the perceptions that were relevant to their status as slaves in the minds of the people around them.

A group is a human collectivity, the members of which recognize both its existence and their own membership in it.[53] Groups can be constructed based on all sorts of criteria, and individuals normally believe themselves to be members of numerous groups (professors, Star Wars fans, women, Americans) without contradiction. When other people make the decision about how to identify an individual, what they use are categories rather than groups.[54] This book is chiefly concerned with the categorization of slaves: their identification by others rather than their self-identification as a group.

Ethnicity is a way of categorizing other people based on culture. From an anthropological perspective, it is a common and widespread aspect of humans' social existence.[55] Race is a way of categorizing people based on their supposedly permanent, fixed, and inherent differences.[56] Those differences are usually assumed to be physical, visible, or biological, but they do not have to be. What matters is the belief that they cannot be changed. Race, unlike ethnicity, is not a common aspect of human experience. It appears only in certain societies and historical periods. When race exists in a society as a way of categorizing people but is not associated with a power hierarchy, it can be referred to as *race-thinking*.[57] When race becomes linked to a power hierarchy, either through explicit ideologies of superiority and inferiority or through institutional structures that implicitly benefit certain racial categories over others, that is *racism*.

This definition of race and racism is broad. In specific historical circumstances, it has overlapped with other categories that we now consider distinct from race, including religion,[58] class,[59] and language.[60] Our belief that physical appearance is a meaningful kind of permanent, fixed, and inherent difference is relatively recent. The word *race* in its current sense, a category of people distinguished from others by certain hereditary physical traits, entered English in the late fifteenth century.[61] The notion that skin color was an important aspect of race emerged in the late sixteenth century, and the ideology of different skin colors as the basis for slavery was not fully developed until the eighteenth and nineteenth centuries.

All of these developments occurred after the period covered by this book. In medieval Latin, the words used to categorize people were *gens*, *generatio*, *genus*, *progenies*, and *natio*. In Arabic, the most common terms of categorization were *jins*, *aṣl*, *naw'*, and *umma*. *Gens* (pl. *gentes*) and *jins* (pl. *ajnās*) are linguistically related.[62] They can be translated in several ways, all building on the concepts of kind, type, group, and kinship. Medieval people created and shared both verifiable genealogies and myths of common ancestry to explain their systems of categories and groups.[63] Some of the most important mythical genealogies made use of the three sons of Noah, the twelve apostles of Jesus, the Homeric heroes, and the founders of Arab tribes, as well as the *gens* of Adam, which encompassed all humanity, the tribe of the free (*banī al-aḥrār*), and the *gentes* of Christianity, Islam, Judaism, and paganism.[64]

In the late medieval Mediterranean, religious categories were often perceived as permanent, fixed, and inherent. Even after conversion, a convert's religion of origin remained relevant and could still be used to categorize him or her. This attitude helps to explain why religion could function as the basis of slave status even though slaves were expected to convert. In this sense, then, it is possible to talk about religion as a racial category in the medieval world.

However, medieval people also engaged in something closer to our form of race-thinking, categorizing each other based on physical differences that they supposed to be permanent, fixed, and inherent. The bodies of knowledge through which these racial categories were constructed were ethnography (the study of different kinds of people throughout the world), physiognomy (the study of physical traits associated with different qualities of personality and character), physiology (the study of the functioning of the human body), and astrology (the study of the effects of heavenly bodies on earthly ones). Ethnography, physiognomy, physiology, and astrology were part of a shared medieval Mediterranean intellectual culture: authoritative treatises were written, translated, and exchanged among Christians, Muslims, and Jews.[65] Medieval scholars debated whether racial categories were truly fixed; for example, whether the children of dark-skinned Ethiopians who moved north would become paler. This debate was largely irrelevant to slavery, though.[66]

In constructing their racial categories, medieval Christians started with the observation that although many human beings resemble one another, none look precisely identical, except for twins.[67] They interpreted the infinite variety of human bodies as a sign of God's boundless creativity and natural fertility.[68] An individual's nature was taken to refer to both his or her unique traits and the shared traits that made him or her recognizable as one human among many. Medieval Islamic scholarly discourse also made a distinction between the diversity of individual bodies and the shared physical characteristics of groups.[69] *Shurūṭ* manuals warned scribes that race (*jins*) and skin color could not substitute for a full physical description (*ḥāliyya*).[70]

Medieval discourse on religious difference was largely binary: humanity was divided into believers and unbelievers, the right religion and the wrong ones. The existence of multiple kinds of Christians and Muslims complicated this binary somewhat, but as discussed in Chapter 1, this had only a limited effect on slavery. In contrast, racial difference was perceived as a broad spectrum ranging from the normative body at the center to the monstrous races that peopled the far reaches of the earth.[71] Whether cyclops, cannibals, and blemmyae were real was beside the point; they represented the extremes of human possibility, the furthest ends of the racial spectrum. The medieval theory of climate was used to place races in intermediate positions along spectrum, usually from north to south.[72] Those living in the frigid northern climate zone were supposed to have pale skin, lank hair, a dull intellect, and a cold temperament. Those living in the tropical southern climate zone were supposed to have dark skin, wooly hair, foolish minds, and a hot temperament. The temperate climate zone in the middle was supposed to produce beautiful, reasonable, and well-balanced people. Since the theory of climate zones was drawn from ancient Greek sources, particularly Hippocrates' *Airs, Waters, Places*, it was part of the intellectual inheritance shared by the entire Mediterranean world. Of course, most medieval authors tended to locate the temperate zone close to their own homes, wherever that might be.

The association between race and climate theory explains why notaries and scribes used racial and geographical categories (*de progenie russiorum* vs. *de partibus Russia*) interchangeably in legal descriptions of slaves.[73] When legislators in Florence tried to define slave status, they struggled to articulate a difference between religious, racial, and geographical categories. Thus they permitted Florentines to own and sell any person "who is not of the Catholic and Christian faith . . . the aforesaid is understood concerning slaves [who were] infidels by origin of their birth, or born from the race of the infidels, even if at the time when they were brought to the said city, court, or district they were of the Christian faith, or even if at some time afterwards they were baptized. . . . [A person] is presumed to have been infidel by origin if he or she arose from infidel places and race."[74]

When Genoa instituted an inspection regime in Caffa in the early fifteenth century to ensure that no Christians were being exported to the Islamic world, the inspectors asked slaves first about their race (*natio*), apparently considered equivalent to asking about their religion.[75] In cases of doubtful status, the question was not whether the slave's race was different from the master's but how far along the spectrum of racial difference the slave fell. The people of the Black Sea were perceived as distant from the people of the Mediterranean: "certainly if it were not for the Genoese who are there, it would not appear that the people [of Caffa] have any lot with us."[76] This is why in Italy, the enslavement of Italian Christians caused outrage, the enslavement of Greek Christians caused discomfort, and the enslavement of Bulgar and Russian Christians was ignored. Although all three categories should have been legally protected from enslavement in Italy, Bulgars and Russians were further along the spectrum of racial difference than Greeks, and therefore it was more socially acceptable to enslave them.

Race and Slavery in the Late Medieval Mediterranean

We have established that racial categories were a factor in determining slave status in the late medieval Mediterranean, even though racial difference was not the ideological basis of slavery. We have also established that late medieval people perceived race not in binary terms but as a profusion of human diversity signifying the endlessly fertile creativity of God in nature. Yet, although the number of racial categories was potentially infinite, only a few of them were strongly associated with slavery in the late medieval Mediterranean. Medieval scholars who produced lists of enslaveable people did not necessarily agree on which races were enslaveable and which were not, but the act of compiling lists demonstrated their belief that it was possible to divide the infinite races of humanity into two categories, the enslaveable and the free.[77]

According to Mamluk-era *shurūṭ* manuals (collections of model contracts), the list of enslaveable people could be divided into Turks and Sūdān. Turks were supposed to be light-skinned northerners originating anywhere from Europe to China. They could be further subdivided into Qiyāṭ, Naymān, Mongol, Kipchak, Khita'i, Circassian, Russian, Alan, Bulgar, Tatar, Āq, Chaghatai, Georgian, Greek, and Armenian categories, among others.[78] Thus a Circassian Turk was not biracial but a light-skinned northerner (a Turk in the general sense) originating from Circassia (a Circassian in the specific sense). To make matters more confusing, Turk could also be used in a specific sense as a synonym for Kipchak. Sūdān (literally meaning "blacks") referred to dark-skinned southerners originating anywhere from Africa to India. They could be subdivided into Ethiopian, Abyssinian, Takrūrī, Nubian, Zaghāwī, Dājūwī, Bajāwī, Indian, Khalanjī, Zanjī, Yemeni, Sarūwī, and *muwallad* (mulatto) categories, among others.[79] The two sets of criteria, skin color and geography, that distinguished the Turks from the Sūdān were linked by the medieval theory of climate.

Legally, misrepresenting the racial category of a slave would not invalidate his or her sale, whereas misrepresenting religion or gender would.[80] According to jurists, this was because religion affected slaves' legal status and gender affected their function, whereas race did neither. However, Mamluk slave-buying guides included lists of enslaveable races and their stereotypical qualities precisely because it would guide the buyer in choosing the right slave for the right function. Unlike *shurūṭ* manuals, Mamluk guides for slave buyers divided the list of enslaveable people into three categories: Arabs, ʿAjam, and Sūdān.[81] Sūdān referred to dark-skinned southern slaves, as before. Arabs rarely appeared as slaves during the Mamluk period, but they may have been included for the sake of ethnographic completeness or as a legacy from earlier models of the genre.[82] ʿAjam could refer to all non-Arabs; to all northern, light-skinned non-Arabs; or to Persians specifically. A fifteenth-century slave-buying manual defined ʿAjam in terms of language: "absolutely everybody who differs from the Arab tongue, such as the Persians and the Turks and the Greeks and the Armenians and the Sūdān and the Berber and the rest of them, although this name specifies the Persian people conventionally."[83]

The recognized subdivisions of ʿAjam shifted over the course of the Mamluk period. In an anonymous thirteenth-century slave-buying guide, ʿAjam included Persians, Turks, Kurds, Rūmī,[84] Armenians, Franks, Alans, Indians (*al-hind*), and Berbers. In the fifteenth century, al-ʿAyntābī added Circassians, Daylamites, Zaranj, and more Indians (*al-sind*). Circassian slaves had served in

Egypt since the thirteenth century or earlier, but their addition to the list of enslaveable races in the fifteenth century was probably a result of their rise to political power in the late fourteenth century. The inclusion of Indians, *al-hind* and *al-sind*, among the ʿAjam is also notable because the *shurūṭ* manuals tended to categorize them as Sūdān.[85]

Contemporary observers noticed certain trends in the racial composition of the Mamluk slave population. Circassian, Rūmī, Kipchak, and Turk were the most common categories used for slaves. Tatar, Mongol, Turkman, Kurd, Armenian, Cypriot, Frankish, Indian (*hind*), and Ethiopian (*ḥabashī*) categories were used less frequently. Chinese, Russian, Samarqandi, and West African (*takrūrī*) categories were represented by single individuals.[86] One notable trend, according to medieval observers, was the shift in the mamluk population from Kipchak Turks to Circassian Turks at the end of the fourteenth century, as discussed in Chapter 5. Another notable trend was the preference of most sultans and amirs for slaves of the same race as themselves. The perception that political factions were based on racial solidarity was widespread in Mamluk sources, even though modern historians have shown that factions presented as racial often included individual mamluks of various races.[87] The two trends were linked by the suggestion that Sultan Barqūq precipitated the shift away from Kipchaks by favoring Circassians like himself.[88] Barqūq's wife, Ird, a Turk, was said to have warned him against this course: "make your army a variegated one of four races, Tatar, Circassian, Anatolian and Turcoman, and then you and your descendants can rest easy," because no single racial faction would be able to dominate Mamluk politics.[89]

Medieval Christian philosophers explored the idea of enslaveable races via Aristotle's theory of natural slavery discussed in Chapter 1. Searching for examples of natural slavery in their own societies led them in a variety of directions. Citizens serving a ruler, artisans, peasants, and barbarians were all identified by medieval philosophers as natural slaves.[90] Medieval philosophers knew that the word *barbarian* signaled linguistic difference: "note that barbarians, according to certain people, are said to be those whose language differs entirely from Latin. Others indeed say that whoever is a foreigner is a barbarian to every other foreigner. . . . But according to he who speaks more truly [i.e., Aristotle], barbarians proper are said to be those who are strong in the strength of the body, are lacking in the strength of reason, and are almost without laws and without the rule of law."[91] In other words, although barbarians were superficially distinguished by language, they were truly set apart from civilized people by their physical strength, lack of reason, and lack of law, all qualities associated with natural slaves.

Where medieval philosophers diverged from Aristotle was their emphasis on barbarian races, characterizing the customs and bodies of entire groups of people as bestial.[92] For example, according to Albertus Magnus, "we call barbarians those who neither law, nor civility, nor the rule of any other discipline disposes to virtue, whom Tullius called forest men in the beginning of *Rhetorica*, conversing with the wild forest beasts in the manner of wild beasts, who are not Greeks or Latins, who are disciplined and fed by a lordly and paternal rule. For such bestial people eat raw meat and drink the blood of humans, they delight to eat and drink from the skulls of humans, they find new kinds of tortures by which they delight to kill people."[93] Such bestial people were located at the far end of the racial spectrum and could be justifiably enslaved by civilized people. In this intellectual context, the long association between Greeks and civilization may have been another reason why medieval Catholics were less comfortable enslaving Greeks than Bulgars or Russians, even though all were Orthodox Christians.

Because the influx of Black Sea slaves to Italy did not begin until the late thirteenth century, Thomas Aquinas and the other great scholastics of the thirteenth century did not link Aristotle's slaves with the Tatars serving in the homes of wealthy Italians.[94] Aristotle himself had identified the Scythians of the ancient Black Sea as a barbarian people prone to natural slavery on the basis of their climate, and both Thomas Aquinas and Albertus Magnus had repeated the connection between Scythians, barbarians, and natural slaves. But it was Italian humanists who equated Scythians and Tatars with natural slaves. According to Giovanni Gioviano Pontano,

> As I heard from the ancients, the custom was that Thracians and also Greeks who inhabit the Black Sea be sold: who, lest they be in the service of the barbarians, merchants sailing the Black Sea, having redeemed them from the Scythians, were offering them for sale. For it seemed more honorable to serve them for a short time, while they repaid the money paid per head, than to be the plunder of barbarians and submissive to perpetual servitude, also with the greatest disgrace of the Christian name. Because today also are saved towards those whom he calls Bulgars and Circassians.[95]

In other words, the Orthodox Christians of the Black Sea (Thracians, Greeks, Bulgars, and Circassians) could be enslaved by Catholics to save them from the Scythians (Tatars), the archetypical barbarians.

Other humanists also liked to use anachronistic classical terms for the contemporary population of the Black Sea. Racial categories formulated a thousand years ago in quite different historical circumstances reappeared not only in private letters but also in official government correspondence and notarial documents.[96] In 1416 and 1417, for example, the Genoese notary Giuliano Canella categorized five different slaves as "Gepids or Zichs."[97] Zich was a widely recognized racial category in the fifteenth century, and it would be possible to find individuals who self-identified as members of that group. Gepid was a racial category dating from the fifth and sixth centuries, a group with no self-identifying members in the fifteenth century.

Being able to categorize slaves by race mattered especially to notaries because it was required by Roman law. The Justinianic Code stated that "those selling slaves should declare their race (*natio*) when making the sale; for the slave's race may often induce or deter a purchaser; therefore, we have an interest in knowing the race; for there is a presumption that some slaves are good, coming from a race with no bad repute, while others are thought bad, since they come from a notorious race."[98] As a result, Italian notaries included race along with gender, age, and name in slave sale contracts and other types of documents. Because race had a predictable place in the boilerplate language for slave sales, it is easy to compile a list of racial categories for slaves commonly used by notaries.

Data about the racial categorization of slaves in Genoa and Venice are presented in Figures 14 and 15 in Chapter 5. Russians, Caucasians (Circassians, Zichs, Abkhaz, Mingrelians), and Tatars made up the great majority of slaves in both cities. The label of "Other" hides a very diverse population. The following racial categories were assigned by the notaries to ten or more slaves: Albanian, Black, Bosnian, Bulgar, Canary Islander, Cuman, Ethiopian, Greek, Hungarian, Jewish, Moor, Saracen,[99] and Turk.[100] Racial categories assigned by the notaries to fewer than ten slaves were Alan,[101] Armenian, Berber, Catalan, Goth,[102] Laz,[103] Libyan, Majar,[104] Meskh,[105] Mongol, Ruthenian, Sarmatian, Serb, Slav, Spanish, Uighur, and Wallach. A few racial categories (*dovagus*, *raamanus*, and *cevia*) do not seem to have equivalents in modern English. Indian and Chinese racial categories appeared only in Caffa and Tana.[106]

When Christian observers categorized mamluks, they used many of the same racial categories as the Genoese and Venetian notaries used for slaves held locally. Mamluks were categorized as Abkhaz, Albanian, Abyssinian, Bulgarian, Circassian, Greek, Mingrelian, Russian, Tatar, Turk, and Wallach.[107] But Christian travelers also noticed mamluks from Germany, Hungary, Catalonia, Aragon, Italy, and Sicily. In 1482–1483, the Dutch traveler Joos van Ghistele met Nāṣir al-Dīn, a mamluk from Danzig, who was a treasury official of the sultan.[108] In 1480–1483, Felix Fabri and Paul Walther de Guglingen met a mamluk named Sefogul, a German from Basel whose relatives Felix knew.[109] Two mamluks, Conrad of Basel and an unnamed Dane, guided the traveler Arnold von Harff in Cairo.[110]

Unfortunately for both Italian notaries and Mamluk scribes, their racial categories were not adequate to describe the complexity and diversity of the people living around the Black Sea. Their hesitation in the face of a human reality that did not fit into neat categories is evident in the sources.[111] Most authors of Mamluk biographical dictionaries did not mention race. When they did, they preferred the broad categories of Turk, Circassian, Rūmī, and Tatar. In a few cases, they disagreed: the amir Bahādir al-Minjakī was either Rūmī or Frankish, and the amir Jaqmaq al-Arghūnshāwī was either Circassian or Turkman.[112] The early fourteenth-century sultan Baybars al-Jashankīr might have been a Turk, or he might have been the first Circassian ruler.[113] Sultan Khushqadam was consistently identified as Greek, but there was debate over whether he, Lājīn, or al-Mu'izz Aybak was the first Greek sultan.[114]

Some Italian notaries left a blank space where race should have appeared in their slave sale contracts.[115] Others put the burden of categorization on the seller, as with a slave "of Goth origin, as she seems to that same Iohannes [the seller] to be from Gothia."[116] The same was true for a slave "who is said to be from Russia"[117] and a slave "of the race of the Russians, as it is asserted by the said slave woman, and whom I sell to you as being of the race of the Russians."[118] The Genoese notary Antonio di Ponzò borrowed the phrase "as is" (*talis qualis est*), a formula for disclaiming responsibility for a slave's health, and repurposed it to disclaim knowledge of a slave's race. A woman whom he could not categorize was sold "of race as is" (*de proienia talis qualis est*).[119] Another notary hedged by describing a slave as "of the Abkhaz or another race."[120]

Notaries also made mistakes in racial categorization. Sometimes they wrote one racial term, then crossed it out and replaced it with another one. Russians and Tatars were most often mistaken for each other in this way.[121] In other cases, notaries gave two racial categories for a single slave: Tatar Russians, Tatar Alans, Tatar Turks, Tatar Circassians, Greek Circassians, Greek Russians, Greek Walachs, Russian Armenians, Russian Bulgars, Russian Circassians, Russian Bosnians, Wallach Bulgars, Bulgar Turks, Bulgar Tatars, Saracen Ethiopians, and Berber Moors.[122] Some combinations can be explained by the dual significance of the term Greek as race or religion. A Russian Greek might therefore be of Russian race and Greek religion. What a notary meant by a Tatar Alan is harder to explain.

Slavery and Physical Appearance

Black Sea slavery was not white slavery. It was not black slavery either. Although both Latin and Arabic sources occasionally described slaves in terms of color, what they intended to convey was not necessarily the color of the slave's skin. To grasp the significance of color in late medieval descriptions requires knowledge of late medieval theories of physiognomy and physiology as well as ethnography.

In Europe, state and ecclesiastical authorities first began keeping lists of people and their descriptions in the late fourteenth century.[123] The initial purpose of the lists was to track undesirables, such as heretics and criminals, who moved from town to town, but they were quickly adapted for tax collection too. Because names were not sufficient to identify wandering heretics and bandits, the list makers added brief descriptions of their clothing, badges and symbols that they wore, marks on their skin, and their color.[124] One of the most notable early lists was a register of slaves created in Florence in 1366.[125] The Florentine register described slaves in terms of color, stature, and marks on the skin.

When late medieval texts referred to a person's color, whether that person was free or a slave, they meant the color of the body rather than the color of the skin. According to the Galenic theory of humoral medicine, all living bodies were composed of a mixture of cold, hot, wet, and dry elements.[126] In the human body, these elements mingled in the form of four fluids: blood, choler (yellow bile), phlegm, and black bile. Complexion (*complexio*) was the state created by a specific mixture of the four fluids. It had a range of meanings. Complexion could refer to an individual's humoral state at a particular moment in time or to an individual's innate and characteristic humoral balance. It could also be used to characterize groups: sex, age, race, climate zone, and astrological sign were all believed to affect complexion.

From a medical perspective, each human being was believed to have a unique personal complexion shaped by both nature and habit. This personal complexion could be affected at any given moment by many factors, including air, exercise, sleep, diet, excretion, and emotion. Each organ within the body also had its own complexion. Physicians sought to determine the personal complexion of each patient, the balance of elements and fluids that was normal for that particular body. Then they could intervene in various ways to restore and maintain the patient's health by restoring and maintaining the correct balance of humors for that patient. The best complexion, from a medical perspective, was a well-balanced one.

Because complexion was an internal rather than external state, medical training required physicians to learn how to read their patients' internal state through external signs. But because humoral balance affected the mind as well as the body, nonphysicians were also interested in reading the external signs to learn about internal qualities of personality and character. This was physiognomy. Over the course of the fourteenth to seventeenth centuries, as both ecclesiastical and state authorities placed increasing importance on listing and identifying people, the dominant meaning of complexion shifted from the internal, concealed blend of humors to the external, visible signs.[127] The emphasis also shifted away from the unique humoral balance of the individual to the categories of complexion associated with categories of people. Strong emphasis on complexion as a permanent group state rather than a transient individual state emerged in the late sixteenth and early seventeenth centuries, at the same time as the new word *race* became widespread in the sense that we use it today.[128]

The principal colors attributed to the human body in Galenic discourse were white, red, yellow, and black, but a healthy body should be mixed in color, ideally a mixture of red and white.[129] The poet Petrarch described his own color as "between white and dark brown" (*inter candidum et subnigrum*), while King Ludwig of Bavaria was compared to the biblical King David, "white and red in color" (*colore candidus et rubicundus*).[130] Healthy young mamluks in training were likewise described as "white and red" (*candidus et rubecundus*).[131] When a slave sale contract mentioned color, notaries tended to place it between the physical description and the health warranty, because it pertained to both clauses. Mixtures such as "whitish brown" (*bruna quasi blanca*), "brown between two colors" (*brunus inter duos colores*), "olive-brown" (*brunam olivegnam*), "blackish olive" (*seminigrum seu ulivignum*), "mixed color" (*coloris lauri*), or "medium color" (*medio collore*) signaled humoral balance and therefore good health.[132] Otherwise, the colors attributed to slaves were black (*nigra, nera*), brown (*bruna, bruneta*), olive (*olivastra, olivegna*), red (*rubera, rosa*), and white (*alba, blanca*). Blackness has received the most scholarly attention because of its implications for the Atlantic trade in African slaves, but blackness meant something subtly different to medieval notaries than it did to modern slavers.[133]

Although the color of slaves is of great interest to us today, it was not particularly interesting to medieval Italian notaries. No more than 3 percent of slave-related documents produced in Venice mentioned slaves' color. In Genoa, thirteenth-century notaries recorded slaves' color more consistently than those in the fourteenth or fifteenth centuries.[134] During the thirteenth century, 38 percent of slave-related documents from Genoa mentioned color. During the fourteenth century, 30 percent of slave-related documents mentioned color, but during the fifteenth century, the figure was only 2 percent. Although the fourteenth-century figure seems significant, 82 percent of those references came from just two notaries, Bartolomeo Gatto and Giovanni Bardi.[135] In the thirteenth century, references to color came from a much larger proportion of notaries. The reason for the shift from general interest in color to interest on the part of just a few notaries to general disinterest to renewed interest in the sixteenth century is unclear.[136] The shift suggests that the relationship between color and slavery did not develop in a linear way.

The Galenic system of humors was equally fundamental to medical theory in the Islamic world.[137] Indeed, it was through Arabic translations of Greek texts that humoral theory reached Latin physicians. As a result of the Galenic emphasis on mixture and balance, the terminology of color in Arabic was complex. The following passage is drawn from a Mamluk *shurūṭ* manual, a guide to writing legal documents. It comes from a chapter explaining how to compose a physical description of the parties to a contract, including their age, stature, forehead, eyebrows, eyes, nose, cheeks, jaw, lips, mouth, teeth, neck, and distinguishing features. For color, it offers the following array of possibilities:

> If a man is very *aswad* (black), he is called *ḥālik* (pitch black). If his black is mixed with red, he is called *daghmān*. If his color is pure, he is called *asḥam*. If the black is mixed with yellow, he is called *aṣḥam*. If his color is muddy, he is called *arbad*. If it is purer than that, he is called *abyaḍ*. If it is fine yellow and leaning towards black, he is called *ādamī* in color.[138] And if it is below *arbad* and above *adama* he is called very *adama*. If it is pure *adama*, he is called *shadīd al-samra* (very brown). And if it is purer than that, he is called *asmar* in color. And if it is purer than that, he is called *raqīq al-samra* (fine brown). If it is purer than that and leaning towards white and red, he is called *ṣāfī al-samra ta'aluhu ḥamra* (pure brown rising to red), and is called *raqīq al-samra bi-ḥamra* (fine brown with red). If his color is very pure he is called *ṣāfī al-samra* (pure brown) and is not called *abyaḍ* (white) because *bayāḍ* is leprosy. If he is completely white, he is called *anṣaḥ*. If there is paleness in his whiteness, he is called *ashqar* (pale). If he is paler than that, he is called *ashkal*. If there is nevertheless increasing red, he is called *ashqar*. If there are nevertheless freckles, he is called *anmash* (freckled). If his color is pure and leaning towards yellow and he is not ill, he is called *asḥab* in color.[139]

Because this passage is about describing the parties to a contract, its range of colors is meant to apply to free people as well as slaves.

With such a rich variety of colors available, restricting scholarly discussion of Mamluk slavery to black and white is misleading. Nevertheless, it has frequently been claimed that the terminology of slavery in Arabic reflects a binary division between black and white. Derivatives of the root *mīm-lām-kāf* (*mamlūk*) supposedly referred to white slaves, whereas derivatives of the root *'ayn-bā-dāl* (*'abd*) supposedly referred to black slaves.[140] The root *rā-qāf-qāf* (*raqīq*) supposedly applied to both white and black slaves. Color-based definitions of these terms, however, tend to come from nineteenth-century dictionaries such as

E. W. Lane's *An Arabic English Lexicon* and not Mamluk dictionaries such as Ibn Manẓūr's *Lisān al-ʿarab*.

When medieval sources are read without the aid of nineteenth-century dictionaries, there are numerous exceptions to the color-based definitions of *mamlūk* and *ʿabd*. The eleventh-century Ḥanafī jurist al-Sarakhsī discussed a hypothetical case in which an *ʿabd* was sold as a Turk but was actually a Greek or an Indian (*sindī*).[141] According to the rule, an *ʿabd* should be black, but Turks and Greeks did not fall under the Sūdān category, and Indians could be either Sūdān or ʿAjam. Al-Asyūṭī's fifteenth-century *shurūṭ* manual refers to the exchange of "a white or black *ʿabd* for a female slave," even though, according to the rule, it should have been a white *mamlūk* and a black *ʿabd*.[142] Another fifteenth-century jurist, al-Suyūṭī, called a group of thirteenth-century amirs *ʿabīd* of the treasury, although as military commanders and former slaves, one would expect them to be white *mamālīk*.[143] Yet not all mamluks were white. Five *mamālīk* were described as brown (*asmar*) in Mamluk biographical dictionaries.[144] There was at least one Ethiopian *mamlūk* whose color was not given and whose brother was also enslaved as a eunuch.[145] A fourteenth-century marriage contract between two slaves referred to the husband, a Nubian (*nūbī*), as a *mamlūk* without describing his color.[146] Color was relevant to how Mamluk masters used their slaves, as discussed in Chapter 3, because it was associated with stereotypes about physical health and temperament. But during the Mamluk period, color was not relevant to determining slave status or the terminology of slavery.

Moreover, color was not correlated with race in the context of late medieval slavery. The theory of climate zones could have been used to link color and race via geographical location, but in practice, one could not predict slaves' color based on their race or their race based on their color. Greek slaves were described in Arabic sources as pale, red, or brown and in Latin sources as white, olive, or brown.[147] The Greek sultan Khushqadam was "light in complexion with a beautiful golden yellow dominating it," according to Ibn Taghrī Birdī, but red in complexion according to Ibn Iyās.[148] Tatars might be white or olive.[149] Circassian slaves were white, olive, brown, or red.[150] Saracens could be white, black, olive, or mixed.[151] In the Florentine slave register of 1366, Moors were more likely to be described as white (seventeen cases) than as black (thirteen cases), and there were also olive and mixed-color Moors.[152] Whiteness was attributed to Abkhaz, Bulgar, Circassian, Russian, Saracen, Slavic, Tatar, and Turkish slaves in the Latin sources; in the Arabic sources, it was attributed to Circassians, Greeks, and Turks.[153] Brownness was attributed to Circassian, Laz, Saracen, and Iberian slaves in Latin; in Arabic, it was attributed to Greeks and Tatars.[154] Blackness was used as a color and a racial category in both Latin and Arabic sources. In addition to Blacks, black color was attributed to Iberian, Ethiopian, Canary Island, Indian, Moorish, and Saracen slaves. In Arabic, it was attributed to Ethiopians, Nubians, Zanjis, Zaghāwis, Bujawis, and Qandaharis.[155]

Finally, color was not the only aspect of physical appearance relevant to slavery. Florentine and Pisan sources frequently mentioned slaves' stature.[156] Some notarial descriptions included hair color.[157] Tatars in Italy (but not in the Mamluk kingdom) were distinguished by the shape of their faces. One of the chief characteristics of the Tatar face was broadness and flatness, including flatness of the nose.[158] Sculpted Tatar heads on two fourteenth-century capitals in the south and west porticoes of the Doge's Palace in Venice offer contemporary images.[159] A Venetian merchant described a Tatar slave as having "a face like a board," that is, flat, and implied that she was ugly.[160] Franco Sacchetti, a Florentine poet, gave a favorable description of a slave woman who "doesn't have a very Tatar face."[161] Felix Fabri judged the Tatar face negatively, as well as the Tatar hairstyle, which reminded him of idiots (*stulti*) in Germany.[162] Pero Tafur claimed that among the Tatars, "the most deformed are of the noblest birth."[163]

The poet and humanist Petrarch linked the perceived ugliness of the Tatar face directly to its association with slavery. In a 1367 letter from Venice to his childhood friend Guido Sette, at that time archbishop of Genoa, he wrote, "Already, a strange, enormous crowd of slaves of both sexes, like a muddy torrent tainting a limpid stream, taints this beautiful city with Scythian faces and hideous filth. If they were not more acceptable to their buyers than they are to me, and if they were not more pleasing to their eyes than to mine, these repulsive youths would not crowd our narrow streets; nor would they, by jostling people so clumsily, annoy foreign visitors, who are accustomed to better sights."[164] Although the features of a Tatar face did not change much when the Tatar being described was free, the associations were less negative.[165] Travelers characterized Mongol women as unattractive but hardworking, able to fight and hold power alongside men. Marco Polo described Tatars at the court of Kubilai Khan as noble and beautiful people. Illustrators of his text portrayed them with the same colors as European nobles.

Descriptions of the faces of Turkish slaves appear in both Italian and Mamluk sources as well. The Italians judged Turks, like Tatars, to be ugly: "[they] have short faces, broad in the upper part and narrow below. Their eyes are very small and very similar to those of that small beast [weasel], which by instinct hunts rabbits in their warrens and underground holes. Their noses are rather like those of the Indians [Ethiopians], and their beards closely resemble those of cats."[166] Mamluk descriptions of Turks portrayed them more positively. According to al-Asyūṭī, a legal description of a Turkish mamluk should mention "whether he has sprouted a moustache, that he is white of complexion, with a prominent forehead, with big deep-black eyes, long lashes, and lids painted with kohl, with a low-bridged nose, flat jaws, ruddy cheeks, red lips, well spaced teeth, with a small mouth, a long neck, of full stature, with small feet."[167] A female Turkish slave should be described as follows: "a young woman, white tinged with red in color, with a prominent forehead, as in the previous description but in feminine form."[168]

Conclusion

Although language and race did not form the ideological basis of late medieval Mediterranean slavery, they played an important role in determining who was and was not enslaved in practice. When it proved difficult or disadvantageous for masters to use religion to categorize their slaves, they turned to language and, especially, to race as substitutes. Yet the strength of race as an intellectual framework is also its weakness. Race subsumes many kinds of difference (ancestry, geography, culture, climate, humoral complexion, physical appearance, astrological sign, etc.) into a single category, and it promises us that this category is fixed, inherent, permanent, natural, and therefore reliable. Racial shorthand was useful to Italian notaries and Mamluk scribes who needed to categorize individual slaves in a few brief but meaningful words.[169] Racial shorthand was also useful for slave buyers who needed help in choosing the right slave for the right purpose and avoiding slaves whose status was doubtful. Cases in which medieval racial categories broke down could usually be ignored because of the power differential inherent in slavery: if the notary or scribe said that a slave was Circassian, the slave's ability to refuse that category was severely limited. Notaries and scribes were also able to gloss over paradoxical dual categories, such as Tatar Alans. Some slaves challenged their racial categorization in court, such as the Greeks who proved they were not Bulgars in Chapter 1. But race was used to confirm the status of others, such as Russian Orthodox slaves in Italy and Turkish Muslim slaves in Egypt, even though they should have been freed on religious grounds.

The fact that medieval people understood race as a spectrum rather than a black–white binary helps explain why some slaves were more successful in petitioning for freedom than others. It also helps explain why modern historians have struggled so much to understand how medieval racial categories worked in the context of slavery. We know that race is culturally constructed and historically contingent, as is slavery, and religion, and color. Nevertheless, today we still find race to be a convenient way to collapse many kinds of difference into a single one. Racial categories are so convenient that we sometimes struggle to understand how others could use them differently than we do. To explain the logic underlying medieval Mediterranean slavery, we have to acknowledge that the racial categories with which we are familiar are not permanent, fixed, inherent, or reliable. In fact, no matter what analytical framework we use, the complexity of human experience means that there will always be individuals and cases that do not fit neatly into our categories.

Chapter 3

Societies with Slaves: Genoa, Venice, and the Mamluk Sultanate

The late medieval Mediterranean was surrounded by societies with slaves.[1] This meant that slavery coexisted with other forms of labor, slave labor was not essential to the economy, slave ownership was not a distinguishing characteristic of the ruling class, and the master–slave relationship was not a model for other hierarchical relationships. In the late medieval Mediterranean, few households had more than two slaves. The majority were women purchased in their teens or twenties. The most notable exception was the household of the Mamluk sultan, which included thousands of enslaved men, women, and eunuchs.

After surveying the demography of slaves and slave ownership, this chapter discusses the services provided by slaves. Although slaves were not economically essential, they performed many important functions. Slaves acted as social and financial assets: their presence added to their masters' prestige, and their value was part of their masters' net worth. They also performed domestic service and manual labor. Male slaves were used for military service by the Mamluks. Wealthy Mamluk notables also had eunuchs to manage the parallel male and female spheres of their households.

Female slaves around the Mediterranean were subject to sexual and reproductive demands as well as demands on their physical labor. Focusing on the sexual and reproductive aspects of the shared culture of Mediterranean slavery reveals three things. First, although historians have paid more attention to the sexual exploitation of slave women in Islamic contexts, sexual exploitation was also common and well documented in Christian contexts. Second, the most important difference between Islamic and Christian practices of slavery had to do with the status of children. Under Christian and Roman law, children inherited the status of their mothers, so the child of a free man and his slave woman would be a slave. In contrast, under Islamic law, if a free man acknowledged paternity of a child by his slave woman, that child was born free and legitimate, and that slave woman became an *umm walad* (mother of a child). She could not be sold and would be manumitted automatically after her master's death. In an Islamic context, therefore, sex with slave women produced heirs, while in a Christian context, it produced property. Third, Christian practices regarding the children of slave women gradually came to resemble Islamic practices over the course of the fourteenth century. In other words, a new aspect of the shared culture of Mediterranean slavery emerged during this period.

In surveying the kinds of service demanded of slaves, this chapter also considers how slave owners' personalities and social positions shaped their slaves' lives. It has been asserted that being a slave in a society with slaves, where small numbers of slaves performed domestic work indoors, was a milder experience than being a slave in a slave society, where large numbers of slaves performed manual labor outdoors. This comparison is not helpful for two reasons. First, it sets up a competition of suffering. Was the pain of grueling manual labor greater or lesser than the pain of rape? That question is neither useful nor historically appropriate: both experiences were terrible, each in its own way. Judging which was "better" is beyond the purview of historians, except to the extent that historical sources make such judgments. Late medieval sources do not. Second, a definitional element of slavery is the overwhelming power, backed by violence, of the master over the slave.[2] A kind master could choose to treat his or her slaves well; a cruel master could choose to treat his or her slaves horribly. Either way, treatment was entirely at the master's discretion and could vary widely within a slaveholding society.

Instead of evaluating masters' treatment of their slaves, this chapter considers the role of masters as social gateways for their slaves. The importance of a master's position and personality in determining an individual slave's experience cannot be overstated. A Tatar boy purchased by a Venetian baker was likely to work in his owner's bakery and run household errands but would probably never ride a horse or wield a spear. A Tatar boy purchased by a Mamluk amir was likely to become an expert horseman and warrior but would probably never bake bread. The fact that these two boys might well have come from the same village is one of the most striking features of the Black Sea slave trade.

The Slave Population

It is hard to estimate the size of the free population in most medieval cities. Estimating the size of the slave population is even harder. Chronicles and travel accounts give rough numbers, but they cannot necessarily be trusted. In states that taxed the possession of slaves, the revenue generated by the tax can be used to estimate the size of the slave population in a given year. However, Genoa is the only late medieval Mediterranean state from which tax data of this kind have been preserved. Starting in 1381, Genoa taxed slave possession at half a florin per slave per year to finance its debts from the Chioggia war.[3] The half-florin tax applied to inhabitants of the city of Genoa, its suburbs, and the nearby towns of Polcevera, Bisagno, and Voltri. It was collected in April and October. In the collection records, noble families were listed by households (*alberghi*) and ordinary people by the neighborhoods (*conestagie*) where they lived. If a slave changed hands or died during the year, the tax was reduced to a quarter-florin.

The half-florin tax, like other Genoese taxes, was collected by tax farmers.[4] Individuals bid at a public auction for the right to collect the half-florin tax for up to three years. The auction was conducted in the Piazza Banchi under the loggia of the palace of the Negro family by a pair of officials called the *consules galleghe*. The winner paid his bid to the state treasury in two to four installments over the course of a year. Meanwhile, he would collect the tax whose revenues he had won. Any money he collected beyond the value of his bid and the cost of collection was his to keep as profit. Thus tax farmers' bids can be seen as specialist investments, and tax farmers often bid on multiple taxes over the course of several years.

Tax farmers tried to bid less than the actual revenue they expected to collect to leave a margin for collection expenses and profit. The rule of thumb is that tax farmers' bids represented about 70 percent of expected revenue, with 10 percent for expenses and 20 percent as profit.[5] When a tax farmer bid 580 lire for the half-florin tax in 1468–1470, he probably expected to collect about 829 lire in revenue. We know that in this year, the tax farmer paid fifty lire, about 6 percent of the expected revenue, to the man who would physically collect the tax for him, leaving 4 percent for other expenses, such as bookkeeping materials.[6] The 70 percent rule can also be checked against data from 1458, the only year for which both the tax farmer's bid and the tax collection register have been preserved.[7] In that year, Gregorio de Cassana bid 900 lire for the half-florin tax. The 70 percent rule suggests that Cassana expected 1,286 lire in revenue from a population of 1,582 slaves. In the 1458 collection register, I counted 2,025 slaves (yielding 1,645 lire, 6 soldi, 3 denari in revenue), and Domenico Gioffrè counted 2,059 slaves (yielding 1,672 lire, 18 soldi, 9 denari in revenue). In this case, the 70 percent rule was too generous: Cassana's bid was only 54 to 55 percent of the revenue he collected. The actual slave population of Genoa in 1458 would have been higher still, because the Fieschi family and the Spinolas of Luccoli were exempt from the half-florin tax in 1458. In the following discussion, therefore, it should be assumed that estimates of the Genoese slave population are rough

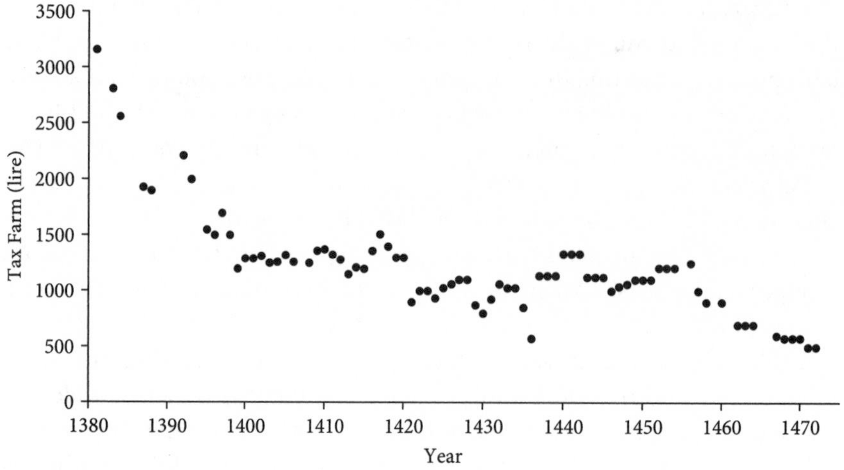

Figure 1. The Half-Florin Tax on Slave Possession in Genoa.

(Gioffrè, *Il mercato*, 69–70; Balard, *La Romanie*, 2:816; ASG, CdSG, N.185,15002, N.185,15006, N.185,15072.)

and more likely to be underestimates than overestimates. Figure 1 shows the winning bids for the half-florin tax between 1381 and 1472.[8]

Analyses of these data have tended to focus on demand rather than supply. The apparent peak in the late fourteenth century (about 7,223 slaves in 1381) is often linked to the Black Death: slaves could have alleviated the sudden labor shortage, and the threat of slave labor could have been used to coerce free servants into accepting lower wages.[9] But because the data set begins in 1381, three decades after the first plague outbreak and two decades after the second outbreak, it is impossible say exactly what the effects were. There is no pre-plague baseline against which to measure 7,223 slaves and decide whether that figure is low or high. Moreover, it is impossible to tell whether any effects of plague on the slave population should be attributed to the first or second outbreak. A close examination of wills, merchant letters, Senate decisions, and guild statutes in Venice has yielded no evidence for change in either the number of slaves or the kinds of labor they performed as a result of the Black Death.[10] Major plague outbreaks recurred in 1421, 1430, and 1436. Those correlate with dips in Figure 1, as plague deaths reduced the number of slaves.[11] After 1430 and 1436, the slave population rebounded to its previous level as masters replaced those who had died. After the 1421 outbreak, though, the slave population only reached 75 percent of its previous level.

Other factors may have affected the slave population of Genoa. In the late fourteenth century, Genoa came under the rule of France. Difficulties in tax collection during the transition may explain the decline in half-florin tax bids between 1380 and 1400.[12] In that case, however, bids should have returned to higher levels after the transition. No demand-based explanation has been offered for the peaks in 1417 (3,451 slaves) and 1440–1442 (3,049 slaves); factors affecting supply are discussed in Chapter 5. Overall, it seems that slaves made up 1 to 2 percent of the total Genoese population in the thirteenth century and 4 to 5 percent in the fifteenth century.[13]

Venetian and Mamluk records do not offer data comparable to Genoa's half-florin tax. While Venice also instituted a three lire tax on slave possession in 1379 to fund its part in the Chioggia war, no records have survived.[14] What remains is anecdotal evidence. The Senate received complaints about a slave shortage in 1459, which matches the Genoese data.[15] In 1483, a Swiss pilgrim reported that Venice had three thousand slaves, about 2.5 percent of its total population.[16] The Mamluks did not tax slave possession, nor were slaves included in the poll tax (*jizya*) paid by non-Muslim subjects.[17] No travelers tried to estimate the slave population of Cairo, much less the entire Mamluk kingdom. Modern scholars have noted shrinking slave retinues (mamluks, concubines, domestic slaves, and slave musicians) in the late fourteenth and early fifteenth centuries.[18] This corresponds to the marked decline in Figure 1 from 1381 into the early 1400s.

Another method of counting the slave population is by household. The bourgeois style of service described by Dennis Romano, in which one household had two or three female servants, was the norm in late medieval Italy.[19] The best evidence for this pattern again comes from Genoa's half-florin tax. In 1458, the half-florin tax was collected by household. As shown in Table 1, 95 percent of households who paid the tax had one or two slaves.[20] None had more than six. This statistical picture is fleshed out by letters between the Genoese merchant Giovanni da Pontremoli and his family during the same year.[21] Seven slaves are mentioned in the letters, but only two belonged to Giovanni.

Evidence from wills indicates a similar pattern in Venice. The famous traveler Marco Polo manumitted one slave in his will in 1324, and the Venetian painter

Table 1. Number of Slaves per Household in Genoa, 1458

No. of slaves per household	*No. of households*	*Percentage of households*
1	1,143	74
2	330	21
3	57	4
4–6	12	1

Source: ASG, CdSG, N.185,01009.

Nicoletto Semitecolo also manumitted one slave in 1386.[22] Panthaleo Iustiniano, a procurator of S. Marco, manumitted three slaves in 1393.[23] Madalutia, the wife of Bernardo Aymo, manumitted two slaves in 1410.[24] Andrea Barbarigo, a fifteenth-century patrician known for frugality, had two slave women in his household and one rented out.[25] Giosafat Barbaro manumitted one slave in 1493.[26] At the upper end of the spectrum, the apothecary Nascimbene de Ferraria mentioned six slaves in his will, but only four were present in his household.[27]

The number of slaves per household in the Mamluk sultanate ranged more widely. ʿAbd al-Laṭīf ibn ʿAbd al-Muḥsin al-Subkī boasted that he had gone through more than a thousand slave women, but elite civilian households more normally counted their slaves in the dozens.[28] At lower social levels and after slave retinues shrank in the late fourteenth century, Mamluk civilian households resembled Italian ones. The households represented in a cache of fourteenth-century documents from Jerusalem had no more than four slaves.[29] Ibn Ṭawq, a professional witness (*shāhid*) in Syria, owned two slave women.[30] In Damascus, the estate of a private secretary of the sultan (*kātib sirr*) included five slaves, and a judge's estate had four.[31] A study of Syrian amirs in the late fifteenth and early sixteenth centuries found that none had more than one *umm walad*.[32]

Military households tended to have more slaves. Each amir commanded a unit composed of both mamluks and free horsemen.[33] The size of the unit depended on the amir's rank: an *amīr mīʾa muqaddam alf* could have one hundred mamluks, an *amīr arbaʿīn* or *amīr ṭablakhāna* could have forty, an *amīr ʿashara* could have ten or twenty, and an *amīr khamsa* could have five. Since the Mamluk army was theoretically composed of twenty-four amirs of one hundred, forty amirs *ṭablakhāna*, twenty amirs of twenty, fifty amirs of ten, and thirty amirs of five, there should have been a total of 26,650 mamluks in the army, both enslaved and manumitted.[34] Each amir registered his mamluks with the *diwān al-jaysh*, which administered the army, and was not supposed to purchase more mamluks than his rank allowed. In practice, powerful amirs could accumulate 150 to 1,000 mamluks.[35] Although a large mamluk corps was prestigious, amirs with too many mamluks risked the sultan's retaliation if they appeared to challenge his power.[36]

In addition to mamluks, middle-ranking military households might have thirty or forty domestic slaves, while prominent amirs had two or three hundred.[37] The number of slave concubines varied. Tankiz, governor of Damascus in the early fourteenth century, had nine, the amir Qawṣūn had sixty, and the amir Bashtak had eighty.[38] Taghrī Birdī, governor of Damascus and father of the chronicler Yūsuf ibn Taghrī Birdī, had eight slave mothers (*ummuhāt awlād*) as well as a group of concubines who had previously belonged to Sultan Barqūq.[39]

Table 2. Number of Mamluks per Sultan

Sultan	*Reign*	*Source*	*Citadel mamluks*	*Total mamluks*
Baybars	1260–1277	al-Yunīnī, Ibn Taghrī Birdī	—	4,000–10,000
Qalawūn	1279–1290	Ibn Iyās	—	6,000–12,000
Muḥammad	1309–1340	Simeonis	10,000	30,000
Barqūq	1382–1389	Frescobaldi, Gucci	—	25,000–800,000
Muḥammad	1421–1422	Lannoy, Piloti	2,000–6,000	10,000
Qāytbāy	1468–1496	Adorno, Ghistele, Fabri, Breydenbach	6,000–10,000	12,000–30,000
Muḥammad	1496–1498	Harff	—	16,000

Sources: Ibn Taghrī Birdī, *Al-Manhal al-ṣāfī*, no. 717; al-Yunīnī, *Dhayl mirāt*, 3:250; Ibn Iyās, *Bidāʾiʿ al-zuhūr*, 1:1:361; Simeonis, *Itinerarium*, 72–73, 79; Frescobaldi, "Pilgrimage," 47; Gucci, "Pilgrimage," 100; Lannoy, *Œuvres*, 116; "Piloti, *Traité*," 54; Adorno, *Itinéraire*, 188; Ghistele, *Voyage*, 31; Breydenbach, *Sanctarum peregrinationum*, fol. 85r; Fabri, *Evagatorium*, 18:25; Harff, *Pilgrimage*, 106–7, 124.

Contemporary estimates of the total slave population of a single military household are rare, but Sunqur, governor of Bahnasā, owned sixty slave concubines, thirty additional slave women, and fifty mamluks at the time of his death in 1335.[40]

The largest Mamluk household was naturally that of the sultan. The sultan's mamluk corps (*al-mamālīk al-sulṭāniyya*) consisted of three groups: mamluks purchased by the reigning sultan (*al-mushtarawāt* or *al-julbān*), mamluks inherited by the reigning sultan from previous sultans (*al-qarāniṣa*), and mamluks inherited or confiscated from amirs who had died or lost favor (*al-sayfiyya*).[41] The citadel of Cairo had twelve barracks (*ṭibāq*) with a capacity of one thousand mamluks each.[42] However, contemporary estimates of the size of the sultan's mamluk corps varied widely, as shown in Table 2. The sultan's mamluk corps were subject to high turnover: several sultans purged the *qarāniṣa* and the *sayfiyya* to consolidate their power. The most notable purges were those of al-Nāṣir Muḥammad in 1310 and al-Nāṣir Faraj in 1411–1412.[43] Their effects on the slave trade remain to be investigated.

In addition, the sultan's household might include anywhere from forty to twelve hundred women, enslaved and free, as well as six hundred eunuchs and an unknown number of domestics.[44] A sultan's chief wife might have her own retinue of up to one thousand slave women.[45] Like other military households, the sultan's household tended to be smaller in the fifteenth century, and fifteenth-century sultans were more likely to be monogamous.[46]

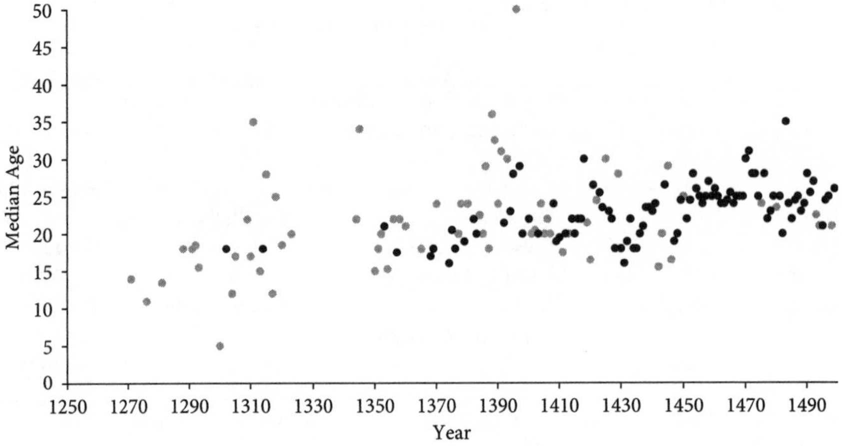

Figure 2. Median Age of Slaves Sold in Genoa. Black points are based on more data (at least ten sales per year) than gray points.

(ASG, CdSG, N.185,00624, N.185,00625; ASG, Not. Ant. 172, 236–39, 253, 258, 265, 273, 286–87, 292, 363, 366–67, 379–82, 396–405, 449, 685, 719, 768; ASG, Notai ignoti, b.xxiii; Balard, "Remarques"; Balard, *La Romanie*; Cibrario, *Della schiavitù*; Amia, *Schiavitù*; Delort, "Quelques précisions"; Epstein, *Speaking*; Ferretto, "Codice diplomatico"; Gioffrè, *Il mercato*; Heers, *Gênes*; Tardy, *Sklavenhandel*; Tria, "La schiavitù"; Verlinden, "Esclavage et ethnographie"; Williams, "Commercial Revolution.")

A third approach to slave demography is to consider the balance of age, gender, and origin. The origins of the Mediterranean slave population are discussed in Chapters 2 and 5. Age was included in Italian slave sale contracts, but notaries habitually rounded slaves' ages to the nearest multiple of two or five.[47] The median age of slaves sold in Genoa and Venice was normally between fifteen and twenty-five years old, as shown in Figures 2 and 3. Girls in their early teens seem to have been the most desirable for domestic work. When Cataruccia Dolfin asked her cousin in Alexandria for a slave, she requested a girl twelve years or older because "you can better use them in this age as you want."[48] Guglielmo Querini also preferred slaves between twelve and fifteen years old for domestic service.[49] Francesco Datini thought that a girl between six and ten would learn his ways more quickly and provide him with better service.[50] Further analysis shows that the slave women for sale tended to be a few years older than men and that the average age of slaves from the Black Sea increased after 1460, when exporting them became more difficult.[51]

Mamluk sale contracts categorized slaves by maturity (nursing, weaned, adolescent, or adult) rather than numerical age. Newly imported mamluks were often described as children (*ṣaghīr*, pl. *ṣugharā'*) below the age of maturity

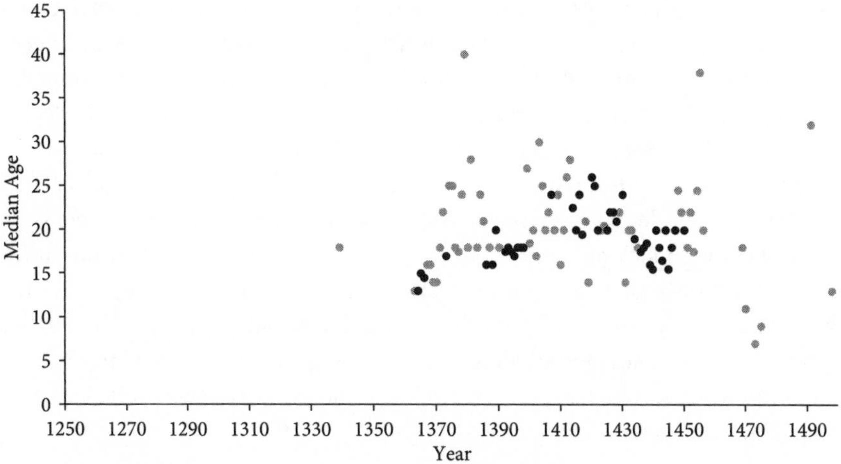

Figure 3. Median Age of Slaves Sold in Venice. Black points are based on more data (at least ten sales per year) than gray points.

(ASVe, Canc. inf., Misc., b.134 bis; ASVe, Canc. inf., Not., b.17; b.19, N.7; b.20, N.8–10; b.23, N.1; b.58–61; b.80, N.7; b.95; b.132, N.9; b.174, N.9; b.211; b.222; b.230, N.1–2; ASVe, PdSM, Misti, b.180; Tamba, *Bernardo de Rodulfis*; Braunstein, "Être esclave"; Cibrario, *Della schiavitù*; Colli, *Moretto Bon*; Dennis, "Un fondo"; Krekic, "Contributo"; Lazari, "Del traffico"; Lombardo, *Nicola de Boateriis*; Verlinden, "Le recrutement des esclaves à Venise"; Zamboni, "Gli Ezzelini.")

(*bulūgh*). The only evidence for numerical age at the time of sale is anecdotal. Jaqmaq al-Arghūnshāwī arrived in Egypt with his mother at age three, Sanqar al-Zaynī was imported around age six, Sultan Khushqadam at age ten, Sultan Shaykh at age twelve, and Sultan Baybars at age fourteen.[52] Taghrī Barmish al-Jalālī and the eunuch Fayrūz al-Nawrūzī al-Rūmī also arrived in Egypt in their teens. The oldest reported were Qawṣūn al-Nāṣirī, who came to Egypt and became a mamluk voluntarily at age eighteen, and Sultan Qāytbāy, who was imported in his early twenties.[53] The chronicler al-Maqrīzī claimed that the willingness of fifteenth-century sultans to accept older mamluks was a sign of decadence, but this may have been an element of his anti-Circassian rhetoric.[54] Fifteenth-century European travelers reported that mamluks in training were between seven and eighteen or between ten and twenty years old.[55]

As for gender balance, it has been argued that the Black Sea slave trade was divided so that boys were sent to Egypt and girls to Italy.[56] Girls were supposed to be beautiful and docile, more suitable than boys for domestic and sexual service.[57] Boys were supposed to be tough because of their steppe upbringing, already skilled at archery and horsemanship, and therefore suitable for military service. The presence of slave women from the Black Sea in Mamluk society has been minimized, except as a "necessary complement" to satisfy the sexual needs of mamluks.[58] Yet the majority of Mamluk as well as Italian slaves were women.[59] During the 1419 plague outbreak in Cairo, the ratio of male to female deaths was 1,065:669 among free people but 544:1,369 among slaves.[60] In Genoa, the half-florin tax records showed male to female ratios of 25:104 in 1413 and 9:100 in 1447.[61] The female majority in the Mamluk slave population may have been missed through lack of attention to civilian households. While Mamluk military households owned both men and women in large numbers, civilian households owned more women than men. The female majority of Black Sea slaves across the Mediterranean is less surprising when considered in terms of supply. As discussed in Chapter 5, the raiders who captured most Black Sea slaves tended to take women and kill men.

Slaves as Social and Financial Assets

All slaves were assets of significant value. Their prices were comparable to those of a house, ten pieces of woolen cloth, 150 kg of wool, 160 kg of grain, 25 to 30 percent of a notary's income, or three years of a sailor's income.[62] Purchasing slaves was an investment. Their value might increase as they learned the language, developed skills, and grew to maturity, but it might also decrease through illness, injury, and aging.

Selling slaves for cash was not the only way to utilize them financially. Slaves could be rented to others, especially craftsmen who could teach them new skills and thereby raise their value.[63] Lactating slaves could be rented as wet nurses for twice as much money as domestic slaves, and their contracts included provisions regarding the quantity and quality of their milk.[64] Because wet nurses were entrusted with the health of babies, they tended to be older than the average slave woman. Slaves could also be bartered in lieu of monetary payment;[65] pledged as collateral against debts;[66] granted to a daughter as part of her dowry;[67] stolen;[68] confiscated by the state;[69] appraised in estate inventories;[70] and inherited in wills.[71] As a result of these activities, it was not unusual for slaves to be jointly owned. For example, one slave in fourteenth-century Jerusalem was inherited collectively by six women (two wives, two sisters, and two young daughters of the deceased).[72] Another slave was jointly purchased by an Egyptian couple and given to their two sons as co-owners.[73] Two Venetian brothers, Petrus and Georgius de Manfredis, had joint ownership of a single slave woman, as did a Genoese couple, Petrus and Isolta de Vignolo, and two Genoese dyers, Damiano of Castagna and Antonius of Rapallo.[74] The fourteen joint owners of one slave sold in Genoa in 1274 were probably the pirate crew who had captured him.[75]

In addition to their monetary value, slaves had social value. A Mamluk saying held that "slaves, even if they consume your wealth, increase your prestige."[76] Slave ownership was a way to display power and wealth. A slave attendant or retinue might accompany their master in public. Italian elites liked to include their slaves in portraits.[77] Slave dancers, singers, lute players, and other musicians entertained guests in elite Mamluk homes.[78] Fourteenth-century amirs had slave orchestras with up to fifty musicians. Slave women also participated in public mourning for Mamluk elites. Civilians who owned mamluks signaled their pretensions to equality with the military ruling class. For example, the treasury clerk ʿAbd al-Bāsiṭ ibn Khalīl was criticized for aspiring beyond his station when he flaunted a retinue of "mamluks of the widely-available kinds."[79] The civilian supervisor of the two shrines in Jerusalem brought his mamluks on hunting excursions and to audiences with the military governor.[80]

When slaves were given as gifts, their value was both monetary and social.[81] Rulers exchanged slaves through diplomatic channels alongside gold, silver, jewels, luxury textiles, and horses. Among the gifts that Sultan Baybars gave Berke, the khan of the Golden Horde, upon the occasion of his conversion to Islam were black male slaves and slave cooks.[82] Tokhta Khan gave Sultan al-Nāṣir Muḥammad eighty male and twenty female slaves, and Janibak Khan made a similar gift to Sultan al-Nāṣir Ḥasan.[83] Mamluk sultans also exchanged slaves with the sultan of Baghdad, the Ottoman sultan, the Ilkhan, and the king of Nubia.[84] One mamluk, Arghūnshāh al-Nāṣiri, was first sent as a gift from China to Persia, then regifted to the Mamluks.[85]

Within the Mamluk kingdom, the sultan and high-ranking amirs exchanged slaves as signs of respect and favor. It was common for the governor of Syria to send large groups of slaves, including mamluks and eunuchs, to the sultan.[86] The amir of Ṣafad also sent a eunuch to Sultan Barqūq, whom Barqūq regifted to his secretary.[87] A more subtle aspect of gifting slaves involved plays on their personal ties. Al-Nāṣir Muḥammad reinforced his relationship with the amir Yalbughā al-Yaḥyāwī by giving him one of a pair of slave sisters and keeping the other for himself.[88] When the amir Tanibak al-Yaḥyāwī discovered that his brother Taybars had been purchased by the governor of Malaṭya, the governor obligingly sent Taybars and a group of other mamluks to Cairo as a gift for the sultan.[89] Refusing to give a slave requested by the sultan could be interpreted as an act of rebellion. When the sultan of Mārdīn substituted two mamluks and a slave woman for a beautiful harpist requested by al-Nāṣir Muḥammad, al-Nāṣir Muḥammad threatened to sack the city.[90]

Finally, in both Mamluk and Italian households, slaves were given as gifts to family members and close friends.[91] Family gifts were often implemented through wills. Lionello Cattaneo gave his slave to a priest before departing on a journey, while Regina Morosini, a Venetian widow, gave a slave to her parish priest because "you have conferred so many services and indulgences on me [that] it would be unfitting if I were ungrateful to you."[92] Doctors also received slaves as gifts from their patients.[93]

Slaves as Domestic and Manual Labor

Most slaves in the late medieval Mediterranean were purchased for domestic service. Their tasks included cooking, cleaning, washing and maintaining clothes and linens, carrying water, buying food, collecting firewood and tending the fire, spinning, sewing, weaving, running errands, caring for and nursing children, tending animals, and personal service.[94] Most worked under a wife's supervision or managed bachelor households.[95] Since Italian households usually had one or two domestic servants, free or enslaved, they were expected to be flexible. Wet nurses were the exception: they were expected to devote themselves fully to childcare. In the Mamluk context, elite households had large numbers of slaves (rarely free women) in domestic service, so they were more likely to specialize.[96] Men in domestic service usually cared for horses (boats in Venice), acted as guards or doormen, and provided personal service for male masters.[97]

Although racial stereotypes seem to have affected the use of domestic slaves in Italy, the evidence is anecdotal. Black men were prized as gondoliers in Venice.[98] Circassians were said to be beautiful and of "great aspect" (*grande aspecto*), and Circassian women were reputed to be very domestic.[99] Tatars were known for loyalty, "since it may be taken as a certainty that no Tartar ever betrayed a master."[100] Tatar women were preferred for wet nursing and hard labor. A Florentine mother advising her son in Naples on the purchase of a female slave recommended "one of the Tartar nation, who are rough and advantageous for long hard work. The Russians, i.e. those from Russia, are more sensitive and more beautiful; but, it seems to me, a Tartar would be better. The Circassians have a passionate nature; although all the others have that too."[101] Yet in 1368, the Venetian Senate considered and ultimately rejected a proposal to ban "any newly purchased male slave of the Tatar language" because many had already been imported and turned out to be "corrupt and wicked of condition, and they cause daily disputes and rumors, and they can easily introduce scandals and errors in this land."[102]

In contrast, Mamluk slave-buying guides included lists of racial stereotypes to help buyers choose the right slave for the right purpose. Black Africans were recommended for domestic work, and mamluks often had black male slaves to look after their horses and collect their food rations from the citadel each day.[103] Alans were also recommended for domestic service. They were described as sturdy, gentle, good-natured, agreeable, and morally upright, but also careless and lazy.[104] Greeks (*rūmī*) were characterized as obedient, sincere, loyal, reliable, and intelligent, but also stingy.[105] Greek men were valued for their education and good manners, whereas Greek women were supposedly accurate and conservative in managing resources and therefore made good housekeepers. Armenians were said to be strong, sound of constitution, and beautiful, but also dishonest, greedy, rude, and dirty.[106] Thus the slave-buying manuals recommended them for hard labor and cautioned that beating or threats might be necessary to make them work.

Eunuchs had a special role as guardians of Mamluk household honor.[107] They served in the dual households of the elite, both in the harem where the women and children lived and in the barracks (*ṭabaqa*) where the young mamluks were trained.[108] In both contexts, they helped integrate other slaves into the household. The *zimāmdār* (head of the harem) and his staff supervised the female slaves, both domestics and concubines. The *muqaddam al-mamālīk* (supervisor of mamluks) and his staff brought up the young mamluks. One of the more famous eunuchs was Sandal al-Manjakī, who served Sultan Barqūq as treasurer and then head of the Sandaliyya barracks.[109] Sandal's mamluk charges revered him for his generosity, piety, abstemiousness, and holiness (*baraka*), despite the temptations of his powerful position. Because castration was not permitted by Islamic law, it usually occurred before slaves were imported to the Mamluk kingdom.[110] Greeks (*rūmī*), Indians (*hindī*), West Africans (*takrūrī*), and Ethiopians (*ḥabashī*) were preferred.[111] Eunuchs from the Black Sea were less common, but a Russian and a Kipchak eunuch were also mentioned.[112]

To the extent that slaves were used for heavy physical labor in the late medieval Mediterranean, they tended to be male. Slave oarsmen, though today strongly associated with galley warfare, were not common until the sixteenth century.[113] Slaves occasionally farmed or built fortifications in Genoa, but this was more common on the islands (Majorca, Sicily, Crete, and Cyprus) than on the mainland.[114] A few Mamluk slaves mined salt and copper in the Sahara.[115] When the fifteenth-century German traveler Bernhard von Breydenbach saw people making bricks on the banks of the Nile, he called them slaves, though they may have been free laborers whom he imagined as slaves in the tradition of Exodus.[116]

Slaves also worked in craft production and in trade. Italian and Mamluk merchants were known to travel with male slaves and authorized them to act as business agents.[117] Islamic law enabled masters to confer a special status, *maʿdhūn*, on slaves so that they could legally conduct business. Artisans were assisted by both male and female slaves.[118] In Cairo, a community of Christian slaves worked as masons and carpenters.[119] Several Venetian guilds (the gold beaters and the makers of velvet and samite) banned slaves from learning trade secrets in case they were later sold outside the guild, but Genoese guilds allowed slaves to learn trade secrets as long as they did not compete with their former masters after manumission.[120] Apothecaries were not permitted to let their slave assistants run the shop or dispense arsenic for fear of poisoning.[121]

Slaves as Soldiers

The best-documented Mamluk slaves were boys in military training.[122] These were the mamluks after whom the Mamluk state was named. New mamluks were housed in special barracks (*ṭabaqa*) under the supervision of eunuchs. A jurist (*faqīh*) visited each day to teach them reading, writing, the Quran, ritual prayer, and the rudiments of Islamic law. Military instructors trained them in horsemanship, archery, and the use of various weapons. The end of training was marked by a graduation or passing-out ceremony (*kharj*).[123] During this ceremony, the sultan would inspect his mamluks and issue each one a suit of formal clothing, a horse, and a sword. Each mamluk also received a document of manumission (*ʿitāqa*). From this moment, he was legally free but enmeshed in a complex system of patronage and factional politics.

The intensity of mamluk training forged bonds of loyalty among boys in the same cohort (*khushdāsh*) and between the boys and their master (*ustādh*). The goal of the mamluk system was for these relationships to replace the ties of biological kinship lost through enslavement.[124] A son might assassinate his father to gain his inheritance, and a civilian bureaucrat might betray a ruler to benefit his own family, but a slave had no kin and therefore no conflicted loyalties. After manumission, masters became patrons, and fellow mamluks became factional allies. A newly graduated and manumitted mamluk would be enrolled as a soldier (*jund*) in his former master's corps and given a salary or a fief (*iqṭa*ʾ) to live on.[125] His subsequent ability to rise through the ranks would depend on the patronage of his former master and the support of his faction as well as his own skill and ambition.[126]

Mamluks of the sultan could expect faster advancement than mamluks of the amirs. More was written about those who attained high ranks like commander (*amīr*), governor (*nāʾib*), or general (*atabak*), but most mamluks remained in obscurity at the rank of soldier (*jund*). They lived in the city where they were stationed, received a salary and rations from the state, and supplemented their income by working or extorting money from civilians.[127] Of the five thousand mamluks associated with Sultan al-Muʿayyad Shaykh, only sixty (1.2 percent) were prominent enough to be named in a biographical dictionary.[128] The most successful Muʿayyadī mamluk, Khushqadam, rose over the course of forty years to become sultan himself. During the same period, his fellow Muʿayyadī mamluk Jānibak Shaykh was not promoted at all. When Khushqadam became sultan, he raised Jānibak Shaykh to the lowest rank of amirs in honor of their metaphorical brotherhood (*khushdāshiyya*). Yet Jānibak Shaykh was unemployed again at the time of his death six or seven years afterward. His biographer described him as "one of the neglected, lost ones."[129]

Mamluks were unique among late medieval Mediterranean slaves in that their manumission was virtually guaranteed and their masters allowed them real opportunities for power and wealth. Their enslavement early in life has been compared to education at a strict boarding school: harsh, but with the prospect of a bright future.[130] Yet, although their careers after manumission have led some to dismiss the legal reality of their slave status, the time that young mamluks spent enslaved was the basis of their class identity. No one could hold a high military post in the Mamluk state without undergoing enslavement and manumission.[131] Although there were free soldiers in the Mamluk army (*ḥalqa*), they were never promoted beyond a certain level. Civilian bureaucrats held important administrative offices, but their career paths were distinct from those for mamluks. If free people wished to join the Mamluk ruling class, they had to become slaves first. One who did so was the amir Qawṣūn.[132] He had come from the Golden Horde to Cairo as a merchant selling leather goods, but Sultan al-Nāṣir Muḥammad saw him in the citadel and persuaded him to sell himself into slavery. The sultan sent 8,000 dirhams to Qawṣūn's brother, and Qawṣūn went to the barracks and began training.

The enslavement of mamluks shaped their youth and had consequences for the rest of their lives.[133] As slaves, mamluks were not allowed to move freely. They stayed in the citadel barracks and needed permission from their eunuch guardians to go down into the city. They possessed no money, privileges, or military equipment of their own; everything was supplied by their master and could be taken away by him. They themselves could be sold, given away, or confiscated at any time. They also could not marry without their master's permission.

The legal effects of slavery did not end with manumission. The jurist al-Suyūṭī, for example, said that an amir could never designate his property as a charitable endowment (*waqf*) like many elite civilians did because of his status as a former slave: "we say that [the *waqf*] reverts to the treasury because its endowers are slaves of the treasury and the permanence of their manumission is subject to consideration."[134] The shaykh Ibn ʿAbd al-Salām refused to swear loyalty to Sultan Baybars until a witness could be found to testify that Baybars had been legally purchased and manumitted.[135] Any question about the legitimacy of a mamluk's sale or manumission had to be rectified at once lest it undermine his authority, as in the case of the general Asandamur explained in Chapter 1.[136]

According to Mamluk racial stereotypes, only Turks (in the generic sense of nomadic, Turkic-speaking people from cold northern climates) were suitable for military training because of their vigorous physical strength and animal aggression.[137] In the late Mamluk period, an exception was made for a new corps of African soldiers who used firearms, apparently because the mamluk cavalry considered firearms beneath them.[138] Racial categories were also used to assign mamluks to barracks in the Cairo citadel. Al-Burjiyya was for Circassians and Alans, while al-Dhahabiyya and al-Zumurrudiyya were for Kipchaks and Khitai.[139] Slave-buying manuals elaborated on the supposed characteristics of specific Turkish races. Kipchaks were said to be moderate in temperament, strong, and powerful, with beautiful, proportionate bodies but grim faces.[140] Those from Khurasān thrived best in Egypt. Kipchak children were said to be clean, healthy, skillful, and beautiful. Kipchak men were said to be good soldiers but merciless, potentially treacherous, and coarse of heart because they ate too much horse meat. They were said not to be skilled in politics, judgment, the crafts, or the sciences.

Circassians were characterized as physically powerful, brave, always ready to strike the first blow, and having a strong sense of group solidarity (*ʿasabiyya*).[141] Yet they were also said to be lacking in wisdom, work ethic, and patience for hardship and long-term warfare. Untrained Circassians were said to be proud and unruly, with no grasp of religion. Yet those trained in knightly skills (*furusiyya*) from a young age were excellent warriors and commanders, while those offered religious education were proficient Muslims and capable of becoming religious scholars (*ʿulamāʾ*). In other words, the worst Circassians were utterly useless, but the best Circassians—those enslaved and trained as mamluks—were suitable for leadership.[142]

Since Galenic theory linked inner qualities of character, outer qualities of complexion, and the characteristic humoral balance of an individual, the inconsistency of the Circassian character stereotype was reflected in a range of possible Circassian complexions. According to al-ʿAyntābī's slave-buying manual, a pale (*ashqar*) Circassian had "no equal in shamelessness, debauchery, evil morals, and lying."[143] A Circassian who was both slender and pale was likely to be active, quick to move and speak, and governed by his passions. A black (*sawād*) Circassian was rash and cowardly to the point that his bad qualities were likely to outweigh his good ones. He might also be greedy and unkind. On the other hand, a Circassian who was white imbued with red (*al-abyaḍ al-musharrib bi-ḥumra*) should be intelligent and opinionated. A brown color (*asmar*) shading into black (*sawād*) and yellow (*ṣufra*) indicated bravery, responsibility, and boldness. Brownish red (*samra ḥumra*) was quick, active, clever, opinionated, powerful, a good companion, and generally more good than bad.

Slavery and Sex

In the late medieval Mediterranean, all female slaves were assumed to be sexually available to their male owners regardless of whether they had been purchased for the express purpose of sexual exploitation.[144] Because women's honor in both Italian and Mamluk society depended on sexual reputation, slave women were categorically dishonored and dishonorable in comparison to free women.[145] Sex between female owners and male slaves did occur, as did homosexual sex between owners and slaves, but it was illicit and acknowledged only in certain contexts.[146] It was the sexual exploitation of female slaves by male owners specifically that was part of the common culture of late medieval Mediterranean slavery.

In Venice and Genoa, sex within marriage was governed by canon law. Baptized slaves could receive all church sacraments, except ordination, and therefore could marry other baptized slaves. Their masters' permission was desirable, but once the sacrament had been performed, a marriage between slaves without their masters' permission would not be dissolved.[147] Marriages between baptized slaves and free people were also permitted, though rare, as long as the free spouse was aware of the enslaved spouse's status. If the free spouse was unaware, the marriage could be annulled.[148]

Sex outside marriage was governed by the *ius commune*, which recognized two kinds of sexual relationships. One was concubinage. Drawing on Roman law, a concubine was defined as an unmarried woman, free or enslaved, who was the sole sexual partner of an unmarried man, who lived in his home, and whom he treated with affection.[149] For young bachelors, elderly widowers, priests, and merchants far from home, a concubine could fulfill many of the functions of a wife, including sex, companionship, and household management.[150] For example, in 1464, a Florentine mother wrote to her unmarried son about his slave concubine Marina, "and how well she looks after you. Hearing such things I find it easy to understand why you want to put off getting married for a year and why they're so slow in finding you a wife. You behave like a man who wants to put off dying or paying his debts for as long as he can. At the moment you've only got one woman in the house and you're well looked after, but when you get married there'll be lots of them and you wonder how you'll get on. So it seems to me you're wise to take your time."[151] Living with a concubine was licit and considered normal for an unmarried man. It usually did not affect his honor, though it did affect the honor of the concubine.[152]

Sex between slave women and married men, and other sexual encounters that did not meet the criteria of concubinage, were illicit but widely tolerated: "although not publicly and openly, access [to slaves] may be had easily and in secret, as we see them daily and touch them."[153] For example, the Milanese ambassador to Venice reported that Doge Pietro Mocenigo, in his seventies at the time, slept with two young and beautiful Turkish slave women.[154] In a dispute over the sale of a slave woman who later died, it was directly stated that the buyer had purchased her "for the sake of satisfying his lust."[155]

The power differential in these encounters was crucial. Slave women had no honor, no legal standing to refuse sex with their masters, and no social protection, except through their masters. Older historiography has put forward a narrative of jealous wives, cheating husbands, and seductive slave women that ignores the fact that slave women did not have the right to resist the sexual advances of their masters or a social network to support them in doing so.[156] The Great Council of Venice did legislate against sex between female slaves and their male masters in 1364 "because the quantity of female slaves in Venice at present is very large and will be greater in the future" and because "female slaves are made lesser and cheaper in price because they are made pregnant and adulterers."[157] However, although the Signori di Notte was charged with enforcing the law, there is no record of any slave owner being prosecuted.[158] Perhaps the social norms that allowed powerful men access to powerless women were too deeply rooted, or perhaps the level of investigation required to verify such a crime was too intrusive for patrician households.

The only practical restriction on the sexual exploitation of slave women limited it to their masters. Sex between slave women and other men was both illicit and socially unacceptable. Masters were forbidden from prostituting their slaves.[159] If a slave woman left her master's house at night or allowed a man into the house to have sex, both parties were punished.[160] To the extent that slave women were recognized as victims of rape, the crime was treated as property damage rather than a violation of honor.[161] Impregnating another man's slave commanded a fine of twenty-five lire in Genoa; if she died as a result of the pregnancy, the fine rose to fifty lire.[162] It might also be necessary to purchase insurance against the expenses and risks of childbirth.[163]

In the Mamluk context, ownership of a slave woman also included unrestricted sexual access to her. Every slave woman was a licit sexual partner for her male master and only for him, regardless of whether she had been purchased for the express purpose of sexual exploitation. Sex with slaves belonging to other people, with jointly owned slaves, and with married slaves was not permitted.[164] Sex and its attendant dishonor were so strongly associated with slave women that they did not veil themselves in public as free women did and could be manumitted with the formula "your sexual organ is free" (*farjuki ḥurrun*).[165] When a notoriously stern market inspector (*muḥtasib*) decided to uphold public morality by forbidding Cairene women from leaving their houses, Sultan Barsbāy made an exception for slave women, as long as they went unveiled.[166] After all, they had no honor to protect, and the measure would prevent free women from going out in disguise.

Like Italian men, Mamluk men used slave women to fulfill many of the functions of a wife without the obligations of marriage.[167] Unlike Italian men, Mamluk men wrote openly about using slave women as a disposable source of sexual gratification. Ibn al-Mujāwir, an early thirteenth-century traveler, recorded a crude story about a man who purchased a slave woman, had sex with her for a week or two, and then tried to annul the contract and get his money back.[168] Al-Qazwīnī had four permanent slave concubines (his *ummuhāt awlād*) and six temporary ones, whom he replaced periodically at slave market. Ibrahīm ibn Aḥmad al-Zar'ī, a fourteenth-century jurist, visited the slave market and the book market on alternate Fridays to acquire pleasures for both body and mind.[169] Al-Zawāwī, a fifteenth-century Sufi, fantasized about receiving a gift of a beautiful Turkish slave woman and 1,000 dinars from the sultan.[170]

Which kinds of slave women were considered most sexually desirable depended on racial stereotyping, fashion, and personal preference. Much recent scholarship has perpetuated the idea that white women were universally considered more desirable than black women, but Sultan al-Nāṣir Muḥammad preferred mulatto (*muwallad*) women, and Sultan al-Ṣāliḥ Ismāʿil preferred black women.[171] Al-Suyūṭī's *Nuzhat al-ʿumr* is a fifteenth-century collection of poetry on the beauty of white, brown, and black skin. In al-ʿAyntābī's slave-buying advice manual, Greek women were considered better housekeepers than sexual partners.[172] The humoral balance of Alan women tended toward the cold humors, so they were not lustful enough. Armenian men were considered more suitable for sex than Armenian women. Turkish women were said to lack gentleness and elegance, but "they accumulate children and treasure-troves of offspring."[173] In a dream, the fifteenth-century Sufi al-Zawāwī asked the Prophet Muḥammad what kind of slave woman to buy as a sexual companion. Muḥammad recommended Ethiopians because they were softhearted and kind, but al-Zawāwī did not take the Prophet's advice. He considered an Indian woman, then decided that he preferred Turks because they were better for childbearing.[174] The fifteenth-century scholar al-Biqāʿī had children by slave women from three different racial categories: Indian, Ethiopian, and Zanj.[175]

Slavery and Reproduction

In the Mamluk context, determining the status of a slave woman's children was fairly straightforward. If a man acknowledged that his slave woman had conceived a child by him, she attained the status of *umm walad* (mother of a child).[176] An *umm walad* could not be sold or given away during the lifetime of her master, and she would be manumitted automatically upon his death. Her master could continue to have sex with her, require her to work, rent her labor, and marry her to another man without her consent. Her child would be considered a free and legitimate heir of her master, but it could be taken away from her and raised by the master's family. Desire for male heirs, especially in the face of high infant mortality, appears frequently in Mamluk sources as a reason for sex with slave women.[177]

It was fairly common for a master to manumit and marry his *umm walad*. Manumission was essential to the transition from slave to wife because marriage between a female slave and her male owner was not permitted. Marriage and slavery were considered two different types of ownership of the body, with different rights and obligations.[178] Ownership in marriage was mutual: both husband and wife had rights over each other's bodies, although those rights were not equal. Ownership in slavery was entirely one-sided: the master exercised extensive rights over the body of the slave, while the slave had no rights at all over the body of the master. The two legal states of slavery and marriage could not coexist because the rights of a slave and the rights of a spouse were incompatible. There was no such thing as a slave wife.[179]

If a slave woman became pregnant and her master did not acknowledge the child as his own, the child was born a slave, and the mother was not an *umm walad*.[180] This may explain why Ibn Baṭṭuṭa's slaves lied to him about the gender of a child born on the road between the Golden Horde and Bukhara, telling him that it was a boy instead of a girl. They admitted the deception after Ibn Baṭṭuṭa had acknowledged and named the child, but he accepted his daughter anyway, writing that "this girl was born under a lucky star, and I experienced everything to give me joy and satisfaction from the time of her birth."[181] The only legal protection offered to slave children was a rule that they could not be sold away from their mothers until the age of separation. Jurists debated where to set this age: some set it at seven or eight years, whereas others marked it by the loss of baby teeth or the onset of puberty.[182]

In the Italian context, determining the status of a slave woman's child was complicated. According to Roman and canon law, children followed the status of their mother. In Lombard law, they followed the status of the inferior parent. Either way, the children of a slave woman would be slaves at birth regardless of their father's status.[183] Thus, if the father-master did nothing, both mother and child would remain his slaves.[184] If he chose to take action, however, he had several options. He could manumit his children, recognize them in his will, petition the papacy to declare them legitimate, provide dowries for them, and even formally adopt them.[185] The slave children of Medici men did especially well.[186] Carlo, the son of Cosimo de'Medici and a Circassian slave named Maddalena, became an abbot. Alessandro, the son of either Lorenzo de'Medici or Giulio de'Medici (Pope Clement VII) and an African slave named Simonetta, became Duke of Florence. This pattern occasionally resulted in a son inheriting his own mother as part of his father's estate.[187] On the other hand, father-masters could anonymously abandon their slave children at a foundling hospital, which would assume them to be free. A single Florentine man, Stefano Moronti, left four children by slave women at the Ospedale degli Innocenti over the course of twelve years.[188] In Genoa, children could be abandoned at the Ospedale dei Poveri Servi Liberti (which tried to restrict its intake of enslaved children in 1481) or with the Greek confraternity in the neighborhood of Santa Maria delle Vigne.[189]

If the father-master chose to manumit and legitimize his children, then the Roman laws of concubinage came into play. The children of concubines were considered natural, one step down from legitimate children produced through marriage or adoption and one step up from spurious children produced through adultery, incest, or other illicit sex.[190] Natural children were easier to make legitimate than spurious children and could become heirs on equal footing with freeborn children.[191]

When father-masters did not make their wishes clear or did not act in time, lawsuits arose. For example, Nicolinus de Presanis moved from Cremona to Caffa, where he had children by a woman named Lucia Christiana, whom he did not marry.[192] Presanis declared their son A. legitimate but then died intestate. In theory, A. should have inherited Presanis' estate, but his family contested A.'s claim on several grounds. One was his mother's status; the family argued that Lucia Christiana had been a slave when A. was conceived, so A. was spurious and could not inherit. Surprisingly, they did not argue that A. himself was a slave through his mother. In an advisory brief, the Genoese lawyer Bartolomeo de Bosco upheld A.'s right to inherit. He argued that Lucia Christiana's slave status had not been satisfactorily proven. Even if she were a slave, "she could be a concubine, and children born from her would be natural."[193] To support his opinion, Bosco cited Roman law on concubinage and canon law on inheritance and slaves' right to marry.[194] The outcome of the case has not survived, but Bosco's brief demonstrates the benefits that concubinage might confer on a slave woman's children. In a similar situation, a Venetian merchant considered tampering with his brother's will to defend the inheritance of his brother's son by a slave concubine in Tana.[195]

A father-master also had options with regard to the slave mother. Freedom for their child came at the expense of the mother–child bond, whether it was adopted by the father-master or left at a foundling hospital.[196] After losing their children, slave mothers could also be exploited to serve the reproductive needs of others as wet nurses.[197] Private households and foundling hospitals employed both free and enslaved wet nurses, but the living conditions of enslaved wet nurses (and thus, according to Galenic medical theory, the quality of their milk) were easier to control. Free families sometimes developed strong ties of affection with the slaves they rented or purchased as wet nurses, ties which they mentioned in wills and acts of manumission.[198]

Over the course of the thirteenth through the fifteenth centuries, Christian practice regarding the children of slave women gradually grew closer to Islamic practice. According to the *Furs de Valencia*, promulgated in the thirteenth century, if a man had a child by his slave, both the mother and the child were free.[199] Slave women in fifteenth-century Valencia sued successfully for freedom on this basis. In Florence, the children of slave mothers and free fathers were free starting in the fourteenth century.[200] Such children were also considered free by Venetians first in Crete and other colonies and later in Venice itself.[201] By the fifteenth century, the Genoese also assumed that the children of free men and slave women were free by default.[202] Interestingly, irregular menstruation came to be considered a redhibitory fault at around the same time, indicating that slave women's reproductive functions (bearing and nursing children) had become essential to their value as commodities.[203] Many reasons (honor, sentiment, a desire for heirs)[204] have been suggested for this evolution toward free status for the children of free men and slave women, but never the possibility that Christians were adopting the Islamic model and beginning to think of their children by slave women as heirs instead of property. It is also telling that while freedom was systematically extended to the children of slave women and free men over the course of the late Middle Ages, it was not extended to the slave women themselves.[205]

Exactly how this Muslim practice might have come to influence Christian practice is unclear, but it could have happened through the slave women. Late medieval Christians were certainly aware of the *umm walad* model.[206] Their slaves were aware too: a master complained in 1382 that his slave woman was claiming to be pregnant "so that I love her and free her," but he did not believe that her pregnancy was real.[207] In 1403, the Genoese authorities felt it necessary to clarify that "if indeed any master carnally knows his slave and she produces a child from the same, we establish nevertheless that slave will not become free for this reason."[208] In other words, it appears that some slave women in the late fourteenth and early fifteenth centuries were trying to claim something like *umm walad* status in Italy.

Even so, the extent to which individual slave women experienced coercion and exercised choice in their sexual lives remains unknowable because no sources have survived in which slave women wrote openly about such things. As we observe from the outside, it is important to remember that coercion and choice were not mutually exclusive. Utter and profound isolation was a defining characteristic of slaves' experience.[209] If at all possible, they were motivated to make or find a place for themselves and reduce their chances of being sold onward and isolated once again. An isolated, enslaved woman thus had a different range of choices and motivations regarding sex than a socially connected, free woman. Some enslaved women coerced into sexual acts, for example, might choose to take contraceptive or abortifacient measures to avoid pregnancy.[210] Others clearly hoped that pregnancy might reduce their isolation and increase their odds of manumission.[211] The prospect of *umm walad* status, in addition to the desire to escape isolation, was a strong incentive for slave women to acquiesce to the sexual demands of their masters. Ḥasbiyat Allah, the slave of the scholar and chronicler al-Biqāʿī, claimed to be pregnant for ten years before finally giving birth to a son. In addition to the security of *umm walad* status, she gained the full and fascinated attention of her master, who tracked her symptoms closely and recorded them both as a medical case study and a wonder tale.[212]

Some masters manipulated their slaves' desire for belonging to control them sexually. When Gasparino Rizzo, a carpenter in Tana, made his will, he manumitted his slave Clara, who had already given birth to one child and was pregnant with a second. However, he stipulated that the children were to be raised by his mother in Venice, while Clara was to remain in Tana. If she married, she would inherit all of his goods in Tana and keep the children until they were old enough to sail to Venice. But if she "wishes to be anyone's *cuma* . . . then she should be expelled from my house in [her] shirt."[213] Whether Clara chose, acquiesced, or was coerced into having sex with Gasparino and bearing his children is not clear from this document. What is clear is that Gasparino used her bond with the children and her poverty to exert control over her sexual life and coerce her into marriage even after his own death and her manumission.

The Gates of Slavery

In addition to gender and race, another factor affecting the experiences of slaves was the social position of their masters. The first owner of a newly imported slave was the gate through which that slave entered slaveholding society, determining the future directions of his or her life.[214] This was especially true in Mamluk society, where many paths were potentially open to slaves but access to certain paths was only available through certain masters.

In Mamluk society, military training was restricted to young male Turks (in the generic sense) purchased by an amir or sultan. Even the most naturally talented boy had no hope of becoming a mamluk if he was purchased by a civilian. Civilian slave owners included caliphs, government ministers (*wazīr*), judges (*qaḍī*), jurists (*faqīh*), professional witnesses (*shāhid*), reciters of the Quran and *ḥadīth*, merchants, chemists, mathematicians, craftsmen, apothecaries, interpreters, tailors, and married and unmarried women.[215] Although the largest concentration of slaves was located at the sultan's court in Cairo, civilians throughout Mamluk territory owned slaves.[216]

A more comprehensive view of slave ownership in Italy is possible because notarial documents, especially those from Genoa, often identified the parties to slave sales according to their occupations as well as their families, neighborhoods, and parish churches. In Venice, the occupations that appeared most frequently in connection with slave ownership were priests, priors and prioresses of hospitals and monasteries, doctors, notaries, government officials, ship captains, and sailors. In Genoa, notaries were the largest group of slave owners, followed by silk workers, merchants, smiths, cobblers, wool merchants, cloth merchants, spice merchants, barbers, priests, monks and nuns, furriers, retail sellers of clothing, and doctors.[217] The large number of slaveholding notaries has been explained both as an expression of classicizing chic among humanists and as a consequence of the source base, because notaries were more likely to draw up notarial documents regarding their slaves.[218] Finally, women constituted 12.7 percent of recorded slave owners in Genoa and 18 percent in Venice, excluding instances of joint ownership.

Surveying the occupations of slave owners also shows that, contrary to the Christian amelioration narrative, individuals at every level of the ecclesiastical hierarchy owned slaves. For historians, perhaps the most important slaveholding priest was Benedetto Bianco, notary and priest of S. Eufemia in the Giudecca in Venice, whose registers preserve hundreds of documents related to slaves, including three that he sold himself.[219] Other slave-owning priests in Venice were Petrus Natal, priest of S. Apostolorum; Iohannis Bono, the priest of S. Mauricio; and Francischinus Pavono, priest of S. Apollinaris.[220] In Genoa, they included Iohannis de Francis de la Landa, priest of S. Maria de Vineis; Oberto de Petra Magolana, priest of S. Margarita de Malaxio; and Iohannis de Portufino, chaplain of S. Pietro in Porta.[221] The bishops of Civitanova, Torcello, Caffa, Chios, and Tabriz all owned slaves.[222] In 1325, Pope John XXII received a Tatar slave as a gift, and in 1488, Pope Innocent VIII received one hundred Moorish slaves.[223] Individual and institutional slave ownership are hard to differentiate in a monastic context, but slaves were present in the following monasteries and convents in and around Genoa: S. Matteo, S. Thoma, S. Barnaba, S. Caterina, S. Agata, S. Lorenzo, S. Marta, S. Columbanus, S. Sepolcro in Sampierdarena, S. Elena in Albaro, S. Maria Pietraminuta, S. Bartolomeo del Fossato, Ss. Iacobus and Philippus de Irchis, S. Andrea in Porta, and S. Andrea di Sarzano.[224] In and around Venice, slaves were present in S. Zacharia, S. Lorenzo, S. Mattheo de Maioribus, and S. Bernard de Murano in Torcello.[225] In addition, individual members of the Cistercian, Dominican, Franciscan, and Hospitaller orders owned slaves.[226] Medieval hospitals were also religious institutions. In Venice, the hospitals of Ss. Peter and Paul, S. Vitus, and the Holy Spirit all had slaves.[227]

Although a slave's first owner was his or her gateway into slaveholding society, most slaves passed through the hands of several owners over the course of their lives. Jaqmaq, the boy whose sale was described at the beginning of Chapter 1, had had at least four owners by the time he arrived in Venice.[228] Such chains of ownership are easiest to trace among mamluks. Many mamluks had two or three owners before manumission, but Jaqmaq al-Arghūnshāwī had seven.[229]

A change of master rarely meant a change of function, although some exceptional slaves underwent drastic changes in both. The first owner of Sultan Baybars was a goldsmith; the first owner of Fāris al-Quṭlūqajāwī was a baker.[230] Both Baybars and Fāris were subsequently purchased by amirs and became mamluks. The mamluk Ṭūghān started out as a donkey driver for the governor of Ṣafad and made his own way into mamluk status.[231] Yashbak, a Circassian boy, was en route to Egypt as a prospective mamluk when his ship was captured by Christians. He was sold in Cyprus, where he served as a slave and learned how to do acrobatics. Years later, after he had been given as a gift to Sultan Barsbāy and trained as a mamluk at last, he integrated his two skill sets by walking on a tightrope from the minaret of al-Ḥasan mosque to a tower of the citadel while shooting a harquebus and a crossbow.[232]

Movement occurred in the other direction as well. Occasionally mamluks were found to have other talents and were allowed to pursue them, ending up as religious scholars, jurists, or poets.[233] Arghūn Shāh al-Dawādār studied Ḥanafī law, serving as head of the chancery (*dawādār*) and governor of Aleppo as well as judging legal cases and studying in Mecca.[234] Ashiqtamur al-Mārdīnī al-Nāṣirī was a successful amir but gained his first promotion through his skill at playing the oud, while ʿAlī al-Mārdīnī began as an oud player and ended up as governor of Damascus.[235]

Even after manumission, masters continued to influence the lives of their slaves.[236] The role of factions and patronage networks in mamluks' careers has already been mentioned. The freedmen of merchants, artisans, scholars, and clerics might go into business for themselves or continue in partnership with their former masters.[237] One freedman named Georgius earned enough by selling clothing in Genoa to purchase another slave, also named Georgius, as his assistant.[238] Sanqar, who belonged to an Aleppan judge, listened to *ḥadīth* alongside his master's sons and eventually became a religious scholar and *ḥadīth* reciter himself.[239] Antonius, freedman of the priest Oberto de Petra Magolana, became a monk.[240] A Franciscan friar named Thermo used a net to catch partridges outside the walls of Tana; with the proceeds, he bought a slave whom he named Partridge (Pernice) and who also became a friar.[241] A child from a noble Circassian family "was sold in Genoa, and having been educated and manumitted from servitude, he entered the Order of Preachers [the Dominican Order]."[242] He eventually returned to Circassia as an archbishop.

After manumission, women often continued to work as paid servants in the households of their former masters. Clara, freedwoman of the Venetian patrician Michael Steno, continued to serve him for a salary of five ducats per year.[243] Sitt Ḥadaq, the nanny (*dāda*) of al-Nāṣir Muḥammad, became the head of his harem (*qahramāna*) and endowed a mosque that still stands in Cairo today.[244] Staying in the same household may sometimes have been a strategy to stay in contact with their free children. For example, the Pratese merchant Francesco Datini decided to adopt Ginevra, his daughter by his slave Lucia. Ginevra was raised by Datini's wife, Margherita, but Lucia remained in the family. She served Margherita until manumission, then married a free servant of the household.[245] Other women preferred to move to a new household. Margarita, the former slave of Bartolomeus Vallaresso, served the widow of Marcus Morosini for a salary of seven ducats per year.[246]

Some freedwomen were able to secure their futures through marriage, especially if their former masters provided a dowry. Marcus Mazole of the Giudecca in Venice gave his freedwoman Magdalena a dowry of forty ducats, enabling her to marry a sailor from Tana and settle in the parish of S. Antonini.[247]

In Genoa, a pair of former slaves were able to marry and buy a house with money advanced by a relative of the woman's former master.[248] When amir Bashtak freed eighty slave women in 1341, he found husbands for them among his mamluks and gave them dowries, clothing, and pearls.[249] A few Italian men married their former slaves themselves.[250] It was not unusual for a Mamluk man to manumit and marry his *umm walad*, and the freedwomen of powerful men were sometimes able to gain wealth and political influence in their own right. Shajar al-Durr was the first former slave to rule Egypt.[251] Julubān, freedwoman and wife of Sultan Barsbāy, arranged the succession of her son Yūsuf.[252] Ittifāq, a second-generation black slave singer trained in the provincial town of Bilbays, was sold to the Head of Singers in Cairo and given to Sultan al-Nāṣir Muḥammad. Her popularity at court catapulted her into a series of marriages to prominent men, including three sultans.[253]

Masters inclined toward beneficence might leave bequests to their former slaves as a reward for past service, a condition of future service, an act of piety, or a display of honor and magnanimity.[254] Marco Polo manumitted his Tatar slave Petrus in his will and left him "everything which he acquired by his own labor in my house."[255] Manfredina, the widow of Nicolaus Perruge of Camogli, left her former slave woman one hundred soldi.[256] Some bequests were very generous. Pietro Ziani, a Venetian patrician, freed his slaves and left them each a house and twenty-five to one hundred lire.[257] Badr al-Dīn ibn 'Abdallah al-Ḥusaynī set up a charitable endowment (*waqf*) to support his servants and former slaves.[258] Lorenza, the widow of Tommaso di Matteo of Florence, freed her slave Ursa and appointed her rectoress of the hospital for poor women endowed by her husband.[259] Antonius Morosini freed his slave Pasqualina and told his grandson to let her and her son stay in the house where she had always lived.[260]

As a result, a few former slaves were able to make bequests and charitable gifts of their own. In her will, the freedwoman of a Mamluk judge left her house as an endowment (*waqf*) to benefit the judge's four granddaughters.[261] Caterina, the freedwoman of Marino Malipiero, left three ducats to her neighbor Antonia and requested her prayers, while Maria, the freedwoman of Giacomo Franco, had her executor arrange nine love feasts (*caritade*) or nine distributions of alms for the poor in her parish.[262] Magdalena, the former slave of Isabella Imperiali, made her will twenty-two years after manumission. She was able to leave a silver belt and a share in Genoa's municipal debt (one *locum* in the Compera Pacis) to her heirs.[263] Shīrīn, a slave concubine of Sultan Barqūq, sponsored the renovation of a ribat in Mecca, Quran readers at Barqūq's madrasa, and endowments for the tomb of her son Faraj.[264] Sūrbāy, a slave concubine of Sultan Jaqmaq, left an estate of 50,000 dinars and parts of the town of Bulāq as well as endowments for a public fountain, two public baths, and seven bridges.[265]

These were best-case scenarios. Many former slaves fell into poverty. When the freedwoman Ghazāl bint ʿAbd Allah died in Jerusalem, her belongings consisted of "a worn-out spare chemise; a blue worn-out and torn coverlet; a worn-out and torn quilt; an old carpet."[266] Manumission often came with onerous conditions, such as a fee or additional years of unpaid service. Sibilina, the first slave from the Black Sea to appear in Genoese records, was manumitted on the condition that she continue to serve for ten years.[267] Lazarus, the freedman of Laurentius de Serigo, had to provide two years of additional service and pay forty ducats in installments over a six-year period.[268] Martinus, freedman of the brothers Damianus and Oliverius de Oliverio of Rapallo, owed them two soldi and six denarii per day for eight years except Sundays and feast days.[269] He was also obligated to serve them, sleep in their house every night (they promised him shelter but not food or clothing), and ask their permission before accepting a salaried position or leaving the city. He was not allowed to steal or play dice. On top of any conditions set by the master, Genoa levied a ten lire tax on manumission (*cabella franchisiarum sclavorum et sclavarum*) payable by the slave.[270]

Moreover, manumission was never guaranteed. Many slaves died without attaining freedom. Even for mamluks and *ummuhāt awlād*, manumission depended on completion of training or the master's acknowledgment of paternity. Islamic law had several contractual forms for establishing the terms of manumission, but they had to be initiated by the master. A slave whose master was not interested in manumission could do nothing. On the Christian side, the *ius commune* allowed slaves to purchase their freedom if the master permitted it. Iohannes purchased his freedom for fifty lire in 1376 with the help of a loan from his sister Lucia and brother-in-law Marcus, both former slaves.[271] On the other hand, a master's promise of manumission was not binding without a written document. Raffael Gentil, a Genoese merchant in Valencia, reneged on a promise to free his slave Magdalena if she had sex with him.[272] Meliadus Baldiccione of Pisa received permission from a bishop to violate an oath not to sell his baptized slave.[273]

The worst-case scenario was a violently abusive master. In such situations, slaves had little recourse. Legally, masters were not allowed to kill their slaves in cold blood and were required to provide them with enough food and clothing for subsistence, but killing a slave through punishment was not a crime.[274] Genoa treated the weapon as evidence of the master's state of mind: a sword implied intent to kill, whereas a whip or stick implied intent to punish.[275] Most slaves were not beaten to death, but violence or the threat of violence was a definitional element of slavery.[276] In a treatise on obedience, the fifteenth-century humanist Giovanni Gioviano Pontano argued that slaves should be managed through fear. Those born in the household (*vernae*) who had never known freedom might love their masters, but "I do not see that those who are captured, sent away from their homeland, spouse, children, [and] parents can love either their captor or their buyer, since he knows that which mortals regard most highly was snatched from him by them: liberty and wealth, with those things which I said [before], wife, children, and relatives."[277]

One strategy pursued by slaves of violent masters was escape, but this was limited by practical considerations. Slaves did not have the right "to go, stay, return, [and] change homes."[278] Venice forbade ship captains from transporting slaves who did not belong to them, and Genoa forbade slaves from traveling more than ten miles beyond the city or on board a ship without permission.[279] As a result, escape to another Italian city was realistic, but return to the Black Sea was not.[280] Still, one slave reached Pera before he was caught, and others may have been successful.[281] In Egypt, escape was hindered by the desert. "[Slaves] talk among themselves of nothing else, they think and speak of nothing else, except in what way and where they might flee," but those who were not caught "came in flight to uninhabited places, and wandering in the mountains and wilderness died of hunger and thirst."[282] Nevertheless, even mamluks sometimes attempted escape.[283] In 1269, four mamluks fled to crusader Acre and another to Tyre.[284]

In the Mamluk kingdom, conversion to Islam was a strategy available to slaves of abusive Jewish or Christian masters. For example, in 1484, the Dominican friar and pilgrim Felix Fabri witnessed the brutal beating of an Ethiopian slave woman by the wife of the Venetian consul in Alexandria. She tried to kill herself, cursed the consul and his wife, became "deluded with anger so that she reviled God and blessed Muhammad, and declared herself about to move to the rite of Muhammad," and finally collapsed unconscious.[285] If her arms and legs had not been tied or if her declaration had been reported to an Islamic judge, she could have been seized from the consul's wife and given to a Muslim household, where she might or might not have been beaten less violently.

Strategies of resistance were dangerous. A few instances of slave revolts on ships are discussed in Chapter 6, but slave revolts on land were rare, except for newly imported mamluks (*julbān*) demanding higher salaries.[286] Some slaves attempted suicide, "for a person sold comes to such miseries that they may tire of living and seek death by all means."[287] Leontios Makhairas, a Cypriot chronicler, reported that slaves would "throw themselves down from the roofs and kill themselves, and some of them cast themselves into pits, and others hanged themselves, for the heavy torments which they made them endure, and because they were famished."[288] An insurance contract for a slave shipped from Porto Pisano in the Sea of Azov to Barcelona stipulated that the insurers were not liable if the slave threw herself into the sea.[289]

Slaves who murdered their masters were executed publicly and gruesomely. A notorious case was that of Bona, slave of the Venetian noble Niccolò Barbo.

When she "made herself pregnant" (*fecisset se impregnari*) by a free servant, Barbo became angry and beat her.[290] She retaliated by purchasing arsenic from an apothecary and mixing it into his food and medicine (he was recovering from a long illness). For his death, she was sentenced to be tied to a stake, dragged by a horse from Santa Croce to San Marco while a crier announced her guilt, then burned to ashes between the two pillars in front of the doge's palace. A few days later, the Great Council restricted the sale and possession of poisonous substances to just two apothecaries. A few months later, they also ordered the Signori di Notte to investigate anyone known for mixing dangerous herbs, "because a short time ago such things seem to have occurred, perpetrated by female slaves or servants."[291] Nevertheless, over the next two decades, a dozen suspiciously similar poisoning accusations were made by Venetian nobles against slave women. These events reveal more about household tensions (and apothecaries' desire to suppress competition from neighborhood healers) than they do about actual murders.[292] Sentencing rested on confessions obtained through torture and systematically presented the slave's motive as revenge. Medieval physicians were usually not able to prove whether a death was caused by poison, but slave owners in Venice clearly feared that their violence toward slaves would be met with violence in return.

Society might limit a violent master's abuse when the law would not.[293] In theory, excessive violence would harm the master's reputation and affect his or her social relationships. In practice, social intervention was too little and too late. For example, when Sultan Barqūq was disturbed by the screams of slave women from the quarters of his deposed predecessor al-Manṣūr Ḥājjī, he intervened several times to stop the beatings. However, Ḥājjī did not permanently cease to beat his slave women until they paralyzed him with poison.[294] In Genoa, the neighbors of Lodisio de Maris Pesagno notified the authorities only after the death of his slave Caterina. She was found hanging in the kitchen with severe injuries and burns all over her body, especially her genitals. The investigators concluded that the cause of death was hanging, so they labeled the incident a suicide and closed the inquiry without questioning Lodisio.[295]

Conclusion

This chapter reveals many aspects of the common culture of slavery in the late medieval Mediterranean as well as some significant differences between Mamluk and Italian practices. Most slaveholding in the late medieval Mediterranean fit the model of societies with slaves: slaves were valuable but not essential to the economy or to ideologies of power. The Mamluk case poses an interesting challenge to the model, however, because the sultans' military and political power was based on slave ownership, but their economic power came from customs and commercial taxes in Alexandria, Damascus, and other ports.

In many respects, slave owners around the late medieval Mediterranean used their slaves in similar ways. Slaves served as social and financial assets. They performed domestic and artisanal labor and participated in trade. Slave women were expected to have sex with their male masters and to give birth to and nurse their children. However, the training of male slaves for military service and the role of eunuchs as mediators between the segregated male and female spheres of elite households were unique to the Mamluks. Moreover, the common culture of slavery underwent change during this period. In Mamluk society, the sexual service of slave women was not solely for their masters' pleasure: their children with their masters were recognized automatically as family members and heirs. In Italian society, all children of slave women were supposed to be property, but in the late fourteenth and fifteenth centuries, Italian father-masters also began to treat their children by slave women as family members and heirs.

This chapter has approached slave labor primarily from the master's perspective. The next chapter, also from the master's perspective, addresses the process of acquiring slaves. In general, when people in the late medieval Mediterranean wanted a slave, they bought one. A few slaves were born or captured locally, but most were enslaved elsewhere and transported to Mediterranean markets. The next chapter therefore explains the process of buying a slave in Genoa, Venice, Cairo, and Alexandria, four of the biggest slave markets in the late medieval Mediterranean.

Chapter 4

The Slave Market and the Act of Sale

The act of selling a slave can be interpreted in several ways. Like any sale, a slave sale was an economic act, an exchange of goods according to a calculated price. Like many sales, it was also a legal act, a transfer of rights and possession. To ensure that the price was fair and the legal transfer was valid, most buyers chose to inspect the physical health and qualities of slaves in the market, adding a medical perspective to the act of sale. Finally, the whole process of marketing, inspection, pricing, and transfer of ownership had social and psychological effects. It reinforced slaves' powerlessness and dishonor within the slaveholding society.[1] The humiliation of sale marked slaves as a class inferior to free people and reinforced the subordination of individual slaves to individual masters during the transfer of ownership.

Unlike other commodities, slaves were not passive objects but human beings with individual will, the capacity to make choices about their actions. Although acting on their own initiative during the sale process was dangerous, slaves could still choose to act or not act in ways impossible for inanimate goods or animals. Slaves in the marketplace were supposed to be passive and dehumanized, yet their humanity and capacity for independent decision-making were essential elements of their value. Their paradoxical status as human commodities had significant effects on their sale.

This chapter describes the sale of a slave in stages: the seller brings the slave into the marketplace; the slave broker matches the seller with a buyer; the buyer inspects the slave; the buyer and seller agree on a price; the buyer and seller ask a notary or scribe to draw up a contract. Actual sales might not include all of these steps, and the steps were not always performed in this order. Nevertheless, this chapter is organized by steps in a process because it exposes many similarities and a few key differences between Mamluk and Italian slave sales.

The Marketplace

Public slave markets were common across the late medieval Mediterranean, but they did not normally take the form of auctions. Settling the affairs of debtors and the deceased did sometimes mean auctioning their estates, including slaves, to convert their assets into cash for quick distribution to creditors or heirs. In Genoa, estate auctions took place in the palace of the commune near the law courts.[2] Venetian estate auctions happened at the Rialto and the church of S. Giorgio. Although the Quarantia Criminal tried to ban all slave auctions in 1366 because they reflected poorly on Venetian honor, slaves were still auctioned at the Rialto in 1369, 1441, and 1446.[3] When a Mamluk judge ordered that the slaves of a deceased eunuch be auctioned in Jerusalem, "they were proclaimed in the markets and in likely venues for bids," not in a single central place.[4]

Most Mamluk slave markets resembled specialized markets for other commodities like swords.[5] They took on one of three physical forms: an open lot or square, a street with slaves standing or sitting along the sides, or an enclosed building (*khān* or *funduq*) with a central courtyard surrounded by shops on the first floor and private rooms on the second floor.[6] In addition, any crowded public space could be used to display slaves. Slaves were sold at fairs and festivals, in mosque and church entrances, in open squares, and in the streets themselves.[7]

Cairo's slave markets were located in the dense commercial district known today as Khān al-Khalīlī. In the late thirteenth and fourteenth centuries, the main market consisted of two rooms next to Khān Masrūr al-Kabīr or among its exterior shops. Male slaves (Turks and Greeks) sat on a bench between the two rooms so that potential buyers could view them.[8] In the fifteenth century, the main market moved to a street, Darb al-Mushtarak, near the Madrasa Ḥusāmiyya.[9] This move brought male and female slaves into the same space. Finally, in November 1514, Sultan Qānṣūh al-Ghawrī moved the slave market again to a different street near the shrine of al-Ḥusayn.[10] This location probably evolved into Wakālat al-Jallāba, the Ottoman-era market for black slaves in Cairo. Having separate markets for white and black slaves was not characteristic of the Mamluk era.

In Alexandria, the primary slave market was located in the Tatar *funduq*. This did not mean that all the sellers were Tatars: when a ship from Libya arrived with thirteen captured sailors, "they led them to the *funduq* of the Tatars and there they held them for sale."[11] Slaves were displayed in the *funduq*'s central courtyard. The fifteenth-century pilgrim Bernhard von Breydenbach described the scene: "we saw the noblest of objects, that is human beings, as slaves for sale at the vilest price. [They were] of both sexes, youths and young men, boys and girls, as well as certain women who had babies hanging at the breast, all of whom were there awaiting sale."[12] A second market for female slaves was located at the *funduq* of the dyers.[13] Slaves were also sold in the Venetian *funduq*, the Catalan *funduq*, and the *fanādiq* of local merchants.[14]

In Genoa and Venice, there were no specialized slave markets.[15] As explained in Chapter 6, the average Italian seller had only one or two slaves available at a time and used a broker to find potential buyers. An exception was Giorgio da Feggino, who had a slave shop in the de' Marini neighborhood of Genoa in 1392.[16] Otherwise, the best evidence for the physical environment of slave sales comes from the dating clauses of sale contracts. For example, Francischa de Arzerono sold a slave to Addano Spinulla "in Genoa in the piazza of St. Luke next to the church."[17] The difficulty is that the place mentioned in the dating clause may not have been the only place associated with the sale. For example, Francischa and Addano might have met in the piazza to discuss the sale, paid the price on the spot in coin, and summoned a notary to draw up the contract. Or they might have discussed the sale in Francischa's house, visited Addano's banker to transfer the money, and stopped by the notary's bench in the piazza to get the contract. From the information given in this document, it is impossible to know which scenario is correct.

Nevertheless, some public spaces saw more slave-related activity than others. In Venice, more than three-quarters of slave sale contracts (386 out of 456) that mentioned a location were drawn up at the Rialto, the area between the Rialto Bridge and what is now the fish market. This was the commercial center of the city as well as a gathering place for notaries, brokers, bankers, money changers, and others who facilitated commercial activity. One was drawn up "in the piazza where the merchants gather and meet," one in the portico of the church of S. Giovanni, and one at the shop of the buyer, a cloth merchant.[18] Slaves may also have been sold in the piazza in front of the church of S. Giorgio.[19] Four were recorded in the office of the *capisestieri* at the Rialto. In 1366, the Quarantia Criminal encouraged slave sales in the New Rialto (*rivoalto novo*) while discouraging them in the rest of the Rialto (*rivoalto magno . . . nec in aliis locis insule rivoalti*) and banning auctions everywhere.[20] Still, a few slave sales occurred in and around Piazza S. Marco, the administrative and political center of the city. These were associated with the piazza itself, the benches of notaries, the communal palace, and the court.

In Genoa, public slave sales were usually recorded at notaries' benches.[21] Their locations were described in relation to the houses of important families in the central business district: Pichemilius and Carlus Ususmaris, Nicolaus Cicogne, Albertinus and Torpetus Marocellus, Barbonus Venti, Angelus de

Nigro, and the Pediculi.[22] Other notaries located the sale at "my bench" without further detail. Sales were also recorded at the communal palace, around the cathedral of S. Lorenzo, next to the hospital of S. Giovanni, and in the piazza of S. Giorgio.

In addition to public markets and gathering places, private houses and shops were also used to arrange sales. Genoese notaries recorded sales in or around a house: on the steps, in the portico, in the loggia, or even in the bedroom. Shops that hosted sales might belong to the seller (like Iohannes de Catara, a woolworker), the buyer (like Nicolaus de Vultabio, a smith), or a witness to the sale (like Nicolaus de Bracellis, a cheesemonger).[23] Slaves owned by monks were sold in monasteries. For both Genoese and Venetians, the choice of a private venue was largely a matter of convenience. Women were no more likely than men to conduct their transactions privately: Agnes, the widow of Marino Foscarini, went to the Rialto to sell a slave to Christina Barisano, a nun from the convent of S. Matteo.[24]

The choice of a private sale venue did have meaning in the Mamluk context. Bypassing the chaos of public slave markets was the prerogative of elite buyers. It may also have been a privilege granted to elite slaves.[25] In early thirteenth-century Aleppo, one merchant brought a selection of slaves to the home of the young ruler so that he and his mother could view them from behind a veil or screen.[26] The Mamluk governor of Aleppo in the early fifteenth century also purchased slaves in the comfort of his home.[27] The sultan al-Muʿayyad Shaykh was interrupted at home during a game of cards by a slave merchant who wanted to show him a particularly impressive boy.[28] Ordinary people were not visited at home by merchants and had to choose their slaves from those available in the public markets.

The Broker

Brokers facilitated trade of all kinds in late medieval cities.[29] Because Genoa and Venice did not have dedicated slave markets, brokers were essential in connecting buyers with sellers. For this reason, a broker (*misseta* or *censarius*) was frequently named among the witnesses to slave sales. The broker's fee was usually incorporated into the price without comment.[30] In Venice, only Victor Pisani of S. Margarita and Clarius Laurentii of S. Marina were identified as specialist slave brokers (*misseta sclavorum*).[31] In Genoa, brokers collected the one florin tax on slave sales and were therefore listed in tax registers.[32] Forty-four percent of slave sales in 1413 involved a broker. The most active by far was Rafael de Stracta (twenty-nine sales). Thirteen other brokers were also named, but none of them mediated more than three or four sales. They were probably general brokers who happened to participate in the slave trade that year.

In Mamluk cities, the distinction between brokers and retail slave traders was fuzzy. This may have occurred because of the Mamluks' specialized slave markets: in Mamluk cities, but not Italian ones, the same individual could sell slaves on his own account in the public market and also broker private transactions among other buyers and sellers for a fee. A *nakhkhās* dealt in slaves and animals as a broker or a retail seller. A *simsār* or a *dallāl* was a general broker, while a *munādin* was a public crier who announced the availability of goods for sale.[33] Mamluk slave brokers were overwhelmingly male, although some employed female assistants. They usually charged 2 percent of the value of the slave, payable by either the buyer or the seller.[34] In 1310, a tax of 50 percent (*nisf al-samsara*) was levied on the broker's fee. Brokers raised their fees, buyers and sellers complained, and the tax was repealed in 1315.

Mamluk slave brokers (*nakhkhās* and *dallāl*) were not considered respectable people like the long-distance traders (*tājir*) who imported slaves from the far corners of the world. Like used car salesmen today, brokers were believed to be experts at hustling and defrauding the unwary.[35] The famous fifteenth-century scholar Ibn Ḥajar al-ʿAsqalānī used a broker to arrange the clandestine purchase of his wife's slave whom he wanted as a concubine.[36] Some brokers' tricks were meant to pass off sick or disabled slaves as healthy, such as concealing diseased spots with a mixture of cress and vinegar.[37] Others, such as dying the hair, whitening the skin, perfuming the breath, and adorning the face with beauty marks and kohl, were intended to make slaves appear more beautiful.[38] Therefore slave-buying advice manuals advised against relying on first impressions or shopping for slaves while in a state of desire.[39] Just as a hungry person did not exercise good judgment in buying food and a naked person was not selective in buying clothes, a lustful person should not buy slave women. A slave's clothing should not affect the decision to buy, nor should the bustle of crowds and the atmosphere of competition in the marketplace.

Because of their bad reputation, slave brokers were rarely named in Mamluk sources. Exceptions are the brokers Muḥammad ibn Quṭlūbughā (*dallāl al-mamālīk*) and Najm al-Dīn Abū Bakr ibn Ghāzī (*dallāl al-mamālīk*) in Cairo, ʿAbdallah ibn Muḥammad al-Ẓafārī al-Mekkī (*dallāl al-raqīq*) in Mecca, and Badr al-Dīn Ḥasan ibn Ma'rūf in Jerusalem, as well as Muḥammad ibn ʿAli al-Shanashī, a professional legal witness (*shāhid*) at a slave market in Cairo.[40] Instead, Mamluk sources tend to discuss brokers anonymously and collectively. *Ḥisba* manuals providing guidance for market inspectors are especially informative since the market inspector was charged with regulating the slave trade. In theory, brokers who violated *ḥisba* regulations could be banned from dealing in slaves.[41] In practice, I have not found evidence of a *nakhkhās* or *dallāl* being banned.

In Mamluk *ḥisba* manuals, brokers were admonished to deal fairly and not use their expertise to commit fraud.[42] First, brokers should confirm the legal status of each slave being offered for sale. If the slave was free, stolen, or likely to escape, the sale would be invalid. Slaves who had already run away could not be sold in absentia. The documents of long-serving slaves, especially those sold by foreigners (*ghurabā'*), should be checked in case a previous owner had placed any restrictions on future sales.

Second, brokers were supposed to inquire into the religious background of each slave until they were absolutely certain of it, not accepting the word of the importer or anyone else with an interest in the sale.[43] Those who had been Muslim before enslavement should be freed. Those who had converted to Islam, as well as children of any religion who might convert, should be sold only to Muslims. Those rules were enforced in practice: Christian travelers who visited Mamluk markets were usually unable to buy slaves.[44] The conversion of slaves was also a matter of contention between Mamluk religious communities. For example, a slave woman over whom two Jewish sisters were disputing escaped her predicament by appearing before a Muslim judge and converting to Islam. The sisters were then required to sell her to a Muslim.[45] Sultan Qāytbāy extorted money from a Jewish man by accusing him of purchasing a Muslim slave woman, even though witnesses testified that she was Jewish and therefore that the sale was legal.[46]

Third, slave brokers were supposed to keep enslaved children with their mothers.[47] Some *ḥisba* manuals set the age of separation at seven or eight years old. Others defined it in terms of the loss of baby teeth, the onset of physical maturity (*bulūgh*), or the consent of both mother and child. Whatever the criterion, enforcement of this rule was mixed. Jaqmaq al-Arghūnshāwī was imported to Egypt with his mother at the age of three and remained with her until he was old enough to begin mamluk training.[48] When Barsbāy ordered the sale of captives taken in his 1425 attack on Cyprus, he stipulated that families not be separated.[49] Yet the fifteenth-century Swiss traveler Felix Fabri described the slave market in Alexandria as filled with "a great clamor and weeping" as families were separated and "the little child is snatched from his mother's lap."[50]

Finally, brokers had to keep a register in which they recorded each sale in case of dispute. The seller's identity was of particular importance and should have been verified by written documents or local guarantors.[51] No Mamluk examples have survived, but a Fatimid slave broker's register was unearthed by an archeological excavation in Fustat.[52] This register contains at least seventeen transactions organized by date. The simplest entries give only the name of the seller, the name of the buyer, and the price. Longer entries include descriptive information about the slave, such as a young Greek boy or an adult female cook.

The Physical Inspection

Physical inspection served two purposes in the sale of a slave. The first was common to all sales: caveat emptor, let the buyer beware. Had the shipment of grain spoiled in transit? Were the cloves at the top of the sack better than those toward the bottom? Inspection enabled the buyer to avoid fraud by checking that the goods matched the seller's description of them. From a Christian legal perspective, inspection was necessary for a valid sale because it affected the just price and subsequent use of the goods.[53] From an Islamic legal perspective, a valid sale required the informed consent of all parties. The buyer's informed consent was signaled by a clause stating that "viewing, cognizance, and agreement in a legal manner" had occurred.[54] Thus inspection was a standard part of the sale process throughout the late medieval Mediterranean.

The second purpose served by inspection was unique to slaves because of their dual status as human beings and commodities. Sale has been described as the phase of enslavement during which slaves' humanity was minimized and their commodity status was dominant, the phase during which they were most socially dead.[55] Yet slave inspection was not just a legal formality but also a demonstration of the total dishonor and powerlessness of one human being in relation to others. The disrespect with which slaves were treated was just as important as violence in establishing and maintaining the power differential between slaves and masters. This power differential was in particular need of reinforcement at the moment of sale, when the slave changed hands from an old master to a new one. Intrusive physical inspection made explicit the profanation of the slave's body, its availability for "use and abuse by everybody," as opposed to the inviolability of the free body.[56] This contrast was most striking for women, because the bodies of free women were normally accorded the greatest degree of respect, while the bodies of enslaved women were the most openly available for abuse.

In addition to reinforcing the powerlessness of slave status, a humiliating inspection was supposed to discourage slaves from intervening in their own sale. The individual will of a slave did not vanish in the marketplace. Despite the rhetoric of slaves as irrational animals or living tools, their ability to carry out tasks that required independent thought was precisely what made them valuable.[57] For this reason, slave inspections were not only concerned with physical health. Mental health and character were also important. At certain points, slaves could choose to cooperate with, acquiesce to, or resist inspection.[58] They could confirm or deny the claims of sellers, and they could encourage or discourage specific buyers. In some cases, they could even give or withhold consent. Although such maneuvering occurred within very narrow constraints and was very dangerous for the slave, buyers and sellers could not afford to ignore it. Humiliating slaves helped stifle their self-assertion during the inspection process.

Carrying out an effective inspection of any commodity was difficult for those without expertise.[59] Inexpert buyers often sought expert advice. In the past, historians have assumed that specialist slave traders and brokers were the experts in slave inspection, but specialist slave traders and brokers were rare in Italian cities and reviled in Mamluk ones.[60] The real experts at inspecting human bodies were physicians, "those who know about temperaments and constitutions."[61]

The poor reputation of Mamluk brokers meant that buyers wanted advice on how to inspect a slave themselves and thus avoid fraud. For this reason, Mamluk physicians wrote manuals to advise prospective slave buyers.[62] The manuals gave step-by-step instructions for inspecting slaves along with sections on the stereotypes associated with various races, advice on controlling slaves, and commonsense advice for the market. The genre evolved from Arabic and Persian commentaries on Greek texts in physiognomy, geography, and the politics of the household.[63] Three slave-buying advice manuals were produced in the late Ayyubid and Mamluk context. *Inspection in Slave-Buying* was an anonymous treatise composed in the early thirteenth century.[64] Ibn al-Akfānī, a physician at the Manṣūrī hospital in Cairo, wrote *The Book of Observation and Inspection in the Examination of Slaves* during the first half of the fourteenth century.[65] *The Apt Statement on Choosing Female and Male Slaves* was composed by al-ʿAyntābī, also a physician at the Manṣūrī hospital but active in the late fifteenth century.[66] All three of these manuals were textually related: it appears that Ibn al-Akfānī's treatise circulated as a preface to the anonymous treatise and that the combined text was a model for al-ʿAyntābī.[67]

In contrast, because specialist slave traders and brokers were rare in Italy, buyers and sellers were equally inexpert. If there was any doubt about a slave's health, the parties might consult a physician. Such was the case of a female slave who died shortly after being purchased by Baptista de Gogis.[68] Since her sale contract had included a guarantee of good health, Baptista sought 150 lire in damages and interest from the seller. A lawyer offering his advice on the case rejected Baptista's claim on several grounds, principally "because Baptista had not made her examination manifest within a month. He had not shown the said slave to be ill at the time of sale, neither within [the month] nor afterwards. If she had been ill, he would have known that beforehand, and he would have had the advice of doctors concerning the individual characteristics of the slave before the sale. Whence it is not possible to say that he was mistaken, nor that the fault was hidden."[69] In other words, Baptista should have consulted a doctor before the sale. Failing that, he should have taken the slave to a doctor within a month of the sale. Because Baptista had entirely neglected to consult a doctor until the slave died, the seller could not be held responsible for concealing the slave's illness.

Despite the translation of several Greek and Arabic texts with slave-buying advice into Latin, no new slave-buying advice manuals were composed in Latin. The most influential of the translated texts was the *Pantegni*, which circulated widely in Europe from the early twelfth century, but it did not generate much commentary because it was used more for reference than for teaching.[70] The pseudo-Aristotelian *Economics* did generate commentary, but it focused on defining slavery rather than choosing or controlling slaves.[71] Bryson's *Management of the Estate*, including his advice on the purchase and management of household slaves, was reworked in Latin and circulated as a Galenic text in the late thirteenth century.[72] A Latin digest was made of Polemon's work on physiognomy.[73] Nevertheless, a Latin genre of slave-buying advice never developed, and slave buyers continued to consult physicians in person.

What, then, was the procedure for inspecting a slave? The answer combines advice from Mamluk slave-buying manuals with a detailed description of an actual slave inspection observed by Felix Fabri, a fifteenth-century Dominican pilgrim passing through Alexandria on his return from Jerusalem.[74] Fabri divided the overall process, which he called handling (*contrectatio*) rather than inspection, into several stages. First, the prospective buyer entered the market, in this case the Tatar *funduq* in Alexandria, and surveyed the crowd of slaves. Once he had settled on a slave, he reached into the crowd and extracted him or her for a more thorough inspection. If the second inspection showed the slave to be satisfactory, he met with the seller to negotiate a price.

The first survey, which Fabri called the consideration (*consideratio*), was based on physiognomy. Mamluk slave-buying advice manuals began with a general assessment of the slave's build, stature, color, skin texture, and proportionality of the limbs. The color of a healthy slave should be pure white tinged with red, pure brown, or a lustrous pitch black.[75] Fabri was very impressed by the ability of Mamluk slave buyers to judge such qualities from a distance: "in that consideration they are the most expert and have the best eye, for there is not a doctor or physician who can be compared to them in recognizing the complexions and states of men."[76] He claimed that experts could evaluate a slave's physical condition, value, skills, and suitability simply by looking at his or her face.

The second phase of inspection, which Fabri called testing for purchase (*probat emendum*), was more comprehensive. According to Fabri, the buyer checked the slave's eyes, tested his or her hearing, touched his or her naked body, and looked at all of his or her limbs and members, including genitals. At the same time, the buyer talked with the slave to assess whether the responses were rational and whether the slave's character was happy, sad, modest, timid, or healthy. Then the slave, still naked, would be compelled to walk, run, and jump to make manifest which were "sick or healthy, male or female, virgin or corrupt."[77]

Mamluk slave-buying advice manuals were more specific about the second phase of inspection. Each manual gave a checklist of body parts to inspect, ordered roughly from head to toe, along with characteristic signs of good and bad health for each.[78] The recommended sequence began with the skin: the buyer ought to look for marks, burns, moles, warts, sores, tattoos, discoloration, or roughness. What appeared to be a mole or tattoo might actually be skin dyed or burned to conceal the marks of leprosy or some other disease. To find out, the buyer should take the slave to a bathhouse and scrub suspicious marks with hot water, vinegar, Meccan potash, or borax.[79] Otherwise the buyer should wait a few days and inspect again, by which time the dye might have faded or the disease might have spread.[80] Next the buyer ought to check the head, the hair and scalp, the whites and pupils of the eyes, the eyelids and eyebrows, the nose, the ears, the lips, the mouth, the teeth and gums, the tongue, the uvula and tonsils, the neck, the lymph nodes, the shoulders, the elbows, the forearms, the hands, the fingers and fingernails, the chest, the breasts, the belly, the back, the legs, the knees, and the feet. Bright light, preferably sunlight, was needed to inspect the eyes, ears, and nose.[81]

In addition, the buyer should test the senses of sight, hearing, and smell as well as the powers of speech and reason. He should check the flexibility of various joints, especially the shoulders and elbows, and observe the slave's motions while walking and running. To evaluate the slave's internal condition, he should take his or her pulse, listen to the sound of his or her voice, and smell his or her breath. Variations in smell between breath through the nose and breath through the mouth could indicate internal disease.

Finally, the buyer should consider the slave's character and skills. Character could be assessed through physiognomy (a black spot under the tongue indicated incorrigibility), ethnography (Greeks were stereotyped as thrifty, Armenians as lazy, etc.), or by talking to the slave and the seller.[82] The buyer should ask why the slave was being sold and not trust the first answer. Slaves habituated to beating or rudeness should be avoided, since their behavior would reflect poorly on their master's ability to govern his household.[83] Relevant skills, such as sewing, baking, cooking, writing, doing sums, speaking various languages, performing music, or dancing, should be demonstrated.[84] Those sold as wet nurses should give milk samples.[85] The mamluk Baylik al-Ẓāhirī demonstrated his literacy by writing a poetic verse in elegant script, while Yalbughā was purchased "because of his skills and his level of reading."[86] The future sultan Ṭaṭar was instructed in the Quran and Ḥanafī law by the merchants who imported him, probably to increase his market value.[87]

Italians did not write slave-buying advice guides, but the qualities they valued are reflected in their letters. In 1372, the young Francesco Datini wrote to his mother figure, Monna Piera, promising her luxuries from Avignon where he was doing business and demanding to be treated as a man when he came home. He intended to buy a slave woman and had definite opinions about the qualities he was looking for: "if you try to say 'send her old' [I would reply that] I don't like their cost and they can't stand the work and on the other hand I don't want to remain empty mouthed as I did last time. . . . If you want a slave I'll send a young and beautiful one who will be good for everything and will not fill the house with spit."[88] In other words, Datini was looking for youth, beauty, energy, good manners, and good cooking. Requests for slaves sent to Biagio Dolfin, the Venetian consul in Alexandria in 1418–1420, emphasized good health, sound limbs, and a good aspect or complexion.[89]

Tests of character and skill, as well as certain physical tests, required the slave's cooperation.[90] It was at these moments that slaves could intervene in the process. They could dispute the seller's description of their skills and condition or "show themselves affable and moderate" to encourage a particular buyer.[91] Such maneuvering was dangerous: slaves in Alexandria who refused to run and jump on command were severely beaten.[92] Shame was also used to control slaves by letting buyers inspect their naked bodies in public spaces. All of the fifteenth-century pilgrims who visited the slave market in Alexandria mentioned that both men and women were stripped for inspection and that they blushed and were visibly ashamed.[93] In Cairo, a fifteenth-century pilgrim encountered "ten children of both sexes, humans for sale, entirely naked and black, sitting in the square like beasts, who were likewise driven with a stick to the place of sale as if they were beasts."[94] A fifteenth-century traveler to Damascus described a slave woman being cried for sale in the street wearing nothing above her waist.[95]

Late medieval European medical treatises identified the genitalia as the shameful or secret parts of both men and women.[96] In the Islamic context, shame zones were defined for men as the area between the navel and the knees and for women as the entire body except for the face, hands, and perhaps the feet and forearms.[97] Doctors were allowed to examine shame zones as part of their medical practice. Whether slave buyers were permitted to do so depended on the genre of the text and the gender of the slave. *Ḥisba* manuals forbade inspecting the shame zones of male slaves, but slave-buying advice manuals recommended it.[98] Inspecting the shame zones of female slaves was permitted as long as it was done privately and in the presence of other women. This was because sexual and reproductive exploitation were licit uses of female slaves and not male slaves. Slave-buying advice treatises agreed that an adult female slave should be sold only during her menstrual period to prove that she had reached puberty but was not pregnant or infertile.[99] To verify this, a woman should inspect and confirm that her menstrual blood was fresh, not old or taken from another woman.[100]

If a slave woman was not menstruating at the time of sale, the law required the buyer to refrain from sexual intercourse with her for one month.[101] If the woman menstruated during that period, she was not pregnant. Purchasing a pregnant slave was discouraged. If she had been impregnated by the seller, she was his *umm walad* and could not legally be sold.[102] If she had been impregnated by someone else, the advice manuals warned that she might hide her condition and try to deceive the buyer into acknowledging paternity. To avoid this, the advice manuals recommended checking all female slaves for pregnancy. Signs included a swollen belly or breasts, paleness, and a craving for salty and sour food.[103] One test was to make the slave lie down on a bed and pull her knees up to her belly. If water sprinkled on her belly caused any movement, she was supposed to be pregnant. Another test was to make the slave drink honey water mixed with rainwater. If pregnant, it would cause her to experience colic or bowel pain.

Because there was no legal equivalent to *umm walad* status in Italy, pregnancy mattered to Genoese and Venetian slave buyers mainly because it increased the risk of injury or death. Thus pregnancy had to be disclosed as a health condition, and a clause might be added to the sale contract assigning liability for the expenses and risks of childbirth.[104] Fifteenth-century Genoese slave owners could buy childbirth insurance. The premium seems to have been 2 to 4 percent, and values of the policies ranged from 100 to 200 lire.[105]

While normative sources like slave-buying advice and *ḥisba* manuals present the inspection of shame zones as a necessity for evaluating slaves' physical health, descriptive sources make clear that it was also for the sexual gratification of the buyer, the bystanders, and often the narrator. Onlookers would gather in the Cairo slave market "because when anyone buys a person, many hurry to see the price and the appraisal."[106] An early thirteenth-century traveler, Ibn al-Mujāwir, ogled slave women in the market at Aden:

> The slave girl is fumigated with an aromatic smoke, perfumed, adorned and a waist-wrapper fastened round her middle. The seller takes her by the hand and walks around the souk with her; he calls out that she is for sale. The wicked merchants appear, examining her hands, feet, calves, thighs, navel, chest and breasts. He examines her back and measures her buttocks in spans. He examines her tongue, teeth, hair and spares no effort. If she is wearing clothes, he takes them off; he examines and looks. Finally he casts a direct eye over her vagina and anus, without her having on any covering or veil.[107]

This woman was being appraised as a concubine, and it is clear from context that Ibn al-Mujāwir told the story because of his own sexual enjoyment of the scene as well as to set up a dirty joke about the small penis of the man who bought her. Prurient interest in the naked bodies of slaves was not restricted to Mamluk markets, but Italian sources were more reticent. Slaves were not inspected publicly in Venice or Genoa, but a Genoese broker arranging the rental of a slave woman as a concubine kept her in his house for fifteen days "and exposed her in the presence of those wanting to see her."[108] Although this was less shameful than exposure in the street, it was more than shameful enough to reinforce the powerlessness and dishonor of her status.

The Price

If the inspection proved satisfactory, the next step was to negotiate a price. Bargaining for slaves was much like bargaining for any other commodity: the buyer might offer five ducats, the seller would demand ten, the buyer would protest that the slave had a defect, and they would haggle "as we do with horses" until they agreed on a price.[109] That price could be affected by many factors. Gender, age, origin, and the overall market price for slaves are the easiest to identify. Skill, health, beauty, personal character, proof of slave status, and virginity or fertility might also affect the value of a particular slave, but patterns are hard to show.

Further analysis of slave prices must be accompanied by several caveats. First, the available data do not constitute a random sample. The thousands of prices preserved in Italian notarial registers and the hundreds of prices in Mamluk sale contracts and narratives may not accurately represent the full range of the slave market. Not all slave sales were recorded, and not all records of slave sales have survived until the present day. Second, the sheer number of currencies circulating in the late medieval Mediterranean makes it difficult to compare prices. The silver asper was favored in the Black Sea, although units of silver by weight (sommi and saggi) and Byzantine hyperpers were also used. Genoa had parallel systems of gold florins and lire, soldi, and denari. Venice primarily used gold ducats and silver grossi. The Mamluks had gold dinars and silver dirhams. To facilitate comparison, I have converted all prices into ducats when necessary, because ducats were the most widely accepted and stable currency of the period.[110] However, ducats were not minted until 1284, and there is not always enough data to account for debasement, inflation, and exchange rate variations. Therefore the following discussion reflects only trends and orders of magnitude of slave prices.

The median price of a slave varied over time, as shown in Figures 4–6. The figure of twenty dinars often cited as the average price of a slave is reasonable

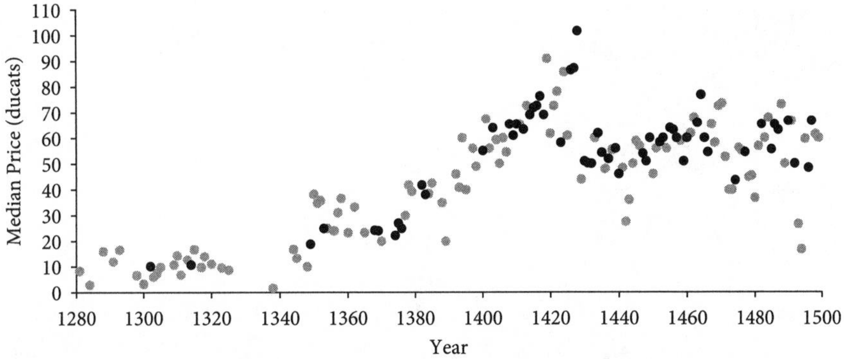

Figure 4. Change in Genoese Slave Prices over Time. Black points are based on more data (at least ten sales per year) than gray points.

(ASG, CdSG, N.185,00624, N.185,00625; ASG, Not. Ant. 172, 194, 221, 236–39, 253, 258, 265, 273, 286–87, 292, 363, 366–67, 379–82, 396–405, 432, 449, 548, 579–80, 645, 685, 719, 724/II, 768, 1034, 1279; ASG, Notai ignoti, b.xxiii; Balard, "Remarques"; Balard, *La Romanie*; Cibrario, *Della schiavitù*; Amia, *Schiavitù*; Delort, "Quelques précisions"; Epstein, *Speaking*; Ferretto, "Codice diplomatico"; Gioffrè, *Il mercato*; Heers, *Gênes*; Karpov, "Venetsianskaia rabotorgovlia"; Tardy, *Sklavenhandel*; Tria, "La schiavitù"; Verlinden, "Esclavage et ethnographie"; Williams, "Commercial Revolution.")

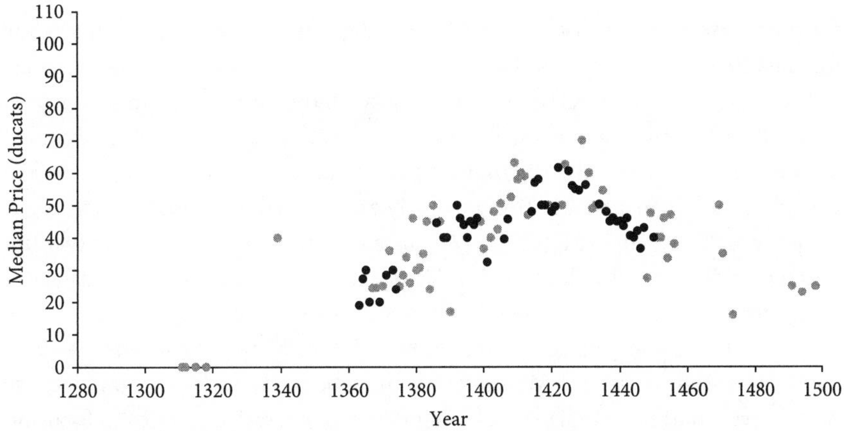

Figure 5. Change in Venetian Slave Prices over Time. Black points are based on more data (at least ten sales per year) than gray points.

(ASVe, Canc. inf., Misc., b.134 bis; ASVe, Canc. inf., Not., b.5, N.16, 26–27; b.12; b.16; b.17; b.19, N.3 and N.7; b.20, N.8–10; b.23, N.1; b.58–61; b.70, N.4; b.80, N.7; b.81; b.91; b.92, N.1–2; b.95; b.121, N.2; b.132, N.9; b.148, N.4 and N.6; b.149, N.1; b.174, N.9; b.182, N.1; b.211; b.222; b.230, N.1–2; b.243, N.3; ASVe, PdSM, Misti, b.180; Tamba, *Bernardo de Rodulfis*; Braunstein, "Être esclave"; Cibrario, *Della schiavitù*; Colli, *Moretto Bon*; Dennis, "Un fondo"; Karpov, "Venetsianskaia rabotorgovlia"; Krekic, "Contributo"; Lazari, "Del traffico"; Lombardo, *Nicola de Boateriis*; Romano, *Housecraft*; Tiepolo, *Domenico*; Verlinden, "Le recrutement des esclaves à Venise"; Zamboni, "Gli Ezzelini.")

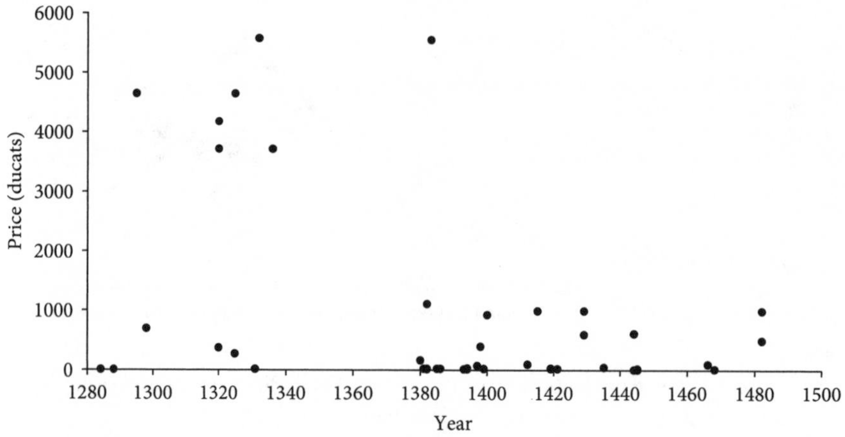

Figure 6. Change in Mamluk Slave Prices over Time. Each point represents one sale.

(Ibn Taghrī Birdī, *Al-Manhal al-ṣāfī*, *Al-Nujūm al-zāhira*; al-Sakhāwī, *Al-Ḍawʾ al-lāmiʿ*; al-Maqrīzī, *Kitāb al-sulūk*; Ashtor, *Histoire*; Ayalon, "L'esclavage"; Ragib, *Actes*; Rapoport, "Women"; Little, "Two Fourteenth–Century Court Records," "Six Fourteenth Century Purchase Deeds"; Verlinden, *L'Esclavage*.)

for the fourteenth century but too high for the thirteenth century and too low for the fifteenth century.[111] In Genoa, the median price was about eight ducats in the thirteenth century, twenty-seven ducats in the fourteenth, and sixty ducats in the fifteenth. Accounting for inflation, slave prices seem to have doubled between 1300 and 1400.[112] The highest price paid for a slave in Genoa was 470 lire (about 313.3 ducats), but this was truly exceptional, because the next highest price was only 165 lire (about 120 ducats).[113] The lowest price was two lire and ten soldi (about 1.7 ducats).[114] In Venice, the median slave price was about thirty-five ducats in the fourteenth century and about forty-eight ducats in the fifteenth. The highest price was one hundred ducats, and the lowest was four soldi (about 0.01 ducats).[115] Mamluk data must be treated with caution because of the very small sample size and the tendency of narrative sources to focus on extreme cases. That being said, the highest price was 6,000 dinars (about 5,580 ducats) for a famous singer.[116] In comparison, even the most expensive mamluk cost only 5,000 dinars (about 4,650 ducats).[117] The lowest price was 200 dirhams (about 9.3 ducats), and the median was 80 ducats.[118]

Thus, all along the price spectrum, from the cheapest slaves to the most expensive, traders could charge more in Mamluk markets than in Genoese or Venetian ones. This was especially true during the first half of the fourteenth century, as shown in Figure 6. The early fourteenth-century Mamluk price spike has sometimes been attributed to the papal embargo policy discussed in Chapter 7,[119] but since Chapter 6 shows that Italian merchants played only a minor role in the mamluk trade, I argue that conspicuous consumption by Sultan al-Nāṣir Muḥammad was more important than papal policy in driving up Mamluk prices. The chronicler al-Maqrīzī claimed that traders who sold mamluks to al-Nāṣir Muḥammad could make profits of 250 to 500 percent.[120] In contrast, traders who exported slaves from Caffa to Genoa in the late thirteenth century could expect profits of 20 to 25 percent, and the accounts of a merchant who shipped slaves from Constantinople to Venice in the early fifteenth century showed profits no greater than 12 percent.[121]

Genoese slave prices remained fairly stable from the 1280s until 1350.[122] A moderate jump from 1349 to 1350 can be attributed to the Black Death, which struck Genoa in 1348.[123] This was followed by a period of growth, exponential in Genoa and linear in Venice, from the 1360s to the 1420s. But in 1428 (Venice) and 1429 (Genoa), slave prices began to decline. In Venice, the decline was steady and gradual, whereas in Genoa, there was a collapse followed by relative stability for the rest of the fifteenth century.[124] A dip in Genoese prices in 1442–1443 may derive from an influx of slaves captured by the Tatars of the Crimean khanate. Another dip in 1493–1494 was due to the expulsion of Jews from Spain in 1492, some of whom ended up enslaved in Genoa.[125] The Ottoman conquest of Constantinople in 1453 did not affect Venetian or Genoese prices, because both states continued to have access to the Black Sea until the 1470s.

In addition to broad trends in slave prices over time, the prices of individual slaves were affected by factors such as age, gender, racial category, and color. As explained in Chapter 3, a numerical age was normally given in Genoese and Venetian sale contracts but not Mamluk ones. The youngest slaves sold independently (without a parent or sibling) in Venice and Genoa were four and five, respectively, while the oldest were in their fifties.[126] The sale of slaves younger than eight or older than forty was rare, though. Figure 7, a plot of the relationship between age and price, shows a curve peaking around age twenty-six in both Venice and Genoa.[127] In their letters, Italian buyers requested slaves between the ages of twelve and fifteen or sixteen because they were old enough to work but still young enough to adapt to life in Italy.[128]

In terms of gender, although the majority of slaves throughout the late medieval Mediterranean were female, women usually commanded higher prices in Genoa and Venice, while men commanded higher prices in the Mamluk market. The median price for women in Genoa was two ducats higher than that for men during the fourteenth century and twenty-four ducats higher in the fifteenth century. In Venice, the median price for women was seven ducats higher than for men in the fourteenth century and eight ducats higher in the fifteenth century. Meanwhile, the median Mamluk prices for women were an

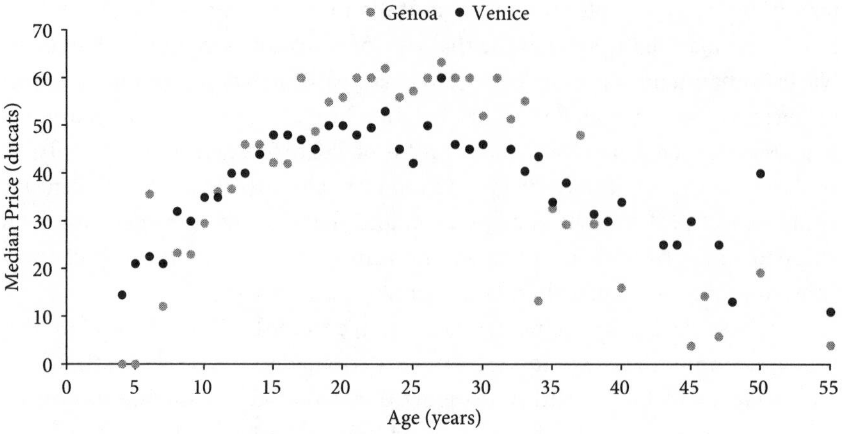

Figure 7. Age Versus Price.

(Amia, *Schiavitù*; ASG, CdSG, N.185,00624, N.185,00625; ASG, Not. Ant. 172, 194, 221, 236–39, 253, 258, 265, 273, 286–87, 292, 363, 366–67, 379–82, 396–405, 432, 449, 548, 579–80, 645, 685, 719, 724/II, 768, 1034, 1279; ASG, Notai ignoti, b.xxiii; ASVe, Canc. inf., Misc., b.134 bis; ASVe, Canc. inf., Not., b.5, N.16, 26–27; b.12; b.16; b.17; b.19, N.3 and N.7; b.20, N.8–10; b.23, N.1; b.58–61; b.70, N.4; b.80, N.7; b.81; b.91; b.92, N.1–2; b.95; b.121, N.2; b.132, N.9; b.148, N.4 and N.6; b.149, N.1; b.174, N.9; b.182, N.1; b.211; b.222; b.230, N.1–2; b.243, N.3; ASVe, PdSM, Misti, b.180; Balard, "Remarques"; Balard, *La Romanie*; Braunstein, "Être esclave"; Cibrario, *Della schiavitù*; Colli, *Moretto Bon*; Delort, "Quelques précisions"; Dennis, "Un fondo"; Epstein, *Speaking*; Ferretto, "Codice diplomatico"; Gioffrè, *Il mercato*; Heers, *Gênes*; Karpov, "Venetsianskaia rabotorgovlia"; Krekic, "Contributo"; Lazari, "Del traffico"; Lombardo, *Nicola de Boateriis*; Romano, *Housecraft*; Tamba, *Bernardo de Rodulfis*; Tardy, *Sklavenhandel*; Tiepolo, *Domenico*; Tria, "La schiavitù"; Verlinden, "Esclavage et ethnographie"; Verlinden, "Le recrutement des esclaves à Venise"; Williams, "Commercial Revolution"; Zamboni, "Gli Ezzelini.")

order of magnitude lower than those for men, 37.2 ducats for women versus 133.3 ducats for men.

This difference arose from the gendered uses of slave labor. Genoese and Venetians wanted slaves primarily for domestic and sexual service. Those kinds of labor were gendered female, and therefore Genoese and Venetians valued women more highly. As shown in Figure 8, male slaves did not appear in the highest price tiers in Genoa and Venice. In contrast, the wealthiest Mamluk slave owners wanted excellent male slaves as mamluks. They also purchased female slaves as domestic servants, concubines, and entertainers but did not value them as highly. Figure 9 shows that the upper price tiers of the Mamluk slave market were dominated by male slaves, but a few female slaves did appear. One would also expect eunuchs in the highest price tier of Mamluk slaves because they were difficult to acquire, but I found only one reference to a price for a Mamluk-era eunuch.[129]

The impact of race on slave prices was debated by medieval as well as modern observers. In the Mamluk case, I was not able to gather enough data or anecdotal evidence to analyze this factor. On the other side of the Mediterranean, the fifteenth-century Venetian crusade strategist Emmanuel Piloti thought that

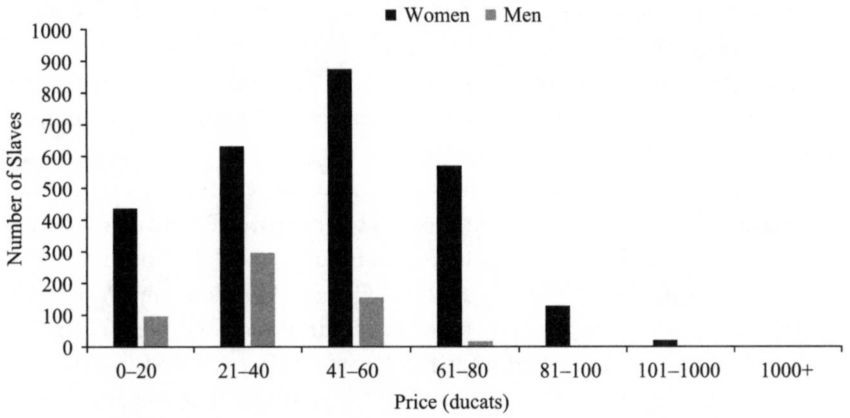

Figure 8. Italian Price Tiers by Gender.

(Amia, *Schiavitù*; ASG, CdSG, N.185,00624, N.185,00625; ASG, Not. Ant. 172, 194, 221, 236–39, 253, 258, 265, 273, 286–87, 292, 363, 366–67, 379–82, 396–405, 432, 449, 548, 579–80, 645, 685, 719, 724/II, 768, 1034, 1279; ASG, Notai ignoti, b.xxiii; ASVe, Canc. inf., Misc., b.134 bis; ASVe, Canc. inf., Not., b.5, N.16, 26–27; b.12; b.16; b.17; b.19, N.3 and N.7; b.20, N.8–10; b.23, N.1; b.58–61; b.70, N.4; b.80, N.7; b.81; b.91; b.92, N.1–2; b.95; b.121, N.2; b.132, N.9; b.148, N.4 and N.6; b.149, N.1; b.174, N.9; b.182, N.1; b.211; b.222; b.230, N.1–2; b.243, N.3; ASVe, PdSM, Misti, b.180; Balard, "Remarques"; Balard, *La Romanie*; Braunstein, "Être esclave"; Cibrario, *Della schiavitù*; Colli, *Moretto Bon*; Delort, "Quelques précisions"; Dennis, "Un fondo"; Epstein, *Speaking*; Ferretto, "Codice diplomatico"; Gioffrè, *Il mercato*; Heers, *Gênes*; Karpov, "Venetsianskaia rabotorgovlia"; Krekic, "Contributo"; Lazari, "Del traffico"; Lombardo, *Nicola de Boateriis*; Romano, *Housecraft*; Tamba, *Bernardo de Rodulfis*; Tardy, *Sklavenhandel*; Tiepolo, *Domenico*; Tria, "La schiavitù"; Verlinden, "Esclavage et ethnographie"; Verlinden, "Le recrutement des esclaves à Venise"; Williams, "Commercial Revolution"; Zamboni, "Gli Ezzelini.")

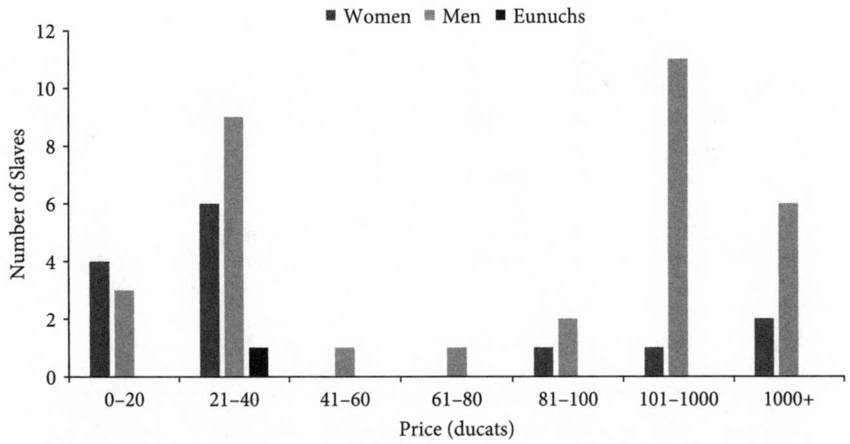

Figure 9. Mamluk Price Tiers by Gender.

(Ibn Taghrī Birdī, *Al-Manhal al-ṣāfī*, *Al-Nujūm al-zāhira*; al-Sakhāwī, *Al-Ḍaw' al-lāmi'*; al-Maqrīzī, *Kitāb al-sulūk*; Ashtor, *Histoire*; Ayalon, "L'esclavage"; Ragib, *Actes*; Rapoport, "Women"; Little, "Two Fourteenth-Century Court Records," "Six Fourteenth Century Purchase Deeds"; Verlinden, *L'Esclavage*.)

Tatars were the most expensive slaves, followed by Circassians, Greeks, Albanians or Slavs, and Africans.[130] Pero Tafur, a fifteenth-century Castilian traveler, thought Tatars fetched the highest prices, but Felix Fabri, a fifteenth-century Swiss Dominican, thought they were the cheapest.[131] Modern scholars have tended to agree with Fabri.[132]

Unfortunately, Piloti's racial categories do not correspond with those used by notaries. Greeks were important to Piloti but rare in sale contracts, whereas Saracens were common in sale contracts but ignored by Piloti. Notaries distinguished between Ethiopians, Moors, and Canary Islanders, but Piloti only recognized Africans. Figure 10 is based on notarial data and therefore privileges the racial categories that were most commonly employed in sale contracts: Tatar, Russian, and Circassian. The figure shows that Tatars fell most often in the lower price tiers (twenty-one to sixty ducats) while Russians and Circassians fell most often in the middle price tiers (forty-one to eighty ducats). Nevertheless, slaves of all three races appeared at least once in every price tier. Therefore race was not the decisive factor in any individual slave's price. Tatars in general might be less expensive than Circassians, but a specific Tatar

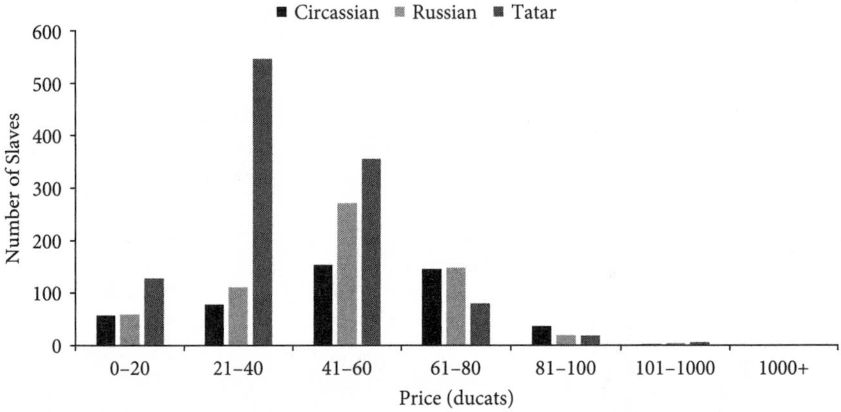

Figure 10. Italian Price Tiers by Race.

(Amia, *Schiavitù*; ASG, CdSG, N.185,00624, N.185,00625; ASG, Not. Ant. 172, 194, 221, 236–39, 253, 258, 265, 273, 286–87, 292, 363, 366–67, 379–82, 396–405, 432, 449, 548, 579–80, 645, 685, 719, 724/II, 768, 1034, 1279; ASG, Notai ignoti, b.xxiii; ASVe, Canc. inf., Misc., b.134 bis; ASVe, Canc. inf., Not., b.5, N.16, 26–27; b.12; b.16; b.17; b.19, N.3 and N.7; b.20, N.8–10; b.23, N.1; b.58–61; b.70, N.4; b.80, N.7; b.81; b.91; b.92, N.1–2; b.95; b.121, N.2; b.132, N.9; b.148, N.4 and N.6; b.149, N.1; b.174, N.9; b.182, N.1; b.211; b.222; b.230, N.1–2; b.243, N.3; ASVe, PdSM, Misti, b.180; Balard, "Remarques"; Balard, *La Romanie*; Braunstein, "Être esclave"; Cibrario, *Della schiavitù*; Colli, *Moretto Bon*; Delort, "Quelques précisions"; Dennis, "Un fondo"; Epstein, *Speaking*; Ferretto, "Codice diplomatico"; Gioffrè, *Il mercato*; Heers, *Gênes*; Karpov, "Venetsianskaia rabotorgovlia"; Krekic, "Contributo"; Lazari, "Del traffico"; Lombardo, *Nicola de Boateriis*; Romano, *Housecraft*; Tamba, *Bernardo de Rodulfis*; Tardy, *Sklavenhandel*; Tiepolo, *Domenico*; Tria, "La schiavitù"; Verlinden, "Esclavage et ethnographie"; Verlinden, "Le recrutement des esclaves à Venise"; Williams, "Commercial Revolution"; Zamboni, "Gli Ezzelini.")

could fall in the highest price tier, while a specific Circassian could fall in the lowest price tier.

Despite its eccentric use of racial categories, Piloti's hierarchy of prices has attracted attention because he placed Africans at the bottom. This confirmed the biases of many nineteenth- and some twentieth-century historians. Their assumptions were shaped by modern ideologies of slavery based on blackness and by orientalist discourses about the superiority of white women, especially Circassians.[133] Returning to the late medieval concepts of race and color explained in Chapter 2, it is clear that Piloti's hierarchy was race based rather than color based. Instead of assuming a correlation between whiteness, Tatarness, and high prices, Figures 11 and 12 show the relationship between color and price without reference to race.

Only Genoese notaries and Mamluk scribes mentioned color often enough to warrant analysis. In the Mamluk data, a clear relationship emerges between color and price: white slaves appear in every price tier, but black slaves appear only in the lowest tiers. In contrast, Genoese notaries identified three prevalent colors: black, white, and olive. White slaves appeared in all tiers, olive slaves were not priced above sixty ducats, and black slaves were not priced above eighty ducats. Thus Genoese buyers valued whiteness most highly, but their preference for white over olive or black affected only the highest price tier. For most slaves in Genoa, color was not the decisive factor in their price.[134] The starkness of the

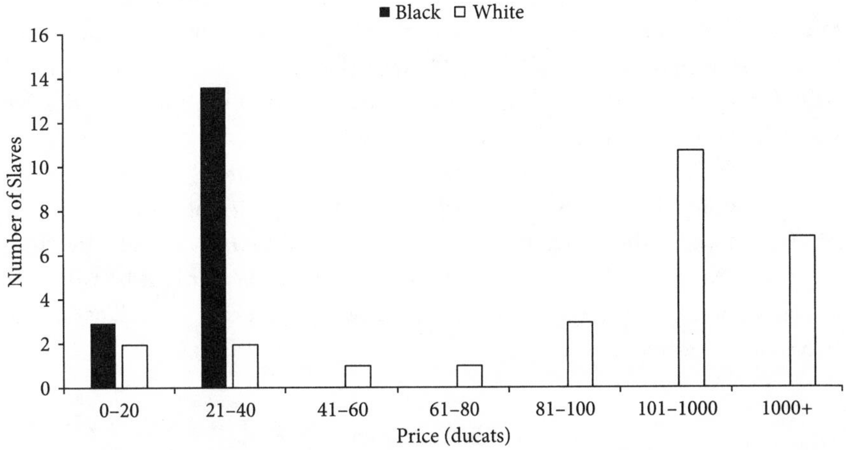

Figure 11. Mamluk Price Tiers by Color.

(Ibn Taghrī Birdī, *Al-Manhal al-ṣāfī*, *Al-Nujūm al-zāhira*; al-Sakhāwī, *Al-Ḍaw' al-lāmi'*; al-Maqrīzī, *Kitāb al-sulūk*; Ashtor, *Histoire*; Ayalon, "L'esclavage"; Ragib, *Actes*; Rapoport, "Women"; Little, "Two Fourteenth-Century Court Records," "Six Fourteenth Century Purchase Deeds"; Verlinden, *L'Esclavage*.)

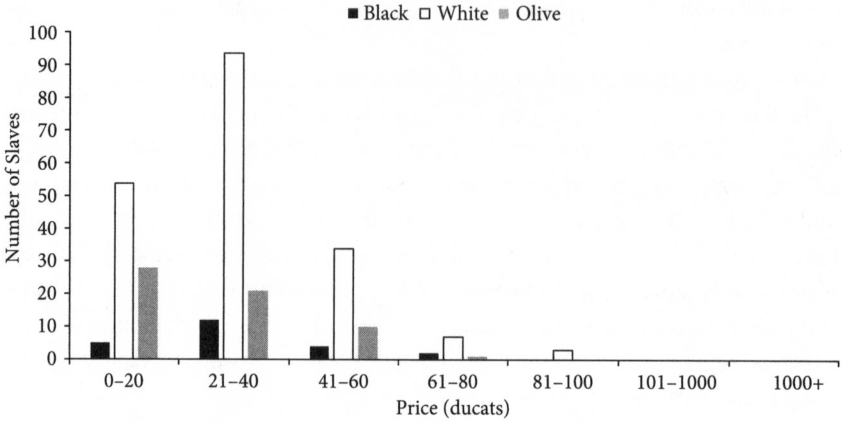

Figure 12. Genoese Price Tiers by Color.

(ASG, CdSG, N.185,00624, N.185,00625; ASG, Not. Ant. 172, 194, 221, 236–39, 253, 258, 265, 273, 286–87, 292, 363, 366–67, 379–82, 396–405, 432, 449, 548, 579–80, 645, 685, 719, 724/II, 768, 1034, 1279; ASG, Notai ignoti, b.xxiii; Balard, "Remarques"; Balard, *La Romanie*; Cibrario, *Della schiavitù*; Amia, *Schiavitù*; Delort, "Quelques précisions"; Epstein, *Speaking*; Ferretto, "Codice diplomatico"; Gioffrè, *Il mercato*; Heers, *Gênes*; Karpov, "Venetsianskaia rabotorgovlia"; Tardy, *Sklavenhandel*; Tria, "La schiavitù"; Verlinden, "Esclavage et ethnographie"; Williams, "Commercial Revolution.")

Mamluk preference for white slaves is partially explained by the fact that mamluks fetched the highest prices and only Turks (in the generic sense), who were often but not always white in color, could become mamluks.

Finally, the relative value of slaves compared to other goods may be easier to grasp through barter than through prices expressed in ducats or dinars. In Genoa, slaves were exchanged for 4,320 or 5,120 kilograms of grain, 93 or 210 palms of silk brocade, 20 palms of black velvet, or six silver cups.[135] One slave was sold for fifteen lire in coin and twenty-five lire in books, namely, the *Office of Our Lady the Virgin Mary* and Seneca's *Letter to Lucilius*.[136] In Venice, slaves were exchanged for twenty *brachia* of black damask or twenty-nine *brachia* of crimson cloth.[137] The Venetian duke of Candia paid four barrels of wine for a slave.[138] A Mamluk *shurūṭ* manual suggested that a slave might be worth "a house, a horse, a mule, a donkey, lengths of cloth, or a pearl" as well as "a dog, two saddles, or impure oil."[139]

The Contract

Once the price had been negotiated, the sale of a slave was usually formalized with a written contract in the presence of witnesses. This placed slaves among high-value goods like land, houses, ships, horses, jewels, and wholesale commodities. Filing notes on the backs of both Italian and Mamluk contracts attest that these documents were meant to be archived. They might be used later to prove ownership or resolve a dispute. The Mamluk chronicler Ibn Iyās recounted one postsale quarrel over a slave that escalated until the buyer hit the broker over the head with a shoe in the middle of a crowded market, causing his death a month later.[140]

Nevertheless, only a few slave sale contracts have survived until the present day. On the Mamluk side, there are two contracts for the same slave owned by a family in Bahnasā in the 1280s, six contracts from Jerusalem in the 1380s–1390s, and one contract from Alexandria in 1419.[141] In the Venetian state archive, there is a file of fifty slave sale contracts, and additional loose contracts can be found in other files there and in Genoa.[142] However, the Genoese and Venetian archives also have thousands of abbreviated contracts copied into notarial registers. Abbreviated contracts give only details unique to each sale (the date and location, the names of buyers and sellers, identifying information for the slave, the price, and the names of witnesses). They are not engrossed with the full legal formulas for sale.

These slave sale contracts, abbreviated or engrossed, can be compared with the model documents in medieval reference works. Handbooks for Italian notaries were called notarial formularies; those used by Mamluk scribes were called *shurūṭ* manuals.[143] Comparison of the surviving Mamluk slave sale contracts with model contracts in the *shurūṭ* manuals shows that the real contracts followed the models closely.[144] The relationship between Italian slave sale documents and Italian notarial formularies has never been investigated.

Most Italian notarial formularies were created by jurists from the legal school at the university in Bologna.[145] Most of them did not include models for the sale of slaves. One might imagine that slave sale contracts would follow models for the sale of serfs because both were unfree, but the three formularies that did mention slaves grouped them with animals. Under the rubric "instrument of sale of horses and of other rational or brute animals," Salatiele presented a model sale contract for horses that could be adapted for male and female slaves (*servi* and *ancillae*), cows, donkeys, mules, and pigs.[146] He explained in his gloss that the notary's two priorities should be to represent the goods accurately and to specify whether the buyer accepted the goods with their faults. In other words, the contractual clauses distinctive to the sale of slaves and animals were the description and the health warranty.

Salatiele's formula for the description was "one male slave, born from such-and-such a slave woman, who is called Stichus, and could be 20 years old."[147] Ventura di San Floriano's formula was "slaves the names of whom are these, namely Ricius and Seius, who are said and agreed to be healthy in body and in mind and also not fugitives."[148] Salatiele's formula adhered closely to the Justinianic Code. Stichus was even one of the stock names for slaves in Roman law. Moreover, Salatiele's formula presumes that Stichus was a *verna*, a slave born into the household with a known slave mother. *Vernae* were common in the Roman world, but medieval slaves were usually born free. Naming free parents in the sale contract would raise questions about the legality of the slave's status. To avoid this, medieval notaries seem to have adapted the Roman formula by replacing parentage with race. This is one of the main differences between formulas for the sale of slaves and of serfs. Serfs' parents were named in their sale contracts.[149]

In practice, Genoese and Venetian notaries described slaves in terms of gender, race, personal name, and approximate age. Occasionally they added comments on color, stature, geographical origin, language, or religion.[150] For example, the Genoese notary Iacobino Nepitelli recorded the sale of "a certain female slave of mine, Mellica by name, white in face, twelve years of age or so, who was from Russian parts."[151] Bartolomeo Gatto described "a certain male slave . . . called Aspertus, of the race of the Tatars, twenty-five years of age or so, white."[152] In Venice, Benedetto Bianco sold "one female slave born of the race of the Tatars, about thirteen years old, whom I bought in Tana, Chesmlich by name and Caterina in baptism,"[153] and Anastasio Christiano described "a certain female slave of mine of the race of the Circassians, eighteen years of age or so, called Cita."[154]

Descriptions of slaves in Mamluk sale contracts followed a similar pattern. Both Italian and Mamluk contracts included the slave's gender, race, and personal name.[155] Where Italian notaries estimated the slave's age in years, Mamluk scribes recorded the slave's level of maturity as nursing, weaned, adolescent, or adult. Mamluk scribes might also add comments about the slave's religion and distinguishing features (*ḥilya*). A simple description was given for "all of the slave girl, Nubian of race, Muslim in religion, adult, named Mubāraka" sold in Jerusalem in 1385.[156] A detailed description was given for a female slave, fifteen years old, Muslim in religion, mulatto (*muwallada*) in origin, named Khulayfa, daughter of Zubayda, "of medium height, virgin, adult . . . red in color, with an aquiline nose and a green tattoo on her chin."[157]

The second clause typical of slave and animal sales was the health warranty. Genoese and Venetian health warranties used formulas like "healthy in mind and body and in all her members, hidden and manifest"[158] or "healthy and clean from danger of all hidden flaws and illnesses up to the present day."[159] *Shurūṭ* manuals also gave formulas for a general warranty of good health, but the only surviving Mamluk contract to include this clause, "free of the faults of slaves," may have used atypical wording because the parties to the sale were a Copt and a Venetian.[160] In some places, the warranty made reference to local custom:

"healthy and clean of all vices and flaws hidden or manifest according to the custom of the city and island of Chios."[161]

Warranties of good health were supposed to protect buyers against fraud. If a slave sold as healthy was in fact sick or injured, the sale could be rescinded. Sultan Baybars was famously returned to the broker (*dallāl*) by one buyer and rejected by another because of a spot or flaw in his eye.[162] Likewise, Francisco Magnano purchased a boy in Genoa guaranteed "healthy and clean of person from all vices and flaws, hidden and manifest, until today" on October 20, 1379, but on October 22, he sued the seller after discovering that the boy "suffered in his left eye."[163] Of 109 slaves sold in Genoa in 1449, 4 were returned because of defects, 3 were returned without a reason, and 1 died within a year of sale.[164] Marco Balanzan even returned a slave from Crete to Constantinople for health reasons.[165] To avoid disputes, there might be a period of refusal during which the seller would automatically assume liability for any faults discovered in the slave. For the Mamluks, the usual period of refusal (*khiyār*) was three days and nights, but it extended to one year for cases of mental illness and leprosy.[166] The Justinianic Code set the period of refusal at either six months or sixty business days, but the customary period of refusal in both Venice and Genoa seems to have been one month.[167] In Genoa, disputes about redhibitory faults were handled by the Officium Mercantie.[168]

Unscrupulous buyers were known to take advantage of the period of refusal to have sex with female slaves and then return them. As described by the early thirteenth-century traveler Ibn al-Mujāwir, "when he has examined, expressed his approval and bought the slave girl, she remains with him for about ten days. When he has taken care of her, had his fill, become bored and tired of her and got what he wanted from her, his lust is at an end. Zayd, the buyer, says to ʿAmr, the vendor, 'Indeed, sir, we have a case to settle in court!' So they attend in front of the judge and one makes a claim against the other, [suggesting there is] a defect [in the slave girl]."[169] The story ended with a crude joke about an Indian slave woman whose buyer tried to rescind the sale after seven days because her vagina was too wide, only to be laughed out of court when the seller countered that the buyer's penis was too small. To deter such cases, a buyer who had sex with a female slave during the period of refusal might lose the right to rescind the sale or might have to compensate the seller for reducing her value.[170]

In Italy, slaves that were acknowledged to suffer from faults could be sold "as is" (*pro tali qualis est*). This form of warranty protected the seller, because it made the buyer aware that the slave was not in perfect health at the time of sale. This was the only legal way to sell slaves with redhibitory faults, faults serious enough to justify rescinding the transaction. Physical inspection at the time of sale was another way to uncover the presence of redhibitory faults. Because Genoese and Venetian sale contracts normally included a health warranty, the terms of the warranty meant that the risk of hidden faults was explicitly assigned to either the buyer (if the slave was sold "as is") or the seller (if the slave was sold as healthy). Physical inspection therefore played a secondary role for buyers trying to avoid lawsuits over redhibitory faults. Because Mamluk sale contracts rarely included a health warranty, the risk of hidden faults was not explicitly assigned to either party. Thus physical inspection was an important step for both parties to avoid lawsuits over redhibitory faults. This small difference in the legal formulas of sale may explain why Mamluk physicians wrote slave-buying manuals and Italians did not.

Mamluk slaves who were known to suffer from faults could be sold with a limited warranty.[171] Slave-buying advice manuals and *shurūṭ* manuals offered long lists of common redhibitory faults.[172] They included blindness, cataracts, and discharge from the eyes; loss of hair from the eyebrows and the presence of hair on the eyelids; deafness; muteness; tuberculosis; bad breath; tooth decay and tooth loss; various skin diseases, including leprosy, mange, and scrofula; joint injuries; pain in the hands, legs, head, knees, stomach, internal organs, or lymph nodes in the neck; ulcers or bleeding hemorrhoids; bed-wetting; and madness. Redhibitory faults mentioned in the *shurūṭ* manuals but not in the slave-buying advice manuals were easy to identify: hunchback, coughing, vomiting, tertian fever, and nonmenstrual vaginal bleeding. Redhibitory faults listed in the slave-buying advice manuals but not in the *shurūṭ* manuals were harder to identify: asthma, migraines, tumors, sores, elephantiasis, varicose and "Medinan" veins, anemia and scurvy, insomnia, dropsy, sciatica, kidney stones, constriction of the uterus, and general imbalance of the humors. Although virginity and menstruation were valued in female slaves, their absence was not a redhibitory fault.[173] Redhibitory faults of character included slander, fornication, drunkenness to the point of vomiting, abstinence from prayer, escape, and criminal behavior.[174]

Italian notarial formularies did not list redhibitory faults associated with slaves, but a list can be compiled from the faults most often disclosed or guaranteed to be absent in actual contracts.[175] In Venice, a warranty against falling sickness (*morbus caducus*) was standard in all slave sale contracts.[176] Falling sickness was a laymen's term referring to any condition that produced a sudden collapse, ranging from epilepsy and apoplectic strokes to insanity and demonic possession.[177] During the later Middle Ages, it was believed to be contagious on par with leprosy.[178] Unlike leprosy, falling sickness was not visually manifest unless the slave happened to collapse during sale. In addition to falling sickness, Genoese and Venetian contracts might warrant against leprosy, incontinence, mental illness, heart disease, fever, or freckled skin.

The faults disclosed in Genoese and Venetian contracts were the loss or blindness of one eye, disease or injury in both eyes, the loss of an ear, scabies, scrofula, disproportionately sized arms, missing fingers or toes, chest pain, lameness, and foot injuries. Undisclosed faults that led to lawsuits included falling sickness, leprosy, attempted suicide, respiratory illness, joint injury, tapeworm, dropsy, and irregular menstruation.[179] Pregnancy could also be a redhibitory fault. For example, Petrus Bono sold a female slave with a warranty of good health to a widow named Gerite on April 13, 1374, but on May 13, he sold the same slave to Paulus Viture with the statement that she was healthy "whether she is pregnant or not pregnant."[180] The first sale was probably rescinded after the slave's pregnancy was discovered, forcing Petrus to resell her with an acknowledgment of her condition.

The only other contracts in which health warranties appeared were for animals.[181] The similarity in their formulas was so great that in at least one case a notary mistook one for the other in the middle of a document. Giovanni Bardi, a notary active in Genoa in the fourteenth century, recorded the sale of "a certain ash-grey mule (*mullam*) of mine with all its vices and flaws, hidden and manifest, as is, to have, hold, and possess and thence do whatever you wish, and this is the slave (*sclava*) which I bought from Antonio de Gravaigo."[182] Since the health warranty and transfer of ownership formulas were exactly the same for mules and slaves, Bardi absent-mindedly slipped from mule to slave in the middle of the document. This mistake suggests that practicing notaries as well as the authors of notarial formularies saw a connection between the sales of animals and slaves.

Apart from descriptions and health warranties, contracts for the sale of slaves used the same formulas as contracts for the sale of other commodities. All sale contracts, Mamluk and Italian, began with a pious invocation. This was followed by the names of the buyer, the seller, and any agents; a statement that the legal act being performed was a sale; and an assertion of the seller's ownership and right to dispose of the goods. Next a contract stated the number of goods being sold (or the fraction, since jointly owned slaves could be sold fractionally) and the description. This was followed by the price, the currency, and arrangements for payment, as well as a variety of warranties and supplementary clauses. It concluded with the date and the names of two witnesses. Italian contracts also mentioned the location, while Mamluk scribes wrote out half the price as well as the whole price in words to prevent tampering.[183]

There remains one final feature unique to slave sale contracts. This was a clause in which slaves acknowledged their status or consented to be sold. In theory, it should not be possible for slaves to act as parties to their own sale, but in practice, clauses of consent and acknowledgment appeared in both Mamluk and

Italian contracts. These clauses had genuine legal weight. When given the opportunity, a daring slave could halt a sale by refusing to acknowledge her status or give consent.[184] Slaves who did acknowledge their status might be precluded from seeking freedom later.[185] Just as slaves had a real though limited capacity to intervene in the inspection process, some slaves had a real though limited capacity to participate in the legal act of sale.

Mamluk contracts emphasized slaves' acknowledgment of their status, while Genoese and Venetian contracts emphasized slaves' consent. Mamluk *shurūṭ* manuals stipulated that adult slaves should acknowledge their slavery and bondage (*al-riqq wa-al-ʿubūdiyya*), but only two of the surviving Mamluk sale contracts include this clause.[186] Italian notarial formularies said nothing about clauses of consent or acknowledgment, yet I have found dozens of slave sale contracts that included one.[187] These clauses were not characteristic of any particular time or place, and their phrasing ranged from simply "present and consenting" to "here present and [the seller's] slave, having confessed to this by right and assenting completely to this sale."[188]

As consent clauses were not mentioned in notarial formularies, why might notaries have chosen to add them? It was not out of concern for the slave's wishes. One possibility was to legitimize the enslavement and first sale of a person who had recently been free. Although notarial formularies rejected the sale of free people as illegal, they did discuss consent in the context of self-sale.[189] This may explain the use of consent clauses when apparently free children were sold into slavery. Examples include Christina, a fifteen-year-old Russian girl sold by her mother in Tana; Nasta, a thirteen-year-old Tatar girl sold by her brother in Tana; and Caterina, a thirteen-year-old Jewish girl who was probably a refugee from Spain, sold in Genoa in 1496.[190]

Another possible function of the consent clause was to legitimize the sale of a person whose status was unclear. This was the situation of Maria, a Greek woman serving Bartolomeo de Azano and his wife, Iohanna, in Kilia, a town on the northern edge of the Danube river delta. The contract for Maria's sale includes a consent clause as well as a unique passage, analyzed in Chapter 1, in which Iohanna and Maria explain the circumstances of the sale.[191] Maria had been either a captive or a slave belonging to Muslims, probably Tatars, in Moncastro. Bartolomeo had ransomed her, and in return, she had served in his household with no written agreement to spell out the duration or conditions of her service. When Bartolomeo abandoned his family for another woman, Iohanna was no longer able to support her two daughters. She sold Maria to a Genoese merchant to raise money.

This sale was possible because Maria's status fell in the gray area between slavery and captivity.[192] Whether or not she was a slave at the time of sale is dubious: she was of Greek and therefore Christian origin, possibly of free birth, had no documented history as a slave, and had been redeemed from Muslims under conditions that normally involved repayment through a fixed period of service or a fixed sum of money. But her account of her history was translated into Latin by Genoese witnesses and put down in writing by a Genoese notary acting on behalf of a Genoese buyer. In the resulting document, Maria does not just consent but actively affirms that she "was and is a slave." The function of the consent clause is clear: it safeguards the buyer's property rights, because it would be difficult for Maria to challenge her status after having affirmed it in a sale contract. A similar document appeared in the same year in Tana: an Alan woman named Silcha acknowledged that Michael of Padua had delivered (*exegit*) her from Coza Saban, a Saracen inhabitant of Tana. In return, she promised to serve him perpetually as a slave.[193] A little more than a year later, Michael sold her to a merchant from Tana for two sommi (about twelve ducats) in profit. Most contracts with consent clauses did not include explanatory details, but these cases illustrate the role that a slave's consent could play in a sale.

Conclusion

Examining each step in the slave sale process shows that Genoese, Venetian, and Mamluk markets operated according to a common pattern, even though their operations were not precisely the same. That pattern is another aspect of the shared late medieval Mediterranean culture of slavery. It emerges even though the Genoese, Venetian, and Mamluk sources dealing with slave markets and slave sales belong to a wide variety of genres, ranging from slave-buying advice manuals to contracts for actual sales.

Slaves were displayed for sale in a distinctive set of physical environments. They included public streets and squares, private homes and shops, and the courtyard and shops of a *funduq*. Mamluk slave sales were more likely to take place in a public space and be facilitated by a retail merchant; Genoese and Venetian slave sales were more likely to take place in a private space and be facilitated by a broker. In either case, a key step in the process was the physical inspection. The prospective buyer, perhaps assisted by a physician or an advice manual, carefully examined the slave's body to ensure that he or she was healthy. The inspection was humiliating for the slave, reinforcing his or her status as a dishonored and powerless outsider. At the same time, slaves as human commodities had a unique ability to intervene in the sale process.

Slave prices in the late medieval Mediterranean reached their peak in the Mamluk market during the early fourteenth century. Genoese and Venetian prices peaked in 1428–1429, but they never exceeded one or two hundred ducats.

The most expensive Mamluk slaves cost thousands of ducats. Women tended to fetch higher prices in Genoa and Venice, whereas both men and women fetched high prices in the Mamluk market. Slaves in their mid-twenties were the most valuable in Genoa and Venice. The Mamluk market showed a strong correlation between whiteness and high prices, while the Genoese market showed a weaker preference for white over olive or black color and for Circassians over Russians or Tatars.

Both Italian and Mamluk jurists made collections of model contracts to guide notaries and scribes in their work. Mamluk *shurūṭ* manuals offered more material on the subject of slave sale than Italian notarial formularies, but both grouped the sale of slaves with that of animals, particularly horses. The resulting contracts were strikingly similar in their structure and language. Both emphasized the description and the health warranty as distinctive elements of a slave sale contract, and both made occasional use of a clause in which slaves acknowledged their status or consented to their sale. There are many more surviving Italian than Mamluk contracts to illustrate the possible uses and variations of these clauses in practice.

Chapter 5

Making Slaves in the Black Sea

How did free people from the Black Sea become commodities in the Mediterranean? Their enslavement is poorly understood. Many Black Sea communities did not keep extensive written records during the late medieval period and, thanks to a history of archive destruction stretching from Timur to the Crimean War, little of what they wrote survives today.[1] Most surviving sources were created by visitors to the Black Sea who took what they wrote home with them. These sources consist mainly of notarial registers and the financial accounts of colonial administrators, but they also include letters, travel narratives, and literary works. Many of their authors were slave owners and therefore had a stake in how slavery was represented, if it was represented at all. Any violence or illegality in the course of enslavement might well go unrecorded.[2] Thus these sources must be interpreted with caution.

Even so, the slave trade was a lucrative enterprise and did generate a paper trail. Too many historians have waved away the processes of enslavement in the Black Sea with sweeping generalizations about poverty and chronic warfare among nameless forest peoples, steppe nomads, or mountain tribes.[3] The inhabitants of the Black Sea were not nameless, unusually poor, or unusually conflict prone in comparison with the inhabitants of the Mediterranean. Instead, it is worth asking how slaving functioned as a social, political, and economic strategy within the Black Sea.[4] A full account would require a book in itself, so this chapter focuses on just two questions in the hope of provoking further discussion. One is the question of child sale. Mediterranean authors alleged that Black Sea parents motivated by poverty, greed, or barbarism voluntarily sold their children into slavery. I have found that although most Black Sea slaves were captives taken in wars or raids, there is also some evidence for child sale.

The second question concerns the relationship between the local and long-distance slave trades. Raiders who took captives in the Black Sea could realize their monetary value through ransom or sale. In effect, either the captives' families could purchase them or a slave trader would do so. This chapter does not discuss ransom. Instead, it focuses on the ports where successful raiders knew slave traders were ready to buy captives. Caffa, a Genoese colony on the Crimean Peninsula, and Tana, a Venetian settlement at the mouth of the Don, were the most important centers of the slave trade in the late medieval Black Sea. Slaves from the Caucasus as well as the Golden Horde were channeled through their markets. Some remained as slaves locally. The others were exported and carried through the Bosporus to Genoa, Venice, and Alexandria or transported across eastern Anatolia to the Mamluk cities of Malaṭya and Aleppo. The regional slave trade that circulated through Caffa and Tana is at the heart of this chapter, whereas Chapter 6 addresses export into the Mediterranean.

Enslavement Through Violence

In the Black Sea, the transition from free to slave status occurred through either violence or sale.[5] Enslavement through violence was a form of social death: captives were at the mercy of their captors, who could choose to kill or save them.[6] Saving them was certainly more lucrative. The sale of captives was an important source of income for soldiers.[7] Captives' families might contact the captors and negotiate a ransom, especially in frontier regions where raids were common and the parties involved knew one another.[8] A few captives might remain in permanent service to their captors. The rest were sold to merchants as slaves. The Catholic bishop of Sevastopol described lines of slaves being led into port by a rope tied around their necks and attached to the tail of a trader's horse.[9] Slaves captured in Poland during the sixteenth and seventeenth centuries walked to the markets of Crimea, sometimes in chains. Many died or were killed because they could not keep up.[10] The majority of the captives were women and children. Although adult men have been the focus of scholarly literature on captivity, women and children were more likely than men to survive a raid and be captured.[11] The fact that slaves in the medieval Mediterranean tended to be female (as shown in Chapter 3) was therefore a matter of supply as well as demand.

Wars in the Black Sea produced slaves in large numbers. The Mongol conquests of the early thirteenth century generated thousands of slaves, enough to support rapid military expansion in Ayyubid Egypt.[12] In his account of the Sixth Crusade, Jean Joinville described Ayyubid mamluk purchases: "when one Eastern ruler defeated another, he took the poor wretches he had conquered and sold them to the merchants, who in their turn came and sold them again to the Egyptians."[13] Among those "poor wretches" were the future Mamluk sultans Baybars and Qalawūn. Civil wars in the Golden Horde in 1299 and 1359–1381, Timur's invasion in the 1390s, and Ottoman wars of expansion in the late fourteenth and fifteenth centuries all generated slaves.

Conquerors could also exact slaves as tribute. Until the late thirteenth century, Russian vassals of the Golden Horde paid a tithe of all their possessions, including people, as tribute. Some of the tithed people were employed as artisans, soldiers, and domestic servants, while others were sold.[14] The Bulgars also sent slaves to the Golden Horde as tribute.[15] In addition, the fourteenth-century Mamluk geographer al-ʿUmarī reported that khans of the Golden Horde would punish political opponents and thieves by seizing and selling their children.[16]

Raids were a regular occurrence in the medieval Black Sea. It is often difficult to distinguish between raids for the purpose of slaving and raids with slaving as a side activity.[17] The Mongols and Tatars of the Golden Horde were notorious as raiders. Tatar raids on Bulgaria, Galicia, Poland, and Russia produced slaves throughout the late medieval period.[18] In the fifteenth century, the Castilian traveler Pero Tafur reported that Tatars "make war on the neighbouring Christians (*naçiones de xpianos*) and take them and sell them in Kaffa."[19] The Athenian humanist Laonikos Chalkokondyles confirmed that Tatars "raid the neighbouring countries, those of the Circassians, Mingrelians and Sarmatians [Russians]. They carry many captives to the Bosporus, the city of Caffa and Lake Maiotis [Sea of Azov], as it is called, and make a living out of selling them cheaply to Venetian and Genoese merchants."[20] The Mamluk encyclopedist al-Qalqashandī also wrote that the Tatars attacked Circassians, Russians, and Alans, "killed their men, and captured their women and children, and imported them to the corners of the earth."[21]

Giosafat Barbaro, a Venetian nobleman, personally witnessed a Tatar-led raid near Tana.[22] Rumors had spread that a band of nomadic Circassians were camping in a wood about three miles away from the city, and a Tatar merchant organized a group to hunt them. Although the hunting party managed to capture or kill about forty Circassians, the Tatar leader was not satisfied and spent an hour chasing those who had escaped. Barbaro also received eight slaves as a gift from Edelmulgh, a Mongol noble, who described them as "part of the booty (*preda*) which I got in Russia."[23]

Some of those captured by the Tatars remained in service to their captors.[24] Mongol nobles had large slave retinues. When the Moroccan traveler Ibn Baṭṭuṭa visited the court of Uzbak Khan in 1333, he noted that each of Uzbak's four wives had several hundred slaves, including mamluks, eunuchs, and female attendants.[25] Uzbak's third wife, the Byzantine princess Bayalun (Maria), returned to her father in Constantinople with a retinue of five hundred mamluks, two hundred slave women, and twenty eunuchs. Mongol soldiers were expected to have two slaves as part of their equipment, along with five horses and thirty sheep.[26] Slaves helped the "wives of the traders and the commonalty" bring sheep and milk to urban markets.[27] The discovery of Mongol graves from this period with multiple bodies suggests that some masters may have been buried with slaves.[28]

Circassians were also notorious raiders. Slaves taken in raids on neighboring villages constituted the lowest level of Circassian society.[29] In the late fourteenth century, the Dominican archbishop of Sultaniyya reported that Circassian nobles "go out from one village to another publicly, or else secretly if they can, and violently seize children and adults of the other village, and immediately sell [them] to merchants by the sea."[30] The future Mamluk sultan Barqūq was seized in this way from the village of Kasā.[31] According to the archbishop, Circassian women also used magic to cause shipwrecks along the coast and enslave the survivors: "they say that God sent [them] to them and they sell a man like a pig."[32]

Giorgio Interiano, a sixteenth-century humanist, described Circassian raids in more detail. Noble boys practiced horsemanship, archery, and hunting from the age of two or three. They spent their lives "hunting wild animals, even more so domestic ones, and also human creatures."[33] Many unfortified Circassian villages were tucked away in the marshes along the eastern coast of the Sea of Azov between Tana and Copa. The nobles made paths through the tall reeds, "and thus through such secret paths they furtively insult the poor peasants and the animals which, with their own children, carry the punishment. But they who export them from one country to another barter and sell them."[34] During the winter, they also crossed the frozen straits to Crimea and raided the Tatars: "a small number of [Circassians] catch a great number of [Tatars] because they are much more agile and better trained in arms and horses and they show more animosity."[35]

Yet Black Sea raiding was not limited to Tatars and Circassians. Lithuanian raiders captured slaves in Russia, Poland, and Prussia for agricultural labor.[36] Turks raided Christian territory "not in hatred of the cross and faith, not for the sake of taking gold and silver, but to capture people and reduce them to servitude" and sell them.[37] Paganino Doria, a Genoese admiral, raided Sozopol and took twenty Greek inhabitants as slaves in 1352.[38] Geoffrey de Thoisy, a commander of the Burgundian fleet assisting the crusaders at Varna in the mid-fifteenth century, raided along the coast to finance his galleys. Among other adventures, he captured four hundred Tatars near Copa and exchanged five of them for supplies in Trebizond.[39]

Slaves could also be acquired on a small scale through kidnapping, but kidnappers risked punishment for slaving outside the context of war. For example, in 1373, a Venetian ship on its way to Tana put in at Porto Pisano and agreed to carry some local Tatars to Caffa. Instead, the pilot and two sailors sold them as slaves.[40] When the Venetian government was informed, it sentenced the sailors to five months in prison and the pilot to three months. Likewise, an Armenian inhabitant of Caffa appealed to the podestà of Genoa in 1397 because he had been illegally detained as a slave by a Genoese man.[41] The podestà declared him free, but within a few weeks, he had been enslaved again by another Genoese man. In 1460, a boy named Giorgio contested his status in Siena. He said that he was of free Christian origin and had been kidnapped at the age of six while playing on a beach: "around ten years ago, I being in the city of Caffa and being with other children by the sea, and a ship of the Genoese being in port, it sent a gondola with several men to land and secretly took me and another boy who was with me, about ten years of age, and then it left from there and brought us to Chios in the east, and I submitted myself."[42] The decision in this case is unknown, but Giorgio may have waited to present his case to Sienese rather than Genoese authorities in the hope that they would be more sympathetic.

Because of such cases, Genoa found it necessary to officially ban the enslavement of Caffans in 1441: "any person of whatever condition, status or rank he may be, whether he be a Genoese or a foreigner, may not dare or presume, publicly or secretly, in the city center or in the outlying areas of Caffa, to buy or cause to be bought, by himself or through an intermediary, any man or woman of the inhabitants of Caffa, of whatever kind or race [*generis vel nationis*] he or she may be."[43] Buying inhabitants of Caffa for export was punished with a fine of 1,000 aspers, with additional fines for government officials and notaries who assisted in the process. Yet just a few years later, a Genoese ship captain employed by the Burgundian crusade fleet kidnapped a group of Caffan women and children. The culprit, Iacobus Bilia (or Jacques de Ville in French sources), was swiftly apprehended: "for when the same Iacobus, secretly and against the laws of Caffa, carried off women and children from there, it was then necessary to arm ships which pursued him. Thus captured he was brought to Caffa. There, because of the continual carrying off of locals, he ought to have been condemned to death, but he was saved by the mercy of the rectors."[44] Instead, the rectors ordered that Iacobus' ship be destroyed.

Enslavement Through Sale

The second way in which people became enslaved was through sale. Historians have generally accepted medieval reports that peasants in the Black Sea voluntarily sold their children as slaves.[45] Some have read ancient or early modern accounts of child sale anachronistically into the Middle Ages.[46] Others have claimed that in the Caucasus, male parental power included the right to sell dependent women and children.[47] A few have linked child sale to *ataliqate*, the practice of sending noble Circassian children to be raised by foster parents, despite the fact that virtually identical fostering practices in western Europe did not result in slavery.[48] Medieval authors suggested a different set of explanations for child sale: Black Sea parents were poor, ambitious, barbaric, or all three.

Desperate poverty was the motive most frequently given for child sale in medieval sources. According to the Mamluk geographer al-ʿUmarī, steppe children were sold to pay oppressive taxes "in a bad year, when plague beset the herds, deep snow fell and severe frost reigned."[49] Both Ibn Khaldūn and al-Qalqashandī commented on Circassian poverty. Al-Qalqashandī was told by a merchant that Kipchaks "sell their children of all ages for want of food."[50] The Dominican archbishop of Sultaniyya wrote that Tatars, "when they have several wives and children, sell some like animals, because they say they cannot feed so many."[51] Men unable to pay their taxes surrendered their "animals, children and wives, and these are sold immediately to merchants, and thus the country is emptied."[52] Petrarch reported that "from where until recently huge quantities of grain would be brought every year by ship into this city, today ships come from there laden with slaves, sold by their parents under pressure of hunger . . . [otherwise] they would be hungrily plucking the scanty grass with their teeth and nails on the stony soil of their Scythia."[53] In light of this evidence, some historians have argued that Black Sea children would have lived more comfortable lives as slaves in the Mediterranean than as free peasants at home.[54]

Another motive behind child sale, according to medieval sources, was greed or ambition. Slave traders offered high prices, and the children sold to Mamluk traders might become wealthy and powerful later.[55] This perspective was adopted by David Ayalon, who described Mamluk slaving as a "peaceful trade, based on common interest and common agreement," in which slave merchants were held in esteem and returned repeatedly to the same families to purchase multiple children.[56] Local rulers were cooperative, because "according to the scale of values of these nomads, the sale of one's own relatives did not seem to have been considered a too big offence."[57] This benign view of Mamluk slaving has support from Mamluk sources, although it is worth repeating that all were composed by slave owners. According to al-Maqrīzī, "the Mongols gave their sons and daughters and relatives to the traders, and they sold them to them desiring the prosperity of Egypt."[58] Ibn Taghrī Birdī said that ʿAlī Bay al-ʿAjamī was imported from Circassia to Egypt by his own uncle.[59] Al-Isḥāqī wrote that the members of a slave caravan on its way to Egypt made wishes on the night of al-Qadr.[60] One boy wished to become sultan; his friend wished to become a great amir; and their camel driver wished for a good death. It turned out that the boy Qāytbāy indeed became sultan, his friend became an amir, and they wondered later in life whether the camel driver's wish had also been granted. Although the story is apocryphal, it implies that slaves from the Black Sea were aware of the mamluk system before they arrived in Egypt.

The recruitment of Qawṣūn as a mamluk also implies that Black Sea people knew about the system. At age eighteen, Qawṣūn traveled from Solgat to Cairo in the retinue of Uzbak Khan's niece, the fiancée of Sultan al-Nāṣir Muḥammad.[61] The sultan noticed Qawṣūn selling leather goods in the royal stables, but he had to be enslaved to become a mamluk. Self-sale was illegal. Therefore the sultan enslaved Qawṣūn by sending money to his relatives in Solgat, and later in his career, Qawṣūn invited them to join him in Egypt. This was not unusual: a number of mamluks and a few former slave women who attained prominent positions invited their relatives to move to Egypt.[62]

By the mid-fourteenth century, non-Mamluk sources were also claiming that Black Sea parents knew about the possible rewards of Mamluk slavery. In 1307, Hayton of Armenia wrote that free people sold themselves as slaves to receive a high price and honor as mamluks.[63] The Byzantine chronicler Nicephorus Gregoras wrote that some families offered their children to slave traders for free.[64] The Dominican archbishop of Sultaniyya reported that he had seen Sultan Barqūq's son and other relatives depart from the Black Sea for Egypt.[65] The Castilian traveler Pero Tafur claimed that according to Black Sea parents, "the selling of children is no sin, for they are a fruit given by God for them to use for profit, and that God will show the children more favour in the places whither they go than with their parents."[66] Concerning Circassians, the humanist Giorgio Interiano explained that "the greater part of the people sold are conducted to Cairo in Egypt, and thus fortune transforms them from the most subjected peasants in the world to some of the greatest positions and lordships of our age, like sultan, amirs, etc."[67] While Mamluk sources portrayed ambitious Tatar and Circassian parents in a positive light, non-Mamluk sources condemned them for valuing wealth and fame above family.

The final motive for child sale suggested by medieval sources was barbarism. Marco Polo wrote that Russians would "borrow money on the security of their children from merchants who come from Khazaria [Crimea], Sudak [Soldaia], and other neighbouring countries, and then spend it on drink, and so they sell their own children."[68] The Burgundian traveler Ghillebert de Lannoy claimed that Russians in Novgorod bought and sold their own women, a sin that good Frankish Christians would never commit.[69] Johannes von Schiltberger, himself a former slave captured in battle, portrayed Circassians as wicked "because they sell their own children to the Infidels, and steal the children of other people and sell them."[70] Alberto Alfieri, a Genoese humanist in Caffa, condemned the locals for polygamy, nature worship, and child sale.[71] The Castilian traveler Pero Tafur claimed that those who sold children at Caffa were fully aware that what they did was wrong: "they use the place for their evil doings and thefts, and their great wickedness, such as fathers selling their children, and brother selling brother. These things, and worse, are done there by all the nations of Persia, and when they leave the city they turn their faces to it, and drawing a bow they shoot an arrow against the wall, saying that they go thus absolved from the sins they have committed."[72]

Many authors went further, claiming that the barbarians of the Black Sea did not practice any religion at all.[73] This was convenient for slave owners: because slave status was based on religious difference, people without a religion could be legitimately enslaved by anyone. Al-Qalqashandī heard from a traveling merchant that the Kipchaks had no religion, even though he also described Islamic institutions in Saray.[74] One wonders if his merchant informant was a slave trader. In al-ʿAyntābī's manual on slave buying, he asserted that Circassians "have no book and no grasp on religion."[75] This was untrue; the vast majority of people in the late medieval Black Sea were Christian or Muslim. Accusing them of barbarism and unbelief was simply a way to justify their enslavement.[76]

Given this context, how seriously should historians take the claims of Mediterranean slave owners concerning child sale? Some corroborating evidence does exist. Within Russia, free people sold themselves into temporary slavery during periods of famine.[77] Notarial documents show six children sold in the Black Sea by adults claiming to be their relatives. All date from 1360. In Tana, Bech sold his fourteen-year-old grandson Iaobluza; Apanas sold his thirteen-year-old sister Nasta; Ocholinato, a widow, sold her fifteen-year-old daughter Christina; and Anecoza sold his fourteen-year-old son Acboga.[78] In addition, Elya pledged his fifteen-year-old son Basil against a loan of 300 aspers.[79] In Kilia, Daoch sold a thirteen-year-old girl named Taytana whom he identified as the daughter of his slave woman.[80] Daoch may have been her father, or he may have captured both Taytana and her mother in a raid. Although these documents confirm that child sale happened in the Black Sea, they do not reveal the motives behind it or how common it might have been.[81] Perhaps child sale was common but not normally recorded in formal contracts; perhaps child sale was rare but occurred in 1360 because the Golden Horde was experiencing a civil war. Without more evidence, it is impossible to be sure.

Caffa and Tana, 1260–1300

The Black Sea slave trade was organized around two ports. Caffa, on the Crimean coast near a mountain pass connecting it with the interior, was a Genoese colony from 1281 to 1475. Tana, in the marshy delta where the Don River flows into the Sea of Azov, was governed by the Golden Horde but was home to a large

Venetian community. Both Caffa and Tana were outlets for various local products as well as western outposts for long-distance trade.[82] The most important local export was grain, much of which went to feed the city of Constantinople, as well as honey, wax, wood, fur, leather, salt, and salted fish. Long-distance commodities were high in value and low in volume, such as silk, spices, and jewels. In return, Mediterranean merchants imported cloth, iron, wine, oil, and gold. Along with Caffa and Tana, Trebizond was a hub for long-distance trade, while Vicina and Kilia were hubs for the grain trade.

By the late thirteenth century, Genoa and Venice already had a history in the Black Sea. Venice had enjoyed commercial privileges in the early thirteenth century because of its role in the Fourth Crusade, while Genoa was excluded from the region. When Genoa supported Michael VIII Paleologus' reestablishment of the Byzantine Empire at Constantinople in 1260, the tables were turned.[83] In 1261, Genoa gained privileges in the Black Sea, and Venice was excluded. The activities of the Genoese during this period are not well documented, but they had settled in Caffa by 1266, in Pera by 1268, and in Soldaia by 1274.[84] Black Sea slaves began to be sold in Genoa in 1275. By 1281, Genoa had appointed a consul, a deputy, and two treasurers to govern Caffa.[85] Genoese merchants then started to settle in Tana in 1280 and in Vicina in 1298.[86]

During the late thirteenth century, Crimea belonged to the Golden Horde, or the Empire of the Tatars in Italian sources. The Golden Horde was one of four successors to the Mongol conquests of the early thirteenth century; the others were the Ilkhanate of Persia, the Chaghatay Khanate in Central Asia, and the Yüan dynasty in China. The Golden Horde's territory, including that of its vassals, extended from the Danube in the west to Khwarazm in the east, beyond the Caspian Sea. The princes of the Rus' were its northern vassals, and in the south it competed with the Ilkhanate for control of the Transcaucasus. The khan's court was nomadic, but Saray was its administrative capital. Crimea was placed under a governor whose seat was Solgat (Qirim, Eski Kirim).

The Genoese colony at Caffa could thus not have existed without the khan's permission. Mengu-Timur Khan apparently granted administrative control over Caffa to Genoa in 1266, although there was no document spelling out the terms of the concession. According to later accounts, Mengu-Timur Khan placed only two restrictions on the Genoese. First, subjects of the Golden Horde in Caffa fell under the jurisdiction of a *tudun*, a judge representing the khan, rather than Genoese jurisdiction.[87] Second, another representative of the khan, the *commercharius*, collected a tax (*gabella canlucorum*) of 3 percent on the value of goods sold in Caffa.[88] Otherwise, Caffa was governed by its Genoese consul.

The Byzantine emperor permitted Venetians to return to the Black Sea in 1268.[89] Because of Genoa's head start, Venice's options were limited. Venetians had had a presence in Soldaia earlier in the century, so a new Venetian consul was appointed there in 1287 or 1288 with a grant of 150 aspers to buy slaves.[90] In 1293, Genoa and Venice went to war. The immediate cause was competition over Ayas (Laiazzo) in Cilician Armenia, another outpost for long-distance trade, but the Venetians also seized the opportunity to occupy Caffa. However, Genoa won the war in 1298 and regained control of Caffa in 1299. The frustrated Venetians eventually settled at Tana, appointing their first consul there in 1326. This was a less desirable location, isolated from other areas of Venetian influence and subject to outbreaks of disease because of the marshes.[91] The Golden Horde did not officially recognize the Venetian presence there until 1333 and never granted Venice jurisdiction over Tana like Genoa had over Caffa.

Instead of establishing settlements or colonies, the Mamluks ensured access to Black Sea goods by cultivating an alliance with the Golden Horde. This policy was initiated by Sultan Baybars. Shortly after his accession, he sent a merchant to Berke Khan.[92] One motive for the alliance was cooperation against a mutual enemy, the Ilkhan of Persia. However, both the Mamluks and the Golden Horde also presented their relationship as an alliance of Muslims against Mongol pagans.[93] In addition, both had an interest in cultivating the slave trade, although it was more important to the Mamluks than to the Golden Horde. The Byzantine emperor initially hesitated to become involved, but in 1263 and 1281, he promised safe passage for diplomats and merchants passing between the Mamluks and the Golden Horde.[94] The details of these agreements are discussed in Chapter 6.

The Mamluk–Byzantine agreement of 1263 did not mention slaves, but the agreement of 1281 did. It referred to merchants with slaves passing through Soldaia (Sūdāq). Soldaia was also named as a gateway to the Golden Horde in other late thirteenth-century and early fourteenth-century Mamluk sources.[95] Genoa and Venice had consuls there, but Soldaia remained under the control of the Golden Horde and provided convenient access to Solgat just half a day's journey away. Solgat was the seat of the Golden Horde's governor and a regional center of Islamic life, boasting a mosque sponsored by Sultan Baybars and a vibrant community of religious scholars.[96] Visitors arrived from the central Islamic lands, and local scholars made the reverse journey to join the scholarly elite.[97] Solgat was also a commercial center: Mamluk merchants came there to sell clothing and to buy slaves (*jawārī wa-mamālīk*) and furs.[98] Both Barqūq and Barsbāy passed through the hands of traders in Solgat on their way from Circassia to Egypt.[99]

Merchants from Syria and Cairo were resident in Caffa too.[100] Their activities were protected by a Mamluk–Genoese treaty of 1290.[101] The Arabic version of the treaty extended safe conduct to Mamluk ambassadors and merchants along with their goods, including male and female slaves (*mamālīkihim wa-jawārihim*).[102] The Latin version extended safe conduct to all Mamluk merchants coming and going with male slaves, mamluks, and female slaves (*sclavos, momolucos et sclavas*).[103] In the event that Mamluk subjects were captured while traveling on enemy ships, their slaves were protected in the Arabic version but not in the Latin version.[104] This discrepancy may indicate that the Genoese wanted to deter Mamluk traders from transporting slaves on the ships of rival powers, namely, the Venetians, while the Mamluks did not want to restrict their shipping options.

More information about the slave trade in Caffa can be gleaned from a cache of notarial documents produced in 1289–1290 by Lamberto de Sambuceto.[105] His registers contain sixty-five acts pertaining to seventy slaves. They depict a population almost equally divided between male and female, with a median age of twelve and a median price of 12.1 ducats.[106] The majority (63 percent) came from the Caucasus, including Circassians, Laz, Abkhaz, and Majar. The remaining slaves were Bulgars, Russians, Cumans, one Hungarian man, and one Indian woman. Lamberto de Sambuceto also made a brief visit to Solgat and drew up one slave sale there, that of an eighteen-year-old Majar woman named Margarita.[107] The preponderance of Caucasian slaves in 1289–1290 is not easily explained, because the Caucasus was stable during this period, while the Golden Horde was experiencing a power struggle between Telebugha, Tokhta, and Nogai as well as factional violence among the Russian vassals.[108]

The slave owners documented by Lamberto di Sambuceto were almost all Italian men, unsurprising for the clientele of an Italian notary. Five women also appeared: Blancha Salvaygo bought one slave and sold another; Jercharona, wife of Muhammad, and Jerana, wife of Crescino of Asti, both sold slaves; and Mabilia, wife of Zino, and Cali of Liminia, wife of Peter the ax master, both bought slaves.[109] The only non-Italian male slave buyers were Greeks, Nicheta Tana from Sinope and Onomacali from Caffa.[110] The male sellers were more diverse. They included Ali Tarali, a Muslim inhabitant of Solgat; Nicheta, a Muslim from the Georgian region of Meskheti; Xaaba, an Armenian candlemaker living in Caffa; Jacobus de Finario, an Italian inhabitant of Constantinople; Michael Chidonios, a Greek from Sinope; Theodoro Romeus, a Greek from Calamita; and Papaiane, a Greek who was probably living in Caffa.[111] Most sales took place in the loggia, with the remainder in private houses, the hospital, or the Genoese *fondaco*. The documents do not state which slaves were exported and which were kept in Caffa.

Caffa and Tana, 1300–1350

The Italian settlements in Caffa and Tana remained insecure during the first decade of the fourteenth century. The Golden Horde was struck by a famine in

1302–1303, which may have increased the number of children sold into slavery.[112] In 1307–1308, Tokhta Khan imprisoned Genoese merchants in Saray and burned Caffa to the ground because the Genoese had been kidnapping Mongol children and selling them as slaves to the Mamluks.[113] Genoese chroniclers portrayed the attack as a punishment for Genoese pride, but the real target of this gesture was the Mamluks. Sultan al-Nāṣir Muḥammad had refused to join an offensive against the Ilkhan in 1307, so Tokhta Khan disrupted the slave supply to pressure him.

The reign of Uzbak Khan (1313–1341) was a golden age for the Golden Horde and its allies. The Genoese rebuilt Caffa in 1313 with a citadel, a cathedral for its newly appointed bishop, shipbuilding facilities, and a lighthouse dedicated to St. Antony.[114] In 1314, Genoa also created a new administrative unit, the Office of the Gazaria, to govern its Black Sea colonies.[115] The term *Gazaria* referred to Genoa's territory along the Crimean coast. One of the earliest acts of this office was to enforce the newly instituted Alexandria Ban (*devetum Alexandrie*). The ban was part of a broader crusade strategy, discussed in Chapter 7, to prohibit Christians from selling war materials to Muslims. As interpreted by Genoa, this meant that no Christians were allowed to transport "any male or female mamluks, Saracens, or other infidels" within the Black Sea.[116] The ban was to be enforced by the consuls of Caffa and Pera, with penalties of fifty lire for each female slave and one hundred lire for each male slave transported illegally. To that end, all ships traveling in the eastern Black Sea were required to stop at Caffa for inspection.

At the same time as it rebuilt Caffa, Genoa extended its influence in Circassia.[117] The biggest Genoese settlements were at Copa and Matrega. The first Catholic bishop of Matrega in 1349 was a former slave who had become a Franciscan after his manumission.[118] The Genoese consul of Copa collected a tax of six aspers on each slave exported.[119] Sevastopol, Batum (Lo Vato), and Faso were also important slave markets on the Circassian coast.[120] Lo Vosporo (Kerch), on the Crimean side of the strait, was also a slave market and, from 1333, the seat of the Catholic metropolitan bishop.[121] Sevastopol is the only one of these ports from which a contemporary description of the slave trade has survived. In 1330, an English Franciscan named Peter who had been appointed bishop of Sevastopol wrote a letter home. He complained that while Catholics idled away in the West,

> in the east the domain of the Christians is diminished and trampled upon daily and maliciously by the Saracens performing now betrayals, now promises, now torments, now offerings, now wars by land and by sea, now selling Christians for a price on market days, where they are

> dragged with a rope tied from the tail of a horse to the neck of those who are sold, because there is none who will help. Rather this is an idle city in which I, though unworthy, have been appointed by the will of the supreme pontiff, where according to a certain rumor one hundred Christian persons are sold to the Saracens, and taken to the land of the Saracens, and are made Saracens. Therefore I oppose the nefarious business with all my might. Nevertheless those ruling here, although they may be Christians, do not obey me in this or in other things, because with regard to the schism they are of the Greeks.[122]

The aspect of the situation that most distressed Peter was not slavery itself but the plight of Christian slaves owned by Muslims. In his description, the Saracens who made war were probably Mongols from the Golden Horde or the Ilkhanate, while the Saracens who purchased slaves were probably Mamluk merchants. The local rulers who refused to help were Orthodox Christians, vassals of the king of Georgia and, by extension, of the Ilkhan and thus doubly unwilling to defer to a Catholic bishop.

In 1322–1323, Sultan al-Nāṣir Muḥammad made peace with the Ilkhan Abū Saʿīd. This undermined the Mamluks' special relationship with the Golden Horde. In the same year, Uzbak Khan sacked Soldaia and killed a Genoese man, Segurano Salvaygo, who acted as a diplomat and possibly a slave trader on behalf of the Mamluks.[123] Both actions were probably meant to punish al-Nāṣir Muḥammad. Uzbak also sent a message to al-Nāṣir Muḥammad expressing his displeasure, to which the sultan replied, "As for what the king [Uzbak] says about having forbidden merchants to buy slaves, we—praise be to Allah!—have no need of slaves."[124] This reply suggests that Uzbak may have banned the export of mamluks in addition to sacking Soldaia, the port where many mamluks embarked, and killing the sultan's representative, who may have been purchasing slaves. It also alludes to the peace treaty with the Ilkhan: if the Mamluks were no longer fighting a border war, fewer mamluks would be killed and fewer new mamluks would be needed to replace them, so protecting the slave trade became less urgent. Nevertheless, mamluks were again being imported to Egypt from the Black Sea in 1336–1337.[125]

The 1320s and 1330s passed quietly enough for Caffa and Tana. The Moroccan traveler Ibn Baṭṭuṭa visited Caffa during this period. He lodged in a mosque, admired the markets, counted two hundred ships in the harbor, and described the city as "one of the world's celebrated ports."[126] In 1333, Uzbak Khan officially recognized the Venetians in Tana and designated an area for them to build, while the pope appointed a bishop for them.[127] Uzbak also created a new slave market when he moved his capital up the Volga from Saray to Saray-Berke.[128] This city was described in Mamluk sources as "a great entrepot for traders and Turkish slaves," and archeologists claim to have identified slave quarters in aristocratic houses there.[129] It had an entire quarter for Mamluk and Iraqi merchants. The only surviving slave-related document from this period, however, is a letter arranging the shipment of one slave from Tana to Venice.[130]

Uzbak Khan died in 1341. Initially, Janibak Khan, his successor, maintained his policies regarding the slave trade, renewing Venice's privileges in Tana and reiterating the prohibition against exporting mamluks to Egypt.[131] But competition between Venice and Genoa for hegemony in the Black Sea was becoming more intense. Then, in September 1343, a Venetian killed a Tatar in the streets of Tana after a private dispute.[132] A mob of Tatars gathered, more were killed on both sides, and the Venetians fled to their ships. The warehouses of Italian merchants were attacked, causing losses of 300,000 florins for the Venetians and 350,000 florins for the Genoese. That winter, the Venetian Senate dispatched ambassadors to Janibak to discuss the release of detained merchants and compensation for their losses.

Meanwhile, the slave trade at Caffa continued. Eight sale contracts have survived from December 1343 to April 1344.[133] Six of the slaves sold were male and three were female, with a median age of fourteen and a median price of 620 aspers (about 18.8 ducats). Four came from the Caucasus, three from Russia, and two from the Golden Horde. Half of the sales were estate auctions, which is unusual. However, because all eight sales come from the register of a single notary, this may simply reflect his sphere of activity. Also unusual was the large proportion of non-Italian slave owners: a spice merchant from Tortosa, a butcher from Simisso, and a man from Tiflis (Tblisi) all bought slaves, while Maria of Lo Vosporo sold one to the consul of Caffa.

In summer 1344, Genoa and Venice set aside their differences and organized a joint embassy to Janibak.[134] In addition, to put economic pressure on Janibak, they agreed that neither Genoese nor Venetians would trade in Tana or any other port east of Caffa. To compensate Venetian merchants for this inconvenience, the Genoese invited them to trade at Caffa under the same terms as Genoese merchants. Both Venice and Genoa wanted to negotiate the release of their citizens and restitution for their losses in Tana, but their long-term interests remained in conflict. The Venetians wanted their privileges in Tana to be reinstated. The Genoese feared that Janibak might force them out of Caffa; at the same time, they hoped to take advantage of the situation to channel Venetian trade through Caffa permanently. The joint negotiations failed, and Janibak besieged Caffa for a second time in summer 1345, but the arrival of the Black Death in 1346 brought him back to the negotiating table. In summer 1347, Janibak made peace with Genoa and confirmed its control of Caffa. In winter 1347, Janibak also made peace with Venice and allowed Venetians to resettle Tana or Lo Vosporo.[135] Venetian galleys therefore returned to Lo Vosporo in 1348 and to Tana in 1349.

Caffa and Tana, 1350–1400

In the wake of their confrontation with the Golden Horde, Genoa and Venice began their campaign for hegemony over the Black Sea in earnest. The reasons for this timing have been debated. Michel Balard has suggested that the labor shortage caused by the Black Death motivated Genoa to monopolize the Black Sea slave trade.[136] Yet the effects of the Black Death on domestic slavery in Italy have been difficult to prove.[137] Moreover, the conflict between Genoa, Venice, and the Golden Horde began well before the Black Death, and Genoa tried to monopolize all Black Sea shipping, not just shipments of slaves.[138] Therefore, although the slave trade was certainly affected by the Genoese–Venetian rivalry in the Black Sea, it was not the primary cause of the conflict.

After making peace with the Golden Horde in 1347, Genoa initiated a series of wars. Between 1348 and 1352, it fought Byzantium over control of Constantinople's grain trade.[139] Genoa's victory not only guaranteed its privileges in the grain trade relative to Greek merchants but also produced large numbers of Greek slaves, most notably 766 Greeks sold after the battle of Heraclea.[140] Meanwhile, Genoa also fought Venice between 1351 and 1354 for control of Black Sea shipping. The peace treaty banned both Venetians and Genoese from trading in Tana for five years. Venice, unwilling to accept Genoese dominance, also forbade its merchants from trading in Caffa for five years.[141] At this time, in 1351, Genoa began to tax Muslim merchants traveling in the northeastern Black Sea regardless of whether they passed through Caffa.[142]

These events disrupted the slave trade but did not halt it, as a few scattered documents attest. Giacomo Vasalo, a resident of Constantinople, purchased a slave in Mesembria (Nesebar) in 1350.[143] In 1351, a Greek innkeeper from Solgat traveled to Caffa and sold a slave to a Genoese man.[144] While Venetians were shut out of both Caffa and Tana between 1354 and 1359, they did receive permission in 1356 from the Golden Horde's governor at Solgat to trade in Provato.[145] The agreement included a provision that when Venetian ships loaded cargo, a Golden Horde representative and a Venetian representative would check for fugitive slaves.

In 1359, Venetian merchants returned to the Black Sea in force. In preparation, Venice had renewed its privileges with the new khan, Berdibak, and with the governor of Solgat, Cotuletamur, so that its subjects could settle in Provato, Soldaia, and Calitra as well as Tana.[146] The notaries who arrived in Tana with the first wave of merchants recorded 221 slave sales between September 1359 and

September 1363.[147] The slave population that they documented was 75 percent female, the median age was fourteen, and the median price was 13.75 ducats. There was a striking change in the origins attributed to the slaves: whereas in 1289–1290, most slaves came from the Caucasus, in 1359–1363, the majority (83 percent) were from the Golden Horde. Circassians, Alans, Russians, Chinese, Greeks, and Jews appeared in small numbers. All of the slave buyers were Italian men, but the sellers were diverse. Nineteen percent were non-Italian inhabitants of Tana, including Abduracoman (ʿAbd al-Raḥmān) the Saracen and Ascelan the Armenian, who each sold four slaves.[148] Six sellers were women, including the Tatar widow Erda, two Saracen widows named Adia, an Armenian widow named Chotlumelich, a Russian widow named Ochinolato, and Katerina of Sevastopol. There were also sellers from Caffa and Pera as well as Porto Pisano and the Golden Horde (including Gazaria and Russia as well as the area around Tana). Finally, a single Venetian named Domenicus of Florentia sold forty-three slaves during September–October 1359 and May–September 1360, appearing and disappearing in sync with the Venetian galleys.

The influx of Tatar slaves in the 1360s is not mysterious. Berdibak Khan's death in 1359 marked the beginning of a twenty-year civil war within the Golden Horde. The conflict was precipitated by a succession struggle among Berdibak's heirs and compounded by the Black Death (which killed at least 25 percent of the population of the Golden Horde between 1346 and 1375), lost tax revenue due to the Italian wars and embargoes, and declining long-distance trade after the overthrow of the Yüan dynasty in China in 1368.[149] Slaves flooded the Black Sea ports, even those that were not normally slaving centers. In 1362, Tatar and Mongol slaves were exported from Cembalo.[150] It was also in 1362–1363 that Barqūq, a future Mamluk sultan, was exported from Circassia via Solgat to Egypt.[151] Kilia, on the northern edge of the Danube delta at the border between the Golden Horde and Dobrudja, normally exported grain to Constantinople and luxury goods upriver to eastern Europe. Yet, in 1360–1361, the Genoese notary Antonio di Ponzò recorded fourteen transactions involving slaves there.[152] Most were sales, but there were also four slaves pledged against various quantities of wax and honey for export.[153] All the buyers were citizens of Genoa, Venice, or Pera. Of the sellers, five were Tatars crossing the border from the Golden Horde. Thoboch, Themir, and Doach were identified by the Golden Horde's administrative units of ten (*decena*), one hundred (*centenarius*), and one thousand (*miliarius*).[154] Tangareth's home was not mentioned. Tandis was a Saracen from Moncastro (Maurocastro, Akkerman), a non-Tatar subject of the Golden Horde. Thoboch, Themir, Tangareth, and possibly Tandis were selling slaves whom they had captured, but Daoch's slave was a thirteen-year-old girl described as "a daughter of a certain slave woman of Daoch himself."[155] Daoch might have captured the mother and daughter together, or the girl might have been Daoch's own daughter.

During the 1360s and 1370s, Genoa took advantage of the Golden Horde's disarray to extend its authority over the Crimean coast and Black Sea shipping. In 1365, Genoa claimed jurisdiction over Soldaia and eighteen smaller Crimean towns.[156] In the 1370s, it established the Office of Heads of St. Antony (Officium capitum sancti Anthonii). This office was charged with collecting taxes on slave sales (*cabella capitum*), slave brokers (*introytus censarie sclavorum*), and slaves kept in a communal warehouse while awaiting export (*introytus domus sclavorum*).[157] The warehouse, known as the slave house (*domus sclavorum*), was located in the slave market (*in bazalle ubi venduntur capita*).[158] The tax on the slave house was auctioned for 7,500 aspers in 1374, but the charge per slave is unknown, and the slave house itself seems to have lasted only ten years. In Tana, slaves were kept in private houses while awaiting export. For example, one resident of Tana agreed to keep a slave he had just sold, a ten-year-old Mongol boy, in his own house at his own risk until the Venetian galleys were ready to depart.[159] Because the sale occurred in September and the galleys usually departed in November, this was a matter of two months. Slaves in Trebizond were also kept by the seller until they were ready to embark.[160]

The tax on slave sales instituted in the early 1370s was thirty-three aspers per slave. In 1374, it was auctioned for 108,413 aspers, which indicates that at least 3,285 slaves were expected to be sold in Caffa that year.[161] However, notarial documentation for this period is thin. In 1371, three slaves of the deceased notary Nicolaus Bosonus were auctioned "by Stephanus de Camilla, bailiff of the commune in Caffa, who reported that he had auctioned the male slave and female slaves mentioned below for several days continuously, publicly, and in a loud voice through the loggia."[162] One additional slave was sold in Licostomo in 1373.[163]

Genoa and Venice went to war again in 1378–1381, this time over the island of Tenedos at the entrance to the Bosporus. The peace included a provision forbidding both Genoese and Venetians from going to Tana for two years, so in 1382, the Venetian galleys used their alternate base at Provato.[164] Meanwhile, the Golden Horde was reunified under Tokhtamysh Khan in 1381. He immediately confirmed Genoa's claim to the Crimean coast from Soldaia to Cembalo, despite the concerns of local Tatars and the governor of Solgat.[165] Their concerns were well founded, as Genoa continued to channel regional trade through Caffa, where it could be taxed. Crimea hovered on the brink of war in 1385–1386, but war was not in the interest of Tokhtamysh Khan, who was confronting Timur in the east, or the Genoese, who were still recovering from their war with Venice. As a result, Tokhtamysh overruled the governor of Solgat and reconfirmed

Genoa's privileges in 1387.[166] This version emphasized economic privileges, including the smooth functioning of the slave trade.[167] Although Tatars and Genoese agreed not to seek compensation from each other for recent acts of violence and robbery, there was an exception for merchants seeking to recover lost goods, including male and female slaves.

While Tokhtamysh Khan facilitated Genoese trade, the Genoese modified their tax system. In 1383, an eight asper tax on slave possession was added to the thirty-three asper tax on slave sales.[168] In 1385–1386, the slave sale tax generated 41,452 aspers, and the slave possession tax generated 4,240 aspers, indicating at least 1,256 slaves sold and at least 530 slaves owned in Caffa that year.[169] In comparison, in Genoa, there were about 636 slaves sold and about 4,417 slaves owned in 1387.[170] After 1385–1386, the taxes on sale and possession were combined into a head tax (*tolta sclavorum* in 1386–1387, *cabella sclavorum* in 1409, *introytus sclavorum* in 1411, *cabella capitum* in 1421 and thereafter).[171] The right to collect the head tax was auctioned in the external loggia of the communal palace in February, June, or September.[172] After the tax farmer had paid his auction bid and covered his expenses, whatever additional revenue he collected was profit. Between 1374 and 1426, the head tax was auctioned once annually. In the 1440s, it was auctioned twice annually, and in 1446, it was auctioned three times. In 1463, it returned to once annually. Each tax farmer's contract lasted a full year, so anywhere between one and three individuals might be collecting the head tax at any given time. Each would hire agents or subfarm the tax to make collection easier. For example, Gregorius Iudex won the head tax auction in February 1442–1443 but subfarmed its collection to nineteen people.[173] The annual revenues generated by the head tax are shown in Figure 13.

In 1385–1386, the only year for which we have separate figures for the taxes on slave sale and possession, the sale tax generated about 90 percent of the total sale-and-possession tax revenue. If the same was true in later years, and if the revenue expected by the tax farmers was 30 percent more than what they bid (as explained in Chapter 3), then the number of slaves sold in Caffa ranged from 532 (in 1465) to 8,545 (in 1446).[174]

Around the same time as it created the head tax on slaves in Caffa, the Genoese authorities also created a head tax on slaves (*cabella capitum*) in Pera. It yielded 900 hyperpers in 1390, 1,250 hyperpers in 1391, and 1,590 hyperpers in 1402.[175] Assuming that Pera's head tax combined two subtaxes on slave sale and possession at the same rates as Caffa's head tax, then I estimate that 370–529 slaves were sold in Pera in 1390, 515–736 slaves in 1391, and 500–714 slaves in 1402. Although no treasury records have survived from Pera after 1402, in 1424, the podestà of Pera was ordered to be more active in collecting the head tax on slaves because revenues had recently declined.[176]

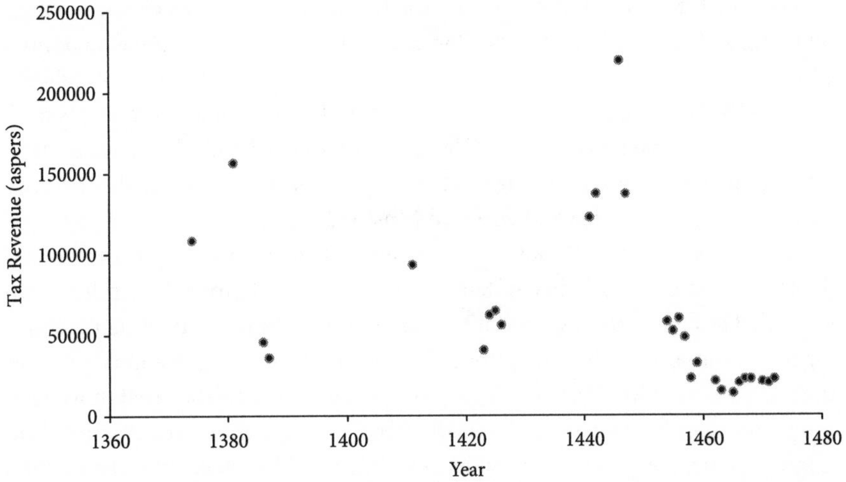

Figure 13. The Head Tax in Caffa.

(ASG, BdSG, Sala 34, 590/1226 bis, fols. 204v, 236v; 590/1227, fol. 209r; 590/1230, fol. 85r; 590/1231, fol. 128v; 590/1232, fols. 127r, 135v; 590/1233, fols. 4v, 6v, 124r, 209v; 590/1234, fols. 49v, 50v, 102v, 124r; 590/1235, fols. 10v, 45r; 590/1236, fols. 9v, 35v; 590/1237, fols. 67r, 79r, 102r; 590/1238, fols. 48r, 92r, 185r; 590/1239, fol. 67r; 590/1240, fols. 95r, 104v; 590/1241, fol. 83r; 590/1242, fols. 43r, 113v; 590/1243, fol. 41v; 590/1246, fol. 115v; 590/1247, fol. 126v; 590/1249, fol. 184v; 590/1251, fol. 181v; 590/1256, fol. 18v; 590/1259, fol. 184v; 590/1260, fol. 130r; Balard, *La Romanie*, 1:301.)

Again during the same period, Genoa reorganized the Office of Heads of St. Antony. It was given a new name, the Office of Saracen Heads of St. Antony (*Officium capitum sarracenorum Sancti Antonii*), and a new charge: to tax Muslim travelers in the eastern Black Sea and Muslim merchants transporting luxury goods. Its agents were stationed "in every place from which heads are exported, whether in Tana or Sevastopol or wherever else the ships go."[177] The reorganization was very effective. By 1381–1382, the Office of Saracen Heads of St. Antony was generating one-third of Caffa's total tax revenue.[178]

There has been much confusion about whether the Saracen heads taxed by the Office of Saracen Heads of St. Antony were slaves.[179] This confusion stems from inconsistencies in the Caffan treasury accounts. Some scribes distinguished between free heads (*capitibus liberis*) and slave heads (*capitibus sclavorum et sclavarum*), while other scribes simply recorded heads (*capitibus*) without mentioning their status. In some entries, it is clear that free and enslaved Muslims in transit were taxed at different rates. In 1441, one treasury scribe noted that free passengers bound for Ottoman territory paid 62 aspers each, while a slave on the same ship paid 254 aspers.[180] However, other scribes obscured the different tax rates by combining all payments from free and enslaved passengers bound for the same destination into a single figure. Finally, it should be noted that the Office of Saracen Heads of St. Antony taxed only Muslims. Christians, enslaved or free, did not pay this tax: the treasury scribe reduced the payment on a cargo of thirty Muslim slaves "on account of one female slave who became Christian."[181] Therefore, although it is tempting to use data from the Office of Saracen Heads of St. Antony to study Mamluk slaving, reliable analysis is more difficult than it appears because of the exclusion of Christian slaves when Mamluks should (in theory) have enslaved mainly Christians as well as the inconsistent identification of free and enslaved Muslims.

There has been additional confusion about the origins and destinations of the ships taxed by the Office of Saracen Heads of St. Antony. When heads are identified as *de Otoman*, should it be read as a possessive "belonging to, bound for the Ottomans" or as a directional "departing from the Ottomans"? I prefer the possessive reading.[182] The directional reading would indicate that more Muslim slaves were being exported to Caffa from Anatolia than the reverse.[183] That is implausible. I have found no evidence of Turks sold as slaves in Caffa or Tana, and therefore it is highly unlikely that any northward trade in Turkish slaves outweighed the southward trade in Tatar slaves.[184] If the possessive reading is correct, then Muslim slaves passing through Caffa were taxed at two different rates, depending on their destination. Muslim slaves bound for Sinope (Sinop), Simisso (Samsūn), Samastro (Amasra), Castamena (Kastamonu), Bursa, and Ottoman territory were taxed at 254 aspers. Those bound for Agi Tarcano (Astrakhan), Malaṭya, Carpa, and Samo were taxed at 206 aspers.[185]

The new Office of Saracen Heads of St. Antony was not popular. Ship captains tried to evade it, and some were caught, such as a captain from Sinope fined for smuggling slaves from Tana to Leffecti in 1384.[186] Venice lodged a formal protest with Genoa in 1384. A Venetian cog had been intercepted because of "the Saracen heads and men of the Tatar empire who are being transported by us to the opposite parts of Turchia, namely from place to place, with their goods."[187] The Senate argued that Genoa's interference violated not only their peace treaty of 1381 but also Venice's commercial privileges renewed by the Golden Horde in 1383. Although Genoa could cite ancient concessions from the Golden Horde as the source of its authority in Caffa, "we [Venetians] can put and take whatever we want in the whole empire of Gazaria, nor is there any exception or prohibition in any way for us in that privilege, and if the intention of the emperor had been that we not remove heads from Tana or from his empire, this would have been declared in the privilege conceded to us."[188] Nevertheless, Venice's protest was ineffective. Rather than starting another war, the Senate informed the consul of Tana and the captains of the Romania galleys that as of March 1385, Venetians should not carry Tatars and Saracens "from the regions of Gazaria and the Sea of Tana to the opposite regions of Turchia."[189] The order was issued secretly to avoid the scandal of public deference to Genoa.

Unfortunately, no notarial registers have survived from Caffa or Tana in the 1370s or 1380s to reflect these changes in the regulation of the slave trade. A few slave owners paid fines to the Caffan treasury: these included Enricus the crossbow maker, Amir the tavern keeper, and Sana Fafea the fisherman.[190] In 1386, the treasury auctioned three slaves, two men and a woman, seized from Saracens.[191] The woman fetched 900 aspers and one man 670 aspers. The other man, Coiha Achali, sold for only 260 aspers, because he was old and infirm. One slave woman was listed in the estate inventory of Isaac or Sava from Syria, who died in Caffa in 1381.[192] This period yields the only reference to a specialist slave trader (*revenditor sclavorum*) in Caffa, suggesting that the slave trade was flourishing.[193] It is also the period when the future sultan Shaykh was imported from Circassia to Egypt.[194]

Sources from the Mediterranean reveal another important change in the Black Sea during the second half of the fourteenth century. This was a shift in the composition of the slave population away from Tatars toward Circassians and Russians. The shift is well known among Mamluk historians. Before 1382, the Mamluk sultanate was held by Turks and their descendants.[195] After 1382, the sultanate was dominated by Circassians.[196] The first Circassian sultan was Barqūq, and the shift is usually attributed to his preference for buying and promoting Circassian mamluks.[197] However, as shown in Figures 14 and 15, notarial documents from Venice and Genoa also show a late fourteenth-century shift in their slave populations from Tatars to Circassians and Russians.[198] The trend is even more striking if other Caucasians (Abkhaz and Mingrelians) are included with the Circassians.

The Italian shift happened in stages. In Genoa, the vast majority of slaves in the 1360s were Tatar. The proportion of Tatars decreased gradually, 6 to 7 percent per decade, until the 1410s, when it plunged to only 24 percent. Meanwhile, the proportion of Caucasians rose as high as 41 percent in the 1410s and the proportion of Russians to 42 percent in the 1440s. Since these data reflect all of the slaves present in Genoa, the 1370s–1400s may have been a transition period during which Tatars imported in the 1360s remained present even though new imports were shifting toward the Caucasus and Russia. In Venice in the 1360s–1370s, Tatars were an even stronger majority (92 percent) of the slave population. The proportion of Tatars decreased to 60 percent in the 1380s and rebounded to 77 percent in the 1390s, but by the 1410s, it had dropped below 35 percent and stayed there. The proportion of Caucasians ranged between 20 percent and 36 percent, but the proportion of Russians was as high as 52 percent. The "other" category of slaves was also more substantial in Venice than in Genoa, especially in the 1400s.

Many factors may have affected this shift.[199] One was the flood of Tatar slaves during the Golden Horde's civil war: when it ended in 1381, the composition of

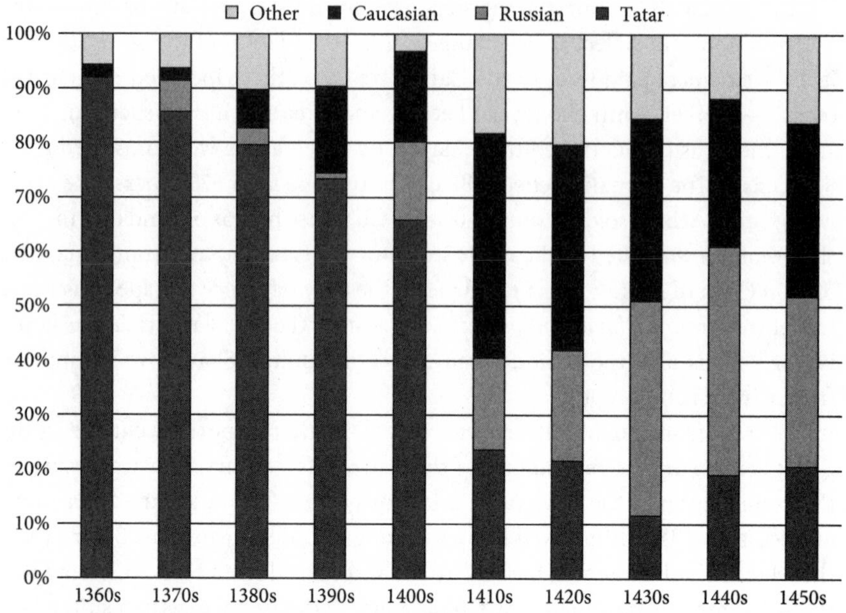

Figure 14. Proportion of Slaves by Race in Genoa.

(ASG, CdSG, N.185,00624, N.185,00625; ASG, Not. Ant. 167, 172, 220, 236–39, 253, 255, 258, 265, 273, 286–87, 292, 360, 363, 366–67, 379–82, 396–405, 449, 685, 719, 768, 1279; ASG, Notai ignoti, b.xxiii, b.xxiv; Balard, "Remarques," "Les génois dans l'ouest," *La Romanie*; Balbi, "La schiavitù"; Belgrano, *Della vita*; Bensa, *Il contratto*; Cibrario, "Nota sul commercio," *Della schiavitù*; Amia, *Schiavitù*; Delort, "Quelques précisions"; Epstein, *Speaking*; Ferretto, "Codice diplomatico"; Gioffrè, *Il mercato*; Haverkamp, "Die Erneuerung"; Heers, *Gênes*; Macchiavello, *I cartolari*; Musso, *Navigazione*; Pandiani, "Vita privata"; Tardy, *Sklavenhandel*; Tria, "La schiavitù"; Verlinden, "Esclavage et ethnographie," "Orthodoxie," "Recrutement des esclaves a Genes"; Williams, "Commercial Revolution.")

the slave supply may simply have returned to normal.[200] To assess this theory, it would be helpful to have data for the early fourteenth century. Another factor may have been the new Office of Saracen Heads of St. Antony. For much of the fourteenth century, Mamluk merchants acquired Tatar slaves in Solgat or Saray-Berke and exported them through Caffa or Tana. In the 1380s, though, Mamluk merchants tried to avoid Genoese surveillance of traffic through Caffa, the Bosporus (Pera), and the Sea of Azov (Copa and Lo Vosporo). One way to do this was to abandon the Golden Horde's slave markets and instead ship slaves from the Circassian coast to Anatolia, where overland routes led to Mamluk territory.

A third factor was Timur's invasion of the Golden Horde in the 1390s. Timur defeated Tokhtamysh Khan once in 1391 and a second time in 1395, after which he devastated the major cities of the region and destroyed their archives.[201] A few Italian notarial documents survive from the early 1390s: a slave woman was auctioned in Tana in 1391, and in Caffa, one slave woman was rented and

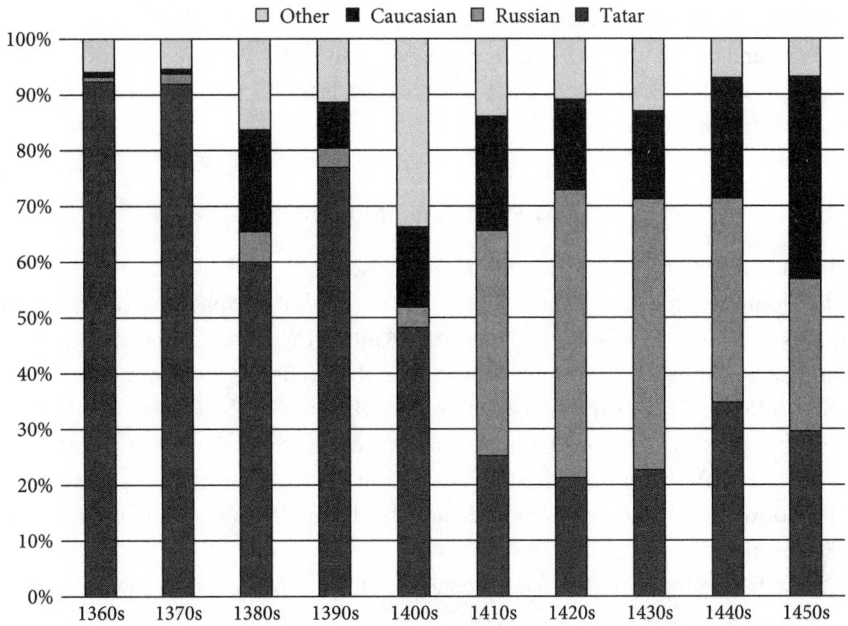

Figure 15. Proportion of Slaves by Race in Venice.

(ASVe, Canc. inf., Misc., b.134 bis and Not., b.17; b.19, N.3, N.7; b.20, N.8, N.10; b.23, N.1; b.58–61; b.80, N.7; b.95; b.132, N.9; b.174, N.9; b.211; b.222; b.230, N.1–2; b.231, N.3; Avog., Raspe, reg. 3646; PdSM, Misti, b.180; Signori di Notte al Criminal, reg. 9–10; Braunstein, "Être esclave"; Cibrario, *Della schiavitù*; Colli, *Moretto Bon*; Lazari, "Del traffico"; Lombardo, *Nicola de Boateriis*; Romano, *Housecraft*; Tamba, *Bernardo de Rodulfis*; Verlinden, "Le recrutement des esclaves à Venise," "La législation.")

another sold in 1394.[202] But in 1395, Timur sacked Tana and enslaved its Italian residents.[203] He then appointed a puppet khan under the tutelage of one of his generals, Edigei, and left the region. In the aftermath, the Great Horde and an assortment of small independent khanates emerged. They all raided their neighbors in Bulgaria, Galicia, Poland, and Russia, which would explain the increased proportion of fifteenth-century slaves categorized as Russian or Ruthenian.[204] Moreover, like Uzbak and Janibak, Edigei "forbade the Tatars from selling their children, so that few imported them to Syria and Egypt."[205] Again, to assess the effectiveness of this policy, it would be helpful to have comparative data from the early fourteenth century.

In any case, Timur's passage through the Caucasus also destabilized Georgia, which had been a stable kingdom, independent or under Mongol sovereignty, since the twelfth century.[206] His first invasion in 1386 was followed by a Circassian revolt in 1390, but his 1397 invasion was especially destructive. Timur's activities caused long-distance trade routes to shift southward, sending the Georgian economy into decline. Noble families began to claim independence.

A second Circassian revolt in 1424 was followed by a Mingrelian revolt in 1462. By the end of the fifteenth century, Georgia had split into three kingdoms and several small principalities. Their leaders were less effective in protecting their subjects from enslavement.

Caffa and Tana, 1400–1450

Timur's invasion changed the political landscape of the Black Sea. The core of the Golden Horde around Saray-Berke remained, but peripheral areas began to break away in the early fifteenth century. Among them was Crimea. The governors of Solgat began to act autonomously in the 1420s. Hajji Giray, who reigned circa 1433–1466, was the first to style himself khan of the Crimean Tatars.[207] He also allied with the resurgent Ottomans. Meanwhile, the Goths, the inland population of Orthodox Christians in Crimea, established their own prince at Theodoro (Mangup) and renewed their traditional ties with the emperor of Trebizond.[208]

Caffa continued to flourish. It remained the port of choice for Mamluk merchants and ambassadors, and its trade continued to enrich Genoa.[209] Yet documentation of the slave trade is scanty, because there are few surviving notarial registers. The treasury auctioned a single Saracen slave in 1410, an Alan man was manumitted in 1411, and a Tatar woman and a Circassian man were sold together in 1424.[210] The Office of Saracen Heads of St. Antony continued to tax Muslims in transit.[211] Tamurbughā, a future Mamluk sultan, was exported from Circassia to Syria in 1419, but the Caffan treasury register for that year has not survived.[212]

Meanwhile, the Venetians rebuilt Tana and renewed their commercial privileges, but the city was sacked again in 1410 and 1418.[213] This did not halt the slave trade. In 1407–1408, Moretto Bon recorded sixteen slave transactions in Tana, seven involving Circassians and seven involving Tatars.[214] Eighty-eight percent of the slaves were female, the median age was twenty, and the median price was 260 bezants (41.5 ducats). All of the buyers were Italian men, but half of the sellers were Saracens or Circassians. An additional forty-two slave transactions were recorded by Donato a Mano between 1410 and 1417.[215] Twenty of those were Russian, eight were Circassian, one was Tatar, and one was Bulgar. Sixty-six percent of the slaves were female, the median age was fourteen (though Donato a Mano was not consistent about recording age), and the median price was 300 bezants (47.9 ducats). Virtually all of the buyers and sellers were Italian men. The three exceptions were sellers: a Jewish man, an Armenian man, and a Saracen man from Urgench. A Tatar slave was sold in 1418, the year of the third sack, and a Bulgarian woman with her young son was sold in 1423.[216] There are also twelve Venetian notarial documents from this period concerning slaves in Trebizond.[217] Trebizond was a second-tier slave market, and the slaves sold there were mainly for local service.

At some point before 1420, Genoa used its hegemony over Black Sea shipping to institute new regulations on the Mamluk slave trade. Early references to the new system appear in the crusade strategy treatise of Emmanuel Piloti, composed in 1420, and in the *Ogdoas* of Alberto Alfieri, composed in 1418–1421.[218] A complete description did not appear until 1434 in a letter to Pope Eugene IV (a Venetian). The Genoese government was concerned that "it had been reported to our dishonor that Christian slaves have been transported by Genoese hands from Caffa to Egypt and other kingdoms of the infidels, which crime is as foreign from us as can be."[219] They explained,

> We have undertaken treaties with the lords of the neighboring regions in which it is appointed that no one may take slaves beyond the boundaries of the Black Sea except in our ships. Bound by that chain, all merchants of all nations are compelled to lead slaves for sale first to Caffa so that there, having found a ship, they may be transferred to where they wish. However the law concerning the broad passage of such slaves orders that first the slaves about to sail be counted. Then with the tax that is imposed on them having been paid, he is allowed to embark them on the ship, who before he may pay it ascends from the port, and both the bishop of Caffa and a band of religious and lay-people [board] it. Having summoned the slaves, he questions the nation of each one, then he inquires into whether each of them wants to become Christian. If any Christian or one who wants to become Christian is found there, he is set down on land and is offered for sale to a Christian man, which is done so that in no way may any Christian be permitted to be taken to the lands of the infidels, but in addition many non-Christians may become faithful.[220]

Other sources make clear that the price paid for the slave convert by his or her new Christian master would be used to compensate his or her previous master.[221] This policy, the Genoese authorities suggested, would encourage people from Trebizond, Tana, Lo Vosporo, and Faso to bring ships full of slaves to Caffa, but none would actually be sent to Egypt. The greed of the locals would benefit the Christian faith, producing many slave converts.

In 1428 or early 1429, the new system was tested. A shipment of slaves for the Mamluks was detained at Caffa because some of the slaves were Christian. The Mamluks retaliated by fining the Genoese community in Alexandria 16,000 ducats.[222] The Genoese consul, with the apparent consent of the Genoese community in Alexandria, paid the fine by taxing all Genoese imports and exports through Alexandria at a rate of 3 percent. Presumably they wished to avoid trouble with the sultan. But the Genoese state ordered the tax revoked in July 1429, arguing that it would set a bad precedent and encourage the greedy to invent new claims for compensation.[223]

Instead of acceding to Mamluk demands, in 1431, Genoa sent ambassadors to Barsbāy to negotiate a treaty covering "both the recent fine of the slaves, and the distribution of spices, and other daily annoyances."[224] The ambassadors were accompanied by "a good interpreter of the Tatar language of Caffa, since [the sultan] was said to be delighted more by this."[225] The first item on the ambassador's agenda was "that the sultan restore the loss suffered by us of those sixteen thousand ducats of gold which were extorted from our merchants as a fine for the slaves of Caffa."[226] If Barsbāy met the Genoese terms, then Genoa would reopen the slave trade:

> Having thus obtained everything mentioned above . . . it pleases us that you grant the trade in slaves [*tractum sclavorum*] from Caffa to the sultan and his people, with them paying the customary and appointed taxes and duties, but always with the preceding declaration, namely that if any of such slaves wants to become a Christian, it should be permitted, provided that the arranged price is paid to his master in Caffa. We will write accordingly to the consul of Caffa, and we will give [these instructions] to the new consul in his orders, that he may arrange and act according to our commissions concerning the trade in such slaves. And for even greater caution, we send two additional letters with you which, when he wants, he may send to the consul of Caffa through one of those Saracens who may be going to Caffa.[227]

The negotiations must have been successful, because the arrangement envisioned in these instructions matches that described in the letter to Pope Eugene IV three years later.

The new inspection system gave Mamluk merchants even more reason to avoid Caffa and instead ship slaves directly from Circassia to Anatolia. To crack down on tax evasion and enforce the inspection system, the Office of Saracen Heads of St. Antony reiterated its ban on direct shipment of slaves from Sevastopol to Turchia in 1430. The text of the decree has been lost, but what has survived is a petition by Batista Matia, burgher of Pera and captain of a small ship, who carried twenty "men of diverse lands and little value" from Batum to Liminia in ignorance of the decree.[228] The council of Caffa pardoned him; perhaps he was not the type of slave smuggler they had intended to catch. In

1435–1436, the future Mamluk sultan Qāytbāy was imported from Circassia to Egypt, but there is no indication of his route.[229]

Resistance to Genoese hegemony over Crimea and Black Sea shipping increased in the 1430s. For example, the port of Cembalo was claimed by both Caffa and the Goths of Theodoro. Venice incited Theodoro to start a war with Caffa in 1422–1424, and although Caffa prevailed, the inhabitants of Cembalo themselves revolted in 1433.[230] A Genoese fleet under Carolo Lomellino suppressed the revolt and pillaged the Crimean countryside, finally attempting to storm Solgat. Their siege failed, and the Crimean khan retaliated against Caffa, wounding the Genoese consul.[231] Goths captured in this war still appeared as former slaves in Caffa in the 1440s, with one as late as 1472.[232]

Nevertheless, Caffa remained the commercial hub of the Black Sea. Pero Tafur, a Castilian traveler who visited in the 1430s, estimated that it was twice as populous as Seville and that "in this city they sell more slaves, both male and female, than anywhere else in the world."[233] Tafur himself purchased three slaves there, two women and one man. The process mirrored that of the Mediterranean slave markets in Chapter 4: "The sellers make the slaves strip to the skin, males as well as females, and they put on them a cloak of felt, and the price is named. Afterwards they throw off their coverings, and make them walk up and down to show whether they have any bodily defect. The seller has to oblige himself, that if a slave dies of the pestilence within sixty days, he will return the price paid."[234]

A cache of slave-related documents drawn up by Niccolo de Varsis and Benedetto de Smeritis has also survived from Tana of the 1430s.[235] Of the ten slaves categorized by race, six were Russian, three were Tatar, and one was Circassian. The majority were women, while the majority of their owners were Italian men. Exceptions were Antonina, wife of Domenico Balotto, who sold a slave to redeem a pledge, and the German Henrich Stangelino of Nuremburg, who manumitted a twenty-year-old Russian man named Stefanus.

The revenue of the Caffan head tax (Figure 13) indicates that the 1440s were a particularly active decade, though there are no surviving notarial registers. The treasury auctioned a fourteen-year-old slave boy on behalf of Santibei the Circassian in 1447.[236] In the same year, the treasury also auctioned three slaves to Coiha (*khwāja*) Ibrahim, a Saracen of Solgat, who resold them to Italian residents of Caffa.[237] Around the same time, the scribes of the Office of Saracen Heads of St. Antony began to record tax payments in the names of merchants rather than ship captains.[238] Examining the data for both merchants and captains reveals no specialist slave traders in the first half of the fifteenth century (1410–1446).[239] Of 170 merchants and captains who were taxed for shipping Muslim slaves, about half (seventy-four) were Italian. The next largest groups were Greeks (thirty-eight) and Saracens (twenty-seven). It was in the 1440s that Saracen merchants and captains, mainly Turks from ports along the Anatolian coast, began to displace the Genoese as shippers of Muslim slaves.[240]

In 1441, Genoa promulgated two new laws for Caffa. In the first, the Statute of Caffa, one provision prohibited the sale or export of any inhabitant of Caffa as a slave. Another provision dealt with fugitive slaves.[241] In general, slaves who escaped and claimed protection from the bishop of Caffa were baptized and resold to Christian buyers. This protected the slave's soul and asserted the superiority of Christianity, while enabling the Caffan authorities to compensate the slave's former owner out of the resale price. Fugitive slaves from Theodoro and the Golden Horde could be resold or manumitted, but fugitive slaves from Solgat were still covered by treaties made in the 1380s. They had to be returned to their owners, who were obligated to pay thirty-five aspers as a reward, or else the owners had to be compensated for the loss of the slave.[242]

The second new law was issued by the Office of the Gazaria. Byzantine and Syrian (Mamluk) ships were forbidden from carrying slaves beyond Chios, that is, from the Bosporus into the Mediterranean.[243] Genoese ships sailing beyond Tenedos, that is, from the Black Sea into the Aegean, were limited in the number of slaves they could carry. A one-deck ship could take thirty slaves, a two-deck ship forty-five slaves, and a three-deck ship sixty slaves, plus one male slave as a personal servant for each merchant on board. However, any ship without other cargo could carry as many slaves as the captain wished. This law defended Genoese dominance of the long-distance slave trade and favored dedicated slave ships over mixed-cargo ships, as explained in Chapter 6. Officials from the Office of the Gazaria were to enforce the new rules by inspecting ships' logs as they returned to Genoa, but it is not clear if this was implemented.

Meanwhile, Tana continued to struggle. Venice experimented with a new settlement in Moncastro in the 1430s.[244] In 1443, an accidental fire burned Tana to the ground, and in 1444, the Senate considered appointing a Venetian consul to Caffa as well as rebuilding Tana yet again. The Venetian patrician Giosafat Barbaro, who lived in Tana from 1436 to 1451, experienced a bustling city but also traveled inland and made friends among the Tatar nobility. He saw slaves taken in raids, as mentioned earlier. He also met a man from Mamluk Cairo, Gulbedin, who lived in Tana and told him stories about hidden treasure.[245]

Caffa and Tana, 1450–1475

Despite the new regulations of the 1440s, Genoese control over shipping in the Black Sea was beginning to fade. The Office of Saracen Heads of St. Antony was abolished in 1449.[246] In 1450, the Byzantine emperor considered levying his own tax on slaves but backed down in the face of Venetian pressure.[247] The Ottoman conquest of Constantinople in 1453 caused short-term panic in Caffa and Tana, but both Genoese and Venetians were able to negotiate safe passage and commercial privileges for their merchants within a year. Mehmed II had good relations with the Mamluks and did not hinder their slave supply, but he also allowed Italians to export slaves as long as they were not Muslims.[248] Nevertheless, many Italians chose to leave the Black Sea in the 1450s.[249] Revenue from the head tax at Caffa plunged (Figure 13), and Venice stopped sending official galley convoys to Tana.

To restore confidence, Genoa handed Caffa over to the Casa di San Giorgio, the institution that managed Genoa's public debt. The Casa di San Giorgio arranged to pay annual tribute to the Ottomans and the Crimean khanate in return for security. This restored Caffa's prosperity until the 1470s but did not protect Genoese settlements in Circassia from Ottoman raids.[250] The Casa di San Giorgio also launched a corruption inquiry. It found that a slave had been misappropriated by the executor of an estate in 1452, and it fined an inhabitant of Caffa for failing to pay taxes on a slave in 1454.[251] It was also during this period, probably in the 1460s, that the future sultan Qānṣūh al-Ghawrī was imported from Circassia or Crimea to Egypt.[252] From 1454 to 1465, the revenue of the Caffan head tax declined (Figure 13). Between 1465 and 1472, the last year of the surviving treasury records, it leveled off. In 1473, one slave was auctioned, and the treasurer and consul of Caffa arranged for eleven slaves to be transported to Genoa by land rather than sea.[253] This was unprecedented, and it indicates that Genoese shipping through the straits was no longer seen as safe.

The final blow fell in 1475. There was a succession dispute among the Crimean Tatars, and the leader of the Shirin clan invited Ottoman intervention.[254] The Ottomans had been seeking a pretext to expand north and seized this opportunity to conquer both Caffa, which they governed directly, and Theodoro, which they granted to the new Crimean khan Mengli-Giray. In the days after Caffa's surrender, the population was disarmed; "foreigners," including Wallachians, Poles, and Georgians, were imprisoned or killed; a census was taken; and Italians were required to hand over half the value of their possessions in cash. Thousands of Italian boys (estimates range from 1,500 to 5,000) and hundreds of girls (perhaps 450) between the ages of seven and twenty were taken captive. All residents of Caffa had their slaves confiscated, three thousand slaves in total, or about 4 percent of the free population at that time.[255] Finally, the remaining Italians were deported to Istanbul. One group revolted and seized control of their ship, but when they reached Kilia (or possibly Moncastro), the local commander sold them as slaves.[256]

This did not mark the end of the slave trade in Caffa. After 1475, it passed into the hands of Ottoman merchants serving Ottoman markets.[257] Mamluk merchants continued to be welcome in the region until 1485, when the Ottomans' expansion to the south brought them into conflict with the Mamluks. The role of the slave trade in their confrontation is discussed in Chapter 6. The Mamluks' precarious position was resolved in 1517, when the Ottomans conquered Egypt and incorporated it into their empire.

Conclusion

Slaves exported from the Black Sea during the late Middle Ages were mostly captured in wars and raids. A few were sold by their own relatives. Long-distance slave traders, Mamluk and Italian, rarely went into the hinterland to capture or buy slaves. Instead, they gathered at regional slave markets, where soldiers and local traders would come to realize the profits of slaving. The slave markets were located in the major cities of the Golden Horde and in ports along the northern and eastern coasts of the Black Sea. The most important were at Caffa and Tana. Tana remained under the control of the Golden Horde, although it had a large Venetian community, but Genoa gained jurisdiction over Caffa in 1281 and governed it as a colony until 1475.

Over the course of the fourteenth century, Genoa used economic power, legal claims, and physical force to exert control over shipping in the Black Sea and channel it through Caffa. From the 1380s, Genoa's hegemony enabled it to tax Muslim travelers and shipments of Muslim slaves. From the 1420s, Genoa tried to inspect all slave shipments to prevent the export of Christian slaves and potential converts. While the taxes and inspections generated hundreds of thousands of aspers in revenue, they also provoked resistance from Venetian, Greek, and Mamluk traders. They may also have played into the widespread shift from Tatar to Circassian slaves in the late fourteenth century. Other possible causes for this shift include the flood of Tatar slaves during the Golden Horde's civil war and Timur's invasion in the 1390s. Genoa's dominance over Black Sea shipping and the slave trade eventually succumbed to Ottoman expansion in the fifteenth century, a process discussed further in Chapter 6.

The goal of this chapter was to explain how free people in the Black Sea became enslaved and fell into the hands of merchants from the Mediterranean. It did not address why the Black Sea was such a rich source of slaves, a topic that deserves its own book. However, it shows that the late medieval Mediterranean slave trade cannot be understood independently of its Black Sea context. On an ideological level, stereotypes of barbarism, poverty, and child sale in the Black Sea helped inhabitants of the Mediterranean rationalize their slave ownership.

On a practical level, social, political, and economic conditions within the Black Sea dictated how slaving would be conducted there and thus how many slaves of what kinds would be available for export each summer. Past scholars have emphasized how Mediterranean demand shaped the slave trade; this chapter emphasizes the role of Black Sea supply. The majority of late medieval slaves were female not only because Mediterranean masters preferred women but also because it was more convenient for raiders in the Black Sea to enslave women and kill men. The shift from Tatar to Circassian slaves occurred in the late fourteenth century not only because Sultan Barqūq favored Circassians but also because the Office of Saracen Heads of St. Antony made it more expensive to export Muslim Tatars around the same time that Timur shattered the political stability of the Caucasus. These and other constraints on the slave traders responsible for connecting Black Sea supply with Mediterranean demand are discussed in Chapter 6.

Chapter 6

Constraining Disorder: Merchants, States, and the Structure of the Slave Trade

In 1393, members of the Venetian Senate complained that the Black Sea slave trade was too disorderly to regulate.[1] Their frustration has been shared by historians. Medieval slave traders are difficult to identify, and their activities are difficult to trace. They never coordinated as a community or formed an institution like the Royal African Company.[2] In fact, few merchants specialized in the slave trade at all, preferring to handle slaves opportunistically and in small numbers. Nevertheless, they managed to export of thousands of slaves from the Black Sea each year.

Trying to grasp the structure of an unstructured trade may sound futile. The key is that all of the merchants who traded in slaves, however sporadically, had to work within certain constraints.[3] These ranged from seasonally prevailing winds to local tax rates, but they can be understood through the lens of political geography. The states that controlled bottlenecks on popular trade routes were able to regulate the passage of slaves. Most obviously, whoever held the Bosporus could regulate shipping between the Black Sea and the Mediterranean. Through a combination of force and legislation, Genoa also made Caffa a shipping hub and thus a point of regulation for the entire Black Sea. The overland Mamluk slave trade could be regulated in the Anatolian–Syrian borderlands. Once such constraints have been identified, it is easier to recognize patterns of choice in the actions of individual merchants.

Historians' desire to name and profile slave traders has been thwarted by the fact that sources in Latin give a different impression of the slave trade, especially the Mamluk slave trade, than Arabic ones. Latin sources indicate that Italians, especially the Genoese, supplied Mamluk slave markets in addition to their own.[4] Their control over this commodity gave them leverage with the sultan to negotiate commercial privileges. Yet Arabic sources show that Mamluk markets were supplied by slave traders from the Islamic world.[5] They competed for the patronage of the sultan, who rewarded them generously for high-quality slaves. These two accounts are mutually exclusive. Who were the primary suppliers of Mamluk slaves, merchants from Italy or from the Islamic world? Did the sultan or the merchants have the upper hand?

Another difficulty arises from historians' tendency to pass judgment on slave traders. Most people today agree that the slave trade is a moral outrage.[6] But historians must set aside generational chauvinism and take seriously the possibility that people in the late medieval Mediterranean would disagree.[7] Were there any medieval sources condemning the slave trade on moral grounds? Did medieval authorities, secular or religious, view the slave trade as evil? Did they try to restrict it on that basis? Historians of Italy, influenced by the narrative of Christian amelioration, generally portray medieval slave traders as "bad Christians" caught up in an urban culture of profit seeking and resistant to the efforts of both religious and secular authorities to rein them in. Because of their presumed involvement in the Mamluk trade, Genoese slave traders have gained an especially bad reputation.[8] Meanwhile, historians of the Mamluks have observed that while retailers selling slaves in public markets had a reputation for fraud, long-distance slave traders were respectable members of society.[9] Do these differences in judgment reflect differences between Latin and Arabic sources or between Italian and Mamluk historiographies?

In this chapter, I argue that generational chauvinism and the search for individual slave traders are both misleading approaches to the study of the late medieval slave trade. Most people who sold slaves in the late medieval Mediterranean did not specialize in the slave trade, did not handle slaves in large numbers, and were nowhere identified as slave traders. A few exceptions are associated with the Mamluk court, but even they did not make slave trading a full-time career. There is no sign that the slave trade was considered inherently wrong in the late Middle Ages. Medieval authorities did not seek to restrict or abolish it on moral grounds; on the contrary, they encouraged it. States benefited by taxing it. Sellers of slaves benefited from state structures (such as laws and treaties) that regulated it. The purpose of this chapter, therefore, is to outline the constraints, both natural and human, that conferred order on the apparently disordered Black Sea slave trade.

The Scale of the Slave Trade

Thousands of slaves were shipped from the Black Sea into the Mediterranean each year. No precise records were kept, but it is possible to estimate the scale of the trade from Genoese tax records and descriptions of the sultan's mamluk corps. For example, the records of a Genoese tax on slave sales in Caffa (see

Chapter 5) shows that about 1,675 slaves were sold there in 1385–1386. A corresponding tax on slave sales in Genoa shows that about 636 slaves were sold there in 1387. Barqūq, the Mamluk sultan, was said to own 2,000–5,000 mamluks, implying purchases of 125–313 mamluks in 1387, if he acquired them at a steady rate. These numbers do not fully describe the flow of slaves. Venice is unaccounted for. Some of the slaves sold in Caffa remained there, whereas some of the slaves sold in Genoa did not come from Black Sea. In addition to his 2,000–5,000 mamluks, Barqūq also had slave women and eunuchs. Mamluk amirs bought significant numbers of slaves too. However, the available numbers do show that the scale of the Black Sea slave trade was in the thousands of slaves per year.[10]

The available numbers also show that the scale of the trade changed over time. Genoa's one florin tax on slave sales provides the best data for tracking these changes. The one florin tax was created in 1380 to finance the interest on government debt accumulated during the Chioggia War. It was not strictly a sales tax: "as often as [a slave] is sold, exchanged, alienated, or transferred from one title to another," the two parties to the transaction each paid one florin.[11] Occasionally, one party paid both florins, for convenience or because the other party was tax exempt.[12] Tax farmers' bids for the one florin tax have survived for almost every year from 1380 to 1472.[13] Collection registers have survived from 1413, 1447, and 1449, but the full collection record would have filled two or three registers per year.[14] For example, the surviving 1413 register lists 136 slaves sold in 130 transactions with cross-references to other registers from the same year that are now lost. Because the tax farmer's bid of 760 lire in 1413 suggests that 434 slaves should have been exchanged, the missing registers help account for the discrepancy.

Figure 16 shows the number of slaves sold in Genoa each year, assuming, as in Chapter 3, that the tax farmers' bids represented about 70 percent of the total revenue they expected to collect. The volume seems to have peaked in the late fourteenth century.[15] While there are no comparable data from Venice, anecdotal evidence indicates the Venetian slave trade also peaked in the late fourteenth century. Venetian merchants complained about a shortage of slaves in 1393, two years before the collapse in Genoese slave sales.[16]

Between 1395 and 1446, the median number of slaves sold per year in Genoa was 350. The years 1421, 1423–1424, and 1436 may have been slow years because of plague outbreaks that killed both masters and slaves, as discussed in Chapter 3. From the 1450s, the number of slave sales in Genoa went into decline. Between 1451 and 1472, the median number of slave sales per year was only eighty-three. In addition, the proportion of slave rentals to slave sales almost tripled from the first half of the fifteenth century to the second half.[17]

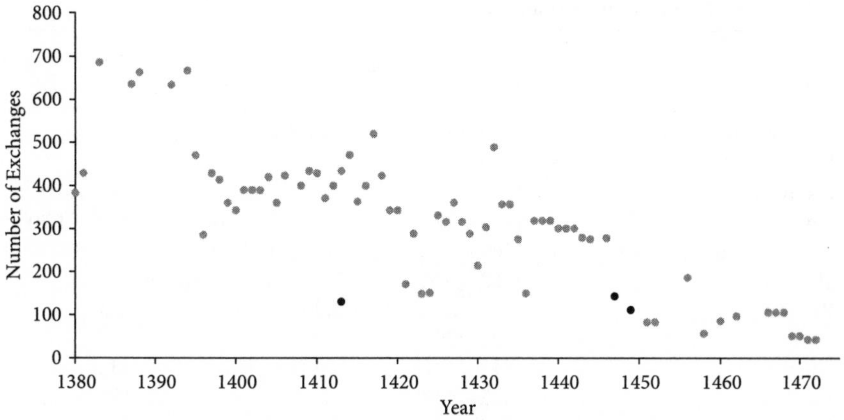

Figure 16. Slave Exchanges per Year in Genoa. Black points are based on collection registers; gray points are based on tax farmers' bids.

(Balard, *La Romanie*, 2:829; Gioffrè, *Il mercato*, 149–50; ASG, CdSG, N.185,00623, N.185,00624, N.185,00625, N.185,15002, N.185,15006, N.185,15072.)

Perhaps this was a strategy to make more efficient use of increasingly scarce slaves. In 1459, the Venetian Senate also complained about a lack of slaves.[18] The cause of this slow decline was Ottoman expansion around the Black Sea, explained in detail later.

No tax data for the Mamluk slave trade have been preserved, but its scale can be estimated based on the number of purchased mamluks (*mushtarawāt*) of each sultan, as shown in Table 3.[19] The table puts Sultan al-Nāṣir Muḥammad's reputation for slave-buying profligacy (Chapter 4) in perspective: he may have paid excessive prices, but he did not purchase mamluks in excessive numbers. Anecdotal evidence also suggests that Mamluk households had fewer slave women in the fifteenth century than in the fourteenth or thirteenth and that a smaller proportion of them were Turks (in the generic sense discussed in Chapter 2).[20] The decrease may have been caused by changing attitudes in favor of monogamy as well as Ottoman interference with Mamluk slave-trading routes.

Comparing the Mamluk and Genoese data shows that the two markets were not closely linked. The peak for Mamluk slave imports was in the 1290s, roughly a hundred years before the peak for Genoese slave imports. The year 1387, analyzed at the beginning of this chapter, was busy in Genoa but slow for the Mamluks. As Genoese slave imports declined over the second half of the fifteenth century, the Mamluks imported many male slaves but few female slaves. Large swathes of the fourteenth century are poorly documented. Nevertheless, it is clear that the number of slaves exported each year from the Black Sea was somewhere in the thousands.

Table 3. *Mushtarawāt* per Sultan

Sultan	*Reign*	*Mushtarawāt*	*Mushtarawāt per year*
Najm al-Dīn Ayyūb	1240–1249	800–1,000	89–111
Baybars	1260–1277	4,000–40,000	235–2,353
Qalawūn	1279–1290	6,000–12,000	545–1,091
Khalīl	1290–1293	<10,000–12,000	3,333–4,000
Muḥammad (3rd reign)	1309–1340	2,000–12,000	65–387
Shaʿbān	1363–1376	200	15
Barqūq	1382–1389, 1390–1399	2,000–5,000	125–313
Shaykh	1412–1421	4,000–5,700	444–633
Barsbāy	1422–1437	<2,000	133
Jaqmaq	1438–1453	4,000	267
Ināl	1453–1461	1,000	125
Khushqadam	1461–1467	3,000–4,000	500–667
Qāytbāy	1468–1496	2,000–8,000	71–286
Qānṣūh	1498–1500	<2,000	1,000
Qānṣūh al-Ghawrī	1501–1516	2,500	167

Sources: Ayalon, "Studies—I," 222–28, "Studies—II," 474.

Physical Geography

The physical geography of land and sea meant that Black Sea slaves could only be transported into the Mediterranean by certain routes. The Bosporus was the sole outlet from the Black Sea into the Mediterranean; all slaves exported by sea had to pass through it. Once they reached the Aegean, they could be taken along any number of routes to Alexandria, Venice, or Genoa, though prevailing winds and currents made some routes easier than others. Moreover, ships needed to stop to replenish their drinking water and supplies, share news, pick up local pilots, and turn over their cargo. These stops shaped their routes.

It has been debated whether Mamluk merchants used their own ships or Italian ones to transport slaves.[21] The possibility of Mamluk commercial shipping in the Black Sea is suggested by a treaty clause dating from 1263 in which the Byzantine emperor permitted two Mamluk ships to pass through the Bosporus each year. Contemporary Byzantine chroniclers believed that Mamluk ships did take advantage of this clause.[22] Another treaty of 1290 also refers to Mamluk merchants traveling with slaves in their vessels.[23] However, after the thirteenth century, there is no evidence for Mamluk ships transporting slaves. Fourteenth-century Mamluk descriptions of the Black Sea are vague.[24]

Venice, in contrast, sent an official galley convoy to Constantinople and the Black Sea each year. The route they took was determined by the Senate. In 1437, the galleys were to stop in Corfu, Modon, Coron, Negroponte, and Constantinople before entering the Black Sea.[25] Within the Black Sea, they normally visited Tana and Trebizond. At the discretion of the captains, they might have also stopped at Moncastro, Sinope, or Simisso. Unofficial Venetian shipping often put in at Candia, the capital of the Venetian colony of Crete.

Genoese ships did not normally travel in convoys, and their captains had more flexibility to choose their routes. They tended to stop in Caffa, Pera, and Chios, all Genoese colonies. They also regularly visited Syracuse, Messina, Gaeta, Naples, and other western Italian ports. These intermediary ports hosted bustling slave markets catering to local buyers, merchants in transit, and pirates and raiders with captives to sell. Those in Constantinople and Pera,[26] Chios,[27] Candia,[28] and Famagusta[29] have received the most scholarly attention, but Bursa,[30] Mytilene,[31] Modon,[32] and Rhodes[33] were also significant. Attempting to unpick the web of local, regional, and long-distance transactions in these ports is futile. A ship bound from Caffa to Genoa might stop in Chios and sell five slaves to locals, buy eight from pirates, and sell thirty to a Catalan merchant for shipment to Majorca. In the documentary record, the connection between the transactions would be invisible because the documents would name the individual buyers and sellers without mentioning the ship on which they sailed. In this context, patterns are more revealing than the details of specific transactions.

In addition to the sea routes, a network of land routes stretched from the southern coast of the Black Sea to the northern edge of Mamluk territory. North–south spurs in the prevailing counterclockwise current of the Black Sea made it easy to cross between Crimea and Sinope.[34] From the ports of Sinope (Sinop), Simisso (Samsūn), Samastro (Amasra), and Bursa, the land routes passed southward to Aleppo.[35] Trebizond (Trabzon) was also a commercial hub, but it was on the eastward route to Tabriz.[36] The greatest barriers to land travel were the Pontic and Taurus mountains. Both ranges ran east–west across Anatolia, the Pontic range along the northern coast and the Taurus range in the south. North–south travel was therefore channeled into a few trunk routes.

One trunk route led from Simisso across the Yesil Irmak River to Amasya and Siwas.[37] At Siwas, the route branched. The southwestern branch reached Aleppo via Qaisariya and Tarsus, whereas the southeastern branch reached Aleppo via Malaṭya and Bahasna. One of these routes was used to take the future sultan Baybars from Soldaia (Sudāq) to Siwas to Damascus in the thirteenth century[38] as well as the future sultan Barsbāy from Circassia to Solgat (Qirim) to Malaṭya in the late fourteenth century.[39] In 1441, Malaṭya was listed in a Genoese tax register as the destination for twenty-nine slaves exported via Caffa and Simisso.[40] Malaṭya was apparently the point of entry into Mamluk territory for many slaves, male and female. Two amirs at Sultan Barqūq's court heard that their siblings had turned up as slaves of the governor of Malaṭya. Both asked the sultan to bring them to Cairo: Tanibak al-Yaḥyāwī wanted to be reunited with his brother Taybars and ʿAlībāy al-Ẓāhirī with his sister Ardbāy. The governor of Malaṭya responded to the sultan with a gift of eighteen mamluks, Taybars among them. He did not send Ardbāy because he had already slept with and impregnated her, making her his *umm walad*.[41] The governor's wife, Fāṭima, also had a Black Sea connection. She was the daughter of a prominent Crimean merchant.

The second trunk route ran southeast from Bursa through Konya, Karaman, and Tarsus to Aleppo. The slave market at the annual fair in Kara Hisar (Afyonkarahisar) may have been associated with this route.[42] Traveling with a returning hajj caravan in 1433, Bertrandon de la Broquière met a group of Circassian slaves heading to Cairo on this route.[43] In Bursa, he also saw Christian men and women for sale in a large hall.[44] According to the Mamluk folk epic *Sirat al-Ẓāhir Baybars*, both Baybars and Qalawūn were imported via this route and not via Siwas.[45]

The Siwas and Bursa routes met along the southern Anatolian coast. Some slaves may have been shipped to Alexandria from Anatolian ports like Ayas, Candeloro (Alanya), or Satalia (Antalya).[46] Most, however, seem to have continued by land to Aleppo.[47] When Sultan Khushqadam wanted to stem the flow of new mamluks (*julbān*) in 1466 because they were causing disturbances in Cairo, he ordered the governor of Aleppo not to admit any slave traders.[48] An amir who forcibly seized a mamluk from a slave trader in Aleppo was taken to Cairo in irons, imprisoned for several days, and exiled.[49] Aleppo also seems to have been a location for the castration of eunuchs. Castration was done by specialists, because it was extremely dangerous. Fayrūz al-Nawrūzī was "imported from his country as a child and sold in the country of Aleppo. Some traders bought him and castrated him," then sold him as a eunuch.[50]

From Aleppo, the trunk route continued south along the Mediterranean coast to Damascus. Damascus was the capital of Mamluk Syria and therefore home to many prominent amirs who would buy slaves in large numbers. Sultan Baybars was initially sold in Damascus.[51] Fakhr al-Dīn ʿUthmān ibn Musāfir, the slave trader who imported Sultan Barqūq, owned a market (*qayṣāriyya*) in Damascus.[52] Muḥammad ibn Suwīd traveled to Syria on account of the slave trade.[53] Gentile Imperiale, a Genoese merchant who imported slaves from Caffa for the sultan, also appeared in Damascus.[54] Slaves who were not sold in Damascus continued south to Gaza and finally to Cairo.

Unlike the Mamluks, Italians rarely used land routes to the Black Sea. Sea routes were generally safer and faster. But when naval wars in the mid-fourteenth century made sea travel less secure, both Genoese and Venetians tried the land routes.[55] Ottoman pressure also motivated Italians to use land routes in the late fifteenth century.[56] The Wallachian and Moldavian routes involved travel up the Danube or Dniester river into central Europe and then across the Alps. Another option was to travel north from the Crimean Peninsula into Russia before turning west. Only one Italian merchant attempted this with slaves: in 1473, just before the Ottoman conquest of Caffa, Angelo Squarzafico agreed to transport eleven slaves by land from Caffa to Genoa.[57]

Political Geography

The physical geography of the eastern Mediterranean placed one set of constraints on slave traders. Political geography added another. These constraints were established by states with control over strategic points along major trade routes. They could change at any time in reflection of changes in the political environment. For the Black Sea slave trade, there were three strategic points: the ports on the northern coast where slaves embarked, the Bosporus, and the Syrian–Anatolian frontier. Previous studies of the political geography of the Black Sea slave trade have focused narrowly on the Bosporus, but all three strategic points mattered.[58]

Most slaves exported from the Black Sea during the later Middle Ages passed through the ports of Caffa or Tana. Tana belonged to the Golden Horde. The impact of regulations and bans on the slave trade imposed by the khans, mentioned in Chapter 5, is difficult to assess. In contrast, Caffa was a colony of Genoa, and the impact of Genoese regulations is easier to trace. Initially, Genoa saw Venice as its main competitor and allowed Mamluk merchants to export slaves freely. The Mamluk–Genoese treaty of 1290 included a clause promising safe conduct for Mamluk merchants and their slaves.[59] However, slaves transported on enemy ships were only protected in the Arabic version of the treaty. In other words, the Genoese permitted Mamluk merchants to export slaves on Genoese ships but not on the ships of rival powers.

Over the course of the fourteenth century, Genoa gained control over shipping within the Black Sea. Conflict over the lucrative grain trade to Constantinople sparked a war between Genoa and Byzantium in 1348.[60] Genoa won, and although Greeks remained active as sailors and ship captains in the Black Sea, they operated under Genoese hegemony. Meanwhile, Genoa also went to war with Venice over Black Sea shipping in 1351 and was victorious again. The terms of the peace treaty banned Venetian merchants from Tana for a five-year period. At the same time, civil war within the Golden Horde enabled Genoa to extend its territorial control along the Crimean coast. As a result, in the 1380s, Genoa was able to channel Black Sea trade through Caffa. There the Office of St. Anthony collected a tax on Muslim travelers, both free people and slaves, regardless of whether they were traveling on Genoese ships. Venice protested that the new policy affected Venetian ships carrying Tatar slaves to the Turks, that is, from Tana to Simisso and Sinope, but to no avail.[61]

In the first half of the fifteenth century, Genoese domination of the Black Sea reached its peak. In the 1420s, Genoa required an inspection of all slaves embarking from Caffa to prevent the export of Christian slaves to the Mamluks. In 1430, the Office of St. Anthony decreed that slaves could not be shipped from Sevastopol (the Circassian coast) to the land of the Turks (Sinope and Simisso). The text of the decree is lost, but presumably its intention was to divert the stream of Circassian slaves destined for the Mamluks to Caffa, where they could be taxed and inspected.[62] In 1441, the Office of the Gazaria forbade Syrian (Mamluk) and Byzantine ships from carrying slaves from the Aegean into the Mediterranean.[63] This would ensure Genoese dominance of the long-distance slave trade without destroying the regional Aegean slave trade. In addition, the number of slaves permitted on Genoese ships sailing from the Black Sea into the Aegean was restricted, encouraging the use of dedicated slave ships rather than mixed-cargo ships. Yet Genoese control over the Black Sea was already beginning to fade. By the time the Ottomans conquered Caffa in 1475, the patterns of Black Sea shipping had already shifted in favor of Ottoman merchants.[64]

The second strategic point along the Black Sea slave-trading routes was the Bosporus, which remained under Byzantine control from 1261 to the 1450s. In the Treaty of Nymphaea, Michael VIII Paleologus rewarded Genoa and Pisa for supporting the reestablished Byzantine Empire at Constantinople by granting them free passage and trade through the Bosporus.[65] He denied similar privileges to Venice until 1268 as punishment for supporting his rival, the Latin emperor of Constantinople.[66] Nevertheless, by the early fourteenth century, both Venetian and Genoese merchants were deeply involved in the Byzantine and Black Sea economies.

Michael VIII Paleologus also allowed Mamluk merchants to pass through the Bosporus as part of his alliance with the Mamluks and the Golden Horde against the Ilkhanate.[67] The first Mamluk–Byzantine treaty, ratified in 1263, permitted two Mamluk ships to enter the Black Sea each year.[68] Although the treaty made no reference to their cargo, contemporary Byzantine chroniclers asserted that the ships were carrying mamluks. George Pachymeres criticized the emperor for undermining the crusader states of Outremer in this way, because "indeed he [the sultan] was unable to bring Scythians safely to himself without sending ships to the Black Sea."[69] Nicephorus Gregoras thought the concession was unintentional: "this matter, since it seemed to be of little moment at the beginning, was easily conceded. Then with the progress of time, it became clear of what kind and how much it was."[70] By the time the emperor recognized the flourishing mamluk trade as a problem, it had become established custom and could no longer be prohibited. Nevertheless, Michael VIII Paleologus clarified his policy on slave exports in a set of mutual oaths exchanged with Qalawūn in 1281. Ambassadors returning from the Golden Horde and merchants returning from Sudāq (Soldaia) could transport slaves through Byzantine territory as long as they paid taxes and did not deal in Christian slaves, "for our law and religious code do not allow us this in the case of Christians."[71] Yet there is no evidence that Byzantine authorities ever halted a slave shipment to protect Christian slaves.

Travel through the Bosporus remained open for Genoese, Venetian, and Mamluk merchants until the mid-fifteenth century. Ottoman encroachment, which had begun in the 1380s, culminated in 1452 with Mehmed II's construction of the Boğazkesen fortress, the Strait- or Throat-Cutter.[72] This fortress overlooked the narrowest point of the Bosporus and enabled Ottoman authorities to inspect all passing ships, but it did not mean that Italians or Mamluks were cut off from the Black Sea.[73] After the conquest of Constantinople in 1453, Genoese and Venetians negotiated fresh commercial treaties and were inserted into the Ottoman *millet* system as autonomous minority communities. The Genoese treaty did not mention slaves; Venetians were explicitly permitted to export slaves as long as they were not Muslim. Italian involvement in the Black Sea slave trade did not end until the Ottomans conquered Caffa and Tana in 1475.[74] The Mamluks continued to enjoy access into the late fifteenth century.[75] Ottoman rulers actively supported the Mamluk slave trade: in 1391 Bayezid I mediated the release of some Mamluk merchants in Caffa,[76] and in 1438, Jaqmaq urged Murad to facilitate the passage of Khwājā Zayn al-Dīn Naksārī, a royal mamluk trader (*tājir al-mamālīk al-sulṭāniyya*), "with whatever mamluks of importable origin he designated in his possession."[77] The Mamluk–Ottoman relationship soured not in 1453 but in the 1480s, when Ottoman expansion to the south reached the Anatolian–Syrian border.

The Anatolian–Syrian border was the third strategic point along the Black Sea slave trade routes, and it was relevant only to the Mamluk slave trade. In the late thirteenth century, Mamluk–Ilkhanid wars prevented the use of this route.[78] Even as relations thawed under the Ilkhan Abū Saʿīd, in 1323, the Ilkhanid governor in Anatolia "forbade traders and others from bringing mamluks to Egypt, and if he heard about someone from the region of the lord of Egypt, he lay in wait for him."[79] After Abū Saʿīd's death in 1335, the Ilkhanate collapsed. The Mamluks were left with a set of buffer states, including Cilician Armenia, Siwas, and Karaman.[80] Although effective Mamluk control rarely stretched beyond Aleppo, vassals and buffer states in the north helped travelers move safely. In 1337, two Mamluk ambassadors to the Golden Horde crossed Anatolia, sailed from Simisso to Crimea, and returned with slaves.[81] News of the Black Death first arrived in Aleppo in 1346–1347 with a Mamluk merchant returning by land from Crimea.[82]

This route remained in use until an Ottoman–Mamluk conflict broke out in 1485. Bayezid II detained Mamluk slave traders and cut the trade routes by both land and sea so that Qāytbāy would be unable to buy mamluks to replace those who died in battle.[83] The peace treaty of 1491 stipulated that "the [Mamluk] sultan could take slaves, iron and any metal from the Black Sea to Syria and to all of his lands."[84] It was in this window, 1492–1493, that the future sultan Qānṣūh was imported from Circassia to Egypt.[85] When the supply of mamluks and Turkish slave women dwindled before the final Ottoman invasion of Egypt in 1516–1517, the Ottoman sultan Selim argued that it was the weakness of the Mamluk currency and not his order that kept slave traders away.[86] Despite Selim's protestations, it was Ottoman control over the trade routes that disrupted the Mamluk slave supply.

One more aspect of the political geography of the slave trade remains to be considered. As part of its crusade strategy, the papacy advocated a Christian embargo against Muslim ports (see Chapter 7). From a papal perspective, therefore, Italian ships transporting Mamluk slaves were smugglers. Acre was a favorite site for this illicit trade before the Mamluks conquered it in 1291.[87] As early as 1246, Pope Innocent IV deplored "certain Genoese, Pisan and Venetian merchants who take Greeks, Bulgars, Russians and Vlachs, all Christians, both male and female, from the regions of Constantinople and travel to the Kingdom of Jerusalem, where they sell them to the highest bidder, even Saracens, in such a way that many of those sold are held as slaves."[88] According to some accounts, Qalawūn's pretext for besieging Acre in 1291 was the killing of "some Muslim traders who had mamluks with them" heading for his court.[89] Whether those killed were slave traders or vegetable sellers (as in another account), thirteenth-century Acre was recognized as a site of illicit slave trading.

After 1291, Acre was part of Mamluk territory and no longer a suitable zone for smuggling. The refugees transferred their activities, including illicit slave shipments, to Famagusta.[90] On September 2, 1301, Octobono Nizola and Michael de Robino invested in a group of Mongol slaves whom Nizola would sell "where God well directed him."[91] Though Nizola could sell the slaves anywhere, Mamluk buyers were nearby and would pay the most. On Friday, September 23,

Lanfranchino Pignatario chartered a Genoese ship, the *St. Anthony*, to carry carrying himself and his goods, including twelve to fifteen slaves, to Alexandria or Damietta the next Thursday.[92] In July 1302, Octobono Nizola appeared again in Famagusta. He chartered a ship called the *St. Anthony*, perhaps the same ship as Pignatario used, to carry five female and six male Mongol slaves from Ayas to Famagusta on behalf of another Genoese merchant named Paschalis de Paschale.[93] In 1307, Manuel Stancono was charged with delivering Daoud, a Muslim slave, to a place and person "whom we know and have ordered."[94] In return, Stancono would be paid the amount stipulated in a contract written in Arabic. This scenario might apply to a slave sale or a ransom, but its secrecy is suspicious.

Ayas (Laiazzo) in Cilician Armenia was another site of illicit trade.[95] Because Armenia was a Christian kingdom, crusade strategists urged merchants to buy silks and spices there instead of in Alexandria. Slaves were available in the Italian community: the protagonist of a Boccaccio story was an Armenian boy kidnapped from Ayas by the Genoese and sold as a slave in Sicily.[96] During the reign of Baybars (1260–1277), slave traders from Persia (*bilād al-ʿajam*) tried to pass through Ayas but were detained.[97] In 1285, therefore, a Mamluk–Armenian treaty stipulated that the king of Armenia could "not forbid anyone, whether a merchant or not, who imports slaves, slave-girls, horses, mules and all kinds of goods, to bring them to the Sultan's territory. . . . He shall open the way for them to import the slaves, slave-girls, horses, mules and other kinds of goods, all nationalities of slaves and nationalities of slave-girls of their various kinds, and not detain any of them."[98] In other words, Armenia was obliged to permit the Mamluk slave trade. Moreover, in a Genoese–Armenian treaty three years later, Genoa promised "if they sell a slave who may be Christian, that they swear not to sell him to Saracens or to any person whom they might believe would sell him to Saracens."[99] However, there was no provision against Genoese merchants selling non-Christian slaves to Muslim merchants. Whether Genoese merchants took advantage of this loophole is unknown.

To sum up, the political geography of the Black Sea enabled Genoa to export slaves freely by sea between 1261 and 1475. Venice was also able to export slaves freely by sea between 1268 and 1475, but from the late fourteenth century, its shipping was constrained by Genoese taxes and regulations at Caffa. The Mamluks were allowed to transport slaves by sea from the 1260s, but their shipping capacity was limited. While conflict with the Ilkhanate blocked the land routes, they used Italian ships to transport slaves by sea. The crusade embargo policy made this risky, though, and so they also resorted to the illicit slave trade through Acre, Famagusta, and Ayas. The situation changed in the second quarter of the fourteenth century. Enforcement of the crusade embargo relaxed around the same time that rapprochement with the Ilkhanate and its subsequent collapse opened the land routes to Aleppo. Mamluk merchants continued to use both land and sea routes until 1485, when the Ottomans exercised their newly won control over all three strategic points (the Black Sea ports, the Bosporus, and the Anatolian–Syrian border) to cut off Mamluk access to Black Sea slaves entirely.

The significance of the land route for the security of the Mamluk slave trade cannot be overemphasized. The crusade embargo was destined for failure, at least with regard to the slave trade, because the Mamluks were only dependent on Italian shipping for a brief period in the early fourteenth century. The Ottoman embargo of 1485 succeeded where the crusade embargo had failed, because the Ottomans controlled the Anatolian–Syrian border as well as the Bosporus and the Black Sea ports.

Incentives and Rewards

Because the Mamluks did not control any of the bottlenecks for the Black Sea slave trade, the sultans used incentives instead of regulation to ensure a steady supply of slaves. Mamluk sultans cultivated their reputation for generosity. In addition to high prices, they offered tax exemptions, privileges, and honors to prominent slave traders. Mamluks who had successful careers sometimes rewarded the traders who had imported them. Like the constraints of political geography, these incentives created patterns of behavior among merchants who traded in slaves.

Mamluk sultans regularly paid above market value for slaves. Al-Nāṣir Muḥammad was especially famous for this: "if the trader brought him an import of mamluks, he gave him more than the value"[100] and "he spent freely on the wishes of the traders in bringing them, and he paid large sums of money for them."[101] Amirs' imitation of his generosity may have driven up prices by 40,000 dirhams per mamluk during the first half of the fourteenth century.[102] Economic troubles during the late fourteenth and fifteenth centuries put a ceiling on the prices that sultans could offer during that era. The merchant who imported the future sultan Shaykh in 1381 was unable to sell him, even though the *atabak* Barqūq was interested, because his asking price was too high.[103] When Shaykh's importer died, another trader snapped him up, lowered the price, and immediately sold him to Barqūq. Still, even at the end of the fifteenth century, the Mamluks were known for their insatiable demand and willingness to pay handsomely for slaves.[104]

Prominent slave traders were also offered a tax exemption (*musāmaḥa*). According to the formula for a *musāmaḥa*, this privilege was granted "in consideration of the mamluks which he purchased by order of the noble gates [i.e., the sultan] for so and so thousand dirhams."[105] Al-Nāṣir Muḥammad, ever extravagant, granted the merchant Ibn al-Ṣawwāf a tax exemption of 100,000 dirhams, 80,000 dirhams in coin, and a golden robe in return for a single mamluk.[106] Merchants with tax exemptions were placed on a list kept by the finance office (*diwān al-khāṣṣ*) and shared with the chancery (*diwān al-inshā'*).[107]

High prices and privileges were a matter of policy as well as economic competition. Sultan Qalawūn circulated a letter to foreign merchants promising that "whoever brings with him male or female slaves, he has a price for them which exceeds what he intended, and the *musāmaḥa* in which he seeks compensation for their value as is usual in the matter of those who import them from nearby countries, so how [much more for traders who import slaves] from distant countries. Because it is our devoted wish to increase our troops, and he who imports them, a duty has been enjoined upon the generous; for he demands much from he who is able to import them."[108] In other words, Qalawūn saw generosity toward slave traders as a policy to increase the size and quality of his army. He instructed his son to act likewise: "let him write a *tawqi'* for the merchant in which he advances from the treasury that which will enable him to cover the cost of his purchase for one trip, and be generous, as it is customary for someone of his station to be, because that is more conducive to his [that merchant's] return. And when a merchant comes to him with our *marsum*, specifying the price of what we bought from him over there, let him pay him the full amount and do not delay from [paying] him his due for even one hour. Rather, take it to him in the shortest time."[109] A policy of prompt and generous payment befit the sultan's high station and encouraged the traders to bring slaves regularly.

In addition to receiving monetary rewards, slave traders were treated with respect and enjoyed a degree of influence at court. During the fifteenth century, Ibrāhīm ibn Qarmash grew close to Sultan Barsbāy and used the relationship to further his brother-in-law's career.[110] Sultan Jaqmaq intervened with foreign rulers on behalf of Muḥammad ibn Musṭafā al-Qaramānī and Zayn al-Dīn Naksārī.[111] Sultan Qāytbāy attended the funeral of Marjan al-Rūmī in 1475.[112] The most honored slave trader of all lived in the fourteenth century. Majd al-Dīn al-Sallāmī was al-Nāṣir Muḥammad's representative to the Ilkhan, visiting Persia for years at a time. His success rested on his good taste and elegant manners. He was said to be "expert in the manners of kings and what befits their minds, skilled in presenting slaves and jewels to them."[113] He negotiated the Mamluk–Ilkhan peace treaty; advised the famous geographer al-'Umarī; fulfilled al-Nāṣir Muḥammad's request for a mamluk who looked like the Ilkhan Abū Sa'īd; and persuaded the lord of Mārdīn, a Mamluk vassal, to give up an excellent slave harpist. In return for his services, al-Nāṣir Muḥammad showered

Majd al-Dīn with gifts: meat, sweets, money, slaves, land, and burial near the sultan's own tomb. After his death, the street where he lived in Cairo was named after him.

Another way of honoring slave traders was to incorporate their names into the names of the mamluks they imported. This was explained by a Mamluk envoy in 1301–1302: "When I was present before [the Ilkhan] King Ghāzān . . . his first question to me was: What is your name? I said: Azdamur. He said: Don't you have three names? I said: Yes. He said: What are they? I said: Husām al-Dīn Azdamur al-Mujīrī. He said: Why al-Mujīrī? So I kissed the earth and said: God save the Khan, we are purchased from the country by traders when we are children, and the trader who buys us names us with his name. The name of my *ustādh* was Mujīr al-Dīn so they gave me the *laqab* al-Mujīrī."[114] A nickname (*laqab*) of this kind signaled a patronage relationship. The names of masters, manumitters, and traders were all considered suitable for a *laqab*.[115] Some mamluks had more than one. Aqbirdī al-Muẓaffarī al-Ẓāhirī was imported by Muẓaffar and manumitted by al-Ẓāhir Barqūq. Uzbak min Ṭuṭukh al-Ashrafī al-Ẓāhirī was imported by Ṭuṭukh, purchased by al-Ashraf Barsbāy, and manumitted by al-Ẓāhir Jaqmaq.[116] The trader's *laqab* came first because the trader was a mamluk's first patron, the link between his original and enslaved identities, just as the manumitter was his final patron and the link between his enslaved and freed identities.[117]

The trader's role as a link to home was more than symbolic. When successful mamluks wanted to reconnect with their families, they sent slave traders to the Black Sea to find them.[118] For example, Sultan Barqūq al-ʿUthmānī's trader was Fakhr al-Dīn ʿUthmān ibn Musāfir. In 1380, two years before he became sultan, Barqūq dispatched Ibn Musāfir to Circassia to find his relatives. The trader returned with a large group, including Barqūq's father, two sisters, a cousin, and several nephews. He also claimed knowledge of Barqūq's original name. Barqūq rewarded him richly: "luck granted [Ibn Musāfir] the importation of the *atabak* Barqūq, and when he died he was a notable of the kingdom. If Barqūq saw him, he would rise in honor of him and treat him with deference and accept his mediation and give him what he asked."[119]

Even merchants who did not import future sultans could benefit from placing slaves with elite buyers. When the mamluk Baylik first arrived in Egypt, his trader touted his literacy to Sultan Baybars. The sultan asked Baylik to demonstrate, and so he wrote a brief verse in Arabic:

> If not for necessity, I would never part from you
> nor be moved around from people to people.[120]

Impressed, Baybars purchased Baylik for a high price. Many years later, when Baylik had become governor of Egypt, the trader fell on hard times. He wrote to Baylik and reminded him of their past bond, suggesting that Baylik's success should be shared:

> We two were together in wretchedness, we endured it
> both our eye and our heart were in dust and pain
> and now the world pays attention to you with what
> you conquer, so do not forget me, your benefactor then.[121]

The strategy was effective; Baylik sent his trader a gift of 10,000 dirhams.

Shipping

All traders who transported slaves by sea were affected by shipping constraints. Those who shipped African slaves across the Atlantic in the seventeenth and eighteenth centuries had ships especially designed to carry the maximum number of slaves while keeping them under the crew's control.[122] Medieval slave traders did not. Little is known about Mamluk slave ships, but Italians transported slaves on ordinary galleys, ships (*nave*), and cogs (*cocche*).

In the early fourteenth century, Venice established a system of official galley convoys to serve popular destinations, such as Jerusalem and Alexandria. The convoy bound for the land of the Romans (Byzantium) was called the Romania galleys.[123] The first Romania galleys departed for Constantinople in 1301. Tana and Trebizond were soon added to their route, followed by Soldaia in 1306, Sinope and Simisso in the 1420s, and Moncastro in the 1430s. The convoy normally consisted of two to four galleys equipped by the Venetian arsenal. The right to load them with cargo was publicly auctioned. Once the winners had been approved, they set up benches in Piazza San Marco to recruit a crew and do business with other merchants. The Romania galleys normally departed in July and returned in late December or early January. If necessary, Venetian naval vessels accompanied them for protection.

The Romania galleys carried many kinds of goods, and their captains regularly took advantage of the opportunity to buy slaves. Andreolo de Bernardo, captain of one of the Romania galleys in 1359, bought three slaves in Tana.[124] Andrea Gradenigo, one of the captains in 1360, bought one slave for himself, while Bertucio Loredano, another of the captains, bought a slave on behalf of the nobleman Bertucio Cornar.[125] Paulo Nani, a captain in 1363, bought two slaves in Tana and a third in Negroponte.[126] Nicolo Bono, a notary who sailed with the Romania galleys in 1363, recorded several slave sales along the way.[127]

The benefits of transporting slaves on the Romania galleys were speed and security. Because they traveled quickly along predictable routes, the galleys minimized living expenses and reduced the mortality rate of slaves in transit.[128] Because they were conservative in their risk assessment, the galleys were also less vulnerable to attack. However, their conservatism meant that in certain years, the galleys did not visit the Black Sea at all. This could cause problems. When it became clear that the Romania galleys would not visit Tana in 1427, a group of merchants petitioned the Senate for a galley to take their slaves to Constantinople.[129] Their petition was rejected, and their slaves were presumably stranded in Tana.

Private ships, Genoese and Venetian, assembled their cargoes in two ways.[130] The captain could rent his entire ship to one group of merchants for a specific itinerary, or the captain could set his own itinerary and accumulate a mixed cargo from various merchants along the way. Renting a ship made sense for wholesale traders sending large quantities of goods to specific destinations. Slaves, however, were usually transported in small numbers on mixed-cargo ships.

Customs records from Genoa illustrate how mixed-cargo ships were able to transport hundreds of slaves each year.[131] As each ship arrived in Genoa, its captain was required to submit a manifest to customs officials and receive their authorization to load and unload cargo.[132] The officials calculated the customs tax (*carato del mare*) owed by each merchant at 5 to 7 percent of the value of his goods. Genoese merchants had six months after their arrival to pay; foreign merchants paid through the captain.[133] To forestall tax evasion, merchants unloading slaves also had to notify the tax farmer of the one florin tax on slave sales.

The result of all the paperwork is a clear picture of how transporting slaves on a mixed-cargo ship worked. For example, ninety-nine slaves belonging to twenty-three different merchants arrived in Genoa on the ship of Antonius and Augustinus de Pinu (see Table 5).[134] Eleven of the merchants shipped just one or two slaves. Another ten shipped three to six slaves. The remaining two merchants, Ambrosius de Flischo and Gregorius de Pinu, shipped fourteen and thirty slaves, respectively. In other words, the great majority of merchants engaged in the slave trade dealt in small numbers of slaves. For this reason, it was unusual for a mixed-cargo ship to carry more than a hundred slaves.[135] Ships within the Black Sea rarely carried more than forty.[136] References to larger cargoes usually apply to convoys rather than single ships. When 306 slaves were brought from Tana to Venice in 1402, they were spread across three cogs.[137]

Slaves on mixed-cargo ships traveled with a variety of other goods. For example, the ship of Ieronimus Catanus arrived in Genoa in 1445 with thirty-six slaves, alum, mastic, cotton, wool, rice, sugar, pepper, ginger, gallnuts, wood, and other items.[138] The slaves belonged to fifteen different merchants, twelve of whom had just one or two slaves. The exceptions were Iacobus de Segnorio with five slaves, Vincentius Pagetinus with six, and Barnabus Ronellus with nine. All of the slaves had been loaded at Chios. Some had been transferred to other ships or sold en route in Naples and Gaeta, but they were still listed on the ship's manifest.

In the late fourteenth century, both Venice and Genoa began to limit the number of slaves that a single ship could carry. In December 1364, the Venetian Senate decided that unarmed ships could carry two slaves per crew member (*salariato*) up to a total of twenty-five slaves, while armed ships could not carry slaves, except for one personal servant per merchant.[139] These limits were so restrictive that Venetians feared the slave trade would be taken over by non-Venetians, so the Senate quickly raised the limit for unarmed ships to three slaves per crew member up to a total of forty slaves and imposed a tax of ten ducats per slave for slaves imported on foreign ships.[140] The new limits expired after two years but were renewed permanently and unanimously in May 1368 "because it is bad and dangerous that any slaves are coming from the market with our galleys in order to transport them anywhere."[141] In July 1368, the Senate also contemplated a ban on shipping any male Tatar slaves to reduce their numbers in Venice.[142]

Venice's limits were prompted by fear of revolt. In 1393, slaves attacked the crew of a Venetian ship in the harbor at Tana. The captain Bernardo Baruto, his scribe, and many of the sailors were killed. It is unclear what happened to the slaves; presumably most of them escaped. The Senate noted that Baruto's ship was carrying two hundred slaves in violation of the legal limit, but it also noted that "the said ship was not at first in clear danger."[143] The crew was able to control the slaves until some of the sailors fell ill. The Senate therefore responded by increasing the fine for violating the limits on slave cargoes but claimed it could do little else because of the disorderly nature of Black Sea slave shipping. Nevertheless, another revolt occurred in 1441 on a ship carrying male slaves from Constantinople to Syracuse.[144] Afterward, the ship ran aground near Messina. Some of the slaves escaped in the ship's boats, but the others died while trying to swim to shore. A slave revolt on the ship of Ieronimus Delfino near Chios in 1445 did not prompt similar regulations from the Genoese authorities.[145]

Another reason for limits on slave shipments may have been to prevent overcrowding and the spread of disease. The evidence for this is ambiguous. When the Greek Orthodox cleric Silvestros Syropoulos sailed from Venice to

Constantinople in 1439, he complained that he had "as much comfort and space as is found for the Circassian or Scythian slaves who are transported by ship from Caffa and Moncastro."[146] He clearly associated slave shipments with overcrowding. On the other hand, Silvestros' galley carried only one hundred passengers, and its crew was smaller than usual. A typical Venetian pilgrim galley carried 170 passengers and 140 crew, and deaths were a regular occurrence.[147] Though slaves may have been disproportionately affected, crowding, disease, and seasickness were common on medieval ships.

Insurance, Freight, and Taxes

Transporting slaves by sea was risky. For this reason, insurance was available for both the usual hazards of sea travel and the particular hazards of shipping slaves. Italian insurers would not cover shipments of slaves to Alexandria, probably because of the crusade embargo.[148] Some refused to cover the risk of a slave's death or escape. Otherwise, premiums ranged from 3 to 7 percent for slaves valued at fifty to one hundred ducats.[149]

One risk was that ships might be captured by pirates or hostile navies.[150] Venice and Genoa regularly intercepted each other's ships. In 1444, for example, the Genoese in Chios seized a Venetian ship sailing from the Crimea to Crete with ninety-five slaves.[151] Three years later, the Venetians in Crete captured two Genoese pirates carrying forty-four slaves.[152] The two incidents were not directly related; this sort of mutual raiding happened frequently. In 1435, a Genoese captain taking slaves from Caffa to Pera tried to evade Venetian galleys by switching to a small bark at Herakleia Pontica and hugging the coast. His slaves were seized instead by a Turkish official in the coastal town of Bosilli.[153]

Storms also posed a serious threat to slave shipping. For example, a Venetian cog carrying slaves from Tana was shipwrecked in 1408.[154] All of its people survived, only to be detained by the Ottomans. An ambassador negotiated the release of the captain and crew, but the slaves were never recovered. Another storm blew a ship carrying slaves from Rhodes to Famagusta off course and delayed it for sixteen days.[155] Winter sailing in the Black Sea was especially dangerous. Venetian galleys only traveled there between April 1 and November 1.[156] Genoese ships ventured out as early as March 15 and as late as December 1. However, ships could be lost to bad weather at any time, even in home waters. A convoy carrying four hundred slaves from Tana had to unload them in Istria because of storms in the Adriatic in August.[157]

Another risk, that of disease, has already been mentioned. While slaves may not have experienced worse crowding than free travelers, both slaves and free travelers frequently fell ill in transit. Plague is the disease most often reported to have killed slaves. Slaves died of plague en route from the Black Sea to Genoa in 1393.[158] In 1400, a ship arriving in Venice lost almost all of its cargo of forty slaves to plague.[159] In 1437, plague killed a slave belonging to Christoforo Guardia before his ship had even left the Black Sea.[160] Eight out of a cargo of twenty-four Abkhaz women and children died of plague on the way to Chios in 1455.[161] No other specific diseases were mentioned in connection with slave shipment, but experienced merchants provided their slaves with shoes and warm clothing, including furs, as part of the cost of shipping them over long distances.[162] The bodies of slaves who died of disease were thrown into the sea.[163]

A final hazard inherent in shipping slaves was resistance. Instances of revolt have already been discussed. There is little evidence of slaves committing suicide while in transit, except for one insurance contract, which stipulated that the insurers were not liable if the slave threw herself into the sea.[164] The chief risk was escape. The most successful were male slaves who jumped overboard near the Anatolian coast and swam to shore. For example, in 1395, the Dominican bishop of Caffa sent two slaves, one man and one woman, to Antonius de Ventura in Genoa.[165] The woman arrived as planned, but the man escaped, prompting Antonius de Ventura to sue the ship captain for the man's value as well as the freight charge paid for his safe delivery. Two male slaves destined for a merchant in Pera escaped from his agent while their ship was still within the Black Sea, assisted by the panic following an outbreak of plague on board.[166]

In addition to insurance and the various ways of losing slaves in transit, merchants who shipped slaves had to compensate ship captains for their services. This was the freight charge (*naulo*). Freight charges could be calculated by value, by weight, or by unit. Table 4 shows the freight charges for goods shipped from Chios to Genoa in 1462.[167] Most goods were charged by weight, but slaves were charged by unit. For the sake of comparison, the freight charge for a slave weighing 130 pounds (1.24 cantars) would be five lire and five soldi, equivalent to 524 pounds of sugar or 786 pounds of rice.[168] The Venetian owners of three ships agreed to charge six ducats per slave carried from Tana to Venice in 1413.[169]

To survive their journey, slaves needed adequate food. This was the charge for board (*mensa*) or living expenses. It was frequently combined with the freight charge. The total cost of shipping one slave from Pera to Genoa, including freight and board, was four lire (about 2.7 ducats) in 1303.[170] In comparison, the total cost of shipping one slave from Famagusta to Alexandria or Damietta in 1301 was four bezants (about 0.9 ducats).[171] In 1395, the cost of shipping seven slaves from Tana to Venice, a journey of six to eight weeks, was only three grossi and three soldi (0.18 ducats), while their living expenses for three days in Venice cost two soldi and seven denari.[172]

Table 4. Freight Charges from Chios to Genoa, 1462

Commodity	*Freight rate*	*Unit*
Cotton	1 lire 5 soldi	cantar
Spices	1 lire 1 soldo	cantar
Wool	16 soldi	cantar
Lead	8 soldi	cantar
Copper	10 soldi	cantar
Rice	14 soldi	cantar
Gall nuts	17 soldi	cantar
Wax	16 soldi	cantar
Caviar, salted sturgeon, salted meat	16 soldi	cantar
Slaves	6 lire 10 soldi	per head
Silk	3 lire	cantar
Crimson	10 soldi	cantar
Carpets	1 ducat	cantar
Sugar, lacquer, indigo	1 lire 1 soldo	cantar
Fur, gold, gems, silk cloth, camel's hair cloth	1.5%	by value

Sources: ASG, Arch. Segr. 575, fol. 46v.

In 1423, the Venetian Senate fixed the cost of shipping a slave from Tana at nine ducats and from Constantinople at seven ducats.[173] Half was the freight charge and half went to living expenses. If a slave died in transit, the freight charge was waived and the living expenses were prorated to the date of her death. Nevertheless, a Venetian merchant paid about one hundred hyperpers (thirty ducats) for shipping a slave from Constantinople to Venice in 1437.[174] In comparison, a free traveler in the 1430s paid twenty ducats for a one-way passage from Venice to Jerusalem with three meals a day.[175] The cost of transporting a slave by the land route from Caffa to Genoa in 1473 was only twenty-five ducats, including food; horses; tolls; taxes, except those charged by Genoa; and some profit.[176]

What kind of food was given to slaves on a ship? In 1455, Gaspare Iudex charged one ducat per slave for twenty Abkhaz women and four children on a mixed-cargo ship from Sevastopol to Chios.[177] For that price, he promised to give them biscuits, cheese, fish, a barrel of wine from Pera, and some cloth for making clothes. The captain of a mixed-cargo ship taking slaves from Famagusta to Egypt gave them only bread, water, and wood (*ligna*), but their owner could send additional food and clothing "for the improvement of the said slaves."[178] Delays could prove disastrous. In 1455, Genoese officials sequestered a ship carrying the possessions of a deceased former consul of Caffa while they audited his accounts. A week after issuing the order, the officials were warned that the cargo included "female slaves who are wasting away and may die" as well as other goods that would be damaged by neglect.[179] Given the circumstances, the officials allowed Georgius Lercarius, the man who had warned them, to take custody of the slaves as long as he returned them or repaid their value upon demand.

Yet another expense associated with the slave trade was taxes. In Genoa, slaves were subject to customs tax and to the one florin sales tax discussed earlier. In Venice, there was no sales tax on slaves. Customs was charged only for slaves on foreign ships, but the rate was high, at ten ducats per slave.[180] Exporting slaves from Venice required a license (*bulleta*) and a fee (four parvi until 1385, five ducats thereafter).[181] Before 1368, the Quarantia Criminal issued the licenses. Between 1368 and 1439, this function was taken over by the heads of the city quarters (*capisestieri*). After 1439, it was handled by the magistrates *delle rason vecchie*. Many slaves in Venice were sold "with license in hand" (*cum bulleta in manu*), meaning that seller had already paid the export license fee.[182] Under Doge Tommaso Mocenigo (1414–1423), the license fee supposedly generated 50,000 ducats, implying ten thousand slaves.[183] No administrative record has survived against which this figure could be checked, and it is unrealistically high. The one florin tax in Genoa indicates that only 149–520 slaves were sold during the same period there.

Mamluk officials probably collected customs taxes on slaves. They definitely taxed slave sales. The sales tax, payable by the buyer, was referred to as *rasm al-sūq*, *ḥaqq al-sūq*, or *wājib al-sūq* in Geniza documents and *rasm sulṭānī* in a 1419 sale contract from Alexandria.[184] It was collected by the supervisor of the office of hospitality and markets (*naẓar dār al-ḍiyāfa wa-al-aswāq*), an official of the chancery, and used to defray the expenses of ambassadors and other visitors to the Mamluk court.[185] The tax rate was proportional to the price of the slave, perhaps 1 to 2 percent, similar to the tax on the sale of animals.[186]

Together, all of these costs increased the price of slaves significantly. A slave woman shipped from Caffa to Genoa in 1395 was valued at 925 aspers (28 ducats).[187] Her combined freight and board charges cost nine libri and seven soldi (13.6 ducats), with an additional 134 aspers (4 ducats) for clothing and export taxes at Caffa and Pera. She does not seem to have been insured. In the end, the costs of shipping made up more than half of her value.

Italian Slave Traders

Few Venetian or Genoese merchants specialized in the slave trade, and many of the slaves they purchased were not meant for resale. As a result, profit was not necessarily the chief motive of merchants who bought slaves, and economic constraints were not the only ones that affected their actions. Some merchants bought slaves for their own use, in which case, they were constrained by their own budgets and preferences. They also bought slaves for relatives and friends, in which case, they were constrained by the terms, formal or informal, of the principal–agent relationship. Moreover, one merchant might buy multiple slaves for different purposes. Therefore, to the extent that the sources allow, the circumstances of each slave sale must be considered individually. Merchants who specialized in slaves were exceptional and should be analyzed as such.

Merchants and travelers in the Black Sea frequently bought slaves for themselves. For example, a fourteenth-century Venetian merchant in Tana bought one slave and enlisted the help of two business associates to pay her shipping expenses, escort her to Venice, and deliver her to his wife.[188] Pero Tafur, a nobleman from Cordoba, acquired three slaves for himself when he passed through Caffa in the 1430s.[189] The Genoese customs register from 1449 shows that thirty-nine people imported slaves for their own use during that year.[190]

Merchants also purchased slaves as agents acting for others. Of the 222 slave sale contracts drawn up by the Venetian notary Benedetto Bianco in Tana, 53 percent of the buyers were agents.[191] This period (1359–1363) may have been atypically busy because the slave trade had just resumed after a decade's hiatus (see Chapter 5). Nevertheless, Bianco's registers provide enough data to show certain patterns. A principal in Venice always worked with a single agent in Tana, and 60 percent of the agents in Tana worked with a single principal in Venice. Sometimes a principal–agent pair collaborated on multiple transactions, such as Nicoleta, a widow in the parish of S. Maria Formosa, who bought two Tatar girls through Marcus Barlo.[192] Another 32 percent of agents served two principals, and the remaining 8 percent served three or more.[193]

In most cases, there was no obvious personal connection between the principals and their agents, but in some cases, they were members of the same family. Andreolus Pachagnelo bought a slave for his father, Marcus; Cristofalus de Vivia bought one for his mother, Agnes; and Nicolaus Superantio bought one for his brother, Marinus.[194] Thomas de Bora did a little of everything: he bought one slave for himself; two for his brothers, Iacobellus and Nicoletus; and one for Marcus de Molino, to whom he was not related.[195] Finally, the notary Benedetto Bianco himself purchased several slaves, one for his own service and three whom he sold after his return to Venice.[196]

Customs records from Genoa show that its merchants also tended to handle slaves in small numbers for various purposes. Returning to the ninety-nine slaves that arrived on the ship of Antonius and Augustinus de Pinu, Table 5 shows that the merchants who imported one or two slaves were most likely to keep them for personal use.[197] Those who imported more than six slaves sold or

Table 5. Slaves on a Mixed-Cargo Ship

Number of slaves per trader	*Number of traders*	*Number of slaves*	*Slaves kept (number)*	*Slaves sold (number)*	*Slaves delivered (number)*	*Slaves reexported (number)*	*Slaves unreported (number)*
1–2	11	14	44% (6)	14% (2)	14% (2)	14% (2)	14% (2)
3–6	10	41	27% (11)	37% (15)	17% (7)	2% (1)	17% (7)
>6	2	44	2% (1)	46% (20)	16% (7)	25% (11)	11% (5)
Total	23	99	18% (18)	36% (37)	16% (16)	16% (16)	15% (15)

Sources: ASG, CdSG, N.185,00625, fols. 31v–35r, 36v–37r.

reexported most of them. Those who imported three to six slaves were most likely to dispose of them in multiple ways. Raynaldus de Lagneto sold one slave, kept one for himself, and delivered one as an agent to his principal. Branca Cataneus delivered three slaves to his principals, sold two, and reexported one to Barcelona. In the end, only one-third of the slaves on the ship were destined for retail sale in Genoa.

Authorization for an agent to buy a slave could be formal or informal. Formal authorization often meant designating a procurator. General procurators were empowered to carry out all kinds of legal transactions on behalf of their principals.[198] Special procurators were empowered only to carry out specific transactions or types of transactions: "you will have full power and ability for me and in my name to sell, alienate, and deliver all and each of my male and female slaves to whomever wishes to buy [them] and then to request an instrument of sale, also to receive the price and to make promises concerning the preservation of indemnity and defense, and to obligate me and my possessions on behalf of the things previously mentioned, and the ability to make contracts and to make promises."[199] Another formal option was a *commenda*, a form of commercial partnership. In 1301, Octobono Nizola entered a *commenda* with Michael de Robino in which each contributed 150 bezants to purchase an unspecified number of Mongol slaves.[200] Nizola would sell the slaves, and the partners would split the profit equally. In 1317, when Ianninus de Aste and Nicolaus de la Porta dissolved their *compania*, they divided the value of seven slaves who were in the possession of Ianninus but belonged to the partnership.[201] In 1395, Ambrosius Rubeus, a cotton worker from Quarto, entered a *commenda* with Petrus de Seputio, a potter from Recco. Seputio gave Rubeus a piece of cobalt blue cloth worth eighteen lire and ten soldi. Rubeus would travel to Caffa on the galley of Iohannis Lomellino and sell the cloth, then use the proceeds to purchase one fourteen- to sixteen-year-old male or female slave. If slaves were not available, he was permitted to invest in other goods.[202] In 1478, one partner in a *societas* agreed to transport two slaves from Genoa to Catalonia, sell them, and reinvest the money in other goods.[203]

Formal agency had to be established through legal documents, but informal agency could be arranged through a conversation or a letter. Guglielmo Querini repeatedly asked his correspondents in Tana to send him Tatar and Russian slaves.[204] Nicolaus de Castilliono, the Genoese consul in Alexandria, wrote to Caffa for slaves rather than buying them locally.[205] Averando and Cosma de'Medici had agents in Venice to purchase slaves fresh from the Black Sea and send them to Florence.[206] Piero Benintendi, the Venetian correspondent of Francesco Datini in Prato, became frustrated with Datini's repeated requests for a slave:

> I am informed about the little slave girl you want, and about the age and everything. And it seems to me that for the time being you could not be well served because for a long time none has come from Romania, and at present anyone who has any, keeps them. Despite this I am still trying to find one, and I have others trying so far as possible, so that you may be served. I am telling you what we are doing—but for the time being I have little hope to succeed. Whenever ships come from Romania, they should carry some [slave girls]; but keep in mind that little slave girls are as expensive as the grown ones, and there will be none that does not cost 50 to 60 florins if we want one of any value. If we find one, we shall do our best.[207]

This letter unveils some of the constraints that personal relationships imposed on the slave trade. Benintendi's efforts to buy a slave were affected not only by economic factors like supply and price but by also personal factors like Datini's nagging and Benintendi's desire to maintain a valuable business relationship. Datini's letters also reveal how he used multiple agents to find a suitable slave. In 1393, the same year as he wrote to Benintendi in Venice, Datini contacted a second agent in Genoa to search for slaves there.[208]

Agents, formal or informal, might be unable to deliver slaves immediately. While waiting, they used the labor and bodies of slaves belonging to their principals, blurring the lines of ownership. In 1384, another of Franceso Datini's correspondents wrote, "I had to buy two slaves for a friend of mine and he ordered them beautiful. And so I bought him two young girls, one of twenty years of age and the other eleven or twelve. And so I kept them here in the house in Caterina our servant's company for around ten days and the younger of twelve years of age never left me for a single night. The other I gave to our young man who stays with us who is called, that is he is nicknamed, the Grater."[209] While awaiting delivery to their master, the two slaves thus worked under the supervision of a free servant, perhaps learning domestic skills or picking up the language. At night the younger girl was kept at home, presumably to protect her from the sexual exploitation experienced by the older woman with the Grater.

Buying slaves through informal agents had many benefits, but there were also drawbacks. In 1360, the Venetian patrician Nicolaus Superantio designated three procurators to find the priest Marino Grisoni in Tana. Grisoni had accepted 800 aspers to purchase female slaves on behalf of Superantio and then vanished with the money.[210] In 1369, Georgius de Mir of Andorra traveled to Caffa and purchased a boy on behalf of Francischino de Raymondo, a gold-beater (*battifolio*) in Genoa. They neglected to draw up a contract for the sale, though, and it was not until 1375 that Georgius' mother finally received payment from Francischino.[211] A formal document would have made it easier to sue the defaulter. In 1395, Iohannis Beffignanus sought arbitration for a dispute with his uncle Raffael, who had failed to pay for two slaves.[212]

Buying slaves through an agent, formal or informal, had several advantages over buying slaves in person. Slaves ordered directly from the Black Sea tended to be cheaper, as little as half of the market price in Italy.[213] The selection of slaves within the Black Sea was greater, and agents could be asked to find slaves with specific qualities. Moreover, only a few Italian cities (Genoa, Venice, Naples) had active retail markets for slaves. Inhabitants of Milan, Bologna, and Florence, much less small towns like Prato, found it easiest to acquire their slaves through agents in the main retail markets.

On the other hand, buying slaves in person had advantages too. For buyers, there was the opportunity to inspect slaves with their own eyes rather than trusting the judgment of an agent. For sellers, there was the opportunity to charge higher prices. Nevertheless, merchants who purchased slaves for retail sale normally handled them as part of a range of commodities. Even wholesale slave traders, those handling more than fifteen slaves at a time, did not deal exclusively in slaves. Francesco Draperio, a Genoese merchant in the eastern Mediterranean in the mid-fifteenth century, sold five hundred slaves through his agent Niccolò de Sestri.[214] During the same period, he also invested in grain, wine, alum, and the tax farms on soap, cotton, carob, and alum. When Paganino Doria arrived in Pera with 766 slaves captured in a raid on Heraclea, most of them (656) were sold through just three merchants (Bartolomeo Lercario of Genoa, Antonio Pallavicino of Genoa, and Enrico di Rustico of Messina), but that did not make slave trading their primary business.[215] Other wholesale slave traders include the partnership of Aragonus Bucharedi of Savona, Nicolaus de Berengeis, and Iacobus Davidis, who sold a lot of seventeen slaves in Genoa in 1349;[216] Domenicus de Florentia, who sold forty-four slaves in forty transactions in Tana in 1359–1360;[217] Tuccio de Pisa, who bought fifty Tatar slaves from four separate sellers in Genoa in 1367;[218] Franciscus de Casali, who sold fifteen Tatar slaves in Genoa in 1368;[219] Antonio and Nicolo Bondumier, who sold dozens of Russian slaves in Venice in the 1380s;[220] Marino Capello di Lodovico, who sold forty-one slaves in Venice between 1437 and 1439;[221] Marcus Sinortum Siculum of Messina, who bought twenty-six slaves in Caffa in 1447;[222] and Domenico de Gattilusio, the lord of Mytilene, who sold fifteen slaves there in 1457.[223]

A few Genoese documents mention the *revenditor sclavorum*, a retail seller of slaves, as a profession. Nicolaus de Sancto Georgio was a *revenditor sclavorum* in Caffa in 1381, as were Facinus de Sancto Salvatore in 1393 and Giovanni de Campi in 1405–1409 in Genoa.[224] In 1435, a *revenditor* named Nicoletus was charged with keeping a slave at home for a month to resolve a dispute over whether she menstruated regularly.[225] In Florence, Bartolomeo Amigi of Genoa and Agostino Davanzi of Ancona were *mercatores sclavorum*.[226] Giorgio da Feggino, though not a *revenditor*, was the only Genoese merchant with a shop dedicated to slaves.[227]

Finally, the roles of retailer and wholesaler were no less flexible than buyer, agent, and owner. Giacomo Badoer, a Venetian merchant resident in Constantinople from 1436 to 1439, participated in the slave trade at every level without identifying himself or being identified by others as a slave trader.[228] He bought two slaves for his own service and rented out a third. In early summer and late autumn, when Black Sea slaves were shipped through the Bosporus, he invested in them as commodities. Some he purchased in partnership and shipped to Venice, Majorca, and Crete. Others he bought with his own funds to send to his friends in Venice, give as gifts, or resell to other merchants. Giacomo never visited Tana or Caffa, but he capitalized very effectively on the stream of slaves passing from the Black Sea into the Mediterranean. At the same time, he also dealt in cloth, oil, wine, spices, wax, furs, and alum. Such flexibility was typical of the late medieval Italian slave trade.

Mamluk Slave Traders

While legal documents and tax records provide most of the evidence for Italians trading in slaves, evidence for Mamluks trading in slaves is mainly anecdotal. The anecdotes, usually about the early lives of prominent mamluks and occasionally their wives, tend to refer only to anonymous merchants (*tājir/tujjār*) or importers (*jallāb*).[229] Even when the merchants' names are given, further information may be unavailable.[230] For this reason, it is difficult to generalize about the Mamluk slave trade. On the other hand, a few slave traders, such as Majd al-Dīn al-Sallāmī and Fakhr al-Dīn ʿUthmān ibn Musāfir, were prominent members of Mamluk society. Their stories help illustrate the possibilities and constraints of the Mamluk slave trade.

One notable characteristic of Mamluk slave traders was their diversity. Genoa's slave markets were supplied mostly by Genoese merchants and Venice's slave markets by Venetians, but the merchants who supplied Cairo came from all over the world. Some were Egyptians, such as Burhān al-Dīn Ibrāhīm ibn ʿUmar al-Maḥallī al-Miṣrī (famous for his great wealth) and Muḥammad ibn Suwīd al-Miṣrī al-Mālikī.[231] Others came from Mamluk Syria. One was Khwājā Shihāb al-Dīn Aḥmad, who was born in Damascus and lived in Aleppo.[232] A Genoese reference to a Muslim slave trader named ʿUmar, acting for the sultan in Caffa, has been connected with Khwājā Zayn al-Dīn ʿUmar ibn Zakarī, a Syrian financier.[233] Fakhr al-Dīn ʿUthmān ibn Musāfir was from Asʿard, a town on the northern Mamluk border near Mārdīn and what is now Diyarbakr, but spent his later life in Damascus.[234] His nicknames indicated that he was both a foreigner (al-ʿAjamī) and an Egyptian (al-Miṣrī). It is likely that Khwājā ʿUthmān (Coiha Octoman) of Malaṭya, who appeared in Genoese tax records exporting ten slaves from Caffa to Simisso, was also a Mamluk slave trader.[235]

Other slave traders came to Cairo from beyond Mamluk borders. Those from the Turkish states of Anatolia included ʿAlāʾ al-Dīn al-Siwāsī from Siwas, Maḥmūd ibn Rustām al-Rūmī al-Bursawī from Bursa, Muḥammad ibn Muṣṭafā al-Qaramānī from Karaman, Marjan al-Rūmī al-Sharīf, and the anonymous traders who brought the future sultan Tamurbughā to Syria.[236] Ibrāhīm ibn Qarmash al-Qirimī al-Qāhirī and his father Qarmash came from Crimea, while Maḥmūd Shāh al-Yazdī al-Dashtī al-Qirimī was linked to both Crimea and the steppe.[237] Majd al-Dīn al-Sallāmī, the best-documented Mamluk slave trader, came from the village of Sallāmiyya near Mosul.[238] Kamāl al-Khitāʾī, who imported slaves from Central Asia, was associated with China.[239] Finally, there were merchants from Genoa, such as Lanfranchino Pignatario, Octobono Nizola, Gentile Imperiale, and Segurano Salvaygo.[240]

A second characteristic of Mamluk slave traders was that they handled slaves in small groups, more than two but fewer than the wholesale limit of fifteen. One trader en route from Circassia to Syria had five or six mamluks, Kamāl al-Khitāʾī brought eight mamluks from Central Asia, Jalāl al-Dīn imported eight mamluks to Aleppo, and thirteen Tatar children were displayed for sale in Cairo by a fourth trader.[241] According to Felix Fabri, a fifteenth-century pilgrim, only sixty slaves were available at one time in the Tatar *funduq* at Alexandria.[242] An exception was the famous fourteenth-century traveler Ibn Baṭṭūṭa. He bought and sold slaves serially as he traveled across Eurasia, acquiring one or two slaves as purchases or gifts, using their services while on the road, then selling them at his destination.[243] In this way, he could access cash without having to carry it on his long journeys. His pattern of buying and selling slaves during a journey was not recognized as slave trading in Mamluk sources, though.

A third characteristic of Mamluk slave traders was that, like Italians, they tended to combine slave trading with other activities. In the Mamluk case, slave trading was closely tied to diplomatic relations with the Golden Horde. Ambassadors often played a dual role as slave traders. This connection appeared early on. In the Mamluk–Genoa treaty of 1290, both ambassadors and merchants were granted safe conduct along with their slaves.[244] In the fourteenth century, the title of ambassador (*al-safīrī*) was used "for some *khwājā* merchants because of their mediation between the kings and their coming and going between the kingdoms to import male and female slaves."[245]

This combination of roles occurred with particular frequency during the reign of al-Nāṣir Muḥammad. Tokhta Khan of the Golden Horde sent an ambassador with eighty mamluks and twenty slave women to al-Nāṣir Muḥammad in 1313–1314.[246] In 1320, the Genoese merchant Segurano Salvaygo was part of an embassy from the Golden Horde that delivered 440 slaves.[247] In 1337, al-Nāṣir Muḥammad sent a merchant, Khwājā ʿUmar, and an amir, Sarṭaqṭāy, as ambassadors to the Golden Horde with a sum of 20,000 dinars to spend on male and female slaves.[248] Majd al-Dīn al-Sallāmī mediated between al-Nāṣir Muḥammad and the Ilkhanate for much of his career. In addition to delivering gifts and negotiating treaties, he "entered the country of the Tatars, traded and did business, and returned with slaves and other kinds of merchandise and wonders of the land."[249] Even at the end of the Mamluk period, Qānim, an official slave trader (*tājir al-mamālīk*), spent a year at the Ottoman court and returned to Cairo in 1450 with many slaves.[250] In 1490, Jānbalāṭ was appointed as an official slave trader (*tājir al-mamālīk*) while already at the Ottoman court as an envoy.[251] In this context, it is interesting to note that the Mamluk tax on slave sales was earmarked to cover the expenses of ambassadors.[252]

Slave trading could also be combined with other careers. Before traveling to the Golden Horde as an ambassador and slave trader, Amir Sarṭaqṭāy was head of the postal service. Jānbalāṭ, who served as slave trader and ambassador to the Ottomans in 1490, became sultan himself in 1500–1501, the only slave trader known to have done so. When the mamluk Ināl Ḍuḍagh was released from prison after joining a revolt in Syria, he repaired his fortunes by traveling to Circassia and importing a group of slaves "in the manner of a trader in mamluks."[253] After selling his slaves to the sultan, he returned to Circassia for another group. Then, restored to the sultan's good graces, he spent the rest of his life in Cairo. Amir Qānim first returned to Circassia in 1426–1427 to bring his own family to Egypt; twenty years later, he was appointed *tājir al-mamālīk* to facilitate the slave trade with the Ottomans.[254] Civilians who traded slaves included

Marjan al-Rūmī, the supervisor of the Bayt Qaraja, and Muḥammad ibn Suwīd, a judge.[255] Ibrāhīm ibn Qarmash al-Qirimī, a slave trader close to Sultan Jaqmaq, was the son of another slave trader, Qarmash al-Qirimī, who worked with Sultan Barqūq.[256]

The meanings of the titles given to prominent Mamluk slave traders have been debated. *Khwājā* was the most frequently used title in the fourteenth century, and it was associated with foreigners.[257] *Khwājā* merchants dealt in various commodities, including slaves, both privately and on behalf of the state. In contrast to the network of *karīmī* merchants, who engaged primarily in the spice trade, *khwājā* traders did not form a network.[258] Some *khwājā* traders also held administrative posts, but an administrative post was not necessary to be a *khwājā*. The titles *tājir sulṭānī* (sultan's trader) and *tājir al-khāṣṣ* (private trader, trader for the treasury) appeared more rarely. Both implied agents acting on behalf of the sultan.[259]

In the fifteenth century, the title *tājir al-mamālīk* (trader of mamluks) appeared. There has been debate about whether it referred to merchants specializing in the mamluk trade, merchants acting as agents to import mamluks for the sultan, or amirs of ten charged with supervising the slave trade.[260] However, it has recently been proposed that *tājir al-mamālīk* was a new administrative post created in the mid-fifteenth century, certainly no later than the 1460s, to supervise the trade in mamluks.[261] I find this theory convincing, because the 1450s and 1460s were when the Ottomans gained control over all of the bottlenecks along the Black Sea trading routes. Managing the slave trade under those circumstances merited the attention of a dedicated official in Cairo. An earlier version of the post may have been *dallāl al-mamālīk* (broker of mamluks), mentioned in the administrative manual of Ibn Shahīn circa 1450.[262] The *dallāl al-mamālīk* could be an amir or a civilian and was grouped with other Cairo-based supervisory posts, such as the head of the postal service (*barīd*), the head of protocol (*mihmandār*), and the governor of the city of Cairo. Individuals with the title *tājir al-mamālīk* were also based in Cairo and could be either civilians (Zayn al-Dīn Naksārī) or low-ranking amirs (Ināl Ḍuḍagh, Damurdāsh, Tanibak Qarā). The title *dallāl al-mamālīk* may have been rejected because of its association with public slave brokers and fraud (see Chapter 4). The title *tājir al-mamālīk*, on the other hand, was sometimes combined with the older *khwājā* (Ibrāhīm ibn Qarmash, Maḥmūd Shāh al-Yazdī).[263]

Regardless of titles, the reigning sultan was the most important client for every Mamluk slave trader. The sultan bought slaves of all kinds in greater numbers than any other individual, and he was able to reward slave traders with public as well as private resources. He bought new mamluks (*mushtarawāt*) with his personal funds and with funds drawn from the treasury.[264] Unmanumitted mamluks of previous sultans (*kuttabiyya*) reverted to the treasury, and the reigning sultan could purchase them as well.[265] Money raised in this way was split between the treasury and the previous sultans' heirs. Records of each sultan's mamluk purchases were kept by the head of the treasury, although none have survived.[266]

As in the Italian case, some Mamluk slave traders acted independently and sold slaves to various clients, while others were agents commissioned by the sultan or an amir.[267] Sultan Qalawūn instructed his son al-Ṣāliḥ concerning the purchase of slaves from independent traders:

> When one of the slave merchants arrives, warn him about selling what is suitable for the *khāṣṣ al-sharīf* [i.e., the sultan's private property] to any of the amirs, whomever he may be. And let him expend the utmost effort possible regarding the warning about that. And when there is among them a thing [*shay'*, i.e., a slave] of excellent race, let him order the conclusion of an agreement over it [*shay'*], and the fixing of a price without delay since that is more attractive to the merchants and more conducive to achieving the goals.[268]

In other words, independent traders with excellent slaves were expected to offer them to the sultan before making them available to anyone else. This was a matter of pragmatism as well as honor; the sultan needed access to the best soldiers to maintain his power. The expectation still existed in the fifteenth century: "before one can sell [slaves], according to the laws of the country, one ought to inform the sultan first."[269] However, the sultan should take care not to antagonize independent traders, because their services were essential.

As a result, there are numerous scenes in the biographies of prominent mamluks in which their slave traders presented them to the sultan and advertised their exceptional qualities. In addition to the mamluk Baylik mentioned previously, Aqbāy was marketed directly to Sultan Shaykh and Qāytbāy to Sultan Barsbāy.[270] Independent traders taking the land route might not go all the way to Cairo to present their slaves, though. In 1406, Khwājā Jalāl al-Dīn brought a group of eight mamluks from Anatolia to Aleppo.[271] The governor of Aleppo demanded to view them and bought six. The two left over were later sold to a cupbearer of the sultan who happened to be delivering gifts to the governor of Aleppo. In the end, the leftover slaves were the most fortunate, because their master, Jaqmaq, eventually became sultan.

In contrast to independent traders, agents were commissioned by the sultan, given money to spend, and instructed about where to go and what slaves to buy. This practice predated the Mamluk era. When the Ayyubid sultan al-Ṣāliḥ

Najm al-Dīn Ayyūb heard that the Mongol conquest of Russia was producing slaves, "he sent merchants by sea with a great sum of money, and had them buy the younger of those Cumans in great quantity."[272] Under the treaty between Michael VIII Paleologus and Baybars, "agents came and went freely in the Black Sea with much gold from the prince of Ethiopia [Egypt], who brought him the maximum number of Scythian youths."[273] When al-Nāṣir Muḥammad wanted new slaves, he "called the traders to him and gave them money, and described to them what was pleasing in male and female slaves, and sent them to the country of Uzbak and Tabriz and Rum and Baghdad and other countries."[274] When he wanted new slave women, "he wrote to the provinces of Egypt to buy mulatto (*muwallad*) slave women and bring them to him."[275] In the fifteenth century, the Genoese trader Gentile Imperiale was commissioned as "a merchant on the part of the sultan to go and buy slaves in Caffa."[276] In Caffa, the traveler Pero Tafur observed that "the Sultan of Egypt has his agents [*factores*] here, and they buy the slaves and send them to Cairo."[277]

Agents were virtually guaranteed a profit by trading with the sultan's money, but they incurred the risk of his displeasure if they failed to carry out his instructions properly. An anonymous merchant who absconded with the money that Baybars had given him for buying male and female slaves in the Golden Horde was tracked down to his hiding place in the Mongol capital of Karakorum.[278] The khan of the Golden Horde, Mengu-Timur, graciously assisted Baybars in recovering him. His punishment is not recorded.

Conclusion

Merchants who decided to ship slaves from the Black Sea into the Mediterranean had to act within certain constraints. Geography, both physical and political, constrained the routes by which they could transport slaves. Seasonal weather patterns constrained the timing. States used treaties and laws to limit the number of slaves that could be shipped, the types of vessels that could carry them, and the routes they could follow. Ship captains decided whether to accept these regulations or flout them. States also used privileges to stimulate the slave trade and taxes to profit from it. Their policies influenced where and how merchants decided to sell slaves. The ability of merchants to deal profitably in slaves was also affected by freight charges, living expenses, war, piracy, disease, and slaves' resistance to shipment. Merchants acting as agents were constrained by the wishes of their principals, some of whom had precise requirements.

To make matters even more complicated, this web of constraints changed over time and affected individual merchants differently. Venice was more conservative than Genoa in its shipping restrictions, and thus Venetian merchants were more likely to find their slaves stranded in Tana at the end of the travel season. Certain merchants were exempt from customs taxes in Genoa or in the Mamluk sultanate; others were ship captains and avoided freight charges by transporting slaves on their own ships. In the 1420s, Genoa was secure enough in its dominance over the Black Sea to stop a shipment of Christian slaves by Muslim merchants. Fifty years later, the Ottomans had gained full control over the Black Sea slave trade routes and chose to cut off first the Italians, then the Mamluks. Tracking all the variations within this complex system may seem overwhelming.

Nevertheless, certain patterns emerge from this shifting web of constraints. The slave trade to Venice and Genoa was conducted by nonspecialists. Some merchants imported slaves for their own use or to oblige their friends and relatives. Others treated slaves as one among many valuable Black Sea commodities. They usually transported their slaves on mixed-cargo ships carrying up to a hundred slaves alongside other goods like cloth, spices, and alum. In a given year, anywhere from fifty to five hundred slaves changed hands in Genoa. The scale of the Venetian slave trade was probably similar.

The slave trade to the Mamluk kingdom was conducted by merchants who specialized in high-value strategic and luxury goods. Although slaves were a significant part of their business, they were not the entirety of it. These merchants also tended to have parallel careers as diplomats and administrators. They came from a variety of backgrounds: some were Mamluk subjects, some were Italian, some were Anatolian, and some came from other parts of the Muslim world. They might operate independently or as agents of the sultan. Many used Italian ships to carry their slaves to Alexandria. Their alternatives were Mamluk shipping, which declined in the late thirteenth century, or traveling overland through Anatolia, which became easier in the mid-fourteenth century. They tended to import slaves in small groups, more than two and fewer than ten. Groups of hundreds of slaves appeared more often in the context of diplomacy and royal gift giving, although the same individuals might be charged with coordinating both the small-scale trade and the large-scale gifts. Because a steady supply of mamluks was necessary for the stability of the Mamluk state, slave traders were rewarded with both profit and honor.

Because the narrative of Christian amelioration maintains that slavery has always been viewed as a moral wrong, historians have tended to assume that medieval states opposed it. It is therefore worth reiterating that all of the states involved in the Black Sea slave trade sought to encourage and not suppress it. Those with control over trade routes, such as the Genoese and the Ottomans, used their authority to tax the slave trade and protect their enslaved coreligionists from export. Those without control over trade routes, such as the Venetians and the Mamluks, shaped the activities of merchants through incentives and legislation.

State policies are what tied the Black Sea slave trade together as a system, and they can only be understood by viewing that slave trade through a Mediterranean lens. Genoa's policy of funneling all slave trade through Caffa makes greatest sense in the context of its Mediterranean rivalries, not only with Venice for commercial success but also with the Mamluks for slave souls. The Mamluk policy of honoring and enriching its most prominent slave traders makes greatest sense in the context of its competition with Genoa and Venice for the best slaves. The fact that some Italian merchants decided to sell slaves in Egypt does not mean that they were manipulating or being manipulated by the Mamluk sultan. Rather, it shows that the Mamluk incentives designed to attract merchants from all over the world, from Iraq and Crimea as well as Genoa, were successful. Chapter 7, therefore, steps back from the details of the slave trade to place it within the context of religious and political conflict in the Mediterranean.

Chapter 7

Crusade, Embargo, and the Trade in Mamluk Slaves

Christians and Muslims were in conflict with one another throughout the late Middle Ages.[1] The key to this struggle, seen as a holy war by both sides, was Egypt. During the twelfth century, Nūr al-Dīn and Saladin had successfully united Egypt and Greater Syria into a single state ruled from Cairo. As a result, the wealth and power of Egypt could be marshaled against crusaders anywhere in Greater Syria, including Jerusalem. From a Christian perspective, it thus became necessary to weaken or defeat the sultan of Egypt to protect the remaining crusader states and mount a new attack on Jerusalem. From a Muslim perspective, the sultans of Egypt were bulwarks of Islam against the crusader threat.

Christian and Muslim observers agreed that the trade in military slaves from the Black Sea was significant in this context, but they disagreed about the reasons why. Muslim observers portrayed the mamluk trade as a way to recruit souls for Islam and protect the Muslim community. Through divine providence, unbelieving slaves became believers and dedicated themselves to the defense of the faith. For Christian observers, the mamluk trade undermined the Christian cause. Renegade mamluks were not only lost to Christianity themselves but also killed Christian knights and thwarted Christian crusades.

Such views were expressed in several contexts. Muslim commentary on the mamluk trade appeared most often in narrative sources assessing the legitimacy and effectiveness of the Mamluk government. Christian commentary usually appeared in treatises on crusade strategy, a genre that proliferated between the fall of Acre in 1291 and the outbreak of the Hundred Years War in 1337.[2] Within the crusade strategy genre, two themes prevailed with respect to mamluks. One was a hope that renegade mamluks would return to Christianity and desert from the Mamluk army. The other was support for a Christian embargo against Egypt. However, popes and crusade strategists disagreed about whether the embargo should be general or limited to war materials, whether slaves should be included, and how it should be enforced. This chapter tracks the development of these two themes, the embargo and the return of renegade mamluks, in crusade strategy treatises and papal statements from the late thirteenth to fifteenth centuries.

In addition, this chapter questions how much weight should be placed on crusade strategy treatises in the study of the mamluk trade. Many historians have concluded on the basis of evidence from crusade strategy treatises that mamluks were imported by "bad Christians," unscrupulous merchants who profited by selling iron, timber, weapons, and other goods to Muslims in violation of papal and civil embargoes.[3] This contrasts with the portrayal of the mamluk trade in Chapter 6, which drew on sources from multiple genres. The comparison reveals that although many of the details provided by crusade strategists were correct, their overall depiction of the mamluk trade was misleading. "Bad Christians" who violated embargoes did exist, and some of them may have dealt in mamluks, but they were not typical mamluk traders. Therefore, although crusade strategy treatises remain valuable for studying the mamluk trade, they must be read alongside sources from other genres.

Mamluks as Slave Converts: The Fortresses of Islam

The first Mamluk sultans, heads of a newly established dynasty of former slaves, found their legitimacy as rulers and their commitment to Islam challenged by their enemies. In response, they emphasized their victories in defense of Islam against both Christian crusaders and pagan Mongols.[4] The transition to Mamluk rule had begun during the Sixth Crusade, so the Mamluks claimed credit for the defeat of Louis IX at al-Manṣūra in 1250. Subsequent sultans campaigned against the remaining crusader strongholds in Syria, culminating in the capture of Acre in 1291. This did not end the crusader threat: in 1365, Peter I of Cyprus attacked Alexandria and held it for six days. In retaliation, Barsbāy conquered Cyprus in 1426 and made the Lusignan rulers his vassals. The Mamluks also claimed credit for halting the Mongol invasion of the Middle East at the battle of ʿAyn Jalūt in 1260 and then defending the Syrian border against the Mongol Ilkhans. They also extended their protection to the holy cities of Mecca and Medina and to the caliph.[5]

The recruitment of new mamluks, essential to the political and military survival of the Mamluk state, was presented as a way to bring more souls to Islam while also protecting the existing Muslim community. This view was expressed by Sultan Qalawūn when he urged long-distance traders to import more slaves because "he [the trader] knows that increasing the armies of Islam is what impels the demand for them [slaves], because . . . whoever brings one of them has removed him from the shadows into the light. He criticizes the unbelief of his past and praises the belief of his present, and he fights for Islam, his kin, and his people."[6] Qalawūn saw the creation of a strong mamluk corps as his legacy: "all kings build something by which they are remembered, whether wealth or land. I raised walls and built protective fortresses for myself, my children, and the Muslims, and [those walls and fortresses] are the mamluks."[7]

Among the scholarly class, the political and religious legitimacy of the Mamluk state was debated.[8] Some condemned them as haughty barbarian usurpers. Others celebrated them as divinely ordained protectors. They saw it as a sign of God's providence that barbarian unbelievers could become valiant defenders of civilization and faith. God had arranged for Tatars (the Mamluks) to defend the lands of Islam against Tatars (the Mongols).[9] From this point of view, the enslavement of mamluks was incidental. As Ibn Khaldūn explained, "it was by the grace of God, praise Him, that He guarded the faith . . . by sending them from this Turkish group and its powerful and abundant tribes defending amirs and faithful protectors, who are imported from the House of War to the House of Islam in the bondage of slavery which hides grace within it . . . not for the purpose of enslavement, but to solidify their group solidarity."[10] In other words, the enslavement of mamluks was a temporary expedient, a blessing in disguise. It was a way to recruit soldiers of the highest caliber and make them complete a strenuous training program. Military excellence, not slavery, was their destiny. Thus mamluks were a class apart from and superior to all other freedmen, a class suited for rulership.

Mamluks as Slave Converts: An Imagined Fifth Column

External opponents of the Mamluks questioned their legitimacy. Mongols and Ottomans expressed contempt for them because of their former enslavement.[11] Christian observers speculated about the sincerity of their conversion. Owing to the common culture of slavery in the late medieval Mediterranean, everyone assumed that mamluks were converts to Islam. Christians, however, tended to assume that they were converts from Christianity specifically.[12] There were a few exceptions. Anselmo Adorno was correct that "it is not the essence of a mamluk that he be a Christian renegade, as others have said, but it is the substance that he be a slave practiced in the use of arms, especially in archery and throwing."[13] Joinville emphasized their eastern origin.[14] Others misunderstood the differences between mamluks, free soldiers (the *ḥalqa*), and other members of the sultan's household.[15] Nevertheless, the majority of Christian observers asserted that mamluks were Christian renegades. Arnold von Harff repeated rumors that mamluks were forced to deny Christ as well as profess Islam:

> It is said in these countries, that when a Christian becomes a mamluk, he must deny our lord Christ and his mother, and also spit on the cross, and allow a cross to be cut on the soles of his feet in order to tread on it in contempt. I say to you: no, that is not true. These mamluks, when they are first captured from Christian countries, are sold to the heathen. Then they are forced to say these words: *holla hylla lalla Mahemmet reschur holla*. In the German language that is: God is God, he shall always remain so, Muhammad is the true prophet sent from God. Then they circumcise him and give him a heathen name.[16]

There were also rumors that sultans Barqūq and Qāytbāy were of Christian origin, and female slaves were assumed to be Christian renegades too.[17] From the Mamluk perspective, this belief that *all* mamluks were originally Christian is truly bizarre. It requires explanation.

The religious ideology of late medieval Mediterranean slavery lies at the heart of this disparity between the sources. Because slaves were expected to convert to the religion of their masters, the slave trade was understood to be a trade in souls as well as bodies. Thus slavery, like holy war or missionary activity, was a way to gain souls for the "right" religion. In the context of the crusades, Christians seem to have been especially prone to view this as a zero-sum game in which any slave converted to Islam must have been lost from Christianity.[18]

This mentality was expressed most clearly by William of Adam, a thirteenth-century crusade strategist. He said that "false Christians, to the irreverence of God, offense of the church, and disgrace of human nature, both strengthen the Babylonian empire and do harm by many and unheard-of crimes by selling to the Saracens men redeemed by the blood of Christ and regenerated by baptism."[19] The word "redeemed" in this passage refers to both sin and slavery. Christian slaves, like all Christians, were redeemed from sin through Christ's death. Selling them to Muslims meant reinflicting sin on them. Just as a ransom payment would be wasted if a ransomed slave were reenslaved, so Christ's redemptive blood would be wasted if a Christian were converted to Islam. Therefore it was the sale of Christian slaves to Muslims, not the practice of slavery itself, that offended God, the Church, and humanity in William of Adam's eyes.

Christians displayed this competitive attitude in their own practices of slavery as well as in their critique of Muslim slavery. In Venice, one slave from Mali named Khayrallah, "blessing of God," was renamed Gratiadeo, "by the grace of God."[20] Another Venetian named his two Tatar slaves after characters from *La chanson de Roland*, an epic poem celebrating a fictional victory by Charlemagne over the armies of Islam.[21] Rather than naming the slaves Marsile and Baligant, the leaders of the Muslim army, he chose Roland and Oliver, the Christian heroes.

This choice positioned the two slaves as fully converted proponents of the Christian cause rather than as defeated enemies, whatever their private beliefs may have been.

This competitive attitude led many Christians to interpret the mamluk system as a plot to increase the number of Muslims at the expense of Christians specifically. According to the fifteenth-century crusade strategist Emmanuel Piloti, each Mamluk sultan had to swear that he would "buy all the creatures of the Christian faith which might be presented to him for sale."[22] Meanwhile, the papacy squandered its money on wars with fellow Christians. "The chief and head of the pagans spends his own treasure to increase and multiply the faith of Muhammad; this is the opposite of what the Roman pope does, the chief of the Christian faith, who spends his ducats to get men-at-arms to destroy Christians."[23] Even worse, Christian merchants were enticed by greed to sell Christian souls to the sultan: "The sultan had the said merchants dressed in robes of cloth-of-gold and had them ride from the castle on horses to the sound of drums, trumpets and fiddles. They go through the city, and the guards of the sultan go crying in a loud voice: 'These lord merchants have brought three hundred souls,' more or less, according to what it might be, 'of the Christian nation and faith to the sultan, and he bought and paid for them, they who will live and die in the faith of Muhammad, so that the faith of Muhammad multiplies and grows and that of the Christians thus loses.'"[24] There is no evidence for such a parade in Mamluk sources. Qalawūn and other sultans depicted themselves as protectors of Islam, built up their armies through slave recruits, and honored slave traders, but they did not seek Christian slaves specifically or parade them through the streets.

Nevertheless, the Christian consensus that all mamluks were renegade Christians had two important results. One was the Christian appropriation of Mamluk achievements. Fifteenth-century travelers to Alexandria claimed that its fortress tower had been built by a mamluk from Oppenheim.[25] Fifteenth-century travelers to Damascus were sure that its castle had been built by a Florentine mamluk and that Sultan Barqūq had been French because the walls of his *khān* were decorated with lilies.[26] Thinking of mamluks as former or crypto-Christians enabled Christian travelers to imagine them as allies in certain respects.[27] Defeat at their hands became more tolerable and respect for them more easily justified.

The other result was a dream that the mamluks might one day desert Islam and return to Christianity.[28] Travelers eagerly reported encounters with individual mamluks who had maintained their faith in secret. The fourteenth-century Franciscan Simon Simonis "participated in spiritual consolation" with the amir of Katiye.[29] The fifteenth-century Dominican Felix Fabri and Franciscan Paul Walther de Guglingen, traveling in the same pilgrim group, both met a mamluk from Basel: "he promised that he wanted to return to the Christian church because he experienced the sect of Muhammad to be bad, just as almost all mamluks speak badly of the sect of Muhammad and say they will return."[30] Fabri also met Hungarian mamluks who asked him to consecrate their marriages and baptize their children. Bernhard von Breydenbach's Hungarian mamluk guide swore that "he had not abjured the faith nor accepted circumcision, but carried his heart faithfully under Saracen clothes."[31] The most dramatic example is Theodōros Metochitēs' oration on the neomartyr Michael of Alexandria. Michael was an Orthodox boy kidnapped from Smyrna, sold as a slave, and trained as a mamluk.[32] As an adult, he contacted a Byzantine ambassador in Cairo in an attempt to reconvert to Christianity, but his plan was betrayed to the authorities. After refusing bribes and resisting torture, he was publicly executed in Alexandria.

In the crusade context, such anecdotes were used to argue that the mamluks might someday defect en masse. This idea appeared in the very first crusade strategy treatise, written by the Franciscan Fidentius of Padua for Pope Nicholas IV in 1291. He explained, "A great part of the army of the sultan of Babylon is Christian. For the sultan received boys and youths from Antioch and Little Armenia and from other Christian places, and he made them Saracens, who became good and energetic knights. It is clearly said and believed that if the Latins give them salaries, they will return willingly to the Christians, because some spark of Christianity remains in them. . . . Also by this the army of the sultan will be diminished, and it will be a work of mercy that the souls of those who were badly seduced through errors are saved."[33] Fidentius of Padua was well informed about the mamluk system. He spent much of his life in Outremer, was fluent in Arabic, and worked closely with the Mamluk command to arrange ransoms for captives from the fall of Antioch in 1268. Therefore, although he hoped for a Christian victory and the salvation of mamluk souls, he also understood that not all mamluks were former Christians and that their loyalty depended on the patronage of their former owners. He may also have been addressing the widespread belief that young Christian men were enticed into becoming mamluks with promises of wealth, power, and carnal pleasure.[34] In any case, he thought that persuading mamluks to defect was possible but would require financial as well as spiritual incentives.

Variations on this idea appeared in fourteenth- and fifteenth-century crusade treatises too. According to the anonymous *Directorium ad passagium faciendum* of 1332, the Mamluk army consisted of "purchased and captured slaves" (*servis empticiis et captivis*) of Greek Christian origin. They had been persuaded to apostatize with promises of freedom and carnal pleasure, but "they cannot entirely forget the gift of Christianity and the faith and grace of baptism which they had received before."[35] A noble Christian leader offering them protection and revenge on their former masters could convince them to hand over the Mamluk fortresses. In 1421, Emmanuel Piloti promised that if the crusaders conquered Alexandria, "all the amirs who are of the Christian nation will return and come to Alexandria" to join them.[36] In 1452, Jean Germain, bishop of Chalon-sur-Saône, assured Charles VII of France that the mamluks were all "children of baptized Christians or renegade Christians, who will return to the Christians easily."[37] In the 1480s, the Dominican Felix Fabri even heard a rumor that Sultan Qāytbāy would return to Christianity.[38] From a Mamluk perspective, the idea that the sultan and his entire mamluk corps would suddenly convert to Christianity seems laughable.[39] Yet from a crusader perspective, because of the assumption that all mamluks were former Christians, it seemed possible.

Crusade Strategy and the Slave Trade, 1290s

The loss of Acre, the last crusader foothold on the Syrian mainland, led directly to the development of the crusade strategy genre. Crusade leaders could no longer make their plans on the ground in consultation with local rulers because the entire eastern Mediterranean coastline was now held against them. Instead, individuals with personal experience of the eastern Mediterranean offered their advice in writing. Their treatises were generally addressed to the pope or the king of France, because they were the most active in planning crusades during the late thirteenth and early fourteenth centuries.

The first crusade strategy treatise was *The Book of the Recovery of the Holy Land* (*Liber recuperationis Terrae Sanctae*) by Fidentius of Padua.[40] Pope Gregory X had asked for written advice on crusading in preparation for the Second Council of Lyons in 1274. As the provincial vicar of the Franciscan Order in the Holy Land since 1266, Fidentius was well qualified to advise. However, he did not complete his treatise until early 1291. He delivered it to Pope Nicholas IV just a few months before the fall of Acre.

In his treatise, Fidentius advocated for a trade embargo against Egypt.[41] Among other benefits, it would prevent the sale of war materials and slaves to the Mamluks. Fidentius saw those two trades as distinct: war materials such as iron, wood, and arms were sold by "bad Christians," while the slave traders were agents of the Mamluk sultan: "For the sultan is accustomed to send some ships annually beyond Constantinople to the Black Sea, and cause youths of those nations which are around that sea to be bought in great quantity, whether those youths who are bought are the sons of pagans or of Christians, because they have a good and strong nature. He has them taken to Egypt, and has them become Saracens. Also he has them instructed in every exercise of fighting and riding. . . . Therefore the galleys of the Christians can impede this, so that no such youths could be brought to Egypt, and it would be a great misfortune for the Saracens."[42] Fidentius recommended a naval blockade because it would disrupt all shipping, that of the "bad Christians" and that of the sultan's agents alike. The idea that the mamluk trade was carried out by Mamluk agents on Mamluk ships during the 1280s is supported by the Byzantine–Mamluk treaty of 1263 and the oaths of 1281 discussed in Chapter 6. The generation of mamluks who captured the crusader strongholds of Syria during Fidentius of Padua's tenure as provincial vicar were probably imported in this way.[43]

After the fall of Acre, Pope Nicholas IV requested more advice on the recovery of the Holy Land.[44] This call produced two more crusade strategy treatises. Charles II of Anjou argued for a naval attack on Alexandria rather than an embargo, but the effects he anticipated were similar. If Alexandria were no longer able to receive ships, both the arms trade by "bad Christians" and the delivery of mamluks from the Black Sea would be disrupted.[45] Like Fidentius of Padua, Charles II did not connect the arms trade with the mamluk trade. The only surviving manuscript of the second treatise, addressed to Philip IV of France by his Genoese doctor, is unfortunately missing its chapters on embargo.[46]

Crusade Strategy and the Slave Trade, 1300–1312

There was a lull in active crusade planning after the pontificate of Nicholas IV, but the atmosphere changed in 1305.[47] Pope Clement V started planning a crusade with Hospitaller and Templar help, and the French court under Philip IV developed a new ideology linking French power with service to Christendom. At the same time, Charles of Valois was working toward the restoration of the Latin kingdom of Jerusalem, and James II of Aragon was preparing to attack Granada. As a result of all this promising activity, no fewer than fifteen crusade strategy treatises were written during the period from 1305 to 1312.

It was this wave of crusade strategists, especially those with ties to Armenia, who first noted a connection between the trade in war materials and the trade in slaves. The port of Ayas (Laiazzo) in Cilician Armenia had become popular with Christian merchants who wanted to buy silks and spices somewhere other than Alexandria. Armenia, a Christian kingdom, was also an unobjectionable destination for Italian shipments of slaves from Caffa. As explained in Chapter 6, because an Armenian–Genoese treaty of 1288 required the Genoese not to sell Christian slaves to Muslims and an Armenian–Mamluk treaty of 1285 required the king of Armenia to permit the export of slaves from his country, it was technically legal for Christian ship captains to import pagan and Muslim slaves from Caffa to Ayas and sell them to Mamluk merchants, who would then export them to Alexandria. However, ship captains who took advantage of this loophole would still qualify as bad Christians in the eyes of crusade strategists.

The first to make the connection between the arms and slave trades may have been Ramon Llull, a Franciscan from Majorca. Along with his famous works on conversion by preaching, Llull wrote frequently on the crusades. In 1305, he argued that a naval blockade was essential to prevent bad Christians from selling slaves to Mamluk merchants: "The Saracens, who originate in the Egyptian and Babylonian region, are neither good nor energetic in arms. But they buy Tatars or Turks and thus from other nations, whom they call mamluks, and with such as these they defend themselves. And therefore they ought not to permit them to go to Babylon in ships with galleys; for such are bought in Greece and are sold by lying Christians for gain."[48] In 1309, he proposed that crusaders disrupt the mamluk trade by reconquering Constantinople. Llull's knowledge about Christian involvement in the mamluk trade may have derived from a visit to Cyprus and Ayas, where slaves were transshipped, or from his friendship with Perceval Spinola, a Genoese noble who lived in Caffa and purchased a slave there in the 1290s.[49]

Around the same time as Ramon Llull, a true expert on trade in the eastern Mediterranean was composing his own treatise.[50] Marino Sanudo the Elder was a Venetian patrician who had conducted business in the eastern Mediterranean for years. The rulers of both Naxos and Andros were his relatives.[51] Like other crusade strategists, he recommended a naval blockade against the Mamluks. However, as a merchant, he was able to describe the most common blockade-running techniques and suggest ways to prevent them. One technique was to hide illegal trade under the cover of legal trade: "in carrying other goods that seem not to breach the ban, under this guise disobedient Christians and also Saracens who sail to Egypt and the lands of the Sultan with wood, iron, pitch and boys seek help from Christians who wish to be obedient."[52] Another technique was transshipment. Sanudo identified Candeloria (Alanya) and Sectalia (Antalya) on the southern Anatolian coast as well as Armenia and the Aegean islands as transshipment points for slaves.[53] In those places, Christian merchants "with a broad conscience" met "defrauders who come with merchandise from the lands of the Sultan" to conduct forbidden trade.[54] To stop them, Sanudo suggested banning all trade with Egypt, forbidding Catholics from living in Egypt so that the sultan could not use them as hostages, enforcing civil penalties for blockade running (such as the seizure of goods), and punishing the Christian rulers of eastern Mediterranean ports.

However, Sanudo's description of the merchants who conducted the slave trade changed between Book I of his treatise, composed in 1306–1307, and Book II, composed in 1312–1313. In 1306–1307, Sanudo said that the sultan used customs revenue from Alexandria to reward his agents, bad Christians and Muslims: "The Sultan and his emirs have this provision, namely that from the aforesaid revenue from the sea he orders special contractors (*speciales mercatores*) to buy small boys from various nations, wherever they can be obtained for money, Christian as well as pagan. These they teach and introduce to military pursuits. . . . They also bring girls, both Christian and pagan, to Egypt and the lands of the Sultan from various peoples, which they use for their carnal pleasure and which they subject to the law of Machomet to the damnation of their souls."[55] Yet, in 1312–1313, Sanudo said that the merchants were bringing slaves to Alexandria on their own initiative: "on account of this trade merchants (*mercatores*) flock there and they bring from the northern shores of the Black Sea boys and girls which the Egyptians call Mamuluchos."[56] A similar shift from agents to independent merchants appeared in the Mamluk sources examined in Chapter 6. In the 1310s, Sultan al-Nāṣir Muḥammad was offering unusually high prices for slaves to display his wealth and stabilize his power base. In both cases, Sanudo reminded his readers that the trade in enslaved girls was just as significant a loss of Christian souls as the trade in enslaved boys.

The shift from agents to independent merchants was also noticed by Hayton (Hetoum), the king of Armenia from 1299 to 1301. Having retired to Cyprus at the end of his reign, he wrote a crusade treatise in 1307 that circulated widely in both Latin and French.[57] In it, Hayton contrasted the Mamluk slave trade with that of the Ayyubids in the 1240s. In the old days, when the Ayyubid sultan realized that the Mongols were selling their captives for low prices, "he sent merchants by sea with a large sum of money, and had them buy Cuman youths in great quantity, who were brought to Egypt."[58] In the Mamluk era, however, "the greater part of the army of the Egyptian Saracens are slaves bought and sold for a price, whom bad Christians, for the love of gain, often bring to Babylon. Or else they are acquired in battles or otherwise, and the Saracens compel them to adhere to their sect and faith."[59] Like Sanudo, Hayton called for an embargo to halt the trade in mamluks.[60]

In 1308, Pope Clement V summoned a general council to be held at Vienne in 1311. The three most important items on the agenda were the crusades, the Templars, and Church reform, so Clement solicited fresh crusade proposals to guide the council's deliberations. One of those who responded was King Henry

II of Cyprus. He reiterated the need for an embargo to prevent bad Christians from selling mamluks to the sultan, but he thought that only the Hospitallers could enforce it. Venice, Pisa, and Genoa were unreliable, because "the men of these communes, as experience has taught, seize others going to the said lands [but] spare their own. Thus their own go with greater freedom and security since they don't expect capture. Then they alone carry more of the said things to the Saracens than all the others, and therefore when they go alone, they profit more."[61] In other words, the good faith of the Italian communes was compromised because too many of their subjects were bad Christians. This accusation was new: Italians had long been criticized for undermining the crusades with petty conflicts, profit seeking, and friendliness toward Muslims but not for trading in slaves.[62]

Not every crusade strategist of this period saw a connection between Italians, bad Christians, the mamluk trade, and the embargo. The Hospitallers argued that an embargo would disrupt the mamluk trade but did not explain how.[63] The anonymous author of *Memoria Terre sancte* supported an embargo so that the Mamluks "will also lose the aid of the men-at-arms who come to them daily by sea from Cumania, because all the Turks of Babylon came from Cumania for the most part by sea."[64] Peter Dubois wrote numerous crusade pamphlets without mentioning the mamluk trade at all.[65] And William of Nogaret's solution to the problem of bad Christians selling children as military slaves was to urge moderate living and military virtues among Christians so that they would no longer need or want to trade with Muslims.[66]

Crusade Strategy and the Slave Trade, 1312–1336

Although both Clement V and Philip IV died shortly after the Council of Vienne, their successors continued to plan crusades. The principal crusade strategist of this period was a Dominican friar, William of Adam. His treatise, *How to Defeat the Saracens*, was written in 1316–1318 and remained in circulation for longer than a century.[67] Spiritual and physical servitude were among its primary themes. William's preface evoked the distress of enslaved Christians forced to convert to Islam: "everyone cries together, beats your ears with inconsolable weeping, and penetrates the heavens with many inner sighs that they suffer not only this harsh yoke on their bodies but also punishment of their spirits, since they are forced to accept and practice an alien law which their fathers did not observe and to forget the Lord their creator, Whom they are forced out of bitter necessity to blaspheme and deny."[68] He explained that these weeping slaves came from the Black Sea and the Aegean and that the traders who profited from their misery were bad Christians from Catalonia, Pisa, Venice, and Genoa.

William of Adam had a great deal to say about the Genoese. Some Genoese citizens, such as Benedetto Zaccaria, were energetic supporters of Christendom. Others were its incorrigible enemies. If they could be persuaded to stop trading with Alexandria and instead become pirates in the Red Sea, their zeal for travel and profit might benefit the crusading cause.[69] At the moment, however, they harbored "the fount of sin" (*caput peccati*), the worst of all the bad Christians, Segurano Salvaygo.[70] Segurano was called the brother of the sultan, and his ships flew the sultan's banner. He might have converted to Islam. He carried messengers from the sultan to the Golden Horde and returned with slaves and other forbidden goods. He was personally responsible for delivering ten thousand boys to the Mamluks, and his bad example encouraged others to do the same.

On the basis of William's account, Segurano has become the face of Genoese slaving.[71] Benjamin Kedar has identified him in Mamluk sources under the name Sakrān.[72] Further investigation has confirmed certain of William's accusations: Segurano was close to the sultan and did serve as a Mamluk agent. He was active in the Mamluk court from 1299 to 1322–1323, except for a period of disfavor in 1309–1310, when al-Nāṣir Muḥammad began his third reign. In 1311–1312, Segurano conducted diplomatic negotiations on behalf of the Mamluks with the Genoese authorities of Chios and James II of Aragon.[73] In 1315–1316, one of his agents in Egypt, a Jew named Isaac, arranged the ransom of an English Hospitaller after thirty-four years of captivity.[74] In 1322–1323, he was executed by Uzbak Khan of the Golden Horde in retaliation for Mamluk insults to a Mongol ambassador.[75]

However, there is little evidence to show that Segurano traded in slaves.[76] Although he conducted business for the head of the Mamluk treasury, he was called "the important Frankish merchant" (*tājiran kabīran min al-afranj*) and not *khwājā* or *tājir al-mamālīk* like most mamluk traders were.[77] Members of the Salvaygo family lived in Caffa, but only one can be shown to have bought slaves. Blanca Salvaygo sold one young girl and purchased another in 1290, probably for her own domestic service.[78] One of Segurano's brothers, perhaps Ambrogio, accompanied an ambassador from Tokhta Khan to al-Nāṣir Muḥammad bringing a message and a gift of male and female slaves in 1313–1314.[79] At the time of his death, Segurano had "prepared a ship loaded with all kinds [of things] from the country of Uzbak," but there is no indication that the cargo included slaves.[80]

The most suggestive evidence for Segurano Salvaygo as a slave trader comes from 1320, when he and an unnamed companion (*rafīq*) joined a diplomatic party from Uzbak Khan tasked with delivering Uzbak's niece as a bride for al-Nāṣir Muḥammad. According to the chronicle of Ibn al-Dawādārī, a single ship carried the ambassadors, the bride, Segurano, his companion, and numerous male and female slaves to Egypt. Of the 2,400 people who traveled, 440 were mamluks. Al-Nāṣir Muḥammad bought 240 of them, and the rest went to amirs. Segurano was accompanying (*ṣuḥba*) the ambassadors and the bridal party in his capacity as a Frankish trader (*al-tājir al-ifranjī*). The sultan sent for "them" and talked with "them," and then sent for the ambassadors to sign the marriage contract. "They" had with them many male and female slaves.[81] The plural ending *-hum* means that "they" were a group of three or more. If only Segurano and his companion were intended, Ibn al-Dawādārī would have used the dual ending *-humā*. This interpretation is supported by a later reference to traders in the plural (*tujjār*) delivering the 440 mamluks. Because Segurano is described as a trader and not an ambassador in this passage, he was probably involved in bringing the slaves from Uzbak to al-Nāṣir Muḥammad. However, the use of plural and not dual grammatical forms means that Segurano and his companion were part of a larger group of traders.

The evidence for Segurano Salvaygo as a slave trader is therefore limited to William of Adam's accusations and Ibn al-Dawādārī's description of the embassy from Uzbak Khan. It is unlikely that he imported ten thousand boys. If this were true, he would have been responsible for providing al-Nāṣir Muḥammad with virtually his entire mamluk corps, according to the estimates in Chapter 6. Yet Chapter 6 also showed that Majd al-Dīn al-Sallāmī was a more important slave trader than Segurano during al-Nāṣir Muḥammad's reign. Therefore, even if William of Adam was correct that Segurano traded in mamluks, he greatly exaggerated his role.

After William of Adam, the crusade strategists of the 1320s and 1330s paid less attention to the mamluk trade. The bishops William Durand and Garcias de Ayerve did not mention slaves.[82] When King Philip VI convened a crusade planning committee in 1332, he received a treatise from the queen's doctor that did not mention slaves and an anonymous treatise that drew heavily on William of Adam but eliminated his comments on the slave trade.[83] King Edward III of England received a crusade treatise from the English Hospitaller who had been ransomed by Segurano Salvaygo's agent, but it also failed to mention the mamluk trade.[84] This loss of interest was due to a combination of factors. None of these crusade strategists were merchants, so they were probably less aware of the mamluk trade. At the same time, the Mamluks and the Ilkhans of Persia were cultivating a better relationship. This enabled the Mamluks to turn their attention to conquering Armenia, which disrupted the transshipment point at Ayas. It also enabled the Mamluks to import mamluks by land through Syria rather than by sea on the ships of bad Christians, making any Christian embargo less effective.

Crusade Strategy and the Slave Trade, 1337–1452

All plans for a crusade ground to a halt in 1337 with the outbreak of the Hundred Years War.[85] Meanwhile, the pope's authority was weakened first by uneasiness with his residence in Avignon and then, from 1378 to 1417, by schism. During this period, the center of crusading attention shifted from attacking the Mamluks to defending against the Ottomans. The form of crusading shifted accordingly from a universal Catholic movement to a league of frontier states. The league members were already well informed about the Ottomans and did not need written advice. Old crusade proposals were still copied for papal, French, and Burgundian libraries, but the only new proposal written in the second half of the fourteenth century was that of Philip of Mézières, the chancellor of Peter I of Cyprus. He did not address the mamluk trade.[86]

Criticism of bad Christians and the mamluk trade reappeared in the fifteenth century. Emmanuel Piloti wrote a crusade strategy treatise in Latin for Pope Eugene IV in 1420, and in 1441, he translated it into French for Philip the Good of Burgundy. Like Sanudo, Piloti was a Venetian merchant. He had been born in Crete, spent long periods in Egypt, and may even have read Sanudo's treatise.[87] Yet the mamluk trade had changed considerably since Sanudo's era. According to Piloti, mamluks came from the Black Sea and from Ottoman territory.[88] Those from the Ottoman markets in Adrianople and Gallipoli were Christian. Additional slaves were channeled through the Aegean and the same Anatolian ports mentioned by Sanudo, Candiloro (Alanya), and Sathalia (Antalya). They were shipped to Egypt in groups of one or two hundred by Muslim merchants (*grans marchans payens*) on their own ships or the ships of bad Christians.[89] In Cairo, they were inspected in the presence of the sultan before purchase. Sale documents were drawn up on the spot, and the merchants were paid in gold.

The Black Sea markets operated differently. There the slave traders were agents (*facteurs et serviteurs*) of the sultan rather than independent merchants.[90] The slaves, categorized as Circassians, Tatars, and Russians, were all said to be *payens*. Because Piloti used the term *payens* for both pagans and Muslims, it is not clear what he meant to say about the slaves' original religion except that it was not Christianity. Traders who wished to export slaves had to stop at Caffa, where the slaves were offered the opportunity to convert to Christianity. Those who accepted remained in Caffa, whereas those who did not were shipped by very bad Christians (*trèsfaulx et trèsmavais crestiens*) to Cairo.[91] Piloti was the first to mention this inspection regime, though it appeared again in sources from the 1420s and 1430s.

In all, Piloti estimated that the Mamluk sultan imported about two thousand souls per year from the Black Sea. This figure has been widely quoted in the secondary literature, although Chapter 6 shows that al-Muʿayyad Shaykh, the sultan during this period, imported 450–650 mamluks per year.[92] Chapter 5 discusses the head tax on slaves in Caffa. If all the tax revenue came from sales, the greatest number of slaves sold per year during the 1420s would have been 2,620 in 1425. Because some of the tax revenue came from slave possession and some of the slaves sold in Caffa were destined for Genoa, Piloti's estimate for the Mamluk trade seems high.

Piloti explained Genoa's acquiescence to the slave trade in the Black Sea as a calculated compromise: "if it were not for the necessity that the Genoese had for the city of Alexandria, they would not let any of the said slaves pass" through Caffa.[93] To break Genoa's dependence on the Mamluks, Piloti recommended conquering Alexandria rather than blockading it.[94] In the meantime, he advised a total ban on travel and trade between Europe and the Holy Land to be enforced by galleys patrolling the Syrian and Anatolian coasts.[95]

The final crusade proposal to mention the mamluk trade was that of Jean Germain, bishop of Chalon-sur-Saône, addressed to Charles VII of France in 1452. Germain made the surprising claim that the mamluks were "commonly Picts and Goths, Greek Christians, conquered by the tricks of the Genoese."[96] If the Genoese stopped raiding other Christians, the trade in mamluks would end.[97] There were Orthodox Goths in Crimea during the mid-fifteenth century, but the reference to Picts indicates that Germain knew little about the ethnography of the Black Sea. No other source suggests that the Genoese habitually raided for slaves instead of buying slaves captured by others. Moreover, Germain's interest in mamluks was behind the times. By 1452, crusade supporters were more concerned about Ottomans than they were about Mamluks.

Embargo as a Crusade Policy

The idea of a Christian embargo to deprive Muslim states of war materials and customs revenue had a long history as papal policy.[98] Although the embargo instituted by the Fourth Lateran Council in 1215 was not the first, its wording became standard:

> We excommunicate and anathematize, moreover, those false and impious Christians who, in opposition to Christ and the Christian people, convey arms to the Saracens and iron and timber for their galleys. We

> decree that those who sell them galleys or ships, and those who act as pilots in pirate Saracen ships, or give them any advice or help by way of machines or anything else, to the detriment of the holy Land, are to be punished with deprivation of their possessions and are to become the slaves (*servos*) of those who capture them. We order this sentence to be renewed on Sundays and feast-days in all maritime towns; and the bosom of the church is not to be opened to such persons unless they send in aid of the holy Land the whole of the damnable wealth which they received and the same amount of their own, so that they are punished in proportion to their offence. If perchance they do not pay, they are to be punished in other ways in order that through their punishment others may be deterred from venturing upon similar rash actions. In addition, we prohibit and on pain of anathema forbid all Christians, for four years, to send or take their ships across to the lands of the Saracens who dwell in the east, so that by this a greater supply of shipping may be made ready for those wanting to cross over to help the holy Land, and so that the aforesaid Saracens may be deprived of the not inconsiderable help which they have been accustomed to receiving from this.[99]

This embargo was reiterated by the First and Second Councils of Lyons, incorporated into canon law, and repeated in papal letters throughout the thirteenth and fourteenth centuries.[100]

Although the papacy actively promoted its embargo policy, it was the Great Council of Venice that first connected it to the slave trade. In 1292, after receiving several letters from Pope Nicholas IV about the embargo, the Great Council granted regulatory authority to the doge, his councilors, and the head of the Quarantia "concerning the pagans and slaves [who are] not to be carried by our subjects to the lands of the sultan."[101] Although this did not constitute a ban on Venetian involvement in the mamluk trade, it shows that the Venetian government saw mamluks as war materials, knew that their subjects were involved in the mamluk trade, and anticipated a need to regulate their activities. In fact, the embargo regulations were about to be loosened rather than tightened. Venice received verbal permission from Pope Benedict XI in 1304 to trade in all goods except those explicitly banned.[102]

The next move to ban the mamluk trade was also initiated by secular powers. At the Council of Vienne in 1311–1312, Pope Clement V had pushed for a new crusade and a stricter embargo. By this point, a number of crusade strategists, including Marino Sanudo, Ramon Llull, and Hayton of Armenia, had pointed out the connection between the trade in war materials and the trade in mamluks, urging the papacy to embargo both. Clement V did not adopt this suggestion, but France did so in 1312, Venice in 1313, and Genoa in 1316. In the French version, Philip the Fair added "male or female youths or orphans" to the list of goods that should not be shipped to the Mamluks and justified it by suggesting that the youths in danger were Christians from his own kingdom.[103] The Venetians copied the terms of Clement V's embargo and added mamluks: "just as it is said that no one can bring the aforesaid things (horses, arms, iron, wood or other things with which the Saracens might oppose Christians), thus it is said and laid down . . . [that no one] can bring mamluks or cause [them] to be brought to the aforesaid parts."[104]

The Genoese embargo was a much more extensive piece of legislation called the Alexandria Ban (*devetum Alexandrie*). References to the Alexandria Ban appeared as early as 1308, though the full version was issued in 1316 and revised in 1317, 1340, and 1365.[105] Among other things, the Alexandria Ban forbade Genoese subjects from transporting the war materials banned by Clement V as well as "mamluks, male or female, or other Saracens, Turks, or infidels from overseas or to any other location subject to the sultan of Babylon to Alexandria."[106] In addition, no one was permitted to transport "any male or female mamluks, Saracens, or other infidels" within the Black or Aegean Seas.[107] The penalty, enforced by the consuls of Pera and Caffa, was one hundred lire for each male slave and fifty lire for each female slave. Nevertheless, one year after the Alexandria Ban was enacted, Pope John XXII accused the Genoese of selling enslaved Christians to Muslims and even capturing free Christians to sell them.[108] His condemnation was expressed in terms of general sinfulness, though: the slave trade was still not covered by the papal embargo.

The papacy finally began to list slaves among the embargoed commodities in the 1330s.[109] However, this change was made only in permits for trade with Muslims. It was not until 1425 that Pope Martin V issued two bulls directly addressing the trade in mamluks. The first was directed against

> Jews of either sex who dwell in Caffa and Tana and other cities beyond the sea, in the lands and places subject to the authority of Christians . . . [who] buy as many persons as they can of either sex of the Circassians, Russians, Alans, Mingrelians and Abkhaz, baptized according to the Greek rite under the profession of the Christian name, and having bought them from the Saracens and other infidels. . . . They cruelly sell them and make the most exact market for them, sometimes [selling] those persons to the lands of the same Saracens and infidels, for this reason, having been led away physically, from which it follows that the Saracens and infidels themselves compel the persons sold to them to apostatize from the catholic faith.[110]

The second bull was virtually identical but addressed to "certain iniquitous children reborn in the font of baptism, despising the name of Christian, and forgetting their own welfare."[111] Jews who engaged in the mamluk trade were to be punished by the local authorities, secular and religious, while Christians were to be excommunicated. The excommunication could be lifted by ransoming the slaves who had been sold or, if that proved impossible, by donating the ransom money to churches, hospitals, or other pious foundations.

Martin V's condemnation of bad Christian slave traders may have been influenced by Emmanuel Piloti's crusade strategy treatise delivered just five years previously. His decision to address Jewish slave traders is odd, because Jews did not participate in the mamluk trade. His thinking may have been affected by canon law on slavery, which had much to say about the evils of Jewish slave ownership in contexts that had nothing to do with the Mamluks.[112] In any case, Martin V's bulls do not seem to have been enforced. There is no evidence of anyone withdrawing from the mamluk trade or being punished for it in the mid-fifteenth century. The next papal embargo on war materials, promulgated by Nicholas V in 1451, did not list mamluks.[113]

The Embargo in Practice

Historians have already shown that papal embargoes and threats of excommunication did not prevent Christian merchants from trading with Muslims.[114] The bans enacted by Genoa, Venice, and France were no more effective than papal ones. Yet their failure was not a matter of mercantile greed or apathetic enforcement. The trade in slaves and other war materials took place within a web of Christian–Muslim interactions, some hostile and others friendly. The governments of Genoa and Venice were cautious in their embargo enforcement to protect their overall political and economic interests throughout the Mediterranean. In particular, they depended on Mamluk markets for access to spices and other luxury goods from the Indian Ocean and East Asia.[115] They competed with each other for Mamluk commercial privileges, and they wrangled with Mamluk authorities over the interpretation of those privileges. The value of Mamluk privileges peaked between the mid-fourteenth and early sixteenth centuries, after the collapse of the overland Silk Road network and before Portuguese ships reached the Indian Ocean. In this context, choosing to enforce restrictions on the mamluk trade could have serious economic consequences.

In December 1303, a Venetian galley was patrolling the eastern Mediterranean to enforce the papal embargo against the Mamluks. Near Crete, the Venetian galley encountered a Genoese ship sailing from Constantinople to Alexandria with a mixed cargo.[116] To avoid confrontation, the Genoese captain entered the port of Candia. He received permission from the Venetian duke of Crete, Guido de Canale, to shelter there, but he despaired of completing his voyage in safety. Instead, he unloaded his cargo, sold it in Candia, and returned to Constantinople. The cargo included thirty-five male and female slaves. They were purchased by another Genoese ship captain named Ottobono della Volta. According to the duke of Crete, "he [della Volta], furtively and secretly, without regard for the honor which we did him [by letting him stay in Candia], bought from him some of the aforementioned slaves, both from those who had been unloaded and from those who remained on the aforementioned ship, against the established good of the Christian faith, our honor, and our ordinances and bans, which we take very seriously indeed."[117] The ordinances and bans were prohibitions on the export of slaves from Crete.[118] No papal or civil bans against the mamluk trade had yet been issued. Moreover, della Volta had not declared any intention of delivering the slaves to Alexandria. Nevertheless, the duke of Crete felt that della Volta had acted against the Christian good as well as Venetian honor. The fact that della Volta purchased the slaves secretly also implies that he knew he was doing something wrong.[119]

Having taken possession of the slaves, della Volta resold them to three different buyers. A Greek man named George purchased fifteen slaves (six male, nine female). Nicholosus, the scribe of Ottobono's ship, purchased three slaves (one male, two female). The remaining seventeen slaves were purchased by Simon of Sicily, a convert from Judaism to Christianity, and Marcus Contarini, his business partner. The numbers of slaves attributed to each buyer vary from document to document, but the total number of slaves is consistent.

When the duke of Crete was informed about the secret sale, he summoned della Volta and demanded that he hand over all thirty-five slaves from Constantinople as well as another seventeen slaves he already had in his possession. The duke also fined della Volta fifty hyperpers per slave. Because there were now fifty-two slaves, the total fine was 2,600 hyperpers. Two of the buyers, George and Nicholosus, relinquished their slaves voluntarily to the duke and were compensated. The third buyer, Simon of Sicily, refused to appear in court for fear of punishment. The duke therefore seized Simon's slaves and manumitted two whom he thought deserved freedom. They may have been Orthodox Byzantines claiming wrongful enslavement.

At this point, Simon of Sicily and Ottobono della Volta decided to resist the confiscation of their slaves. They went to the Mamluk amir of Alexandria and reported that the duke of Crete had seized a cargo of mamluks (*mamulucos*) destined for the sultan of Egypt. This was a serious allegation, and the amir of Alexandria took action immediately. He wrote first to the duke of Crete asking him to send the slaves to Alexandria. The duke replied with an explanation of the situation and the laws against exporting slaves from Crete, but the amir was not satisfied. He arrested the duke's grandson, Franciscus de Canal, who was in Alexandria as a merchant. The duke then appealed to the doge of Venice for help. He wrote that he did not believe the slaves from Constantinople were mamluks belonging to the sultan, but he also promised to carry out whatever instructions the doge sent.

Around the same time, the amir of Alexandria also wrote to the doge of Venice.[120] He explained that the slaves belonged to a merchant of the sultan named Solomon Muhammad. Solomon Muhammad had shipped them to the sultan, but the ship had been detained at Crete and the slaves confiscated. From a Mamluk perspective, this violated the treaties governing commerce between Mamluk and Venetian citizens. It was a delicate issue, because commercial relations between Venice and the Mamluks had just been renewed in 1302.[121] The amir therefore asked the doge to make amends. The implied threat was that if the doge failed to defend the property rights of Mamluk merchants, the sultan might withdraw his protection from Venetian merchants. Finally, the amir assured the doge that the good of Christianity was not at stake, because "not one of these mamluks is a Christian on account of whom you could have any occasion for reproof of your faith."[122]

The doge received two more letters about the confiscated slaves. One was a report from the Venetian consul in Alexandria summarizing della Volta's complaint to the amir and asking the doge to resolve the matter quickly. The other was a petition from della Volta against the duke of Crete. Della Volta complained that he had been fined not only for his own slaves but also for the slaves belonging to George, Nicholosus, and Simon. He protested that he had not transported their slaves anywhere, nor had they paid the freight charges that they owed him, and he was unable to pay a fine of more than 2,000 hyperpers.

The doge responded favorably to della Volta's petition. Roughly nine months after the slaves had first arrived on Crete, della Volta returned to the island with a sealed letter instructing the duke to make restitution for the confiscated slaves. The letter was formally opened and its contents executed by the duke in the presence of his own notaries and the local Genoese consul. In addition, the duke sent a letter to the amir of Alexandria apologizing for having detained the sultan's slaves and offering him 1,200 bezants in compensation. Presumably the amir of Alexandria then released the duke's grandson from prison. The fate of the slaves was not reported. They had probably been sold locally while the diplomatic incident was unfolding, because detaining them would have entailed significant expense for their food and shelter.

This incident reveals much about the early fourteenth-century trade in mamluks. It conforms to the structure of the slave trade established in previous chapters. The slaves probably came from the Black Sea and were shipped through Constantinople to Alexandria. They belonged to a Mamluk slave trader acting on behalf of the sultan, yet they were transported on a Genoese ship with a mixed cargo. The same trader dealt in both male and female slaves and shipped them together. The amir of Alexandria's remark concerning the slaves' religion is especially telling. Although he was not convinced that the laws against exporting slaves from Crete should apply to a shipment of Mamluk slaves accidentally stranded there, he did recognize that Christian rulers would be reluctant to allow Christian slaves to be shipped to Muslims and sought to reassure the doge on this point. His appreciation of the religious significance of the slave trade reflects the underlying common culture of slavery in the late medieval Mediterranean.

The behavior of the Genoese ship captain also conforms to the blockade evasion tactics described by Marino Sanudo.[123] Sanudo began his treatise a few years after this incident, and his ideas for suppressing blockade runners may have been shaped by his knowledge of it. Because Sanudo was a politically active Venetian patrician with business interests in the eastern Mediterranean, he would probably have been aware of this conflict between the Mamluks and the duke of Crete. Sanudo's first tactic against blockade runners was an absolute ban on trade with the Mamluks, so that every ship could be stopped no matter what its apparent cargo. His second tactic was to enforce civil penalties against blockade runners. In this case, neither the Genoese ship captain nor Ottobono della Volta was punished to the extent allowed by the law, and della Volta successfully protested the penalties he did receive. Finally, Sanudo suggested that Catholics should no longer reside in Mamluk territory so that they could not be used as hostages. The imprisonment of the duke of Crete's grandson was certainly effective in pressuring the Venetians to give way in this case.

Yet Sanudo's advice was never adopted because it did not serve Venice's long-term interests. The Venetian state found itself in a paradoxical situation. On one hand, Venice wanted to enforce papal policies and its own laws. On the other hand, Venice wanted a strong commercial partnership with the Mamluks and a monopoly on their trade with Europe.[124] The risks of strict law enforcement were too high compared to the benefits of a good relationship with the Mamluks. When Marcus Contarini, a Venetian patrician, was caught in Negroponte in 1316 with a cargo of slaves, he was able to claim that they were destined for Rhodes and receive a pardon from the Great Council.[125] In 1447, the duke of Crete even sent a cargo of slaves confiscated from Genoese pirates to the Mamluk sultan as a gift "in order to gratify his mind towards the favors and benefits of the Venetians who do business in Alexandria and Syria."[126]

Genoa was able to intervene in the Mamluk slave trade more successfully. Comparing the Crete incident with another disputed slave shipment illustrates why. As described in Chapter 5, Genoa established an inspection regime in Caffa sometime before 1420 to ensure that no Christian slaves were exported to Mamluk markets. As a result, in 1428 or early 1429, Genoese inspectors actually detained a shipment of slaves bound for the Mamluks.[127] As with the slaves detained in Crete, the Mamluks retaliated against Genoese merchants in Alexandria, fining them 16,000 ducats. At first, the Genoese consul in Alexandria tried to smooth over the dispute by paying the fine, but his superiors in Genoa reversed this decision and sent ambassadors to negotiate with Sultan Barsbāy. Rather than making concessions in the slave trade to protect their standing in the spice trade, the ambassadors used Genoa's leverage over the slave trade to demand concessions from the sultan. If Barsbāy canceled the fine and fulfilled other Genoese requests with regard to the spice trade, then Genoa would allow the slave trade to resume:

> Having thus obtained everything mentioned above . . . it pleases us that you grant the trade in slaves (*tractum sclavorum*) from Caffa to the sultan and his people, with them paying the customary and appointed taxes and duties, but always with the preceding declaration, namely that if any of such slaves wants to become a Christian, it should be permitted, provided that the arranged price is paid to his master in Caffa. We will write accordingly to the consul of Caffa, and we will give [these instructions] to the new consul in his orders, that he may arrange and act according to our commissions concerning the trade in such slaves. And for even greater caution, we send two additional letters with you which, when he wants, he may send to the consul of Caffa through one of those Saracens who may be going to Caffa.[128]

The implied threat was that if the sultan did not satisfy the Genoese ambassadors, Genoa could cut off the trade in mamluks permanently.

When compared with the dispute in Crete, this incident in Caffa reflects both a different era in the slave trade and a different balance of power with the Mamluks. Because of its jurisdiction over Caffa and therefore over the Black Sea slave trade, Genoa had real leverage over the Mamluks.[129] Venice did not. Yet Genoa, like Venice, had a merchant community in Alexandria that was vulnerable to retaliation, and so it had to use its leverage judiciously. Genoa, too, was caught in the paradox of trying to enforce civil and papal policies against the Mamluks while also maintaining a friendly commercial relationship. However,

Genoa's possession of a colony in the Black Sea gave it an advantage over the Mamluks, Venice, and the papacy in determining the shape of the Black Sea slave trade.

Conclusion

Neither the papal embargo policy nor the urging of crusade strategists prevented Italian merchants from engaging in the mamluk trade. This persistence was not due to their greed as "bad Christians" or to apathetic enforcement by maritime powers but rather to the broader economic and political forces at work in the Mediterranean. Venice, Genoa, and the Mamluks all recognized the significance of the mamluk trade in the context of holy war. In principle, Venice and Genoa supported the efforts of crusaders and the papacy to undermine Mamluk power. In practice, they were willing to enforce specific policies, such as the embargo on war materials, for limited periods of time. The Mamluks, however, held the trump card: access to the lucrative market in spices and other eastern goods at Alexandria.

Most (but not all) of the crusade strategists who argued for the suppression of the mamluk trade had an accurate understanding of its structure. Their descriptions of the roles played by Mamluk and Italian merchants, the importance of Italian shipping, and the preferred transshipment points evolved over time, in harmony with the information compiled from other sources in Chapter 6. However, the crusade strategists exaggerated the role of "bad Christians" like Segurano Salvaygo in comparison with Mamluk merchants and those from the Golden Horde. They largely ignored the parallel trade in female slaves and the impact of the land route to Mamluk Syria. They assumed that all mamluks were converts from Christianity, but none made a connection between the Circassian slaves sold to the Mamluks and the Circassian slaves sold in Italian markets. For all of these reasons, historians who relied on crusade strategy treatises to study the mamluk trade have been misled. This body of sources, while fascinating and useful, is not sufficient to construct a well-balanced description of the trade in mamluks.

Conclusion

In 1483–1484, a group of German pilgrims passed through Alexandria. One, the Franciscan friar Paul Walther de Guglingen, did not mention its slave market. Another, Bernhard von Breydenbach, dean and chamberlain of the archiepiscopal seat of Mainz, mentioned that "we saw the most noble objects, that is men, for sale for the lowest price."[1] The third, Felix Fabri, a Dominican friar from Ulm, reacted more strongly. In that market, "we found the most precious merchandise, which however was being sold for a low price. That merchandise was rational creatures of God, made in the image of God, people of either sex."[2] The sight of the market in human beings "whom Christ bought with his precious death" upset Fabri.[3] He described the scene in detail, criticized the insatiable desire of slave owners for ever more slaves to display their wealth, and expressed sympathy for the slaves whose own desire was to escape suffering.

On its surface, Fabri's discomfort may seem to prefigure modern attitudes toward slavery. Considered within the broader context of late medieval Mediterranean slavery, though, this interpretation is unconvincing. Slavery was legal and socially acceptable throughout the Mediterranean, in Venice and Genoa as well as in Alexandria and Cairo. It was a universal threat, a misfortune that could befall anyone; masters one day might find themselves enslaved the next. While this did not necessarily cause masters to treat their slaves more humanely, it did mean that no group of people was perceived as categorically destined for enslavement in the way that Africans came to be seen in the early modern world.

In theory, the legitimacy of slave status was based on religious difference. Christians were not permitted to enslave fellow Christians, Muslims were not permitted to enslave fellow Muslims, and Jews were not permitted to enslave fellow Jews, but unbelievers could be enslaved without question. Slaves' conversion to the religion of their masters was not only expected but used as a justification for slavery. In practice, language and race operated as a shorthand for categorizing specific individuals as enslaveable or not enslaveable. Reliance on this shorthand led to the enslavement of Muslim Turks by Muslim Arabs as well as Greek, Bulgarian, Russian, Circassian, and various other Orthodox Christians by Italian Christians. At the time, it was only the enslavement of Greeks by Italians that gave rise to controversy.

The common culture of slavery in the late medieval Mediterranean was visible in the slave trade too. Merchants imported slaves from the Black Sea to Mamluk and Italian ports in small numbers, fewer than ten per merchant. Most of them were transported on mixed-cargo Italian ships carrying up to a hundred slaves belonging to multiple merchants. At their Mediterranean destinations, slaves were sometimes sold at auction, but usually they were displayed for sale in markets, public spaces, shops, and private homes. Brokers facilitated sales and helped buyers inspect their slaves for illness and other faults, although their advice could not always be trusted. Notaries and scribes drew up contracts to finalize sales of this unique merchandise, merchandise which was able to intervene in the sale process by interacting with buyers and sellers and by acknowledging or consenting to the act of sale.

Having completed the act of sale, masters throughout the Mediterranean used their slaves in much the same ways. Slaves were financial assets that could be rented, sold, pledged, and insured. They were also social assets that enabled the master to display his or her wealth and power over others. Slaves performed manual and domestic labor. Slave women, often neglected by scholarship that assumes the archetypical slave to be male, made up the majority of slaves during this period. The exploitation of their sexual and reproductive capacities in addition to their labor power was not a matter of whim; it was an essential element of their masters' power over their bodies. Even after manumission, masters continued to exercise authority over their former slaves as patrons and frequently as employers.

Nevertheless, the existence of a common culture of slavery in the late medieval Mediterranean should not obscure the fact that there were significant differences between Mamluk and Italian practices of slavery. The Mamluk sultan and his amirs trained male slaves for military service. Elite Mamluk masters favored eunuchs as supervisors within their households. Their children by slave women were born into free rather than slave status, and their slave mothers were given *umm walad* status and a path to freedom. Italian masters did not use military slaves or eunuchs. Although there was a trend in the fourteenth and fifteenth centuries for father-masters to assume the freedom of their children by slave women, this was a deviation from the *ius commune* and did not confer any benefit on slave mothers. In the Mamluk sphere, merchants who traded in slaves on behalf of the sultan were respected, whereas those who served the public were reviled as fraudsters. In the Italian sphere, trading in slaves did not affect a merchant's reputation either way. Slaves were seen as a commodity like any other. The exceptions were Italian merchants who sold slaves to the Mamluks, opening themselves to allegations of enabling the forced conversion of Christian souls to Islam.

This much can be understood through comparison. An integrated approach, treating Italian and Mamluk slavery as two branches of a single system, is required to grasp the apparently chaotic structure of the slave trade between the Black Sea and the Mediterranean. Within the Black Sea, slaves were produced through violent capture and through sale by their relatives. They were taken to urban markets where their enslavers realized their value by selling them. No network of professionals emerged to organize those markets because the merchants who traded in slaves tended not to be specialists. Instead, states became involved, competing to ensure their merchants' access to slaves and tax their transactions. Genoa and Venice became rivals for control over Black Sea ports and shipping routes: their goals were tax revenue, access to slaves, and shipping business for their citizens. The Mamluks' chief concern was a steady supply of slaves to maintain the stability of their military and political system. They cultivated alliances with the Golden Horde, the Byzantines, and later the Ottomans so that they could import slaves securely by land as well as by sea.

The central role of religious difference in the ideology of slavery meant that state involvement in the slave trade had religious significance as well. In the hostile religious atmosphere of the late medieval Mediterranean, the Black Sea slave trade became inextricably entangled with the crusade movement. The resounding success of Mamluk soldiers against crusader armies, as well as a competitive attitude between Christians and Muslims for control over slave souls, led Christian crusade strategists to include slaves in their proposed embargo against the Mamluks. In comparison to secular powers like France, Venice, and Genoa, the papacy was relatively late to add slaves to its list of banned goods. In the case of the slave trade, the failure of the embargo was not due to apathy or corruption. In part, it was a matter of logistics. Setting aside a brief period in the early fourteenth century when the Anatolian–Syrian border was too dangerous to cross, Italian ship captains never had a monopoly on Mamluk access to Black Sea slaves. In the late thirteenth century, Mamluk merchants used their own ships in addition to Italian ones. By the mid-fourteenth century, Mamluk merchants were traveling along the land route through Anatolia as well as the sea route through the Bosporus. Yet even to the extent that Genoa and Venice were able to control the Mamluk slave trade, they were more interested in restricting it than in halting it. Italian control over Black Sea ports in the late fourteenth and early fifteenth centuries was counterbalanced by Mamluk control over the spice trade. Since Genoa and Venice were unwilling to withdraw their merchants from Alexandria and Damascus, they could not refuse the Mamluk state's demand for slaves.

What do we gain by situating Felix Fabri's reaction to the market for "that most precious merchandise" within a Mediterranean context? Despite Fabri's expressions of sympathy for the slaves in Alexandria, he did not sympathize with the slaves he encountered in Venice. The possibility of abolition never seems to have crossed his mind. To the contrary, the humanity of those "rational creatures of God" was exactly what made them precious merchandise. As rational beings, slaves could perform tasks requiring intelligence, will, and judgment. As beings created in God's image, slaves had souls worth struggling for. The prices they commanded and the services they provided made slaves profitable for merchants and taxable by states. The sensitivity of their status as human beings meant that their sale was carefully regulated and subject to the most delicate of diplomatic negotiations. In other words, late medieval slavery was not an afterthought or an aberration. It lay at the heart of Mediterranean society, politics, and religion. A complex web of slavery, captivity, trade, and ransom tied disparate parts of the Mediterranean together. While Fabri's concern for the Tatars and Ethiopians sold in Alexandria gets the attention of modern readers, it is his lack of concern for their sisters and brothers, the Tatars and Ethiopians sold in Venice, that is typical of slavery in the late medieval Mediterranean.

Abbreviations

ASG	Archivio di Stato di Genova
ASLSP	*Atti della società ligure di storia patria*
ASVE	Archivio di Stato di Venezia
BMV	Biblioteca Marciana, Venice
BNF	Bibliothèque nationale de France, Paris
BSOAS	*Bulletin of the School of Oriental and African Studies*
CPFSV	Comitato per la pubblicazione delle fonti relativi alla storia di Venezia
CRSC	Centre de recherche scientifique de Chypre
DK	Dār al-Kutub al-Miṣriyya, Cairo
HMAK	Al-Hay'a al-miṣriyya al-ʿāmma lil-kitāb
IFAO	Institut français d'archéologie orientale du Caire
IJMES	*International Journal of Middle East Studies*
IMG	Istituto di medievistica, Università di Genova
JESHO	*Journal of the Economic and Social History of the Orient*
JMEMS	*Journal of Medieval and Early Modern Studies*
JRAS	*Journal of the Royal Asiatic Society*
JSAI	*Jerusalem Studies in Arabic and Islam*
MTTTN	Al-Mu'assasa al-miṣriyya al-ʿāmma lil-ta'alīf wa-al-tarjama wa-al-ṭibaʿa wa-al-nashr
MSR	*Mamluk Studies Review*
RESE	*Revue des études sud-est européennes*

Notes

Introduction

1. ASVe, Canc. inf., Not., b.19, N.7, reg. 5, item 111. Items 95 and 106 are the two other slaves.

2. Ibn Taghrī Birdī, *Al-Manhal al-ṣāfī*, 4:275–312, no. 849; Ibn Taghrī Birdī, *Al-Nujūm al-zāhira*, 15:258; Ibn Iyās, *Badāʾiʿ al-zuhūr*, 2:198–99. Jaqmaq died in 1453, in his eighties. I estimate that he was born in the early 1370s and reached Egypt in the mid- to late 1380s.

3. Verlinden, *L'Esclavage*; Balard, "Remarques"; Gioffrè, *Il mercato*; Constable, "Muslim Spain"; Stuard, "To Town to Serve"; Evans, "Slave Coast"; Livi, *Sardi*; Lewis, *Race*; Marmon, *Eunuchs*; Fleet, *European and Islamic Trade*.

4. Attempts have been made using Latin or Arabic sources separately. Ehrenkreutz, "Strategic Implications"; Amitai, "Diplomacy"; Verlinden, "Medieval 'Slavers'"; Verlinden, "Mamelouks"; recently, Amitai and Cluse, *Slavery*.

5. This common culture of slavery originated before the thirteenth century. It is beyond the scope of this book to determine whether it emerged from shared legal and philosophical discourses (e.g., Salaymeh, *Beginnings*, 84–104), from a long history of reciprocal slave trading (e.g., McCormick, *Origins of the European Economy*; Constable, "Muslim Spain"), from parallel evolution (e.g., Patterson, *Slavery and Social Death*), or from some combination of these (e.g., Fancy, *Mercenary Mediterranean*, 53–97).

6. See Trivellato, "Renaissance Italy," and O'Connell, "Italian Renaissance," for Italy's place in recent historiography of the Mediterranean. Historians of the Mamluks have not embraced the Mediterranean framework in the same way.

7. Customs tax: ASG, BdSG, Sala 38, 1552, 1553. Sales tax: ASG, CdSG, N.185,00623, N.185,00624, N.185,00625. Possession tax: ASG, CdSG, N.185,00101, N.185,01009.

8. Friedberg, *Corpus iuris canonici*; Watson, *Digest*; Sauli, *Leges municipales*; *Liber iurium*; Desimoni, *Leges genuenses*; Thiriet, *Régestes*; Passeggieri, *Summa totius artis notariae*.

9. Holt, *Early Mamluk Diplomacy*; Sacy, *Pièces*; Adam, *How to Defeat the Saracens*; Sanudo, *Book of the Secrets*; Piloti, *Traité*.

10. Fabri, *Evagatorium*; Broquière, *Le Voyage*; Boccaccio, *Decameron*; Petrarch, *Prose*; Balard, "Giacomo Badoer"; Nigro, *Francesco di Marco Datini*; Strozzi, *Lettere*; Pontano, "De obedientia."

11. Müller, *Die Kunst des Sklavenkaufs*; Swain, *Economy*; Swain, *Seeing the Face*.

12. Ibn Buṭlān, "Risāla jāmiʿa"; Ghersetti, *Trattato generale*. Ibn Buṭlān is also known as Ibn ʿAbdūn.

13. The anonymous manual has never been published. It is available in a single manuscript, missing its last chapters and colophon, at the Dār al-Kutub. The manual of Ibn al-Akfānī (also known as al-Anṣārī) survives in a single manuscript fragment at the BNF. It has been published in Barker, "Purchasing a Slave." The manual of al-ʿAyntābī (also known as al-Amshāṭī) exists in several manuscripts and has been published as al-ʿAyntābī, *Al-Qawl al-sadīd*.

14. Al-Subkī, *Fatāwā*; al-Suyūṭī, *Al-Ḥāwī lil-fatāwī*; al-Anṣārī, *Al-Iʿlām wa-al-ihtimām*.

15. Al-Asyūṭī, *Jawhar al-ʿuqūd*; al-Jarawānī, *Al-Kawkab al-mushriq*.

16. Ibn Bassām, *Nihāyat al-rutba*; Ibn al-Ukhuwwa, *Maʿālim al-qurba*; al-Shayzarī, *Kitāb nihāyat al-rutba*. Ibn Taymiyya, *al-Ḥisba fī al-islām*, does not have a chapter on slaves.

17. Holt, *Early Mamluk Diplomacy*; Sacy, *Pièces*.

18. Little, "Six Fourteenth Century Purchase Deeds"; Ragib, *Actes*; Bauden, "L'achat." No slave sale contracts from the Mamluk period have emerged from the Cairo Geniza.

19. Ibn Iyās, *Bidāʾiʿ al-zuhūr*; Ibn Taghrī Birdī, *Al-Nujūm al-zāhira*; Ibn al-Dawādārī, *Kanz al-durar*; Ibn ʿAbd al-Ẓāhir, *Tashrīf al-ayām*.

20. Al-Maqrīzī, *Kitāb al-khiṭaṭ*; Ibn Shahīn, *Zoubdat kachf*.

21. Al-Sakhāwī, *Al-Ḍawʾ al-lāmiʿ*; Ibn Taghrī Birdī, *Al-Manhal al-ṣāfī*; Ibn Ḥajar, *Al-Durar al-kāmina*.

22. Brunschvig, *Deux récits*; Ibn Baṭṭuṭa, *Travels*.

23. Halperin, "Missing."

24. An exception is Kramarovsky, "Golden Horde."

25. ASG, BdSG, Sala 34, 590/1225–62.

26. ASG, Not. Ant. 273, 318; ASVe, Canc. Inf., Not., b.19, N.3, N.7; b.117, N.6; b.121, N.2; b.231, N.3; Balard, *Gênes et l'Outre-Mer*, vol. 1; Bratianu, *Actes*; Colli, *Moretto Bon*; Khvalkov, "Slave Trade"; Prokofieva, "Akti"; Verlinden, "Le recrutement des esclaves à Venise."

27. Tafur, *Travels*; Lockhart et al., *I Viaggi*; Lech, *Das mongolische Weltreich*.

28. Clarkson, *History*, ch. 1; Allard, *Les esclaves*, 474, 489; Yanoski, *De l'abolition*, 111; Bongi, "Le schiave," 217.

29. Bongi, "Le schiave," 216, 235; Wallon, *Histoire*, ch. 9 and 10; Biot, *De l'abolition*, 441–42; Cibrario, *Della schiavitù*, 3:264–65; Molmenti, *La storia*, 2:570; Lazari, "Del traffico," 467, 475, 497.

30. Davis, *Problem*, 13–24 vs. Miller, *Problem*, 24, 148.

31. Harper, *Slavery*, 209–14, calls it the amelioration thesis; Finley, *Ancient Slavery*, 80–85, 100–101, calls it the moral-spiritual approach. See also Glasson, *Mastering Christianity*, ch. 7; Brown, "Christianity"; Heers, *Esclaves*, 10–12; Verlinden, *L'Esclavage*, 1:7–10.

32. Marx, "German Ideology," 149–54.

33. Williams, *Capitalism and Slavery*; Genovese and Fox-Genovese, "Janus Face"; Brown, *Moral Capital*, 11–16; Miller, *Problem*, 119–62. See also Harper, *Slavery*, 4.

34. Schiel and Hanß, "Semantics," 11–13; Cavaciocchi, *Serfdom and Slavery*; Amitai and Cluse, *Slavery*, 12; Hellie, "Recent Soviet Historiography."

35. Verlinden, *L'Esclavage*, 1:14–15; Miller, *Problem*, 121–30.

36. Rio, *Slavery*; Bensch, "From Prizes of War"; Pelteret, *Slavery*.

37. McKee, "Domestic Slavery," provides a historiographical survey; Verlinden, *L'Esclavage*; Gioffrè, *Il mercato*; Williams, "From the Commercial Revolution"; Heers, *Esclaves* and *Gênes*.

38. Bensch, "From Prizes of War"; Haverkamp, "Die Erneuerung."

39. Stuard, "Ancillary Evidence"; Gillingham, "Women, Children"; Klapisch-Zuber, "Women Servants."

40. Helmholz, "Law of Slavery"; Winroth, "Neither Slave nor Free"; Gilchrist, "Saint Raymond of Peñafort"; Gilchrist, "Medieval Canon Law"; Landau, "Hadrians IV. Dekretale"; Rio, "Freedom and Unfreedom"; Weigand, *Die Naturrechtslehre*.

41. Karras, *Slavery and Society*; Pelteret, *Slavery*; Wyatt, *Slaves and Warriors*; Holm, "Slave Trade"; McCormick, *Origins*.

42. Brown, *Moral Capital*; Arnesen, "Recent Historiography"; Finley, *Ancient Slavery*; Harper, *Slavery*, 210, 320–25; Harrill, *Manumission of Slaves*, 178–82.

43. In a world where slavery still exists, historians can and should denounce it. They should also help antislavery activists understand the history of slavery and the various ways that history has shaped present discourses. At the same time, historians must also maintain their professional commitment to resist generational chauvinism: the idea that people today are inherently better or wiser than people in the past. This is especially important when past worldviews clash uncomfortably with present ones. "AHR Forum: Crossing Slavery's Boundaries."

44. Wallon, *Histoire*, 3:466; Yanoski, *De l'abolition*, 143; Biot, *De l'abolition*, 427, 429–30, 441; Cibrario, *Della schiavitù*, 3:178, 283; Heyd, *Histoire*, 2:559; Golubovich, *Biblioteca*, 3:173; Haverkamp, "Die Erneuerung," 147–48; Depping, *Histoire*, 1:57, 179, 208.

45. Brown, *Moral Capital*, 3–8, 28–29; Drescher, *Abolition*, ch. 10 and 13. See also Wyatt, *Slaves and Warriors*, 1–20, about the effects of the Christian amelioration narrative on the study of slavery in medieval Britain.

46. "Iudex non debet simpliciter iudicare secundum conscientiam, sed debet eam informare secundum allegata, et probata ad facti veritatem pertinentia." Bosco, *Consilia*, 135, cons. 78.

47. Gioffrè, *Il mercato*, Abkhaz table, 1430.

48. Epstein, "A Late Medieval Lawyer," 64. See also McKee, "Inherited Status."

49. Similarly, Wallace, *Premodern Places*, 186, expresses surprise that medieval people did not think the Black Death might be divine punishment for the Genoese slave trade in the Black Sea.

50. Talbi, "Law and Economy"; Popovic, *Revolt*.

51. Gordon and Hain, *Concubines and Courtesans*; Perry et al., "Roundtable"; Ali, *Marriage*; Schneider, *Kinderverkauf*; El Hamel, *Black Morocco*; Troutt Powell, *A Different Shade*; Zilfi, *Women and Slavery*.

52. Troutt Powell, "Will That Subaltern Ever Speak," 250. Mamluk-focused studies include Guo, "Tales"; Rapoport, "Ibn Ḥağar"; Marmon, *Eunuchs*; Little, "Six Fourteenth Century Purchase Deeds"; Ayalon, "L'esclavage"; al-ʿArīnī, *Al-Mamālīk*; Rabie, "Training"; Sobers Khan, "Slaves, Wealth and Fear"; Muhammad, "Al-Raqīq."

53. This is a vast field, but see Miller, *Problem*; Patterson, *Slavery and Social Death*; Meillassoux, *Anthropology of Slavery*; Miers and Kopytoff, *Slavery in Africa*; Hall, *A History of Race*; Toru and Philips, *Slave Elites*.

54. Pipes, *Slave Soldiers*, 63–73; and Crone, *Slaves on Horses*, 81, argue that Islamic ideas of political legitimacy caused freemen to cede the political arena to slaves, and as a result, they judge Islam negatively. But military slavery has been practiced in non-Muslim societies: Miller, *Problem*, 53; Bernand and Stella, *D'Esclaves a soldats*; Freed, "Origins"; Arnold, "German Knighthood"; Keupp, *Dienst und Verdienst*. More nuanced analyses of military slavery in specific Muslim societies include Mazor, *Rise and Fall*; Gordon, *Breaking of a Thousand Swords*; Toru and Philips, *Slave Elites*; Ali, *Malik Ambar*.

55. Rabbat, "Changing Concept," 89–90; Crone, *Slaves on Horses*, 78–79, 622n. The claim in Pipes, *Slave Soldiers*, 18–21, that military slaves manumitted themselves informally is incorrect.

56. Ayalon, "L'Esclavage"; al-ʿArīnī, *Al-Mamālīk*; Rabie, "Training."

57. Drescher, *Abolition*, 275–77, 380–86; Troutt Powell, *A Different Shade*, ch. 4.

58. El Hamel, *Black Morocco*, 17–55; Okeowo, "A Mauritanian Abolitionist's Crusade"; vs. Trabelsi, "Memory"; Mirza, "Remembering," 304; Zilfi, *Women and Slavery*, ch. 4; Toledano, *As If Silent and Absent*, ch. 1.

59. Middle East Media Research Institute, "Islamic State"; "Open Letter," sec. 11 and 12.

60. "AHR Forum: Crossing Slavery's Boundaries." Examples include Rosenthal, *Muslim Concept*, 33; Mez, *Renaissance of Islam*, 156; Mukhtar, *Bughiyyat al-murīd*, 102.

Chapter 1

1. Sigmund, *St. Thomas Aquinas*, 38–39; Minnis, *From Eden*, 114–17.

2. Minnis, *From Eden*, 134.

3. Rustomji, *Garden*, 91–96.

4. Rustomji, *Garden*, 111–15; Rustomji, "Are Houris Heavenly Concubines?"

5. Antoninus, *Summa*, title 3, ch. 6, part iv; Rotman, "Captif ou esclave?"; Hershenzon, "Towards a Connected History," 2; Kosto, *Hostages*, 11–14, 163–98.

6. Bensch, "From Prizes of War," 67–74; Hershenzon, "Towards a Connected History," 3–4, characterizes proximity and hope of ransom as unique to the Mediterranean system of bondage, but his survey is limited to the western and central Mediterranean.

7. Sobers Khan, *Slaves Without Shackles*, 126; Friedman, *Encounter Between Enemies*; Dursteler, *Venetians in Constantinople*, 72–77; Dávid and Fodor, *Ransom Slavery*; Arbel, "Slave Trade," 158; Lyons and Lyons, *Ayyubids*, 2:104–5, 113, 133; Kizilov, "Slaves."

8. Nevertheless, ransomed captives returning home were often suspected of conversion. Bensch, "From Prizes of War," 70–74, 81–83.

9. Perry, "Conversion," 135.

10. Brunschvig, "ʿAbd"; El Hamel, *Black Morocco*, 21–36.

11. Passeggieri, *Summa totius artis notariae*, fols. 411r–415v. The others were gender (male, female, hermaphrodite); birth (born, about to be born); legal capacity (empowered, under another's power); birth status (legitimate, natural, neither); and age (adult, child).

12. Monleone, *Iacopo da Varagine*, 212. See also Antoninus, *Summa*, title 3, ch. 6, parts iv–vi for the fifteenth century. In part iii, he explained that *servi* of God, sin, or a lord or jurisdiction were not "properly or strictly" *servi*.

13. Siraisi, "*Libri morales*," 113; Fioravanti, "Servi, rustici, barbari," 405.

14. Epstein, *Speaking*, 18–19; Haverkamp, "Die Erneuerung," 140; Constable, "Muslim Spain," 271.

15. Stuard, "Ancillary Evidence," 8.

16. Balletto, "Schiavi," 661; Pontano, "De obedientia," 204.

17. Helmholz, "Law of Slavery," B; Rio, *Slavery*; Gilchrist, "Saint Raymond," 304–6.

18. Gillingham, "Women, Children," 68.

19. Bellomo, *Common Legal Past*, 152–54.

20. Friedberg, *Corpus iuris canonici*; Ordinary Gloss in Kelly, "Corpus Juris Canonici." Canon law compilations after the *Liber extra* say little about slavery. A helpful introduction is Brundage, *Medieval Canon Law*.

21. Nielsen, *Secular Justice*, 46, 95.

22. Ali, *Marriage*, analyzes legal analogies between slavery and marriage. Schneider, *Kinderverkauf*, is devoted to child sale and debt slavery. Heffening, "Zum Aufbau," discusses slavery and *furūʿ al-fiqh*.

23. Brunschvig, "ʿAbd," 3a; Helmholz, "Law of Slavery," A; Rosenthal, *Muslim Concept*, 31–32; Weigand, *Die Naturrechtslehre*, 64–65; Pahlitzsch, "Slavery," 163–64; *Corpus iuris canonici*, C.12 q.2 c.68; X.3.19.3 gloss on *commutari*; X.4.9.3 gloss on *favore libertatis*; X.5.11.1.

24. Varkemaa, *Conrad Summenhart*, 88.

25. "Restituens eos natalibus antiquis, & iuri ingenuitatis, et denuncians eos cives Roma. atque restituens eos iuri primęvo secundum quem omnes homines liberi nascebantur." Passeggieri, *Summa totius artis notariae*, fols. 179r–180r and gloss.

26. "حراً من أحرار الملسمين، له ما لهم وعليه ما عليهم." Al-Asyūṭī, *Jawhar al-ʿuqūd*, 2:533.

27. "Omnes, tam servi quam liberi, de terra sunt creati et nudi et plorando nati . . . omnes, tam liberi quam servi, eundem locum habent scilicet eundem mundum, eandem terram, eundem aerem . . . omnes, tam liberi quam servi moriuntur, in cinerem resolvuntur et putrescunt . . . omnes, tam liberi quam servi, habent unum Dominum . . . omnes, tam liberi quam servi, ad iudicium Dei venient." Monleone, *Iacopo da Varagine*, 213–15.

28. Marmon, "Domestic Slavery," 1–2.

29. "Si dominus iubet ea, que non sunt contraria sacris scripturis, subiciatur domino seruus. Sin uero contraria precipit, magis obediat spiritus quam corporis domino." *Corpus iuris canonici*, C.11 q.3 c.93.

30. Brunschvig, "ʿAbd," 3d; Helmholz, "Law of Slavery," C3; *Corpus iuris canonici*, X.1.18.

31. Johansen, "Valorization," 91; Helmholz, "Law of Slavery," C3; Gilchrist, "Saint Raymond," 322.

32. Rosenthal, *Muslim Concept*, 81–92; Epstein, *Speaking*, 20–21; Antoninus, *Summa*, title 3, ch. 6.

33. Minnis, *From Eden*, 285–86n144; Helmholz, "Law of Slavery," A; Epstein, *Speaking*, 141; *Corpus iuris canonici*, C.12 q.2 c.68; dictum Gratiani on C.33 q.3 d.4 c.12. Augustine argued that neither sin nor slavery was natural to humanity. Killoran, "Aquinas and Vitoria," 88, 92. Guy of Rimini argued that the idea of natural slavery violated the Golden Rule and natural love. Dunbabin, "Reception," 728.

34. Genesis 16 and 21, esp. 21:10; Williams, "From the Commercial Revolution," 56; *Corpus iuris canonici*, D.47 c.9; D.56 c.9; C.32 q.2 c.12 and q.4 c.2.

35. Exodus; Gilchrist, "Saint Raymond," 310; Epstein, *Speaking*, 22; *Corpus iuris canonici*, C.1 q.4 c.11; C.23 q.5 c.49; X.5.6.13 gloss on *libera* and *ancilla*; Simeonis, *Itinerarium*, 55.

36. Genesis 9–10; Antoninus, *Summa*, title 3, ch. 6, part iii; Glasson, *Mastering Christianity*, 44–45; Braude, "Sons of Noah"; Gilchrist, "Saint Raymond," 302.

37. El Hamel, *Black Morocco*, 18–20.

38. Rosenthal, *Muslim Concept*, 30–32, 91.

39. Dunbabin, "Reception," 723–37; Fioravanti, "Servi, rustici, barbari," 403; Siraisi, "*Libri morales*," 113, on the pseudo-Aristotelian *Economics*.

40. Fioravanti, "Servi, rustici, barbari," 405–25.

41. Minnis, *From Eden*, 98.

42. Brunschvig, "ʿAbd," 2b; Helmholz, "Law of Slavery," A, C4; Pahlitzsch, "Slavery," 163–64; Monleone, *Iacopo da Varagine*, 212–15; Antoninus, *Summa*, title 3, ch. 6, parts iii–x; Passeggieri, *Summa totius artis notariae*, gloss on fol. 412r–v; Masi, *Formularium florentinum*, 10; Roberti, *Un formulario inedito*, 85; *Corpus iuris canonici*, D.1 c.9; D.8 c.1; C.3 q.7 c.1, dictum Gratiani and gloss on *moribus*; X.1.3.13; X.5.40.10.

43. Brunschvig, "ʿAbd," 3a; Borkowski and du Plessis, *Textbook*, 94; Thomas, *Textbook*, 392–93; Gilchrist, "Saint Raymond," 323–24; Antoninus, *Summa*, title 3, ch. 6, part iii; Passeggieri, *Summa totius artis notariae*, fol. 412r–v; *Corpus iuris canonici*, D.1 c.7; C.15 q.8 c.3 gloss on *ingenuae, hereditatem*; C.32 q.3 c.1; C.32 q.4 c.9 gloss on *nec sanguinis*; X.1.18.8; X.4.10.1.

44. Schneider, *Kinderverkauf*. See also Little, *A Catalogue*, 380, doc. 683.

45. Borkowski and du Plessis, *Textbook*, 91; Varkemaa, *Conrad Summenhart*, 94–101; *Corpus iuris canonici*, C.29 q.2 c.7 gloss on *divortii*; X.3.21.2 gloss on *lex*.

46. Passeggieri, *Summa totius artis notariae*, fols. 412r–v, 434r, allowed self-sale for persons over age twenty, aware of their free status, consenting to sale, and receiving a share of the price. See also Salatiele, *Ars notariae*, 1:19, 2:16, 2:116; Antoninus, *Summa*, title 3, ch. 6, part iv; Gigli, *I sermoni evangelici*, 95.

47. Borkowski and du Plessis, *Textbook*, 92; *Corpus iuris canonici*, D.32 c.10; D.34 c.7; D.35 c.8; D.81 c.30 gloss on *et venundentur*; C.15 q.8 c.3; C.32 q.2 c.11; C.32 q.4 c.9; C.36 q.1 c.3; Cossar, "Clerical 'Concubines,'" 115–16; Antoninus, *Summa*, title 3, ch. 6, part iv.

48. Brunschvig, "ʿAbd," 3b; *Corpus iuris canonici*, C.1 q.3 c.6; C.12 q.2 c.67; X.3.19.4.

49. Salatiele, *Ars notariae*, 1:156–58; Ibn al-Ukhuwwa, *Maʿālim al-qurba*, ch. 41; al-Qalqashandī, *Subḥ al-aʿshā*, 4:32.

50. Brunschvig, "ʿAbd," 3e, 3g; Rosenthal, *Muslim Concept*, 25–26; Marmon, "Domestic Slavery," 3; Ali, *Marriage*, 8, 192; Helmholz, "Law of Slavery," C; *Corpus iuris canonici*, C.3 q.5 c.8 and c.11; C.3 q.11 c.4; C.6 q.1 c.17; C.13 q.2 c.5 and gloss; C.32 q.2 c.12; C.32 q.4 c.9; C.33 q.3 d.1 c.19; X.2.20.45; X.3.49.6; X.4.9.2; X.5.3.7; X.5.38.2; X.5.40.10 gloss on *si liber*.

51. *Ma'dhūn* status. Brunschvig, "ʿAbd," 3h; Marmon, "Domestic Slavery," 6.

52. Patterson, *Slavery and Social Death*, 37.

53. Fynn-Paul, "Empire," 4–5; Fancy, *Mercenary Mediterranean*, 72–74; Verlinden, *L'Esclavage*, 1:18–21; Pahlitzsch, "Slavery," 164.

54. Schneider, *Kinderverkauf*, 14; Perry, "Daily Life," 5, 23.

55. *Corpus iuris canonici*, D.54 c.13, X.5.6; Glancy, "To Serve Them All the More," 38–41; Blumenthal, *Enemies and Familiars*, 13–17.

56. Gioffrè, *Il mercato*, 54–56.

57. Except Muslims in the crusader states or Greeks in Sicily. Verlinden, "Orthodoxie," 441–43; Kedar, *Crusade*, 212.

58. Friedman, *Tolerance and Coercion*, 106–20.

59. Schiel, "Slaves' Religious Choice," 36–37, 42–44.

60. "No dee esser libero chi non crede nella ricomperazione di Cristo . . . la maggior parte sono come a battezzare buoi. E non si intende pure per lo battesimo essere cristiano; e non se' tenuto di liberarlo, benchè sia cristiano, se non vuogli. Non dico, che se il vedi buono e che abbia voglia d'essere buono cristiano, che tu non facci mercè di liberarlo; e così faresti male e peccato, avendo schiavo o

schiava di rea condizione, come la maggior parte sono, benchè fosse cristiano, di liberarlo." Gigli, *I sermoni evangelici*, 94–95, sermon 29; Stuard, "To Town to Serve," 46. See also Glancy, "To Serve Them All the More"; Antoninus, *Summa*, title 3, ch. 6, part iii.

61. Zilfi, *Women and Slavery*, 207–8.

62. Chrissis, *Crusading in Frankish Greece*, 262–67; Carr, *Merchant Crusaders*, 17–31; Fleet, *European and Islamic Trade*, 37–58; Pahlitzsch, "Slavery," 164–65; Verlinden, "Le recrutement des esclaves à Venise," 87–89; Jorga, "Notes et extraits," 8 (1900): 102–3.

63. Köpstein, *Zur Sklaverei*, 60.

64. Talbot, *Correspondence*, 97, doc. 46.

65. "Aliqui ianuenses induzerunt aliquos pueros et puellas grecas de Constantinopoli et de aliis terris Romanie, promittentes eis multa bona facere, ut cum eis Januam venirent; et multi et multe venerunt et cum fuerunt in civitate Janue vendiderunt eos et eas pro sclavis, quod est iniquum." Belgrano, "Prima serie," 113, 115; Laiou, *Constantinople and the Latins*, 184–85.

66. Laiou, *Constantinople and the Latins*, 273.

67. "Ut omnes Graeci, qui fuerunt venditi a Latinis ubicumque sunt, liberentur, et de caetero ut non vendantur Graeci, et si quidam vendiderint vel emerint eos, vel vadant contra eos, sint excommunicati." Raynaldus, *Annales ecclesiastici*, 25:161–62, no. 24.

68. Hoade, "Itinerary of an Anonymous Englishman," 60; Golubovich, *Biblioteca*, 4:447.

69. "Li Greci portano maggiore odio a noi Latini che alli Saracini, e per lo grande odio sono partiti dalla Chiesa Romana; e come noi facciamo della Chiesa di Roma capo per li Cristiani el Papa, vicario di Dio, così li Greci fanno vicario per loro, in quel luogo del Papa, sì fanno lo Patriarca di Constantinopoli; e costui fa li vescovi . . . Ogni domenica si communica lo Papa, con tutti quelli che l'ubidiscono; ma lo Papa sì fa questo a loro, ch'elli sì concede che altri gli pigli, e poi sì gli venda per ischiavi. E io più volte vidi gli mercatanti che n'avevano una grande schiera, e così gli menavano a vendere al mercato, a modo come fussono bestie; e quando lo mercatante se ne vuole spacciare di questa trista mercatanzia, sì gli fa gridare al banditore; e chi più danari ne profera, a colui sono venduti. O Greci, che fusti signori del mondo, e ora siete fatti schiavi, rivenduti per lo mondo, aprezzati a modo di bestie!" Poggibonsi, *Libro d'Oltramare*, 146. In Poggibonsi, *A Voyage*, 124, the editors suggest that it was the negligent patriarch of Constantinople who allowed his people to be enslaved. I interpret the passage to mean that the Roman pope did not protect Greeks because he was not in communion with them.

70. William of Adam, *How to Defeat the Saracens*, 44–45 for Greek intransigence, 80–81 for Greek slaves' suffering.

71. "De nacione Grecorum seu qui fuerint Ermines, Albanesos, Rossos, Bugros, Bloschs vel de partibus aut regionibus Constantinopolitano imperatori subiectis." Verlinden, "Orthodoxie," 434–37. See also Ferrer i Mallol, "Esclaus i lliberts," 174–88.

72. Thiriet, *Régestes*, doc. 1697; ASVe, Senato, Deliberazioni, Misti, reg. 52, fol. 96r. A Greek slave was definitely sold in Modon in 1363. ASVe, Canc. inf., Not., b.19, N.3, fol. 8r.

73. Blumenthal, *Enemies and Familiars*, 34–35; Delort, "Quelques précisions," 223; Tomassetti, *Bullarum diplomatum*, 5:130–32.

74. Broquière, *The Voyage*, 95; Broquière, *Le Voyage*, 149.

75. Barker, "Christianities in Conflict," 52–57.

76. Preiser-Kapeller, "Zwischen Konstantinopel und Goldener Horde," 200; Jaimoukha, *Circassians*, 148–49; Zevakin and Penčko, "Ricerche," 88; Lemercier-Quelquejay, "Cooptation," 22–24; Allen, *A History*, 132.

77. Zevakin and Penčko, "Ricerche," 83; Richard, *La papauté*, 230–55. Origo, "Domestic Enemy," 360n22; and Gioffrè, *Il mercato*, 24, interpreted this letter to mean that Circassians had adopted Christianity en masse.

78. Jaimoukha, *Circassians*, 137–50; Allen, *A History*, 119. Christian churches and cemetaries were in use throughout the late medieval period. Kouznetsov and Lebedynsky, *Les chrétiens disparus*, 38.

79. Kouznetsov and Lebedynsky, *Les chrétiens disparus*, 38; and Ibn Baṭṭuṭa, *Travels*, 516, on the existence of Christian Turks. Vasiliev, *Goths*, 175, dismisses these reports.

80. Ruthenians shifted from the Greek to the Latin rite in the late fourteenth century. Subtelny, *Ukraine*, 55–74.

81. Tafur, *Travels*, 147; Broquière, *The Voyage*, 98.

82. Kern, "Der 'Libellus de notitia orbis,'" 106; Marino, *El Libro*, 107. Vasiliev, *Goths*, 219–21, is skeptical.

83. Gioffrè, *Il mercato*, Goth table; Argenti, *Occupation*, 1:625 and 3:627–28, 658, docs. 168, 221; Balletto, "Schiavi," 664–65, 667–68, 678; Heers, *Gênes*, 656; Balard, *Gênes et l'Outre-mer*, 2:51–52, doc. 17; ASG, BdSG, Sala 34, 590/1233, fols. 138r, 186r.

84. Bongi, "Le schiave," 220; Haverkamp, "Die Erneuerung," 138; Gioffrè, *Il mercato*, 21; Fynn-Paul, "Empire," 35–37; Heyd, *Histoire*, 2:560; Balard, *La Romanie*, 2:793–94, 797.

85. Northrup, "Military Slavery," 120; Haarmann, "Ideology," 183; Ayalon, "Mamlūkiyyāt," 338.

86. Ayalon, "L'esclavage," 22; Ayalon "Mamlūk Novice," 6; Heyd, *Histoire*, 2:555. Other cases of Muslims enslaving Muslims appear in Brunschvig, "ʿAbd," 3a; El Hamel, *Black Morocco*, 9; Mez, *Renaissance of Islam*, 158–59; al-ʿArīnī, *Al-Mamālīk*, 129–30; Fancy, *Mercenary Mediterranean*, 116.

87. Al-Qalqashandī, *Subḥ al-aʿshā*, 4:456–58; Ibn Baṭṭuṭa, *Travels*, 472, 495, 516; *Al-Maqṣad al-rafīʿ*, fols. 265r, 266v–267r; al-Maqrīzī, *Kitāb al-khiṭaṭ*, 3:694; al-ʿAyntābī, *Al-Qawl al-sadīd*, 56; *Al-Taḥqīq fī shirāʾ al-raqīq*, fol. 41; Ibn Shaddād, *Tārīkh al-malik*, 127.

88. Ibn Taghrī Birdī, *Al-Manhal al-ṣāfī*, 4:68, no. 769; al-Sakhāwī, *Al-Ḍawʾ al-lāmiʿ*, 3:33–34, no. 143.

89. Al-Sakhāwī, *Al-Ḍawʾ al-lāmiʿ*, 10:289–90, no. 1134; al-Maqrīzī, *Kitāb al-khiṭaṭ*, 4:159.

90. Herzog, "First Layer," 139.

91. Ayalon, "Names," 211, argues that this patronymic concealed slaves' non-Muslim fathers.

92. Al-Subkī, *Fatāwā*, 2:281–85.

93. Lewis, *Race*, 57–58; Hunwick, "Islamic Law and Polemics," 43–68.

94. *Corpus iuris canonici*, D.54 c.13; X.5.6.1; X.5.6.4; X.5.6.19; Passeggieri, *Summa totius artis notariae*, fol. 434r; Antoninus, *Summa*, title 3, ch. 6, part v; Perry, "Conversion," 135–38.

95. William of Adam, *How to Defeat the Saracens*, 80–81. See also Gregory X's letter of 1272 castigating the Genoese for enabling the Mamluks to capture Christians, separate children from their mothers, and force them to convert. These were not Christians from the Black Sea though. Tomassetti, *Bullarum diplomatum*, 4:11–13.

96. William of Adam, *How to Defeat the Saracens*, 82–83.

97. William of Adam, *How to Defeat the Saracens*, 24–25. This attitude reinforced medieval crusade and missionary movements. Bensch, "From Prizes of War," 83; Fisher, "Muscovy," 585.

98. Tafur, *Travels*, 133; Tafur, *Andaças*, 162.

99. "Apud nos & christiani serviunt. Nam ut de maioribus accepi Thraces quoque & Graecos qui pontum incolerent venundari mos fuit: qui ne servitia barbarorum essent, mercatores Euxinum navigantes, redemptos illos a Scytis, venales faciebant. Honestius enim visum est tantisper servire eos, dum solutam pro capite suo pecuniam rependerent, quam praedam esse barbarorum perpetuaeque obnoxios servituti, cum maximo etiam Christiani nominis opprobrio. . . . Haec igitur tanta humani generis iniuria, ius gentium effectum est." Pontano, "De obedientia," 201–2.

100. Heers, *Jacques Coeur*, 137–39.

101. The Bulgars mentioned here were mercenaries. Makhairas, *Recital*, 1:464–67; Arbel, "Slave Trade," 163; Dincer, "Enslaving Christians," 7. The biblical reference is Deut. 15:12.

102. Melichar, "God, Slave, and a Nun."

103. Bongi, "Le schiave," 132–35; Costamagna, *Il notaio*, 104–5, 109; Petrucci, *Notarii*, 36.

104. For Genoa, see Sauli, *Leges municipales*; *Liber iurium*; Desimoni, *Leges genuenses*. For Venice, see Verlinden, "La législation," 2:147–72.

105. "Intelligantur . . . sclavi et sclave illi qui per aliquam personam, tamquam sclavi vel sclave possessi fuerint seu detempti." Desimoni, *Leges genuenses*, 937–38.

106. Sauli, *Leges municipales*, 373.

107. "Que teneatur et habeatur pro sclava per dominum vel dominam ipsius. Et que reputetur et habeatur pro sclava a vicinia dicti domini vel domine." Desimoni, *Leges genuenses*, 951–52.

108. Verlinden, "La législation," 165. In an exceptional case, the juridical manumission of two slaves was arranged through a complaint to the Signori di Notte. Lockhart et al., *I Viaggi*, 89.

109. "Que leviter vendite sunt et vendi possent et tractari pro sclavis, quod esset pessime factum et contra Deum et honorem nostri dominii . . . quia sunt christiani, et non vendere nec vendi facere eas ullo modo." Verlinden, "La législation," 154.

110. Verlinden, "La législation," 162.

111. Verlinden, "La législation," 157.

112. "Rustice et rudis intellectus . . . nulla utilitas nec proficuum ex eis sequi possit." Verlinden, "La législation," 157–58.

113. Verlinden, "La législation," 159.

114. Tria, "La schiavitù," 223–24, doc. 91. Doc. 88 is similar.

115. Corrao, *Acta curie*, 77–78.

116. Gioffrè, *Il mercato*, Greek table; Verlinden, "Orthodoxie," 451; Barker, "Christianities in Conflict," 61–63.

117. "Maria ungara constituta in iure et in presentia spectabilium dominorum Sindicatorum comunis Ianue." Tria, "La schiavitù," 207–8, doc. 75.

118. "Dictam Mariam fuisse et esse Ungaram et Christianam et per consequens liberam et francham, retinereque non posse pro serva, immo pro libera et francha habendam esse et haberi debere." Tria, "La schiavitù," 207–8, doc. 75.

119. In theory, a Christian slave sold illegally should be declared free and the owner should be compensated by the seller. Antoninus, *Summa*, title 3, ch. 6, part v. In Valencia, slaves were sold with a warranty that they were "catiu de bona guerra," captives from a good war. Pirates who took slaves illegally were executed. Blumenthal, *Enemies and Familiars*, 20–21, 33. In Perpignan, slaves were sold with a warranty "non fuit de palia domini regis," that they were not subjects of the king of Aragon. Winer, *Women*, 136.

120. Tria, "La schiavitù," 208–9, doc. 76.

121. "Ad locandum et pensionandum ipsam Mariam in civitate Ianue illi vel illis persone vel personis bone condicionis et fame et pro ea mercede et precio quo melius haberi potuerit." Tria, "La schiavitù," 210–11, doc. 78. Benedicta, a Hungarian slave woman, paid her compensation by working as a wet nurse. Cluse, "Frauen," 94–95.

122. "Quod cristiani non possunt vendi nec obligari." ASG, Not. Ant. 1279, doc. 514.

123. Gioffrè, *Il mercato*, Moor table (1487).

124. "Se esse christianam ac liberam et pro libera se gerens et de progenie Ungarorum que vendi non potest pro sclava tam de iure quam ex forma ordinamentorum civitatis Janue." Tria, "La schiavitù," 189–90, doc. 59.

125. Balard, *La Romanie*, 2:798 (Georgius); Gioffrè, *Il mercato*, Hungarian table (Elena); Tria, "La schiavitù," 207–8, doc. 75 (Caterina). Appeals by Catholic Sards from Sardinia fall before the chronological range of this project. Livi, *Sardi*.

126. "Dictum sclavum se presentasse in Syo coram domino potestate Syi in eius curia, asserens se esse christianum ab nacione catolicum et nunquam fuisse sclavum ymo liberum, francum et hominem sui iuris. Qui dominus potestas Syi, visis testibus productis per dictum sclavum liberavit ipsum." Balard, *Notai genovesi in Oltremare: Atti rogati a Chio*, 126–28, doc. 43.

127. Gioffrè, *Il mercato*, Armenian table.

128. Gioffrè, *Il mercato*, Albanian table (Anastasia, Magdalena).

129. "Francham et liberam et natam a parentibus liberis et de progenie christianorum et propterea non posse nec debere in servitute detineri." ASG, Not. Ant. 1279, doc. 379; Gioffrè, *Il mercato*, Albanian table (1483, 1482).

130. Tria, "La schiavitù," 213–14, doc. 81.

131. Bongi, "Le schiave," 222. I have not seen the original source.

132. Greek slaves also contested their status successfully in Valencia. Blumenthal, *Enemies and Familiars*, 36–40.

133. "Ex grecis parentibus sit procreata." ASG, Not. Ant. 403, fols. 192v–193r.

134. "Vendi nec emi minusque retineri pro sclava ut iuri et equitati consuevit . . . ne anima dicti quondam Ilarii propter huiusmodi retentionem patiatur." Gioffrè, *Il mercato*, 41, without citation.

135. Tria, "La schiavitù," 169, 217–18, docs. 39, 84 (Genoa); Balard, *La Romanie*, 2:797 (Caffa).

136. "Quod omnes Greci liberi sint et pro liberis habeantur et tractentur in civitate Ianue et districtu." Balard, *La Romanie*, 1:304.

137. Balard, "Les genois et les regions bulgares," 96.

138. Gioffrè, *Il mercato*, 46–47.

139. Barker, "Christianities in Conflict," 61–63.

140. Gioffrè, *Il mercato*, 24, Mingrelian table (1479), Abkhaz table (1487).

141. Little, "Two Fourteenth-Century Court Records," 28–47, in Jerusalem. For Ayyubid-era cases, see Perry, "Conversion," 144–48, in Cairo and Perry, "Daily Life," 23, in ʿAydhāb.

142. Ibn Taghrī Birdī, *Al-Manhal al-ṣāfī*, 3:143–51, no. 588. See also nos. 769, 782, 784; Popper, "Egypt and Syria," 19:25–26; al-ʿArīnī, "Al-Fāris," 56; Ayalon, "L'esclavage," 21–22.

143. Brunschvig, "ʿAbd," 2b.

144. "Deplanximus miseriam talium hominum, laudantes deum, creatorem nostrum, qui nos hucusque a talibus custodivit, rogantesque eum obnixe, ut nos custodiret ab hiis miseriis et cum salute nos ad terram fidelium reduceret." Guglingen, *Fratris Pauli Waltheri*, 230.

145. Even enemies of the same religion sometimes enslaved each other rather than accept ransoms. In 1335, Genoese sold defeated Catalans to Muslims in al-Andalus. Lopez, *Su e giù*, 278–79.

146. Runciman, *A History*, 3:325–26; Cipollone, "La Bolla *Adaperiat dominus*"; Loiseau, "Frankish Captives." For slaving in earlier crusades, see Gillingham, "Crusading Warfare"; Friedman, *Encounter Between Enemies*.

147. Setton, *Papacy*, 1:272.

148. Makhairas, *Recital*, 1:677–79; al-Sakhāwī, *Al-Ḍawʾ al-lāmiʿ*, 3:4–5 and 34, 6:214, 12:50, nos. 20, 144, 297, 715; Ibn Taghrī Birdī, *Al-Manhal al-ṣāfī*, 3:255–76, no. 651; Ibn Taghrī Birdī, *Al-Nujūm al-zāhira*, 14:300; Ibn Iyās, *Bidāʾiʿ al-zuhūr*, 2:423; ASVe, Canc. inf., Not., b.211, reg. IV, fols. 13v, 55r, 65v, 67r, 69v.

149. Schwoebel, *Shadow*; Schiltberger, *Bondage*; Broquière, *The Voyage*, 131; Adorno, *Itinéraire*, 472; Breydenbach, *Sanctarum peregrinationum*, fol. 94r; a fascinating fictional account is Pamuk, *White Castle*.

150. Riley-Smith, *Crusades*, 258; Luttrell, "Slavery," 81–100; Greene, *Catholic Pirates*.

151. Fabri, *Evagatorium*, 18:152.

152. Blumenthal, *Enemies and Familiars*, 54.

153. Tafur, *Travels*, 97–99.

154. Verlinden, "Orthodoxie," 452.

155. "Ne subito rapiatur a piratis, et in perpetuam ac miserrimam servitutem redigatur, quod saepe fit." Fabri, *Evagatorium*, 2:146.

156. Poggibonsi, *A Voyage*, 5.

157. Oikonomidès, *Hommes d'affaires*; Thomas, *Diplomatarium*, 1:127.

158. Raymond and Lopez, *Medieval Trade*, 317.

159. Heyd, *Histoire*, 2:472.

160. Jorga "Notes et extraits," 7 (1899): 66–67, 74–75; Lane, *Venice*, 287.

161. Ibn Taghrī Birdī, *Al-Manhal al-ṣāfī*, 5:63–65, no. 887.

162. Ciocîltan, *Mongols*, 177.

163. Ibn al-Furāt, *Tārīkh al-duwal*, 9:1:33; Frenkel, "Some Notes," 203.

164. Thomas, *Diplomatarium*, 1:127.

165. Riley-Smith, *Crusades*, 260; Roger of Stanegrave, "L'Escarboucle d'armes," 293–387.

166. Morozzo della Rocca, *Lettere*, 29, 118; Balbi and Raiteri, *Notai genovesi*, 136–37, doc. 76.

167. Heers, *Gênes*, 143.

168. Musso, *Navigazione*, 230–32, doc. 1; Cali/Theodora in Barker, "Christianities in Conflict."

169. Prokofieva, "Akti," no. 20.

170. "In perpetuum, salvo tamen quod si pater suus eum rescatare voluerit aut aliquis suorum propincorum, eum restituere tenearis." Morozzo della Rocca, *Benvenuto de Brixano*, 81, doc. 220, also docs. 226 and 236; Lombardo, *Nicola de Boateriis*, 64–66, doc. 60.

171. Dincer, "Enslaving Christians," 8–9.

172. Thomas, *Textbook*, 392.

173. Gilchrist, "Saint Raymond," 307–10.

174. Gilchrist, "Saint Raymond," 309–10. Examples are Gioffrè, *Il mercato*, Greek table (1486, 1498); Köpstein, *Zur Sklaverei*, 101; ASVe, Canc. inf., Not., b.211, reg. IV, fol. 55r.

175. ASVe, Canc. inf., Not., b.211, reg. IV, fols. 13v, 55r.

176. Tria, "La schiavitù," 212–13, doc. 80.

177. Verlinden, "La législation," 170.

178. "Et est illa sclava quam dictus Bartholomeus vir suus redemit a Sarracenis in loco Asperi Castri, in quo loco erat sclava, prout asserunt predicte Iohana et Maria sclava; que Maria asserit predicta vera esse, et quod eciam veritas est quod ipsa Maria fuit seu est sclava ipsius Iohane et dicti Bartholomei propter redempcionem predictam, licet veritas est quod de predictis non apparet instrumentum aliquod seu scriptura aliqua. Et predictam vendicionem fecit idem Iohana, prout asserit, propter necessitatem denariorum quam habet pro substentacione vite sue et filiarum suarum duarum, eo quia dicit quod dictus Bartholomeus vir suus non facit nec fecit, iam sunt plures menses elapsi, eidem Iohane aliquid bonum nec eciam pro dictis filiabus suis, set manet in Maocastro cum quadam femina quam tenet, ac eciam pro solvendo summum unum argenti cuidam presbitero cui dicta Iohana tenetur, prout asserit." Balard, *Gênes et l'Outre-Mer*, 2:83–86, doc. 41. A *sommum* was a unit of weight for unminted silver. Asprocastro, Maurocastro, and Moncastro were the same city. Iliescu, "Nouvelles éditions," 114n5.

179. Precival bought a second slave in Kilia. Balard, *Gênes et l'Outre-Mer*, 2:147, doc. 86. He made both purchases in September, when ships bound for Italy would normally depart from the Black Sea to avoid winter storms.

180. Antonio di Ponzò had returned to Genoa by 1363. Balard, *Gênes et l'Outre-Mer*, 2:10–11.

181. Blumenthal, *Enemies and Familiars*, 89–92.

182. Johnson, "On Agency."

183. Fabri, *Evagatorium*, 18:37, 167.

Chapter 2

1. Bartlett, *Why Can the Dead*; Meri, "Aspects of Baraka."

2. Some medieval Christians had themselves tattooed or branded with the sign of the cross, but Christian masters might also tattoo or brand their slaves with crosses to make them easier to identify. Groebner, *Who Are You?*, 110.

3. Groebner, *Who Are You?*, 82; Constable, "Clothing," 290; Jotischky, "Mendicants," 93. On hiding one's religion by changing clothes, see Broquière, *The Voyage*, 35–38, 46; Adler, "Rabbi Meshullam," 176.

4. Varthema, *Travels*, 63; Schiltberger, *Bondage*, 100.

5. Tamba, *Bernardo de Rodulfis*, 109–10, doc. 100.

6. Constable, "Clothing," 292; Geary, "Ethnic Identity," 19–20; Bartlett, "Medieval and Modern Concepts," 52–53; Phillips, *Before Orientalism*, 175; Haverkamp, "Die Erneuerung," 133; Morony, "Religious Communities," 156–60; Haarmann, "Ideology."

7. "الجارية النوبية الجنس المدعوة مباركة المراة النصرانية." vs. "una schiaveta negra saracina d'anni 14 in circa." Bauden, "L'achat," 274, 298.

8. Kafadar, "A Rome of One's Own."

9. Byzantine sources used Scythian. Pahlitzsch, "Slavery," 166. China and India were sometimes also identified with Scythia. Gómez, *Tropics*, 345–354.

10. Heng, "Invention."

11. Delort, "Quelques précisions," 221; Cibrario, *Della schiavitù*, 3:178; Origo, "Domestic Enemy," 338–39; Haarmann, "Ideology," 183; Northrup, *From Slave to Sultan*, 67; Ayalon, "Mamlūk," 17.

12. Ibn Baṭṭuṭa, *Travels*, 420, 455; Broquière, *The Voyage*, 46.

13. Brunschvig, *Deux récits*, 20–22.

14. Brunschvig, *Deux récits*, 21.

15. Brunschvig, *Deux récits*, 83–84.

16. Constable, "Muslim Spain," 271.

17. Geary, "Ethnic Identity," 20.

18. "Multi et diversarum linguarum populi christiani qui nobiscum in fide non ambulant nec doctrina." Brocardus, "Directorium," 2:382.

19. Poggibonsi, *A Voyage*, 54; Poggibonsi, *Libro d'Oltramare*, 62. See also Schiltberger, *Bondage*, 78.

20. Poggibonsi, *A Voyage*, 89; Poggibonsi, *Libro d'Oltramare*, 105.

21. Alfieri, *Education*, 170–71.

22. Harff, *Pilgrimage*, 4; Harff, *Die Pilgerfahrt*, 3–4.

23. "Non videtur ei de terra egipti se videtur ei de galbo propter loquelam suam." Williams, "From the Commercial Revolution," 127–28.

24. "Origine et lingua Latinus." Thomas, *Diplomatarium*, 1:251, doc. 128.

25. "De lingua tartarea." Verlinden, "La législation," 2:163.

26. Interiano, *La vita*, fol. 3v.

27. Blumenthal, *Enemies and Familiars*, 214.

28. Epstein, *Speaking*, 26, 30. See also Blumenthal, *Enemies and Familiars*, 140–41.

29. Epstein, *Speaking*, 31; Balard, "Remarques," 648.

30. "In tartaro Caron, in nostra lingua Paulus." ASVe, Canc. inf., Misc., b.134 bis, series 1, item 13. "Nomine Chotlu et in latino deinceps vocatam Christinam." ASVe, Canc. inf., Not., b.19, N.7, reg. 1, fol. 4r.

31. "In sua lingua Stoilana, gratia baptismi Marta." ASVe, PdSM, Misti, b.180, Pergamene (July 16, 1401). "Nundum baptizata et vocatur in sua lingua Achzoach et in baptismo debet nuncupari Bona." Tamba, *Bernardo de Rodulfis*, 70–71, doc. 63.

32. "Vocata ad batismum et in latino Margarita." ASVe, Canc. inf., Not., b.20, N.9, reg. 1, fol. 4v.

33. "Faretela batezare e porete nome a vostro modo." Delort, "Quelques précisions," 221.

34. Verlinden, "Le recrutement des esclaves à Venise," 102; Schiel, "Slaves' Religious Choice," 34–35.

35. Cluse, "Zur Repräsentation," 396; Balard, "Remarques," 648.

36. ASVe, Canc. inf., Not., b.230, N.1, reg. 1, fol. 77r and reg. 3, fol. 27v.

37. "Vocatam in sua lingua Catarina et in batismate Antonia." ASVe, Canc. inf., Not., b.20, N.10, fol. 15v.

38. "Vocatam in sua lingua Serafina in idiomate autem nostro Magdalena." ASVe, Canc. inf., Not., b.60, protocol 1446–1449, fol. 42r.

39. Verlinden, *L'Esclavage*, 2:460; Heyd, *Histoire du commerce*, 2:558; Schiel, "Slaves' Religious Choice," 38.

40. Delort, "Quelques précisions," 226.

41. Bratianu, *Actes*, docs. 205, 208, 249, 265, 266; Balard, *Gênes et l'outre-mer*, 1:275, doc. 708.

42. ASVe, Canc. inf., Not., b.19, N.7, reg. 2, fol. 24r, item 144; Ferretto, "Codice diplomatico," 2:167; Balard, *La Romanie*, 2:793.

43. Verlinden, *L'Esclavage*, 2:931–32.

44. ASVe, Canc. inf., Not., b.19, N.7, reg. 2, fols. 33r, 34v, items 185, 194; reg. 5, items 4, 51.

45. Ayalon, "Mamlūk," 12.

46. Ayalon, "Names," 195–96.

47. The origin of Barqūq's name was debated. Ibn Taghrī Birdī, *Al-Manhal al-ṣāfī*, 3:285, no. 657.

48. Gioffrè, *Il mercato*, Tartar and "Slaves Without Race" tables; Balard, *Romanie*, 1:305; ASVe, Canc. inf., Not., b.19, N.7, reg. 5, items 21, 29, 43, 77, 111; b.20, N.8, reg. 2, fol. 6r; b.92, N.2, reg. 1, fol. 14v, 15r; b.230, N.1, reg. 3, fol. 14r; ASG, Not. Ant. 397, fol. 17v.

49. Ibn Taghrī Birdī, *Al-Manhal al-ṣāfī*, 4:271–312, nos. 847 and 849.

50. Ayalon, "Names," 210–11; ʿAshūr, *Al-ʿAṣr al-mamālīkī*, 134; Lutfi, *Al-Quds*, 235. Jewish freedwomen and converts in medieval Egypt were called "daughters of Abraham." Perry, "Conversion," 136.

51. Ayalon, "Names," 219–23.

52. Shaw, *Necessary Conjunctions*, 15.

53. Jenkins, *Rethinking Ethnicity*, 25.

54. Jenkins, *Rethinking Ethnicity*, 14, 55–57.

55. Some people experience ethnicity as a core element of their sense of self and their social world, while others do not. Even in societies where ethnicity does not entail many social consequences, some form of ethnic categorization is still often present. Jenkins, *Rethinking Ethnicity*, 48–49, 52.

56. Jenkins, *Rethinking Ethnicity*, 23, 77–85; Fredrickson, *Racism*; Heng, "Invention," 325.

57. Taylor, *Race*, 16–18.

58. Fredrickson, *Racism*, 168; Nirenberg, *Communities of Violence*; Ziegler, "Physiognomy," 198.

59. Freedman, *Images*; Ziegler, "Physiognomy," 188.

60. Nineteenth-century philologists posited two language families, the Semitic and the Indo-European/Aryan, which they perceived as fundamental to the culture and character of their speakers. Olender, *Languages of Paradise*.

61. Groebner, *Who Are You?*, 140; Goetz, *Baptism*; Glasson, *Mastering Christianity*, ch. 2.

62. Edzard, *Polygenesis*, 36. Thanks to Josephine van den Bent for this citation.

63. Bartlett, "Medieval and Modern Concepts," 44–45; Geary, "Ethnic Identity," 19; Lewis, *Race*, 43–44; Ayalon, "Circassians," 137; Braude, "Sons of Noah"; Reuter, "Whose Race," 101; Pohl, "Introduction," 4.

64. Bartlett, "Medieval and Modern Concepts," 45; al-Sarakhsī, *Kitāb al-Mabsūṭ*, 13:12–13; al-Sakhāwī, *Al-Ḍawʾ al-lāmiʿ*, 3:74. Religious communities described in terms of common ancestry: Geary, "Ethnic Identity," 23; Verlinden, "Le recrutement des esclaves à Venise," 175; Poggibonsi, *A Voyage*, 54; Golubovich, *Biblioteca*, 3:223; Alfieri, *Education*, 176–77; Brocardus, "Directorium," 385; Piloti, *Traité*, 35; Ibn ʿAbd al-Ẓāhir, *Tashrīf al-ayām*, 205; Theiner, *Vetera monumenta*, 1:769–70, doc. 1041.

65. Biller, "Proto-Racial Thought"; Ziegler, "Physiognomy," 190–93; Groebner, *Who Are You?*, 137–38; Jordan, "Why 'Race'?," 165; Reuter, "Whose Race," 102; Haarmann, "Ideology," 177; Earle, *Body of the Conquistador*; Akbari, *Idols in the East*, 157, 169.

66. I have found two slaves categorized in a way that implies racial change. The first was "once of the race of the Tatars" (*olim de genere tartarorum*). ASVe, Canc. inf., Not., b.117, N.6, reg. 3, fol. 6r. The other was a Tatarized Russian (*rosa atartarada*). Dorini and Bertelè, *Il Libro dei conti*, 588, 591.

67. Groebner, *Who Are You?*, 26–28.

68. Groebner, *Who Are You?*, 120; Ziegler, "Physiognomy," 182.

69. Pormann and Savage-Smith, *Medieval Islamic Medicine*, 45.

70. Al-Asyūṭī, *Jawhar al-ʿuqūd*, 1:96–97; Sobers Khan, *Slaves Without Shackles*, 239–40.

71. Akbari, *Idols in the East*, 160–61; Phillips, *Before Orientalism*, 174.

72. Gómez, *Tropics*, 48–53, 69; Lewis, *Race*, 45–48; Haarmann, "Ideology," 179; Akbari, *Idols in the East*, 156; Biller, "Proto-Racial Thought," 158; Ziegler, "Physiognomy," 185.

73. Cluse, "Zur Repräsentation," 395.

74. "Qui non sint catholicae fidei et christianae. . . . Et praedicta intelligantur de sclavis et servis infidelibus ab origine suae nativitatis, seu de genere infidelium natis etiam si tempore quo ad dictam civitatem, comitatum, vel districtum, ducerentur essent christianae fidei, seu etiam si postea quandocumque fuerint baptizati . . . praesumatur ab origine fuisse infidelis si fuerit de patribus et genere infidelis oriundus." Rodocanachi, "Les esclaves," 388.

75. ASG, Arch. Segr., 1781, fols. 530v–531r.

76. Tafur, *Travels*, 134.

77. A few slaves were categorized simply as saleable. "De progenie que vendi liceat." Amia, *Schiavitù*, 160. "De progenie vendibile." ASG, Not. Ant. 719/I, doc. 189. "De progenie tartarorum vel alia natione que vendi possit." Amitai and Cluse, *Slavery*, 17. Heers, *Gênes*, 656.

78. Al-Asyūṭī, *Jawhar al-ʿuqūd*, 1:96–97; Little, "Six Fourteenth Century Purchase Deeds," 304.

79. Lewis, *Race*, 50.

80. Al-Asyūṭī, *Jawhar al-ʿuqūd*, 1:70; al-Sarakhsī, *Kitāb al-Mabsūṭ*, 13:12–13.

81. Al-ʿAyntābī, *Al-Qawl al-sadīd*; *Al-Taḥqīq fī shirāʾ al-raqīq*.

82. For Arab slaves, see Rapoport, "Women," 14; ʿAbd al-Raziq, *La femme*, 50.

83. Al-ʿAyntābī, *Al-Qawl al-sadīd*, 49. Similarly *Al-Taḥqīq fī shirāʾ al-raqīq*, fol. 32. "اعلم أن العجم على الإطلاق، يطلق على مَن خالف لسانَ العربية، كالفرس والترك والروم والأرمن والسودان والبربر وغيرهم، غير أن هذا الاسم خص بأهل فارس اصطلاحاً."

84. Literally, *al-rūm* were Romans. During the thirteenth and fourteenth centuries, though, the term underwent a shift in connotation from Byzantine or ex-Byzantine Christians to members of an urban social and cultural elite who lived in former Byzantine lands and were able to speak and write refined Turkish. Kafadar, "A Rome of One's Own," 11.

85. Al-Asyūṭī, *Jawhar al-ʿuqūd*, 1:96–97 vs. al-ʿAyntābī, *Al-Qawl al-sadīd* and *Al-Taḥqīq fī shirāʾ al-raqīq*.

86. Ibn Taghrī Birdī, *Al-Manhal al-ṣāfī*, no. 374 (Chinese); Marmon, *Eunuchs*, 69 (Russian); al-Sakhāwī, *Al-Ḍawʾ al-lāmiʿ*, 3:173 no. 668 (West African), 10:289–90 no. 1134 (Samarqandi).

87. Levanoni, "Al-Maqrizi's Account," 96–101; Mazor, *Rise and Fall*, 166–70.

88. Al-Qalqashandī, *Subḥ al-aʿshā*, 4:458; al-Maqrīzī, *Kitāb al-khiṭaṭ*, 3:781. Levanoni, "Al-Maqrizi's Account," 93–105; Ayalon, "Mamlūk," 16.

89. Popper, "History," 13:163.

90. Fioravanti, "Servi, rustici, barbari"; Gómez, *Tropics*, 53–56.

91. "Nota quod barbari, secundum quosdam, dicuntur illi quorum idioma discordat omnino a latino. Alii vero dicunt quod quilibet extraneus est barbarus omni alio extraneo. . . . Sed secundum quod verius dicitur, barbari proprie dicuntur illi qui in virtute corporis vigent, in virtute rationis deficiunt, et sunt quasi extra leges et sine regimine juris." Thomas Aquinas, cited in Fioravanti, "Servi, rustici, barbari," 423.

92. Fioravanti, "Servi, rustici, barbari," 424–25.

93. "Barbaros enim dicimus qui nec lege, nec civiltate, nec alicuius disciplinae ordine disponuntur ad virtutem, quos Tullius in principio Rhetoricae silvestres homines vocat, more ferarum cum silvestribus feris conversantes, quales non sunt Graeci vel Latini, qui disciplinati sunt et connutriti regimine dominativo et paterno. Tales enim bestiales crudas carnes comedunt et sanguinem humanum bibunt, de craneis hominum comedere et bibere delectantur, nova suppliciorum genera inveniunt quibus delectantur homines interficere." Albertus Magnus, cited in Fioravanti, "Servi, rustici, barbari," 424–25. Stereotypes of barbarian bestiality played into poisoning accusations against slave women. Schiel, "Mord," 208–9.

94. Fioravanti, "Servi, rustici, barbari," 426–27; Verlinden, *L'Esclavage*, 2:24–25.

95. "Ut de maioribus accepi Thraces quoque & Graecos qui pontum incolerent venundari mos fuit: qui ne servitia barbarorum essent, mercatores Euxinum navigantes, redemptos illos a Scytis, venales faciebant. Honestius enim visum est tantisper servire eos, dum solutam pro capite suo pecuniam rependerent, quam praedam esse barbarorum perpetuaeque obnoxios servituti, cum maximo etiam Christiani nominis opprobrio. Quod hodie quoque servatur adversus eos quos Burgaros, & Cercasios vocat." Pontano, "De obedientia," 201–2.

96. Alfieri, *Education*, 34–35; Brocardus, "Directorium," 386–88, 463; Heers and de Groer, *Itinéraire*, 196–97; Jorga, "Notes et extraits," 6:106, 127–28 and 7:40; Pachymeres, *De Michaele*, 176; Chalkokondyles, *Laonikos Chalkokondyles*, 285–89; Petrarch, *Seniles* 10.2; Germain, "Le discours," 322; Balbi, *L'epistolario*, 107–9; Thomas, *Diplomatarium*, 1:268; Interiano, *La vita*, fol. 2v, as well as the introduction by the famous printer Aldus Manutius.

97. Gioffrè, *Il mercato*, 22; Wirth, "Gepiden."

98. Digest 21.1.31. Watson, *Digest*, 2:613, translates *natio* variously as "nationality," "race," and "people." I have modified his translation to render *natio* consistently as "race."

99. Saracen combined the ethnic category Arab with the religious category Muslim. It also implied a sedentary lifestyle. Akbari, *Idols in the East*, 155; Constable, "Muslim Spain," 274.

100. In the fifteenth century, Turk replaced Saracen as the generic term for Muslims. Carr, *Merchant Crusaders*, 60.

101. Al-Lāwūn or al-Aṣ, they lived near the Dariyal (Dar-i-Alan) Pass. Allen, *A History*, 30–31.

102. Vasiliev, *Goths*.

103. They lived in what is now Daghestan. Lemercier-Quelquejay, "Cooptation," 30–32.

104. Majar or Maniar was a city on the Kuma River near modern Budyonnovsk. Balard, *La Romanie*, 2:793. Tardy, *Sklavenhandel*, 149, argued that the *maniar* were Hungarian (Magyar) inhabitants of the Caucasus.

105. Meskhia was just east of Trebizond in the kingdom of Georgia. King, *Black Sea*, 11, 126.

106. Balard, *Gênes et l'outre-mer*, 1:150–51, doc. 388; Bratianu, *Actes*, docs. 161, 326; ASVe, Canc. inf., Not., b.19, N.7, reg. 2, fol. 3r, item 17.

107. Heers and de Groer, *Itinéraire*, 198; Webb, "A Survey of Egypt and Syria," 382–85; Fabri, *Evagatorium*, 3:371–72, 18:34; Breydenbach, *Sanctarum peregrinationum*, fol. 85r; Harff, *Pilgrimage*, 102, 120; Verona, *Liber*, 102; Ghistele, *Voyage en Egypte*, 34; Varthema, *Travels*, 63–64. In these texts, Abyssinia was the land of Prester John. I have not found any evidence for the claim by Ashtor, *A Social and Economic History*, 282, that Sultan Lajīn had been a Teutonic knight.

108. Ghistele, *Voyage en Egypte*, 30.

109. Fabri, *Evagatorium*, 3:371–72, 18:34; Guglingen, *Fratris Pauli Waltheri*, 231.

110. Harff, *Pilgrimage*, 102.

111. Modern scholars have also struggled to explain cases in which geographical origin, racial category, language, and name did not line up as expected. Verlinden, *L'Esclavage*, 2:931–32; Khvalkov, "Slave Trade in Tana," 112.

112. Ibn Taghrī Birdī, *Al-Manhal al-ṣāfī*, 3:435–36 and 4:271–74, nos. 710 and 847 vs. al-Sakhāwī, *Al-Ḍaw' al-lāmi'*, 3:74–75, nos. 288 and 289.

113. Ibn Taghrī Birdī, *Al-Manhal al-ṣāfī*, 3:467–73, no. 718.

114. Al-Sakhawi, *Al-Ḍaw' al-lāmi'*, 3:175–76, no. 681; Popper, "History," 23:19; Ibn Iyās, *Bidā'i' al-zuhūr*, 2:378–79, 456; al-Isḥāqī, *Akhbār al-uwal*, 141.

115. Balard, *Gênes et l'outre-mer*, 1:351, doc. 854; ASG, Not. Ant. 719/III, doc. 3; ASVe, Canc. inf., Not., b.117, N.6, reg. 3, fol. 2v.

116. "De proienia gotie ut eidem Iohani videtur de Gotia." Balard, *Gênes et l'outre-mer*, 2:51–52, doc. 17; see also Dennis, "Un fondo," 429–30.

117. "Qui dicitur fuisset de partibus Roscie." ASG, Not. Ant. 172, fol. 51r.

118. "De progenie rubeorum ut asseritur per dictam sclavam et quam tibi vendo tamquam de progenie rubeorum." ASG, Not. Ant. 237, fol. 265r.

119. Pistarino, *Notai genovesi*, 3–6, docs. 1–2.

120. "De avogasorum vel alio genere." Verlinden, "Le recrutement des esclaves à Venise," 143.

121. ASVe, Canc. inf., Not., b.19, N.7, reg. 2, fols. 4v, 24r, 29v, 35r, items 32, 143, 164, 200; b.59, protocol 1444–1445 (December 3, 1445); b.230, N.1, reg. 3, fols. 6v, 14r, and 18r; reg. 4, fol. 40r; Verlinden, "Le recrutement des esclaves à Venise," 97; ASG, Not. Ant. 379, fol. 121r–v; Not. Ant. 396, fols. 175r–v, 120r–v; Not. Ant. 402, fols. 127v–128r, 195r–v; Not. Ant. 719/I, doc. 154; ASG, Notai ignoti, b.xxiv.3; Boccaccio, *Decameron*, 449–50; Morozzo della Rocca, *Benvenuto de Brixano*, 96, doc. 259.

122. ASVe, Canc. inf., Not., b.19, N.7, reg. 2, fol. 2v; b.60, protocol 1446–1449, fol. 69v; b.231, N.3, reg. 2, fols. 7v–8r; ASVe, Canc. inf., Misc., b.134 bis, series 1, item 37; Verlinden, "Le recrutement des esclaves à Venise," 134, 158, 170; ASG, Not. Ant. 380, fol. 176r–v; Not. Ant. 381, fol. 106r; Not. Ant. 397, fols. 205r, 248r–v; Not. Ant. 719/III, doc. 25; Balard, "Les génois," 2:24; Toniolo, *Notai genovesi*, 74–75, doc. 22; Tria, "La schiavitù," docs. 42, 98; Colli, *Moretto Bon*, doc. 29; Gioffrè, *Il mercato*, 29.

123. Groebner, *Who Are You?*, 75. Compare with Sobers Khan, *Slaves Without Shackles*, 240.

124. Groebner, *Who Are You?*, 80, 97; Cluse, "Zur Repräsentation," 395–96.

125. Groebner, *Who Are You?*, 108–10; Livi, *La schiavitù domestica*.

126. Pormann and Savage-Smith, *Medieval Islamic Medicine*, 43–45; Siraisi, *Medieval and Early Renaissance Medicine*, 101–6; Kaye, *A History of Balance*, ch. 3–4; Ziegler, "Physiognomy," 192–98.

127. Groebner, *Who Are You?*, 139, 144.

128. Groebner, *Who Are You?*, 140; Hannaford, *Race*, 5.

129. Ziegler, "Physiognomy," 183.

130. Groebner, *Who Are You?*, 130.

131. Breydenbach, *Sanctarum peregrinationum*, fol. 85r.

132. Balard, "Remarques," 646; Cibrario, *Della schiavitù*, 3:198–99; Bratianu, *Actes*, doc. 270; Cluse, "Zur Repräsentation," 394; Gioffrè, *Il mercato*, Moor table (1476); Pavoni, *Notai genovesi*, 106–7, doc. 79.

133. Black slaves in either the medieval or modern sense were rare in Europe before the fifteenth century. Balard, *La Romanie*, 2:787, found 5 percent of the fourteenth-century Genoese slave population to be black. According to Lane, *Venice*, 350, the first direct association between slavery and dark skin did not appear in Venice until 1490. Epstein, *Speaking*, 23, 80–81; Blumenthal, *Enemies and Familiars*; McKee, "Implications," 111; Winer, *Women*, 141–42.

134. Verlinden, "Le recrutement des esclaves a Genes," 42; Balard, "Remarques," 646; Williams, "From the Commercial Revolution," 60–63, 140–44; Balard, *La Romanie*, 2:787.

135. ASG, Not. Ant. 379–382 (Giovanni Bardi), 396–405 (Bartolomeo Gatto).

136. References to color remained common in Pisa and Florence, the hinterland of the Italian slave trade. Amia, *Schiavitù*, 178–80; Cluse, "Zur Repräsentation," 393.

137. Pormann and Savage-Smith, *Medieval Islamic Medicine*, 43–45.

138. Al-Asyūṭī spells it *ādamī* (human) rather than *adamī* (skinlike, leathery). The noun in the following sentence is *adama* (skin or leather).

139. Al-Asyūṭī, *Jawhar al-ʿuqūd*, 2:574–75.

إذا كان الرجل شديد السواد. قيل: حالك. فإن خالط سواده حمرة. قيل: دغمان. فإن صفا لونه. قيل: أسحم. فإن خالط السواد صفرة. قيل: أصحم. فإن كدر لونه. قيل: أربد. فإن صفا عن ذلك. قيل: أبيض. فإن رقّت الصفرة، ومال إلى السواد. قيل: آدمي اللون. فإن كان دون الأربد وفوق الأُدمة. قيل: شديد الأدمة، فإن رق من الأدمة. قيل: شديد السمرة. فإن صفا عن ذلك. قيل: أسمر اللون. فإن صفا عن ذلك. قيل: رقيق السمرة. فإن صفا عن ذلك ومال إلى البياض والحمرة. قيل: صافى السمرة تعلوه حمرة. ويقال: رقيق السمرة بحمرة. فإن صفا لونه جدا. قيل: صافي السمرة، ولا يقال: أبيض. لأن البياض هو البرص. فإن خلص بياضه. قيل: أنصح. وإن كان فى بياضه شقرة. قيل: أشقر. فإن زاد على ذلك. قيل: أشكل. فإن كان مع ذلك حمرة زائدة قيل: أشقر. فإن كان مع ذلك نمش. قيل: أنمش. فإن صفى لونه ومال إلى الصفرة من غير علة. قيل: أسحب اللون.

140. Lewis, *Race*, 56; Ayalon, "Mamlūkiyyāt," 324; Ragib, *Actes*, 2:24; Petry, *Civilian Elite*, 405.

141. Al-Sarakhsī, *Kitāb al-Mabsūṭ*, 13:13.

142. Al-Asyūṭī, *Jawhar al-ʿuqūd*, 1:97.

143. Al-Suyūṭī, *Al-Ḥāwī lil-fatāwī*, 1:156. Military slaves were called *ʿabīd* in Iberian sources without implying blackness. Fancy, *Mercenary Mediterranean*, 87; Tibi, *Tibyān*, 253n467.

144. Ibn Taghrī Birdī, *Al-Manhal al-ṣāfī*, BNF arabe 2072, fols. 14r (Qarājā al-ʿUmarī al-Nāṣirī), 14r–15r (Qardamdash al-Aḥmadī), 38v (Sultan Kitbughā); al-Sakhāwī, *Al-Ḍawʾ al-lāmiʿ*, 6:214 no. 714 (Qarājā al-Ashrafī), 6:216 no. 722 (Qaraqjā al-Ḥasanī al-Ẓāhirī).

145. Al-Sakhāwī, *Al-Ḍawʾ al-lāmiʿ*, 3:84–85 no. 330. Joos van Ghistele saw Abyssinian mamluks in Egypt, although he may have misunderstood the term *mamlūk*. Ghistele, *Voyage en Egypte*, 34. Felix Fabri met a dark-skinned mamluk dragoman, but he also was imprecise in his use of the term *mamlūk*. Fabri, *Evagatorium*, 18:147.

146. ʿAbd al-Raziq, "Un document," 309–10.

147. Ibn Taghrī Birdī, *Al-Manhal al-ṣāfī*, BNF arabe 2071, fols. 206r–207r; BNF arabe 2072, fols. 52v–55v; al-Sakhāwī, *Al-Ḍawʾ al-lāmiʿ*, 6:214 no. 714; Ibn Iyās, *Bidāʾiʿ al-zuhūr*, 2:378–79; Epstein, *Speaking*, 108.

148. Popper, "History," 23:81; Ibn Iyās, *Bidāʾiʿ al-zuhūr*, 2:456.

149. Epstein, *Speaking*, 108, found black, brown, fair, and red Tatars. A chronicler from Lübeck described a Romani group as "black as Tatars" (*nigri ut tartari*). Groebner, *Who Are You?*, 117.

150. Balletto, "Schiavi," 683; Bratianu, *Actes*, docs. 183, 190, 191, 199, 204, 205, 224, 249, 257, 265, 270, 271, 309; Interiano, *La vita*, fol. 6r.

151. Gioffrè, *Il mercato*, 31.

152. Livi, *La schiavitù domestica*.

153. Bratianu, *Actes*, docs. 193, 199, 329; Amia, *Schiavitù*, docs. 24, 62; Desimoni, "Actes passés," docs. 76, 110; ASG, Not. Ant. 396, fols. 103v–104r; Not. Ant. 405/I, fols. 23v–24r; Ibn Taghrī Birdī, *Al-Manhal al-ṣāfī*, 3:467–73 and 4:68, nos. 718 and 769; al-Sakhāwī, *Al-Ḍaw' al-lāmiʿ*, 10:281 no. 1105.

154. Bratianu, *Actes*, docs. 183, 187, 270; Desimoni, "Actes passés," doc. 91; Ferretto, "Codice diplomatico," 1:110n286; Balard, *Gênes et l'outre-mer*, 1:276, doc. 711; al-Sakhāwī, *Al-Ḍaw' al-lāmiʿ*, 6:214 no. 714; Ibn Taghrī Birdī, *Al-Manhal al-ṣāfī*, BNF arabe 2072, fol. 38v.

155. Al-ʿAyntābī, *Al-Qawl al-sadīd*, 58–62; *Al-Taḥqīq fī shirā' al-raqīq*, fols. 48–52.

156. Cluse, "Zur Repräsentation," 394.

157. ASG, Not. Ant. 381, fol. 106r; Bratianu, *Actes*, docs. 88, 188, 265.

158. Ziegler, "Physiognomy," 187. This differed from the Mongol racial category created by Blumenbach. Phillips, *Before Orientalism*, 172. Verlinden attempted to apply Blumenbach's categories to Black Sea slaves in an early article. Verlinden, "Esclavage et ethnographie."

159. The current capitals are eighteenth-century copies. The fourteenth-century original from the south facade is on display in the Museo dell'Opera. The original from the west facade has been lost. Saviello, "Zu einer Bildtopographie," 103–5. See also Suckow, "Adalberts Traum," 365.

160. "Un viso che pare un tavolaccio." Delort, "Quelques précisions," 220–21. See also Broquière, *The Voyage*, 114; Tafur, *Travels*, 136; *Viaggi fatti da Vinetia*, 15, 73, 76.

161. "Non à il viso molto tartarescho." Delort, "Quelques précisions," 221.

162. Fabri, *Evagatorium*, 18:40.

163. Tafur, *Travels*, 136.

164. Wallace, *Premodern Places*, 191.

165. Phillips, *Before Orientalism*, 101–2, 182.

166. Simeonis, *Itinerarium*, 78–79.

167. Little, "Six Fourteenth Century Purchase Deeds," 305; al-Asyūṭī, *Jawhar al-ʿuqūd*, 1:97.

168. Little, "Six Fourteenth Century Purchase Deeds," 304; Al-Asyūṭī, *Jawhar al-ʿuqūd*, 1:97.

169. Sobers Khan, *Slaves Without Shackles*, 112–13.

Chapter 3

1. Versus slave societies. Berlin, *Many Thousands Gone*, 8; Finley, *Ancient Slavery*, 79–80.

2. Patterson, *Slavery and Social Death*, 4–5.

3. Gioffrè, *Il mercato*, 65–75; ASG, Arch. Segr. 562, fols. 76r–78v. The Genose florin of account was equivalent to 25 soldi. Spufford, *Handbook*, 109–15.

4. Heers, *Gênes*, 130–31; Tucci, *Le imposte*, 44.

5. Sieveking, "Aus Genueser Rechnungs- und Steuer-büchern," 48; Gioffrè, *Il mercato*, 73.

6. Gioffrè, *Il mercato*, 77.

7. Gioffrè, *Il mercato*, 73–75; ASG, CdSG, N.185,01009. A temporary increase in the tax rate was called a *salsa*. In 1458, a *salsa* increased the half-florin tax rate from twelve soldi six denari to sixteen soldi three denari. Amia, *Schiavitù*, 191; Sieveking, "Aus Genueser Rechnungs- und Steuerbüchern," 21, 35.

8. Data from Gioffrè, *Il mercato*, 69–70; Balard, *La Romanie*, 2:816. I checked their numbers against archival records for the following years: ASG, CdSG, N.185,15002, fol. 30r (1381); N.185,15003, fol. 15v (1384); N.185,15006, fol. 54v (1387); N.185,15072, fol. 3 (1422), fol. 15 (1423), fol. 32 (1424), fol. 45 (1425), fol. 63 (1426), fol. 82 (1427), fol. 93 (1428), fol. 111 (1429), fol. 119 (1430), fol. 135 (1431), fol. 151 (1432), fol. 162 (1433, 1434). I found discrepancies in 1429 (875 lire vs. 975 lire

in Gioffrè) and 1433–1434 (2,050 lire over two years vs. 1,050 lire for 1433 and 1,025 lire for 1434 in Gioffrè).

9. Cluse, "Frauen," 89; Balard, *La Romanie*, 1:299, 2:796; Origo, "Domestic Enemy," 324; Klapisch-Zuber, "Women Servants," 68; Rodocanachi, "Les esclaves," 386; vs. McKee, "Implications," 103.

10. Schiel, "Die Sklaven und die Pest," 374.

11. Gioffrè, *Il mercato*, 68, 71–72. Tax revenues in 1435–1436 were so badly affected by the plague that state officials allowed the tax farmers to pay less than their original bids.

12. Balard, *La Romanie*, 2:817.

13. Epstein, *Speaking*, xii; Gioffrè, *Il mercato*, 79; McKee, "Implications," 103.

14. Amia, *Schiavitù*, 191.

15. Bongi, "Le schiave," 244.

16. Fabri, *Evagatorium*, 18:432.

17. Rabie, *Financial System*, 108.

18. Ayalon, "Studies on the Structure—I," 204, 226; Rapoport, "Women," 13–14; Ashtor, *A Social and Economic History*, 283.

19. Romano, *Housecraft*, xx–xxi.

20. ASG, CdSG, N.185,01009. Balard, "Remarques," 666.

21. Gioffré, *Lettere di Giovanni da Pontremoli*, 207, 215–17, docs. 144, 148, 149.

22. Lazari, "Del traffico," 472–73.

23. Tamba, *Bernardo de Rodulfis*, 18–22, doc. 12.

24. ASVe, Canc. inf., Not., b.229, reg. 3, fol. 16r–v.

25. Romano, *Housecraft*, 90–93.

26. Lenna, "Giosafat Barbaro," 102–5.

27. Two had run away. Lombardo, *Nicola de Boateriis*, 224–28, doc. 212.

28. Rapoport, "Ibn Ḥağar," 339.

29. Lutfi, *Al-Quds*, 307.

30. Ibn Ṭawq, *Al-Taʿlīq*. Thanks to Amina Elbendary for sharing this source.

31. Little, "Two Fourteenth-Century Court Records," 18–19.

32. Rapoport, "Ibn Ḥağar," 340.

33. Ayalon, "Studies on the Structure—II," 459–64, 473–74.

34. Ibn Shahīn, *Zoubdat kachf*, 113.

35. Ibn Taghrī Birdī, *Al-Manhal al-ṣāfī*, nos. 588, 618, 680, 741, 760, 1154, 1228.

36. Ayalon, "Studies on the Structure—II," 464; Ibn Taghrī Birdī, *Al-Manhal al-ṣāfī*, nos. 536, 657, 1137.

37. Harff, *Pilgrimage*, 107, 124.

38. Rapoport, "Women," 9–10; ʿAbd al-Raziq, *La femme*, 54.

39. Ibn Taghrī Birdī, *Al-Manhal al-ṣāfī*, 4:31–43, no. 760.

40. Al-Jazarī, *Tārīkh ḥawādith*, 3:920–21.

41. Al-ʿArīnī, "Al-Fāris," 47. In addition to the sultan's mamluks, the army included free soldiers (*ajnad al-ḥalqa*) and the amirs' mamluks (*ajnad al-umara'*). Ibn Shahīn, *Zoubdat kachf*, 116.

42. Ibn Shahīn, *Zoubdat kachf*, 27.

43. Levanoni, *A Turning Point*, 28–31.

44. ʿAbd al-Raziq, *La femme*, 50; Ibn Shahīn, *Zoubdat kachf*, 121–22; al-Maqrīzī, *Kitāb al-sulūk*, 2:2:546; Simeonis, *Itinerarium*, 77; Bellorini and Hoade, *Visit to the Holy Places*, 49–50.

45. ʿAbd al-Raziq, *La femme*, 64–65; Ibn Taghrī Birdī, *Al-Manhal al-ṣāfī*, nos. 662, 858, 1288.

46. Rapoport, "Ibn Ḥağar," 336–42.

47. Gioffrè, *Il mercato*, 109; Balard, "Remarques," 654.

48. Christ, *Trading Conflicts*, 130.

49. Heers, *Esclaves*, 179.

50. Cluse, "Frauen," 103.

51. Cluse, "Frauen," 90, 94; Verlinden, "Le recrutement des esclaves à Venise," 126, 128, 140, 159; Gioffrè, *Il mercato*, 111–12, 117–18.

52. Khowaiter, *Baibars*, 6; Ibn Taghrī Birdī, *Al-Manhal al-ṣāfī*, 4:68 no. 769, 4:271–74 no. 847, 6:84 no. 1119, BNF arabe 2071, fols. 221v–223r; al-Sakhāwī, *Al-Ḍaw' al-lāmi'*, 3:175–76, 308–11, nos. 681, 1190; 6:176–77, no. 600.

53. Al-Maqrīzī, *Kitāb al-khiṭaṭ*, 4:224–26; al-Sakhāwī, *Al-Ḍaw' al-lāmi'*, 6:201–11, no. 697.

54. Al-Maqrīzī, *Kitāb al-khiṭaṭ*, 3:692, 694; Levanoni, "Al-Maqrizi's Account," 101–2.

55. Ghistele, *Voyage*, 31; Piloti, *Traité*, 34.

56. Heers, *Gênes*, 370; Gioffrè, *Il mercato*, 30, 76; Balard, *La Romanie*, 1:294, 296; McKee, "Implications," 103; Balard, "Giacomo Badoer," 558; Clerget, *Le Caire*, 342; Spuler, *Die Goldene Horde*, 385.

57. Verlinden, "Le recrutement des esclaves à Venise," 184; Rodocanachi, "Les esclaves," 385; Bongi, "Le schiave," 218–19; Heyd, *Histoire du commerce*, 2:561; Stuard, "Ancillary Evidence," 19; Bauden, "L'achat," 300; Zevakin and Penčko, "Ricerche," 42.

58. Northrup, "Military Slavery," 124; Ayalon, "Mamlūk," 16.

59. Heers, *Esclaves*, 286; Verlinden, "Le recrutement des esclaves à Venise"; Lutfi, *Al-Quds*, 307; Balard, "Remarques," 650; Gioffrè, *Il mercato*, 79, 178; Rapoport, "Women," 9; McKee, "Implications," 103; Delort, "Quelques précisions," 227–28; Balletto, "Schiavi," 693.

60. Al-Maqrīzī, *Kitāb al-sulūk*, 4:1:492.

61. ASG, CdSG, N.185,00623, N.185,00625.

62. Gioffrè, *Il mercato*, 142–43; Doosselaere, *Commercial Agreements*, 216.

63. Balard, *La Romanie*, 2:823; Argenti, *Occupation*, 1:619; Romano, *Housecraft*, 90–91; Verlinden, *L'Esclavage*, 2:906–7; Balard, "Remarques," 673.

64. 'Abd al-Raziq, *La femme*, 83–84; Cluse, "Frauen," 96–101; Winer, "Conscripting the Breast."

65. Balletto, "Schiavi," 668.

66. Pistarino, *Notai genovesi*, 63–65, doc. 39; Paviot, "La piraterie bourguignonne," 2:206; Little, *A Catalogue*, 192–93, doc. 51; Prokofieva, "Akti," nos. 41, 105.

67. ASVe, Canc. inf., Not., b.20, N.8, reg. 6, fol. 5v; b.61, reg. 1453–54 (October 2, 1453); ASG, Not. Ant. 719/II, doc. 108; ASG, CdSG, N.185,00625, fols. 23v–24r; Tria, "La schiavitù," 154, doc. 23.

68. Boldorini, *Caffa e Famagosta*, doc. 89.

69. Marmon, "Domestic Slavery," 10; Ibn Taghrī Birdī, *Al-Manhal al-ṣāfī*, nos. 593, 598, 668, 927, 1073, 1124, 1194.

70. ASG, Not. Ant. 432, docs. 16, 24, 33, 60, 109; ASVe, Notarile Testamenti 733, doc. 15.

71. Tamba, *Bernardo de Rodulfis*, docs. 369, 374; ASG, Not. Ant. 380, fols. 43v–44r, 60v–61r, 112r–113r.

72. Little, "Six Fourteenth Century Purchase Deeds," 326–28.

73. Ragib, *Actes*, 1:34–37, no. XII. See also no. XIII, appendix nos. III–V.

74. ASVe, Canc. inf., Not., b.132, N.9, fol. 119r; Gioffrè, *Il mercato*, Russian table (1453); ASG, CdSG, N.185,00625, fol. 14v. Fuertes and Ruiz, "Los esclavos," 23, mention a slave owned by a wife whose husband had the right of usufruct. Usufruct (*ius utendi et fruendi*) is the right to use and enjoy, that is, share with others. Varkemaa, *Conrad Summenhart's Theory*, 210, 223.

75. Balard, "Remarques," 630.

76. Marmon, "Domestic Slavery," 10; Patterson, *Slavery and Social Death*, 79.

77. Lowe, "Lives," 17–18.

78. Marmon, "Domestic Slavery," 9, 12; Rapoport, "Women," 9; 'Abd al-Raziq, *La femme*, 55, 66–67, 85. On slave singers especially, see Nielson, "Gender and the Politics of Music."

79. "المماليك من سائر الأجناس." Ibn Taghrī Birdī, *Al-Manhal al-ṣāfī*, 7:137 no. 1358. See also 7:345, no. 1475; BNF arabe 2071, fol. 113v; Little, *Catalogue*, 212, doc. 349; al-Maqrīzī, *Kitāb al-sulūk*, 2:3:679.

80. Ibn Taghrī Birdī, *Al-Manhal al-ṣāfī*, 7:228, no. 1405.

81. Groebner, *Liquid Assets*, 1–14; Behrens-Abouseif, *Practicing Diplomacy*, 61–65, 133–34.

82. Al-'Aynī, *'Iqd al-jumān*, 1:362.

83. Ibn al-Dawādārī, *Kanz al-durar*, 9:280; Labib, *Handelsgeschichte*, 110.

84. Ibn Taghrī Birdī, *Al-Manhal al-ṣāfī*, 1:252; Schiltberger, *Bondage*, 7, 33; Ibn Iyās, *Bidāʾiʿ al-zuhūr*, 5:61; Har-El, *Struggle for Domination*, 213; Devonshire, "Relation," 24–25; Perry, "Daily Life," 30–33.

85. Ibn Taghrī Birdī, *Al-Manhal al-ṣāfī*, no. 374.

86. Ibn Taghrī Birdī, *Al-Manhal al-ṣāfī*, nos. 365, 651, 983.

87. Ibn Taghrī Birdī, *Al-Manhal al-ṣāfī*, nos. 983.

88. The sisters were Tulū and Urdū. Ibn Ḥajar, *Al-Durar al-kāmina*, no. 862.

89. Popper, "History," 18:1–2.

90. Al-Maqrīzī, *Kitāb al-sulūk*, 2:1:240–41. See also Ibn Taghrī Birdī, *Al-Manhal al-ṣāfī*, no. 470 and BNF arabe 2071, fol. 162r.

91. Tamba, *Bernardo de Rodulfis*, 327, 342, docs. 369, 374; Tiepolo, *Domenico*, 23–24, doc. 11; ASVe, Canc. inf., Not., b.20, N.10, fol. 1v; b.58, reg. 1438–1441, fol. 18v; b.80, N.7, reg. 1, fol. 6r; Ibn Taghrī Birdī, *Al-Manhal al-ṣāfī*, nos. 367, 796, 784, 1073; Ragib, *Actes*, nos. XII, XIII; Tria, "La schiavitù," 143, 222–23, docs. 10, 90; ASG, Not. Ant. 380, fols. 60v–61r, 112r–113r; Not. Ant. 399, fols. 111r–112r; Khvalkov, "Slave Trade," 116.

92. "Michi plurima contulleritis servitia et osequia indignum esset si contra vos ingratam essem." Tamba, *Bernardo de Rodulfis*, 280–81, doc. 311; Gioffrè, *Il mercato*, "Slaves Without Race" table (1411). See also Tria, "La schiavitù," 156–57, doc. 27.

93. Zamboni, *Gli Ezzelini*, 249, 410–11.

94. Epstein, *Speaking*, 132; Klapisch-Zuber, "Women Servants," 60; Marmon, "Domestic Slavery," 9; Rapoport, "Women," 12, 16, 18; Gioffrè, *Il mercato*, 89–90; Romano, *Housecraft*, 171; Stuard, "Ancillary Evidence," 22; Datini, *Letters*, 40–42, 44, 134, 169, 378.

95. Klapisch-Zuber, "Women Servants," 58; Rapoport, "Women," 23.

96. Marmon, "Domestic Slavery," 9; al-ʿAynī, *ʿIqd al-jumān*, 1:362; Ibn Shahīn, *Zoubdat kachf*, 122; al-Sakhāwī, *Al-Ḍawʾ al-lāmiʿ*, 12:66–67, no. 404 (specializing in geomancy).

97. Epstein, *Speaking*, 133, 135; Klapisch-Zuber, "Women Servants," 60; Romano, *Housecraft*, 171; Marmon, "Domestic Slavery," 9; al-Maqrīzī, *Kitāb al-khiṭaṭ*, 2:582; Harff, *Pilgrimage*, 108, 182; Lewis, *Race*, 68; Sobers Khan, "Slaves, Wealth, and Fear," 157.

98. Molmenti, *La storia di Venezia*, 2:570; Romano, *Housecraft*, 170.

99. Interiano, *La vita e sito*, fols. 5v–6r.

100. Tafur, *Travels*, 133.

101. "Qualche tartera di nazione, che sono per durare fatica vantaggiate e rustiche. Le rosse, cioè quelle di Rossia, sono più gentili di compressione e più belle; ma, a mio parere, sarebbero meglio tartere. Le circasse, è forte sangue; benché tutte l'abbino questo." Strozzi, *Lettere*, 475. See also Gioffrè, *Il mercato*, 103; Balard, *La Romanie*, 2:822; Cluse, "Frauen," 103.

102. "Aliquis sclavus masculus de lingua tartarea emptus de novo . . . prave et male condicionis et cottidie faciant brigas et rumores, et de levi possent inducere scandala et errores in hac terra." ASVe, Senato, Deliberazioni Misti, reg. 32, fol. 134r.

103. Lewis, *Race*, 56, 59, 68; Harff, *Pilgrimage*, 108, 112, 182; Sobers Khan, "Slaves, Wealth, and Fear," 157; El Hamel, *Black Morocco*, 62–86.

104. Al-ʿAyntābī, *Al-Qawl al-sadīd*, 56.

105. Al-ʿAyntābī, *Al-Qawl al-sadīd*, 52.

106. Al-ʿAyntābī, *Al-Qawl al-sadīd*, 55.

107. Frederick II was accused of keeping eunuchs in imitation of Muslim rulers. Tanner, *Decrees*, 281–82 (Lyons I).

108. Ayalon, "L'esclavage," 14–15; Marmon, *Eunuchs*, 11–12; *Al-Maqṣad al-rafīʿ*, fols. 124r–127r.

109. Ibn Taghrī Birdī, *Al-Manhal al-ṣāfī*, no. 1223.

110. Ibn al-Ukhuwwa, *Maʿālim al-qurba*, 76; Lewis, *Race*, 10; Brunschvig, "ʿAbd," 3a.

111. Marmon, *Eunuchs*, 126n48 and 133n103.

112. Marmon, *Eunuchs*, 69, 71.

113. Epstein, *Speaking*, 135; Makris, *Studien*, 110.

114. Epstein, *Speaking*, 133, 137; Gioffrè, *Il mercato*, 90, 94; Balard, "Remarques," 651; Arbel, "Slave Trade," 160–61; Mummey, "Enchained in Paradise," 126–27.

115. Lewis, *Race*, 56.

116. Breydenbach, *Sanctarum peregrinationum*, fol. 84v.

117. Marmon, "Domestic Slavery," 13; Goitein, "Slaves," 4; Gioffrè, *Il mercato*, 84–85, 89–90; Greci, "Datini Correspondence," 438; ASVe, Canc. inf., Not., b.88, N.11, reg. 2, fol. 15v.

118. ʿAbd al-Raziq, *La femme*, 82; Balard, *La Romanie*, 2:804, 821, 823; Bensch, "From Prizes of War," 84; Schiel, "Mord," 222.

119. Loiseau, "Frankish Captives."

120. Gioffrè, *Il mercato*, 91; Verlinden, "La législation," 2:161; Lazari, "Del traffico," 482–83.

121. Epstein, *Speaking*, 97–98; Schiel, "Mord," 202, 220–22.

122. Al-Maqrīzī, *Kitāb al-khiṭaṭ*, 3:691–95, is the classic description. Ayalon, "L'esclavage," and Ayalon, "Mamlūk"; al-ʿArīnī, *Al-Mamālīk*, and al-ʿArīnī , "Al-Fāris"; Rabie, "Training."

123. Al-ʿArīnī, "Al-Fāris," 55–56; Ayalon, "L'esclavage," 17; Popper, "Egypt and Syria," 17:144.

124. Al-ʿArīnī, *Al-Mamālīk*, 218; Ayalon, "L'esclavage," 9–14; Rabie, "Training"; Rabbat, "Changing Concept," 93–95, 97; Levanoni, *A Turning Point*, 14–19.

125. Al-ʿArīnī, "Al-Fāris," 60–61; Levanoni, *A Turning Point*, 19–20.

126. Irwin, "Factions"; Steenbergen, *Order out of Chaos*; Mazor, *Rise and Fall.*

127. Irwin, "Factions," 240–41; Rabbat, *Citadel*, 293.

128. Irwin, "Factions," 240.

129. "كان من المهملين المنهمكين." Al-Sakhāwī, *Al-Ḍawʾ al-lāmiʿ*, 3:60, no. 244.

130. Northrup, "Military Slavery," 129; Pipes, *Slave Soldiers*, 13–23.

131. Ayalon, "L'esclavage," 54; al-ʿArīnī, *Al-Mamālīk*, 125–26; Petry, *Protectors or Praetorians?*, 73. There were a few exceptions. Ibn Taghrī Birdī, *Al-Manhal al-ṣāfī*, nos. 224, 331, 1238, 1378.

132. Levanoni, *A Turning Point*, 34–36; Ibn Taghrī Birdī, *Al-Manhal al-ṣāfī*, BNF arabe 2072, fols. 36v–37v; al-Maqrīzī, *Kitāb al-khiṭaṭ*, 4:224–26. Similarly al-Sakhāwī, *Al-Ḍawʾ al-lāmiʿ*, 2:312, no. 985.

133. Al-Maqrīzī, *Kitāb al-khiṭaṭ*, 3:692–93; Rabie, "Training," 154; Ayalon, "L'esclavage," 16; Northrup, *From Slave to Sultan*, 195.

134. "قلنا إن مرجعه الى بيت المال لأن واقفيه أرقاء بيت المال وفي ثبوت عتقهم نظر." Al-Suyūṭī, *Al-Ḥāwī lil-fatāwī*, 1:156. Thanks to Leonor Fernandes for sharing this reference.

135. Ibn Taghrī Birdī, *Al-Manhal al-ṣāfī*, 7:289, no. 1439.

136. Ibn al-Furāt, *Tārīkh al-duwal*, 7:285, 8:222; Popper, "Egypt and Syria," 13:10–11, 17:144, 18:2, 19:25–26.

137. Lewis, *Race*, 68; Rabbat, "Changing Concept," 82; Frenkel, "Some Notes," 190–92; Ayalon, "Mamlūkiyyāt," 325–26. This was not true of all systems of military slavery. Bacharach, "African Military Slaves"; Eaton, "Rise and Fall."

138. Lewis, *Race*, 68; Marmon, "Black Slaves." In 1446, African slaves created an imitation court outside Cairo. Some contemporaries portrayed it as a revolt, others as a festival. The sultan disbursed it and shipped the slaves to the Ottomans. Sobers Khan, "Slaves, Wealth, and Fear."

139. Al-Maqrīzī, *Kitāb al-khiṭaṭ*, 3:692–94; al-ʿArīnī, "Al-Fāris," 51; Rabbat, "Changing Concept," 95–96; Irwin, "Factions," 233; Levanoni, "Al-Maqrizi's Account," 96–101.

140. Al-ʿAyntābī, *Al-Qawl al-sadīd*, 50–51.

141. Al-ʿAyntābī, *Al-Qawl al-sadīd*, 52–54.

142. Ibn Taghrī Birdī, *Al-Manhal al-ṣāfī*, no. 1279; Ayalon, "Circassians," 144. Al-Maqrīzī castigated Sultan Barqūq and all Circassians for greed and corruption, but his rhetoric reflects his unhappiness with the political transition under Barqūq as well as actual instances of corruption. Levanoni, "Al-Maqrizi's Account," 101–3.

143. "الأشقر لا نظير له في القحة والفجور والشر والأخلاق والكذب." Al-ʿAyntābī, *Al-Qawl al-sadīd*, 54.

144. Klapisch-Zuber, "Women Servants," 72; Stuard, "Ancillary Evidence," 10–11; Pistarino, "Tra liberi e schiave," 360; Ali, *Marriage*; Johansen, "Valorization," 84; Perry, "Daily Life," ch. 3.

145. Stuard, "Ancillary Evidence," 17; Cluse, "Zur Repräsentation," 389–90; Johansen, "Valorization," 80; Blumenthal, *Enemies and Familiars*, 169–82; Karras, *Unmarriages*, 6–7; Rapoport, "Ibn Ḥağar," 344. Negative commentary on the morals of slave women has crept into the secondary scholarship as well: Amia, *Schiavitù*, 157; Lazari, "Del traffico," 477–81; Gioffrè, *Il mercato*, 96.

146. In the Islamic context, licit sex implied male control, so a free woman could not claim sexual ownership of her male slave. Ali, *Marriage*, 12–15. In the Catholic context, free women who knowingly married unfree men lost their freedom. Friedberg, *Corpus iuris canonici*, C.29 q.2 c.3 vs. Pahlitzsch, "Slavery," 166. Homosexual sex is discussed in Marmon, "Domestic Slavery," 4; Rabbat, "Changing Concept," 95; Ayalon, "L'esclavage," 14; Irwin, "Ali al-Baghdadi," 46; Ruggiero, *Boundaries of Eros*, 115–16; Sabaté, "Gli schiavi," 404–5. Accusations of homosexuality were a trope of Christian polemics against Islam, so comments by Christian pilgrims on Mamluk sex should be interpreted cautiously. Boswell, *Christianity*, 279–83; Daniel, *Islam*, 164–69.

147. Gilchrist, "Medieval Canon Law," and Gilchrist, "Saint Raymond of Peñafort," 319; Winroth, "Neither Slave nor Free," 107–8; Landau, "Hadrians IV. Dekretale"; Sahaydachny, "*De coniugio seruorum*."

148. Friedberg, *Corpus iuris canonici*, C.29 q.2 c.3; Pistarino, "Tra liberi e schiave," 365–73.

149. Brundage, "Concubinage," 118–28; Harper, *Slavery*, 314–19; Karras, *Unmarriages*, 95, 147; Zorgati, *Pluralism*, ch. 5. Concubinage also existed in Jewish law and practice, though there was a late medieval move to suppress it. Perry, "Daily Life," ch. 3.

150. Ruggiero, *Boundaries of Eros*, 14–15, 162; Karras, *Unmarriages*, 84; McKee, "Implications," 105; Balletto, "Schiavi," 686; Cossar, "Clerical 'Concubines'"; Pedani, "Mamluk Documents," 139; Orlandi, "Catalonia Company," 352; Colli, *Moretto Bon*, doc. 27; Ashtor, *Levant Trade*, 408; Bresc, *Le livre de raison*, 51.

151. Strozzi, *Selected Letters*, 111.

152. Karras, *Unmarriages*, 7, 17; Cossar, "Clerical 'Concubines,'" 111–12; Blumenthal, "Masters," 239. Versus Orlandi, "Catalonia Company," 352.

153. Karras, *Unmarriages*, 70, 97; Ruggiero, *Boundaries of Eros*, 40, 107.

154. Molmenti, *La storia di Venezia*, 2:571.

155. "Explende libidinis suae causa." Bosco, *Consilia*, 495; Cluse, "Frauen," 104.

156. Origo, "Domestic Enemy," is the quintessential example vs. McKee, "Implications," 104; Harper, *Slavery*, 284. Rapoport, "Ibn Ḥağar," takes a more nuanced approach.

157. "Quia maxima quantitas sclavarum est ad presens Venecium et est futura maior . . . quod sclave efficiuntur minoris et vilioris pretii quia pregnantur et adulteres efficiuntur." ASVe, Maggior Consiglio, Deliberazioni, reg. 19 (Novella), fol. 103r (September 17, 1364).

158. Ruggiero, *Boundaries of Eros*, 40. Signori di Notte records for this era are spotty.

159. Epstein, *Speaking*, 133; Verlinden, "La législation," 153–54; Desimoni, *Statuto*, 30–31.

160. Cessi, *Deliberazioni*, 3:179–80, doc. 89; ASVe, Signori di Notte al Criminal, reg. 1A, fols. 3v, 6v–7v.

161. Ruggiero, *Boundaries of Eros*, 19–21, 40–41; Klapisch-Zuber, "Women Servants," 72.

162. Gioffrè, *Il mercato*, 98.

163. Heers, *Esclaves*, 216–21; Tria, "La schiavitù," 156, 166–67, 184, docs. 26, 37, 53; ASG, Not. Ant. 292, fols. 203v–204r; 379, fol. 147v; 404/I, fol. 96r; 719/III, doc. 97.

164. Brunschvig, "'Abd," 2a, 3e; Marmon, "Domestic Slavery," 4, 6; Rapoport, "Ibn Ḥağar"; Ali, *Marriage*, 6; Johansen, "Valorization," 71–112; Rapoport, "Women," 23.

165. Marmon, "Domestic Slavery," 4, 12. Compare with Williams, "From the Commercial Revolution," 231.

166. Popper, "Egypt and Syria," 18:147.

167. Guo, "Tales."

168. Ibn al-Mujāwir, *A Traveller*, 162.

169. Rapoport, "Ibn Ḥağar," 339; Rapoport, "Women," 11.

170. Katz, *Dreams*, 117, 120.

171. Al-Maqrīzī, *Kitāb al-sulūk*, 2:2:546; Ibn Taghrī Birdī, *Al-Manhal al-ṣāfī*, 2:426, no. 452.

172. Al-ʿAyntābī, *Al-Qawl al-sadīd*, 55–56.

173. "إلا أنهن كنز الأولاد ومعادن النسل." Al-ʿAyntābī, *Al-Qawl al-sadīd*, 50–51.

174. Katz, *Dreams*, 118.

175. Guo, "Tales," 117–18.

176. Brunschvig, "ʿAbd," 3f, 3l; Mirza, "Remembering"; al-Jarawānī, *Al-Kawkab al-mushriq*, 359. *Umm walad* status began at pregnancy, not at birth.

177. Rapoport, "Ibn Ḥağar," 333–34; Guo, "Tales," 121. Recently, the Islamic State (ISIS) has used the sexual exploitation of slave women for pleasure as a recruiting tool. Since *umm walad* status and the birth of heirs would restrict the exchange of slaves for pleasure, ISIS has systematically forced birth control on the women held by its fighters. Callimachi, "To Maintain Supply." Although birth control existed in the Middle Ages, it was nowhere near as effective as modern methods. With respect to slavery, then, ISIS' policy of suppressing the *umm walad* is one of its most significant departures from Islamic legal tradition.

178. Brunschvig, "'Abd," 3e–f; Johansen, "Valorization," 77, 89; Ali, *Marriage*, 49–62; Katz, *Dreams*, 89–93, 117–20. In contrast, Pontano, "De obedientia," links marriage and servitude via Aristotle.

179. Slave wives existed in colloquial language, although not in law, in nineteenth-century Egypt. Troutt Powell, *A Different Shade of Colonialism*. That was not the case in Mamluk Egypt.

180. Three legal schools assumed that a slave woman's master had fathered her child unless it was impossible for him to have done so at the time she became pregnant. Otherwise, a crime must have been committed, because a slave woman was only allowed to have sex with her master. In contrast, the Ḥanafī legal school required the father to claim paternity. Brunschvig, "ʿAbd," 3f.

181. Ibn Baṭṭuṭa, *Travels*, 539, 556.

182. Ibn al-Ukhuwwa, *Maʿālim al-qurba*, 20, 57, 75; al-Shayzarī, *Book*, 102; Ibn Bassām, *Nihāyat al-rutba*, 150.

183. Desimoni, *Leges genuenses*, 951; Friedberg, *Corpus iuris canonici*, C.15 q.8 c.3, C.32 q.3 c.1, C.32 q.4 c.9, C.32 q.4 c.15, X.1.18.8, X.4.10.1; Passeggieri, *Summa totius artis notariae*, fol. 412r–v and gloss; Antoninus, *Summa*, title 3, ch. 6, part vi, offers a loophole if the slave mother is a *socia*.

184. Iulianus Vinacia gave his own daughter by a slave woman to a priest. Tria, "La schiavitù," 156–57, doc. 27.

185. Balard, *La Romanie*, 2:822; Blumenthal, *Enemies and Familiars*, 260; Prokofieva, "Akti," no. 128; ASG, Not. Ant. 399, fol. 31r–v.

186. McKee, "Domestic Slavery," 323n27; Brackett, "Race and Rulership."

187. Epstein, *Speaking*, 131.

188. Klapisch-Zuber, "Women Servants," 69.

189. Heers, *Esclaves*, 227; Cluse, "Frauen," 99.

190. Brundage, "Concubinage," 127; Cossar, "Clerical 'Concubines,'" 119; Passeggieri, *Summa totius artis notariae*, fol. 415r.

191. Karras, *Unmarriages*, 96, 146–47; Belgrano, *Della vita*, 407–8.

192. Bosco, *Consilia*, 135–42, cons. 78; Epstein, "A Late Medieval Lawyer," 49–68; McKee, "Inherited Status," 47.

193. "Potuit esse concubina, et filii nati ex ea sunt naturales." Bosco, *Consilia*, 136.

194. Bosco, *Consilia*, 136, favoring Friedberg, *Corpus iuris canonici*, X.4.9 over C.32 q.4.

195. Morozzo della Rocca, *Lettere*, 33–40, docs. 14–15.

196. Blumenthal, "Masters," 236; Cluse, "Frauen," 99; Winer, *Women*, 151.

197. Cluse, "Frauen," 96–103; Winer, "Conscripting the Breast"; Blumenthal, "Masters," 237; Guo, "Tales," 115; ʿAbd al-Raziq, *La femme*, 83–84.

198. Cluse, "Frauen," 97–98.

199. Blumenthal, *Enemies and Familiars*, 174.

200. McKee, "Inherited Status," 45; Karras, *Unmarriages*, 92.

201. McKee, "Inherited Status."

202. Bosco, *Consilia*, 135–42, cons. 78.

203. Cluse, "Frauen," 108.

204. Blumenthal, *Enemies and Familiars*, 173–74; Blumenthal, "Masters," 237, 245–52; McKee, "Inherited Status," 48–50. The situation could have evolved in other ways: in medieval Japan, boys took the father's status and girls took the mother's status. Nelson, "Slavery," 474.

205. It was the opposite in Ragusa: enslaved wet nurses were automatically freed upon the death of their masters, but their children remained enslaved. Stuard, "To Town to Serve," 43.

206. Daniel, *Islam*, 158; Ghistele, *Voyage*, 20–21.

207. Cassandro, "Aspects of the Life," 15.

208. "Si vero aliquis dominus carnaliter cognoverit sclavam suam, que partum produxerit ex eodem, statuimus quod nichilominus ipsa sclava propterea libera non existat." Desimoni, *Leges genuenses*, c.952.

209. Miller, *Problem*, 32–33, 66–67.

210. On medieval contraception and abortion in general, see Green, *Making Women's Medicine Masculine*, 222, 235, 312; Pormann and Savage-Smith, *Medieval Islamic Medicine*, 107, 148.

211. Pistarino, "Tra liberi e schiave," 361; Blumenthal, *Enemies and Familiars*, 172–93.

212. Guo, "Tales," 109–13. See also Rapoport, "Ibn Ḥağar," 334–35.

213. "Velet esse cuma alicuius . . . tunc sit expulsa de domo mea in chamixia." Prokofieva, "Akti," no. 128.

214. Miers and Kopytoff, *Slavery in Africa*, 40; Miller, *Problem*, 93. This was why manumitted slaves took the family names of their former masters. Heers, *Gênes*, 568; Epstein, *Speaking*, 26; Ayalon, "Names," 213–17.

215. Ibn Taghrī Birdī, *Al-Manhal al-ṣāfī*, nos. 264, 463, 802, 849, 957, 959, 1020, 1358, 1405; al-Sakhāwī, *Al-Ḍaw' al-lāmi'*, 5:242–43, no. 829 and 6:48, no. 131; Rapoport, "Women," 11; Ibn Baṭṭuṭa, *Travels*, 55; Tafur, *Travels*, 73.

216. Little, "Six Fourteenth Century Purchase Deeds"; and Little, "Two Fourteenth-Century Court Records"; Lutfi, *Al-Quds*, 307, for Jerusalem. Ragib, *Actes*, nos. XII, XIII, for Bahnasā.

217. Balard, "Remarques," 664, found that drapers and spice merchants were most common in the thirteenth century.

218. Balbi, *Simon Boccanegra*, 211; Gioffrè, *Il mercato*, 82–83; Balard, *La Romanie*, 2:819; Epstein, *Speaking*, 112–13; Wallace, *Premodern Places*, 192.

219. ASVe, Canc. inf., Not., b.19, N.7, reg. 3, fols. 2r, 3r, 4r.

220. ASVe, Canc. inf., Not., b.19, N.7, reg. 1, fol. 4r and reg. 3, fol. 4r; b.80, N.7, reg. 1, fol. 1r; b.230, N.1, reg. 3, fol. 16v.

221. Tria, "La schiavitù," 156–57, doc. 27; Gioffrè, *Il mercato*, Russian table; Macchiavello, *I cartolari*, doc. 83.

222. ASG, Not. Ant. 402, fol. 108r–v; Tria, "La schiavitù," 212, doc. 79; Verlinden, "La législation," 164, 172; Verlinden, "Le recrutement des esclaves à Venise," 149.

223. Spuler, *Die Goldene Horde*, 386; Rodocanachi, "Les esclaves," 389.

224. Pistarino, "Tra liberi e schiave," 355; Gioffrè, *Il mercato*, Russian table (1406, 1428, 1459), Circassian table (1424), Bulgarian table (1424), Hungarian table (1487), Moor table (1474, 1492); ASG, CdSG, N.185,00624; ASG, Not. Ant. 719/III, doc. 97; ASVe, Canc. inf., Not., b.59, prot. 1444–1445, fol. 53v.

225. ASVe, Canc. inf., Not., b.59, prot. 1442–1443 (September 28, 1442); b.80, N.7, reg. 1, fol. 8v; b.222, fol. 4r–v; Verlinden, "Le recrutement des esclaves à Venise," 152.

226. Gioffrè, *Il mercato*, Russian table (1436); ASG, Notai ignoti, b.xxiv.3; ASG, Not. Ant. 397, fol. 137r; ASG, Not. Ant. 398, fol. 70r–v; *Viaggi fatti da Vinetia*, 8; Luttrell, "Slavery." The Teutonic Knights enslaved Tatars captured in Lithuania. Spuler, *Die Goldene Horde*, 386.

227. ASVe, Canc. inf., Misc., b.134 bis, series 1, items 33, 41; ASVe, Canc. inf., Not., b.17, reg. 1, fol. 7r–v; b.59, reg. 1445 (August 14, 1445); b.60, prot. 1446–1449, fols. 41r–v, 60v.

228. ASVe, Canc. inf., Not., b.19, N.7, reg. 5, item 77.

229. Ibn Taghrī Birdī, *Al-Manhal al-ṣāfī*, 4:271–74, no. 847.

230. Ibn Taghrī Birdī, *Al-Manhal al-ṣāfī*, 3:447, no. 717, and BNF arabe 2071, fols. 206r–207r; al-Sakhāwī, *Al-Ḍawʾ al-lāmiʿ*, 6:164, no. 547.

231. Ibn Taghrī Birdī, *Al-Manhal al-ṣāfī*, no. 1282.

232. Frenkel, "Some Notes," 196.

233. Al-ʿArīnī, "Al-Fāris," 52; al-Maqrīzī, *Kitāb al-khiṭaṭ*, 3:693; Ibn Taghrī Birdī, *Al-Manhal al-ṣāfī*, no. 583, 602, 1151, 1162, 1260.

234. Ibn Taghrī Birdī, *Al-Manhal al-ṣāfī*, no. 367.

235. Ibn Taghrī Birdī, *Al-Manhal al-ṣāfī*, no. 470, and BNF arabe 2071, fol. 162r.

236. Forand, "Relation"; Marmon, "Domestic Slavery," 14–17; Brunschvig, "ʿAbd," 3k; Helmholz, "Law of Slavery," B.

237. Balard, *La Romanie*, 2:826, 882; Gioffrè, *Il mercato*, 92, "Slaves Without Race" table (1401).

238. Gioffrè, *Il mercato*, Russian table (1437).

239. Ibn Taghrī Birdī, *Al-Manhal al-ṣāfī*, no. 1119.

240. Macchiavello, *I cartolari*, doc. 83.

241. *Viaggi fatti da Vinetia*, 8.

242. "Fuit venditus Ianue, eruditusque et liberatus a servitute intravit ordinem Predicatorum." Kern, "Der 'Libellus de notitia orbis,'" 111.

243. ASVe, Canc. inf., Not., b.20, N.8, reg. 6, fol. 8r; see also Balard, "Remarques," 679.

244. She was probably Sudanese. Williams, "Mosque"; ʿAbd al-Raziq, *La femme*, 60–61.

245. Datini, *Letters*, 8–9. Lucia had several more children with her husband.

246. ASVe, Canc. inf., Not., b.20, N.8, reg. 6, fol. 7r.

247. Verlinden, "Le recrutement des esclaves à Venise," 103–4. See also Prokofieva, "Akti," nos. 56, 128, 148.

248. Gioffrè, *Il mercato*, "Slaves Without Race" table (1463, 1472).

249. ʿAbd al-Raziq, *La femme*, 54.

250. Williams, *From the Commercial Revolution*, 318.

251. Ibn Taghrī Birdī, *Al-Manhal al-ṣāfī*, no. 1182; Rapoport, "Women," 8.

252. Ibn Taghrī Birdī, *Al-Manhal al-ṣāfī*, no. 858 and BNF, arabe 2072, fol. 109r; al-Sakhāwī, *Al-Ḍawʾ al-lāmiʿ*, 12:68–69, 117, 127, nos. 417, 710, 779; Popper, "Egypt and Syria," 23:67.

253. Al-Ṣāliḥ Ismaʿīl, al-Kāmil Shaʿbān, and al-Muẓaffar Ḥājjī. Rapoport, "Women," 11.

254. Romano, *Housecraft*, 161–65; Cluse, "Frauen," 92; Brunschvig, "ʿAbd," 2a–b; Lewis, *Race*, 4.

255. "Omnia quae adquisivit in domo mea suo labore." Lazari, "Del traffico," 472–73.

256. ASG, Not. Ant. 255, fol. 147r.

257. Luzzato, *Studi di storia economica*, 130.

258. Rabie, *Financial System*, 132.

259. Romano, *Housecraft*, 180.

260. Braunstein, "Être esclave," 91.

261. Rabie, "Ḥujjāt tamlīk wa-waqf," late Ayyubid period.

262. Romano, *Housecraft*, 172.

263. ASG, Not. Ant. 403, fol. 112r–v.

264. Ibn Taghrī Birdī, *Al-Manhal al-ṣāfī*, no. 1199.

265. Al-Sakhāwī, *Al-Ḍawʾ al-lāmiʿ*, 12:66, no. 403.

266. Ghazāl's daughter Fāṭima inventoried her belongings. Lutfi, *Al-Quds*, 46–48.

267. Verlinden, "Le recrutement des esclaves a Genes," 50.

268. ASVe, Canc. inf., Not., b.121, N.2, reg. 2, fol. 4r.

269. Tria, "La schiavitù," 148–49, doc. 17.

270. Tucci, *Le imposte*, 42; Cibrario, *Della schiavitù*, 208–10; ASG, Not. Ant. 645, docs. 33, 35.

271. ASG, Not. Ant. 397, fol. 193r–v. See also ASG, Not. Ant. 401, fols. 180v–181r; Balard, "Remarques," 678.

272. Blumenthal, *Enemies and Familiars*, 219.

273. Bongi, "Le schiave," 222.

274. Brunschvig, "ʿAbd," 3b; Gilchrist, "Saint Raymond of Peñafort," 318; Helmholz, "Law of Slavery," C4.

275. Desimoni, *Leges genuenses*, 959–62.

276. Patterson, *Slavery and Social Death*, 4–5.

277. "Qui vero captus sit, amissa patria, coniuge, liberis, parentibus, qui amare aut raptorem, aut emptorem possit, non video; cum sciat erepta sibi ab illis ea, quae prima mortales ducunt, libertatem, et divitias: et cum his quos dixi, uxorem, liberos, cognatos." Pontano, "De obedientia," 202.

278. "Ire, stare, redire, mutare domos." Tria, "La schiavitù," 169, doc. 39.

279. Verlinden, "La législation," 149–51; Desimoni, *Leges genuenses*, 937–38, 782–83.

280. Amia, *Schiavitù*, 158; ASVe, Avog., Raspe, reg. 3646, fols. 9–10; ASVe, Canc. inf., Not., b.58, reg. 1442–1443, fol. 96r; ASG, Not. Ant. 397, fols. 36, 176–77, 203; Not. Ant. 402, fol. 7.

281. Delort, "Quelques précisions," 238.

282. "Nihil aliud inter se tractant, non aliud cogitant et loquuntur, nisi quo modo et quo fugiant . . . in fuga ad loca inhabitata veniunt, et montibus et solitudinibus errantes fame et situ pereunt." Fabri, *Evagatorium*, 18:167.

283. Fabri, *Evagatorium*, 18:26; Ibn Taghrī Birdī, *Al-Manhal al-ṣāfī*, nos. 407, 767; Ibn Taghrī Birdī, *Al-Nujūm al-zāhira*, 14:349.

284. Lyons and Lyons, *Ayyubids*, 1:168–69, 2:132–34. The rulers of Acre and Tyre angered Sultan Baybars by keeping the mamluks and letting them convert to Christianity.

285. "Ira dementata fuit, ut Deum blasphemaret et Machometum benediceret, seque ad ritum Machometi migraturum proclameret, quod et fecisset." Fabri, *Evagatorium*, 18:167–68. See also Perry, "Conversion."

286. Qasim, *ʿAṣr salāṭīn al-mamālīk*, 242; ʿAbd al-Rahim, "Al-Mamālīk al-julbān," 112. Cypriot fears of slave revolt never materialized. Arbel, "Slave Trade"; Dincer, "Enslaving Christians."

287. "Ad tantas enim miserias homo venditus devenit, ut vivere taedeat et mors omnibus modis quaeratur." Fabri, *Evagatorium*, 18:168.

288. Makhairas, *Recital*, 1:464–67.

289. Piattoli, "L'assicurazione," 873–74.

290. ASVe, Avog., Raspe, reg. 3646, fols. 81v–82r; Schiel, "Mord," 201–2.

291. "Quia a pauco tempore citra visa fuerunt esse occursa de talibus rebus perpetratis per sclavas vel servas." ASVe, Signori di Notte al Criminal, reg. 1A, fols. 45v–46r.

292. Schiel, "Mord." See also Meek, "Men, Women"; Tria, "La schiavitù," 222, doc. 89.

293. Toledano, *As If Silent and Absent*, ch. 3.

294. Popper, "Egypt and Syria," 13:103–4. Ḥājjī may have targeted his black slave women: al-Sakhāwī, *Al-Ḍawʾ al-lāmiʿ*, 3:87, no. 340. Aqūsh al-Ashrafī was also notorious for beating his slave women. Ibn Taghrī Birdī, *Al-Manhal al-ṣāfī*, 3:27–30, no. 518. The mother of Yalbughā al-Yaḥyāwī was smothered by her slave women in 1349. Al-Maqrīzī, *Kitāb al-sulūk*, 2:3:799–800.

295. Epstein, *Speaking*, 63–64.

Chapter 4

1. Meillassoux, *Anthropology of Slavery*, 11.

2. ASG, Not. Ant. 449, doc. 47; Tria, "La schiavitù," 192–93, doc. 62; Gioffrè, *Il mercato*, Russian table (1439); ASG, Not. Ant. 253, fol. 132r. Auctions in Caffa took place in the communal palace, near the law courts, and in the *loggia*. Balbi and Raiteri, *Notai genovesi*, docs. 46, 52, 54; ASG, Not. Ant. 273, fol. 230v; Balletto, "Caffa," 219, 224–25.

3. ASVe, Quarantia criminal, Parti II, reg. 29, fol. 74v. Verlinden, "Le recrutement des esclaves à Venise," 117, incorrectly described this as a ban on all slave sales. Auctions appear in Molmenti, *La storia*, 1:131; Lombardo, *Nicola de Boateriis*, 307, doc. 300; Lazari, "Del traffico," 480; Braunstein, "Être esclave," 90; ASVe, Canc. inf., Not., b.149, N.1, reg. 5, fol. 73v.

4. Little, "Two Fourteenth-Century Court Records," 32–33.

5. On slave markets, see Barker, "Purchasing a Slave." On other specialized markets in Cairo, see al-Maqrīzī, *Kitāb al-khiṭaṭ*; Qāsim, *ʿAṣr salāṭīn al-mamālīk*, ch. 9.

6. Ragib, "Les marchés," 722–23; Constable, *Housing the Stranger.*

7. For fairs, *Al-Taḥqīq fī shirāʾ al-raqīq*, fol. 15; al-ʿAyntābī, *Al-Qawl al-sadīd*, 36. For entries, Ragib, "Les marchés," 723–24. For squares, Fabri, *Evagatorium*, 18:36–37, 40; Guglingen, *Fratris Pauli Waltheri*, 230; Ghistele, *Voyage*, 20. For streets, Broquière, *The Voyage*, 84.

8. Al-Maqrīzī, *Kitāb al-khiṭaṭ*, 2:246. There is no evidence that female slaves were sold there, despite Raymond and Wiet, *Les Marchés*, 94–95; Mukhtar, *Bughiyyat al-murīd*, 86, or that auctions happened there, despite Ragib, "Les marchés," 756. The slave market in Bursa also had benches. Broquière, *The Voyage*, 84.

9. Al-Maqrīzī, *Kitāb al-khiṭaṭ*, 3:94, 127; al-Khāṣikī, *Al-Tuḥfa al-fākira*, fols. 40v, 54r; al-Sakhāwī, *Al-Ḍawʾ al-lāmiʿ*, 10:159, no. 643; Ibn al-Furāt, *Tārīkh al-duwal*, 8:101. Barker, "Purchasing a Slave," 6–9, describes Cairo's slave markets in greater detail.

10. Ibn Iyās, *Badāʾiʿ al-zuhūr*, 4:404–5, 5:94; Denoix, Depaule, and Tuchscherer, *Le Khan al-Khalili*, 2:52; Seif, *Khan al-Khalili*, 54; Walz, "Wakalat al-Gallaba"; al-Jabartī, *ʿAbd al-Raḥmān al-Jabartī's History*, 2:314; Wiet, *Les Marchés*, Appendix II; Clerget, *Le Caire*, 2:343.

11. "Duxerunt autem eos in fonticum Tartarorum et eos ibi venales habuerunt." Fabri, *Evagatorium*, 18:152.

12. "Nobilissimas res, id est homines, vilissimo precio vidimus venales utriusque sexus, iuvenes et iuvenculas, pueros et puellas, mulieres etiam quasdam qui parvulos habebant ad ubera pendentes, qui omnes ibi sui expectabant venditionem." Breydenbach, *Sanctarum peregrinationum*, fol. 88r. Fabri, *Evagatorium*, 18:164; Harff, *Pilgrimage*, 95.

13. It burned during the Cypriot sack of Alexandria in 1365. Al-Nuwayrī, *Kitāb al-ilmām*, 2:166.

14. ASVe, Canc. inf., Not., b.211, reg. IV, fols. 55r, 65v, 67r, 69v; b.222, fols. 32r, 40r; b.230, N.1, reg. 1, fol. 31r; Sennoune, "Fondouks, Khans et Wakalas," 469.

15. Venice did not have a market (*forum*) for slaves. Fabri, *Evagatorium*, 18:432.

16. Belgrano, *Della vita*, 86.

17. "Actum Ianua in platham Sancti Luce iuxta ecclesiam." ASG, Not. Ant. 397, fol. 21r–v.

18. "In platea ubi congregantur et conveniuent mercatores." Verlinden, "Le recrutement des esclaves à Venise," 105; ASVe, Canc. inf., Misc., b.134 bis, series 1, item 4; Not. b.19, N.7, reg. 1, fol. 17v.

19. Rodocanachi, "Les esclaves," 393.

20. ASVe, Quarantia criminal, Parti II, reg. 29, fol. 74v.

21. Petrucci, *Notarii*, 26.

22. ASG, Not. Ant. 258, 287, 379 (Venti); 379–81 (Marocellus brothers); 396–405/I (Ususmaris brothers, Cicogne); 719 (de Nigro); Ferretto, "Codice diplomatico" (Pediculi).

23. Ferretto, "Codice diplomatico," 2:166, no. 362; ASG, Notai Antichi 685/II, docs. 18, 55.

24. ASVe, Canc. inf., Not., b.80, N.7, reg. 1, fol. 8v.

25. Clerget, *Le Caire*, 344; Mez, *Renaissance of Islam*, 160.

26. Ibn Taghrī Birdī, *Al-Manhal al-ṣāfī*, 3:447–67, no. 717.

27. Ibn Taghrī Birdī, *Al-Manhal al-ṣāfī*, 4:68, no. 769.

28. Ibn Taghrī Birdī, *Al-Nujūm al-zāhira*, 6:374.

29. Favier, *Gold and Spices*, 72–74; Blumenthal, *Enemies and Familiars*, 58–62.

30. ASG, Not. Ant. 403, fols. 187v–188r, makes the seller responsible for all expenses.

31. Both active in the 1410s. Victor Pisani: ASVe, Canc. inf., Not., b.230, N.2, reg. 4, fol. 3v and b.230, N.1, reg. 3, fols. 18v, 20r. Clarius Laurentii: ASVe, Canc. inf., Not., b.230, N.1, reg. 3, fols. 6v, 9r, 15r.

32. ASG, CdSG, N.185,00623. Heers, *Esclaves*, 181, observes that the brokers Isnard Boniface and Jean Dyenas were named frequently in connection with slave sales in Marseilles in 1380.

33. Shatzmiller, *Labour*, 262–63; Ragib, *Actes de vente*, 2:48.

34. Rabie, *Financial System*, 105. Ragib, *Actes*, 2:51–53, says the broker's fee was 10 percent.

35. The most famous treatises on slave market fraud were Ibn Buṭlān's "Risāla jāmiʿa," from eleventh-century Baghdad; and al-Saqaṭī, *Un Manuel hispanique de hisba*, from thirteenth-century Spain. See also Ragib, "Les marchés," 728–34, 759–61; Rosenberger, "Maquiller."

36. Rapoport, "Ibn Ḥağar," 332, suggests that the slave avoided being sold until Ibn Ḥajar's agent appeared, but it would have been easier for the broker to rig the sale.

37. Barker, "Purchasing a Slave," 18, 21; al-ʿAyntābī, *Al-Qawl al-sadīd*, 105.

38. Barker, "Purchasing a Slave," 18, 21; *Al-Taḥqīq fī shirāʾ al-raqīq*, fol. 15; al-ʿAyntābī, *Al-Qawl al-sadīd*, 108.

39. *Al-Taḥqīq fī shirāʾ al-raqīq*, fols. 14–15; al-ʿAyntābī, *Al-Qawl al-sadīd*, 36, 38.

40. Al-Sakhāwī, *Al-Ḍawʾ al-lāmiʿ*, 5:70, no. 255; 8:214–15, no. 559; 12:115, no. 696; al-Maqrīzī, *Kitāb al-sulūk*, 2:2:546; Little, "Six Fourteenth Century Purchase Deeds," 317.

41. Ragib, "Les marchés," 727.

42. Ibn Bassām, *Nihāyat al-rutba*, 149–50; Ibn al-Ukhuwwa, *Maʿālim al-qurba*, 19, 50.

43. Al-Shayzarī, *Book*, 103; Ibn Bassām, *Nihāyat al-rutba*, 149; Brunschvig, "ʿAbd," 3b; Friedmann, *Tolerance and Coercion*, 106–20.

44. Ghistele, *Voyage*, 21; Fabri, *Evagatorium*, 18:25, 37; Breydenbach, *Sanctarum peregrinationum*, fol. 84r.

45. Goitein, "Slaves," 13; Goitein, *A Mediterranean Society*, 1:136.

46. Ibn al-Ṣayrafī, *Inbāʾ al-haṣr*, 518–19.

47. Brunschvig, "ʿAbd," 3b; al-Shayzarī, *Book*, 102; Ibn al-Ukhuwwa, *Maʿālim al-qurba*, 20, 57; Ibn Bassām, *Nihāyat al-rutba*, 150. Preventing the separation of children from their fathers was discussed but not mandated.

48. Ibn Taghrī Birdī, *Al-Manhal al-ṣāfī*, 4:271–74, no. 847. See also al-Sakhāwī, *Al-Ḍawʾ al-lāmiʿ*, 10:275, no. 1078; 12:5, no. 24; Ghistele, *Voyage*, 21.

49. Ibn Iyās, *Bidāʾiʿ al-zuhūr*, 2:101.

50. "Clamor magnus et fletus . . . parvulus a sinu matris rapitur." Fabri, *Evagatorium*, 18:166.

51. Al-Shayzarī, *Book*, 102; Ibn Bassām, *Nihāyat al-rutba*, 149.

52. Richards, "Fragments."

53. Langholm, *Merchant in the Confessional*.

54. "النظر والمعرفة والمعاقدة الشرعية." or equivalent. Little, "Six Fourteenth Century Purchase Deeds," 298–99; al-Nuwayrī, *Nihāyat al-arab*, 9:36; Guellil, *Damaszener Akten*, 115; al-Asyūṭī, *Jawhar al-ʿuqūd*, 1:60, 75.

55. Patterson, *Slavery and Social Death*, 38; Udovitch, *Partnership and Profit*, 114.

56. Johansen, "Valorization," 74; Patterson, *Slavery and Social Death*, 10–12.

57. Aristotle, *Politics*, I.ii.4–6; Patterson, *Slavery and Social Death*, 32.

58. Johnson, *Soul by Soul*, 16–17. The choice of most slaves not to resist inspection was rational, given the violence they could expect, and did not diminish their agency. Johnson, "On Agency."

59. Mamluk experts wrote guides to horses and gems as well as slaves. Italians who wrote commercial advice manuals did not discuss slaves. Pegolotti, *La Pratica della mercatura*.

60. Delort, "Quelques précisions," 221; Verlinden, "Le recrutement des esclaves à Venise," 101; Ragib, "Les marchés," 744.

61. Al-ʿAyntābī, *Al-Qawl al-sadīd*, 36; Ibn Bassām, *Nihāyat al-rutba*, 149–50, 152; al-Shayzarī, *Book*, 103; al-Jarawānī, *Al-Kawkab al-mushriq*, 73; Barker, "Purchasing a Slave"; Ferragud, "Role of Doctors." Lay medical experience was also valued. Blumenthal, "Domestic Medicine."

62. Müller, *Die Kunst des Sklavenkaufs*. Al-Zawāwī, a Sufi, received advice about slave inspection from the Prophet Muḥammad himself in a dream. Katz, *Dreams*, 119.

63. Müller, *Die Kunst des Sklavenkaufs*; Swain, *Economy*; Hoyland, "Physiognomy"; Ghaly, "Physiognomy"; Ghersetti, "De l'achat"; Mourad, *La physiognomie*.

64. *Al-Taḥqīq fī shirāʾ al-raqīq*.

65. Barker, "Purchasing a Slave."

66. Al-ʿAyntābī, *Al-Qawl al-sadīd*.

67. Müller, *Die Kunst des Sklavenkaufs*, 109–11, 177.

68. Bosco, *Consilia*, 493–95, cons. 301. See also ASG, Not. Ant. 401, fols. 67v–68r, in which the buyer and seller dispute the doctor's inspection fee.

69. "Quia Baptista non liquidavit executionem suam intra mensam, cum intra eum non probauerit, nec etiam postea, quod dicta sclaua tempore venditionis esset infirma, et cum si fuisset infirma, id presciuerit, et ante venditionem super accidentibus sclauae habuerit consilium medicorum. Vnde non potest dicere, se errasse, nec vitium occultum." Bosco, *Consilia*, 495. In support of his opinion, Bosco cited ch. 21 of the *Digest* on fraud. He also noted that Baptista had had sex with the slave and had used ointment to treat her for scabies, possibly worsening her condition.

70. Ferragud, "Role of Doctors," 146; Jordan, "Fortune," 295–96.

71. Siraisi, "Libri morales," 113–14.

72. McVaugh, "Armengaud Blaise"; Swain, *Economy*, 498–503.

73. Foerster, *Scriptores physiognomonici*, 1:clxxvii and 2:157–58; Swain, *Seeing the Face*.

74. Fabri, *Evagatorium*, 18:165–66; the passage is translated in full in Barker, "Purchasing a Slave." See also Harff, *Pilgrimage*, 95; Breydenbach, *Sanctarum peregrinationum*, fol. 88r; Ghistele, *Voyage*, 21; Guglingen, *Fratris Pauli Waltheri*, 230.

75. Barker, "Purchasing a Slave," 18, 21.

76. "In illa consideratione sunt oculatissimi et expertissimi, non enim est medicus aut physicus, qui valeat eis comparari in cognoscendis complexionibus et conditionibus hominum." Fabri, *Evagatorium*, 18:165.

77. "Infirmus vel sanus, masculus vel foemella, virgo aut corrupta." Fabri, *Evagatorium*, 18:165.

78. Al-ʿAyntābī, *Al-Qawl al-sadīd*, had a separate chapter on physiognomy.

79. Ibn Bassām, *Nihāyat al-rutba*, 150; Barker, "Purchasing a Slave," 18, 21; al-ʿAyntābī, *Al-Qawl al-sadīd*, 105.

80. Al-ʿAyntābī, *Al-Qawl al-sadīd*, 105; Ibn Bassām, *Nihāyat al-rutba*, 150.

81. Ibn Bassām, *Nihāyat al-rutba*, 151; Barker, "Purchasing a Slave," 19, 22; al-ʿAyntābī, *Al-Qawl al-sadīd*, 108.

82. Ragib, "Les marchés," 738; *Al-Taḥqīq fī shirāʾ al-raqīq*, ch. 2; al-ʿAyntābī, *Al-Qawl al-sadīd*, ch. 1–2.

83. Al-ʿAyntābī, *Al-Qawl al-sadīd*, 36, 39.

84. Ragib, "Les marchés," 752–53; Al-ʿAyntābī, *Al-Qawl al-sadīd*, 36.

85. Al-ʿAyntābī, *Al-Qawl al-sadīd*, 111–12.

86. Ibn Taghrī Birdī, *Al-Manhal al-ṣāfī*, 3:513, no. 749; al-Isḥāqī, *Akhbār al-uwal*, 133 (Baylik). Al-Sakhāwī, *Al-Ḍawʾ al-lāmiʿ*, 10:289–90, no. 1134 (Yalbughā). A similar story circulated about Baybars. Frenkel, "Some Notes," 193.

87. Ibn Taghrī Birdī, *Al-Manhal al-ṣāfī*, 6:397–405, no. 1248.

88. Cassandro, "Aspects of the Life," 9.

89. Christ, *Trading Conflicts*, 131n62–63, 133n73.

90. Al-ʿAyntābī, *Al-Qawl al-sadīd*, recommended feeding the slave acidic foods to check dental health (p. 109), taking a urine sample to check kidney function (p. 114), and making the slave grip the buyer's forearm to check strength (p. 110). Other texts suggested observing the slave while he or she was asleep to check for bed-wetting, tooth-grinding, somnabulism, sleeping on the stomach, and other faults. Ragib, "Les marchés," 748.

91. "Affabiles et modigeratos se exhibent." Fabri, *Evagatorium*, 18:166.

92. Fabri, *Evagatorium*, 18:165. See also Blumenthal, *Enemies and Familiars*, 79.

93. Fabri, *Evagatorium*, 18:165; Breydenbach, *Sanctarum peregrinationum*, fol. 88r; Ghistele, *Voyage*, 21.

94. "Decem parvulos utriusque sexus, homines venales, nudos penitus et nigros, sedentes in foro sicut bestie, qui cum virga simul pelluntur ad locum venditionis ac si essent bestie." Guglingen, *Fratris Pauli Waltheri*, 230.

95. Broquière, *The Voyage*, 84.

96. Green, "From 'Diseases of Women.'"

97. Johansen, "Valorization," 75, 88. A lustful gaze at the uncovered shame zones of another person was permitted only for married couples and the male owner of a female slave.

98. Barker, "Purchasing a Slave," 18, 21; al-ʿAyntābī, *Al-Qawl al-sadīd*, 112; Ibn Bassām, *Nihāyat al-rutba*, 150.

99. Barker, "Purchasing a Slave," 18, 20; al-ʿAyntābī, *Al-Qawl al-sadīd*, 38. Al-Nuwayri, *Nihāyat al-arab*, 9:35, described female slaves as menstruating (المعصر) rather than adolescent (المراهق).

100. Ibn Bassām, *Nihāyat al-rutba*, 149; *Al-Taḥqīq fī shirāʾ al-raqīq*, fol. 20.

101. This was known as *istibrāʾ*. Al-Jarawānī, *Al-Kawkab al-mushriq*, 273; al-Asyūṭī, *Jawhar al-ʿuqūd*, 2:197; Lagardère, *Histoire et société*, 6:161. The duration of *istibrāʾ* was usually one menstrual cycle but could be one to three months for women with irregular cycles. Brunschvig, "ʿAbd," 3b, 3f.

102. Al-Asyūṭī, *Jawhar al-ʿuqūd*, 1:58; al-Jarawānī, *Al-Kawkab al-mushriq*, 359; Ibn al-Ukhuwwa, *Maʿālim al-qurba*, 57; al-Anṣārī, *Al-Iʿlām wa-al-ihtimām*, 110; Puente, "Entre la esclavitud," 348n44.

103. *Al-Taḥqīq fī shirāʾ al-raqīq*, fol. 20; al-ʿAyntābī, *Al-Qawl al-sadīd*, 38, 115; Ragib, "Les marchés," 742.

104. In ASVe, Canc. inf., Not., b.132, N.9, fol. 119r, the buyer was liable for the risks of labor, but the child would belong to the seller. In ASVe, Canc. inf., Not., b.230, N.2, reg. 1, fol. 34v, the seller was liable.

105. Gioffrè, *Il mercato*, 99–100; Balletto, "Schiavi," 683–84; Cluse, "Frauen," 102.

106. "Quia, quando aliquis emit hominem, accurrunt multi, ut pretium et appretiatum videant." Fabri, *Evagatorium*, 18:37.

107. Ibn al-Mujāwir, *A Traveller*, 162; Löfgren, *Arabische Texte*, 1:66.

108. "Et eam exposuit palam volentibus eam videre." Gioffrè, *Il mercato*, 97n30.

109. "Sicut nobiscum fit cum equis." Fabri, *Evagatorium*, 18:166 (also 18:37, 40); Breydenbach, *Sanctarum peregrinationum*, fol. 84v; Alighieri, *Purgatorio*, canto 20, ll. 80–81.

110. Spufford, *Handbook*; Bacharach, "The Dinar versus the Ducat." Dinars and ducats were roughly equal in value.

111. Ragib, "Les marchés," 758; Goitein, *A Mediterranean Society*, 1:139; Ashtor, *Histoire*, 208; Lewis, *Race*, 13.

112. Cluse, "Frauen," 90.

113. ASG, Not. Ant. 449, doc. 5; Gioffrè, *Il mercato*, Tartar table (1423). The 470 lire price is excluded from Figure 4 in order not to flatten the scale.

114. Balard, *La Romanie*, 2:787.

115. Verlinden, "Le recrutement des esclaves à Venise," 84, 131.

116. Ibn Taghrī Birdī, *Al-Manhal al-ṣāfī*, 3:367–372, no. 668.

117. Ashtor, *Histoire*, 362.

118. Ragib, *Actes*, no. XII.

119. Ashtor, *Histoire*, 363; Bauden, "L'achat," 301.

120. Al-Nāṣir Muḥammad would pay up to 100,000 dirhams for a mamluk who had cost only 20,000–40,000 dirhams. Al-Maqrīzī, *Kitāb al-khiṭaṭ*, 3:694; al-Maqrīzī, *Kitāb al-sulūk*, 2:2:525.

121. Balard, *La Romanie*, 1:297; Balard, "Giacomo Badoer," 562 (Majorca shipments were more profitable).

122. There was a dip in prices c.1275 when Black Sea slaves first reached the Genoese market, but prices rose again in the 1280s as the Iberian slave supply dried up. Balard, "Remarques," 662.

123. Balard, *La Romanie*, 2:802–3, argued that the Black Death caused a two-year price spike.

124. Apparent dips in 1338 and 1389 in Genoa and the spike in 1409 in Venice are based on one or two prices per year and may not be significant, whereas the dips in 1442–1443 and 1493–1494 are based on four or five prices per year.

125. Gioffrè, *Il mercato*, 54–56.

126. Youngest slaves: Verlinden, "Le recrutement des esclaves à Venise," 172; Balard, "Remarques," 656–67. Oldest slaves: Gioffrè, *Il mercato*, Tartar table (1459); Circassian table (1495); Moor table (1490); Verlinden, "Le recrutement des esclaves à Venise," 155; ASVe, Canc. inf., Not., b.92, N.1, fol. 25r–v; b.230, N.1, reg. 3, fol. 46v.

127. Others have argued that slaves peaked in value in their late teens or early twenties. Rodocanachi, "Les esclaves," 394; Bongi, "Le schiave," 224–25; Karras, *Unmarriages*, 86; Gioffrè, *Il mercato*, 141; Argenti, *Occupation*, 1:617–18; Balard, *La Romanie*, 2:812–13. Fitting curves to my data yields a different result: $y = -0.0872x^2 + 4.5026x - 4.5059$ for Genoa with a maximum at 25.8177, $y = -0.0513x^2 + 2.6722x + 12.414$ for Venice with a maximum at 26.0448.

128. Luzzato, *Studi di storia economica*, 191; Christ, *Trading Conflicts*, 130.

129. Little, "Two Fourteenth-Century Court Records," 33; Hogendorn, "Location."

130. Piloti, *Traité*, 15.

131. Tafur, *Travels*, 133 vs. Fabri, *Evagatorium*, 18:40.

132. Verlinden, "Le recrutement des esclaves à Venise," 126, 140, 159; Gioffrè, *Il mercato*, 129; Balard, *La Romanie*, 2:811. But Argenti, *Occupation*, 1:617–18, sides with Piloti.

133. Gioffrè, *Il mercato*, 125–26; Bongi, "Le schiave," 224–25; Rodocanachi, "Les esclaves," 394; Verlinden, "Le recrutement des esclaves à Venise," 160; Balard, *La Romanie*, 2:811. This pattern was noted by McKee, "Implications," 101, 104. See also Painter, *History of White People*.

134. Balard, "Remarques," 647, found that black and white women were priced similarly.

135. Gioffrè, *Il mercato*, 20, Russian table (1428, 1462) (54 and 64 mine of grain); Moor table (1470); "Slaves Without Race" table (1488); Jewish table (1498).

136. Delort, "Quelques précisions," 241n1.

137. ASVe, Canc. inf., Misc., b.134 bis, series 1, item 44 and series 2, item 7.

138. Lazari, "Del traffico," 494.

139. "بدار او فرس او بغل او حمار او عروص قماش او لؤلؤ او غير ذلك . . . كلب او سرجين او زيت نجس." Al-Asyūṭī, *Jawhar al-ʿuqūd*, 1:97–98.

140. Ibn Iyās, *Bidāʾiʿ al-zuhūr*, 4:115.

141. Ragib, *Actes*; Little, "Six Fourteenth Century Purchase Deeds"; Bauden, "L'achat."

142. ASVe, Canc. inf., Misc., b.134 bis.

143. The three best-studied Mamluk *shurūṭ* manuals are al-Nuwayrī, *Nihāyat al-arab*; al-Jarawānī, *Al-Kawkab al-mushriq*; and al-Asyūṭī, *Jawhar al-ʿuqūd*. See also Guellil, *Damaszener Akten*.

144. Little, "Six Fourteenth Century Purchase Deeds," 334; Bauden, "L'achat," 293, 316; Ragib, *Actes*, vol. 2. See also Hallaq, "Model Shurut Works," 128.

145. Orlandelli, "Genesi dell' 'ars notariae'"; Costamagna, *Il notaio*, 104–5.

146. "Instrumentum venditionis equorum et aliorum animalium tam rationalibus quam brutorum." Salatiele, *Ars notariae*, 1:156–58, 2:235. Al-Jarawānī, *Al-Kawkab al-mushriq*, 54–55, placed slaves (*al-raqīq*) and animals (*al-ḥayawān*) under the same rubric. San Floriano, *Cartolarius*, fol. 10r, gave one model for the sale of slaves, horses, houses, and land. See Williams, "From the Commercial Revolution," 244–50.

147. "Unum servum, natum ex tali ancilla, qui vocatur Stichus, et potest esse etatis xx annorum." Salatiele, *Ars notariae*, 2:235, imitating Watson, *Digest*, 1:202.

148. "Masnata nomina quorum sunt haec scilicet Ricius et Seius quos dixit et convenit esse sanos corpore et mente et nec etiam fugitivos." San Floriano, *Cartolarius*, fol. 10r.

149. "De venditione hominum vel colonorum et servitorum: Talis vendidit tali integre videlicet: personas M. et P. fratrum filiorum quondam talis de tali loco . . . vel Martinum filium I., et P. filium talis de loco tali . . ." Masi, *Formularium florentinum*, 102–3. Salatiele, *Ars notariae*, 2:298–99, gives a model for manumission but not sale.

150. Pisan and Florentine notaries noted stature more often. Cluse, "Zur Repräsentation," 393–94.

151. "Quamdam sclavam seu ancillam meam nomine Mellicam albam in facie etatis annorum xii vel circa qua fuit de partibus Ruscie." ASG, Not. Ant. 172, fol. 3v.

152. "Quidam sclavum . . . vocatum Aspertus de proienie tartarorum etatis annorum xxv vel circa album." ASG, Not. Ant. 405/I, fol. 38r.

153. "Unam sclavam ortam progenie tartarorum annorum circha tresdecim quam emi in Tana nomine Chesmelich et in baptismo Kattrinam." ASVe, Canc. inf., Not., b.19, N.7, reg. 3, fol. 3r.

154. "Quamdam meam sclavam de genere zarchassiorum etatis annorum xviii vel circa vocatam Citam." ASVe, Canc. inf., Not., b. 60, prot. 1446–1449, fol. 33r.

155. Little, "Six Fourteenth Century Purchase Deeds," 304–6; al-Jarawānī, *Al-Kawkab al-mushriq*, 54–55; al-Asyūṭī, *Jawhar al-ʿuqūd*, 1:97–98; al-Nuwayrī, *Nihāyat al-arab*, 9:35; Guellil, *Damaszener Akten*, 114.

156. Little, "Six Fourteenth-Century Purchase Deeds," 299.

157. Ragib, *Actes*, 1:37, 40. The same slave also appears in 1:36, 92, 95.

158. "Mente et corpore sanam et omnibus suis membris tam occultis quam manifestis." ASVe, Canc. inf., Misc., b.134 bis, item 31. See also Fuertes and Ruiz, "Los esclavos," 13–14; Cibrario, *Della schiavitù*, 200–203; Balard, "Remarques," 642; Bongi, "Le schiave," 225; Blumenthal, *Enemies and Familiars*, 67.

159. "Sanam et nitidam de pericula ab omnibus magagnis et infirmitatibus occultis usque in presentem diem." ASG, Not. Ant. 402, fol. 8r–v.

160. "المبراة من عيوب الرقيق." Bauden, "L'achat," 274, 283–85. See also al-Jarawānī, *Al-Kawkab al-mushriq*, 55; Guellil, *Damaszener Akten*, 114; al-Nuwayrī, *Nihāyat al-arab*, 9:35.

161. "Sanam et nitidam ab omnibus viciis et magagnis occultis vel manifestis secundum consuetudinem civitatis et insule Chii." Argenti, *Occupation*, 1:617.

162. Thorau, *Lion of Egypt*, 28.

163. "Sanum et nitidum de persona ab omnibus viciis et magagnis occultis et manifestis usque hodie." ASG, Not. Ant. 400, fol. 121r–v; "patitur in occullo sinistro," fols. 122v–123r.

164. ASG, CdSG, N.185,00625, fols. 3v, 4v–5v, 10v, 11v, 13v, 16v, 19v.

165. Verlinden, "Traite des esclaves," 802.

166. This was Mālikī and customary law. Ḥanafīs, Shāfiʿīs, and Ḥanbalīs did not allow a period of refusal. Ragib, *Actes*, 2:98; *Al-Taḥqīq fī shirāʾ al-raqīq*, fol. 16; al-Asyūṭī, *Jawhar al-ʿuqūd*, 1:71; Brunschvig, "ʿAbd," 3b.

167. D 21.1.19 vs. D 21.1.31; Watson, *Digest*, 2:608 vs. 2:613. ASVe, Canc. inf., Not., b.17, reg. 1, fol. 1r; Gioffrè, *Il mercato*, 56; Bosco, *Consilia*, 493–95, cons. 301; Zamboni, *Gli Ezzelini*, 419–20, doc. F (six months); Tria, "La schiavitù," 199–200, doc. 68 (ten days).

168. Cluse, "Frauen," 105–10. Dispute resolution procedures have also been studied in Valencia (Ferragud, "Role of Doctors"; Blumenthal, "Domestic Medicine") and Catalonia (Sabaté, "Gli schiavi," 392–93) but not Venice.

169. Ibn al-Mujāwir, *A Traveller*, 162; Löfgren, *Arabische Texte*, 1:66.

170. Slave singers were not sold with a period of refusal because of their association with sex. Al-Asyūṭī, *Jawhar al-ʿuqūd*, 1:58, 69–70. Similarly D 21.1.23; Watson, *Digest*, 2:609.

171. Al-Jarawānī, *Al-Kawkab al-mushriq*, 55; Guellil, *Damaszener Akten*, 114; al-Nuwayrī, *Nihāyat al-arab*, 9:35. For Ḥanafīs, the limited warranty implied freedom from redhibitory faults. For Ḥanbalīs, it implied freedom from faults, except those stated. For Mālikīs, it implied freedom from faults, except those known to the buyer. Al-Asyūṭī, *Jawhar al-ʿuqūd*, 1:71.

172. Al-Jarawānī, *Al-Kawkab al-mushriq*, 55; al-Asyūṭī, *Jawhar al-ʿuqūd*, 1:70; Guellil, *Damaszener Akten*, 115; Barker, "Purchasing a Slave"; al-ʿAyntābī, *Al-Qawl al-sadīd*; Ibn Bassām, *Nihāyat al-rutba*, 151–52.

173. Al-Asyūṭī, *Jawhar al-ʿuqūd*, 1:70. Shāfiʿīs did consider absence of menstruation, bad breath, bed-wetting, and fornication as redhibitory faults in women because it affected their sexual use.

174. The four legal schools disagreed about criminal behavior. Al-Asyūṭī, *Jawhar al-ʿuqūd*, 1:71.

175. D.21.1; Watson, *Digest*, 2:602–19, deals with redhibitory faults in slaves.

176. Cluse, "Frauen," 105; Winer, *Women*, 139; Rodocanachi, "Les esclaves," 395; Cibrario, *Della schiavitù*, 200.

177. Temkin, *Falling Sickness*, 86. A contract from fifth-century Egypt with warranties against epilepsy and demon attacks can be found in Hoogendijk, "Byzantinischer Sklavenkauf."

178. Temkin, *Falling Sickness*, 115–17; Tria, "La schiavitù," 218–19, doc. 85.

179. Cluse, "Frauen," 106–9.

180. "Et quae gravida et non gravida." ASVe, Canc. inf., Not., b.20, N.9, reg. 1, fol. 6v. See also Molmenti, *La storia*, 2:571; Cluse, "Frauen," 102.

181. Masi, *Formularium florentinum*, 17, 85; Roberti, *Un formulario inedito*, 64; Passeggieri, *Summa totius artis notariae*, fol. 63; *Summa artis notariae*, fol. 6r–v.

182. "Quamdam meam mullam bochardam cum omnibus suis viciis, mendis et magagnis ocultis et manifestis et pro tali qualis est, ad habendum, tenendum et possidendum et quicquid inde volueris faciendum, et est illa sclava quam emi ab Anthonio de Gravaigo." ASG, Not. Ant. 379, fol. 44v.

183. This practice began in the Mamluk period. Bauden, "L'achat," 294.

184. Goitein, "Slaves," 14.

185. Lagardère, *Histoire et société*, 3:175; Blumenthal, *Enemies and Familiars*, 37.

186. Al-Asyūṭī, *Jawhar al-ʿuqūd*, 1:97; al-Jarawānī, *Al-Kawkab al-mushriq*, 54–55; al-Nuwayrī, *Nihāyat al-arab*, 9:35; Guellil, *Damaszener Akten*, 114. A Central Asian *shurūṭ* manual required witnesses and included a formula for slave parents to acknowledge their children's status. Muḥammad, "Al-Basīṭ fī al-shurūṭ," 251–52. Similar clauses appeared in Geniza documents. Goitein, "Slaves," 13–14. The two Mamluk examples are Little, "Six Fourteenth Century Purchase Deeds," 317; Ragib, *Actes*, 1:39. See also Little, *A Catalogue*, 380, doc. 683.

187. Examples are ASVe, Canc. inf., Misc., b.134 bis, series 2, item 1; ASG, Not. Ant. 137, fols. 160v–161r; 380, fol. 159v; 397, fols. 238v–239r; 1034, doc. 522; Amia, *Schiavitù*, 239, doc. 28; Raymond and Lopez, *Medieval Trade*, 116, doc. 44; Williams, "From the Commercial Revolution," 412–13, doc. 13.

188. "Presentem et consentientem." ASG, Not. Ant. 273, fol. 185v. "Hic presentis et sclavum suum huic recto fuisse confitentis ac huic vendicione totaliter assentientis." ASVe, Canc. inf., Not. b.19, N.7, reg. 2, fol. 39v, item 235.

189. Passeggieri, *Summa totius artis notariae*, fol. 412r–v; Antoninus, *Summa*, title 3, ch. 6, part iv; Varkemaa, *Conrad Summenhart's Theory*, 94–101.

190. ASVe, Canc. inf., Not., b.19, N.7, reg. 2, fols. 21v and 23r, items 125 and 135; Gioffrè, *Il mercato*, 56.

191. Balard, *Gênes et l'Outre-Mer*, 2:83–86, doc. 41.

192. Balletto, "Schiavi," 667; Mummey, "Enchained in Paradise," 133.

193. ASVe, Canc. inf., Not., b.19, N.7, reg. 2, fol. 43r and loose leaf between fols. 10v and 11r.

Chapter 5

1. Halperin, "Missing"; Allen, *A History*, 121; Jaimoukha, *Circassians*, 37; Petkov, *Voices*.

2. Epstein, *Speaking*, 71.

3. Balard, *La Romanie*, 1:292–96, 300; Balard, "Gênes et la mer Noire," 44; Małowist, "Kaffa," 108; Heers, *Esclaves*, 88; Verlinden, *L'Esclavage*, 2:916; Irwin, *Middle East*, 70.

4. Miller, *Problem*, 8–9.

5. Compare with Meillassoux, *Anthropology of Slavery*.

6. Patterson, *Slavery and Social Death*.

7. Heers, *Esclaves*, 66; Heers, *Gênes*, 365; Fisher, "Muscovy," 577–79; Spuler, *Die Goldene Horde*, 384.

8. Khvalkov, "Slave Trade," 113–14; Kizilov, "Slaves," 193; Hershenzon, "Towards a Connected History," 3–4.

9. Kunstmann, "Studien," 817–18.

10. Fisher, "Muscovy," 583. Compare with Wright, *Strategies* on the trans-Saharan slave trade.

11. Gillingham, "Women, Children," 62.

12. Ayalon, "Studies on the Structure—II," 474; Frenkel, "Some Notes," 188; Northrup, *From Slave to Sultan*, 65; Khowaiter, *Baibars*, 3–4.

13. Joinville, *Chronicles*, 234–35.

14. Martin, *Medieval Russia*, 149; Małowist, "Social and Economic Life," 300; al-Maqrīzī, *Kitāb al-khiṭaṭ*, 3:779–80.

15. Martin, *Treasure*, 192n132.

16. Lech, *Das mongolische Weltreich*, 140.

17. Gillingham, "Women, Children," 61.

18. Spuler, *Die Goldene Horde*, 384; Fisher, "Muscovy," 580–83; Martin, *Medieval Russia*, 317; Hellie, *Slavery*, 22; Fine, *Late Medieval Balkans*, 180, 195, 225; Quirini-Popławska, "Venetian Involvement," 284–86.

19. Tafur, *Travels*, 134; Tafur, *Andanças*, 164.

20. Chalkokondyles, *Laonikos Chalkokondyles*, 295.

21. "قتل رجالهم، وسبى نساءهم، وذراريهم، وجلب إلى أقطار الأرض." Al-Qalqashandī, *Subḥ al-aʿshā*, 4:474.

22. Lockhart et al., *I Viaggi*, 81–82.

23. Lockhart et al., *I Viaggi*, 88.

24. Spuler, *Die Goldene Horde*, 384–86; Vernadsky, *A History of Russia*, 3:213–14.

25. Ibn Baṭṭuṭa, *Travels*, 2:484–86, 498.

26. Spuler, *Die Goldene Horde*, 377.

27. Ibn Baṭṭuṭa, *Travels*, 2:481.

28. Spuler, *Die Goldene Horde*, 248.

29. Jaimoukha, *Circassians*, 156–61; Suny, *Making*, 42–43; Lemercier-Quelquejay, "Cooptation," 25–26, 28; Zevakin and Penčko, "Ricerche," 39–40; Elie de La Primaudaie, *Études*, 237–38.

30. "De una villa exeunt ad aliam publice et violenter rapiunt filios et homines alterius ville, sive etiam furtive si possent, et statim vendunt mercatoribus in maritimis." Kern, "Der 'Libellus de notitia orbis,'" 110–11.

31. Ibn Iyās, *Bidāʾiʿ al-zuhūr*, 1:2:319.

32. "Dicunt quod deus misit ipsis et vendunt hominem pro porco." Kern, "Der 'Libellus de notitia orbis,'" 111.

33. "Ala preda di fiere salvatiche e piu di domestiche: et etiam di creature humane." Interiano, *La vita*, fol. 4r.

34. "E cosi furtivamente per simili passi secreti insultano i poveri villani. et li animali de liquali con li proprij figlioli ne portano la pena. pero che straportati da un paese ad unaltro li Barattano e vendeno." Interiano, *La vita*, fol. 4r.

35. "Poco numero di loro caccia gran gente di quella: perche sono molto piu agili e meglio in ordine di arme e di cavalli et demonstrano piu animosita." Interiano, *La vita*, fol. 5v.

36. Rowell, *Lithuania Ascending*, 73–76.

37. "Non in odium crucis et fidei, non propter aurum et argentum capiendum, sed ut homines capiant et in suam servitutem redigant." Fabri, *Evagatorium*, 18:167.

38. Balard, "Les genois et les regions bulgares," 90.

39. Wavrin, *Anchiennes chroniques*, 157; Paviot, "La piraterie," 2:206; Taparel, "Un épisode," 21.

40. Karpov, *La navigazione*, 61.

41. Balard, *La Romanie*, 2:793–94.

42. "Già, circha anni dieci, essendo io alla città di Chafa et dessendo io chon altri fanciulli in sulla marina e dessendo una nave di gienovesi in porto, misse in terra la ghondola chon alquanti huomini et segretamente presero me et un altro fanciullo, ch'era chon mecho, d'età d'anni dieci o circha et dinde ci levaro et chondusserci a Scio di levante et ine m'achonciai." Prunai, "Notizie e documenti," 415. Similarly Blumenthal, *Enemies and Familiars*, 36–37.

43. "Aliqua persona cujuscumque conditionis status seu gradus existat. siue sit januensis sine extranea. non possit audeat vel presumat publice vel secrete in ciuitate vel in anteburgis caphe emere sue emi facere per se vel interpositam personam aliquem hominem vel feminam habitatorum caphe cujuscumque generis vel nationis existat." "Statuto di Caffa," 635.

44. "Nam cum Iacobus ipse clam contraque leges Caphe: mulieres parvulosque inde asportaret: necesse fuit mox armare navigia: que illum insequerentur. Captus itaque Capham productus est.

Ibique cum perper asportationem familiarum capite damnandus esset: clementia tamen rectorum conservatus est." ASG, Arch. Segr. 1789, fols. 341v–342r, no. 1198. Paviot, "La piraterie," 2:206; Karpov, "Une ramification," 188; Jorga, "Notes et extraits," 8:52; Desimoni and Belgrano, "Documenti ed estratti," 424, doc. 86.

45. Balard, *La Romanie*, 1:292–96, 2:796; Heers, *Gênes*, 370; Elie de La Primaudaie, *Études*, 139; Gioffrè, *Il mercato*, 14; Origo, "Domestic Enemy," 326; Heyd, *Histoire*, 2:178, 556; Małowist, "New Saray," 337; Bongi, "Le schiave," 220; Raymond and Lopez, *Medieval Trade*, 115; Ayalon, "Mamlūk Novice," 2–3; Frenkel, "Some Notes," 203; Quirini-Popławska, "Venetian Involvement," 283–84.

46. Małowist, "Kaffa," 108; Hellie, *Slavery*, 370; King, *Black Sea*, 117–18; Ayalon, "Mamlūk Novice," 4.

47. Małowist, "Kaffa," 108; Elie de La Primaudaie, *Études*, 139, 237; Khvalkov, "Slave Trade," 111; Heyd, *Histoire*, 2:556; Bongi, "Le schiave," 220.

48. Broadbridge, "Sending Home," 14; Jaimoukha, *Circassians*, 175–77; Popper, "History," 12. Compare with Kosto, *Hostages*, 74–77; Corbier, *Adoption*; Boswell, *Kindness*.

49. Lech, *Das mongolische Weltreich*, 140.

50. "أنهم يبيعون أولادهم في بعض السنين لضيق العيش." Al-Qalqashandī, *Subḥ al-aʿshā*, 4:458, also 4:461.

51. "Quando habent plures uxores et filios aliquos vendunt sicut et animalia, quia dicunt se tot non posse nutrire." Kern, "Der 'Libellus de notitia orbis,'" 108.

52. "Animalia, filios et uxores, ac illi statim vendunt mercatoribus et sic evacuata est patria." Kern, "Der 'Libellus de notitia orbis,'" 107–8.

53. Wallace, *Premodern Places*, 191.

54. Allen, *A History*, 284; Spuler, *Die Goldene Horde*, 371; Hellie, *Slavery*, 370; Popper, "History," 16:8; Ayalon, "Mamluk," 3; Labib, *Handelsgeschichte*, 108, 328.

55. Labib, *Handelsgeschichte*, 328; Heyd, *Histoire*, 2:556; al-ʿArīnī, "Al-Fāris," 49; Petry, *Twilight*, 28–29; Amitai, "Mamluks of Mongol Origin," 121; Fahmī, *Ṭuruq al-tijāra*, 220.

56. Ayalon, "Names," 211–12.

57. Ayalon, "Great Yāsa," 125.

58. "أعطى المغل أولادهم وبناتهم واقاربهم للتجار، وباعوهم منهم رغبة في سعادة مصر." Al-Maqrīzī, *Kitāb al-sulūk*, 2:2:525, also al-Maqrīzī, *Kitāb al-khiṭaṭ*, 3:694.

59. Popper, "History," 19:44.

60. Al-Qadr is the holiday celebrating the revelation of the Quran. Al-Isḥāqī, *Akhbār al-uwal*, 141.

61. Al-Shujāʿī, *Taʾrikh al-malik*, 39–40.

62. Broadbridge, "Sending Home"; Barker, "Reconnecting"; Popper, "History," 17:165; Diem, *Arabische Privatbriefe*, doc. 47.

63. Hayton, "Flos," 222, 341.

64. Gregoras, *Byzantina historia*, 1:101–2.

65. Kern, "Der 'Libellus de notitia orbis,'" 111–12. The story cannot be true: the son in question, al-Nāṣir Faraj, was born to Barqūq and a Greek (*rūmī*) slave in Egypt. However, Barqūq did bring a group of relatives, including his nephews, to Egypt in 1380. Barker, "Reconnecting," 91; al-Sakhāwī, *Al-Ḍawʾ al-lāmiʿ*, 6:168, no. 562.

66. Tafur, *Travels*, 132–33; Tafur, *Andanças*, 161.

67. "La maior parte di dicti populi venduti: sono conducti al Chairo in egypto. et cosi la fortuna li transmuta da i piu subditi villani del mondo a deli magiori stati e signorie del nostro seculo: como Soldano: Armiraglij etc." Interiano, *La vita*, fol. 4r–v.

68. Polo, *Travels*, 334.

69. Lannoy, *Œuvres*, 33–34.

70. Schiltberger, *Bondage*, 50.

71. Alfieri, *Education*, 164.

72. Tafur, *Travels*, 132; Tafur, *Andanças*, 161.

73. Hayton, "Flos," 283, 337; Alfieri, *Education*, 164; Sanudo, *Book of the Secrets*, 384; Lull, "Projet," 124; Marino, *El Libro del conoscimiento*, 80–81.

74. Al-Qalqashandī, *Subḥ al-aʿshā*, 4:456–58; also Ayalon, "Mamlūk Novice," 6.

75. "ليس لهم كتاب ولا مسكة في دين." Al-ʿAyntābī, *Al-Qawl al-sadīd*, 53.

76. Similarly Glancy, "To Serve Them All the More," 45.

77. Hellie, *Slavery*, 343, 350–53.

78. ASVe, Canc. inf., Not., b.19, N.7, reg. 2, fols. 17v, 21v, 23r–v, items 102, 125, 135, 138.

79. ASVe, Canc. inf., Not., b.19, N.7, reg. 2, fol. 23v, item 141. For other examples of people, including children, given as financial surety, see Kosto, *Hostages*, 121–28.

80. Pistarino, *Notai genovesi*, 175–77, doc. 97.

81. Child sale also happened in the Mediterranean, but in that context, it was clearly atypical. Gioffrè, *Il mercato*, 55; Tria, "La schiavitù," 156–57, doc. 27; Cibrario, *Della schiavitù*, 196.

82. Balard, *La Romanie*, 2:719–33; Balard, "Gênes et la mer Noire," 33–45; Canale, *Della Crimea*, 1:315–23.

83. Giurescu, "Genoese," 587; Papacostea, "Quod non iretur," 202–3; Manfroni, "Le relazione," 796, doc. 1.

84. Martin, *Medieval Russia*, 143; Williams, "From the Commercial Revolution," 162; Bratianu, *Recherches*, 221.

85. Bratianu, *Recherches*, 206, 221; Balard, "Remarques," 637–38.

86. Karpov, "Genois et Byzantines," 33; Balard, "Les génois dans l'ouest," 2:26.

87. Balard, *La Romanie*, 1:459.

88. Bratianu, *Recherches*, 247; Jorga, "Notes et extraits," 4:36.

89. Jorga, "Notes et extraits," 4:28; Vernadsky, *A History of Russia*, 3:187–88; Quirini-Popławska, "Venetian Involvement," 262–66.

90. Quirini-Popławska, "Venetian Involvement," 266.

91. Marino, *El Libro del conoscimiento*, 96–97; Thiriet, *La Romanie vénitienne*, 347.

92. In 1261–1262. Ciocîltan, *Mongols*, 90.

93. Morgan, *Mongols*, 158–66.

94. Amitai, "Diplomacy."

95. Frenkel, "Some Notes," 195–96; Ibn al-Dawādārī, *Kanz al-durar*, 8:99, 9:12; Ibn Baṭṭuṭa, *Travels*, 19; *Al-Maqṣad al-rafīʿ*, fols. 266v–267r.

96. Fisher, *Crimean Tatars*, 3; Baybars also gave Berke a Quran codex written by the caliph ʿUthmān. Behrens-Abouseif, *Practicing Diplomacy*, 62.

97. Ibn Baṭṭuṭa, *Travels*, 2:471–72, 479–80; Popper, "History," 13:58; Ibn Taghrī Birdī, *Al-Manhal al-ṣāfī*, nos. 274, 298, 1523 and BNF arabe 2072, fol. 101v; al-Sakhāwī, *Al-Ḍawʾ al-lāmiʿ*, 5:315, 6:62, 6:138–39, 6:146, 8:143–45, 10:311, nos. 209, 335, 431, 457, 1039, 1185; Lutfi, *Al-Quds*, 234.

98. Al-Dimashqī, *Nukhbat al-dahr*, 327.

99. Ibn Taghrī Birdī, *Al-Manhal al-ṣāfī*, 3:255–76, no. 651; Ibn Iyās, *Bidāʾiʿ al-zuhūr*, 1:2:319.

100. The Syrians may have been Franks or Mamluk subjects. Balard, *La Romanie*, 1:201, 286–87; Bratianu, *Actes*, docs. 238, 298, 319.

101. Ibn ʿAbd al-Ẓāhir, *Tashrīf al-ayām*, 166–69; Sacy, *Pièces*, 33–52, drawn from *Liber iurium duplicatum* (ASG, Codici Membranacii, Codice C, fols. 235r–236v). Comparison and English translation in Holt, "Qalawun's Treaty," 101–8; Holt, *Early Mamluk Diplomacy*, 141–51. Amitai, "Diplomacy," misses the reference to slaves in the Latin version.

102. Ibn ʿAbd al-Ẓāhir, *Tashrīf al-ayām*, 166.

103. Sacy, *Pièces*, 40.

104. Holt, *Early Mamluk Diplomacy*, 148; Ibn ʿAbd al-Ẓāhir, *Tashrīf al-ayām*, 167; Sacy, *Pièces*, 41.

105. Balard, *Gênes et l'Outre-Mer*, vol. 1; Bratianu, *Actes*.

106. Balard, *La Romanie*, 1:296, said men were priced higher than women during this period, but I found the median price to be 12.4 ducats for women vs. 12.1 ducats for men. The age range was similar to that in Genoa. Balard, "Remarques sur les esclaves," 655.

107. Balard, *Gênes et l'Outre-Mer*, vol. 1, doc. 635. If she was resold in Caffa in July 1290, one of the documents must have reported her age incorrectly.

108. Martin, *Medieval Russia*, 171–72.

109. Balard, *Gênes et l'Outre-Mer*, vol. 1, docs. 685, 767, 770, 844, 854.

110. Bratianu, *Actes*, docs. 167, 238.

111. Bratianu, *Actes*, docs. 194, 318; Balard, *Gênes et l'Outre-Mer*, vol. 1, docs. 373, 579, 593, 594, 714.

112. Spuler, *Die Goldene Horde*, 385.

113. Spuler, *Die Goldene Horde*, 406; Balard, *La Romanie*, 1:202; Heyd, *Histoire*, 2:558; Ciocîltan, *Mongols*, 168–72; al-ʿArīnī, *Al-Mamālīk*, 57.

114. Balard, "Gênes et la mer Noire," 36; Balard, "Constantinople," 195; Golubovich, *Biblioteca*, 3:38–58, 4:230–33.

115. Jorga, "Notes et extraits," 4:29. The name of the office was established in 1341.

116. "Aliquos mumuluchos mares uel feminas Sarracenos uel alios infideles." Sauli, *Leges municipales*, 372, 378.

117. Zevakin and Penčko, "Ricerche," 25–35; Leskov and Lapushnian, *Art Treasures*, 20, 28.

118. Preiser-Kapeller, "Zwischen Konstantinopel und Goldener Horde," 208.

119. Zevakin and Penčko, "Ricerche," 40.

120. Heers, *Gênes*, 365; Balard, *La Romanie*, 1:141; Elie de La Primaudaie, *Études*, 240, 245, 247; Canale, *Della Crimea*, 1:169, 2:30.

121. Małowist, "New Saray," 338; Canale, *Della Crimea*, 1:313; Theiner, *Vetera monumenta*, 1:348–49, doc. 458.

122. "In oriente quotidie dominium christianorum diminuitur (et) conculcatur malignanter agentibus Saracenis nunc proditionibus nunc promissionibus nunc tormentis nunc donariis nunc bellis per terram et per mare, nunc emendo pretio christianos in nundinis ubi trahuntur cauda equi fune ligato ad collum illis qui venduntur, quia non est qui adjuvet. Quin immo est hic vana civitas, in qua praepositus sum voluntate summi pontificis licet immeritus, ubi secundum famam quondam venditi sunt centum personarum christianorum Saracenis, et translati ad terram Saracenorum, et facta sunt Saraceni. Ego autem pro viribus nefario negotio contradico. Et tamen hic dominantes, licet christiani sint, mihi non obediunt in his et in aliis, quia de schismate sunt Graecorum." Kunstmann, "Studien," 817–18.

123. Vernadsky, *A History of Russia*, 3:197; Tizengauzen, *Sbornik materialov*, 1:493.

124. Ciocîltan, *Mongols*, 190. See also Spuler, *Die Goldene Horde*, 385.

125. Ibn Taghrī Birdī, *Al-Manhal al-ṣāfī*, 6:342–44, no. 1217.

126. Ibn Baṭṭuṭa, *Travels*, 2:471.

127. Thomas, *Diplomatarium*, 1:243–44, doc. 125; Golubovich, *Biblioteca*, 4:423; Papacostea, "Quod non iretur," 205. The tax rate in Tana was 3 percent, as in Caffa.

128. Martin, *Medieval Russia*, 142; Małowist, "New Saray," 328.

129. "هي فرضة عظيمة للتجار ورقيق الترك." Al-Qalqashandī, *Subḥ al-aʿshā*, 4:457; Małowist, "New Saray," 331; Ibn Baṭṭuṭa, *Travels*, 2:516.

130. Morozzo della Rocca, *Lettere*, 19. Quirini-Popławska, "Venetian Involvement," 266, says that the notary Corrado de Sidulo recorded slave sales in Caffa in 1329.

131. Al-Shujāʿī, *Taʾrikh al-malik*, 98; Thomas, *Diplomatarium*, 1:259–63, docs. 133–35.

132. Thomas, *Diplomatarium*, 1:268; Karpov, "Genois et Byzantins," 35–37.

133. Balard, *La Romanie*, 1:299; ASG, Not. Ant., 273, fols. 200r, 204v, 227r, 230v; Balbi and Raiteri, *Notai genovesi*, docs. 46, 52, 54.

134. Papacostea, "Quod non iretur," 206–12; Thomas, *Diplomatarium*, 1:279–85, 302, 327–29.

135. Thomas, *Diplomatarium*, 1:311–13, doc. 167.

136. Balard, *La Romanie*, 1:299.

137. Schiel, "Die Sklaven und die Pest."

138. Papacostea, "Quod non iretur."

139. Laiou, "Byzantine Economy"; Oikonomidès, *Hommes d'affaires*, 46–49.

140. Balard, *La Romanie*, 1:303.

141. Ermanno, *Venezia—Senato*, doc. 781.

142. Balard, *La Romanie*, 1:132; Karpov, "Rabotorgovlia," 140. Thanks to Thomas Kitson for translating this article.

143. Petkov, *Voices*, 508, doc. 234.

144. Verlinden, "Esclavage et ethnographie," 1:291. Musso, "Gli Orientali," 106, lists a slave in an estate inventory.

145. Golubovich, *Biblioteca*, 2:197; Karpov, *La navigazione*, 80–81; Thomas, *Diplomatarium*, 2:24–25, doc. 14.

146. Thomas, *Diplomatarium*, 2:47–52, docs. 24, 25.

147. Most came from Benedetto Bianco (ASVe, Canc. inf., Not., b.19, N.7); Verlinden, "Le recrutement des esclaves à Venise." Others came from Nicolo Bono (ASVe, Canc. inf., Not., b.19, N.3) and Marcus Marzella (ASVe, Canc. inf., Not., b.117, N.6). See also ASVe, Canc. inf., Misc., b.134bis, ser. 1, items 5 and 7.

148. ASVe, Canc. inf., Not., b.19, N.7, reg. 2, items 3, 20, 92, 120, 147, 161, 178, 191, 192, 213, 225, 226; reg. 5, items 1, 2, 3, 11, 17, 18, 19, 21, 22, 29, 33, 34, 40, 42, 74, 76–77, 91, 95, 106, 111, 113, 146, 153; ASVe, Canc. inf., Not., b.19, N.3, fol. 8r.

149. Martin, *Medieval Russia*, 202.

150. ASVe, Canc. inf., Not., b.117, N.6, reg. 1, fol. 3r, items 121, 122.

151. Al-Sakhāwī, *Al-Ḍawʾ al-lāmiʿ*, 3:10–12, no. 48.

152. Pistarino, *Notai genovesi*; Balard, *Gênes et l'Outre-Mer*, vol. 2; Balard, "Les génois dans l'ouest," 2:28–29; Małowist, "Kaffa," 109; Giurescu, "Genoese," 598; Fine, *Late Medieval Balkans*, 272, 367; Baraschi, "Tatars"; Papacostea, "De Vicina à Kilia," 76–79.

153. One slave was pledged against five cantars (238.25 kilograms) of wax, two slaves and one house were pledged against one cantar (47.65 kilogram) of wax, and one slave and one house were pledged against thirty cantars (1429.5 kilograms) of honey. These numbers, while inconsistent, show that slaves and houses were among the most valuable possessions of Kilia's residents. Balard, *Gênes et l'Outre-Mer*, vol. 2, docs. 39, 43, 122.

154. The numbers refer to households or to adult men in a unit. Martin, *Medieval Russia*, 149.

155. Pistarino, *Notai genovesi*, 175–77, doc. 97.

156. Jorga, "Notes et extraits," 4:29; Vasiliev, *Goths*, 178–82.

157. Balard, *La Romanie*, 1:299–300.

158. Balard, "Esclavage en Crimée," 11; ASG, BdSG, Sala 34, 590/1225, fol. 89v and 590/1226, fols. 272v, 245v.

159. ASVe, Canc. inf., Not. b.19, N.7, reg. 2, fol. 36r; Verlinden, "Le recrutement des esclaves à Venise," 99.

160. Karpov, "Venetsianskaia rabotorgovlia," 202. Thanks to Thomas Kitson for glossing this.

161. Balard, "Esclavage en Crimée," 12–13.

162. "Per Stephanum de Camilla, placerium communis in Caffa, qui retulit dictos sclavum et sclavas infrascriptos pluribus diebus continuis incallegasse et incantasse publice et alta voce per logiam." Balletto, "Caffa 1371," 224.

163. Balbi and Raiteri, *Notai genovesi*, doc. 10.

164. Stöckly, *Le système*, 111.

165. Vasiliev, *Goths*, 177, 180–81.

166. The three treaties of 1380, 1381, and 1387 are in Sacy, *Pièces*, 53–58, 62–64. See also Desimoni, "Trattato," 162–65; Basso, "Il 'Bellum de Sorcati.'"

167. Basso, "Il 'Bellum de Sorcati,'" 15–16.

168. Balard, "Esclavage en Crimée," 13, says the eight asper tax appeared in 1381–1382.

169. ASG, BdSG, Sala 34, 590/1226bis, fol. 236v; Balard, *La Romanie*, 1:301.

170. Balard, *La Romanie*, 2:816, 829; ASG, CdSG, N.185,15006, fols. 26v, 54v.

171. ASG, BdSG, Sala 34, 590/1226bis, fols. 204v, 236v and 590/1227, fols. 133v, 209r and 590/1229, fol. 168r.

172. ASG, BdSG, Sala 34, 590/1224–1262. Balard, "Esclavage en Crimée," 10, and Stello, "La traite," 174, incorrectly assume that both the thirty-three asper and eight asper taxes applied to slaves sold.

173. ASG, BdSG, Sala 34, 590/1233, fols. 124r, 125r.

174. Six hundred to thirty-two hundred slaves per year in Balard, "Esclavage en Crimée," 14.

175. ASG, BdSG, Sala 34, 590/1303, fol. 34r and 590/1304, fol. 24v and 590/1305, fol. 61v; Balard, *La Romanie*, 1:306–7. He reports 2,500 lire from 1374, which I could not verify.

176. Jorga, "Notes et extraits," 5:158.

177. "In quocumque loco unde capita extrahuntur et tam in tanai quam savastopoli et alibi qui navigia expediant." ASG, BdSG, Sala 34, 590/1308bis, fol. 3v; Balard, *La Romanie*, 1:299; Verlinden, "Mamelouks," 740.

178. 1,125 sommi, 27 saggi, and 14 carati. Balard, *La Romanie*, 1:300.

179. I agree with Stello, "Caffa," 382–83; Stello, "La traite," 174. See also Balard, "Esclavage en Crimée," 16; Balard, *La Romanie*, 1:299; Karpov, "Rabotorgovlia"; Jorga, "Notes et extraits," 4:48; Verlinden, "Medieval 'Slavers,'" 3.

180. ASG, BdSG, Sala 34, 590/1233, fol. 120v.

181. "Pro quadam sclava que effecta est christiana." ASG, BdSG, Sala 34, 590/1233, fol. 118v.

182. Karpov, "Rabotorgovlia," 143.

183. Balard, "Esclavage en Crimée," 16; Stello, "La traite," 177–78; Stello, "Caffa," 387–88. Stello notes that the route from Caffa to Pera is underrepresented, but that route may not have been preferred by Muslim travelers.

184. Christian Greeks would not have been taxed. I found no Greek slaves sold in Caffa and exactly one Greek slave sold in Tana. ASVe, Canc. inf., Not., b.19, N.7, reg. 2, fol. 5v, item 38.

185. Karpov, "Rabotorgovlia," 143, identified Samo as the Aegean island of Samos. Balard, "Esclavage en Crimée," 16, thought it might be Samogetes (Russia) or Sam on the Caspian Sea.

186. Balard, *La Romanie*, 1:132, 299.

187. "Testarum saracenorum et homini imperii tartarorum qui transportantur per nostros ad oppositas partes turchie, silicet de loco ad locum, cum bonis suis." ASVe, Senato, Deliberazioni, Misti, reg. 39, fol. 19r; Thiriet, *Régestes*, docs. 683, 686.

188. "Quod in toto imperio Gazarie posimus ponere et trahere quicquid vollumus, nec fit nobis in ipsis privilegiis aliuqa exceptio vel prohibitio ullo modo, et si intentio imperatori fuisset quod non extraheremus testas de Tana vel de eius imperio, in privilegiis nobis concessis, hoc fuisset declaratur." ASVe, Senato, Deliberazioni, Misti, reg. 39, fol. 19r.

189. "De partibus Gazarie et maris tane ad oppositas partes Turchie." ASVe, Collegio, Secreti, Registro 1382–1385, fol. 71v, dated 1384 *more veneto*. See also ASVe, Secreta, Libri Commemoriali, reg. 8, fol. 125v; Thomas, *Diplomatarium*, 2:245, doc. 141.

190. ASG, BdSG, Sala 34, 590/1226 and 590/1226bis.

191. ASG, BdSG, Sala 34, 590/1226bis, fols. 121v, 190v.

192. Balard, *La Romanie*, 1:350.

193. ASG, BdSG, Sala 34, 590/1226, fol. 37v.

194. Ibn Taghrī Birdī, *Al-Manhal al-ṣāfī*, 6:263–312, no. 1194.

195. Exceptions were Baybars al-Jashankīr (probably Circassian) and Lājīn (*rūmī*). Ibn Taghrī Birdī, *Al-Manhal al-ṣāfī*, 3:467–73 and 5:210–11, nos. 718 and 985.

196. Exceptions were Khushqadam and Tamurbughā (both *rūmī*). Ibn Taghrī Birdī, *Al-Manhal al-ṣāfī*, 5:210–11, no. 985; al-Sakhāwī, *Al-Ḍawʾ al-lāmiʿ*, 3:40–41, no. 167.

197. Al-Qalqashandī, *Subḥ al-aʿshā*, 4:458; al-Maqrīzī, *Kitāb al-khiṭaṭ*, 3:781; Popper, "History," 13:173; Ibn Taghrī Birdī, *Al-Manhal al-ṣāfī*, 3:285–342, no. 657; Ayalon, "Circassians," 139–42.

198. Cluse, "Frauen," 91, for Genoa and Cluse, "Zur Repräsentation," 393, for Pisa.

199. Ayalon, "Mamluk," 7, attributed the shift to depopulation of the Kipchak steppe by the Mongol invasions of the 1230s and subsequent slaving. Ashtor, *Levant Trade*, 82–83, argued that the shift actually occurred in the 1320s, when peace with the Ilkhanate opened the Anatolian land route to Mamluk merchants. Gioffrè, *Il mercato*, 14, attributed the shift to Timur's invasion.

200. Al-ʿArīnī, "Al-Fāris," 48.

201. Martin, *Medieval Russia*, 203; Halperin, "Missing"; Małowist, "New Saray," 334–36.

202. ASG, Not. Ant. 318, fols. 39r, 40r–v; Tzavara, "Morts en terre étrangère," 202.

203. Małowist, "New Saray," 337; Elie de La Primaudaie, *Études*, 121; Thiriet, *Délibérations*, doc. 933.

204. Spuler, *Die Goldene Horde*, 384; Fisher, "Muscovy," 580–83; Martin, *Medieval Russia*, 317; Hellie, *Slavery*, 22; Fine, *Late Medieval Balkans*, 180, 195, 225; Quirini-Popławska, "Venetian Involvement," 284–86.

205. "منع الطتر من بيع أولادهم بحيث قل جلبهم الى الشام ومصر." Al-Sakhāwī, *Al-Ḍawʾ al-lāmiʿ*, 2:325, no. 1061.

206. Suny, *Making*, 40–46; Allen, *A History*, 123–27.

207. Fisher, *Crimean Tatars*, 3–4; Vásáry, "Crimean Khanate," 16; Inalcik, *An Economic and Social History*, 1:276.

208. Vasiliev, *Goths*, 182, 187–88.

209. Al-Qalqashandī, *Subḥ al-aʿshā*, 4:460–61; Heyd, *Histoire*, 2:557; Musso, "Gli orientali," 103–5; Cosmo, "Mongols and Merchants," 396.

210. ASG, BdSG, Sala 34, 590/1227, fol. 85v; Gioffrè, *Il mercato*, Tartar table; Musso, "Gli orientali," 105–6.

211. Stello, "La traite," 174–75.

212. Al-Sakhāwī, *Al-Ḍawʾ al-lāmiʿ*, 3:40–41, no. 167.

213. Jorga, "Notes et extraits," 4:238, 506–7 (1410 sack by Poulad-beg Khan), 594 (1418 sack by Kerimberi Khan); Małowist, "New Saray," 337–38.

214. Colli, *Moretto Bon*; Khvalkov, "Slave Trade," 110–11.

215. Prokofieva, "Akti"; ASVe, Canc. inf., Not. b.121, N.2, reg. 2; ASVe, Notarile testamenti 733.

216. ASVe, Canc. inf., Not., b.231, N.3, reg. 2, fol. 1v; Verlinden, "Le recrutement des esclaves à Venise," 107.

217. Balard, "Gênes et la mer Noire," 36, 49; Karpov, "Venetsianskaia rabotorgovlia." Three of the documents are published in Colli, *Moretto Bon*.

218. Piloti, *Traité*, 52–54; Alfieri, *Education*, 176–78.

219. "Fuisse in nostram infamiam relatum per Ianuensium manus transvehi seruos christianos e Caffa in Egiptum et alia infidelium regna quod crimen quantum a nobis alienum sit." ASG, Arch. Segr., 1781, fol. 530v, doc. 1410.

220. "Inivimus federa cum dominis regionum vicinarum, in quibus appositum est necui liceat servos extra maris pontici terminos deferre, nisi in navibus nostris. Quo vinculo ligati coguntur omnes omnium illarum nationum mercatores venales seruos primum Caffam deducere ut ibi navem nacti trayciantur quo volunt. Lex autem super eiusmodi seruorum transitu lata iubet primum dinumerari seruos navigaturos. Deinde persoluto vectigali quod his impositum est licet illos navem conscendere. Que priusquam solvat e portu ascendit et illam caffensis episcopus et religiosis et laicis comitatus. Et vocatis seruis sciscitatur nationem singulorum. Exquirit deinde an quis eorum velit christianus fieri. Siquis ibi christianus invenitur aut qui velit christianus fieri, deponitur in terram, atque venundatur homini christiano, quo fit ut non modo nullus christianus permittatur portari ad infidelium terras, sed plurimi insuper non christiani fideles fiant." ASG, Arch. Segr., 1781, fols. 530v–531r. Published in Stello, "Caffa," 391–92.

221. ASG, Arch. Segr., 2707A/1, doc. 25.

222. ASG, Arch. Segr., 2707A/1, doc. 25; Sacy, *Pièces*, 71–74. Jorga says 9,000 ducats in some passages and 16,000 ducats in others. "Notes et extraits," 6:51–52 vs. 97.

223. There are two finished versions of this letter dated July 18, 1429 and one draft dated July 4, 1429. The draft is ASG, Arch. Segr., 1779 (Litterarum), fols. 184v–185r. The finished versions are ASG, Arch. Segr., 513 (Diversorum), fols. 53v–54r and 1779 (Litterarum), fol. 187r–v. Jorga dates the Diversorum version to 1428 instead of 1429, probably because the register jumps forward a year between fols. 22v and 23r. Jorga, "Notes et extraits," 5:372–73, 6:56.

224. "Tam in avania recenti sclavorum, quam in datione specierum, et aliis quotidianis molestiis." Sacy, *Pièces*, 71–74; ASG, Arch. Segr., 2707A/1, doc. 25.

225. "Bonum interpretem lingue tartare caffensis, quoniam ea plus delectari dicitur." Jorga, "Notes et extraits," 6:97.

226. "Ut nobis Soldanus restituat sive nostris damnum passis illos ducatos auri sedecim millia qui a nostris mercatoribus pro avania sclavorum Caffae extorti sunt." Sacy, *Pièces*, 72.

227. "Obtentis itaque omnibus suprascriptis . . . placet nobis ut Soldano ac suis tractum sclavorum ex Caffa concedatis, ipsis solventibus dritus et cabellas consuetas et ordinatas, hac tamen declaratione semper praecedente, quod scilicet si quis eiusmodi sclavorum vellet christianus fieri, id ei liceat, dummodo eius domino solvatur precium in Caffa constitutem. Scribimus namque consuli Caffae, et novo consuli in mandatis dabimus ut de tractatu talium sclavorum disponat ac faciat iuxta commissiones vestras. Et ad uberiorum cautelam binas vobis litteras mittimus annexas, quas, cum voluerit, consuli Caffae transmittat per aliquem ex his saracenis qui Caffam iturus sit." ASG, Arch. Segr., 2707A/1, doc. 25. The wording in Sacy, *Pièces*, 74, differs slightly. Ashtor, *Levant Trade*, 308, reported a similar incident in 1452, but the document he cites (ASVe, Canc. inf., Not., b.211, reg. 2, fols. 14–17) is a dispute about slaves intended for the Genoese consul in Alexandria and not for the sultan.

228. "Homines . . . diversorum [locorum] et terrarum pauco extimationis." Fleet, "Caffa, Turkey," 385–86; Karpov, "Rabotorgovlia," 142.

229. Al-Sakhāwī, *Al-Ḍawʾ al-lāmiʿ*, 6:201–11, no. 697.

230. Vasiliev, *Goths*, 201–10; Małowist, "Kaffa," 102.

231. Jorga, "Notes et extraits," 6:416.

232. ASG, BdSG, Sala 34, 590/1233, fols. 138r, 177r, 186r and 590/1259, fol. 109v.

233. Tafur, *Travels*, 132–33; Tafur, *Andanças*, 161.

234. Tafur, *Travels*, 133; Tafur, *Andanças*, 162.

235. Khvalkov, "Slave Trade," 114; ASVe, Canc. inf., Not., b.231, N.3, reg. 1, fol. 3r–v. Quirini-Popławska, "Venetian Involvment," 274, adds Cristoforo Perscini.

236. ASG, BdSG, Sala 34, 590/1235, fol. 57v.

237. ASG, BdSG, Sala 34, 590/1235, fols. 21v, 54v.

238. Karpov, "Rabotorgovlia," 140.

239. Stello, "La traite," 176.

240. Balard, "Esclavage en Crimée," 15; Karpov, "Rabotorgovlia," 144.

241. "Statuto di Caffa," 634–35.

242. Desimoni, "Trattato," 164.

243. Heers, *Gênes*, 313; Canale, *Della Crimea*, 1:322. Heyd, *Histoire*, 2:559, interpeted this as a health measure. Epstein, *Speaking*, 99, interpreted these as ships of one, two, and three masts rather than decks. Verlinden, "Medieval 'Slavers,'" 5–6, thought the rules applied to Genoese galleys from Byzantium and Syria rather than galleys belonging to Byzantines and Syrians.

244. Jorga, "Notes et extraits," 6:135, 7:65, 7:416. Thiriet, *La Romanie vénitienne*, 428, dates the Venetian consul in Caffa after 1453.

245. Lockhart et al., *I Viaggi*, 69.

246. Balard, "Esclavage en Crimée," 11–12.

247. Jorga, "Notes et extraits," 8:67–68.

248. Gioffrè, *Il mercato*, 19; Heyd, *Histoire*, 2:317.

249. Małowist, "Kaffa," 114.

250. Vigna, "Codice diplomatico," 317–18, doc. 129. There was a scare in 1470 when the Ottomans demanded 8,000 ducats in tribute instead of 3,000. Małowist, "Kaffa," 123.

251. ASG, BdSG, Sala 34, 590/1236, fol. 35r; Boldorini, *Caffa*, 73–74, doc. 89.

252. Qānṣūh al-Ghawrī's name may derive from the Crimean village of Gavri (Plotinnoye). Oleksandr Halenko, email message to author, June 4, 2017, citing a 1542 Ottoman tax register held in Istanbul, Başbakanlık Archives, Tapu Ve Tahrir defterleri, no. 214; Petry, *Twilight*, 124.

253. ASG, BdSG, Sala 34, 590/1261, fol. 111v; Musso, "I Genovesi e il Levante," 2:167–69.

254. Fisher, *Crimean Tatars*, 7–11, 34; Małowist, "Kaffa," 128–30; Vasiliev, *Goths*, 246.

255. Similar to Genoa and Venice. Zevakin and Penčko, "Ricerche," 90.

256. Babinger, *Mehmed the Conqueror*, 344.

257. Inalcik, *An Economic and Social History*, 283–85; Fisher, "Muscovy," 583; Karpov, "Rabotorgovlia," 144.

Chapter 6

1. ASVe, Senato, Deliberazioni Misti, reg. 42, fol. 135r.

2. Smallwood, *Saltwater Slavery*.

3. This approach is derived from New Institutional Economics and the notion of slaving as a strategy rather than a system. North, *Institutions*; Miller, *Problem*, 8–9.

4. Heyd, *Histoire*, 2:558; Verlinden, "Mamelouks," 741–42; Ciocîltan, *Mongols*, 94–95; Heers, *Esclaves*, 104; Cahen, *Pre-Ottoman Turkey*, 321; Abu-Lughod, *Before European Hegemony*, 213–14. Some have argued that Venetians controlled the Mamluk slave trade. Apellániz Ruiz de Galarreta, *Pouvoir et finance*, 39, 42–43, 59; Fahmī, *Ṭuruq al-tijāra*, 221; Miller, *Problem*, 65; Quirini-Popławska, "Venetian Involvement," 270–72. Jews owned slaves but did not trade them widely during this period. Perry, "Daily Life," 25–28; Goitein, *A Mediterranean Society*, 1:140, 452n10; Stello, "Le traite," 176.

5. Ayalon, "L'esclavage," 1–4; Ayalon, "Mamlūk," 10; al-ʿArīnī, *Al-Mamālīk*, 73–76; Sato, "Slave Traders"; Amitai, "Diplomacy," 355.

6. Although they cannot always articulate why. O'Connell Davidson, *Modern Slavery*.

7. "AHR Forum: Crossing Slavery's Boundaries."

8. Heyd, *Histoire*, 2:177, 443; al-ʿArīnī, *Al-Mamālīk*, 57; Fahmī, *Ṭuruq al-tijāra*, 222; Davis, *Problem*, 43; Labib, *Handelsgeschichte*, 328; Ashtor, *Levant Trade*, 11; Epstein, *Speaking*; Balard, *La Romanie*, 1:298; Cluse, "Frauen," 90; Cluse, "Role," 462; Runciman, *A History*, 3:357; Setton, *Papacy*, 2:46–48; Ehrenkreutz, "Strategic Implications," 342–43. Even Miller, *Problem*, 30, 65, 137–38, attributed medieval slaving to private, mercantile ambition.

9. Sato, "Slave Traders"; Muḥammad, "Al-Raqīq," 103.

10. The transatlantic slave trade was one or two orders of magnitude larger, involving tens of thousands of slaves per year and hundreds of thousands at its peak. "Trans-Atlantic Slave Trade Database."

11. "Totiens quotiens vendetur permutabitur vel alienabitur seu aliquo titulo in alium transferretur." Tucci, *Le imposte*, 41; Sieveking, "Aus Genueser Rechnungs- und Steuer-büchern," 21. Among the taxed transactions were gifts, dowries, and swaps. ASG, CdSG, N.185,00624, fols. 3v, 10v, 25v; N.185,00625, fols. 23v–24r.

12. ASG, Not. Ant. 367, fol. 153r; Gioffrè, *Il mercato*, 148.

13. Fourteenth-century data come from Balard, *La Romanie*, 2:829. I checked his figures for 1380 (ASG, CdSG, N.185,15002, fol. 5v), 1381 (ASG, CdSG, N.185,15002, fol. 25v), and 1387 (ASG, CdSG, N.185,15006, fol. 26v). Fifteenth-century data come from Gioffrè, *Il mercato*, 149–50. I checked his figures for 1422–1434 (ASG, CdSG, N.185,15072, fols. 5, 27, 41, 44, 63, 79, 96, 110, 119, 144, 150, and 170). There were discrepancies in 1422 (505 lire vs. Gioffrè's 500), 1425 (580 lire vs. Gioffrè's 560), 1429 (505 lire vs. Gioffrè's 550), and 1432 (855 lire vs. Gioffrè's 851). The Genoese florin of account was equivalent to 25 soldi or 0.8 lire. Spufford, *Handbook*, 109–15. When Gioffrè analyzed the half-florin tax, he used this exchange rate, but for the one florin tax, he switched to 0.75 lire per florin without explanation. I use 0.8 lire per florin for both taxes.

14. ASG, CdSG, N.185,00623 (1413), N.185,00624 (1447), N.185,00625 (1449); Gioffrè, *Il mercato*, 147–64.

15. Balard, *La Romanie*, 2:830, agrees; McKee, "Implications," 102, says it peaked in the mid-fifteenth century.

16. Raymond and Lopez, *Medieval Trade*, 402–3, doc. 195.

17. Gioffrè, *Il mercato*, 94. I counted 59 rentals vs. 492 sales in 1400–1449 but 176 rentals vs. 526 sales in 1450–1499.

18. Heyd, *Histoire*, 2:562.

19. Ashtor, *A Social and Economic History*, 282, estimated that early Mamluk sultans bought eight hundred mamluks per year, whereas late sultans bought two hundred to three hundred. Petry, *Civilian Elite*, 22, estimated that Circassian sultans bought four hundred to five hundred mamluks per year.

20. Rapoport, "Ibn Ḥağar," 341–42.

21. Ehrenkreutz, "Strategic Implications," 338; Amitai, "Diplomacy," 363; Amitai, "Between the Slave Trade," 410; Fuess, "Rotting Ships." See also Müller, "Venezia," 140. Khalilieh, "An Overview," does not include Mamluk-era material.

22. Pachymeres, *De Michaele*, 177–79; Gregoras, *Byzantina historia*, 1:101–2.

23. Holt, *Early Mamluk Diplomacy*, 147.

24. Ibn Taghrī Birdī, *Al-Manhal al-ṣāfī*, no. 504; al-Qalqashandī, *Subḥ al-aʿshā*, 4:469.

25. ASVe, Senato, Deliberazioni Misti, reg. 60, fols. 11r–12v.

26. Köpstein, *Zur Sklaverei*; Balard, "Giacomo Badoer"; Balard, *La Romanie*, 1:306–7; Verlinden, "Traite des esclaves"; Verlinden, "Encore la traite."

27. Balard, *La Romanie*, 1:308–9; Balletto, "Schiavi"; Argenti, *Occupation*, 1:615–25.

28. Zachariadou, *Trade*, 160–63; McKee, "Inherited Status"; Verlinden, "La Crete"; Noiret, *Documents*; Pettenello and Rauch, *Stefano Bono*; Thiriet, *La Romanie vénitienne*, 314–15.

29. Dincer, "Enslaving Christians"; Arbel, "Slave Trade"; Mas Latrie, *Histoire de l'île de Chypre*; Desimoni, "Actes passés a Famagouste"; Lombardo, *Nicola de Boateriis*.

30. Inalcik, "Bursa."

31. Roccatagliata, *Notai genovesi in Oltremare: Atti rogati a Pera e Mitilene*.

32. Guglingen, *Fratris Pauli Waltheri*, 82; Thiriet, *Régestes*, doc. 1697.

33. Luttrell, "Slavery."

34. King, *Black Sea*, 16.

35. Cahen, *Pre-Ottoman Turkey*, 321–24; Inalcik, *An Economic and Social History*, 1:220; Wirth, "Alep," 46–47 and fig. 3; Har-El, *Struggle*, 38; Popper, "Egypt and Syria," 15:51–53 and map 18; Sinclair, *Eastern Turkey*, 2:293–95; Fahmī, *Ṭuruq al-tijāra*, 149. The existence of this route is postulated in Stello, "La traite," 177–79; Balard, "Esclavage en Crimée," 15; Karpov, "Rabotorgovlia."

36. Twelve slaves in Trebizond are described in Karpov, "Venetsianskaia rabotorgovlia."

37. Cahen, *Pre-Ottoman Turkey*, 322–23, notes a significant Genoese presence in Siwas in the late thirteenth century with strong connections to Sinope, Simisso, and the Black Sea.

38. Thorau, *Lion of Egypt*, 28.

39. Ibn Taghrī Birdī, *Al-Manhal al-ṣāfī*, 3:255–76, no. 651; Popper, "History," 18:1–2.

40. ASG, BdSG, Sala 34, 590/1233, fol. 120v. Ten male and female slaves were also taken from Caffa to Simisso by Coiha (*khwājā*) Octoman de Malatia in 1446. ASG, BdSG, Sala 34, 590/1234, fol. 28r.

41. Popper, "History," 18: 1–2, 164.

42. Brunschvig, "Coup d'oeil," 66; Popper, "Egypt and Syria," 15:51, route XVIII.

43. Broquière, *Le Voyage*, 108.

44. Broquière, *Le Voyage*, 135.

45. Herzog, "First Layer," 144.

46. Stello, "Caffa," 389; Amitai, "Between the Slave Trade," 415; Sanudo, *Book of the Secrets*, 59–61; Piloti, *Traité*, 138.

47. Ibn Taghrī Birdī, *Al-Manhal al-ṣāfī*, 4:68–74, 6:84, nos. 769, 1119; Amitai, "Between the Slave Trade," 414. During the Ayyubid period, the Aleppan slave market yielded 100,000 dirhams in tax

revenue. Sauvaget, *Alep*, 1:253. It remained significant under the Ottomans. Inalcik, *An Economic and Social History*, 1:56.

48. Al-ʿAdwī, "Miṣr fī ʿahd al-sulṭān Khushqadam," 71.

49. Popper, "History," 13:8.

50. "جلب من بلاده صغيرا وابيع بالبلاد الحلبية فاشتراه بعض التجار وخصاه." Ibn Taghrī Birdī, *Al-Manhal al-ṣāfī*, BNF arabe 2071, fols. 221v–223r; al-Sakhāwī, *Al-Ḍawʾ al-lāmiʿ*, 6:176–77, no. 600; Hogendorn, "Location."

51. Ibn Taghrī Birdī, *Al-Manhal al-ṣāfī*, 3:447–67, no. 717. See also Marmon, *Eunuchs*, 113.

52. Sato, "Slave Traders," 144.

53. Al-Sakhāwī, *Al-Ḍawʾ al-lāmiʿ*, 9:72, no. 191.

54. Broquière, *Le Voyage*, 68. He also ransomed an Italian in Tunis in 1384. Orlandi, "Catalonia Company," 366.

55. Karpov, "Genois et Byzantins," 36; Balard, "Le génois dans l'ouest," 31.

56. Małowist, "Kaffa," 108–10; Inalcik, *An Economic and Social History*, 1:276–78.

57. Epstein, *Purity Lost*, 62; Musso and Jacopino, "I Genovesi," 2:167–69.

58. Ehrenkreutz, "Strategic Implications"; Amitai, "Diplomacy"; Cahen, *Pre-Ottoman Turkey*, 321; Labib, *Handelsgeschichte*, 329; Saunders, "Mongol Defeat."

59. Ibn ʿAbd al-Ẓāhir, *Tashrīf al-ayām*, 166–67; Sacy, *Pièces*, 40–41; Holt, *Early Mamluk Diplomacy*, 141–51; Holt, "Qalawun's Treaty."

60. Laiou, "Byzantine Economy"; Oikonomidès, *Hommes d'affaires*, 46–49.

61. ASVe, Senato, Deliberazioni Misti, reg. 39, fol. 17v; Thiriet, *Régestes*, docs. 683, 686; Balard, "Esclavage en Crimée," 10.

62. Fleet, "Caffa, Turkey," 375, 381, argues that there was no north–south route, that the slaves were intended for Anatolian copper mines, and that the decree was a protectionist measure to ensure Genoa's supply of slaves.

63. Heers, *Gênes*, 313; Canale, *Della Crimea*, 1:322. Also discussed in Chapter 5.

64. Inalcik, *An Economic and Social History*, 1:283–85.

65. Manfroni, "Le relazioni."

66. Setton, *Papacy*, 1:100.

67. Labib, *Handelsgeschichte*, 103–8; Vernadsky, *Mongols and Russia*, 151–65.

68. Amitai, "Diplomacy," 363.

69. Pachymeres, *De Michaele*, 176.

70. Gregoras, *Byzantina historia*, 1:101–2.

71. Holt, *Early Mamluk Diplomacy*, 124.

72. Inalcik, *An Economic and Social History*, 1:273.

73. Heyd, *Histoire*, 2:317; Inalcik, *An Economic and Social History*, 1:190–94; Jorga, "Notes et extraits," 8:24–25.

74. Italians began to develop alternative sources of slaves in Dalmatia, Iberia, and West Africa in the mid-fifteenth century. Bruscoli, "Bartolomeo Marchionni"; Evans, "Slave Coast"; Gioffrè, *Il mercato*, 27–38.

75. Har-El, *Struggle*, 66; Fleet, *European and Islamic Trade*, 7–8.

76. Har-El, *Struggle*, 66, citing Feridun Beg, *Munseat al-Selatin*, 1:114–16. Har-El identifies the merchants as slave traders, but the original letters do not.

77. "بما عيناه بصحبه من الممالك الاجلاب الجنس." Feridun, *Munseat al-Selatin*, 1:200–201.

78. Ehrenkreutz, "Strategic Implications," 336; Amitai, *Mongols and Mamluks*, but in "Between the Slave Trade," 414–16, he shows that the war did not entirely halt cross-border trade.

79. "وأنه منع التجار وغيرهم من جمل المماليك الي مصر واذا سمع باحد من جهة صاجب مصر اخرق به." Al-Maqrīzī, *Kitāb al-sulūk*, 2:1:293.

80. Har-El, *Struggle*, 27–28; Sinclair, *Eastern Turkey*, 1:110, 2:379–82; also Wing, "Submission."

81. Zetterstéen, *Beiträge*, 194. Ibn Baṭṭuṭa traveled to Saray via Sinope. He planned to sail from Sinope to Kerch but landed elsewhere along the coast and went inland to Solgat. Ibn Baṭṭuṭa, *Travels*, 2:465–71.

82. Ibn al-Wardī, *Tatimmat al-mukhtaṣar*, 2:489.

83. Har-El, *Struggle*, 198; Ibn Iyās, *Badāʾiʿ al-zuhūr*, 3:266; Petry, *Protectors or Praetorians?*, 32.

84. "Che potesse il Soldano del mar Maggior cauare schiavi, ferri, & ogni metallo per condurre in Soria, & per tutti i suoi paesi." Guazzo, *Cronaca*, fol. 330r.

85. Ibn Iyās, *Badāʾiʿ al-zuhūr*, 3:404.

86. Ayalon, "Mamlūk," 5; Muḥammad, "Al-Raqīq," 261; Rapoport, "Ibn Ḥağar," 341–42.

87. Northrup, *From Slave to Sultan*, 156; Jacoby, "Supply," 114; Jacoby, "L'expansion." Antioch may have served a similar function before 1268. Golubovich, *Biblioteca*, 2:60.

88. "Nonnullis mercatoribus Januensibus Pisanis et Venetis, qui, de partibus Constantinopolitanis navigantes in regnum Hierosolymitanum, quamplures Graecos, Bulgaros, Ruthenos et Blacos, Christianos, tam mares quam feminas, secum in navibus detulerunt, eosque venales quibuslibet, etiam Sarracenis, exponunt, ita quod multi de talibus detinentur a suis emptoribus tamquam servi." Williams, "From the Commercial Revolution," 124. Acre taxed slave sales. Jacoby, "Acre-Alexandria," 14–15. Edward I did not witness Genoese merchants selling slaves in Acre; the original source mentions Venetians and not slaves. Dandolo, *Chronicon*, 1:318, no. 380.

89. "بعض التجار من المسلمين كان معهم مماليك." Ibn al-Furāt, *Tārīkh al-duwal*, 8:96. Holt, "Mamluk–Frankish Diplomatic Relations," 288–89.

90. Riley-Smith, *Crusades*, 238–39; Schein, *Fideles*, 77; Raiteri, "La schiavitù," 699–702; Pavoni, *Notai genovesi* (1982), 201–2, doc. 163, for illegal Catalan shipping.

91. "Quo Deus eidem melius administraverit." Pavoni, *Notai genovesi* (1982), 224–25, doc. 184.

92. Pavoni, *Notai genovesi* (1982), 124–26, 183–85, and 195, docs. 95, 148, and 157.

93. Pavoni, *Notai genovesi* (1987), 296–97, doc. 248.

94. "Quem scimus et ordinavimus." Balard, *Notai genovesi* (1984), 137–39, doc. 67.

95. Jacoby, "Supply," 120–22.

96. Balletto, *Notai genovesi*; Sebellico, *Felice de Merlis*; Golubovich, *Biblioteca*, 2:60; Sanudo, *Book of the Secrets*, 59–61; Boccaccio, *Decameron*, V.7.

97. Amitai, "Between the Slave Trade," 414.

98. Holt, *Early Mamluk Diplomacy*, 101–2; Ibn ʿAbd al-Ẓāhir, *Tashrīf al-ayām*, 100.

99. "Si emunt sclauum qui sit crispianus quod iurent ipsum non uendere sarracenis uel alicui persone quod credant quod ipsum uendant sarracenis." *Liber iurium*, 8:183d–184a.

100. "فكان التاجر إذا أتاه بالجلبة من المماليك بذل له فيها أغلى القيم." Al-Maqrīzī, *Kitāb al-sulūk*, 2:2:524.

101. "بذل الرغائب للتجار في حملهم إليه، ودفع فيهم الأموال العظيمة." Al-Maqrīzī, *Kitāb al-khiṭaṭ*, 3:694.

102. Al-ʿArīnī, "Al-Fāris," 49.

103. Al-Sakhāwī, *Al-Ḍawʾ al-lāmiʿ*, 3:308–11, no. 1190.

104. Fabri, *Evagatorium*, 18:166; Tafur, *Travels*, 74.

105. "بنظير المماليك الذين ابتاعهم برسم الأبواب الشريفة بكذا وكذا ألف درهم." Al-Qalqashandī, *Subḥ al-aʿshā*, 13:39.

106. Al-Maqrīzī, *Kitāb al-khiṭaṭ*, 4:655. See also ʿAbd al-Raziq, *La femme*, 53.

107. Labib, *Handelsgeschichte*, 259–60.

108. Ibn ʿAbd al-Ẓāhir, *Tashrīf al-ayām*, 237; al-Qalqashandī, *Subḥ al-aʿshā*, 13:341. "من أحضر معه منهم مماليك وجواري، فله في قيمتهم ما يزيد علي ما يريد، والمسامحة بما يتعوضه بثمنهم علي المعتاد في أمر من يجلبهم من البلد القريب، فكيف من البلد البعيد: لأن رغبتنا مصروفة إلي تكثير الجنود، ومن جلب هؤلاء فقد أوجب حقا علي الجود؛ فليستكثر من يقدر علي جلبهم."

109. Northrup, *From Slave to Sultan*, 190. See also Joinville, *Chronicles*, 234–35.

110. Ibn Taghrī Birdī, *Al-Manhal al-ṣāfī*, 5:258–61, no. 1003.

111. Abu-Manneh, "Georgians," 111; Har-El, *Struggle*, 74.

112. Al-Sakhāwī, *Al-Ḍawʾ al-lāmiʿ*, 10:153, no. 608.

113. "خبيرا بأخلاق الملوك وما يليق بخواطرها، دربا بما يتحفه بها من رقيقها وجواهرها." Al-Ṣafadī, *Aʿyān al-ʿaṣr*, 1:523–24, no. 270. Labib, *Handelsgeschichte*, 71–72; Muḥammad, "Al-Raqīq," 103; al-Maqrīzī, *Kitāb al-khiṭaṭ*, 3:132–33; al-Maqrīzī, *Kitāb al-sulūk*, 2:1:240–41; Ibn Taghrī Birdī, *Al-Manhal al-ṣāfī*, 3:367–72, no. 668; al-ʿUmarī, *Masālik al-abṣār*, 146.

114. Zetterstéen, *Beiträge*, 101.

115. Ayalon, "Names," 213–17. Some mamluks with the same trader considered themselves brothers (*khushdash*). Ibn Taghrī Birdī, *Al-Manhal al-ṣāfī*, 2:309 and 4:31–43, nos. 368 and 760.

116. Ibn Taghrī Birdī, *Al-Manhal al-ṣāfī*, 2:346–47 and 2:489–90, nos. 394 and 493.

117. Ayalon, "Names," 215; al-ʿArīnī, *Al-Mamālīk*, 73, 207.

118. Sato, "Slave Traders," 143–47; Broadbridge, "Sending Home"; Barker, "Reconnecting."

119. Ibn Taghrī Birdī, *Al-Nujūm al-zāhira*, 11:220.

"نالته السعادة لجلبه الأتابك برقوق ومات وهو من أعيان المملكة. وكان برقوق إذا رآه قام له من بُعد وأكرمه
وقبل شقاعته وأعطاه ما طلب."

According to Ibn Furāt, it was Ibn Musāfir's brother ʿAlī who brought Barqūq's relatives to Cairo. Frenkel, "Some Notes," 203.

120. "لو لا الضرورة ما فارقتكم ابدا * ولا تنقلت من ناس الي ناس" Ibn Taghrī Birdī, *Al-Manhal al-ṣāfī*, 3:512–15, no. 749.

121. Ibn Taghrī Birdī, *Al-Manhal al-ṣāfī*, 3:512–15, no. 749.

"كنا جميعين في بؤس نكاده * والعين والقلب منافي قذى وأذى
والآن أقبلت الدنيا عليك بما * تهرى فلا تنسني إن الكرام اذا"

122. Smallwood, *Saltwater Slavery*, 65–100.

123. Karpov, *La navigazione*, 69–71, 86–88; Stöckly, *Le systeme*, 101–18; Lane, *Venice*, 69–70, 129, 348.

124. ASVe, Canc. inf., Not., b.19, N.7, reg. 2, fols. 5v and 7r, items 38, 48, and 49.

125. ASVe, Canc. inf., Not., b.19, N.7, reg. 2, fols. 37r and 42r, items 218 and 250.

126. ASVe, Canc. inf., Not., b.19, N.7, reg. 5, items 35, 100, 117. See also Canc. inf., Misc., b.134 bis, series 1, item 11.

127. Verlinden, "Le recrutement des esclaves à Venise," 97–98; ASVe, Canc. inf., Not., b.19, N.3, fol. 8r–v.

128. Karpov, *La navigazione*, 157.

129. ASVe, Senato, Deliberazioni Misti, reg. 56, fol. 16v.

130. Heers, *Gênes*, 310–12; Byrne, *Genoese Shipping*, 29–30.

131. Bensch, "From Prizes of War," 79–81. Comparable practices by the personnel of the Dutch East India Company are described in Rossum, "To Sell Them in Other Countries," 609.

132. Day, *Les douanes*, iv; Tucci, *Le imposte*, 37–38; Byrne, *Genoese Shipping*, 61; Gioffrè, *Il mercato*, 153. Records survive for 1445 and 1458 (ASG, BdSG, Sala 38, 1552 and 1553). The records for 1425 and 1495 are now lost.

133. A few Genoese merchants were exempt from customs. ASG, BdSG, Sala 38, 1552, f.281v.

134. ASG, CdSG, N.185,00625, fols. 31v–35r, 36v–37r.

135. Verlinden, "Medieval 'Slavers,'" 1–2, 6–7, mentions ships with 100 and 114 slaves. Majorca-bound ships sometimes carried more, which explains the high proportion of Tatar slaves there. Mummey, "Enchained in Paradise," 122.

136. Stello, "La traite," 175.

137. Cassandro, "Aspects of the Life," 15. See also Verlinden, "Medieval 'Slavers,'" 2.

138. ASG, BdSG, Sala 38, 1552, fols. 142r–146r; Heers, *Gênes*, 650.

139. ASVe, Senato, Deliberazioni Misti, reg. 31, fol. 87r.

140. ASVe, Senato, Deliberazioni Misti, reg. 31, fols. 128v–129r.

141. "Quia malum et periculosum est, quod cum galeis nostris a mercato venentur aliqui sclavi pro conducendo ipsos aliquo." ASVe, Senato, Deliberazioni Misti, reg. 32, fol. 126r; Thiriet, *Régestes*, doc. 463; Karpov, *La navigazione*, 157.

142. ASVe, Senato, Deliberazioni Misti, reg. 32, fol. 134r.

143. "Dicta navis fuit non semel in manifestissimo periculo." ASVe, Senato, Deliberazioni Misti, reg. 42, fol. 135r.

144. Nehlsen-Stryk, *L'Assicurazione*, 240–44.

145. Gioffrè, *Il mercato*, 170–71.

146. Syropoulos, *Les mémoires*, 533.

147. Casola, *Canon Pietro*, 160–61. See also Elkan, "Rabbi Meshullam," 195; Hoade, "Itinerary of an Anonymous Englishman," 76; Simeonis, *Itinerarium*, 93.

148. Pavoni, *Notai genovesi* (1982), 183–85, doc. 148; Nehlsen-Stryk, *L'Assicurazione*, 240–44.

149. Piattoli, "L'assicurazione"; Bensa, *Il contratto*, 129; Verlinden, *L'Esclavage*, 2:908–9; Verlinden, "Medieval 'Slavers,'" 1; Gioffrè, *Il mercato*, "Slaves Without Race" table.

150. Morosini, *Cronaca veneta*, fol. 494 (January 20, 1428); Gioffrè, *Il mercato*, 20–21; Heers, *Gênes*, 298–307; Zachariadou, *Trade*; Balard, "Remarques," 631. Slaves transported overland risked seizure by local authorities. Musso and Jacopino, "I Genovesi," 168–69.

151. Thiriet, *Régestes*, doc. 2626.

152. ASVe, Senato, Deliberazioni Mar, reg. 2, fol. 188v; Thiriet, *Régestes*, doc. 2736.

153. Karpov, "New Documents," 40–41.

154. ASVe, Senato, Deliberazioni Misti, reg. 48, fols. 60r, 62r; Jorga, "Notes et extraits," 4:293, 301–2, 317.

155. Hoade, "Itinerary of an Anonymous Englishman," 58.

156. Karpov, *La navigazione*, 41.

157. ASVe, Senato, Deliberazioni Misti, reg. 56, fol. 120v; Thiriet, *Régestes*, doc. 2072.

158. Origo, "Domestic Enemy," 331.

159. McKee, "Domestic Slavery," 315.

160. Gioffrè, *Il mercato*, 157.

161. Verlinden, "Medieval 'Slavers,'" 7; Heers, *Gênes*, 371.

162. Dorini and Bertelè, *Il Libro dei conti*, 358, 362, 588, 624; Christ, *Trading Conflicts*, 134.

163. Balard, *La Romanie*, 2:827.

164. Piattoli, "L'assicurazione," 873–74.

165. ASG, Not. Ant. 402, fol. 108r–v.

166. Gioffrè, *Il mercato*, 157.

167. ASG, Arch. Segr., 575, fol. 46v.

168. The Genoese cantar weighed 47.65 kilograms. My calculations yield 105 soldi per cantar for slaves, but Heers claimed that slaves were charged at 60 soldi in good money or 75 soldi in current money per cantar. Heers, *Gênes*, 269 and 317–18.

169. ASVe, Canc. inf., Not., b.174, reg. 1, fol. 8v.

170. Balard, *La Romanie*, 2:827.

171. Pavoni, *Notai genovesi* (1982), 183–85, doc. 148.

172. Spufford, *Handbook*, 86, gives a rate of eighteen grossi per ducat. The slaves belonged to the estate of Pietro Stornello, a Venetian merchant in Tana who dealt mainly in cloth. Back in Venice, one slave was sold within a month for three grossi, four soldi, and one denari, covering the shipping cost for all seven. The rest took several months to sell. ASVe, PdSM, Misti, b.127a, fol. 13r. Thanks to Alan Stahl for suggesting this source.

173. ASVe, Senato, Deliberazioni Misti, reg. 54, fol. 102r.

174. Dorini and Bertelè, *Il Libro dei conti*, 90–91, 347, 588.

175. Tafur, *Travels*, 47.

176. Musso and Jacopino, "I Genovesi," 168.

177. Verlinden, "Medieval 'Slavers,'" 7; Heers, *Gênes*, 371.

178. "Pro melioramento pro dictis sclavis." Pavoni, *Notai genovesi* (1982), 183–85, doc. 148.

179. "Sclaue que consumuntur et possent decedere." Vigna, "Codice diplomatico," 395.

180. Cecchetti, "La donna," 325; Tafur, *Travels*, 157–58.

181. The Quarantia Criminal registers note each *bulleta*. A few are printed in Verlinden, "La législation," 2:170–72. No records survive for *bullete* issued by the *capisestieri*. McKee, "Domestic Slavery," n47. The fees appear in ASVe, Senato, Deliberazioni Misti, reg. 39, fol. 41r; Verlinden, "La législation," 2:153, 161.

182. ASVe, Canc. inf., Not., b.132, N.9, fol. 11r; b.211, reg. III, fol. 4v; b.230, N.1, reg. 3, fols. 6r, 16v, 40v-41r; b.230, N.1, reg. 4, fol. 33r; Verlinden, "Le recrutement des esclaves à Venise," 107, 109, 149, 154.

183. Bauden, "L'achat," 298; Bongi, "Le schiave," 242; Heers, *Esclaves*, 173–74; Depping, *Histoire*, 1:177, says it was 30,000 ducats. Stahl, "Deathbed Oration," 290, observes that different versions of Mocenigo's oration give different numbers for the output of the Venetian mint, so the numbers for the license fee may vary too.

184. Bauden, "L'achat," 297–98; Goitein, "Slaves," 12.

185. Al-Qalqashandī, *Subḥ al-aʿshā*, 4:32; Popper, "Egypt and Syria," 15:98.

186. Ragib, *Actes*, 2:54.

187. ASG, Not. Ant. 449, docs. 158, 223.

188. Morozzo della Rocca, *Lettere*, 19–20.

189. Tafur, *Travels*, 133.

190. ASG, CdSG, N.185,00625, fols. 23v, 31v–40r. Slaves for personal use were exempt.

191. None of the sellers were agents. ASVe, Canc. inf., Not., b.19, N.7; Verlinden, "Le recrutement des esclaves à Venise." Of fifty-nine slave sales documented by Lamberto di Sambuceto in Caffa in 1289–1290, only 8 percent involved agents.

192. Verlinden, "Le recrutement des esclaves à Venise," 198, docs. 152, 177; ASVe, Canc. inf., Not., b.19, N.7, reg. 5, items 33, 60.

193. Frignanus Contar, Henricus Barbarigo, Iohanis Trevisano, Marcus Zacharia, Nicolaus Baxeio, Thomas de Bora.

194. Verlinden, "Le recrutement des esclaves à Venise," 187 and 190, docs. 31, 64, 66; ASVe, Canc. inf., Notai, b.19, N.7, reg. 2, fols. 1r, 29v, and 30r, items 2, 167, and 169.

195. Verlinden, "Le recrutement des esclaves à Venise," 196, docs. 129, 132, 134, 145; ASVe, Canc. inf., Not., b.19, N.7, reg. 5, items 9, 12, and 16.

196. Verlinden, "Le recrutement des esclaves à Venise," 194, 199, and 200, docs. 155, 218, and 223; ASVe, Canc. inf., Not., b.19, N.7, reg. 3, fols. 2r, 3r, and 4r.

197. ASG, CdSG, N.185,00625, fols. 31v–35r, 36v–37r.

198. ASG, Not. Ant. 402, fols. 17v–18r, 110r–111r, 159r–v, 182r–v.

199. "Pro me meoque nomine plenissimam virtutem et potestam habeatis vendendi, alienandi et traddendi omnes et singulos sclavos et sclavas meas quibuslibet emere volentibus et instrumentum venditionis exinde rogandi, precium quoque recipiendi et de conservatione indemnitatis et deffensionis promittendi ac me et bona mea pro premissis obligandi, cartas facere valendi et promittendi." Tamba, *Bernardo de Rodulfis*, 311, doc. 351. See also ASG, Not. Ant. 402, fol. 57r–v; ASVe, Canc. inf., Not., b. 229, reg. 2, fol. 26r.

200. Pavoni, *Notai genovesi* (1982), 224–25, doc. 184.

201. Verlinden, "Le recrutement des esclaves à Venise," 89. ASVe, Canc. inf., Misc., b.134 bis, series 1, item 23.

202. ASG, Not. Ant. 402, fols. 171v–172r. The document does not explain the division of profits.

203. Gioffrè, *Il mercato*, 156. See also Luzzato, *Studi di storia economica*, 188.

204. Heers, *Esclaves*, 179.

205. ASVe, Canc. inf., Not., b. 211, reg. 2, fol. 16v. The Venetian consul in Alexandria received requests for African slaves. Christ, *Trading Conflicts*, 129–34; Bauden, "L'achat," 298; Pedani, "Mamluk Documents," 140–42.

206. Rodocanachi, "Les esclaves," 387.

207. Raymond and Lopez, *Medieval Trade*, 402–3, doc. 195; Piattoli, "Lettere," 130–31.

208. Cluse, "Frauen," 103.

209. Cassandro, "Aspects of the Life," 15.

210. ASVe, Canc. inf., Not. b.19, N.7, reg. 2, fol. 36v.

211. ASG, Not. Ant. 400, fols. 61v–62r.

212. ASG, Not. Ant. 449, doc. 159.

213. Balard, *La Romanie*, 2:827.

214. Heers, *Gênes*, 404–5.

215. Balard, *La Romanie*, 1:303.

216. ASG, Not. Ant. 287, fols. 87v–88r.

217. Domenicus de Florentia used multiple notaries, so the full extent of his activity is unknown. ASVe, Canc. inf., Not. b.19, N.7, reg. 2, fols. 1r, 2r, items 2, 7; Verlinden, "Le colonie."

218. Heers, *Esclaves*, 180.

219. ASG, Not. Ant. 379, fol. 131r.

220. Luzzato, *Studi di storia economica*, 151. See also Khvalkov, "Slave Trade," 111.

221. Quirini-Popławska, "Venetian Involvement," 282–83.

222. ASG, BdSG, Sala 34, 590/1235, fol. 15r.

223. Roccatagliata, *Notai genovesi in Oltremare: Atti rogati a Pera e Mitilene*, 2:94–95, doc. 42.

224. Gioffrè, *Il mercato*, 154; ASG, BdSG, Sala 34, 590/1226, fol. 37v.

225. Tria, "La schiavitù," 172, doc. 43.

226. See also Piero Bartolo in Florence and Nicolo and Lando Lemmi in Lucca. Heers, *Esclaves*, 180.

227. Belgrano, *Della vita*, 86.

228. Balard, "Giacomo Badoer"; Verlinden, *L'Esclavage*, 2:904–10; Verlinden, "Traite des esclaves"; Dorini and Bertelè, *Il libro dei conti*; Schiel, "Slaves' Religious Choice," 39–41; Quirini-Popławska, "Venetian Involvement," 269.

229. Ibn Taghrī Birdī, *Al-Manhal al-ṣāfī*, nos. 365, 651, 749, 847, 1248; Ibn Bassām, *Nihāyat al-rutba*, 149.

230. Traders for whom we have little more than a name are ʿAbd al-Wāḥid ibn Buddāl (al-Maqrīzī, *Kitāb al-khiṭaṭ*, 4:544); Shaykh (Ibn Taghrī Birdī, *Al-Manhal al-ṣāfī*, 3:502); Sālim (al-Sakhāwī, *Al-Ḍawʾ al-lāmiʿ*, 10:289); ʿAlāʿ āl-Dīn ʿAlī (Ibn Iyās, *Bidāʾiʿ al-zuhūr*, 2:308); Nāṣir al-Dīn (Ibn Taghrī Birdī, *Al-Manhal al-ṣāfī*, 2:351–52, 4:143, BNF arabe 2072, fol. 43v; al-Sakhāwī, *Al-Ḍawʾ al-lāmiʿ*, 10:290–91); Damurdash (al-Sakhāwī, *Al-Ḍawʾ al-lāmiʿ*, 4:12); Ṭuṭukh (Ibn Taghrī Birdī, *Al-Manhal al-ṣāfī*, 2:346; al-Sakhāwī, *Al-Ḍawʾ al-lāmiʿ*, 3:53–54, 5:150); Qābūn (al-Sakhāwī, *Al-Ḍawʾ al-lāmiʿ*, 6:175); Sharif (Ibn Taghrī Birdī, *Al-Manhal al-ṣāfī*, 3:82); Kazlak/Kizil (Ibn Taghrī Birdī, *Al-Nujūm al-zāhira*, 15:258; al-Sakhāwī, *Al-Ḍawʾ al-lāmiʿ*, 10:290); ʿAbd al-Raḥmān (Ibn Taghrī Birdī, *Al-Manhal al-ṣāfī*, 2:438); Khalīl (Ibn Taghrī Birdī, *Al-Manhal al-ṣāfī*, 4:205); Jubān/ʿUthmān Jubān (Ibn Taghrī Birdī, *Al-Manhal al-ṣāfī*, 3:351).

231. Al-Sakhāwī, *Al-Ḍawʾ al-lāmiʿ*, 5:29 and 9:72, no. 191; Ibn Taghrī Birdī, *Al-Manhal al-ṣāfī*, 3:285; Popper, "History," 14:116.

232. Al-Sakhāwī, *Al-Ḍawʾ al-lāmiʿ*, 2:147, 3:176–77, nos. 415, 682. He may also have imported Shukurbāy al-Aḥmadiyya, concubine of Sultan Faraj and wife of Sultan Khushqadam.

233. ASVe, Canc. inf., Not., b. 222, reg. 1, fols. 14v–15r; Apellániz Ruiz de Galarreta, *Pouvoir et finance*, 74–75. ʿUmar ibn Zakarī died in 1393. A procurator was appointed to settle his affairs in Caffa in January 1401.

234. Sato, "Slave Traders," 143.

235. ASG, BdSG, Sala 34, 590/1234, fol. 28r.

236. Al-Maqrīzī, *Kitāb al-khiṭaṭ*, 3:170; Ibn Taghrī Birdī, *Al-Manhal al-ṣāfī*, 4:156, no. 797; al-Sakhāwī, *Al-Ḍawʾ al-lāmiʿ*, 3:40, 10:136, 10:153, nos. 551, 608; Abu-Manneh, "Georgians," 111.

237. Al-Sakhāwī, *Al-Ḍawʾ al-lāmiʿ*, 1:118; Ibn Taghrī Birdī, *Al-Manhal al-ṣāfī*, 6:263.

238. Al-Maqrīzī, *Kitāb al-khiṭaṭ*, 3:132–33.

239. Frenkel, "Some Notes," 197.

240. Pavoni, *Notai genovesi* (1982), 183–85, 224–25, docs. 148, 184; Broquière, *Le Voyage*, 68; Labib, *Handelsgeschichte*, 75–76.

241. Broquière, *Le Voyage*, 108; Frenkel, "Some Notes," 197; Ibn Taghrī Birdī, *Al-Manhal al-ṣāfī*, 2:346–47, 3:203–6, 4:68–74, 5:326–29, nos. 394, 621, 769, 1029; Fabri, *Evagatorium*, 18:40. Another trader displayed ten slaves in Cairo. Guglingen, *Fratris Pauli Waltheri*, 230.

242. Fabri, *Evagatorium*, 18:164.

243. Ibn Baṭṭuṭa, *Travels*, 2:444–46, 448–49, 454, 459, 473, 500–501, 517; 3:539, 548, 556, 584–85, 596, 605.

244. Holt, *Early Mamluk Diplomacy*, 147.

245. "لبعض التجار الخواجكية لسفارتهم بين الملوك وترددهم في الممالك لجلب المماليك والجواري." Al-Qalqashandī, *Subḥ al-aʿshā*, 6:15.

246. Ibn al-Dawādārī, *Kanz al-durar*, 9:280.

247. Ibn al-Dawādārī, *Kanz al-durar*, 9:302.

248. Al-Maqrīzī, *Kitāb al-sulūk*, 2:2:423; Zetterstéen, *Beiträge*, 194.

249. "يدخل إلى بلاد التتار، ويتجّر ويتبضّع، ويعود بالرقيق وغيره من أنواع المتاجر وغرائب البلاد." Al-Ṣafadī, *Aʿyān al-ʿaṣr*, 1:523, no. 270; Yudkevich, "Nature," 428.

250. Frenkel, "Some Notes," 197; al-Sakhāwī, *Al-Ḍawʾ al-lāmiʿ*, 6:200–201, no. 695.

251. Al-Sakhāwī, *Al-Ḍawʾ al-lāmiʿ*, 3:62–63, no. 253.

252. Popper, "Egypt and Syria," 15:98.

253. "على قاعدة تجار المماليك." Ibn Taghrī Birdī, *Al-Manhal al-ṣāfī*, 3:206, no. 621.

254. Frenkel, "Some Notes," 197; al-Sakhāwī, *Al-Ḍawʾ al-lāmiʿ*, 6:200–201, no. 695.

255. Al-Sakhāwī, *Al-Ḍawʾ al-lāmiʿ*, 9:72 and 10:153, nos. 191, 608.

256. Al-Sakhāwī, *Al-Ḍawʾ al-lāmiʿ*, 1:118. The *laqab* for the son's mamluks was al-Ibrāhīmī. The father's mamluks had the *laqab* al-Qarmashī.

257. Al-Qalqashandī, *Subḥ al-aʿshā*, 6:13.

258. Mortel, "Mercantile Community," 19–20; Sato, "Slave Traders," 145–46, 154–56.

259. Labib, *Handelsgeschichte*, 328.

260. Al-ʿArīnī, "Al-Fāris," 49; Ayalon, "L'esclavage ," 3–4; Shatzmiller *Labour*, 136–37; Frenkel, "Some Notes," 198.

261. Ito, "Slave Traders and Mamluks."

262. Ibn Shahīn, *Zoubdat kachf*, 115. I found one person with this title. Al-Sakhāwī, *Al-Ḍawʾ al-lāmiʿ*, 12:115.

263. Al-Sakhāwī, *Al-Ḍawʾ al-lāmiʿ*, 1:118, 3:308.

264. Al-ʿArīnī, "Al-Fāris," 50.

265. Ayalon, "L'esclavage," 5.

266. Ibn Taghrī Birdī, *Al-Manhal al-ṣāfī*, 1:196, no. 97. The commerce office (*matjar*) also bought and sold goods, possibly including slaves, on behalf of the state. Rabie, *Financial System*, 92–94.

267. Rapoport, "Women," 9.

268. Northrup, *From Slave to Sultan*, 190.

269. "Avant qu'on puisse les vendre, on doit, suivant les lois du pays, en avertir le sultan en premier lieu." Ghistele, *Voyage*, 21. See also al-Maqrīzī, *Kitāb al-khiṭaṭ*, 3:692.

270. Ibn Taghrī Birdī, *Al-Manhal al-ṣāfī*, 3:513; Ibn Taghrī Birdī, *Al-Nujūm al-zāhira*, 6:374; Petry, *Twilight*, 28.

271. Ibn Taghrī Birdī, *Al-Manhal al-ṣāfī*, 4:68, no. 769.

272. "Misit cum magna summa pecunie mercatores per mare, et fecit emi de illis Cumanis junioribus in maxima quantitate." Hayton, "Flos," 226, 344–45. See also Ghistele, *Voyage*, 35.

273. Pachymeres, *De Michaele*, 177.

274. Al-Maqrīzī, *Kitāb al-sulūk*, 2:2:524 (also 3:694).
"طلب التجار إليه وبذل لهم المال، ووصف لهم حلى المماليك والجوارى، وسيرهم إلى بلاد أزبك وتوريز والروم وبغداد وغير ذلك من البلاد."

275. "كتب الي اعمال مصر ببيع الجواري المولدات وحملهن اليه." Al-Maqrīzī, *Kitāb al-sulūk*, 2:2:546.

276. "Marchant de par le souldan pour aler acheter des esclaves en Caffa." Broquière, *Le Voyage*, 68; BNF, MS français 9087, fol. 175v. Kline, *Voyage*, 41, mistranscribes Caffa as Haifa.

277. Tafur, *Travels*, 133; Tafur, *Andanças*, 161–62.

278. Ibn Shaddād, *Tārīkh al-malik*, 308.

Chapter 7

1. Housley, *Later Crusades*; Cobb, *Race for Paradise*.

2. Leopold, *How to Recover*; Schein, *Fideles*; Dürrholder, *Die Kreuzzugspolitik*; Delaville le Roulx, *La France en Orient*. Atiya, *Crusade*, is less reliable.

3. Ehrenkreutz, "Strategic Implications"; Amitai, "Diplomacy," 356; Heyd, *Histoire*, 2:443, 555–63; Labib, *Handelsgeschichte*, 328; Depping, *Histoire*, 1:57; Ashtor, *Levant Trade*, 11; Mansouri, "Les communautés marchandes," 89–101; Setton, *Papacy*, 2:46; Epstein, *Purity Lost*, 166; Apellániz Ruiz de Galarreta, *Pouvoir et finance*; Schein, *Fideles*, 80.

4. Broadbridge, *Kingship*; Hillenbrand, *Crusades*, 225–48; Haarmann, "Yeomanly Arrogance."

5. When the Mongols sacked Baghdad in 1258, they killed the reigning ʿAbbasid caliph al-Mustaʿṣim. A new caliph, al-Mustanṣir, appeared in Cairo in 1261. His authority was not widely accepted outside the Mamluk kingdom.

6. Al-Qalqashandī, *Subḥ al-aʿshā*, 13:341.
"ويعلم أن تكثر جيوش الإسلام هو الحاث علي طلبهم: لأن . . . ومن أحضر منهم فقد أخرج من الظلمات إلي النور؛ وذم الكفر أمسه وحمد الإيمان يومه، وقاتل عن الإسلام عشيرته وقومه."

7. Al-Maqrīzī, *Kitāb al-khiṭaṭ*, 3:692.
"كل الملوك عملوا شيئا يذكورون به ما بين مال وعقار، وأنا عمّرت أسوارا، وعملت حصونا مانعة لي ولأولادي وللمسلمين وهم المماليك."

8. Haarmann, "Ideology," 181–83; Ayalon, "Mamlūkiyyāt," 340–49; Rabbat, "Representing the Mamluks"; Levanoni, "Al-Maqrizi's Account," 103–4; Frenkel, "Some Notes," 188, 191–92; al-Qalqashandī, *Subḥ al-aʿshā*, 4:458; Ibn Shahīn, *Zoubdat Kachf*, 142.

9. This idea was taken to its logical extreme in Poliak, "Influence."

10. Ibn Khaldūn, *Kitāb al-ʿibār*, 5:371.
"كان من لطف الله سبحانه ان تدارك الايمان . . . بأن بعث لهم من هذه الطائفة التركية فقبائلها العزيزة المتوافرة أمراء حامية وانصارا متوافية يجلبون من دار الحرب الي دار الاسلام في مقادة الرق الذي كمن اللطف في طيه . . . لا لقصد الاستعباد انما هو اكثاف للعصبية."

11. Broadbridge, *Kingship*; Har-El, *Struggle for Domination*, 205.

12. Harff, *Pilgrimage*, 120; Tafur, *Travels*, 74; Fabri, *Evagatorium*, 3:328, 18:92; Breydenbach, *Sanctarum peregrinationum*, fol. 32r; Guglingen, *Fratris Pauli Waltheri*, 140, 225; Varthema, *Travels*, 13; Casola, *Canon Pietro*, 279–80; Ghistele, *Voyage*, 34–35. *Mammelu* was a synonym for *apostate* in fifteenth-century Burgundy. Haarmann, "Mamluk System," 7.

13. "Non enim est de essentia mamaluci quod sit renegatus christianus, uti aliqui dixerunt, sed est de substantia quod sit servus in usu armorum execitatus maxime in sagittando et jacendo." Adorno, *Itinéraire*, 198.

14. Joinville, *Chronicles*, 234–35.

15. Verona, *Liber*, 80; Bellorini and Hoade, *Visit*, 48, 106, 162; Harff, *Pilgrimage*, 93.

16. The translation is mine but draws on Harff, *Pilgrimage*, 122. "Item man sayt in desen lande, wan eyn cristen verleunt der eyn mammeloick wyrt, so moyss he vnsen here Jhesum verluckende mit sijner moder ind dar zoe off dat cruytz spijen ind laissen sich eyn cruytz vnder die voesse snijden durch smaeheyt dar off zo treden. ich sage dir, neyn dat en is nyet waer. dese mammeloicken, as sij yerst gefangen werdent vss cristen landen, so werdent sij verkoufft den heyden. dan werden sij dar zoe gedrongen dat sij dese woert sprechen moissen: holla hylla lalla Mahemmet reschur holla; dat is zo dutzschen gesprochen: got is got, sall ewych blijuen, Machemet is der gewaer boede gesant van goede. dan besnijden sij yen ind geuen yem eynen heydenschen namen." Harff, *Die Pilgerfahrt*, 105. The phrase the mamluks are forced to say is the *shahāda*, usually translated as "there is no god but God, and Muhammad is his Prophet."

17. Haarmann, "Mamluk System," 6–16; Tafur, *Travels*, 73; Ghistele, *Voyage*, 37–38.

18. Bensch, "From Prizes of War," 82–83; Stantchev, *Spiritual Rationality*, 27–29.

19. William of Adam, *How to Defeat the Saracens*, 28–29.

20. ASVe, Canc. inf., Not., b.174, N.9, reg. 2, fol. 4r.

21. Delort, "Quelques précisions," 224.

22. "Que touctes créatures de la foy crestienne que luy seront présentées pour vendre, qu'il promecte de les acheter toutes." Piloti, *Traité*, 52.

23. "Leur chief et teste de payens despent le sien trésor en croître et multipliquer la foy de Mahommet; qu'est le contraire de ce que fait le pape de Rome qu'est chief de la foy crestienne, que

despent ses ducas pour faire gens d'armes à destruire crestiens." Piloti, *Traité*, 54. See also Tafur, *Travels*, 74.

24. "Le souldain fait vestir lesditz marchans de robes de drap d'or, et les fait chevaulchier de chasteau sur chevaulx à son de tambours, de trompettes et de ménestriers, et vont par la ville, et les gardes du souldain à haulte vois vont disent: 'Ces seigneurs marchans ont amené trois cens ammes, ou plus, ou moins, à ce qu'il sera, de la nation et foy crestienne au souldain, et il les a achettées et poyées, lesquelles vivront et moriront en la foy de Mahommet, à ce que la foy de Mahommet multiplique et croisse, et celle de crestiens voise fallant.'" Piloti, *Traité*, 53.

25. Fabri, *Evagatorium*, 18:176; Breydenbach, *Sanctarum peregrinationum*, fol. 88v.

26. Adorno, *Itinéraire*, 330; Varthema, *Travels*, 9; Broquière, *The Voyage*, 22.

27. Haarmann, "Mamluk System," 21.

28. A few mamluks did flee to the crusader states (in 1269) and to Christian Ethiopia (in the early fifteenth century). Ibn Taghrī Birdī, *Al-Nujūm al-zāhira*, 14:349; Lyons and Lyons, *Ayyubids*, 1:168–69, 2:132–34.

29. Simeonis, *Itinerarium*, 104–5.

30. "Promisit, quod redire ad ecclesiam Christi vellet, quia male sensit de secta Machometi, sicut paene omnes Mamaluci male loquuntur de secta Machometi et redire se dicunt, ut patebit." Fabri, *Evagatorium*, 18:34. Guglingen, *Fratris Pauli Waltheri*, 231.

31. "Non erat neque eum fidem abnegaverat neque circuncisione accepat sed cor gerebat fidele sub sarracenica veste." Breydenbach, *Sanctarum peregrinationum*, fol. 84r.

32. Pahlitzsch, "Slavery," 167–70.

33. "Pars magna militie Soldani Babilonie est Xpistianorum. Nam Soldanus accepit pueros et juvenes de Antiochia et de Armenia Minori et de aliis partibus Xpistianorum, et fecit eos Sarracenos, qui facti sunt boni et strenui milites. Et manifeste dicitur et creditur quod si Latini darent eis stipendia, libenter redirent ad Xpistianos, quia remansit in eis aliqua sintilla Xpistianitatis. . . . Et ex hoc etiam Soldani exercitus minuetur, et erit opus misericordie quod anime ipsorum salventur qui male abducti fuerant per errores." Golubovich, *Biblioteca*, 2:60.

34. Harff, *Pilgrimage*, 115, 240; Fabri, *Evagatorium*, 18:93; Poggibonsi, *A Voyage*, 89; Lull, "Projet," 129.

35. "Non tamen possunt donum christianitatis et fidem atque baptismi graciam, que ante susceperant, penitus oblivisci." Brocardus, "Directorium," 512.

36. "Tous lez armiraulx qui sont esté de nation crestienne retourneront et venront en Alexandrie." Piloti, *Traité*, 218.

37. "Enfanz de chrestiens baptizez ou chrestiens renyez, qui legerement se retourneront devers les chrestiens." Germain, "Le discours," 329.

38. Fabri, *Evagatorium*, 3:186. He noted Qāytbāy's improvements to Jerusalem's water supply as confirmation.

39. The popular Mamluk romance *Sīrat al-Malik al-Ẓāhir Baybars* demonized Aybak, one of the hero Baybars' rivals, by portraying him as a crypto-Christian and ally of the crusaders. This portrayal had no basis in fact and was not meant to cast suspicion on mamluks as a class. Herzog, "First Layer," 142–43.

40. Earlier crusade treatises dealt with preaching, ideology, and finance, but not with strategy. Schein, *Fideles*, 22.

41. Golubovich, *Biblioteca*, 2:46–49.

42. "Nam Soldanus solitus mittere annuatim aliquas naves ultra Constantinopolim ad Mare Majus, et de juvenibus nationum illarum, que morantur circa illud mare, facit emi in magna quantitate, sive illi juvenes qui emuntur sint filii paganorum, sive Xpistianorum, quia naturam bonam habent et fortem, et facit eos adduci in Egiptum, et facit eos fieri Sarracenos, facit etiam doceri eos in omni exercitio pugnandi et equitandi. . . . Igitur galee Xpistianorum possunt impedire ista, ita quod nulli tales juvenes adduci poterunt in Egiptum, et erit magnum incomodum Sarracenis." Golubovich, *Biblioteca*, 2:48 (2:13 for bad Christians).

43. Pachymeres, *De Michaele*, 178–79, predicted that the treaties would endanger Outremer.

44. *Dirum amaritudinis* (August 13, 1291); Leopold, *How to Recover*, 8.

45. Bratianu, "Le conseil," 353–54.

46. Kohler, "Traité."

47. Leopold, *How to Recover*, 27–28; Housley, *Later Crusades*, 25–26; Schein, *Fideles*, 181.

48. "Saraceni, qui in terra aegyptiaca uel babylonica oriuntur, in armis non sunt strenui neque boni. Sed Tartaros siue Turcos, et sic de aliis nationibus, ipsi emunt, quos Molucos uocant, et cum illis talibus se defendunt. Et ideo nauis cum galeis in Babyloniam non permitterent ipsos ire; nam tales emuntur in Graecia et uenduntur propter lucrum per falsidicos christianos." Lull, "De fine," 281; Lull, "Projet," 109.

49. Golubovich, *Biblioteca*, 1:368–69; Hillgarth, *Ramon Lull*, xxv; Cluse, "Role," 444–45.

50. The first book was composed in 1306–1307, the second in 1312–1313, and the third in 1319–1321; the completed work began to circulate in 1322. Sanudo, *Book of the Secrets*, 13.

51. Laiou, "Marino Sanudo Torsello," 374.

52. Sanudo, *Book of the Secrets*, 57; Sanudo, *Liber secretorum*, 27.

53. Sanudo, *Book of the Secrets*, 59–61.

54. Sanudo, *Book of the Secrets*, 60; Sanudo, *Liber secretorum*, 29.

55. Sanudo, *Book of the Secrets*, 56; Sanudo, *Liber secretorum*, 27.

56. Sanudo, *Book of the Secrets*, 80; Sanudo, *Liber secretorum*, 42–43.

57. Leopold, *How to Recover*, 29–30; Schein, *Fideles*, 212.

58. "Misit cum magna summa pecunie mercatores per mare, et fecit emi de illis Cumanis junioribus in maxima quantitate, qui portati fuerunt in Egiptum." Hayton, "Flos," 344–45.

59. "Major pars exercitus Sarracenorum Egipti sunt servi empti precio et venditi, quos mali Christiani, causa lucrandi aliquid, in Babiloniam sepe portant, aut in preliis vel aliter acquisti, quos Sarraceni compellunt eorum secte et fidei adherere." Hayton, "Flos," 341.

60. Hayton, "Flos," 354.

61. "Hujusmodi homines communitatum, sicut experiencia docuit, alios euntes ad dictas terras capiunt, suis parcunt, et ideo sui licentius et securius vadunt, cum capcionem non dubitent, et tunc ipsi soli plus portant de dictis rebus Sarracenis quam omnes alii, quare cum soli vadant, plus lucrantur." Mas Latrie, *Histoire*, 2:119.

62. Schein, "From 'Milites Christi,'" 683; Cluse, "Role," 451.

63. Kedar and Schein, "Un project," 225; Cluse, "Role," 446.

64. "Perderent eciam succursum gentium armatarum que eis cotidie de Comenia per mare veniunt, quia omnes Turqui de Babilonia venerunt de Comania pro majori parte per mare." My translation, drawing on Cluse, "Role," 449.

65. Dubois, *Recovery*, 201.

66. Nogaret, "Quae sunt advertenda," 200.

67. The three surviving manuscripts are all associated with the Council of Basel in 1431–1449. William of Adam, *How to Defeat the Saracens*, 2, 11, 23. Union with the Greeks was on the agenda in Basel, and William of Adam's extended attacks on Byzantium may have interested the attendees. Leopold, *How to Recover*, 195.

68. William of Adam, *How to Defeat the Saracens*, 22–25.

69. William of Adam, *How to Defeat the Saracens*, 110–11.

70. William of Adam, *How to Defeat the Saracens*, 32–35.

71. Heyd, *Histoire*, 2:558; Labib, *Handelsgeschichte*, 75–76; Balard, *La Romanie*, 1:298; Epstein, *Purity Lost*, 162–66; Stantchev, *Spiritual Rationality*, 84; Ciocîltan, *Mongols*, 176–77.

72. Kedar, "Segurano-Sakran Salvaygo."

73. Ibn Abī al-Faḍā'il, *Histoire*, 3:198–99; Kedar, "Segurano-Sakran Salvaygo," 91.

74. Stanegrave, "L'Escarboucle," 37, 311–12.

75. Tizengauzen, *Sbornik materialov*, 1:493.

76. I agree with Yudkevich, "Nature," 428–31.

77. Tizengauzen, *Sbornik materialov*, 1:493; Ibn al-Dawādārī, *Kanz al-durar*, 9:280, 302.

78. Balard, *Gênes et l'Outre-Mer*, 1:306 and 346, docs. 767 and 844.

79. Ibn al-Dawādārī, *Kanz al-durar*, 9:280.

80. "جهز مركبا موسوقا من بلاد ازبك من كل الاصناف." Tizengauzen, *Sbornik materialov*, 1:493.

81. Ibn al-Dawādārī, *Kanz al-durar*, 9:302.

"حضر صحبتهم سكران التاجر الإفرنجي ورفيقه، استحضرهم مولانا السلطان عز نصره وتحدث معهم. وكان معهم عدة مماليك وجوار. ثم استحضر مولانا السلطان الرسل وذلك الرجل المقعد، وعقدوا العقد الشريف."

82. Dürrholder, *Die Kreuzzugspolitik*, 103–17.

83. Housley, *Later Crusades*, 34; Brocardus, "Directorium"; Leopold, *How to Recover*, 43–44.

84. Stanegrave, "L'Escarboucle," 321–23.

85. Housley, *Later Crusades*, 39; Leopold, *How to Recover*, 42, 190.

86. Leopold, *How to Recover*, 188; Mézières, *Le Songe*; Palmer, *England, France*, 180–210.

87. Leopold, *How to Recover*, 199.

88. North Africa was a third source of slaves, but not mamluks. Piloti, *Traité*, 135.

89. Piloti, *Traité*, 53, 138–41.

90. Piloti, *Traité*, 53–54.

91. Piloti, *Traité*, 143.

92. Piloti, *Traité*, 54. Piloti's figure spread via Heyd, *Histoire*, 2:558.

93. "Et se ne fust la nécessité que Genevois ont de la cité d'Alexandrie, ilz ne lasseroyent passer nesuns desdis esclaves." Piloti, *Traité*, 143.

94. Piloti, *Traité*, 160–61.

95. Piloti, *Traité*, 130–31.

96. "Communement Pictes et Gethes, chrestiens grecz, conquis par les ruses des Genevoys." Germain, "Le discours," 329.

97. Germain, "Le discours," 339.

98. Stantchev, *Spiritual Rationality*.

99. Lateran IV, canon 71 in Tanner, *Decrees*, 1:270.

100. Lyons I, canon 5 and Lyons II, canon 1; Friedberg, *Corpus iuris canonici*, X.5.6.6, X.5.6.17; Potthast, *Regesta pontificum*, vol. 2, no. 20959; Menache, "Papal Attempts," 236–59; Setton, *Papacy*, 1:262–63; Schein, *Fideles*, 151; Cluse, "Role," 439–40.

101. "Super paganis et sclavis non portandis per nostros fideles ad terras Soldani." Cessi, *Deliberazioni*, 3:318, no. 28. The letters are found in Langlois, *Les registres*, 2:641–42, 901–2, nos. 4403, 6789, 6794–98.

102. ASVe, Secreta, *Libri Commemoriali*, reg. 1, fols. 13r, 172v; Predelli, *I libri commemoriali*, 1:37–38, docs. 161, 166.

103. "Masculos vel femellas impuberes vel pupillos." Laurière, *Ordonnances*, 1:505–6; Cluse, "Role," 453–54.

104. "Sicut dicitur nullus possit portare predicta (sc. equos, arma, ferrum, lignamina vel alia cum quibus Saraceni possent impugnare christianos), ita dicitur et ponatur . . . nec etiam possit portare vel portari facere mamuluchos ad partes predictas." Verlinden, "La législation," 150. The Avogaria del commun banned the transport of slaves on the Alexandria galleys in 1412, but this was not enforced effectively. Christ, *Trading Conflicts*, 134.

105. Belgrano, "Prima serie," 111, 113; Laiou, *Constantinople and the Latins*, 184–85.

106. "Mumulicos siue mumulichas mares uel feminas neque aliquos Saracenos Turcos uel infidelles in Alexandriam de ultra mare uel ad aliquem alium locum subditum Soldano Babilonie." Sauli, *Leges municipales*, 372.

107. "Aliquos mumuluchos mares uel feminas Sarracenos uel alios infideles." Sauli, *Leges municipales*, 372.

108. Raynaldus, *Annales ecclesiastici*, 24:60.

109. Stantchev, *Spiritual Rationality*, 146–47; Thomas, *Diplomatarium*, 1:277, 306–7.

110. "Iudaei utriusque sexus, qui in Caffensi et Cannensi ac aliis ultramarinarum partium civitatibus, terris et locis christianorum ditioni subiectis commorantur . . . Zichorum, Rossorum, Alanorum, Mingrellorum et Anogusiorum [sic], sub christiani nominis professione iuxta Graecorum

ritum baptizatorum, personas utriusque sexus, quotquot possunt, emunt, et emptas Saracenis alisque infidelibus . . . crudeliter vendunt ac exactissimas mercantias de eis faciunt, personas ipsas nonnunquam ad eorumdem Saracenorum et infidelium terras, ob eam causam, corporaliter abducendo, ex quo inde sequitur quod Saraceni et infideles ipsi personas easdem sic eis venditas fidem catholicam abnegare compellunt." Tomassetti, *Bullarum*, 4:718–20.

111. "Nonnulli iniquitatis filii baptismatis fonte renati, christianum nomen contemnentes, propriaeque salutis immemores." Tomassetti, *Bullarum*, 4:720–21.

112. Friedberg, *Corpus iuris canonici*, D.54 c.13, D.54 c.18, C.17 q.4 c.34.

113. Tomassetti, *Bullarum*, 5:105–6.

114. Studies of blockade running have focused on iron, timber, and weapons. Constable, "Clothing"; Jacoby, "Supply"; Odena, "Les 'Alexandrini'"; Burns, "Renegades." Venice's rejection of two legates sent by Pope John XXII to enforce the embargo is discussed in Besta, *Riccardo Malombra*; Ortalli, "Venice and Papal Bans"; Stantchev, *Spiritual Rationality*, 133–45.

115. Abu-Lughod, *Before European Hegemony*, 137–49, 212–16, 239–41; Christ, *Trading Conflicts*.

116. This story is based on letters in ASVe, Secreta, *Libri commemoriali*, vol. 1, fols. 53r, 71v–72r; Thomas, *Diplomatarium*, 1:23–32, docs. 12–18. The register with the Senate decisions concerning this incident, vol. 2 of the series Senato Deliberazioni Misti Registri, was destroyed in a fire in the sixteenth century. Its rubrics were published by Giomo, "Le Rubriche," 18:59; 19:111, 112; 20:293.

117. "Qui furtive et occulte non respiciens honorem quem fecerimus ei emit de predictis sclavis tam ex illis qui exoneratus fuerant quam de illis de remanserunt in supradicta nave contra bonum statum fidei christiane honorem vostrem et ordinamenta bannaque nostra, quod quidem habuimus valde grave ex neccessitate quam ex hominibus habebamus tam pro illis quos amiseramus exterremotu quam pro malicis serviciis que nos facere opportebat." ASVe, Secreta, *Libri commemoriali*, vol.1, fol. 53r.

118. Older laws against exporting slaves from Crete and assisting fugitive slaves were recopied into the register as part of this case. ASVe, Secreta, *Libri commemoriali*, vol. 1, fol. 72v.

119. In 1301, della Volta had openly registered his purchase of an Armenian slave with a notary in Famagusta. Pavoni, *Notai genovesi*, 106–7, doc. 79.

120. This letter appears in Latin translation. ASVe, Secreta, *Libri commemoriali*, vol. 1, fol. 53r.

121. Menache, "Papal Attempts," 248–49.

122. "De istis mamuluchis non est aliquis christianus propter quod possitis habere reprehensionem aliquam occasionem fedei vostro." ASVe, Secreta, *Libri commemoriali*, vol. 1, fol. 53r.

123. Sanudo, *Book of the Secrets*, 56–57.

124. Abu-Lughod, *Before European Hegemony*, 215.

125. Thiriet, *Régestes*, doc. 361. Contarini was investigated by papal legates in 1322 for violating the embargo, but that investigation did not refer to the 1316 slave cargo. ASVe, Secreta, *Libri Commemoriali*, reg. 2, fols. 155r–157r; Predelli, *I libri commemoriali*, 1:260–61, doc. 415.

126. "Pro gratificando mentem suam ad favores et commoda venetorum qui in Alexandria et Siria mercantui." ASVe, Senato, Deliberazioni, Mar, reg. 2, fol. 188v. Thiriet, *Régestes*, vol. 3, doc. 2736.

127. Another shipment of mamluks appears to have been detained successfully and diverted to Cyprus sometime during the reign of Sultan Barsbāy (1422–1437). Frenkel, "Some Notes," 196.

128. "Obtentis itaque omnibus suprascriptis . . . placet nobis ut Soldano ac suis tractum sclavorum ex Caffa concedatis, ipsis solventibus dritus et cabellas consuetas et ordinatas, hac tamen declaratione semper praecedente, quod scilicet si quis eiusmodi sclavorum vellet christianus fieri, id ei liceat, dummodo eius domino solvatur precium in Caffa constitutem. Scribimus namque consuli Caffae, et novo consuli in mandatis dabimus ut de tractatu talium sclavorum disponat ac faciat iuxta commissiones vestras. Et ad uberiorum cautelam binas vobis litteras mittimus annexas, quas, cum voluerit, consuli Caffae transmittat per aliquem ex his saracenis qui Caffam iturus sit." ASG, Arch. Segr., 2707A/1, doc. 25. The wording in Sacy, *Pièces*, 74, differs slightly.

129. Apellániz Ruiz de Galarreta, *Pouvoir et finance*, 39, 42–43, 59, argued that it was the Venetians who used the slave trade for leverage in the spice trade.

Conclusion

1. "Nobilissimas res, id est homines, vilissimo precio vidimus venales." Breydenbach, *Sanctarum peregrinationum*, fol. 88r.

2. "Invenimus merces pretiosissimas, quae tamen vili pretio vendebantur. Merces illae erant rationabiles Dei creaturae, ad imaginem Dei factae, homines utriusque sexus." Fabri, *Evagatorium*, 18:164.

3. "Quos Christus emit sua pretiosa morte." Fabri, *Evagatorium*, 18:165.

Bibliography

Archival Sources

Cairo, Dār al-Kutub al-Miṣriyya (DK)

Al-Taḥqīq fī shirā' al-raqīq. Taimuriyya, Faḍā'il wa-radhā'il, no. 48

Genoa, Archivio di Stato di Genova (ASG)

Giuseppe Felloni has created an online catalog for the Banco di San Giorgio and Casa di San Giorgio collections at http://www.lacasadisangiorgio.it/main.php?do=cenni

Archivio Segreto (Arch. Segr.)

513	*Libri diversorum*, register 17, years 1428–1430
562	*Libri diversorum*, register 67, years 1457–1458
575	*Libri diversorum*, register 80, years 1462–1463
1779	*Litterarum*, register 3, years 1427–1431
1781	*Litterarum*, register 5, years 1431–1434
1789	*Litterarum*, register 13, years 1446–1450
2707A/1–3	*Instructiones et relationes*, register 1

Banco di San Giorgio (BdSG)

Sala 34, 590/1225–1262	Caffa *massaria*, years 1374–1472
Sala 34, 590/1303–1305	Pera *massaria*, years 1389–1390, 1390–1391, 1402
Sala 38, 1552–1553	*Caratorum veterum*, years 1445, 1458

Casa di San Giorgio (CdSG)

N.185,00623	One florin tax, year 1413
N.185,00624	One florin tax, year 1447
N.185,00625	One florin tax, year 1449
N.185,00101	Half-florin tax, years 1453–1457
N.185,01009	Half-florin tax, year 1458
N.185,15002	*Vendita delle gabelle*, years 1380–1381
N.185,15003	*Vendita delle gabelle*, year 1384
N.185,15006	*Vendita delle gabelle*, year 1387
N.185,15072	*Vendita delle gabelle*, years 1422–1430

Codici Membranacii, Codice C (*Liber iurium duplicatum*)

Manoscritti membranacei, nos. 7, 17, 18

Notai Antichi (Not. Ant.)

111	Fredericus de Platealonga
120/I	Simone de Albario
167	Lanfranco de Nazario
172	Iacobinus Nepitelli
194	Iohanis de Sollano
220–21, 236–39	Thome de Casanova
253	Parentino de Quinto
255	Raffael Beffignanus

258	Deloffé de Anneto
265	Franciscus de Silva
273	Nicolo Beltramis
286–87, 292	Benvenuto de Bracelli
318	Ioanni de Ogniboni
360	Raffaele de Guaso
363	Antonio Turco
366/I-367	Ianoti Besignani
379–82	Giovanni Bardi
396–405/I	Bartolomeo Gatto
432	Christoforo Revellino
449	Oberto Foglietta
548	Giovanni Labaino
579–80	Antonio Fazio
645	Battista Crosa
685/II	Andrea Testa
719/I-III	Bartolomeo Risso
724/II	Oberto Foglietta
768/I	Parisola Batista
992	Lorenzo Costa
1034	Nicolo Raggi
1279	Giovanni Costa

Notai ignoti, xxiii and xxiv

Paris, Bibliothèque nationale de France (BNF)

Broquière, Bertrandon de la. *Le Voyage d'Outremer.* MS français 9087.

Ibn Sāʿid al-Akfānī, Muḥammad. *Al-Naẓar wa-al-taḥqīq fī taqlīb al-raqīq.* MS arabe 2234, fols. 148r–151r.

Ibn Taghrī Birdī, Jamāl al-Dīn Yusūf. *Al-Manhal al-ṣāfī wa-al-mustawfā baʿd al-wāfī.* MS arabe 2068–72.

Khāṣikī, Āqbughā al-. *Al-Tuḥfa al-fākira fī al-dhakr rusūm khuṭūṭ al-Qāhira.* MS arabe 2265.

Al-Maqṣad al-rafīʿ al-munshāʾ al-ḥāwī ilā ṣanāʿat al-inshāʾ. MS arabe 4439.

Venice, Biblioteca Marciana (BMV)

Imola, Petrus de. *Apparatus notularum sive summa artis notariae.* MS Lat. V 128 (3376).

Morosini, Antonio. *Cronaca veneta.* MS Ital., Cl. VII, 2049.

San Floriano, Ventura di. *Cartolarius seu formulae notariorum.* MS Lat. V 45 (3011).

Summa artis notariae. MS Lat. V 120 (2918).

Venice, Archivio di Stato di Venezia (ASVe)

Sources marked online are at http://www.archiviodistatovenezia.it/web/index.php?id=63

Avogaria di comun, Raspe (Avog., Raspe)

3643	years 1361–1378
3645	years 1393–1406
3646	years 1406–1417

Cancelleria inferiore, Miscellanea notai diversi, b.134 bis. (Canc. inf., Misc.)

Cancelleria inferiore, Notai (Canc. inf., Not.)

5, N.16	Francesco Alberegno
5, N.26	Andriucio fu Bonajunte
5, N.27	Iohannis de Argoiotiis
12	Odoricus Brutus
16	Suriano Belli
17	Giovanni Barbafella, Belanzinis de Antonio
19, N.3	Nicolò Bono
19, N.7	Benedetto Bianco

20, N.8	Borolo Antonio
20, N.9	Giovanni Bon
20, N.10	Bartholomeus quondam Benvenuto
23, N.1	Iohanis Burgi
58–61	Anastasio Christiano
68, N.1	Marino Doto
70, N.4	Darvasi Basilio
80, N.7	Nicolò Foscolo
81	Philosofis de Domenicis
88, N.11	Iacobus Spada
91	Gibillino de Giorgio
92, N.1	Gibillino de Giorgio
92, N.2	Pietro Girarolo
95, I	Francesco de Gibillino
117, N.6	Marcus Marzella
121, N.2	Donato a Mano
132, N.9	Marciliano de Naresi
148, N.4	Palma Giacomo fu Guglielmo
148, N.6	Pietro Pelacan
149, N.1	Victor Pomino
174, N.9	Cristoforo Rizo
182, N.1	Soje de Iacopo
182, N.4	Petrus Sancto
211	Nicolò Turiano
222	Antonio de Vataci
229	Leonardo de Valle
230, N.1	Nicolo Venier
230, N.2	Bartolomeo de Virisellis
231, N.3	Nicolaus de Varsis
243, N.3	Luca de Zuffi
243, N.21	Antonio Zio

Collegio, Secreti (online), register 1382–1385
Maggior Consiglio, Deliberazioni (online), registers 10 (Presbiter), 19 (Novella)
Notai di Candia, b.2, N.1 (Franciscus Avonal)
Notarile Testamenti, b.733 (Donato a Mano)
Procuratori di San Marco, Misti (PdSM, Misti)
127a estate of Pietro Stornello
180–81 estate of Biagio Dolfin
Quarantia criminal (online), Parti II, register 29 (years 1366–1370)
Secreta, Libri Commemoriali, registers 1, 2, 8
Senato, Deliberazioni Misti (online), registers 31, 32, 38, 39, 42, 48, 52, 54, 56, 60
Senato, Deliberazioni Mar (online), register 2
Signori di Notte al Criminal, registers 1A, 7, 9, 10
Signori di Notte al Civil, b.1bis, capitolare A (years 1348–1545)

Published Sources

ʿAbd al-Raḥīm, Hadiyya Imām ʿAlī. “Al-Mamālīk al-julbān wa-dawruhum fī ʿaṣr dawlat al-mamālīk al-jarākisa min sana 784–922 H./1382–1517 M.” Master’s thesis, Cairo University, 2003.

ʿAbd al-Raziq, Ahmad. “Un document concernant le mariage des esclaves au temps des Mamlūks.” *JESHO* 13 (1970): 309–14.

———. *La femme au temps des Mamlouks en Égypte.* Cairo: IFAO, 1973.

Abril Fuertes, José, and José Mingorance Ruiz. "Los esclavos en la documentación notarial de Jerez de la Frontera (1392–1550)." *Historia, instituciones, documentos* 39 (2012): 9–37.

Abu-Lughod, Janet. *Before European Hegemony: The World System A.D. 1250–1350.* Oxford: Oxford University Press, 1989.

Abu-Manneh, Butrus. "The Georgians in Jerusalem in the Mamluk Period." In *Egypt and Palestine: A Millennium of Association*, ed. Amnon Cohen and Gabriel Baer, 102–12. Jerusalem: Yad Izhak Ben-Zvi, 1984.

Adam, William of. *How to Defeat the Saracens*, ed. Giles Constable. Washington, DC: Dumbarton Oaks Research Library and Collection, 2012.

Adler, Elkan, trans. "Rabbi Meshullam ben R. Menahem of Volterra, 1481." In *Jewish Travellers: A Treasury of Travelogues from 9 Centuries*, 156–208. New York: Hermon Press, 1966.

Adorno, Anselm. *Itinéraire d'Anselme Adorno en Terre Sainte (1470–1471)*, ed. Jacques Heers and Georgette de Groer. Paris: Centre national de la recherche scientifique, 1978.

ʿAdwī, Wafāʾ ʿAlī Ibrahīm Muḥammad al-. "Miṣr fī ʿahd al-sulṭān Khushqadam (865–872 H./1461–1467 M.)." Master's thesis, Cairo University, 2009.

"AHR Forum: Crossing Slavery's Boundaries." *American Historical Review* 105 (2000): 451–84.

Akbari, Suzanne Conklin. *Idols in the East: European Representations of Islam and the Orient.* Ithaca: Cornell University Press, 2009.

Alfieri, Alberto. *Education, Civic Virtue, and Colonialism in Fifteenth-Century Italy: The Ogdoas of Alberto Alfieri*, trans. Carla Weinberg and E. Ann Matter. Tempe: ACMRS, 2011.

Ali, Kecia. *Marriage and Slavery in Early Islam.* Cambridge: Harvard University Press, 2010.

Ali, Omar. *Malik Ambar: Power and Slavery Across the Indian Ocean.* Oxford: Oxford University Press, 2016.

Alighieri, Dante. *The Divine Comedy*, trans. John Ciardi. New York: New American Library, 2003.

Allard, Paul. *Les esclaves chrétiens depuis les premiers temps de l'église jusqu'a la fin de la domination romaine en occident.* Paris: Didier, 1876.

Allen, W. E. D. *A History of the Georgian People from the Beginning down to the Russian Conquest in the Nineteenth Century.* London: Kegan Paul, 1932.

Amia, Amerigo d'. *Schiavitù romana e servitù medievale.* Milan: Ulrico Hoepli, 1931.

Amitai, Reuven. *Mongols and Mamluks: The Mamluk–Ilkhanid War, 1260–1281.* Cambridge: Cambridge University Press, 1995.

———. "Diplomacy and the Slave Trade in the Eastern Mediterranean: A Re-examination of the Mamluk–Byzantine–Genoese Triangle in the Late Thirteenth Century in Light of the Existing Early Correspondence." *Oriente Moderno* 88 (2008): 349–68.

———. "Mamluks of Mongol Origin and Their Role in Early Mamluk Political Life." *MSR* 12 (2008): 119–38.

———. "Between the Slave Trade and Diplomacy: Some Aspects of Early Mamluk Policy in the Eastern Mediterranean and the Black Sea." In Amitai and Cluse, *Slavery*, 401–22.

Amitai, Reuven, and Christoph Cluse, eds. *Slavery and the Slave Trade in the Eastern Mediterranean (c.1000–1500 CE).* Turnhout: Brepols, 2017.

Anṣārī, Zakariya al-. *Al-Iʿlām wa-al-ihtimām bi-jamʿ fatāwā shaykh al-islām*, ed. Aḥmad ʿUbayd. Damascus: Dār al-Taqwa, 2007.

Ansgar Kelly, Henry. "Corpus Juris Canonici (1582)." http://digital.library.ucla.edu/canonlaw/ (accessed March 18, 2017).

Antoninus. *Summa theologica.* Vol. 3. Nuremberg: Anton Koberger, 1477–1479.

Apellániz Ruiz de Galarreta, Francisco. *Pouvoir et finance en Méditerranée pré-moderne: Le deuxième état mamelouk et le commerce des épices (1382–1517).* Barcelona: CSIC, 2009.

Arbel, Benjamin. "Slave Trade and Slave Labor in Frankish Cyprus (1191–1571)." *Studies in Medieval and Renaissance History* 14 (1993): 149–90.

Argenti, Philip. *The Occupation of Chios by the Genoese and Their Administration of the Island, 1346–1566.* Cambridge: Cambridge University Press, 1958.

ʿArīnī, Sayyid al-Bāz al-. *Al-Mamālīk*. Beirut: Dār al-nahdiyya al-ʿarabiyya, 1967.

———. "Al-Fāris al-mamlūkī." *Dirāsāt fī tārīkh al-ʿuṣūr al-wusṭā* 1 (n.d.): 47–72.

Aristotle. *Politics*, trans. H. Rackham. Cambridge: Harvard University Press, 1977.

Arnesen, Eric. "The Recent Historiography of British Abolitionism: Academic Scholarship, Popular History, and the Broader Reading Public." In *British Abolitionism and the Question of Moral Progress in History*, ed. Donald Yerxa, 99–119. Columbia: University of South Carolina Press, 2012.

Arnold, Benjamin. *German Knighthood, 1050–1300*. Oxford: Clarendon Press, 1985.

Ashtor, Eliyahu. *Histoire des prix et des salaires dans l'Orient médiéval*. Paris: SEVPEN, 1969.

———. *A Social and Economic History of the Near East in the Middle Ages*. Berkeley: University of California Press, 1976.

———. *Levant Trade in the Later Middle Ages*. Princeton: Princeton University Press, 1983.

ʿAshūr, Saʿīd ʿAbd al-Fattāḥ. *Al-ʿAṣr al-mamālīkī fī Miṣr wa-al-Shām*. Cairo: Dār al-nahḍa al-ʿarabīyya, 1965.

Asyūṭī, Shams al-Dīn Muḥammad al-. *Jawhar al-ʿuqūd wa-muʿīn al-quḍāa wa-al-muwaqqiʿīn wa-al-shuhūd*, ed. Muḥammad Ḥāmid al-Fiqqī. Cairo: Maṭbaʿat al-sunna al-Muḥammadiyya, 1955.

Atiya, Aziz. *The Crusade in the Later Middle Ages*. New York: Klaus Reprint Corp., 1965.

Ayalon, David. "The Circassians in the Mamlūk Kingdom." *Journal of the American Oriental Society* 69 (1949): 135–47.

———. "L'esclavage du mamelouk." *Oriental Notes and Studies* 1 (1951): 1–66.

———. "Studies on the Structure of the Mamluk Army—I." *BSOAS* 15 (1953): 203–28.

———. "Studies on the Structure of the Mamluk Army—II." *BSOAS* 15 (1953): 448–76.

———. "The Great Yāsa of Chingiz Khān: A Re-examination." *Studia Islamica* 36 (1972): 113–58.

———. "Names, Titles and 'Nisbas' of the Mamluks." *Israel Oriental Studies* 5 (1975): 189–232.

———. "Mamlūkiyyāt." *JSAI* 2 (1980): 321–49.

———. "Mamlūk: Military Slavery in Egypt and Syria." In *Islam and the Abode of War: Military Slaves and Islamic Adversaries*, 1–21. Aldershot: Ashgate Variorum, 1994.

———. "The Mamlūk Novice: On His Youthfulness and on His Original Religion." In *Islam and the Abode of War: Military Slaves and Islamic Adversaries*, 1–8. Aldershot: Ashgate Variorum, 1994.

ʿAynī, Badr al-Dīn Maḥmūd al-. *ʿIqd al-jumān fī tārīkh ahl al-zamān*, ed. Muḥammad Amīn. 4 vols. Cairo: HMAK, 1987–1992.

ʿAyntābī, Maḥmūd ibn Aḥmad al-. *Al-Qawl al-sadīd fī ikhtiyār al-imāʾ wa-al-ʿabīd*, ed. Muḥammad ʿIsā Sāliḥiyya. Beirut: Muʾassasat al-risāla, 1996.

Babinger, Franz. *Mehmed the Conqueror and His Time*. Princeton: Princeton University Press, 1978.

Bacharach, Jere. "The Dinar versus the Ducat." *IJMES* 4 (1973): 77–96.

———. "African Military Slaves in the Medieval Middle East: The Cases of Iraq (869–955) and Egypt (868–1171)." *IJMES* 13 (1981): 471–95.

Balard, Michel. "Remarques sur les esclaves à Gênes dans le seconde moitié du XIIIe siècle." *École française de Rome, Mélanges d'archéologie et d'histoire* 80 (1968): 627–80.

———. *Gênes et l'Outre-Mer*. 2 vols. Paris: Mouton, 1973–1980.

———. "Les Génois dans l'ouest de la Mer Noire au XIVe siècle." In Berza and Stănescu, *Actes du XIVe congrès*, 2:21–32.

———. *La Romanie génoise (XIIe-début du XVe siécle)*. 2 vols. Genoa: Società ligure di storia patria, 1978.

———. *Notai genovesi in Oltremare: Atti rogati a Cipro da Lamberto di Sambuceto (11 ottobre 1296–23 giugno 1299)*. Genoa: IMG, 1983.

———. *Notai genovesi in Oltremare: Atti rogati a Cipro da Lamberto di Sambuceto (31 marzo 1304–19 luglio 1305, 4 gennaio-12 luglio 1307), Giovanni de Rocha (3 agosto 1308–14 marzo 1310)*. Genoa: IMG, 1984.

———. *Notai genovesi in Oltremare: Atti rogati a Chio da Donato di Chiavari (17 Febbraio–12 Novembre 1394)*. Genoa: IMG, 1988.

———. "Gênes et la mer Noire (XIIIe–XVe siècles)." In *La mer Noire et la Romanie génoise (XIIIe–XVe siècles)*, 31–54. London: Variorum Reprints, 1989.

———. “Les genois et les regions bulgares au XIVe siecle.” In *La Mer Noire et la Romanie génoise (XIIIe–XVe siècles)*, 87–97. London: Variorum Reprints, 1989.

———. “Esclavage en Crimée et sources fiscales génoises au XVe siècle.” *Byzantinische Forschungen* 22 (1996): 9–17.

———. “Giacomo Badoer et le commerce des esclaves.” In *Milieux naturels, espaces sociaux*, ed. E. M. Mornet, 555–64. Paris: Publications de la Sorbonne, 1997.

———. “Constantinople et les ports pontiques: Topographie, liens entre le port et la ville, fonctions.” In *Les ports et la navigation en Méditerranée au Moyen Âge*, ed. Ghislaine Fabre, Daniel Le Blévec, and Denis Menjot, 191–200. Lattes: Association pour la connaissance du patrimonie en Languedoc Roussillon, 2009.

Balard, Michel, Laura Balletto, and Christopher Schabel. *Gênes et l'outre-mer: Acts notaries de Famagouste et d'autres localités du Proche-Orient (XIVe–XVe s.)*. Nicosia: CRSC, 2013.

Balard, Michel, William Duba, and Christopher Schabel. *Actes de Famagouste du notaire génois Lamberto di Sambuceto (décembre 1299–septembre 1300)*. Nicosia: CRSC, 2012.

Balbi, Giovanna. “La schiavitù a Genova tra i secoli XII e XIII.” In *Mélanges offerts a René Crozet*, ed. Pierre Gallais and Yves-Jean Riou, 2:1025–29. Poitiers: Société des études medievales, 1966.

———, ed. *L'epistolario di Iacopo Bracelli*. Genoa: Fratelli Bozzi, 1969.

———. *Simon Boccanegra e la Genova del '300*. Genoa: Marietti, 1991.

Balbi, Giovanna, and Silvana Fossati Raiteri. *Notai genovesi in Oltremare: Atti rogati a Caffa e a Licostomo, sec. XIV*. Genoa: Istituto internazionale di studi liguri, 1973.

Balletto, Laura. “Caffa 1371.” In *Genova, Mediterraneo, Mar Nero (secc. XIII–XV)*, 195–268. Genoa: Civico istituto colombiano, 1976.

———. *Notai genovesi in Oltremare: Atti rogati a Laiazzo da Federico di Piazzalunga (1274) e Pietro di Bargone (1277, 1279)*. Genoa: IMG, 1989.

———. “Schiavi e manomessi nella Chio dei genovesi nel secolo XV.” In Ferrer i Mallol and Mutgé i Vives, *De l'esclavitud*, 659–94.

Baraschi, Silvia. “Tatars and Turks in Genoese Deeds from Kilia (1360–1361).” *RESE* 25 (1987): 61–67.

Barker, Hannah. “Reconnecting with the Homeland: Black Sea Slaves in Mamluk Biographical Dictionaries.” *Medieval Prosopography* 30 (2015): 87–104.

———. “Purchasing a Slave in Fourteenth-Century Cairo: Ibn al-Akfānī's *Book of Observation and Inspection in the Examination of Slaves*.” *MSR* 19 (2016): 1–24.

———. “Christianities in Conflict: The Black Sea as a Genoese Slaving Zone in the Later Middle Ages.” In Fynn-Paul and Pargas, *Slaving Zones*, 50–69.

Bartlett, Robert. “Medieval and Modern Concepts of Race and Ethnicity.” *JMEMS* 31 (2001): 39–56.

———. *Why Can the Dead Do Such Great Things? Saints and Worshippers from the Martyrs to the Reformation*. Princeton: Princeton University Press, 2013.

Basso, Enrico. “Il ‘Bellum de Sorcati’ ed i trattati del 1380–87 tra Genova e l'Orda d'Oro.” *Studi genuensi* 8 (1990): 11–26.

Batou, Jean, and Henryk Szlajfer, trans. *Western Europe, Eastern Europe and World Development, 13th–18th Centuries*. Leiden: Brill, 2010.

Bauden, Frédéric. “L'achat d'esclaves et la rédemption des captifs à Alexandrie d'après deux documents arabes d'époque mamelouke conservés aux Archives de l'État à Venise (ASVe).” *Mélanges de l'Université Saint-Joseph* 58 (2005): 269–325.

Behrens-Abouseif, Doris. *Practicing Diplomacy in the Mamluk Sultanate: Gifts and Material Culture in the Medieval Islamic World*. London: I. B. Tauris, 2014.

Belgrano, Luigi. *Della vita privata dei genovesi*. Genoa: Istituto Sordo-Muti, 1875.

———. “Prima serie di documenti riguardanti la colonia di Pera.” *ASLSP* 13 (1877): 97–317.

Bell, Peter, Dirk Suckow, and Gerhard Wolf, eds. *Fremde in der Stadt: Ordnungen, Repräsentationen und soziale Praktiken (13.–15. Jahrhundert)*. Frankfurt: Peter Lang, 2010.

Bellomo, Manlio. *The Common Legal Past of Europe, 1000–1800*. Washington, DC: Catholic University of America Press, 1995.

Bellorini, Theophilus, and Eugene Hoade, eds. *Visit to the Holy Places of Egypt, Sinai, Palestine and Syria in 1384.* Jerusalem: Franciscan Press, 1948.
Bensa, Enrico. *Il contratto di assicurazione nel medio evo.* Genoa: Tipografia marittima editrice, 1884.
Bensch, Stephen. "From Prizes of War to Domestic Merchandise: The Changing Face of Slavery in Catalonia and Aragon, 1000–1300." *Viator* 25 (1994): 63–91.
Berkey, Jonathan. "The Muhtasibs of Cairo Under the Mamluks: Towards an Understanding of an Islamic Institution." In *Mamluks in Egyptian and Syrian Politics and Society,* ed. Michael Winter and Amalia Levanoni, 245–76. Leiden: Brill, 2004.
Berlin, Ira. *Many Thousands Gone: The First Two Centuries of Slavery in North America.* Cambridge: Belknap Press, 1998.
Bernand, Carmen, and Alessandro Stella, eds. *D'Esclaves a soldats: Miliciens et soldats d'origin servile XIIIe–XXIe siecles.* Paris: L'Harmattan, 2006.
Berza, M., and E. Stănescu. *Actes du XIVe congrès international des études byzantines, Bucarest, 6–12 September 1971.* Bucharest: Editura academiei republicii socialiste România, 1975.
Besta, Enrico. *Riccardo Malombra, professore nello studio di Padova, consultore di stato in Venezia.* Venice: Fratelli Visentini, 1894.
Biller, Peter. "Proto-Racial Thought in Medieval Science." In Eliav-Feldon, Isaac, and Ziegler, *Origins,* 157–80.
Biot, Edouard. *De l'abolition de l'esclavage ancien en occident.* Paris: J. Renouard, 1840.
Bliznyuk, Svetlana. *Die Genuesen auf Zypern, Ende 14. und im 15. Jahrhundert.* Frankfurt: Peter Lang, 2005.
Blumenthal, Debra. *Enemies and Familiars: Slavery and Mastery in Fifteenth-Century Valencia.* Ithaca: Cornell University Press, 2009.
———. "Domestic Medicine: Slaves, Servants and Female Medical Expertise in Late Medieval Valencia." *Renaissance Studies* 28 (2014): 515–32.
———. "Masters, Slave Women and Their Children: A Child Custody Dispute in 15th-Century Valencia." In Schiel and Hanß, *Mediterranean Slavery,* 229–56.
Boccaccio, Giovanni. *Decameron,* trans. G. H. McWilliam. New York: Penguin Books, 1984.
Boldorini, Alberto. *Caffa e Famagosta nel Liber mandatorum dei revisori dei conti di San Giorgio (1464–1469).* Genoa: Consiglio nazionale delle ricerche, 1965.
Bongi, Salvatore. "Le schiave orientali in Italia." *Nuova antologia di scienze, lettere ed arti* 2 (1866): 215–46.
Borkowski, Andrew, and Paul du Plessis. *Textbook on Roman Law.* Oxford: Oxford University Press, 2005.
Bosco, Bartolomeo de. *Consilia.* Lodano: Franciscum Castellum, 1620.
Boswell, John. *Christianity, Social Tolerance, and Homosexuality.* Chicago: University of Chicago Press, 1981.
———. *The Kindness of Strangers: The Abandonment of Children in Western Europe from Late Antiquity to the Renaissance.* New York: Pantheon Books, 1988.
Brackett, John. "Race and Rulership: Alessandro de'Medici, First Medici Duke of Florence, 1529–1537." In *Black Africans in Renaissance Europe,* ed. T. F. Earle and K. J. P. Lowe, 303–25. Cambridge: Cambridge University Press, 2005.
Bratianu, G. I. *Actes des notaires génois de Péra et de Caffa de la fin du treizième siècle (1281–1290).* Bucharest: Cultura Nationala, 1927.
———. *Recherches sur le commerce génois dans la Mer Noire au XIIIe siècle.* Paris: Libraire orientaliste Paul Geuthner, 1929.
———. "Le conseil du Roi Charles: Essai sur l'internationale chrétienne et les nationalités à la fin du moyen âge." *RESE* 19 (1942): 291–361.
Braude, Benjamin. "The Sons of Noah and the Construction of Ethnic and Geographical Identities in the Medieval and Early Modern Periods." *William and Mary Quarterly* 54 (1997): 103–42.

Braunstein, Philippe. "Être esclave à Venise à la fin du Moyen Âge." In *Couleurs de l'esclavage sur les deux rives de la Méditerranée (Moyen Âge-XXe siècle)*, ed. Roger Botte and Alessandro Stella, 85–103. Paris: Éditions Karthala, 2012.

Bresc, Henri. *Le livre de raison de Paul de Sade (Avignon, 1390–1394)*. Paris: Èditions du comitè des travaux historiques et scientifiques, 2013.

Breydenbach, Bernhard von. *Sanctarum peregrinationum in montem Syon ad Christi sepulcrum in Hierusalem opus*. Speyer: Peter Drach, 1502.

Broadbridge, Anne. *Kingship and Ideology in the Islamic and Mongol Worlds*. Cambridge: Cambridge University Press, 2008.

———. "Sending Home for Mom and Dad: The Extended Family Impulse in Mamluk Politics." *MSR* 15 (2011): 1–18.

Brocardus. "Directorium ad passagium faciendum." In *Recueil des historiens des croisades: Documents arméniens*, 368–518. Paris: Imprimerie nationale, 1906.

Broquière, Bertrandon de la. *Le Voyage d'Outremer*, ed. Charles Schefer. Paris: Ernest Leroux, 1892.

———. *The Voyage d'Outremer*, trans. Galen Kline. New York: Peter Lang, 1988.

Brown, Christopher. "Christianity and the Campaign Against Slavery and the Slave Trade." In *Enlightenment, Reawakening and Revolution 1660–1815*, ed. Stewart Brown and Timothy Tackett, 517–35. Cambridge: Cambridge University Press, 2006.

———. *Moral Capital: Foundations of British Abolitionism*. Chapel Hill: University of North Carolina Press, 2006.

Brundage, James. "Concubinage and Marriage in Medieval Canon Law." In *Sexual Practices and the Medieval Church*, ed. James Brundage and Vern Bullough, 118–28. Buffalo: Prometheus Books, 1982.

———. *Medieval Canon Law*. London: Longman, 1995.

Brunschvig, Robert, trans. *Deux récits de voyage inédits en Afrique du Nord au XVe siècle: Abdalbasit b. Halil et Adorne*. Paris: Maisonneuve et Larose, 1936.

———. "Coup d'oeil sur l'histoire des foires à travers l'Islam." In *La Foire*, 43–75. Brussels: Libraire encyclopedique, 1953.

———. "ʿAbd." In *The Encyclopaedia of Islam*, ed. H. A. R. Gibb, J. H. Kramers, E. Lévi-Provençal, and J. F. Schacht, 2nd ed., 1:24–40. Leiden: Brill, 1960.

Bruscoli, Francesco Guidi. "Bartolomeo Marchionni and the Trade in African Slaves in the Mediterranean World at the End of the Fifteenth Century." In Cavaciocchi, *Serfdom and Slavery*, 377–88.

Burns, R. I. "Renegades, Adventurers and Sharp Businessmen: The Thirteenth-Century Spaniard in the Cause of Islam." *Catholic Historical Review* 58 (1972): 341–66.

Byrne, Eugene. *Genoese Shipping in the Twelfth and Thirteenth Centuries*. Cambridge: Mediaeval Academy of America, 1930.

Cahen, Claude. *Pre-Ottoman Turkey: A General Survey of the Material and Spiritual Culture and History c.1071–1330*, trans. J. Jones-Williams. New York: Taplinger, 1968.

Callimachi, Rukmini. "To Maintain Supply of Sex Slaves, ISIS Pushes Birth Control." *New York Times*. https://www.nytimes.com/2016/03/13/world/middleeast/to-maintain-supply-of-sex-slaves-isis-pushes-birth-control.html (accessed August 7, 2018).

Canale, Michele Giuseppe. *Della Crimea del suo commercio e dei suoi dominatori dalle origini fino ai di nostri*. Genoa: R. Inst. de'Sordo-Muti, 1855.

Carr, Mike. *Merchant Crusaders in the Aegean, 1291–1352*. Woodbridge: Boydell and Brewer, 2015.

Casola, Pietro. *Canon Pietro Casola's Pilgrimage to Jerusalem in the Year 1494*, trans. M. Margaret Newett. Manchester: Manchester University Press, 1907.

Cassandro, Michele. "Aspects of the Life and Character of Francesco di Marco Datini." In Nigro, *Francesco di Marco Datini*, 3–52.

Cavaciocchi, Simonetta, ed. *Serfdom and Slavery in the European Economy, 11th–18th Centuries*. Fondazione istituto internazionale di storia economica F. Datini, Atti delle Settimane di Studi 45. Florence: Firenze University Press, 2014.

Cecchetti, B. "La donna nel medioevo a Venezia." *Archivio Veneto* 31 (1886): 33–69, 307–49.

Cessi, Roberto. *Deliberazioni del Maggior Consiglio di Venezia.* Bologna: Nicola Zanichelli, 1934.

Chalkokondyles, Laonikos. *Laonikos Chalkokondyles: A Translation and Commentary of the "Demonstrations of Histories" (Books I–III)*, trans. Nicolaos Nicoloudis. Athens: Historical Publications St. D. Basilopoulos, 1996.

Chrissis, Nikolaos. *Crusading in Frankish Greece: A Study of Byzantine–Western Relations and Attitudes, 1204–1282.* Turnhout: Brepols, 2012.

Christ, Georg. *Trading Conflicts: Venetian Merchants and Mamluk Officials in Late Medieval Alexandria.* Leiden: Brill, 2012.

Cibrario, Luigi. "Nota sul commercio degli schiavi a Genova nel secolo XIV." In *Opusculi del cavaliere Luigi Cibrario*, 78–81. Turin: Stabilimento tipografico fontana, 1841.

———. *Della schiavitù e del servaggio.* Milan: Stabilimento Civelli, 1868.

Ciocîltan, Virgil. *The Mongols and the Black Sea Trade in the Thirteenth and Fourteenth Centuries*, trans. Samuel Willcocks. Leiden: Brill, 2012.

Cipollone, Giulio. "La Bolla *Adaperiat dominus* (1272) e l'Ordo Trinitatis et captivorum." *Archivium historiae pontificae* 21 (1983): 229–44.

Clarkson, Thomas. *The History of the Rise, Progress and Accomplishment of the Abolition of the African Slave-Trade by the British Parliament.* New York: n.p., 1836.

Clerget, Marcel. *Le Caire, étude de géographie urbaine et d'histoire économique.* Cairo: E. and R. Schindler, 1934.

Cluse, Christoph. "Frauen in Sklaverei: Beobachtungen aus genuesischen Notariatsregistern des 14. und 15. Jahrhunderts." In *Campana pulsante convocati: Festschrift anlässlich der Emeritierung von Prof. Dr. Alfred Haverkamp*, ed. Frank Hirschmann and Gerd Mentgen, 85–124. Trier: Kliomedia, 2005.

———. "Zur Repräsentation von Sklaven und Sklavinnen in Statuten und Notariatsinstrumenten italienischer Städte um 1400." In Bell, Suckow, and Wolf, *Fremde in der Stadt*, 383–408.

———. "The Role of the Slave Trade in the De recuperanda Treatises around 1300." In Amitai and Cluse, *Slavery*, 437–69.

Cobb, Paul. *The Race for Paradise: An Islamic History of the Crusades.* Oxford: Oxford University Press, 2014.

Colli, Sandro de'. *Moretto Bon, Notaio in Venezia, Trebisonda e Tana (1403–1408).* Venice: CPFSV, 1963.

Constable, Olivia Remie. "Muslim Spain and Mediterranean Slavery: The Medieval Slave Trade as an Aspect of Muslim–Christian Relations." In *Christendom and Its Discontents: Exclusion, Persecution, and Rebellion, 1000–1500*, ed. Scott Waugh and Peter Diehl, 264–84. Cambridge: Cambridge University Press, 1996.

———. *Housing the Stranger in the Mediterranean World.* Cambridge: Cambridge University Press, 2003.

———. "Clothing, Iron, and Timber: The Growth of Christian Anxiety About Islam in the Long Twelfth Century." In *European Transformations: The Long Twelfth Century*, ed. Thomas Noble and John Van Engen, 279–313. Notre Dame: University of Notre Dame Press, 2012.

Corbier, Mireille, ed. *Adoption et fosterage.* Paris: Éditions de Boccard, 1999.

Corrao, Pietro, ed. *Registri di lettere ed atti (1328–1333).* Acta curie felicis urbis Panormi 5. Palermo: Municipio di Palermo, 1986.

Cosmo, Nicola di. "Mongols and Merchants on the Black Sea Frontier in the Thirteenth and Fourteenth Centuries: Convergences and Conflict." In *Mongols, Turks, and Others: Eurasian Nomads and the Sedentary World*, ed. Reuven Amitai and Michal Biran, 391–424. Leiden: Brill, 2005.

Cossar, Roisin. "Clerical 'Concubines' in Northern Italy During the Fourteenth Century." *Journal of Women's History* 23 (2011): 110–31.

Costamagna, Giorgio. *Il notaio a Genova tra prestigio e potere.* Rome: Consiglio nazionale del notariato, 1970.

Crone, Patricia. *Slaves on Horses: The Evolution of the Islamic Polity.* Cambridge: Cambridge University Press, 1980.

Dandolo, Andrea. *Chronicon Venetum*, ed. L. A. Muratori. Bologna: Nicola Zanichelli, 1928.

Daniel, Norman. *Islam and the West.* Oxford: Oneworld, 1993.

Datini, Margherita. *Letters to Francesco Datini*, ed. Carolyn James and Antonio Pagliaro. Toronto: ITER, 2012.

Dávid, Géza, and Pál Fodor. *Ransom Slavery Along the Ottoman Borders (Early Fifteenth–Early Eighteenth Centuries).* Leiden: Brill, 2007.

Davis, David Brion. *The Problem of Slavery in Western Society.* Oxford: Oxford University Press, 1966.

Day, John. *Les douanes de Gênes, 1376–1377.* Paris: SEVPEN, 1963.

Delaville le Roulx, Joseph. *La France en Orient au XIVe siècle.* Paris: E. Thorin, 1885.

Delort, Robert. "Quelques précisions sur le commerce des esclaves à Genes vers la fin du XIVe siècle." *Mélanges d'archéologie et d'histoire publiés par l'Ecole française de Rome* 78 (1966): 215–50.

Dennis, George. "The Correspondence of Rodolfo de Sanctis, Canon of Patras, 1386." In *Byzantium and the Franks, 1350–1420*, 285–321. London: Variorum Reprints, 1982.

———. "Un fondo sconosciuto di atti notarili Veneti in San Francisco." In *Byzantium and the Franks, 1350–1420*, 425–32. London: Variorum Reprints, 1982.

Denoix, Sylvie, Jean-Charles Depaule, and Michel Tuchscherer. *Le Khan al-Khalili et ses environs: Un centre commercial et artisanal au Caire du XIIIe au XXe siècle.* Cairo: IFAO, 1999.

Depping, G. B. *Histoire du commerce entre le Levant et l'Europe depuis les croisades jusqu'à la fondation des colonies d'Amérique.* Paris: Imperimerie royale, 1830.

Desimoni, Cornelio. "Actes passés a Famagouste de 1299 à 1301 par devant le notaire génois Lamberto di Sambuceto." *Archives de l'Orient Latin* 2 (1884): 3–120.

———. *Statuto dei padri del comune della repubblica genovese.* Genoa: Stabilimento Fratelli Pagano, 1885.

———. "Trattato dei genovesi col Chan dei Tartari nel 1380–1381 scritto in lingua volgare." *Archivio storico italiano* 20 (1887): 162–65.

———. *Leges genuenses.* Monumenta Historia Patriae 18. Turin: E. Regio Typographeo, 1901.

Desimoni, Cornelio, and L. T. Belgrano. "Documenti ed estratti inediti o poco noti riguardanti la storia del commercio e della marina ligure." *ASLSP* 5 (1867): 357–548.

Devonshire, Henriette. "Relation d'un voyage du sultan Qaitbay en Palestine et en Syrie." *Bulletin de l'institut français d'archéologie orientale* 20 (1922): 1–43.

Diem, Werner. *Arabische Privatbriefe des 9. bis 15. Jahrhunderts aus der österreichischen Nationalbibiothek in Wien.* Wiesbaden: Harrassowitz, 1996.

Dimashqī, Shams al-Dīn Abī ʿAbd Allah Muḥammad al-. *Nukhbat al-dahr fī ʿajāʾib al-barr wa-al-baḥr*, ed. Aḥmad Ayyūb, Ṭalāl al-Ḥadīthī, and Ghasān al-Nāṣīr. Damascus: Dār Nūr, 2013.

Dincer, Aysu. "Enslaving Christians: Greek Slaves in Late Medieval Cyprus." *Mediterranean Historical Review* 31 (2016): 1–19.

Doosselaere, Quentin van. *Commercial Agreements and Social Dynamics in Medieval Genoa.* New York: Cambridge University Press, 2009.

Dorini, Umberto, and Tommaso Bertelè. *Il Libro dei conti di Giacomo Badoer (Constantinople 1436–1440).* Rome: Istituto poligrafico dello stato italiano, 1956.

Drescher, Seymour. *Abolition: A History of Slavery and Antislavery.* Cambridge: Cambridge University Press, 2009.

Dubois, Pierre. *The Recovery of the Holy Land*, trans. Walther Brandt. New York: Columbia University Press, 1956.

Dunbabin, Jean. "The Reception and Interpretation of Aristotle's *Politics*." In *The Cambridge History of Later Medieval Philosophy*, ed. Norman Kretzmann, Anthony Kenny, and Jan Pinborg, 723–37. Cambridge: Cambridge University Press, 1982.

Dürrholder, Gottfried. *Die Kreuzzugspolitik unter Papst Johann XXII (1316–1334).* Freiburg: Heitz und Mündel, 1913.

Dursteler, Eric. *Venetians in Constantinople: Nation, Identity and Coexistence in the Early Modern Mediterranean*. Baltimore: Johns Hopkins University Press, 2006.

Earle, Rebecca. *The Body of the Conquistador: Food, Race and the Colonial Experience in Spanish America, 1492–1700*. New York: Cambridge University Press, 2012.

Eaton, Richard. "The Rise and Fall of Military Slavery in the Deccan, 1450–1650." In *Slavery and South Asian History*, ed. Indrani Chatterjee and Richard Eaton, 115–35. Bloomington: Indiana University Press, 2006.

Edzard, Lutz. *Polygenesis, Convergence and Entropy: An Alternative Model of Linguistic Evolution Applied to Semitic Linguistics*. Wiesbaden: Harrassowitz, 1998.

Ehrenkreutz, Andrew. "Strategic Implications of the Slave Trade Between Genoa and Mamluk Egypt in the Second Half of the Thirteenth Century." In Udovitch, *Islamic Middle East*, 335–45.

El Hamel, Chouki. *Black Morocco: A History of Slavery, Race, and Islam*. Cambridge: Cambridge University Press, 2013.

Eliav-Feldon, Miriam, Benjamin Isaac, and Joseph Ziegler, eds. *The Origins of Racism in the West*. Cambridge: Cambridge University Press, 2009.

Elie de La Primaudaie, F. *Études sur le commerce au Moyen Age: Histoire du commerce de la Mer Noire et des colonies génoises de la Krimée*. Paris: Comptoir des Imprimeurs-Unis, 1848.

Epstein, Steven. "A Late Medieval Lawyer Confronts Slavery: The Cases of Bartolomeo de Bosco." *Slavery and Abolition* 20 (1999): 49–68.

———. *Speaking of Slavery: Color, Ethnicity, and Human Bondage in Italy*. Ithaca: Cornell University Press, 2001.

———. *Purity Lost: Transgressing Boundaries in the Eastern Mediterranean, 1000–1400*. Baltimore: Johns Hopkins University Press, 2006.

Ermanno, Orlando. *Venezia—Senato, Deliberazioni miste, Registro XXVIII (1357–1359)*. Venice: Istituto veneto di scienze, lettere ed arti, 2009.

Evans, Daniel. "The Slave Coast of Europe." *Slavery and Abolition* 6 (1985): 41–58.

Fabri, Felix. *Evagatorium in Terrae Sanctae, Arabiae et Egypti peregrinationem*, ed. Conrad Hassler. 3 vols. Stuttgart: Societatis literariae stuttgardiensis, 1843–1849.

Fahmī, Naʿīm Zakī. *Ṭuruq al-tijāra al-dawliyya wa-maḥaṭṭātuhā bayna al-sharq wa-al-gharb*. Cairo: HMAK, 1973.

Fancy, Hussein. *The Mercenary Mediterranean: Sovereignty, Religion, and Violence in the Medieval Crown of Aragon*. Chicago: University of Chicago Press, 2016.

Favier, Jean. *Gold and Spices: The Rise of Commerce in the Middle Ages*. New York: Holmes and Meier, 1998.

Feridun Beg, Ahmed. *Munseat al-Selatin*. Istanbul: n.p., 1857–1859.

Ferragud, Carmel. "The Role of Doctors in the Slave Trade During the Fourteenth and Fifteenth Centuries Within the Kingdom of Valencia (Crown of Aragon)." *Bulletin of the History of Medicine* 87 (2013): 143–69.

Ferrer i Mallol, Maria Teresa. "Esclaus i lliberts orientals a Barcelona. Segles XIV i XV." In Ferrer i Mallol and Mutgé i Vives, *De l'esclavitud*, 167–212.

Ferrer i Mallol, Maria Teresa, and Josefina Mutgé i Vives, eds. *De l'esclavitud a la llibertat: Esclaus i llibertats a l'edat mitjana*. Barcelona: Consell Superior d'Investigacions Científiques, 2000.

Ferretto, A. "Codice diplomatico delle relazioni fra la Liguria, la Toscana e la Lunigiana ai tempi di Dante: 1265–1321." *ASLSP* 31, nos. 1 and 2 (1901–1903): 1:1–452 and 2:1–501.

Fine, John. *The Late Medieval Balkans: A Critical Survey from the Late Twelfth Century to the Ottoman Conquest*. Ann Arbor: University of Michigan Press, 1987.

Finley, Moses. *Ancient Slavery and Modern Ideology*. New York: Viking Press, 1980.

Fioravanti, Gianfranco. "Servi, rustici, barbari: Interpretazioni medievali della Politica aristotelica." *Annali della scuola normale superiore di Pisa. Classe di lettere e filosofia*, 3rd ser., 11 (1981): 399–429.

Fisher, Alan. "Muscovy and the Black Sea Slave Trade." *Canadian-American Slavic Studies* 6 (1972): 575–94.

———. *The Crimean Tatars*. Stanford: Hoover Institution Press, 1978.

Fleet, Kate. *European and Islamic Trade in the Early Ottoman State: The Merchants of Genoa and Turkey.* Cambridge: Cambridge University Press, 1999.
———. "Caffa, Turkey and the Slave Trade: The Case of Batista Macio." In *Europa e Islam tra i secoli XIV e XVI*, ed. Michele Bernardini, Clara Borrelli, Anna Cerbo, and Encarnación Sánchez García, 1:373–89. Naples: Istituto universitario orientale, 2002.
Foerster, Richard. *Scriptores physiognomonici graeci et latini.* Leipzig: B. G. Tuebner, 1893.
Forand, Paul. "The Relation of the Slave and the Client to the Master or Patron in Medieval Islam." *IJMES* 2 (1971): 59–66.
Fredrickson, George. *Racism: A Short History.* Princeton: Princeton University Press, 2002.
Freed, John. "The Origins of the European Nobility: The Problem of the Ministerials." *Viator* 7 (1976): 211–41.
Freedman, Paul. *Images of the Medieval Peasant.* Stanford: Stanford University Press, 1999.
Frenkel, Yehoshua. "Some Notes Concerning the Trade and Education of Slave-Soldiers During the Mamluk Era." In Amitai and Cluse, *Slavery*, 187–212.
Friedberg, Emil. *Corpus iuris canonici.* Graz: Akademische Druck- u. Verlaganstalt, 1959.
Friedman, Yohanan. *Tolerance and Coercion in Islam: Interfaith Relations in the Muslim Tradition.* New York: Cambridge University Press, 2003.
Friedman, Yvonne. *Encounter Between Enemies: Captivity and Ransom in the Latin Kingdom of Jerusalem.* Leiden: Brill, 2002.
Fuess, Albrecht. "Rotting Ships and Razed Harbors: The Naval Policy of the Mamluks." *MSR* 5 (2001): 45–71.
Fynn-Paul, Jeff. "Empire, Monotheism, and Slavery in the Greater Mediterranean Region from Antiquity to the Early Modern Era." *Past and Present* 205 (2009): 3–40.
Fynn-Paul, Jeff, and Damian Pargas, eds. *Slaving Zones: Cultural Identities, Ideologies, and Institutions in the Evolution of Global Slavery.* Leiden: Brill, 2018.
Gantner, Clemens, Walter Pohl, and Richard Payne, eds. *Visions of Community in the Post-Roman World: The West, Byzantium and the Islamic World, 300–1100.* Farnham: Ashgate, 2012.
Geary, Patrick. "Ethnic Identity as a Situational Construct in the Early Middle Ages." *Mitteilungen der anthropologischen Gesellschaft in Wien* 113 (1983): 15–26.
Genovese, Eugene, and Elizabeth Fox-Genovese. "The Janus Face of Merchant Capital." In *Fruits of Merchant Capital: Slavery and Bourgeois Property in the Rise and Expansion of Capitalism*, 3–25. Oxford: Oxford University Press, 1983.
Germain, Jean. "Le discours du voyage d'oultremer au très victorieux roi Charles VII, prononcé, en 1452, par Jean Germain, évêque de Chalon," ed. Charles Schefer. *Revue de l'Orient Latin* 3 (1895): 303–42.
Ghaly, Mohammed. "Physiognomy: A Forgotten Chapter of Disability in Islam: The Discussions of Muslim Jurists." *Bibliotheca orientalis* 66 (2009): 162–98.
Ghersetti, Antonella. "De l'achat des esclaves: entre examen médical et physiognomie. Le chapitre 46 du Kitāb al-dalā'il d'Ibn Bahlūl (Xe s.)." In *Essays in Honour of Alexander Fodor on His Sixtieth Birthday*, ed. K. Dévényi and T. Iványi, 83–94. Budapest: Eötvös Loránd University, 2001.
———, trans. *Trattato generale sull'acquisto e l'esame degli schiavi.* Catanzaro: Abramo, 2001.
Ghistele, Joos van. *Voyage en Egypte de Joos van Ghistele, 1482–1483*, ed. Renée Bauwens-Préaux. Cairo: IFAO, 1976.
Gigli, Ottavio, ed. *I sermoni evangelici, le lettere, ed altri scritti inediti o rari di Franco Sacchetti.* Florence: Felice Le Monnier, 1857.
Gilchrist, John. "The Medieval Canon Law on Unfree Persons: Gratian and the Decretist Doctrines c.1141–1234." *Studia Gratiana* 19 (1976): 271–302.
———. "Saint Raymond of Peñafort and the Decretalist Doctrine on Serfdom." *Escritos del Vedat* 7 (1977): 299–328.
Gillingham, John. "Women, Children and the Profits of War." In *Gender and Historiography: Studies in the Earlier Middle Ages in Honour of Pauline Stafford*, ed. Janet Nelson, Susan Reynolds, and Susan Johns, 61–74. London: Institute of Historical Research, 2012.

———. "Crusading Warfare, Chivalry, and the Enslavement of Women and Children." In *The Medieval Way of War: Studies in Medieval Military History in Honor of Bernard S. Bachrach*, ed. Gregory Halfond, 133–51. Burlington: Ashgate, 2015.

Gioffrè, Domenico. *Il mercato degli schiavi a Genova nel secolo XV.* Genoa: Fratelli Bozzi, 1971.

———. *Lettere di Giovanni da Pontremoli mercante genovese 1453–1459.* Genoa: IMG, 1982.

Giomo, Giuseppe. "Le Rubriche dei Libri 'Misti' del Senato perduti." *Archivio Veneto* 18–20 (1879–1880): 18:40–69 and 315–38; 19:90–117; 20:81–95 and 293–313.

Giurescu, Constantin. "The Genoese and the Lower Danube in the XIIIth and XIVth Centuries." *Journal of European Economic History* 5 (1976): 587–601.

Glancy, Jennifer. "'To Serve Them All the More': Christian Slaveholders and Christian Slaves in Antiquity." In Fynn-Paul and Pargas, *Slaving Zones*, 23–49.

Glasson, Travis. *Mastering Christianity: Missionary Anglicanism and Slavery in the Atlantic World.* Oxford: Oxford University Press, 2012.

Goetz, Rebecca. *The Baptism of Early Virgina: How Christianity Created Race.* Baltimore: Johns Hopkins University Press, 2012.

Goitein, S. D. "Slaves and Slavegirls in the Cairo Geniza Records." *Arabica* 9 (1962): 1–20.

———. *A Mediterranean Society: The Jewish Communities of the Arab World as Portrayed in the Documents of the Cairo Geniza.* Vol. 1, *Economic Foundations.* Berkeley: University of California Press, 1967.

Golubovich, Girolamo. *Biblioteca bio-bibliografica della Terra Santa e dell'Oriente francescano.* 5 vols. Florence: Quaracchi, 1906–1927.

Gómez, Nicolás Wey. *The Tropics of Empire: Why Columbus Sailed South to the Indies.* Cambridge: MIT Press, 2008.

Gordon, Matthew. *The Breaking of a Thousand Swords: A History of the Turkish Military of Samarra (A.H. 200–275/815–889 C.E.).* Albany: State University of New York Press, 2001.

Gordon, Matthew, and Kathryn Hain, eds. *Concubines and Courtesans: Women and Slavery in Islamic History.* Oxford: Oxford University Press, 2017.

Greci, Roberto. "The Datini Correspondence from Bologna, Ferrara and Parma." In Nigro, *Francesco di Marco Datini*, 433–46.

Green, Monica. "From 'Diseases of Women' to 'Secrets of Women': The Transformation of Gynecological Literature in the Later Middle Ages." *JMEMS* 30 (2000): 5–39.

———. *Making Women's Medicine Masculine: The Rise of Male Authority in Pre-Modern Gynaecology.* Oxford: Oxford University Press, 2008.

Greene, Molly. *Catholic Pirates and Greek Merchants: A Maritime History of the Mediterranean.* Princeton: Princeton University Press, 2010.

Gregoras, Nicephorus. *Byzantina historia*, ed. Ludovic Schopen. Bonn: Weberi, 1829.

Groebner, Valentin. *Liquid Assets, Dangerous Gifts: Presents and Politics at the End of the Middle Ages*, trans. Pamela Selwyn. Philadelphia: University of Pennsylvania Press, 2002.

———. *Who Are You? Identification, Deception, and Surveillance in Early Modern Europe*, trans. Mark Kyburz and John Peck. New York: Zone Books, 2007.

Guazzo, Marco. *Cronaca di M. Marco Guazzo.* Venice: Francesco Bindoni, 1553.

Guellil, Gabriela Linda, ed. *Damaszener Akten des 8./14. Jahrhunderts nach at-Tarsusis Kitab al-Iʿlam: Eine Studie zum arabischen Justizwesen.* Bamberg: Aku, 1985.

Guglingen, Paul Walther de. *Fratris Pauli Waltheri Guglingensis itinerarium in Terram Sanctam ad Sanctam Catharinam*, ed. M. Sollweck. Tübingen: Litterarischen Verein in Stuttgart, 1892.

Guillén, Fabienne, and Salah Trabelsi, eds. *Les esclavages en Méditerranée: Espaces et dynamiques économiques.* Madrid: Casa de Velázquez, 2012.

Guo, Li. "Tales of a Medieval Cairene Harem: Domestic Life in al-Biqāʿī's Autobiographical Chronicle." *Mamluk Studies Review* 9, no. 1 (2005): 101–22.

Haarmann, Ulrich. "Ideology and History, Identity and Alterity: The Arab Image of the Turk from the Abbasids to Modern Egypt." *IJMES* 20 (1988): 175–96.

———. "Yeomanly Arrogance and Righteous Rule: Faẓl Allāh ibn Rūzbihān Khunjī and the Mamluks of Egypt." In *Iran and Iranian Studies: Essays in Honor of Iraj Afshar*, ed. Kambiz Eslami, 109–24. Princeton: Zagros, 1998.

———. "The Mamluk System of Rule in the Eyes of Western Travelers." *MSR* 5 (2001): 1–24.

Hall, Bruce. *A History of Race in Muslim West Africa, 1600–1960.* Cambridge: Cambridge University Press, 2011.

Hallaq, Wael. "Model Shurut Works and the Dialectic of Doctrine and Practice." *Islamic Law and Society* 2 (1995): 109–34.

Halperin, Charles. "The Missing Golden Horde Chronicles and Historiography in the Mongol Empire." *Mongolian Studies* 23 (2000): 1–15.

Hanawalt, Barbara, ed. *Women and Work in Preindustrial Europe.* Bloomington: Indiana University Press, 1986.

Hannaford, Ivan. *Race: The History of an Idea in the West.* Washington, DC: Woodrow Wilson Center Press, 1996.

Har-El, Shai. *Struggle for Domination in the Middle East: The Ottoman-Mamluk War, 1485–91.* Leiden: Brill, 1995.

Harff, Arnold von. *The Pilgrimage of Arnold von Harff*, trans. Malcolm Letts. London: Hakluyt Society, 1946.

———. *Die Pilgerfahrt des Ritters Arnold von Harff*, ed. Eberhard von Groote. Hildesheim: Georg Olms, 2004.

Harper, Kyle. *Slavery in the Late Roman World, AD 275–425.* Cambridge: Cambridge University Press, 2011.

Harrill, J. Albert. *The Manumission of Slaves in Early Christianity.* Tübingen: J. C. B. Mohr, 1995.

Haverkamp, Alfred. "Die Erneuerung der Sklaverei im Mittelmeerraum während des hohen Mittelalters." In Herrmann-Otto, *Unfreie Arbeits- und Lebensverhältnisse*, 130–66.

Hayton. "Flos historiarum terre orientis." In *Recueil des historiens des croisades, Documents arméniens*, 2:113–254. Paris: Imprimerie nationale, 1906.

Heers, Jacques. *Livre de comptes de Giovanni Piccamiglio homme d'affaires génois, 1456–1459.* Paris: SEVPEN, 1959.

———. *Gênes au XVe siècle: Activité économique et problèmes sociaux.* Paris: SEVPEN, 1961.

———. *Esclaves et domestiques au Moyen Âge dans le monde méditerranéen.* Paris: Hachette Littératures, 1996.

———. *Jacques Coeur: 1400–1456.* Paris: Perrin, 1997.

Heffening, W. "Zum Aufbau der islamischen Rechtswerke." In *Studien zur Geschichte und Kultur des Nahen und Fernen Ostens: Paul Kahle zum 60. Geburtstag*, 101–18. Leiden: Brill, 1935.

Hellie, Richard. "Recent Soviet Historiography on Medieval and Early Modern Russian Slavery." *Russian Review* 35 (1976): 1–32.

———. *Slavery in Russia, 1450–1725.* Chicago: University of Chicago Press, 1982.

Helmholz, R. H. "The Law of Slavery and the European Ius Commune." In *The Legal Understanding of Slavery: From the Historical to the Contemporary*, ed. Jean Allain, 17–39. Oxford: Oxford University Press, 2012.

Heng, Geraldine. "The Invention of Race in the Middle Ages." *Literature Compass* 8 (2011): 315–50.

Herrmann-Otto, Elisabeth, ed. *Unfreie Arbeits- und Lebensverhältnisse von der Antike bis in die Gegenwart: Eine Einführung.* Hildesheim: Georg Olms, 2005.

Hershenzon, Daniel. "Towards a Connected History of Bondage in the Mediterranean: Recent Trends in the Field." *History Compass* 15 (2017): 1–13.

Herzog, Thomas. "The First Layer of the Sirat Baybars: Popular Romance and Political Propaganda." *MSR* 7 (2003): 137–48.

Heyd, W. *Histoire du commerce du Levant au Moyen-Âge*, trans. Raynaud Furcy. Amsterdam: A. M. Hakkert, 1967.

Hillenbrand, Carole. *The Crusades: Islamic Perspectives.* New York: Routledge, 2000.

Hillgarth, J. N. *Ramon Lull and Lullism in Fourteenth-Century France.* Oxford: Clarendon Press, 1971.

Hoade, Eugene, trans. "Itinerary of an Anonymous Englishman (1344–5)." In *Western Pilgrims*, 47–76. Jerusalem: Franciscan Printing Press, 1952.
Hogendorn, Jan. "The Location of the 'Manufacture' of Eunuchs." In Toru and Philips, *Slave Elites*, 41–70.
Holm, Poul. "The Slave Trade of Dublin, Ninth to Twelfth Centuries." *Perita* 5 (1989): 317–45.
Holt, P. M. "Qalawun's Treaty with Genoa in 1290." *Der Islam* 57 (1980): 101–8.
———. "Mamluk–Frankish Diplomatic Relations in the Reign of Qalawun (678–89/1279–90)." *JRAS* 2 (1989): 278–89.
———. *Early Mamluk Diplomacy (1260–1290): Treaties of Baybars and Qalawun with Christian Rulers*. Leiden: Brill, 1995.
Hoogendijk, Francisca. "Byzantinischer Sklavenkauf." *Archiv für Papyrusforschung und verwandte Gebiete* 42 (1996): 225–34.
Housley, Norman. *The Later Crusades, 1274–1580: From Lyons to Alcazar*. Oxford: Oxford University Press, 1992.
Hoyland, Robert. "Physiognomy in Islam." *JSAI* 30 (2005): 361–402.
Hunwick, John. "Islamic Law and Polemics over Race and Slavery in North and West Africa (16th–19th Century)." In *Slavery in the Islamic Middle East*, ed. Shaun Marmon, 43–68. Princeton: Markus Wiener, 1999.
Ibn ʿAbd al-Ẓāhir, Muḥī al-Dīn. *Tashrīf al-ayām wa-al-ʿuṣūr fī sīrat al-malik al-Manṣūr*, ed. Murād Kāmil. Cairo: Wizārat al-thaqāfa wa-al-irshād al-qawmī, 1961.
Ibn Abī al-Fadāʾil, Mufaddal. *Histoire des sultans mamlouks*, trans. E. Blochet. Paris: Fermin-Didot, 1929.
Ibn Bassām. *Nihāyat al-rutba fī ṭalab al-ḥisba*, ed. Husām al-Dīn al-Sāmraʾī. Baghdad: al-Maʿarif Press, 1968.
Ibn Baṭṭuṭa, Muḥammad. *The Travels of Ibn Battuta*, trans. H. A. R. Gibb. New Dehli: Munshiram Manoharlal, 1999.
Ibn Butlān, Abī al-Ḥasan. "Risāla jāmiʿa li-funūn nāfiʿa fī shirā al-raqīq wa-taqlīb al-ʿabīd." In *Nawādir al-Makhṭūṭāt*, ed. ʿAbd al-Salām Hārūn, 383–420. Cairo: Al-Hayʾa al-ʿāmma li-quṣūr al-thaqāfa, 1954.
Ibn al-Dawādārī, Abū Bakr. *Kanz al-durar wa-jamīʿ al-ghurar*, ed. Hans Roemer, Saʿīd ʿAbd al-Fattāḥ ʿAshūr, and Ulrich Haarmann. 9 vols. Freiburg: Schwarz, 1960–1972.
Ibn al-Furāt, Nāṣir al-Dīn Muḥammad. *Tārīkh al-duwal wa-al-mulūk*, ed. Qusṭanṭīn Zurayq. Beirut: American University Press, 1939.
Ibn Ḥajar al-ʿAsqalānī, Shihāb al-Dīn Aḥmad. *Al-Durar al-kāmina fī aʿyān al-miʾa al-thāmina*. 4 vols. Hyderabad: Maṭbaʿat majlis dairat al-maʿarif al-ʿuthmāniyya, 1972–1976.
Ibn Iyās, Muḥammad ibn Aḥmad. *Bidāʾiʿ al-zuhūr fī wiqāʾiʿ al-duhūr*, ed. Paul Kahle and Muḥammad Muṣṭafā. 5 vols. Cairo: HMAK, 1982–1984.
Ibn Khaldūn, Yusūf. *Kitāb al-ʿibār wa-diwān al-mubtadāʾ wa-al-khabar fī ayām al-ʿarab wa-al-ʿajam wa-al-barbar*. 7 vols. Beirut: Dār al-kitāb al-lubnānī, 1956–1961.
Ibn al-Mujāwir, Abū Bakr ibn Muḥammad. *A Traveller in Thirteenth-Century Arabia: Ibn al-Mujāwir's Tārīkh al-mustabṣir*, trans. G. Rex Smith. Aldershot: Ashgate, 2008.
Ibn al-Ṣayrafī, ʿAlī ibn Dawūd. *Inbāʾ al-haṣr bi-ibnāʾ al-ʿaṣr*, ed. Ḥasan Ḥabashī. Cairo: Dār al-fikr al-ʿarabī, 1970.
Ibn Shaddād, Muḥammad ibn ʿAlī. *Tārīkh al-malik al-ẓāhir*, ed. Aḥmad Ḥuṭayṭ. Wiesbaden: Franz Steiner, 1983.
Ibn Shahīn, Khalīl. *Zoubdat Kachf al-Mamalik*, ed. Paul Ravaisse. Paris: E. Leroux, 1894.
Ibn Taghrī Birdī, Jamāl al-Dīn Yusūf. *Al-Manhal al-ṣāfī wa-al-mustawfā baʿd al-wāfī*, ed. Muḥammad Amīn and Saʿīd ʿAbd al-Fattāḥ ʿAshūr. 7 vols. Cairo: HMAK, 1986.
———. *Al-Nujūm al-zāhira fī mulūk Miṣr wa-al-Qāhira*. 16 vols. Cairo: MTTTN, 1963–1972.
Ibn Ṭawq, Aḥmad. *Al-Taʿlīq: Yawmiyyāt Shihāb al-Dīn Aḥmad ibn Ṭawq*, ed. Jaʿfar al-Muhājir. 4 vols. Damascus: Institut français de Damas, 2002–2004.
Ibn Taymiyya, Aḥmad. *Al-Ḥisba fī al-islām*, ed. Muḥammad Mubārak. Cairo: Dār al-kutub al-ʿarabiyya, 1967.

Ibn al-Ukhuwwa, Muḥammad ibn Aḥmad. *Maʿālim al-qurba fī aḥkām al-ḥisba*, ed. Reuben Levy. London: Luzac, 1938.

Ibn al-Wardī, Zayn al-Dīn ʿUmar. *Tatimmat al-mukhtaṣar fī akhbār al-bashar*, ed. Aḥmad Rifʿat al-Badrawī. Beirut: Dār al-maʿrifa, 1970.

Iliescu, Octavian. "Nouvelles éditions d'actes notariés instrumentés au XIVe siècle dans les colonies génoises des bouches du Danube—Actes de Kilia et de Licostomo." *RESE* 15 (1977): 113–30.

Inalcik, Halil. "Bursa and the Commerce of the Levant." *JESHO* 3 (1960): 131–47.

———. *An Economic and Social History of the Ottoman Empire*. Cambridge: Cambridge University Press, 1997.

Interiano, Giorgio. *La vita e sito de'Zichi chiamati Ciarcassi: Historia notabile*. Venice: Aldus Manutius, 1505.

Irwin, Robert. "Factions in Medieval Egypt." *JRAS* 2 (1986): 228–46.

———. *The Middle East in the Middle Ages: The Early Mamluk Sultanate, 1250–1382*. Carbondale: Southern Illinois University Press, 1986.

———. "Ali al-Baghdadi and the Joy of Mamluk Sex." In *Mamluks and Crusaders: Men of the Sword and Men of the Pen*, 45–57. Burlington: Ashgate Variorum, 2010.

Isḥāqī, Muḥammad ibn ʿAbd al-Muʿṭī al-. *Akhbār al-uwal fīman taṣarraf fī Miṣr min arbāb al-duwal*, ed. Muḥammad Muhannā. Cairo: al-Maṭbaʿa al-azhariyya al-miṣriyya, 1893.

Ito, Takao. "Slave Traders and Mamluks." Paper presented at the School of Mamluk Studies, Chicago, June 23–25, 2016.

Jabartī, ʿAbd al-Raḥman al-. *ʿAbd al-Raḥmān al-Jabartī's History of Egypt*, trans. Thomas Philipp and Moshe Perlmann. Stuttgart: Franz Steiner, 1994.

Jacoby, David. "L'expansion occidentale dans le Levant: Les vénitiens á Acre dans la seconde moitié du treiziéme siécle." *Journal of Medieval History* 3 (1977): 225–64.

———. "The Supply of War Materials to Egypt in the Crusader Period." *JSAI* 25 (2001): 102–13.

———. "Acre-Alexandria: A Major Commercial Axis of the Thirteenth Century." In *Come l'orco della fiaba: Studi per Franco Cardini*, ed. Marina Montesano, 151–68. Florence: SISMEL, 2010.

Jaimoukha, Amjad. *The Circassians: A Handbook*. Richmond: Curzon, 2001.

Jarawānī, Muḥammad ibn ʿAlī al-. *Al-Kawkab al-mushriq fīmā yaḥtāj ilayhi al-muwaththiq li-ʿālim al-shurūṭ*, ed. Souad Saghbini. Berlin: EB, 2010.

Jazarī, Muḥammad ibn Ibrahīm al-. *Tārīkh ḥawādith al-zamān*, ed. ʿUmar Tadmūrī. Sidon: al-Maktaba al-ʿaṣriyya, 1998.

Jenkins, Richard. *Rethinking Ethnicity: Arguments and Explorations*. London: Sage, 2008.

Johansen, Baber. "The Valorization of the Human Body in Muslim Sunni Law." *Princeton Papers in Near East Studies* 4 (1996): 71–112.

Johnson, Walter. *Soul by Soul: Life Inside the Antebellum Slave Market*. Cambridge: Harvard University Press, 1999.

———. "On Agency." *Journal of Social History* 37 (2003): 113–24.

Joinville, Jean. *Chronicles of the Crusades*, trans. Margaret Shaw. Harmondsworth: Penguin, 1963.

Jordan, Mark. "The Fortune of Constantine's *Pantegni*." In *Constantine the African and ʿAli ibn al-ʿAbbas al-Magusi: The Pantegni and Related Texts*, ed. Charles Burnett and Danielle Jacquart, 286–302. Leiden: Brill, 1994.

Jordan, William Chester. "Why 'Race'?" *JMEMS* 31 (2001): 165–74.

Jorga, N. "Notes et extraits pour servir a l'histoire des croisades au XVe siècle." *Revue de l'Orient Latin* 4–8 (1896–1901): 4:25–118, 226–320, 503–622; 5:108–212, 311–88; 6:50–143, 370–434; 7:38–107, 375–429; 8:1–115, 267–311.

Jotischky, Andrew. "The Mendicants as Missionaries and Travellers in the Near East in the Thirteenth and Fourteenth Centuries." In *Eastward Bound: Travel and Travellers, 1050–1550*, ed. Rosamund Allen, 88–106. Manchester: Manchester University Press, 2004.

Kabadayi, M. Erdem, and Tobias Reichardt, eds. *Unfreie Arbeit: Ökonomische und kulturgeschichtliche Perspektiven*. Hildesheim: Georg Olms, 2007.

Kafadar, Cemal. "A Rome of One's Own: Reflections on Cultural Geography and Identity in the Lands of Rum." *Muqarnas* 24 (2007): 7–25.

Karpov, Sergei. "Rabotorgovlia v iuzhnom prichernomor'e v pervoi polovine XV v. (preimushchestvenno po dannym massarii Kaffy)." *Vizantiiskii Vremennik* 46 (1986): 139–45.

———. "New Documents on the Relations Between the Latins and the Local Populations in the Black Sea Area (1392–1462)." *Dumbarton Oaks Papers* 49 (1995): 33–41.

———. "Une ramification inattendue: les Bourguignons en Mer Noire au XVe siècle." In *Coloniser au Moyen Âge*, ed. Michel Balard and Alain Ducellier, 186–89. Paris: Armand Colin, 1995.

———. "Genois et Byzantins face a la crise de Tana de 1343." *Byzantinische Forschungen* 22 (1996): 33–42.

———. *La navigazione veneziana nel Mar Nero XIII–XV sec.* Ravenna: Edizioni del Girasole, 2000.

———. "Venetsianskaia rabotorgovlia v Trapezunde (konets XIV–nachalo XV v.)." *Vizaniiskie ocherki* (n.d.): 191–207.

Karras, Ruth Mazo. *Slavery and Society in Medieval Scandinavia.* New Haven: Yale University Press, 1988.

———. *Unmarriages: Women, Men, and Sexual Unions in the Middle Ages.* Philadelphia: University of Pennsylvania Press, 2012.

Katz, Jonathan. *Dreams, Sufism, and Sainthood: The Visionary Career of Muhammad al-Zawawi.* Leiden: Brill, 1996.

Kaye, Joel. *A History of Balance, 1250–1375: The Emergence of a New Model of Equilibrium and Its Impact on Thought.* Cambridge: Cambridge University Press, 2014.

Kedar, Benjamin. "Segurano-Sakran Salvaygo: Un mercante genovese al servizio dei sultani mamalucchi, c. 1303–1322." In *Fatti e idee di storia economica nei secoli XII–XX: Studi dedicati a Franco Borlandi*, 75–91. Bologna: Società editrice il mulino, 1977.

———. *Crusade and Mission: European Approaches Towards the Muslims.* Princeton: Princeton University Press, 1984.

Kedar, Benjamin, and Sylvia Schein, eds. "Un project de 'passage particulier' proposé par l'ordre de l'Hôpital, 1306-1307." *Bibliotheque de l'Ecole des Chartes* 137 (1979): 211–26.

Kennedy, Hugh, ed. *The Historiography of Islamic Egypt (c.950–1800).* Leiden: Brill, 2001.

Kern, Anton. "Der 'Libellus de notitia orbis' Iohannes' III. (de Galonifontibus?) O.P. Erzbischofs von Sulthanyeh." *Archivium fratrum praedicatorum* 8 (1938): 82–123.

Keupp, J. U. *Dienst und Verdienst: Die Ministerialen Friedrich Barbarossas und Heinrichs VI.* Stuttgart: Anton Hiersemann, 2002.

Khalilieh, Hassan. "An Overview of Slaves' Juridical Status at Sea in Romano-Byzantine and Islamic Laws." In *Histories of the Middle East: Studies in Middle Eastern Society, Economy and Law in Honor of A. L. Udovitch*, ed. Roxani Margariti, Adam Sabra, and Petra Sijpesteijn, 73–100. Leiden: Brill, 2011.

Khowaiter, Abdul-Aziz. *Baibars the First: His Endeavours and Achievements.* London: Green Mountain Press, 1978.

Khvalkov, Ievgen. "The Slave Trade in Tana: Marketing Manpower from the Black Sea to the Mediterranean in the 1430s." *Annual of Medieval Studies at CEU* 18 (2012): 104–18.

Killoran, John. "Aquinas and Vitoria: Two Perspectives on Slavery." In *The Medieval Tradition of Natural Law*, ed. Harold Johnson, 87–101. Kalamazoo: Medieval Institute, 1987.

King, Charles. *The Black Sea: A History.* Oxford: Oxford University Press, 2004.

Kizilov, Mikhail. "Slaves, Money Lenders, and Prisoner Guards: The Jews and the Trade in Slaves and Captives in the Crimean Khanate." *Journal of Jewish Studies* 58 (2007): 189–210.

Klapisch-Zuber, Christiane. "Women Servants in Florence During the Fourteenth and Fifteenth Centuries." In Hanawalt, *Women and Work*, 56–80.

Kohler, Charles. "Traité du recouvrement de la Terre Sainte adressé, vers l'an 1295, a Philippe le Bel par Galvano de Levanto, médecin génois." *Revue de l'Orient Latin* 6 (1898): 343–69.

Köpstein, Helga. *Zur Sklaverei in ausgehenden Byzanz.* Berlin: Akademie, 1966.

Kosto, Adam. *Hostages in the Middle Ages*. Oxford: Oxford University Press, 2012.

Kouznetsov, Vladimir, and Iaroslav Lebedynsky. *Les chrétiens disparus du Caucase*. Paris: Editions Errance, 1999.

Kramarovsky, Mark. "The Golden Horde and the Levant in the Epoch of Fr. Petrarca: Trade, Culture, Handcrafts." *Rivista di Bizantinistica* 3 (1993): 249–80.

Krekić, Barisa. "Contributo allo studio degli schiavi levantini e balcanici a Venezia (1388–1398)." In *Dubrovnik, Italy and the Balkans in the Late Middle Ages*, 379–94. London: Variorum Reprints, 1980.

Kunstmann, Friedrich. "Studien über Marino Sanudo den aelteren." *Konigliche bayerische Akademie der Wissenschaften; Philosophische, philologische und historische Klasse* 7 (1855): 696–819.

Labib, Subhi. *Handelsgeschichte Ägyptens im Spätmittelalter (1171–1517)*. Wiesbaden: Franz Steiner, 1965.

Lagardère, Vincent. *Histoire et société en occident musulman au Moyen Age: Analyse du Mi'yar dal-Wansarisi*. Madrid: Casa de Velázquez, 1995.

Laiou, Angelika. "Marino Sanudo Torsello, Byzantium and the Turks: The Background to the Anti-Turkish League of 1332–1334." *Speculum* 45 (1970): 374–92.

———. *Constantinople and the Latins: The Foreign Policy of Andronicus II, 1282–1328*. Cambridge: Harvard University Press, 1972.

———. "The Byzantine Economy in the Mediterranean Trade System: Thirteenth–Fifteenth Centuries." In *Gender, Society and Economic Life in Byzantium*, 177–222. Brookfield: Ashgate Variorum, 1992.

Landau, Peter. "Hadrians IV. Dekretale 'Dignum Est' (X.4.9.1) und die Eheschliessung Unfreier in der Diskussion von Kanonisten und Theologen des 12. und 13. Jahrhunderts." *Studia Gratiana* 12 (1967): 511–53.

Lane, F. C. *Venice, a Maritime Republic*. Baltimore: Johns Hopkins University Press, 1973.

Langholm, Odd. *The Merchant in the Confessional: Trade and Price in the Pre-Reformation Penitential Handbooks*. Leiden: Brill, 2003.

Langlois, Ernest. *Les registres de Nicolas IV*. Paris: E. Thorin, 1905.

Lannoy, Ghillebert de. *Œuvres de Ghillebert de Lannoy: Voyageur, diplomate et moraliste*, ed. Charles Potvin. Louvain: P. et J. Lefever, 1878.

Laurière, Eusèbe. *Ordonnances des roys de France de la troisième race*. Paris: Imprimerie royale, 1723.

Lazari, Vincenzo. "Del traffico e delle condizioni degli schiavi in Venezia nei tempi di mezzo." *Miscellanea di storia italiana* 1 (1862): 463–501.

Lech, Klaus. *Das mongolische Weltreich: Al-'Umari's Bericht über die Reiche der Mongolen in seinem Werk Masalik al-absar fi mamalik al-amsar*. Wiesbaden: Harrassowitz, 1968.

Lemercier-Quelquejay, Chantal. "Cooptation of the Elites of Kabarda and Daghestan in the Sixteenth Century." In *The North Caucasus Barrier: The Russian Advance Towards the Muslim World*, ed. Marie Bennigson-Broxup, 18–44. London: Hurst, 1996.

Lenna, Niccolò di. "Giosafat Barbaro (1413–94) e i suoi viaggi nella regione Russa (1436–51) e nella Persia (1474–78)." *Nuovo archivio veneto* n.s. 28 (1914): 5–105.

Leopold, Anthony. *How to Recover the Holy Land: The Crusade Proposals of the Late Thirteenth and Early Fourteenth Centuries*. Aldershot: Ashgate, 2000.

Leskov, A. M., and V. L. Lapushnian. *Art Treasures of Ancient Kuban: Catalog of Exhibition*. Moscow: Ministry of Culture of the USSR, 1987.

Levanoni, Amalia. *A Turning Point in Mamluk History: The Third Reign of al-Nasir Muhammad ibn Qalawun (1310–1341)*. Leiden: Brill, 1995.

———. "Al-Maqrizi's Account of the Transition from Turkish to Circassian Mamluk Sultanate: History in the Service of Faith." In Kennedy, *Historiography*, 93–105.

Lewis, Bernard. *Race and Slavery in the Middle East: An Historical Inquiry*. Oxford: Oxford University Press, 1990.

Liber iurium reipublicae genuensis. Monumenta Historia Patriae 7–8. Turin: E. Regio Typographeo, 1854–1857.

Little, Donald. "Six Fourteenth Century Purchase Deeds for Slaves from al-Ḥaram aš-Šarīf." *Zeitschrift der deutschen morgenländischen Gesellschaft* 131 (1981): 297–337.

———. "Two Fourteenth-Century Court Records from Jerusalem Concerning the Disposition of Slaves by Minors." *Arabica* 29 (1982): 16–49.

———. *A Catalogue of the Islamic Documents from al-Ḥaram aš-Šarīf in Jerusalem*. Beirut: Orient-Institut der deutschen morgenländischen Gesellschaft, 1984.

Livi, Carlo. *Sardi en schiavitù nei secoli XII–XV*. Florence: F. Cesare, 2002.

Livi, Ridolfo. *La schiavitù domestica nei tempi di mezzo e nei moderni*. Padua: CEDAM, 1928.

Lockhart, Laurence, Raimondo Morozzo della Rocca, and Maria Francesca Tiepolo. *I Viaggi in Persia degli ambasciatori veneti Barbaro e Contarini*. Rome: Istituto poligrafico dello stato, 1973.

Löfgren, Oscar. *Arabische Texte zur Kenntnis der Stadt Aden im Mittelalter*. Uppsala: Almqvist och Wiksells Boktryckeri-A.-B., 1936.

Loiseau, Julien. "Frankish Captives in Mamluk Cairo." *Al-Masaq* 23 (2011): 37–52.

Lombardo, Antonio. *Nicola de Boateriis, notaio in Famagosta e Venezia (1355–1365)*. Venice: CPFSV, 1973.

Lopez, Robert. *Su e giù per la storia di Genova*. Genoa: IMG, 1975.

Lowe, Kate. "The Lives of African Slaves and People of African Descent in Renaissance Europe." In *Revealing the African Presence in Renaissance Europe*, ed. Joaneath Spicer, 13–34. Baltimore: Walters Art Museum, 2012.

Lull, Ramon. "Projet de Raymond Lull 'De Acquisitione Terrae Sanctae,'" ed. Eugene Kamar. *Studia Orientalia Christiana: Collectanea* 6 (1961): 3–132.

———. "De fine." In *Raimundi Lulli Opera Latina*, ed. Aloisius Madre, 233–91. Turnhout: Brepols, 1981.

Lutfi, Huda. *Al-Quds al-Mamlûkiyya: A History of Mamlûk Jerusalem Based on the Ḥaram Documents*. Berlin: Klaus Schwarz, 1985.

Luttrell, Anthony. "Slavery at Rhodes: 1306–1440." In *Latin Greece, the Hospitallers and the Crusades, 1291–1400*, 81–100. London: Variorum Reprints, 1982.

Luzzato, Gino. *Studi di storia economica veneziana*. Padua: CEDAM, 1954.

Lyons, U., and M. C. Lyons. *Ayyubids, Mamlukes and Crusaders: Selections from the Tarīkh al-Duwal wa'l-Mulūk of Ibn al-Furāt*. Cambridge: W. Heffer, 1971.

Macchiavello, Sandra. *I cartolari del notaio Simone di Francesco de Compagnono (1408–1415)*. Genoa: Società ligure di storia patria, 2006.

Makhairas, Leontios. *Recital Concerning the Sweet Land of Cyprus Entitled "Chronicle,"* trans. Richard Dawkins. Oxford: Clarendon Press, 1932.

Makris, Georgios. *Studien zur spätbyzantinischen Schiffahrt*. Genoa: IMG, 1988.

Małowist, Marian. "Kaffa: The Genoese Colony in the Crimea and the Eastern Question (1453–1475)." In Batou and Szlajfer, *Western Europe, Eastern Europe*, 101–32.

———. "New Saray, Capital of the Golden Horde." In Batou and Szlajfer, *Western Europe, Eastern Europe*, 325–38.

———. "Social and Economic Life in Timur's Empire." In Batou and Szlajfer, *Western Europe, Eastern Europe*, 287–324.

Manfroni, Camillo. "Le relazione fra Genova, l'Impero Bizantino e i Turchi." *ASLSP* 28 (1896): 575–856.

Mansouri, Mohamed Tahar. "Les communautés marchandes occidentales dans l'espace mamlouk (XIIIe–XVe siècle)." In *Coloniser au Moyen Âge*, ed. Michel Balard and Alain Ducellier, 89–101. Paris: Armand Colin, 1995.

Maqrīzī, Taqī al-Dīn Aḥmad al-. *Kitāb al-sulūk li-maʿrifat duwal al-mulūk*, ed. M. M. Ziyāda and Saʿīd ʿAbd al-Fattāḥ ʿAshūr. 4 vols. Cairo: Lajnat al-taʾlīf wa-al-tarjama wa-al-nashr, 1934–1973.

———. *Kitāb al-khiṭaṭ wa-al-athār fī Miṣr wa-al-Qāhira*, ed. Ayman Fu'ad Sayyid. 5 vols. London: al-Furqan Islamic Heritage Foundation, 2002–2004.

Marino, Nancy. *El Libro del conoscimiento de todos los reinos*. Tempe: ACMRS, 1999.

Marmon, Shaun. *Eunuchs and Sacred Boundaries in Islamic Society.* Oxford: Oxford University Press, 1995.

———. "Domestic Slavery in the Mamluk Empire: A Preliminary Sketch." In *Slavery in the Islamic Middle East*, ed. Shaun Marmon, 1–23. Princeton: Markus Wiener, 1999.

———. "Black Slaves in Mamlūk Narratives: Representations of Transgression." *Al-Qantara* 28 (2007): 456–63.

Martin, Janet. *Treasure of the Land of Darkness: The Fur Trade and Its Significance for Medieval Russia.* Cambridge: Cambridge University Press, 1986.

———. *Medieval Russia, 980–1584.* Cambridge: Cambridge University Press, 1993.

Marx, Karl. "The German Ideology." In *The Marx-Engels Reader*, ed. Robert Tucker, 148–75. New York: W. W. Norton, 1978.

Mas Latrie, M. L. de. *Histoire de l'île de Chypre sous le règne des princes de la maison de Lusignan.* Paris: Imprimerie nationale, 1852.

Masi, Gino, ed. *Formularium florentinum artis notariae (1220–1242).* Milan: Società editrice vita e pensiero, 1943.

Mazor, Amir. *The Rise and Fall of a Muslim Regiment: The Manṣūriyya in the First Mamluk Sultanate, 678/1279–741/1341.* Göttingen: V&R unipress, 2015.

McCormick, Michael. *Origins of the European Economy: Communications and Commerce, A.D. 300–900.* Cambridge: Cambridge University Press, 2001.

McKee, Sally. "Inherited Status and Slavery in Renaissance Italy and Venetian Crete." *Past and Present* 182 (2004): 31–54.

———. "The Implications of Slave Women's Sexual Service in Late Medieval Italy." In Kabadayi and Reichardt, *Unfreie Arbeit*, 101–14.

———. "Domestic Slavery in Renaissance Italy." *Slavery and Abolition* 29 (2008): 305–26.

McVaugh, M. R. "Armengaud Blaise as a Translator of Galen." In *Texts and Contexts in Ancient and Medieval Science*, ed. E. Sylla and M. R. McVaugh, 115–33. Leiden: Brill, 1997.

Meek, Christine. "Men, Women and Magic: Some Cases from Late Medieval Lucca." In *Women in Renaissance and Early Modern Europe*, ed. Christine Meek, 43–66. Dublin: Four Courts Press, 2000.

Meillassoux, Claude. *The Anthropology of Slavery: The Womb of Iron and Gold*, trans. Alide Dasnois. Chicago: University of Chicago Press, 1991.

Melichar, Petra. "God, Slave and a Nun: A Case from Late Medieval Cyprus." *Byzantion* 79 (2009): 280–91.

Melis, Frederigo. *Origini e sviluppi delle assicurazioni in Italia (secoli XIV–XVI).* Rome: Istituto nazionale delle assicurazioni, 1975.

Menache, Sophia. "Papal Attempts at a Commercial Boycott of the Muslims in the Crusader Period." *Journal of Ecclesiastical History* 63 (2012): 236–59.

Mensching, Günther. "Die Rechtfertigung von Unfreiheit im Denken des Hochmittelalters." In Herrmann-Otto, *Unfreie Arbeits- und Lebensverhältnisse*, 117–29.

Meri, Joseph. "Aspects of Baraka (Blessings) and Ritual Devotion Among Medieval Muslims and Jews." *Medieval Encounters* 5 (1999): 46–69.

Mez, Adam. *The Renaissance of Islam*, trans. Salahuddin Khuda Bakhsh and D. S. Margoliouth. Patna: Jubilee, 1937.

Mézières, Philippe de. *Le Songe du vieil pelerin*, ed. G. W. Coopland. Cambridge: Cambridge University Press, 1969.

Middle East Media Research Institute. "Islamic State (ISIS) Releases Pamphlet on Female Slaves." https://www.memri.org/jttm/islamic-state-isis-releases-pamphlet-female-slaves (accessed August 7, 2018).

Miers, Suzanne, and Igor Kopytoff, eds. *Slavery in Africa: Historical and Anthropological Perspectives.* Madison: University of Wisconsin Press, 1977.

Miller, Joseph. *The Problem of Slavery as History: A Global Approach.* New Haven: Yale University Press, 2012.

Minnis, Alistair. *From Eden to Eternity: Creations of Paradise in the Later Middle Ages*. Philadelphia: University of Pennsylvania Press, 2016.

Mirza, Younus. "Remembering the Umm al-Walad: Ibn Kathir's Treatise on the Sale of the Concubine." In Gordon and Hain, *Concubines and Courtesans*, 297-323.

Molmenti, Pompeo. *La storia di Venezia nella vita privata dalle origini alla caduta della repubblica*. Bergamo: Istituto italiano d'arti grafiche, 1911.

Monleone, Giovanni, ed. *Iacopo da Varagine e la sua cronaca di Genova*. Rome: Istituto storico italiano, 1941.

Morgan, David. *The Mongols*. Oxford: Blackwell, 1986.

Morony, Michael. "Religious Communities in the Early Islamic World." In Gantner, Pohl, and Payne, *Visions of Community*, 155–63.

Morozzo della Rocca, Raimondo. *Benvenuto de Brixano, notaio in Candia, 1301–1302*. Venice: Alfieri, 1950.

———. *Lettere di Mercanti a Pignol Zucchello (1336–1350)*. Venice: CPFSV, 1957.

Mortel, Richard. "The Mercantile Community of Mecca During the Late Mamlūk Period." *JRAS*, 3rd ser., 4 (1994): 15–35.

Mourad, Youssef. *La physiognomie arabe et le Kitab al-Firasa de Fakhr al-Din al-Razi*. Paris: Geuthner, 1939.

Muḥammad, Amānī Muḥammad ʿAbd al-ʿAzīz. "Al-Basīṭ fī al-shurūṭ." Master's thesis, Cairo University, 2010.

Muḥammad, Labība. "Al-raqīq wa-al-tijāra fī Miṣr wa-al-Shām fī ʿaṣr dawlat salāṭīn al-mamālīk, 648–923 H./1250–1517 M." Master's thesis, Cairo University, 1993.

Mukhtar, Muḥammad. *Bughiyyat al-murīd fī shirāʾ al-jawārī wa-taqlīb al-ʿabīd*. Cairo: Muḥammad Mukhtar, 1996.

Müller, Hans. *Die Kunst des Sklavenkaufs nach arabischen, persischen und türkischen Ratgebern vom 10. bis zum 18. Jahrhundert*. Freiburg: Klaus Schwarz, 1980.

Müller, R. C. "Venezia e i primi schiavi neri." *Archivio Veneto*, 5th ser., 113 (1979): 139–42.

Mummey, Kevin. "Enchained in Paradise: Slave Identities on the Island of Majorca, ca. 1360–1390." In *Mediterranean Identities in the Premodern Era: Entrepôts, Islands, Empires*, ed. John Watkins and Kathryn Reyerson, 121–38. Farnham: Ashgate, 2014.

Musso, Gian Giacomo. "Gli orientali nei notai genovesi di Caffa." In *Ricerche di archivio e studi storici in onore di Giorgio Costamagna*, 97–110. Rome: Centro di ricerca editore, 1974.

———. *Navigazione e commercio genovese con il Levante nei documenti dell'Archivio di Stato di Genova (secc. XIV–XV)*. Rome: Ministero per i beni culturali e ambientali, 1975.

Musso, Gian Giacomo, and Maria Silva Jacopino. "I Genovesi e il Levante tra medioevo ed eta moderna." In *Genova, la Ligure e l'Oltremare tra medioevo ed età moderna: Studi e ricerche d'archivio*, ed. Maria Silva Jacopino and Raffaele Belvederi, 67–183. Genoa: Fratelli Bozzi, 1976.

Nehlsen-von Stryk, Karin. *L'Assicurazione marittima a Venezia nel XV secolo*, trans. Carla Vinci-Orlando. Rome: Il Veltro, 1988.

Nelson, Thomas. "Slavery in Medieval Japan." *Monumenta Nipponica* 59 (2004): 463–92.

Nielsen, Jorgen. *Secular Justice in an Islamic State: Maẓālim under the Baḥrī Mamlūks, 662/1264–789/1387*. Leiden: Nederlands Instituut voor het Nabije Oosten, 1985.

Nielson, Lisa. "Gender and the Politics of Music in the Early Islamic Courts." *Early Music History* 31 (2012): 233–59.

Nigro, Giampiero, ed. *Francesco di Marco Datini: The Man, The Merchant*. Florence: Firenze University Press, 2010.

Nirenberg, David. *Communities of Violence: Persecution of Minorities in the Middle Ages*. Princeton: Princeton University Press, 1996.

Nogaret, William of. "Quae sunt advertenda pro passagio ultramarino." In *Notices et extraits des documents inedits relatifs a l'histoire de France sous Philippe le Bel*, ed. E. P. Boutaric, 199–205. Paris: Imprimerie national, 1862.

Noiret, Hippolyte. *Documents inédits pour servir à l'histoire de la domination vénitienne en Crète de 1380 a 1485*. Paris: Thorin et fils, 1892.

North, Douglass. *Institutions, Institutional Change, and Economic Performance*. Cambridge: Cambridge University Press, 1990.

Northrup, Linda. "Military Slavery in the Islamic and Mamluk Context." In Kabadayi and Reichardt, *Unfreie Arbeit*, 115–31.

———. *From Slave to Sultan: The Career of al-Mansur Qalawun and the Consolidation of Mamluk Rule in Egypt and Syria (678–689 A.H./1279–1290 A.D.)*. Stuttgart: Franz Steiner, 1998.

Nuwayrī, Shihāb al-Dīn Aḥmad al-. *Nihāyat al-arab fī funūn al-adab*. 31 vols. Cairo: MTTTN, 1964–1992.

Nuwayrī al-Iskandarānī, Muḥammad ibn Qāsim al-. *Kitāb al-ilmām bi-al-iʿlām fīmā jarrat bihu al-aḥkām wa-al-umūr al-maqḍīyya fī waqʿat al-Iskandarīyya*, ed. Aziz Atiya. 7 vols. Hyderabad: Maṭbaʿat majlis dairat al-maʿarif al-ʿuthmāniyya, 1968–1976.

O'Connell, Monique. "The Italian Renaissance in the Mediterranean, or, Between East and West." *California Italian Studies Journal* 1 (2010): 1–30.

O'Connell Davidson, Julia. *Modern Slavery: The Margins of Freedom*. New York: Palgrave Macmillan, 2015.

Odena, J. Trenchs. "Les 'Alexandrini,' ou la désobéissance aux embargos conciliaires ou pontificaux contre les Musulmans." In *Islam et chrétiens du Midi (XIIe–XIVe s.)*, 169–94. Toulouse: Edouard Privat, 1983.

Oikonomidès, Nicolas. *Hommes d'affaires grecs et latins à Constantinople (XIIIe–XVe siècles)*. Montreal: Institut d'études médiévales Albert-le-Grand, 1979.

Okeowo, Alexis. "A Mauritanian Abolitionist's Crusade Against Slavery." *New Yorker*. http://www.newyorker.com/magazine/2014/09/08/freedom-fighter (accessed September 18, 2014).

Olender, Maurice. *The Languages of Paradise: Race, Religion and Philology in the Nineteenth Century*, trans. Arthur Goldhammer. Cambridge: Harvard University Press, 2008.

"Open Letter to Al-Baghdadi." http://www.lettertobaghdadi.com/ (accessed March 18, 2017).

Origo, Iris. "The Domestic Enemy: The Eastern Slaves in Tuscany in the Fourteenth and Fifteenth Centuries." *Speculum* 30 (1955): 321–66.

Orlandelli, Gianfranco. "Genesi dell' 'ars notariae' nel secolo XIII." *Studi medievali*, 3rd ser., 6 (1965): 329–66.

Orlandi, Angela. "The Catalonia Company: An Almost Unexpected Success." In Nigro, *Francesco di Marco Datini*, 347–76.

Ortalli, Gherardo. "Venice and Papal Bans on Trade with the Levant: The Role of the Jurist." *Mediterranean Historical Review* 10 (1995): 242–58.

Pachymeres, George. *De Michaele et Andronico Palaeologis libri tredecim*, trans. Immanuel Bekker. Bonn: Weberi, 1835.

Pahlitzsch, Johannes. "Slavery and the Slave Trade in Byzantium in the Palaeologan Period." In Amitai and Cluse, *Slavery*, 163–84.

Painter, Nell Irvin. *The History of White People*. New York: W. W. Norton, 2010.

Palmer, J. J. N. *England, France, and Christendom, 1377–99*. Chapel Hill: University of North Carolina Press, 1972.

Pamuk, Orhan. *The White Castle*. New York: Braziller, 1991.

Pandiani, Emilio. "Vita privata genovese nel rinascimento." *ASLSP* 47 (1915): 1–411.

Papacostea, Şerban. "De Vicina à Kilia. Byzantins et génois aux bouches du Danube au XIVe siècle." *RESE* 16 (1978): 65–79.

———. "'Quod non iretur ad Tanam.' Un aspect fondamental de la politique génoise dans la mer Noire au XIVe siècle." *RESE* 17 (1979): 201–17.

Passeggieri, Rolandinus. *Summa totius artis notariae Rolandini Rodulphini Bononiensis*. Bologna: Arnaldo Forni, 1977.

Patterson, Orlando. *Slavery and Social Death: A Comparative Study*. Cambridge: Harvard University Press, 1982.

Paviot, Jacques. "La piraterie bourguignonne en Mer Noire à la moitié du XVe siècle." In *Horizons marins, itinéraires spirituels (Ve–XVIIIe siècles)*, 2:203–15. Paris: Publications de la Sorbonne, 1987.

Pavoni, Romeo. *Notai genovesi in Oltremare: Atti rogati a Cipro da Lamberto di Sambuceto (6 luglio–27 ottobre 1301)*. Genoa: IMG, 1982.

———. *Notai genovesi in Oltremare: Atti rogati a Cipro da Lamberto di Sambuceto (gennaio-agosto 1302)*. Genoa: IMG, 1987.

Pedani, Maria Pia. "The Mamluk Documents of the Venetian State Archives: Historical Survey." *Quaderni di studi arabi* 20–21 (2002–2003): 133–46.

Pegolotti, Francesco Balducci. *La Pratica della Mercatura: Book of Descriptions of Countries and of Measures of Merchandise*, trans. Allan Evans. Cambridge: Medieval Academy of America, 1936.

Pelteret, David. *Slavery in Early Medieval England: From the Reign of Alfred Until the Twelfth Century*. Rochester: Boydell and Brewer, 1995.

Perry, Craig. "The Daily Life of Slaves and the Global Reach of Slavery in Medieval Egypt, 969–1250 CE." PhD diss., Emory University, 2014.

———. "Conversion as an Aspect of Master–Slave Relationship in the Medieval Egyptian Jewish Community." In *Contesting Inter-Religious Conversion in the Medieval World*, ed. Yaniv Fox and Yosi Yisraeli, 135–59. London: Routledge, 2017.

———. "Roundtable: Locating Slavery in Middle Eastern and Islamic History." *IJMES* 49 (2017): 133–72.

Petkov, Kiril. *The Voices of Medieval Bulgaria, Seventh-Fifteenth Century: The Records of a Bygone Era*. Leiden: Brill, 2008.

Petrarch, Francesco. *Prose*, ed. Guido Martellotti. Milan: R. Ricciardi, 1955.

Petrucci, Armando. *Notarii: Documenti per la storia del notariato italiano*. Milan: Giuffrè, 1958.

Petry, Carl. *The Civilian Elite of Cairo in the Later Middle Ages*. Princeton: Princeton University Press, 1981.

———. *Twilight of Majesty: The Reigns of the Mamluk Sultans al-Ashraf Qaytbay and Qansuh al-Ghawri in Egypt*. Seattle: University of Washington Press, 1993.

———. *Protectors or Praetorians? The Last Mamluk Sultans and Egypt's Waning as a Great Power*. Albany: State University of New York Press, 1994.

Pettenello, Gaetano, and Simone Rauch. *Stefano Bono, notaio in Candia (1303–1304)*. Venice: CPFSV, 2011.

Phillips, Kim. *Before Orientalism: Asian Peoples and Cultures in European Travel Writing, 1245–1510*. Philadelphia: University of Pennsylvania Press, 2014.

Piattoli, Livio. "L'assicurazione di schiavi imbarcati su navi ed i rischi di morte nel medioevo." *Rivista del diritto commerciale e del diritto generale delle obbligazioni* 32 (1934): 866–74.

Piattoli, R. "Lettere di Piero Benintendi." *ASLSP* 60 (1932): 1–173.

Piloti, Emmanuel. *Traité d'Emmanuel Piloti sur le passage en Terre Sainte (1420)*, ed. Pierre-Hermann Dopp. Louvain: E. Nauwelaerts, 1958.

Pipes, Daniel. *Slave Soldiers and Islam: The Genesis of a Military System*. New Haven: Yale University Press, 1981.

Pistarino, Geo. "Tra liberi e schiavi a Genova nel Quattrocento." *Anuario de estudios medievales* 1 (1964): 353–74.

———. *Notai genovesi in oltremare: Atti rogati a Chilia da Antonio di Ponzò (1360–61)*. Genoa: Università di Genova, Istituto di paleografia e storia medievale, 1971.

Poggibonsi, Niccolò da. *Libro d'Oltramare*, ed. P. B. Bagatti. Jerusalem: Tipografia dei Francescani, 1945.

———. *A Voyage Beyond the Seas (1346–1350)*, ed. Theophilus Bellorini and Eugene Hoade. Jerusalem: Franciscan Printing Press, 1945.

Pohl, Walter. "Introduction: Ethnicity, Religion and Empire." In Gantner, Pohl, and Payne, *Visions of Community*, 1–23.

Poliak, A. N. "The Influence of Chingiz-Khan's Yasa upon the General Organization of the Mamluk State." *BSOAS* 10 (1942): 862–76.

Polo, Marco. *The Travels*, trans. Ronald Latham. London: Penguin Books, 1958.

Pontano, Giovanni Gioviano. "De obedientia." In *Opera Ioannis Iouiani Pontani*. Lyons: Barthélemy Trot, 1514.

Popovic, Alexandre. *The Revolt of African Slaves in Iraq in the 3rd/9th Century*. Princeton: Markus Wiener, 1999.

Popper, William. *Egypt and Syria Under the Circassian Sultans, 1382–1468 A.D.* University of California Publications in Semitic Philology 13–14, 17–19, and 22–24. Berkeley: University of California Press, 1954–1963.

——. *The History of Egypt, 1382–1469 A.D.* University of California Publications in Semitic Philology 15–16. Berkeley: University of California Press, 1955–1957.

Pormann, Peter, and Emilie Savage-Smith. *Medieval Islamic Medicine*. Edinburgh: Edinburgh University Press, 2007.

Potthast, August. *Regesta pontificum romanorum*. Graz: Akademische Druck- und Verlagsanstalt, 1957.

Predelli, Riccardo, ed. *I libri commemoriali della republica di Venezia*. 4 vols. Venice: A spese della società, 1876.

Preiser-Kapeller, Johannes. "Zwischen Konstantinopel und Goldener Horde: Die byzantinischen Kirchenprovinzen der Alanen und Zichen im mongolischen Machtbereich im 13. und 14. Jahrhundert." In *Caucasus During the Mongol Period*, ed. Jürgen Tubach, Sophia Vashalomidze, and Manfred Zimmer, 199–216. Wiesbaden: Reichert, 2012.

Prokofieva, Nina. "Akti venetsianskogo notariya v Tane Donato a Mano (1413–1419)." *Prichernomorie v srednie veka* 4 (2000): 36–174.

Prunai, Giulio. "Notizie e documenti sulla servitù domestica nel teritorio senese (Secc. VIII–XVI)." *Bulletino senese di storia patria* 7 (1936): 133–82, 245–98, 398–438.

Puente, Christina de la. "Entre la esclavitud y la libertad: consecuencias legales de la manumisión según el derecho mālikí." *Al-Qantara* 21 (2000): 339–60.

Qalqashandī, Abū al-ʿAbbās Aḥmad al-. *Subḥ al-aʿshā fī ṣanāʿat al-inshāʾ*. 14 vols. Cairo: Al-Maṭbaʿa al-amīriyya, 1913–1919.

Qāsim, Qāsim ʿAbduh. *ʿAsr salāṭīn al-mamālīk: Al-Tārīkh al-siyāsī wa-al-ijtimāʿī*. Cairo: ʿAyn lil-dirāsat wa-al-buḥūth al-insāniyya wa al-ijtimāʿiyya, 1998.

Quirini-Popławska, Danuta. "The Venetian Involvement in the Black Sea Slave Trade (14th to 15th Centuries)." In Amitai and Cluse, *Slavery*, 255–98.

Rabbat, Nasser. "The Changing Concept of Mamluk in the Mamluk Sultanate in Egypt and Syria." In Toru and Philips, *Slave Elites*, 81–98.

——. *The Citadel of Cairo: A New Interpretation of Royal Mamluk Architecture*. Leiden: Brill, 1995.

——. "Representing the Mamluks in Mamluk Historical Writing." In Kennedy, *Historiography*, 59–75.

Rabie, Hassanein. "Ḥujjāt tamlīk wa-waqf." *Majallat al-jamʿiyya al-miṣriyya lil-dirāsāt al-tārīkhiyya* 12 (1964–1965): 191–202.

——. *The Financial System of Egypt, AH 564–741/AD 1169–1341*. London: Oxford University Press, 1972.

——. "The Training of the Mamluk Faris." In *War, Technology and Society in the Middle East*, ed. V. J. Parry and M. E. Yapp, 153–63. London: Oxford University Press, 1975.

Ragib, Yusuf. "Les marchés aux esclaves en terre d'Islam." In *Mercati e mercanti nell'alto medioevo: L'Area euroasiatica e l'area mediterranea*, 721–66. Spoleto: Presso la sede del centro, 1993.

——. *Actes de vente d'esclaves et d'animaux d'Egypte médiévale*. Cairo: IFAO, 2002.

Raiteri, Silvana Fossati. "La schiavitù nelle colonie genovesi del Levante nel Basso Medioevo." In Ferrer i Mallol and Mutgé i Vives, *De l'esclavitud*, 695–716.

Rapoport, Yossef. "Women and Gender in Mamluk Society: An Overview." *MSR* 11 (2007): 1–48.

——. "Ibn Ḥağar al-ʿAsqalānī, His Wife, Her Slave-Girl: Romantic Triangles and Polygamy in 15th Century Cairo." *Annales islamologiques* 47 (2013): 327–52.

Raymond, André, and Gaston Wiet. *Les Marchés du Caire: Traduction annotée du texte de Maqrizi.* Cairo: IFAO, 1979.

Raymond, Irving, and Robert Lopez. *Medieval Trade in the Mediterranean World.* New York: Columbia University Press, 1955.

Raynaldus, Odoricus, ed. *Annales ecclesiastici.* Bar-le-Duc: Guerin, 1880.

Reuter, Timothy. "Whose Race, Whose Ethnicity? Recent Medievalists' Discussions of Identity." In *Medieval Polities and Modern Mentalities*, ed. Janet Nelson, 100–110. Cambridge: Cambridge University Press, 2006.

Richard, Jean. *La papauté et les missions d'Orient au Moyen Age (XIIIe–XVe siècles).* Rome: École française de Rome, 1977.

Richards, D. S. "Fragments of a Slave Dealer's Day-Book from Fustat." In *Documents de l'Islam médiéval*, ed. Yusuf Ragib, 89–96. Cairo: IFAO, 1991.

Riley-Smith, Jonathan. *The Crusades: A History.* London: Bloomsbury, 2014.

Rio, Alice. *Slavery After Rome, 500–1100.* Oxford: Oxford University Press, 2017.

Roberti, Melchiorre. *Un formulario inedito di un notaio padovano del 1223.* Venice: R. Istituto nel Palazzo Loredan, 1906.

Roccatagliata, Ausilia. *Notai genovesi in Oltremare: Atti rogati a Chio (1453–1454, 1470–1471).* Genoa: IMG, 1982.

———. *Notai genovesi in Oltremare: Atti rogati a Pera e Mitilene.* 2 vols. Genoa: IMG, 1982.

Rodocanachi, E. "Les esclaves en Italie du XIIIe au XVIe siècle." *Revue des questions historiques* 79 (1906): 383–407.

Romano, Dennis. *Housecraft and Statecraft: Domestic Service in Renaissance Venice, 1400–1600.* Baltimore: Johns Hopkins University Press, 1996.

Rosenberger, Bernard. "Maquiller l'esclave (al-Andalus XIIeme–XIIIeme siecles)." In *Les soins de beauté: Moyen Age, début des tempes modernes*, ed. Denis Menjot, 319–46. Nice: Faculté des lettres et sciences humaines, 1987.

Rosenthal, Franz. *The Muslim Concept of Freedom Prior to the Nineteenth Century.* Leiden: Brill, 1960.

Rossi, Franco. *Servodio Peccator, notaio in Venezia e Alessandria d'Egitto (1444–1449).* Venice: CPFSV, 1983.

Rossum, Matthias van. "'To Sell Them in Other Countries and to Make Their Profit': The Dynamics of Private Slave Trade and Ownership Under the Dutch East India Company (VOC)." In Cavaciocchi, *Serfdom and Slavery*, 593–618.

Rotman, Youval. "Captif ou esclave? Entre marché d'esclaves et marché de captifs en Méditerranée médiévale." In Guillén and Trabelsi, *Les esclavages*, 25–46.

Rowell, S. C. *Lithuania Ascending: A Pagan Empire Within East-Central Europe, 1295–1345.* Cambridge: Cambridge University Press, 1994.

Ruggiero, Guido. *The Boundaries of Eros: Sex Crime and Sexuality in Renaissance Venice.* Oxford: Oxford University Press, 1985.

Runciman, Steven. *A History of the Crusades.* London: Cambridge University Press, 1951.

Rustomji, Nerina. *The Garden and the Fire: Heaven and Hell in Islamic Culture.* New York: Columbia University Press, 2008.

———. "Are Houris Heavenly Concubines?" In Gordon and Hain, *Concubines and Courtesans*, 266–77.

Sabaté, Flocel. "Gli schiavi davanti alla giustizia nella Catalogna bassomedievale." In Cavaciocchi, *Serfdom and Slavery*, 389–406.

Sacy, Silvestre de. *Pièces diplomatiques tirées dans archives de la république de Gènes.* Notices et extraits des manuscrits de la bibliothèque du roi 11. Paris: n.p., 1827.

Ṣafadī, Khalīl ibn Aybak al-. *Aʿyān al-ʿaṣr wa-aʿwān al-naṣr*, ed. Fuat Sezgin. 3 vols. Frankfurt: Institut für Geschichte der arabisch-islamischen Wissenschaften, 1990.

Sahaydachny, Antonina Nina. "*De coniugio seruorum*: A Study of the Legal Debate About the Marriage of Unfree Persons Among Decretists and Decretalists from A.D. 1140–1215." PhD diss., Columbia University, 1994.

Sakhāwī, Shams al-Dīn Muḥammad ibn ʿAbd al-Raḥmān al-. *Al-Ḍawʾ al-lāmiʿ fī aʿyān al-qarn al-tāsiʿ*, ed. Ḥusām al-Dīn al-Qudsī. 12 vols. Cairo: Maktabat al-Qudsī, 1934.

Salatiele. *Ars notariae*, ed. Gianfrano Orlandelli. Milan: Giuffrè, 1961.

Salaymeh, Lena. *The Beginnings of Islamic Law: Late Antique Islamicate Legal Traditions.* Cambridge: Cambridge University Press, 2016.

Sanudo, Marino. *Liber secretorum fidelium crucis super Terrae Sanctae recuperatione et conservatione*, ed. Joshua Prawer. Toronto: Toronto University Press, 1972.

———. *The Book of the Secrets of the Faithful of the Cross, Liber Secretorum Fidelium Crucis*, trans. Peter Lock. Farnham: Ashgate, 2011.

Saqaṭī, al-. *Un Manuel hispanique de hisba*, ed. G. S. Colin and E. Lévi-Provençal. Paris: E. Leroux, 1931.

Sarakhsī, Muḥammad ibn Aḥmad al-. *Kitāb al-Mabsūṭ.* 30 vols. Cairo: Maṭbaʿat al-saʿāda, 1906–1913.

Sato, Tsugitaka. "Slave Traders and Karimi Merchants During the Mamluk Period: A Comparative Study." *MSR* 10 (2006): 141–56.

Sauli, L., ed. *Leges municipales.* Monumenta Historia Patriae 2. Turin: E. Regio Typographeo, 1838.

Saunders, J. J. "The Mongol Defeat at Ain Jalut and the Restoration of the Greek Empire." In *Muslims and Mongols: Essays on Medieval Asia by J. J. Saunders*, ed. G. W. Rice, 67–76. Christchurch: Whitcoulls, 1977.

Sauvaget, Jean. *Alep: Essai sur le développement d'une grande ville syrienne, des origines au milieu du XIXe siècle.* 2 vols. Paris: Libraire orientaliste Paul Geuthner, 1941.

Saviello, Alberto. "Zu einer Bildtopographie des Fremden. Völkerdarstellungen an der Piazza di San Marco in Venedig." In Bell, Suckow, and Wolf, *Fremde in der Stadt*, 89–115.

Schein, Sylvia. "From 'Milites Christi' to 'Mali Christiani': The Italian Communes in Western Historical Literature." In *I comuni italiani nel regno crociato di Gerusalemme*, ed. Gabriella Airaldi and Benjamin Kedar, 681–89. Genoa: IMG, 1986.

———. *Fideles Crucis: The Papacy, the West and the Recovery of the Holy Land, 1274–1314.* Oxford: Clarendon Press, 1991.

Schiel, Juliane. "Die Sklaven und die Pest. Überprüfung Forschungsnarrativs am Beispiel Venedig." In Cavaciocchi, *Serfdom and Slavery*, 365–76.

———. "Mord von zarter Hand. Der Giftmordvorwurf im Venedig." In Schiel and Hanß, *Mediterranean Slavery*, 201–28.

———. "Slaves' Religious Choice in Renaissance Venice: Applying Insights from Missionary Narratives to Slave Baptism Records." *Archivio veneto* 146 (2015): 23–45.

Schiel, Juliane, and Stefan Hanß, eds. *Mediterranean Slavery Revisited (500–1800), Neue Perspektiven auf mediterrane Sklaverei (500–1800).* Zürich: Chronos, 2014.

———. "Semantics, Practices and Transcultural Perspectives on Mediterranean Slavery." In Schiel and Hanß, *Mediterranean Slavery*, 11–24.

Schiltberger, Johannes. *The Bondage and Travels of Johann Schiltberger, a Native of Bavaria, in Europe, Asia, and Africa, 1396–1427*, trans. J. Buchan Telfer. Cambridge: Cambridge University Press, 2010.

Schneider, Irene. *Kinderverkauf und Schuldknechtschaft: Untersuchungen zur frühen Phase des islamischen Rechts.* Stuttgart: Franz Steiner, 1999.

Schwoebel, Robert. *The Shadow of the Crescent: The Renaissance Image of the Turk (1453–1517).* Nieuwkoop: B. de Graaf, 1967.

Sebellico, Andreina Bondi. *Felice de Merlis, prete e notaio in Venezia ed Ayas (1315–1348).* Venice: CPFSV, 1973–1978.

Seif, Ola Rashad. "The Khan al-Khalili District: Development, Topography and Context from the 12th to the 21st Century." Master's thesis, American University in Cairo, 2005.

Sennoune, Oueded. "Fondouks, khans et wakalas a Alexandrie a travers les recits de voyageurs." *Annales islamologiques* 38 (2004): 453–89.

Setton, Kenneth. *The Papacy and the Levant (1204–1571).* 4 vols. Philadelphia: American Philosophical Society, 1976–1978.

Shatzmiller, Maya. *Labour in the Medieval Islamic World*. Leiden: Brill, 1994.

Shaw, David. *Necessary Conjunctions: The Social Self in Medieval England*. New York: Palgrave Macmillan, 2005.

Shayzarī, ʿAbd al-Raḥmān ibn Naṣr al-. *Kitāb nihāyat al-rutba fī ṭalab al-ḥisba*, ed. Sayyid al-Bāz al-ʿArīnī. Cairo: MTTTN, 1946.

——. *The Book of the Islamic Market Inspector*, ed. R. P. Buckley. Oxford: Oxford University Press, 1999.

Shujāʿī, Shams al-Dīn al-. *Tārīkh al-malik al-Nāṣir Muḥammad ibn Qalāwūn al-Ṣāliḥī wa-awlādihi*, ed. Barbara Schäfer. Wiesbaden: Franz Steiner, 1977.

Sieveking, Heinrich. "Aus Genueser Rechnungs- und Steuer-büchern: ein Beitrag zur mittelalterlichen Handels- und Vermögensstatistik." *Sitzungsberichte der philosophisch-historischen Klasse der kaiserlichen Akademie der Wissenschaften* 162 (1909): 1–110.

Sigmund, Paul. *St. Thomas Aquinas on Politics and Ethics*. New York: W. W. Norton, 1988.

Simeonis, Simon. *Itinerarium Symonis Semeonis ab Hybernia ad Terram Sanctam*, trans. Mario Esposito. Dublin: Dublin Institute for Advanced Studies, 1960.

Sinclair, Thomas. *Eastern Turkey: An Architectural and Archaeological Survey*. 4 vols. London: Pindar Press, 1987–1990.

Siraisi, Nancy. "The *Libri morales* in the Faculty of Arts and Medicine at Bologna: Bartolomeo da Varignana and the Pseudo-Aristotelian Economics." *Manuscripta* 30 (1976): 105–18.

——. *Medieval and Early Renaissance Medicine: An Introduction to Knowledge and Practice*. Chicago: University of Chicago Press, 1990.

Smallwood, Stephanie. *Saltwater Slavery: A Middle Passage from Africa to American Diaspora*. Cambridge: Harvard University Press, 2007.

Sobers Khan, Nur. "Slaves, Wealth and Fear: An Episode from Late Mamluk-Era Egypt." *Oriens* 37 (2009): 155–61.

——. *Slaves Without Shackles: Forced Labour and Manumission in the Galata Court Registers, 1560–1572*. Berlin: Klaus Schwarz, 2014.

Spufford, Peter. *Handbook of Medieval Exchange*. London: Offices of the Royal Historical Society, 1986.

Spuler, Bertold. *Die Goldene Horde: Die Mongolen in Russland, 1223–1502*. Wiesbaden: Harrassowitz, 1965.

Stahl, Alan. "The Deathbed Oration of Doge Mocenigo and the Mint of Venice." In *Intercultural Contacts in the Medieval Mediterranean*, ed. Benjamin Arbel, 284–301. London: Frank Cass, 1996.

Stanegrave, Roger of. "L'Escarboucle d'armes de la conquête précieuse de la Terre sainte de promission." In *Projets de Croisade (v.1290–v.1330)*, ed. Jacques Paviot, 293–387. Paris: L'Académie des inscriptions et belles-lettres, 2008.

Stantchev, Stefan. *Spiritual Rationality: Papal Embargo as Cultural Practice*. Oxford: Oxford University Press, 2014.

"Statuto di Caffa: Codice diplomatico delle colonie tauro-ligure." *ASLSP* 7 (1879): 575–681.

Steenbergen, Jo van. *Order out of Chaos: Patronage, Conflict and Mamluk Socio-political Culture, 1341–1382*. Boston: Brill, 2006.

Stello, Annika. "La traite d'esclaves en mer Noire (premiere moitie du XVe siecle)." In Guillén and Trabelsi, *Les esclavages*, 171–80.

——. "Caffa and the Slave Trade During the First Half of the Fifteenth Century." In Amitai and Cluse, *Slavery*, 375–98.

Stöckly, Doris. *Le système de l'incanto des galées du marché à Venise (fin XIIIe–milieu XVe siècle)*. Leiden: Brill, 1995.

Strozzi, Alessandra. *Lettere di una gentildonna fiorentina del secolo xv ai figliuoli esuli*, ed. Cesare Guasti. Florence: G. C. Sansoni, 1877.

——. *Selected Letters of Alessandra Strozzi: Bilingual Edition*, trans. Heather Gregory. Berkeley: University of California Press, 1997.

Stuard, Susan Mosher. "To Town to Serve: Urban Domestic Slavery in Medieval Ragusa." In Hanawalt, *Women and Work*, 39–55.

———. "Ancillary Evidence for the Decline of Medieval Slavery." *Past and Present* 149 (1995): 3–28.

Subkī, Taqī al-Dīn al-. *Fatāwā al-Subkī.* Cairo: Maktabat al-Qudsi, 1937.

Subtelny, Orest. *Ukraine: A History.* Toronto: University of Toronto Press, 2000.

Suckow, Dirk. "Adalberts Traum und Fellussos Besen. Zur (Un-)Sichtbarkeit von Sklaven im Bild (12.–16. Jahrhundert)." In Bell, Suckow, and Wolf, *Fremde in der Stadt*, 355–82.

Suny, Ronald. *The Making of the Georgian Nation.* Bloomington: Indiana University Press, 1994.

Suyūṭī, Jalāl al-Dīn ʿAbd al-Raḥman al-. *Nuzhat al-ʿumr fī al-tafḍīl bayna al-bīḍ wa-al-sūd wa-al-sumr*, ed. ʿAbd al-Amīn Mahdī al-Ṭāʿī. Baghdad: Dār Ibn Nadīm, 1990.

———. *Al-Ḥāwī lil-fatāwī fī al-fiqh wa-ʿulūm al-tafsīr wa-al-ḥadīth wa-al-uṣūl wa-al-naḥw wa-al-iʿrāb wa-sāʾir al-funūn.* Beirut: Dār al-Jabīl, 1992.

Swain, Simon, ed. *Seeing the Face, Seeing the Soul: Polemon's Physiognomy from Classical Antiquity to Medieval Islam.* Oxford: Oxford University Press, 2007.

———. *Economy, Family, and Society from Rome to Islam: A Critical Edition, English Translation, and Study of Bryson's Management of the Estate.* Cambridge: Cambridge University Press, 2013.

Syropoulos, Silvestros. *Les mémoires du grand ecclésiarque de l'Église de Constantinople Sylvestre Syropoulos sur le Concile de Florence (1438–1439)*, trans. V. Laurent. Rome: Pontificium institutum orientalium studiorum, 1971.

Tafur, Pero. *Andaças é viajes de Pero Tafur por diversas partes del mundo avido (1435–1439).* Madrid: Miguel Ginesta, 1874.

———. *Travels and Adventures, 1435–1439*, trans. Malcolm Letts. London: G. Routledge, 1926.

Talbi, Mohamed. "Law and Economy in Ifrīqiya (Tunisia) in the Third Islamic Century: Agriculture and the Role of Slaves in the Country's Economy." In Udovitch, *Islamic Middle East*, 209–49.

Talbot, Alice-Mary. *The Correspondence of Athanasius I, Patriarch of Constantinople.* Washington, DC: Dumbarton Oaks, 1975.

Tamba, Giorgio. *Bernardo de Rodulfis: Notaio in Venezia (1392–1399).* Venice: CPFSV, 1974.

Tanner, Norman, trans. *Decrees of the Ecumenical Councils.* 2 vols. Washington, DC: Georgetown University Press, 1990.

Taparel, Henri. "Un épisode de la politique orientale de Philippe le Bon: Les bourguignons en Mer Noire (1444–1446)." *Annales de Bourgogne* 55 (1983): 5–29.

Tardy, Lajos. *Sklavenhandel in der Tartarei: Die Frage der Mandscharen*, trans. Mátyás Esterházy. Szeged: Universitas szegediensis de Attila József nominata, 1983.

Taylor, Paul. *Race: A Philosophical Introduction.* Cambridge: Polity Press, 2013.

Temkin, Owsei. *The Falling Sickness: A History of Epilepsy from the Greeks to the Beginnings of Modern Neurology.* Baltimore: Johns Hopkins University Press, 1971.

Tenenti, Alberto. "Gli schiavi de Venezia alla fine del cinquecento." *Rivista storica italiana* 67 (1955): 52–69.

Theiner, Augustino. *Vetera monumenta Poloniae et Lithuaniae gentiumque finitimarum historiam illustrantia.* Rome: Typis vaticanis, 1860–1864.

Thiriet, Freddy. *Régestes des délibérations du Sénat de Venise concernant la Romanie.* 3 vols. Paris: Mouton, 1958–1961.

———. *La Romanie vénitienne au Moyen-Age: Le développement et l'exploitation du domaine colonial vénitien (XIIe–XVe siècles).* Paris: E. de Boccard, 1959.

———. *Délibérations des assemblées vénitiennes concernant la Romanie.* 2 vols. Paris: Mouton, 1966–1972.

Thomas, George. *Diplomatarium veneto-levantinum sive acta et diplomata res venetas graecas atque levantis illustrantia.* 2 vols. Venice: Monumenti storici publicati dalla R. deputazione veneta di storia patria, 1880–1889.

Thomas, J. A. C. *Textbook of Roman Law.* Amsterdam: North-Holland, 1976.

Thorau, Peter. *The Lion of Egypt: Sultan Baybars I and the Near East in the Thirteenth Century.* London: Longman, 1995.

Tibi, Amin. *The Tibyān: Memoirs of ʿAbd Allāh b. Buluggīn, Last Zirid Amir of Granada*. Leiden: Brill, 1986.

Tiepolo, Maria Francesca. *Domenico Prete di S. Maurizio, notaio in Venezia (1309–1316)*. Venice: CP-FRSV, 1970.

Tizengauzen, V. G., ed. *Sbornik materialov otnosjascichsja k istorii Zolotoj ordy*. St. Petersburg: S. G. Stroganova, 1884.

Toledano, Ehud. *As If Silent and Absent: Bonds of Enslavement in the Islamic Middle East*. New Haven: Yale University Press, 2007.

Tomassetti, Aloysius. *Bullarum diplomatum et privilegiorum sanctorum romanum pontificum*. Turin: Augustae Taurinorum, 1859.

Toniolo, Paola Piana. *Notai genovesi in Oltremare: Atti rogati a Chio da Gregorio Panissaro (1403–1405)*. Genoa: Accademia ligure di scienze e lettere, 1995.

Toru, Miura, and John Edward Philips. *Slave Elites in the Middle East and Africa*. London: Kegan Paul International, 2000.

Trabelsi, Salah. "Memory and Slavery: The Issues of Historiography." *International Social Science Journal* 58 (2006): 237–43.

Trans-Atlantic Slave Trade Database. http://slavevoyages.org/assessment/estimates (accessed August 31, 2016).

Tria, Luigi. "La schiavitù in Liguria (ricerche e documenti)." *ASLSP* 70 (1947): 1–253.

Trivellato, Francesca. "Renaissance Italy and the Muslim Mediterranean in Recent Historical Work." *Journal of Modern History* 82 (2010): 127–55.

Troutt Powell, Eve. *A Different Shade of Colonialism: Egypt, Great Britain, and the Mastery of the Sudan*. Berkeley: University of California Press, 2003.

———. "Will That Subaltern Ever Speak? Finding African Slaves in the Historiography of the Middle East." In *Middle East Historiographies: Narrating the Twentieth Century*, ed. Israel Gershoni, Amy Singer, and Y. Hakan Erdem, 242–61. Seattle: University of Washington Press, 2006.

Tucci, Raffaele di. *Le imposte sul commercio genovese fino alla gestione del Banco di San Giorgio*. Bergamo: C. Nava, 1931.

Tzavara, Angeliki. "Morts en terre étrangère. Les Vénitiens en Orient (seconde moitié du XIVe-première moitié du XVe siècle)." *Thesaurismata* 30 (2000): 189–239.

Udovitch, Abraham. *Partnership and Profit in Medieval Islam*. Princeton: Princeton University Press, 1970.

———. *The Islamic Middle East, 700–1900*. Princeton: Darwin Press, 1981.

ʿUmarī, Shihāb al-Dīn Aḥmad al-. *Masālik al-abṣār fī mamālik al-amṣar*, ed. Dorothea Krawulsky. Beirut: Al-Markaz al-islāmī lil-buḥūth, 1986.

Varkemaa, Jussi. *Conrad Summenhart's Theory of Individual Rights*. Leiden: Brill, 2012.

Varthema, Ludovico di. *The Travels of Ludovico di Varthema*, trans. John Winter Jones. New York: Burt Franklin, 1863.

Vásáry, István. "The Crimean Khanate and the Great Horde (1440s–1500s): A Fight for Primacy." In *The Crimean Khanate Between East and West (15th–18th Century)*, ed. Denise Klein, 13–26. Wiesbaden: Harrassowitz, 2012.

Vasiliev, Alexander. *The Goths in the Crimea*. Cambridge: Medieval Academy of America, 1936.

Verlinden, Charles. "Esclavage et ethnographie sur les bords de la Mer Noire (XIIIe et XIVe siècles)." In *Miscellanea historica in honorem Leonis van der Essen*, 1:287–298. Brussels: Éditions universitaires, 1947.

———. "Le colonie vénitienne de Tana, centre de la traite des esclaves au XIVe et au début du XVe siècle." In *Studi in onore di Gino Luzzatto*, 2:1–25. Milan: Giuffrè, 1950.

———. "La Crete, debouche et plaque tournante de la traite des esclaves aux XIVe et XVe siecles." In *Studi in onore di Amintore Fanfani*, 3:593–669. Milan: Giuffrè, 1962.

———. "Traite des esclaves et traitants italiens à Constantinople (XIIIe–XVe siècles)." *Le Moyen Age* 69 (1963): 791–804.

———. "Orthodoxie et esclavage au bas Moyen Age." In *Mélanges Eugène Tisserant*, 5:427–56. Vatican City: Biblioteca apostolica vaticana, 1964.

———. "Le recrutement des esclaves à Venise aux XIVe et XVe siècles." *Bulletin de l'institut historique belge de Rome* 39 (1968): 83–202.

———. "Medieval 'Slavers.'" In *Economy, Society, and Government in Medieval Italy*, ed. David Herlihy, Robert Lopez, and Vsevolod Slessarev, 1–15. Kent: Kent State University Press, 1969.

———. "La législation vénitienne du bas Moyen Âge en matière d'esclavage (XIIIe–XVe siecles)." In *Ricerche storiche ed economiche in memoria di Corrado Barbagallo*, ed. Luigi de Rosa, 2:147–72. Naples: Edizioni scientifiche italiane, 1970.

———. "Mamelouks et traitants." In *Économies et sociétés au Moyen Age: Mélanges offerts à Edouard Perroy*, 737–47. Paris: Publications de la Sorbonne, 1973.

———. "La traite des esclaves dans l'espace byzantin au XIVe siècle." In Berza and Stănescu, *Actes du XIVe congrès*, 2:281–84.

———. "Le recrutement des esclaves a Genes du milieu du XIIe siecle jusque vers 1275." In *Fatti e idee di storia economica nei secoli XII–XX: Studi dedicati a Franco Borlandi*, 37–57. Bologna: Società editrice il mulino, 1977.

———. *L'Esclavage dans l'Europe médiévale*. 2 vols. Ghent: Rijksuniversiteit te Gent, 1977.

———. "Encore la traite des esclaves et les traitants italiens à Constantinople." *Bulletin de l'institut historique belge de Rome* 59 (1989): 107–20.

Vernadsky, George. *A History of Russia*. Vol. 3, *The Mongols and Russia*. New Haven: Yale University Press, 1953.

Verona, Jacopo da. *Liber peregrinationis di Jacopo da Verona*, ed. Ugo Monneret de Villard. Rome: Libreria dello Stato, 1950.

Viaggi fatti da Vinetia, alla Tana, in Persia, in India, et in Constantinopoli. Venice: Figlivoli di Aldo, 1545.

Vigna, Amadeo. "Codice diplomatico delle colonie tauro-ligure durante la signoria dell'Ufficio di S. Giorgio (1453–1475)." *ASLSP* 6–7 (1868): 6:1–981; 7:1:1–901; 7:2:5–442.

Wallace, David. *Premodern Places: Calais to Surinam, Chaucer to Aphra Behn*. Malden: Blackwell, 2004.

Wallon, Henri. *Histoire de l'esclavage dans l'antiquité*. Paris: Imprimerie royale, 1847.

Walz, Terence. "Wakalat al-Gallaba: The Market for Sudan Goods in Cairo." *Annales islamologiques* 13 (1977): 217–45.

Watson, Alan. *The Digest of Justinian*. Philadelphia: University of Pennsylvania Press, 1985.

Wavrin, Jehan de. *Anchiennes chroniques d'Engleterre*, ed. Mlle. Dupont. Paris: Jules Renouard, 1863.

Webb, John. "A Survey of Egypt and Syria, Undertaken in the Year 1422 by Sir Gilbert de Lannoy." *Archaeologia, or Miscellaneous Tracts Relating to Antiquity* 21 (1827): 281–444.

Weigand, Rudolf. *Die Naturrechtslehre der Legisten und Dekretisten von Irnerius bis Accursius und von Gratian bis Johannes Teutonicus*. Munich: Max Hueber Verlag, 1967.

Weiss, Gillian. *Captives and Corsairs: France and Slavery in the Early Modern Mediterranean*. Stanford: Stanford University Press, 2011.

Williams, Caroline. "The Mosque of Sitt Hadaq." *Muqarnas* 11 (1994): 55–64.

Williams, Eric. *Capitalism and Slavery*. Chapel Hill: University of North Carolina Press, 1944.

Williams, John. "From the Commercial Revolution to the State Revolution: The Development of Slavery in Medieval Genoa." PhD diss., University of Chicago, 1995.

Winer, Rebecca. *Women, Wealth, and Community in Perpignan, c.1250–1300: Christians, Jews, and Enslaved Muslims in a Medieval Mediterranean Town*. Aldershot: Ashgate, 2006.

———. "Conscripting the Breast: Lactation, Slavery and Salvation in the Realms of Aragon and Kingdom of Majorca, c.1250–1300." *Journal of Medieval History* 34 (2008): 164–84.

Wing, Patrick. "Submission, Defiance, and the Rules of Politics on the Mamluk Sultanate's Anatolian Frontier." *JRAS* 25, no. 3 (2015): 377–88.

Winroth, Anders. "Neither Slave nor Free: Theology and Law in Gratian's Thoughts on the Definition of Marriage and Unfree Persons." In *Medieval Church Law and the Origins of the Western*

Legal Tradition, ed. Wolfgang Müller and Mary Sommar, 97–109. Washington, DC: Catholic University of America Press, 2006.

Wirth, Eugen. "Alep et les courants commerciaux entre l'Europe et l'Asie du XIIe au XVIe siècles." *Revue du monde musulman et de la Méditerranée* 55 (1990): 44–56.

Wirth, G. "Gepiden." *Lexikon des Mittelalters*. http://apps.brepolis.net/BrepolisPortal/default.aspx (accessed April 9, 2014).

Wright, Marcia. *Strategies of Slaves and Women: Life-Stories from East/Central Africa*. New York: Lilian Barber Press, 1993.

Wyatt, David. *Slaves and Warriors in Medieval Britain and Ireland, 800–1200*. Leiden: Brill, 2009.

Yanoski, Jean. *De l'abolition de l'esclavage ancien au Moyen Âge, et de sa transformation en servitude de la glèbe*. Paris: Imprimerie royale, 1860.

Yudkevich, Jenia. "The Nature and Role of the Slave Traders in the Eastern Mediterranean during the Third Reign of Sultan al-Nāṣir Muḥammad b. Qalāwūn (1310–1341 CE)." In Amitai and Cluse, *Slavery*, 423–36.

Yule, Henry. *Cathay and the Way Thither, Being a Collection of Medieval Notices of China*. Nendeln: Kraus Reprint, 1967.

Zachariadou, Elisavet. *Trade and Crusade: Venetian Crete and the Emirates of Menteshe and Aydin (1300–1415)*. Venice: Istituto ellenico di studi bizantini e postbizantini, 1983.

Zamboni, Filippo. *Gli Ezzelini, Dante e gli schiavi*. Florence: Tipografia di Salvadore Landi, 1897.

Zetterstéen, Karl von. *Beiträge zur Geschichte der Mamlūkensultane in den Jahren 690–741 der Higra nach arabischen Handschriften*. Leiden: Brill, 1919.

Zevakin, E. S., and A. Penčko. "Ricerche sulla storia delle colonie genovesi nel Caucaso occidentale nei secoli XIII–XV." In *Miscellanea di studi storici*, 7–98. Genoa: Fratelli Bozzi, 1969.

Ziegler, Joseph. "Physiognomy, Science, and Proto-Racism 1200–1500." In Eliav-Feldon, Isaac, and Ziegler, *Origins*, 181–99.

Zilfi, Madeline. *Women and Slavery in the Late Ottoman Empire: The Design of Difference*. New York: Cambridge University Press, 2010.

Zorgati, Ragnhild Johnsrud. *Pluralism in the Middle Ages*. New York: Routledge, 2012.

Index

Acknowledgments

The ideas in this book have evolved over the last eleven years in conversation with many friends and colleagues. At Columbia, I benefited greatly from the help and advice of Adam Kosto and Richard Bulliet as well as Neslihan Senocak, Christopher Brown, Evan Haefeli, Robert Somerville, Joel Kaye, Martha Howell, Morris Rossabi, Caterina Pizzigoni, and Consuelo Dutschke. I also want to thank Steve Schoenig, Liam Moore, Mike Heil, Jeffrey Wayno, Jay Gundacker, Debby Shulevitz, Tzafrir Barzilay, Hannah Elmer, Ethan Yee, Jake Purcell, Deborah Hamer, Jeun Hee Cho, Ariel Rubin, Ariel Lambe Mercik, Andy Whitford, Carolyn Arena, Justin Dumbrowski, Owen Miller, Christine Simpson, and the members of the Medieval Latin Reading Group for their support and encouragement along the way.

At Rhodes College, I enjoyed many stimulating conversations with Etty Terem, Chuck McKinney, Jonathan Judaken, Rhiannon Graybill, Clara Pascual-Argente, Judy Haas, Lori Garner, Stephanie Elsky, and the students in my 2015 and 2017 seminars on Slavery in the Premodern World. Ellen Kanavos helped me clean up the loose ends. Shaun Marmon, Jessica Goldberg, Wim Blockmans, Sergei Karpov, Craig Perry, Won Hee Cho, Marina Rustow, Juliane Schiel, Mirko Sardelic, Jeffrey Fynn-Paul, Felicia Roşu, Damian Pargas, Marlis Saleh, Stephan Conermann, and the members of MEDMED-L helped me refine and develop my ideas in various ways. Jerry Singerman and the anonymous reader for University of Pennsylvania Press guided and vastly improved this project in its later stages. I would like to express my appreciation to the Schoff Fund at the University Seminars at Columbia University and to the Institute for Humanities Research at Arizona State University for their help in publication. Material in this work was presented to the University Seminar on Medieval Studies.

My writing and archival research were funded by Columbia University, Rhodes College, the Council of American Overseas Research Centers, the American Research Center in Egypt, the Foreign Language and Area Studies Program, the Center for Arabic Study Abroad in Cairo, the Mellon Summer Institute in Italian Paleography, the American Historical Association, the Gladys Krieble Delmas Foundation, and the Charlotte W. Newcombe Foundation. In Italy, the staff of the Archivi di Stati in Genoa and Venice were very generous. Thanks especially to Alessandra Schiavon, to Giuseppe Felloni, and to Sandra Origone and Laura Balletto of the Università degli Studi di Genova. In Egypt, I would have accomplished nothing without the staff of the American Research Center in Egypt, especially Djodi Deutsch and Mme. Amira, and the advice of Hassanein Rabie and Jere Bachrach. Hoda Zeidan, Khalid Yossef, Abdelrahman El Refaiy, and Elisa Wynne-Hughes weathered the beginning of the Arab Spring with me.

Finally, my family have supported me at every step along the way. Thank you for all of your patience; I could never have gotten here without you. There are not enough words in the world to express my gratitude to Toby: *grazie mille, alf shukran, ehara koe i a ia*. Any flaws that remain, hidden or manifest, are my own responsibility.